Contents at a glance

Contents

What do you think of this book? We want to hear from you!

Microsoft is interested in hearing your feedback so we can continually improve our
books and learning resources for you. To participate in a brief online survey, please visit:

www.microsoft.com/learning/booksurvey/

Chapter 5   Maintain a core SharePoint environment   401

What do you think of this book? We want to hear from you!

Microsoft is interested in hearing your feedback so we can continually improve our books and learning resources for you. To participate in a brief online survey, please visit:

www.microsoft.com/learning/booksurvey/

Introduction

Although this book was written primarily to help you prepare for Exam 70-331: "Core Solutions of Microsoft SharePoint Server 2013," it is also intended to be a reference that you can refer to during your experiences with SharePoint Server 2013. In many cases, the steps to perform a task are shown to help you feel comfortable with related questions on the exam as well as provide a reference on how to perform the task in a real-life situation. The level of detail in this book will often exceed what is required on the exam because it is an advanced solutions exam. This does not mean there will not be specific questions about steps required to perform a task or requirements needed to install a service application. It does mean that you do not need to focus on being able to spell out a command correctly or know exactly what parameter to pass it. You should focus on the concepts, the overall steps involved with a task, and the components needed for a solution. If you focus on these concepts and go through the tasks in this book, you will be well on your way to passing the exam.

This book is generally intended for exam candidates who have four or more years working with SharePoint Server and related technologies such as SQL Server and Windows Server. The candidate should have hands-on experience with a multiserver SharePoint farm in the capacities of planning, implementing, and maintaining. This includes but is not limited to the areas of high availability, disaster recovery, capacity planning, and exposure to SharePoint Online. Despite having multiple years of experience with a multiserver SharePoint farm, it is doubtful that exam candidates will have experience with all the technologies covered by the exam, and they should focus on the areas in which they have the least exposure. Also, any feature that has been added to SharePoint Server 2013 will likely receive additional coverage on the exam.

This book will help you prepare for the exam, but nothing can take the place of real-life experience. In an effort to make the exams closer to measuring knowledge of the product, they are going more and more to case studies and getting away from simple multiple choice questions. You will still see a number of traditional multiple choice questions, but you will also see questions in which you have to place steps in order and questions in which you have to choose the right set of items from a large list of possible answers. In these cases, practicing the actual implementation of the functionality covered in this book will help you far more than just trying to memorize what is involved.

This book covers every exam objective, but it does not cover every exam question. Only the Microsoft exam team has access to the exam questions, and Microsoft regularly adds new questions to the exam, making it impossible to cover specific questions. You should consider this book a supplement to your relevant real-world experience and other study materials. If you encounter a topic in this book that you do not feel completely comfortable with, use the links you'll find in the text to find more information and take the time to research and study the topic. Great information is available on MSDN, TechNet, and in blogs and forums.

Microsoft certifications

Microsoft certifications distinguish you by proving your command of a broad set of skills and experience with current Microsoft products and technologies. The exams and corresponding certifications are developed to validate your mastery of critical competencies as you design and develop, or implement and support, solutions with Microsoft products and technologies both on-premise and in the cloud. Certification brings a variety of benefits to the individual and to employers and organizations.

> **MORE INFO** **ALL MICROSOFT CERTIFICATIONS**
>
> For information about Microsoft certifications, including a full list of available certifications, go to *http://www.microsoft.com/learning/en/us/certification/cert-default.aspx*.

Acknowledgments

There are many whom I need to acknowledge in this book, both friends and family. Without the patience, support, and insight of these folks, this book would not exist. First and foremost, this book is for Marlene: Thanks for putting up with the late night writing marathons, working weekends, and the "how does this sound" conversations. For Samantha: Keep checking the oil; that car will run forever. For Kate: "Spoilers!" and "Don't Blink."

Beyond family, I have a few folks to thank for allowing me to bounce tech questions off of them: David Frette ("...it's a custom what?"), Steve Buck ("...sure, PKI is easy!"), Dante Marcuccio ("...I know it's in there somewhere"), Brian Culver ("...you busy?"), and Angelo Palma ("...hey, you should blog that"). You guys keep SharePoint fun.

Errata and book support

We've made every effort to ensure the accuracy of this book and its companion content. Any errors that have been reported since this book was published are listed on our Microsoft Press site:

http://aka.ms/ER70-331/errata

If you find an error that is not already listed, you can report it to us through the same page.

If you need additional support, send an e-mail Microsoft Press Book Support at *mspinput@microsoft.com*.

Please note that product support for Microsoft software is not offered through these addresses.

We want to hear from you

At Microsoft Press, your satisfaction is our top priority, and your feedback our most valuable asset. Please tell us what you think of this book at:

http://www.microsoft.com/learning/booksurvey

The survey is short, and we read every one of your comments and ideas. Thanks in advance for your input!

Stay in touch

Let's keep the conversation going! We're on Twitter: *http://twitter.com/MicrosoftPress*.

Preparing for the exam

Microsoft certification exams are a great way to build your resume and let the world know about your level of expertise. Certification exams validate your on-the-job experience and product knowledge. While there is no substitution for on-the-job experience, preparation through study and hands-on practice can help you prepare for the exam. We recommend that you round out your exam preparation plan by using a combination of available study materials and courses. For example, you might use the Exam Ref and another study guide for your "at home" preparation, and take a Microsoft Official Curriculum course for the classroom experience. Choose the combination that you think works best for you.

Note that this Exam Ref is based on publically available information about the exam and the author's experience. To safeguard the integrity of the exam, authors do not have access to the live exam.

## CHAPTER 1

Design a SharePoint topology

When you begin to design your Microsoft SharePoint implementation, there are two key traits to consider: flexibility and scalability. A flexible SharePoint environment enables the structure and layout to change with minimal impact to users; a scalable SharePoint environment allows for the necessary growth to meet changing business requirements.

> **IMPORTANT**
>
> **Have you read page xix?**
>
> It contains valuable information regarding the skills you need to pass the exam.

This section covers the taxonomical, navigational, and structural considerations that should be addressed before implementing your SharePoint environment.

Objectives in this chapter:

- Objective 1.1: Design information architecture
- Objective 1.2: Design a logical architecture
- Objective 1.3: Design a physical architecture
- Objective 1.4: Plan a SharePoint Online (Microsoft Office 365) deployment

Objective 1.1: Design information architecture

As human beings, we encounter metadata in our daily lives. We describe items by their physical appearance, their location, or their purpose. We meet other people and learn their names, their titles, and what their roles are within an organization.

As information workers, we seek to capture metadata and make it reusable. Sometimes we simply write a single piece of metadata (such as a phone number) down on a piece of paper; more often we associate other metadata, such as the location, name, and role of the person whose phone number we wrote down.

Sometimes the information captured is of benefit to only a single individual, but this is usually not the case; more often, we see information being shared between ourselves and others in our organization.

As you will see in this objective, planning the design of the information you seek to capture will improve your chances of it being reused and searchable.

This objective covers how to:

- Design an intersite navigational taxonomy.
- Design site columns and content types.
- Design keywords, synonyms, best bets, and managed properties.
- Plan information management policies.
- Plan managed site structure.
- Plan term sets.

Designing an intersite navigational taxonomy

The core navigational elements of SharePoint navigational taxonomy are sites and site collections. A site is the smallest element in this taxonomy and is composed of lists and libraries; a site collection is a grouping of sites that are functionally, navigationally, and administratively related to one another.

Sites within a site collection are automatically related to one another by a parent-child relationship (see Figure 1-1). The first site that is created within a site collection is referred to as the top-level site and it often defines the navigational relationship with all its subsites (child/grandchild/great-grandchild and so on).

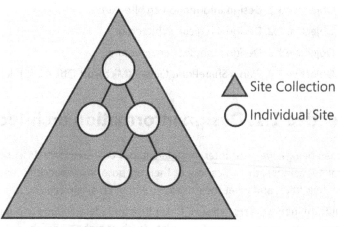

FIGURE 1-1 A site collection and its sites.

If you possess a single site collection for your navigational taxonomy, site navigation is easily configurable. In sites that have the publishing feature enabled, it's a simple task to move the sites around to suit the needs of the business as the organization changes and grows—to a point.

Scalability issues

The initial issue with placing all content within a single site collection is not apparent to users. They are readily adopting the new environment, adding new sites, permission groups, workflows, branding, and content. This site collection is stored within the confines of a single content database; and, more importantly, cannot be scaled across multiple content databases.

As the site collection continues to grow, other issues begin to surface, affecting users and admins alike. These issues include the following:

- **Security groups**   As site owners begin creating new sites and subsites, they have the option to specify that the site will not inherit permissions (this is not the default). Each new site can, in theory, add up to three new permission groups: visitors, members, and owners; the sheer number of additional groups can quickly become unwieldy to administer.

- **Permissions inheritance**   As the volume of data within a site collection increases, the surface area affected by a permissions change becomes larger. A minor permissions change near the top of a site collection can potentially expose sensitive data at a lower level site, list, or library.

- **Taxonomical changes**   Structural taxonomy changes in site columns and content types begin to affect the granular sites as well, especially if the parent column or content type is heavily altered.

- **Recycle bins**   Individual sites recycle bins remain fairly easy to administer for the site owners, but the site collection recycle bins begin to have thousands and thousands of documents that must be sorted through by the site collection administrator (SCA) in the event of a restore request.

- **SQL backup and restore**   As the sheer volume of content increases within the site collection (and its related content database), backup and restoration times increase in duration along with the amount of data that can be influenced by a database corruption.

Navigational terms

When speaking of navigation, there are four terms that should be defined: global, current, structural, and managed navigation.

Current and global navigation refer to the two major navigation page areas present in traditional web design (also known as the "inverted L"), as shown in Figure 1-2.

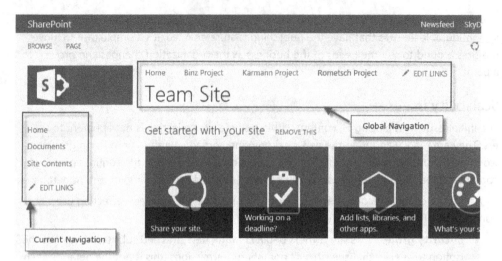

FIGURE 1-2 Global and current navigation.

When discussing intersite navigation taxonomy, this section will be concentrating on the global navigation section, although the current navigation section might be occasionally mentioned.

SharePoint 2013 provides two distinct ways to generate navigation for a SharePoint site or sites, structural and managed navigation. Structural navigation is a defined structure that possesses both automatically generated elements (for example, new links generated when a new list, library, or subsite is added to a site) and manually generated links (perhaps linking to a distinct site collection).

A newer component of SharePoint is the capability to build a metadata structure that assigns the navigational taxonomy to a site. As you might imagine, this structure is fluid, enabling multiple sites and site collections to be unified into a navigational structure that can be subscribed to by a site or site collection.

EXAM TIP

Each of these navigational types has merit. For a group of users who are unfamiliar with creating and maintaining terms and term sets, structural navigation might be a more appropriate choice.

Because the managed navigation option is the newer of the two navigational types, be familiar with how to create this structure within the Term Store Management Tool.

Designing a basic taxonomy

We have already shown that there is an implied parent-child relationship present within a site collection, so designing an intersite taxonomy is then dependent on how navigational relationships can be configured between distinct site collections.

Defining the relationship between sites or site collections is less about the technical details and more about the philosophy of how the SharePoint farm will be used. Toward the end of this section, the technical actions required to configure site collection relationships will be addressed.

Prior to setting up these relationships, other considerations should be discussed:

- Who are the audiences for the respective web applications/sites?
- Will publishing site collections be separated from collaborative site collections?
- What purpose does each web application/site serve?
- What is the preferred URL for each site/site collection?

Org chart navigation

One of the easiest site taxonomies to build echoes the organizational chart. Users visiting the site are immediately greeted with a navigational menu system that starts with each major unit in the company (human resources, information technology, accounting, and so on). This design might be sufficient for a smaller organization with few subdepartments, but tends to be inflexible in a larger organization.

As an example, take the situation in which a user needs to view the status of their 401K benefits. Depending on how large the organization is, the navigation could go something like this:

Intranet → North America → Business Units → Human Resources → Retirement Benefits → 401K Status

If a person needs to get to that site on a regular basis, they might wind up choosing to do either of these:

- Bookmark the 401K site
- Search for the 401K site

One of the constants in business is change; organizational structures are not exempted from this fact:

- **New acquisitions**   As a business grows, other businesses are often purchased and folded into the structure.
- **Departmental change**   As departments grow within an organization, it is not uncommon to see them split into two different units (for example, accounting becomes accounts receivable and accounts payable).

As you recall from the last section, people might choose to bookmark or search for a site that is nested deeply within the navigation structure. Altering that navigational structure to accommodate change in the org chart might result in the following:

- Broken bookmarks
- Errant search results (depending on how up-to-date your search index is)

Functional navigation

The challenge is not to necessarily make the navigational hierarchy about the structure of the company; instead, you might consider making the hierarchy about the actions taken by a person visiting the site.

Designing the site navigation around activities enables the site to be flexible in purpose. For example, instead of building an HR header that lists all the HR subdepartments, you might instead build a header that lists a series of actions such as these:

- New to the company? A site that is dedicated to the onboarding process of a new employee, which enables them to do the following:
  - Complete all necessary HR and IT forms
  - Kick off workflows and requests for items such as telephones, computer accounts, and so on
- Check retirement status
- Check leave/vacation status

As you can see, these navigation items function as verbs; they have action and intent behind them. If users decide that they would rather visit the HR site to see what items are presented by that team, the HR header link will take them to the HR site.

It becomes apparent that deciding which items get promoted to the navigation requires some interaction with the respective business units. Before proceeding to meet with these groups, develop an arsenal of requirements, gathering questions such as these:

- What are the major components of your business unit?
- What functions do you see your group(s) serving?
- When people call your group, what are the three most common things that they are looking for?
- If people within the organization were to search for your groups, what are the top 10 terms you might see them using?

When you meet with these units, it is important to throw the rule book out: a large white board, some sticky notes (to foster navigation activities), and an open forum is all that is necessary to foster a solid navigational design. Challenge the members of the group to act not as managers or information workers but instead to act as a normal business user would when navigating the site.

Later in this objective, managed site structure will be discussed; in that topic, we will compare the two types of navigation available, managed and structural. These navigation types are discussed at length and compared from a functional standpoint.

Designing site columns and content types

There are two distinct types of columns within SharePoint: list columns and site columns. From a functional perspective, they are identical, with one major difference: site columns are reusable.

List columns

As an example, let's consider a new list for a small company's building management that will be used to assign a new desk to a worker. The company currently has two offices, one in Houston and one in San Antonio, and has only one building in each city. The plan is for the organization to eventually expand into other states.

The requirement is to capture a simple series of metadata elements, and for each office to maintain its own list:

- User name
- Office location
- Phone number
- City
- State
- Zip code

Within each office's list, you could build simple list columns to capture each of these distinct pieces of metadata (also known as information types), shown in Table 1-1.

TABLE 1-1 List columns and information types

List Column Name	Information Type
User name	Person or group
Office location	Choice, enforce unique values
Phone	Choice, enforce unique values
City	Choice
State	Choice
Zip code	Choice

Adding values to each list requires you to visit that list to make changes. Not too bad for one or two lists, but as the company begins to add sites (and lists), maintenance of the multiple list columns could become error-prone.

Site columns

The next step on the path to reusable metadata is to build site columns instead of list columns and associate the site columns to list or library. The major benefit of moving from list columns to site columns is extensibility; what was once a piece of metadata that could be associated with only one list can now be associated to many.

Site columns are created the same way as list columns are, but with one major difference: they are hierarchical in nature. When a site column is instantiated on a particular site, that site and all its child sites inherit the site column and its properties.

Figure 1-3 shows the inheritance of two site columns. This example is purposely oversimplified, but you can see the inheritance of site columns based on where they were initially created.

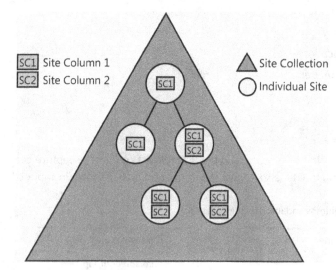

FIGURE 1-3 Site column inheritance.

Site columns are hierarchical:

- A site column that is created at the top-level site in a site collection (SC1) is available to all sites in the site collection.
- A site column created at a subsite level (SC2) is available to that site and its child sites.

After a site column is created, a list can be assigned that column (along with its information type and all metadata). If the metadata associated with the information type changes (for instance, adding a new color choice), this change can be propagated throughout any list that had previously been assigned that site column.

Both list columns and site columns are defined by the type of content they possess (also referred to as the column's information type). Most of these information types are scoped to the particular list or site column, meaning that metadata contained within the column is available only to sites residing in a particular site collection.

This site collection limitation presents a real problem: If you build multiple site collections (and you should be), you must now have a mechanism to make metadata available beyond the site collection boundary without having to build the same information type over and over again in each new site collection.

Fortunately, SharePoint provides a model for presenting information types in multiple site columns across multiple site collections; this model is called the managed metadata service. The MMS allows for the creation of a both local and global term sets, as you will soon see in the "Planning term sets" topic. A global term set can be used to store metadata (terms) for them to be reused and maintained in list and site columns across multiple site collections.

Content types

So far, you have been working with one column at a time: a name, a color, and a product type. Although it is perfectly viable to build each list or library and then assign distinct list or site columns, this does not allow you to manage groupings of similar items in a list or library. To address this need, SharePoint provides the notion of content types.

A content type defines the attributes of a list item, document, or folder. These attributes not only provide descriptive information about the item (metadata and properties) but also provide activities that can be associated with each item (workflows, information management policies, document templates, and other features).

Content types behave in a hierarchical fashion and are inherited from each parent site to its child within the same site collection, as shown in Figure 1-4.

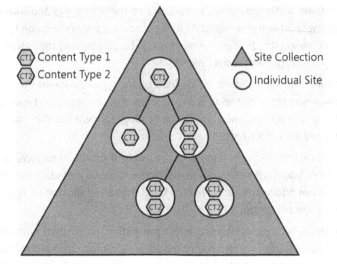

FIGURE 1-4 Content type inheritance.

The hierarchy of content types behaves similarly to the hierarchy of site columns, meaning the following:

- A content type that is created at the top-level site in a site collection (CT1) is available to all sites in the site collection.
- A site column created at a subsite level (CT2) is available to that site and its child sites.

After a content type is created, a list or library can be assigned that content type. If the content type is changed (for instance, a new retention policy stage or new site column), these changes can be propagated throughout any list or library that had previously been assigned that content type.

It should be noted that all content types are related: documents, items, pages, lists, libraries, and more are all part of a large ecosystem of content types.

For example, when you provision a new document library, the default content type provisioned is Document. If you were to want to build a hierarchy of legal documents and have contracts as one of the available content types, its content type hierarchy might look something like Figure 1-5.

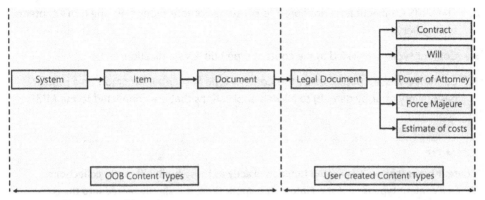

FIGURE 1-5 Content type hierarchy.

In this case, you might assign a core set of site columns to the legal document content type and then assign workflows, retention policies, and more site columns to the individual child content types (contract, will, and so on).

Any site collection created within a SharePoint environment is automatically populated with a series of content types that themselves are composed of out-of-the-box (OOB) site columns. The number and type of content types provisioned depend on the two different factors:

- **Site template**   The template you choose when provisioning a new site will determine what content types are created.
- **Features**   The features you select to add to an existing SharePoint site/site collection can also provide new content types.

The key here is to remember the scope. So far, we have a series of site columns that can inherit managed metadata, but the content type is still limited in application scope to the site collection.

If this structure is to be truly extensible, it's time to learn how to apply content types from outside the site collection. For that, we will use the Managed Metadata Service (MMS) and a concept known as a content type hub.

Content type hub

Although content types can easily be defined within the boundaries of a site collection, you haven't yet seen any provision for creating a content type that can be used in multiple site collections. This situation is quickly remedied by the use of a content type hub.

A content type hub is aptly named and is simply a normal site collection that has been specified to provide content types to other site collections.

Content types are syndicated by the MMS; the process is fairly straightforward:

1. The MMS is configured to allow the content type hub to be the only source for centralized content type syndication.

2. The MMS Connection is configured to consume content types from the hub's content type gallery.

3. Content types are placed in the content type hub for syndication.

4. Content types are published by the Content Type Subscriber timer job on a regular basis (every hour by default) to all web applications that are connected to the MMS application.

EXAM TIP

Content types that are syndicated function exactly as those built within site collections. When a content type is published into a web application, it is simply placed into the content type gallery of each site collection for use.

External content types

External content types incorporate Business Connectivity Services (BCS) functionality to enable external data to be represented within SharePoint sites. These content types are metadata that represent the following:

- Connectivity information to data
- Data definitions for the data
- Behaviors applied to data

Information that is provided via the use of external content types is reusable, mimicking the behavior of normal content types within a site or site collection. Workers interacting with an external content type do not have to be aware of the underlying data type, connection type, or security present in the content type.

As the ultimate goal is to present external content exactly the same as internal content contained within SharePoint itself, external content types act the same as any other data presented in and consumed by both Microsoft Office and SharePoint. This includes the ability to search the content as well as taking it offline in Microsoft Outlook 2013.

External content types are highly useful after they are configured, allowing for the creation of lists and data columns within SharePoint that function identically to their native SharePoint counterparts.

As the information represented by external content types is provided by BCS, it only stands to reason that there would be some specific web parts created for this purpose:

- **Business Data List**   Displays a list of entity instances from a business application presented by BCS, such as a customer or order list
- **Business Data Item**   Displays the details of an item from a business application presented by BCS, such as a particular customer or order
- **Business Data Item Builder**   Creates a BCS item, providing it to other web parts

- **Business Data Related List** Displays a list of related items from a business application presented by BCS, such as all orders related to a particular customer
- **Business Data Actions** Displays a list of actions available to a portal user, such as sending e-mail or editing customer information

External content type and item pickers are also available for use within SharePoint along with profile pages, which can display details about a particular item. If more functionality is desired than what is presented by the OOB tools, development using external content types is available via the following:

- SharePoint object model
- Client object model
- Representational State Transfer (REST) URLs

> **NOTE SHAREPOINT DESIGNER (SPD) 2013 AND EXTERNAL CONTENT TYPES**
>
> SharePoint Designer (SPD) has always been a tool that is heavily integrated with the SharePoint platform. In certain governance situations, it might make sense to limit the use of SPD, but note that there are some things that SPD does exceptionally well that are beyond the scope of other toolsets. Designing SharePoint/BCS external content types is one of those functional requirements that heavily promotes the use of SPD for knowledge worker design specialists.

Designing keywords, promoted results, and managed properties

Search has always been a keystone technology within SharePoint, and an already-adept search functionality has been heavily improved by the integration of FAST search. FAST search (an additional technology that can be installed alongside SharePoint Server 2010) is now a core technology within SharePoint Server 2013 and provides additional functionality not present within SharePoint Server 2010 search.

As you might have noticed from the title of this section, we are not heavily focused on the technicalities of search at this point; instead, we will lightly cover search architecture, choosing to focus on how search queries and results are "shaped" via the use of keywords, promoted results, and managed properties.

Core search components

Search can be broken down into six major components: Search Administration, Crawl, Content Processing, Analytics Processing, Indexing, and Query Processing.

The relationship between these components can be seen in Figure 1-6.

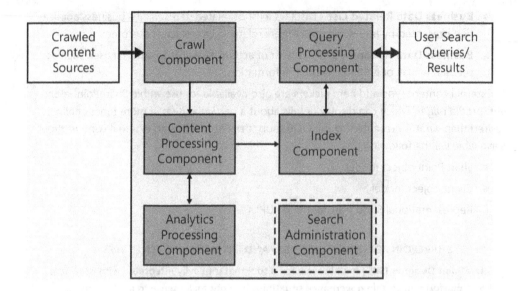

FIGURE 1-6 Search component relationships.

As you can see, the six components together accomplish two major tasks: crawls and queries. At one end of the process, content sources (such as file shares and SharePoint content) are crawled by the Crawl component; on the other end, the information has been broken down by search and is available for querying by users.

> **MORE INFO** **SEARCH IN SHAREPOINT SERVER 2013**
>
> For a detailed description of each search component and database, visit the TechNet article "Overview of Search in SharePoint Server 2013" at *http://technet.microsoft.com/en-us/ library/jj219738.aspx.*

The Search Administration component simply provides for the administration of the search components, also providing for the creation and initialization of new search components. Unlike the rest of the components, Search Administration does not provide any information transfer to or from any of the other components.

The Crawl component simply performs a crawl of the content available in the content sources; this is usually accomplished via the use of an indexing connector or protocol handler and depends on the type of file being crawled (Word, Excel, Acrobat, and so on).

After the content has been crawled, it is passed on from the Crawl component to the Content Processing component. Several operations are carried out within this step, one of which is the mapping of crawled properties to managed properties (which is discussed shortly). Additionally, items that have been crawled are turned into artifacts in this stage for inclusion within the search index. Link and URL information is stored in the link database and then processed and forwarded to the Analytics Processing component.

There are two major types of analysis present in the Analytics Processing component: search analytics and usage analytics.

- Search analytics focuses on the analysis of content being crawled and added to the search index. Items that are analyzed within search analytics improve search relevance and recall; these include metrics such as click distance, social tags and distance, and so on.

- Usage analytics focuses on user actions within search, providing a statistical analysis of usage counts (such as viewed or clicked items), recommendations (based on the user's interactions within the site), and activity ranking (the tracking of usage events) to influence search relevancy.

After analytics processing is complete, search relevance for items such as links and URLs are returned back to the Content Processing component.

After content is received from the Content Processing component, the Index component writes this content to the search index. This component also receives requests for information contained in the search index and returns result sets to the Query Processing component.

The Query Processing component receives and analyzes incoming search queries, which improve the precision, recall, and relevance of the search result sets. The resulting queries are sent to the Index component, which returns a set of search results (that are also processed) for a particular query to the front-end server.

EXAM TIP

Search is a critical component of any SharePoint 2013 farm. A thorough understanding of each search component's role within the farm helps determine which component(s) are assigned to a particular server.

Making search meaningful

Now that you have a basic understanding of the SharePoint 2013 search mechanisms, you see how everyday business users can improve search results for their particular section of a SharePoint installation.

From a design perspective, it's fairly straightforward to build a basic search engine—such a system can crawl, parse, and index content; it can also perform basic search ranking by the frequency with which a word or phrase occurs.

As content in this basic search engine grows, however, it becomes more and more difficult to find specific content within the growing search index. A high-value search result might be hard to locate when it is surrounded (and perhaps outranked) by other documents with similar search terms; for instance, a document displaying this year's 401K plan should appear first in search but might instead be displayed after documents detailing previous years' 401K plans.

Fortunately, business users who generate SharePoint lists and documents can influence search results for the content they generate.

Keywords

Within a SharePoint 2013 site, descriptive metadata (words or phrases) can be directly assigned to any list item or document; these words and phrases are called keywords. These keywords are generated as a folksonomy, meaning that they are created by individual users on a site.

Although terms are stored within a series of term sets, enterprise keywords are stored within a single term set within the managed metadata service. This specialized term set is nonhierarchical and simply called the "keyword set." As with the managed terms, enterprise keywords are stored in the term store database.

Adding keywords to a list item or document is fairly straightforward, but requires a bit of configuration prior to use.

The basic configuration process requires two steps:

1. The MMS Connection must be configured to be the default storage location for keywords.

2. The enterprise keywords site column can then be added to content types.

> **IMPORTANT** **MISSING DEFAULT TERM STORE**
>
> When you are adding new keywords, you might see this message: The Site Does Not Contain A Default Keywords Term Store. This occurs when you have not yet selected the default storage location for keywords within your SharePoint environment.

To configure the default storage location, follow these steps:

1. Open Central Administration and select **Application Management**.

2. Under Service Applications, select **Manage Service Applications.**

3. Select the **MMS Connection**.

4. From the ribbon, choose the **Properties** link.

5. On the Edit Managed Metadata Service Connection page, select the check box for **This Service Application Is The Default Storage Location For Keywords** (see Figure 1-7).

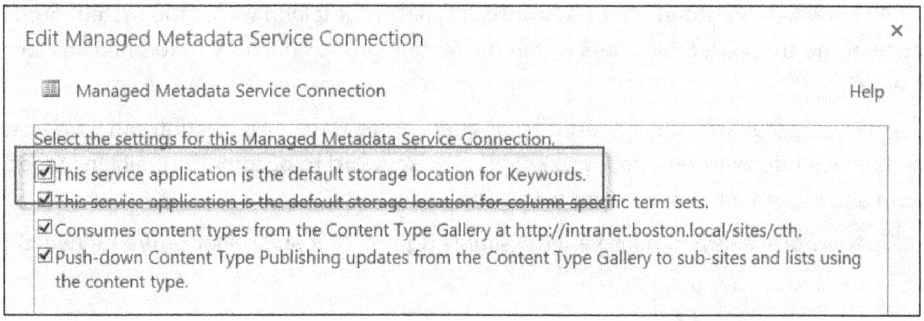

FIGURE 1-7 Default storage location for keywords.

Next, the enterprise keywords column must be added to a list or document library; this column allows for multiple values. After this column has been added, new keywords can be added to the list item (see Figure 1-8).

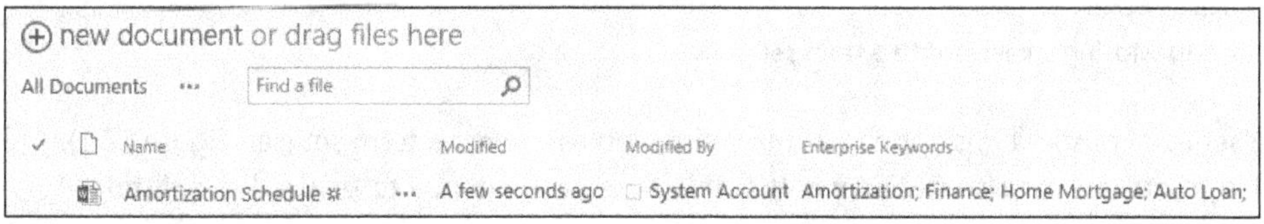

FIGURE 1-8 Keywords added to the list item.

After keywords are added to a list item or document, they are automatically added to the Managed Metadata term store (see Figure 1-9).

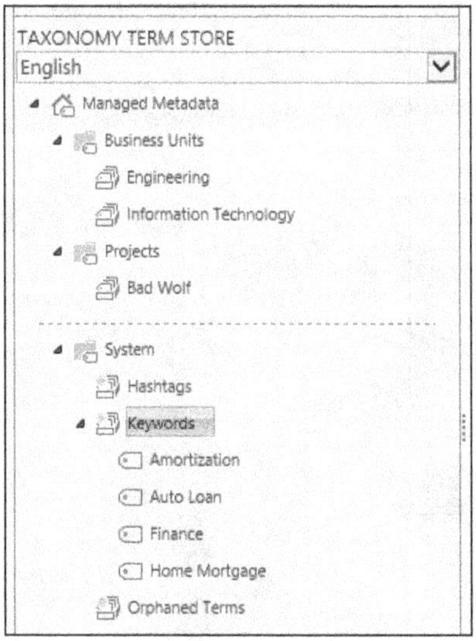

FIGURE 1-9 Taxonomy term store.

All keywords are stored in the keyword set that is contained within the System group; none of the specialized term sets within the System group enables you to build any sort of hierarchy.

Keywords that are regularly used by business users in the organization can be reviewed and moved into term sets; doing so enables the keyword to become centrally managed as a term and moved into appropriate term sets.

To transform a keyword into a term, simply right-click it and select **Move Keyword** (see Figure 1-10).

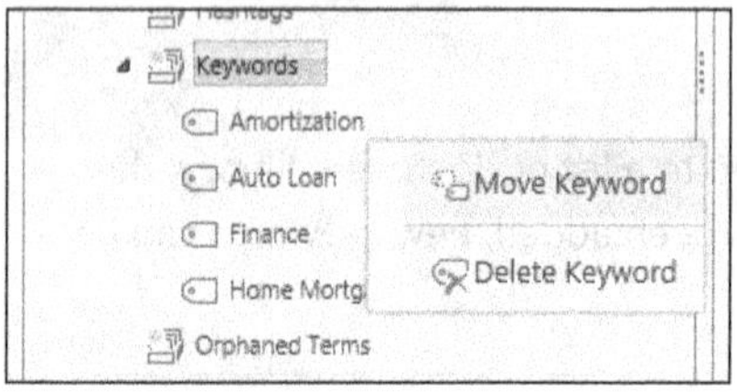

FIGURE 1-10 Moving a keyword to a term set.

A series of destinations appear; at this point, you can select a term set (see Figure 1-11). At this point, you can also decide whether this word can continue to be used as a distinct keyword outside of the new term set.

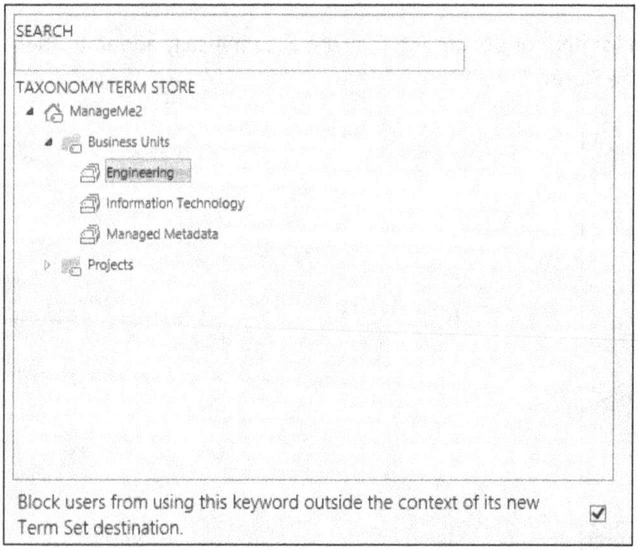

FIGURE 1-11 Choosing a destination term store.

Note that this conversion is one-way; after the keyword is changed into a term, it cannot be converted back to a keyword.

Promoted results

In previous versions of SharePoint, there was a concept known as a best bet, which was simply a search result that was promoted within the search results to be a preferred search result for a particular search topic. For instance, when a user would type in a search query that included a keyword such as "HR" or "Human Resources," the search results could be configured to display a best bet at the top of the search results that would promote the URL of the Human Resources web site.

In SharePoint 2013, best bets have been replaced by promoted results. Although the two act in a very similar fashion, there is one distinct difference between the two—how they are triggered.

Best bets used a combination of keywords and synonyms to trigger the display of a preferred result for a search. If multiple keywords were to be specified (but they were not synonyms of one another), multiple keyword entries were required. Additionally, a best bet could itself be triggered to have start, end, and review.

Promoted results improves on this concept specifically based on how they are triggered. Instead of using keywords as triggers, promoted results are triggered by query rules. These rules can be configured for use at one of two levels:

- At the site collection level:
  - Specified within Site Collection Administration → Site Query Rules
  - Scoped to the entire site collection
- At the site level:
  - Specified within Search → Query Rules
  - Scoped to the particular site

After the new query rule has been added, the process of adding a new promoted result in SharePoint 2013 is almost identical to that of creating a new best bet in SharePoint 2010. Adding a promoted result is shown in Figure 1-12.

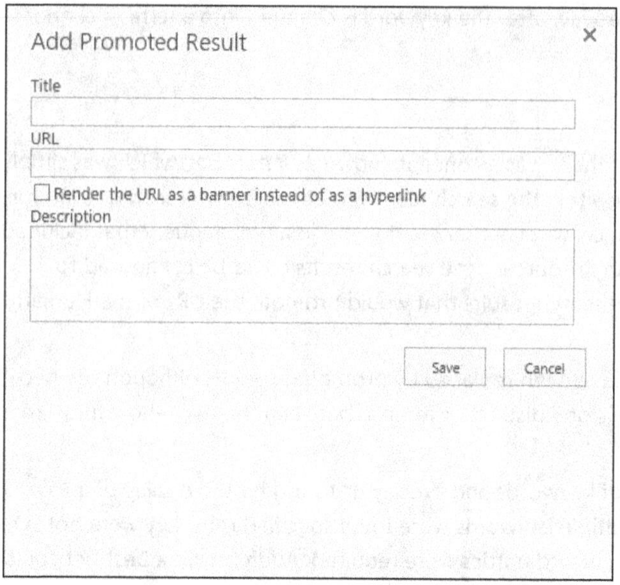

FIGURE 1-12 Adding a promoted result.

As with best bets, a promoted result can display a message and a link to a location or item.

A new field has been added to the promoted result: Render The URL As A Banner Instead Of As A Hyperlink. It provides for the display of a banner about a topic instead of a normal text URL.

Building a new query rule to contain the promoted result requires three actions:

1. Selecting an appropriate search context

2. Specifying the query condition(s); choices include the following:

    A. Query Matches Keyword Exactly

    B. Query Contains Action Term

    C. Query Matches Dictionary Exactly

    D. Query Mode Common in Source

    E. Result Type Commonly Clicked

    F. Advanced Query Text Match

3. Specifying the resulting action(s):

    A. Add a Promoted Result Above Search Results

    B. Add a Result Block Displaying A Specific Portion Of Search Results

    C. Change The Ranked Results By Changing The Query

> **IMPORTANT** **ALTERING EXISTING QUERY RULES**
>
> Simply stated, SharePoint 2013 does not enable you to alter any of the built-in query rules. If you want to build a query based on an existing rule, you must first copy it and then alter the copy; the original's edit menu is always grayed out.

CREATING A SAMPLE PROMOTED RESULT

Let's go through the process of creating a simple promoted result. The requirements for this example are as follows:

- The Human Resources site (http://hr.boston.local) has to be displayed within search as a promoted result when users specify one of the following search phrases:

  - 401K

  - Benefits

  - Vacation

  - Hiring

  - Termination

  - Recruiting

  - Leave

- To keep this simple, the accompanying query rule will require an exact match between the query and the keyword.

- You will not show the promoted result as a banner, merely displaying it instead as a URL for the users to click.

- The query will be scoped to your particular site, not the entire site collection.

First, you must build the query itself. To begin, do the following:

1. In the upper-right corner of the screen, select Settings (gear icon).

2. Scroll down and select Site Settings.

3. On the Site Settings page, scroll to the Search section and select Query Rules.

   If you want to instead build a query that affects the entire site collection, from Site Collection Administration, select Search Query Rules.

4. On the Manage Query Rules page, select the Local SharePoint results (System) context (note that there are several other contexts in an OOB configuration).

5. A series of queries appear beneath the query rule section; unless you have already built some queries, these rules are built in and cannot be edited.

6. Select the New Query Rule selection beneath the context selection.

7. On the Add Query Rule page, make the following selections:

A. In the General Information section, choose the following:

  - Rule Name: HR Promotion

B. In the Query Conditions section, choose the following:

  - Query Conditions: Query Matches Keyword Exactly

  - Query Exactly Matches One Of These Phrases (Semi-Colon Separated): 401K; Benefits; Vacation; Hiring; Termination; Recruiting; Leave

Now that the context and query conditions have been set, it's time to build the promoted result, as follows:

1. In the Actions section, select Add Promoted Result.

2. Note that although Add New Promoted Result is selected, you can also choose to select an existing promoted result and make changes.

3. Add the following items:

   A. Title: Human Resources

   B. URL: *http://hr.boston.local*

   C. Render The URL As A Banner: Leave unselected

   D. Description: The HR Team Is Available To Assist With All Your Human Resources Requirements

4. Click **Save**.

5. Click the **Publishing** menu item (below the Actions section). In this section, you can do the following:

   A. Choose to activate/deactivate the rule (note that you are not activating/deactivating the promoted result)

   B. Set the following fields:

   - Start Date

   - End Date

   - Review Date

   - Contact for this Query Rule

After you click **Save** to complete the creation of the query rule, you should see the completed query rule on the Manage Query Rules page (see Figure 1-13).

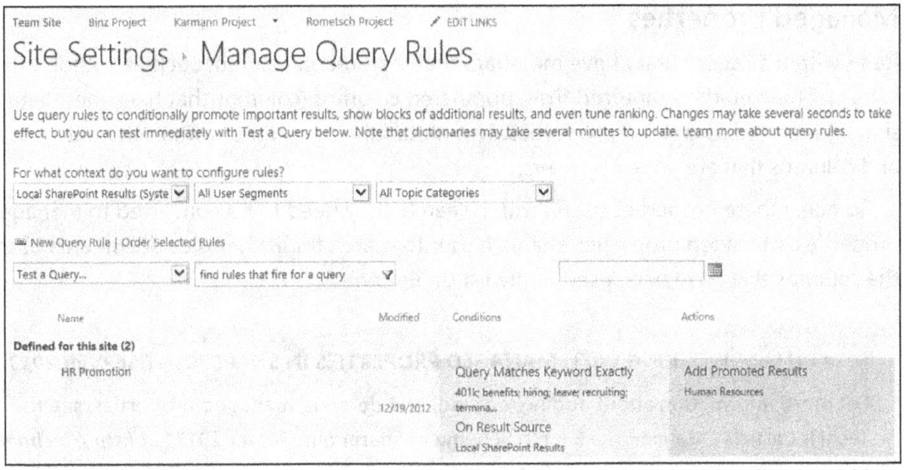

FIGURE 1-13 Manage Query Rules page.

At this point, you can return to the main page for your site and verify that your promoted results are working as expected. Type any of the following search terms and click the search icon (see Figure 1-14):

- 401K
- Benefits
- Vacation
- Hiring
- Termination
- Recruiting
- Leave

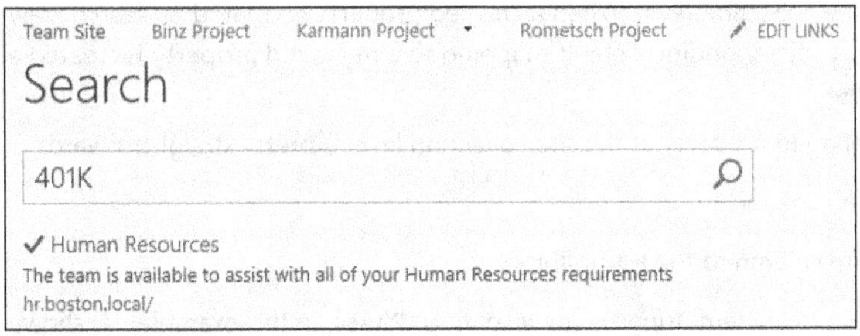

FIGURE 1-14 Successfully promoted result in search.

Managed properties

Items within a list or library have metadata that is stored in columns such as author, title, and subject. The metadata captured from populated columns (columns that have metadata assigned) is stored as crawled properties. This metadata is captured from both built-in columns and columns that are added by users.

To make these properties useful within search, they need to be converted to managed properties. Managed properties enable a user to search for list items or documents based on the columns that have been used in the list or library.

> **MORE INFO** **WORKING WITH MANAGED PROPERTIES IN SHAREPOINT SERVER 2013**
>
> For more information about adding, editing, and deleting managed properties, see the TechNet article "Manage the Search Schema in SharePoint Server 2013" at *http://technet. microsoft.com/en-us/library/jj219667.aspx.*

So, for instance, if you want to perform an advanced search based on documents in which the author of the item is Bob Ford, and the title contains the word "Equipment," the crawled properties for each of these columns must first be mapped to a corresponding managed property.

In SharePoint 2010, the mapping between crawled properties and managed properties had to be created manually in the search service application. After the mapping was created, a full search had to complete before the managed properties could be used in a custom search results page (rendered via XSLT). For some environments, this might cause issues because a full crawl of the search corpus could take several days.

Thankfully, the creation of a managed property is quite a bit more streamlined within SharePoint 2013. The ability to create a managed property within Central Administration still exists, but it is also possible (and very likely, as you will see in a moment) to build a managed property at the site collection level. When a crawled property is created by search crawls of the list or library, a corresponding default mapping to a managed property is created at the site collection level.

Creating a managed property at the site collection level is pretty straightforward:

1. Create a site column.

2. Add the site column to the list or library.

3. Add value(s) to an item using the new column (**Phase**, in this example), as shown in Figure 1-15.

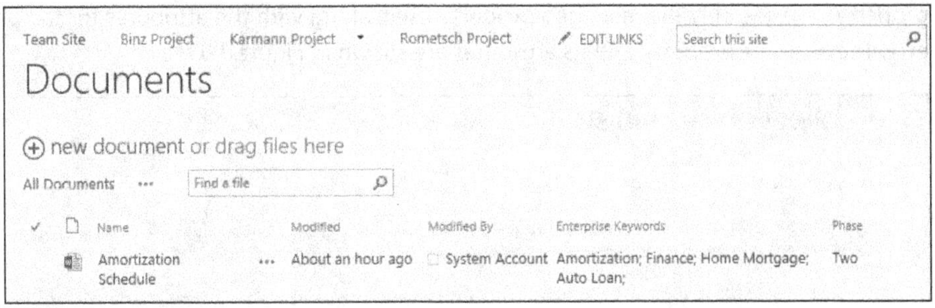

FIGURE 1-15 New site column: Phase.

4. After a search crawl occurs:

   A. A crawled property is created from the site column.

   B. A managed property is created and mapped to the crawled property.

5. To review the newly created properties:

   A. From Site Settings, Site Collection Administration, select Search Schema.

   B. On the page that follows, you can choose to see the crawled properties (see Figure 1-16).

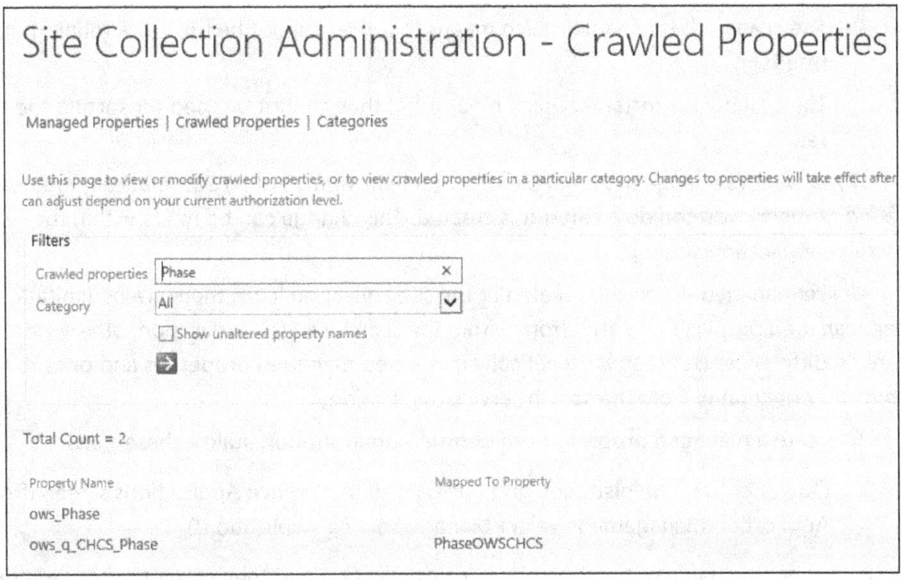

Site Collection Administration - Crawled Properties

Managed Properties | Crawled Properties | Categories

Use this page to view or modify crawled properties, or to view crawled properties in a particular category. Changes to properties will take effect after can adjust depend on your current authorization level.

Filters

Crawled properties   Phase   ×
Category   All   ∨
                     ☐ Show unaltered property names
                     ➡

Total Count = 2

Property Name	Mapped To Property
ows_Phase	
ows_q_CHCS_Phase	PhaseOWSCHCS

FIGURE 1-16 Crawled properties (site collection level).

In the previous screen shot, you see both the crawled properties (ows_Phase and ows_q_CHCS_Phase) and the managed property (PhaseOWSCHCS). If you choose to see just the managed properties (by selecting its link and then entering the name of the managed property) you see only the managed property itself, along with the attributes for the property. The example property and its attributes are shown in Figure 1-17.

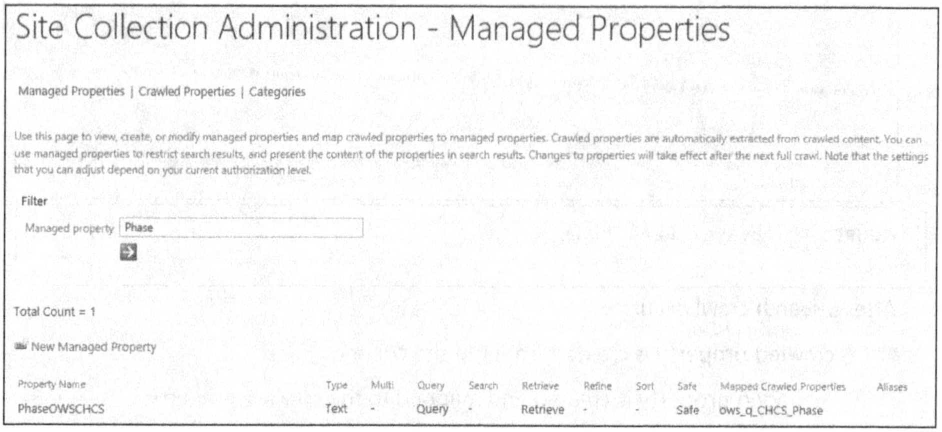

Site Collection Administration - Managed Properties

Managed Properties | Crawled Properties | Categories

Use this page to view, create, or modify managed properties and map crawled properties to managed properties. Crawled properties are automatically extracted from crawled content. You can use managed properties to restrict search results, and present the content of the properties in search results. Changes to properties will take effect after the next full crawl. Note that the settings that you can adjust depend on your current authorization level.

Filter

Managed property Phase

Total Count = 1

New Managed Property

Property Name	Type	Multi	Query	Search	Retrieve	Refine	Sort	Safe	Mapped Crawled Properties	Aliases
PhaseOWSCHCS	Text	-	Query	-	Retrieve	-	-	Safe	ows_q_CHCS_Phase	

FIGURE 1-17 Managed properties (site collection level).

If you decide to create a new managed property at the site collection level, there are a few restrictions:

- They can be of the type Text or Yes/No (Boolean).
- They cannot be refinable, which means that they cannot be used as a refiner for search results.
- They cannot be sortable, which means that they cannot be used for sorting the result set.

If you want to change the refinable or sortable attributes of an automatically created managed property, you can do so after it is created. This change can be made within the search service application settings.

Unlike managed properties created at the site collection level, there are no limitations on managed properties created from within the search service application; otherwise, there are no differences between automatically generated managed properties and ones that are manually generated from the search service application.

To create a managed property from Central Administration, follow these steps:

1. Open Central Administration and navigate to the Service Applications screen (from Application Management, select Manage Service Applications).

2. Select the name of the Search Service Application and then select the Manage menu item from the ribbon.

3. Under the Queries and Results navigation menu, select Search Schema.

At this point, configuration is identical to the menus found in the site collection administration. None of the attributes limitations exists for managed properties created in the search service application.

Planning information management policies

In an increasingly litigious corporate world, the ability to regulate the lifecycle of content is no longer an optional feature for an electronic content management (ECM) system; it has become a core requirement.

SharePoint 2013 provides specific functionality designed to regulate the creation, interaction, and disposition of content. An information management policy is a set of rules that can be assigned to any given piece of content. These rules (also known as policy features) then define behaviors, such as the retention schedule, auditability, or markings (bar codes and labels) for a given piece of content.

> **MORE INFO   INFORMATION MANAGEMENT POLICY PLANNING REFERENCE**
>
> For more details on the creation and use of information management policies, see the TechNet article "Plan for Information Management Policy in SharePoint Server 2013" at *http://technet.microsoft.com/en-us/library/cc262490.aspx*.

There are four sets of policy features available in SharePoint Server 2013: retention, auditing, bar codes, and labels.

Retention policy features

Documents that have to comply with legal regulations often have a retention requirement. This requirement essentially regulates the amount of time that a document can (or should) be legally discoverable within any given ECM system.

After a retention policy feature has been enabled in SharePoint, a retention stage must be added to describe how the item will be managed according to the information management policy. This retention stage requires two elements to be valid: an event and an action. A third element, recurrence, is utilized only when certain actions are selected.

EXAM TIP

Although one stage is the requirement for a retention policy to be considered valid, it is possible to build multiple stages as your business needs require.

An event describes what causes the stage to activate and can either be based on a date property or a custom retention formula (developed via custom code and grayed out by default). The date property is composed of a time period values + a set number of years as defined by your company's file plan. The time period values will be one of these three values:

- **Last Modified**   The date the item was last changed
- **Created Date**   The date the item came into existence, or
- **Declared Record**   The date that an item was declared a legal record

An action defines what happens to the item after the event has taken place and is one of the following:

- **Move to recycle bin**   Relocates the item to the site's recycle bin.
- **Permanently delete**   Bypasses the recycle bin functionality and permanently discards the item.
- **Transfer to another location**   Moves the item to a pre-defined destination location that must be registered for a site.
- **Start a workflow**   Can run a workflow; this option is not available for a site collection policy (discussed in the next section), but is available for a retention schedule based on a list or a content type.
- **Skip to next stage**   Causes the item to skip to the next retention stage.
- **Declare record**   Sets the item to be a legal record, defined "in place" for the site; requires the In Place Records feature to be enabled in the site.
- **Delete previous drafts**   Removes all prior draft (minor) versions of a document; activates the recurrence element, enabling the stage to be repeated based on a periodic schedule.
- **Delete all previous versions**   Removes all prior major and minor versions of a document; activates the recurrence element, enabling the stage to be repeated based on a periodic schedule.

Auditing policy feature

A vital element in any information management policy, auditing enables key personnel to monitor how a document is interacted with and by whom. When the auditing policy feature is enabled, any combination of the following five events can be audited:

- Opening or downloading documents, viewing items in lists, or viewing item properties
- Editing items
- Checking out or checking in items
- Moving or copying items to another location in the site
- Deleting or restoring items

Barcode policy feature

Due to legal regulation and other concerns, documents are sometimes still rendered as paper documents. Printed versions of these documents must still be managed; thus SharePoint's information policies include the barcode policy feature. When enabled, this feature creates a unique identifier value for a document and then inserts a bar code image of that value in the document. Although the default bar codes are compliant with the Code 39 standard (ANSI/AIM BC1-1995, Code 39), you can use the policies object model to add other bar code providers.

Labeling policy feature (deprecated in SharePoint 2013)

The labeling policy feature is provided in SharePoint 2013 for backward compatibility and should not be actively used in new SharePoint sites. The purpose of this policy feature was to enable fixed text and/or document properties to be applied to the printed version of a document.

Assigning an information management policy

Information management policies can be assigned three different ways:

- Policy features can be associated with a site collection policy template; that policy template can be associated with a content type, list, or library.
- Policy features can be associated directly with a content type; the content type can then be added to lists and libraries.
- Policy features can be associated directly with a list or library.

Note the hierarchy in the three different applications of information management; the more direct the application of policy features, the more difficult the administration of the features would be across multiple libraries, lists, or sites.

Another benefit of applying the policy features via site collection policy templates is the prevention of lower-level policy overrides. After the policy has been applied at a high level (the top of the site collection), all subordinate levels utilizing the same content type must inherit the information management policies present in the top-level content type.

Each of the four policy features can be disabled via Central Administration. To disable any of the features, go into Central Administration. From Security, Information Policy, select Configure Information Management Policy.

Creating a new site collection policy

To create a new site collection policy, follow these steps:

1. In the upper-right corner of the screen, select **Settings** (gear icon).

2. Scroll down and select **Site Settings**.

3. On the Site Settings page, scroll to the Site Collection Administration section.

4. Select the **Content Type Policy Templates** section.

5. On the Policies page, click **Create** to begin creating a new information management policy (note that you can also import an existing policy).

6. Type the name of the new policy (and optionally an administrative description of the policy).

7. Type a policy statement. This statement appears to users when they interact with items subject to this policy.

8. Choose and configure any or all policy features as applicable.

EXAM TIP

Site collection policies are scoped to a single site collection. For the sake of consistency, it is possible to export a policy from one site collection and then import it to another for reuse. Be familiar with the steps required in this process.

Planning a managed site structure

SharePoint Server 2010 introduced a new concept to navigation, namely the use of metadata for navigation within lists and libraries. By assigning metadata to individual items (using the term store, which we will be covering in the next section), the content of larger lists and libraries could be more easily navigated and displayed (similar to how views can be used) by using filters on one or more pieces of metadata.

SharePoint Server 2013 expands on this concept, introducing the notion of metadata-based navigation. Using the MMS, a navigational structure can be generated on a fairly dynamic basis, tying multiple sites and site collections together into an organized (and exceptionally flexible) structure.

Metadata-based navigation specifically addresses two key navigational considerations found in previous versions of SharePoint: complex URLs and site collection boundaries.

Complex URLs

In prior versions of SharePoint, it was not uncommon to see complex URLs for pages such as /Lists/Posts/Post.aspx?ID=132 or /Pages/Default.aspx. This sort of URL is not only unfriendly to users trying to remember the location of a particular page but also difficult to integrate into an effective Search Engine Optimization (SEO) strategy.

When attempting to simplify these navigational structures, administrators often would result to non-SharePoint technologies such as the URL rewrite module (found in Internet Information Services [IIS]) to simplify URLs into friendlier URLs. Using this rewriting technology, a structure such as /pages/default.aspx could be more simply represented as /default.aspx.

As with any other technology, the additional administration required for the rewrites to take place could theoretically cause problems, including the following:

- **An administrator's IIS experience level**   Some advanced knowledge of IIS was required for installing and troubleshooting the rewrite module.
- **Regular expressions (Regex)**   The IIS rewrite module relies on the pattern-matching capability of regular expressions to take a particular URL structure (for example, /pages/default.aspx) and rewrite it (for example, /default.aspx).
- The notion that the rewrites happen outside of SharePoint's control, potentially causing issues with navigation, search, and so on if configured incorrectly.

Site collection boundaries

There was also the additional issue of navigation across multiple site collections. When a user navigated within the boundaries of a single site collection, the structure was uniform and consistent, using the global and current site navigational model provided by the SharePoint Server publishing functionality.

The use of a single site collection is easy but not scalable; thus the need for multiple site collections. After multiple site collections were put into use (mostly for the purposes of scalability), a user would encounter an entirely new navigational structure in each distinct site collection.

Path-based navigation

When two site collections need to be included in the same navigational structure, path-based site collections can be used. These site collections are related via the use of managed paths. Two distinct types of managed paths were used: explicit and wildcard.

Explicit managed paths enable two site collections to be put into the same URL path. For instance, if you had a site collection at http://your.url.com/, you could create an explicit managed path (for example, /yoursite) to store another site collection at http://your.url.com/yoursite.

Wildcard managed paths enable one site collection to be the "implied" parent of several site collections. Doing so requires two things:

- All site collections are nested under a path that itself is not a site.
- All site collections in the wildcard are at the same URL level.

If you had a site collection at http://your.url.com/, you could build a wildcard managed path (/projects) to contain all your projects, each in its own site collection. So the projects would be located at http://your.url.com/projects/project1, /project2, /project3, and so on. If a user decided, however, to navigate directly to http://your.url.com/projects, there would be a problem; there is no site at that level, only the wildcard managed path.

> **MORE INFO** **DEFINING MANAGED PATHS**
>
> For more information about creating and implementing new managed paths, review the TechNet article "Define managed paths in SharePoint Server 2013" at *http://technet.micro-soft.com/en-us/library/cc261845.aspx.*

Using metadata for managed navigation

SharePoint Server 2013 introduces a new concept: the idea that navigational metadata can be stored as a descriptive element within the term store. Instead of having to nest site collections under one another for a clean navigational structure and then having to replicate the desired navigation set across each site collection, it is now possible to arrange sites and site collections within a clean, user-friendly, SEO-friendly structure.

After you have designed your navigational metadata structure, SCAs can utilize the metadata control within each site collection to "subscribe" to the navigational structure; conversely, it is also possible for the site administrators to build their own navigational structure in the term store.

Here's the best part: After they are created, these structures are extremely flexible, allowing for changes to be made without the need for potential disruptions (managed paths, backup/restores, and so on).

Implementing managed navigation

Managed navigation is dependent on one or more term sets. A term set is nothing more than a grouping of terms within the term store. Each term set defines a navigational structure, and multiple navigational structures can be utilized, even within a single site collection (if desired).

Within a site, global and current navigation can each utilize a term set for navigation. Note that global and current navigation cannot utilize two separate term sets—only one term set can be specified on the navigation settings page of a site. The individual terms can be set to show in global navigation, current navigation, or both (as you will see shortly).

By default, a SharePoint site utilizes structural navigation; if you have used prior versions of SharePoint, this interface is familiar (see Figure 1-18).

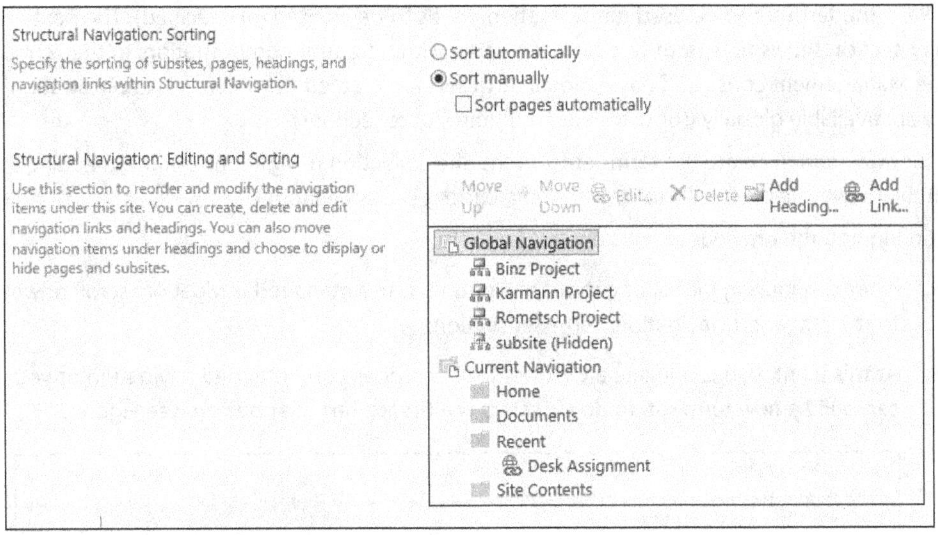

Structural Navigation: Sorting

Specify the sorting of subsites, pages, headings, and
navigation links within Structural Navigation.

○ Sort automatically
◉ Sort manually
   ☐ Sort pages automatically

Structural Navigation: Editing and Sorting

Use this section to reorder and modify the navigation
items under this site. You can create, delete and edit
navigation links and headings. You can also move
navigation items under headings and choose to display or
hide pages and subsites.

Move Up   Move Down   ⚒ Edit...   ✕ Delete   Add Heading...   Add Link...

- Global Navigation
  - Binz Project
  - Karmann Project
  - Rometsch Project
  - subsite (Hidden)
- Current Navigation
  - Home
  - Documents
  - Recent
    - Desk Assignment
  - Site Contents

FIGURE 1-18 Structural navigation.

Converting a site from structural to managed navigation requires only a few steps:

1. In the upper-right corner of the screen, select Settings (gear icon).

2. Scroll down and select Site Settings.

3. On the Site Settings page, scroll to the Look and Feel section and select Navigation.

4. On the Navigation Settings page, you can change global or current navigation from
   structural to managed navigation (see Figure 1-19).

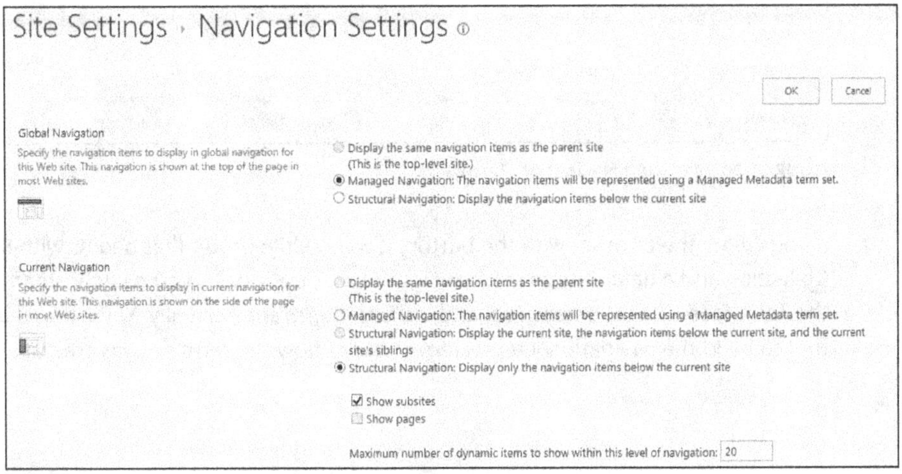

Site Settings › Navigation Settings ①

[OK] [Cancel]

Global Navigation

Specify the navigation items to display in global navigation for
this Web site. This navigation is shown at the top of the page in
most Web sites.

○ Display the same navigation items as the parent site
  (This is the top-level site.)
◉ Managed Navigation: The navigation items will be represented using a Managed Metadata term set.
○ Structural Navigation: Display the navigation items below the current site

Current Navigation

Specify the navigation items to display in current navigation for
this Web site. This navigation is shown on the side of the page
in most Web sites.

○ Display the same navigation items as the parent site
  (This is the top-level site.)
○ Managed Navigation: The navigation items will be represented using a Managed Metadata term set.
○ Structural Navigation: Display the current site, the navigation items below the current site, and the current
  site's siblings
◉ Structural Navigation: Display only the navigation items below the current site

☑ Show subsites
☐ Show pages

Maximum number of dynamic items to show within this level of navigation: [20]

FIGURE 1-19 Navigation settings.

Next, the term set to be used for navigation needs to be created (or specified). The next major section shows how term sets can be created within Central Administration, in the Term Store Management console. If navigational term sets are created from Central Administration, they are available globally (for use across multiple site collections).

For now, we will create the term set from the site collection navigation settings, meaning that they are available locally (only within the current site collection).

Continuing the previous set of steps:

5. After configuring global or current navigation to use managed navigation, scroll down to the Managed Navigation: Term Set section.

6. At this point, you can locate a term set that describes your intended navigation or you can build a new term set; to do so, select the Create Term Set button (see Figure 1-20).

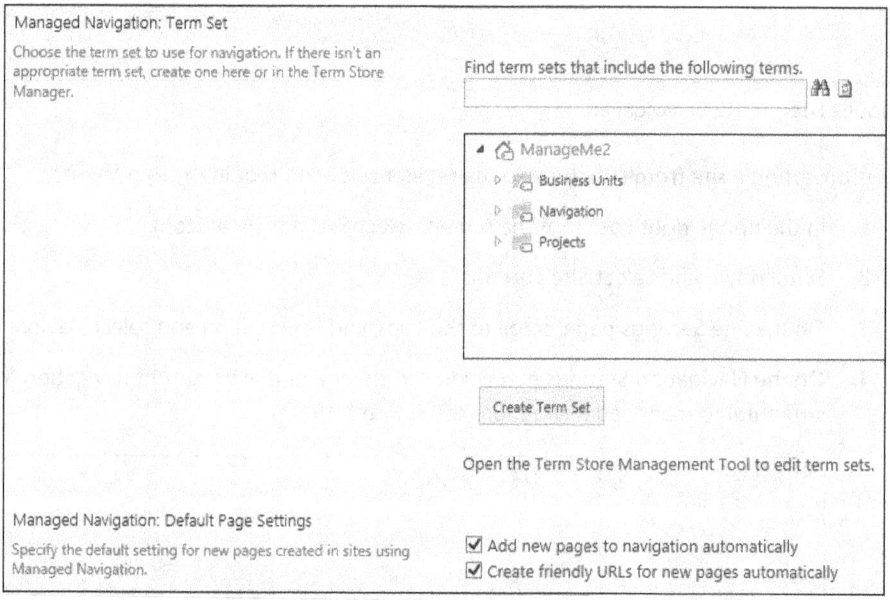

FIGURE 1-20 Managed Navigation: Term Set.

7. If you create the term set with the button, it will build a group that begins with Site Collection and a default term set (see Figure 1-21); optionally, you could instead open the Term Store Management Tool and build the term set manually. You have to use the tool to build the navigational terms regardless of how the term set was created.

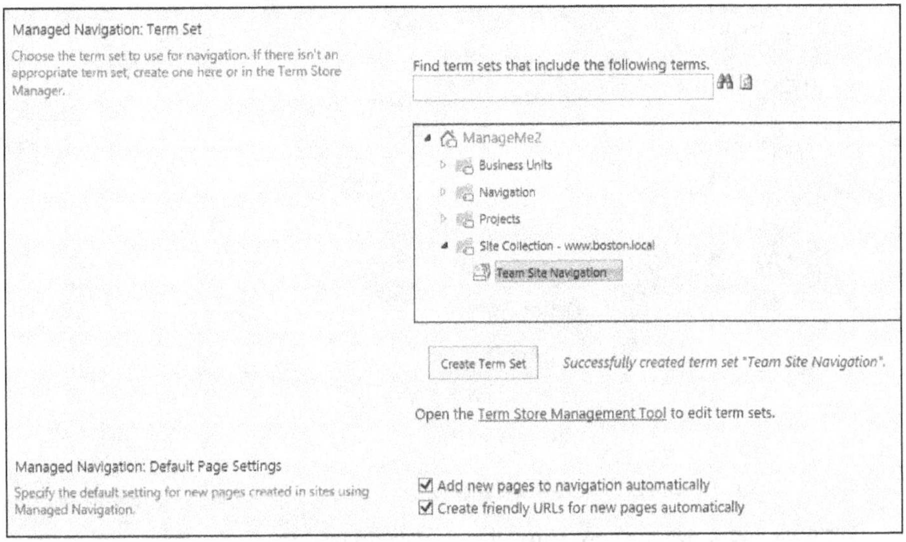

Managed Navigation: Term Set

Choose the term set to use for navigation. If there isn't an appropriate term set, create one here or in the Term Store Manager.

Find term sets that include the following terms.

▲ 🏠 ManageMe2
  ▷ 📑 Business Units
  ▷ 📑 Navigation
  ▷ 📑 Projects
  ▲ 📑 Site Collection - www.boston.local
    📑 Team Site Navigation

Create Term Set   *Successfully created term set "Team Site Navigation".*

Open the Term Store Management Tool to edit term sets.

Managed Navigation: Default Page Settings

Specify the default setting for new pages created in sites using Managed Navigation.

☑ Add new pages to navigation automatically
☑ Create friendly URLs for new pages automatically

FIGURE 1-21 Create a new term set for managed navigation.

8. Open the Term Store Management Tool.

9. When you open the term set and select Intended Use, note that the set is already configured for site navigation; if the set was created from Central Administration, you need to select this check box (see Figure 1-22).

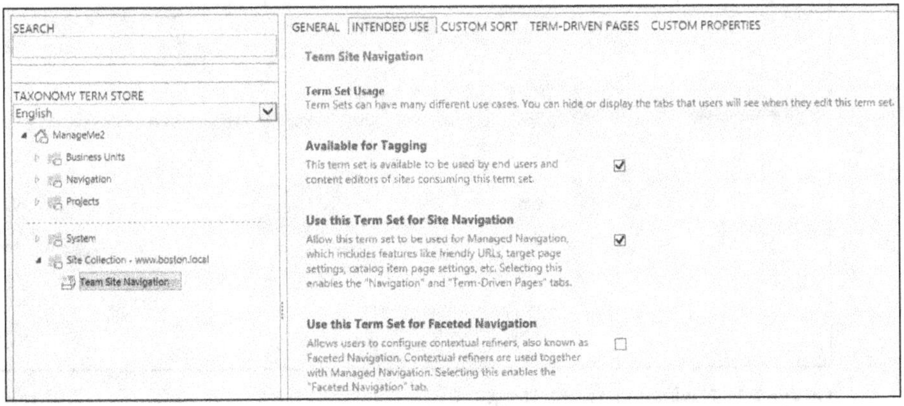

FIGURE 1-22 New term set, built for navigation.

10. Creating a new term is as simple as selecting the drop-down menu and selecting Create Term (see Figure 1-23).

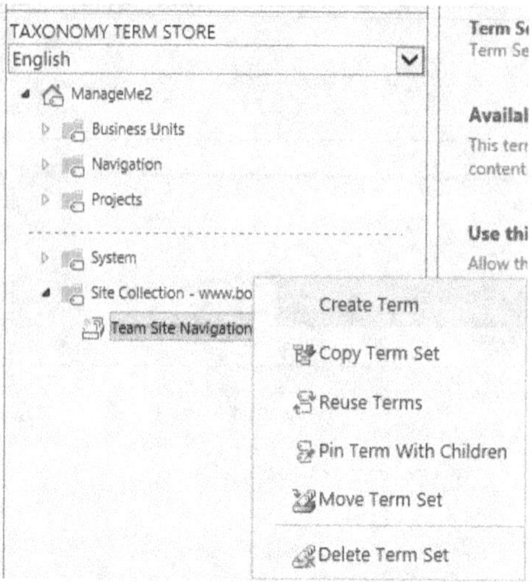

FIGURE 1-23 Creating a new term in the navigational term set.

11. Within each node (term), you can specify whether the term is for use in global or current navigation menus; you can also use the term as a link/header or as a term-driven web page (see Figure 1-24).

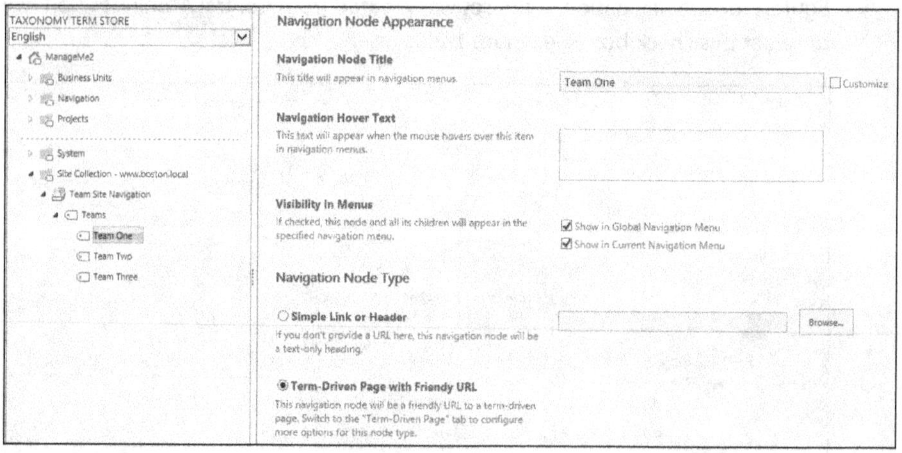

FIGURE 1-24 Navigation node settings.

12. Choosing each node type to be a simple link or header, the finished navigation looks like Figure 1-25.

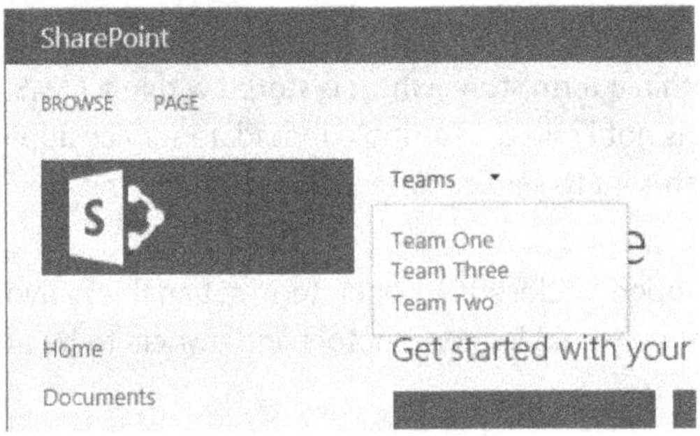

FIGURE 1-25 Completed metadata navigation.

EXAM TIP

Regardless of which navigation type you choose, the ability to create a reliable navigational structure is a critical component in site hierarchy design. Be familiar with the structural navigation concepts (such as managed paths) as well as metadata navigation configuration requirements.

Planning term sets

Term sets are part of the larger set of MMS functionality present in a SharePoint Server 2013 ECM solution. MMS encompasses two distinct groupings of metadata: taxonomy and folksonomy.

- **Taxonomy** The more formalized of the two groupings, taxonomy is hierarchical and deliberate in nature and includes terms and term sets.
- **Folksonomy** The more casual of the two groupings, folksonomy imparts items with metadata via the use of tags/keywords; no hierarchy can be implied or defined.

A term set is nothing more than an intelligent grouping of related terms; terms are nothing more than metadata that can be associated with items in a SharePoint list or library.

EXAM TIP

SharePoint administrators are often not the people who define term sets. Most term sets start as tags and keywords (folksonomy) and are then promoted to a more formal status as part of a term set (taxonomy). Be familiar with how this transition takes place.

Terms

One of the more interesting behaviors of terms is that they can be nested, up to seven levels deep. Additionally, you can designate certain levels of terms as "unavailable for tagging," meaning that you will be using them only for navigational purposes (such as grouping topics by letter, for example, A–F, G–J, and so on).

Term sets

Term sets with SharePoint are stored within a term store, which is stored within a MMS application. A SharePoint implementation is not limited to a single metadata service application; multiple service applications might be present to service different legal or organizational functions.

Term sets can have a status of either open or closed. An open term set enables anyone to contribute a new term; a closed term set only enables contributors and owners to be able to add a new term.

> **IMPORTANT** **SHAREPOINT METADATA HIERARCHY**
>
> MMS Application(s) → Taxonomy Term Store (organized by language) → Term Set Group → Term Sets → Terms

Defining term set functionality

As human beings, we use metadata on a regular basis. We have logical groupings of metadata that describe our existence, such as these:

- **Colors** Red, orange, yellow, green, blue, indigo, violet
- **Sizes** X-small, small, medium, large, X-large
- **Fabrics** Polyester, cotton, wool, silk

In these examples, colors, sizes, and fabrics could all be valid term sets; their values would be considered as terms with a SharePoint environment. Additionally, these term sets could be grouped into a larger term set group, such as clothing.

Local versus global term sets

As term sets are being designed, it is important to consider the audience who will be consuming the metadata. During this design phase, questions such as these often arise:

- Does everyone in the enterprise need access to a particular term?
- Is the term specific in scope?
- Who should be managing the term set?
- What is the desired "footprint" of the term set?

A SharePoint MMS application is associated to a web application via the service application proxy. Terms provided via the proxy can be assigned to items within the desired SharePoint web application; the only consideration that must be made is one of scope.

Term sets are assigned by way of the Term Set Management Tool, which can be utilized at two distinct levels: site collection administration and Central Administration. Term sets created via site collection administration are called local term sets; those created via Central Administration are called global term sets.

Often, terms are generated specifically for the use of a single component/entity of the business; term sets that are scoped to a single site collection are known simply as local term sets.

Storing terms in a local term set simply means that the terms are available for use only within the site collection in which they are generated (although the term set is stored centrally within the MMS application). Such an arrangement might be preferable for items intended to be limited to one segment of the business and/or requiring less formal information management oversight (such as working with an enterprise librarian).

The creation and management of local term sets is done by site collection owners and administrators using the Term Store Management Tool.

Term sets that apply to a large section of the business are generally designed by an information management team. These term sets are often more formalized and are intended for application across multiple sites and site collections within a web application.

The creation and management of global term sets can be done by farm administrators, or (preferably) alongside appropriately trained business stakeholders who have been granted access via the MMS instance management page in Central Administration.

Core term set planning

The process of creating an information taxonomy can seem daunting, even in a relatively small business. The key to a successful metadata planning effort is to approach the information plan one piece at a time.

Members of a particular business unit often volunteer to be early adopters of this information management strategy and are willing advocates for a successful ECM implementation. Traditionally, this is the point at which IT has often attempted to interface with the business stakeholders directly, presumably to try and assess any technical pitfalls that could arise.

As it turns out, it is a common misconception to assume that term set designers have to be technical in order to design an effective metadata taxonomy; truthfully, they do not. Working with an enterprise librarian or design team, it is quite preferable to involve this group of term set designers in planning simply because they have firsthand knowledge of the products and processes that are pertinent to their segment of the business.

> **MORE INFO**   **TERM SET PLANNING WORKSHEETS**
>
> Microsoft provides two distinct metadata planning worksheets in Microsoft Excel format. The term sets planning worksheet (*http://go.microsoft.com/fwlink/p/?LinkId=163486&clcid=0x409*) provides a basic worksheet that can be implemented manually; the detailed term set planning worksheet (*http://go.microsoft.com/fwlink/p/?LinkId=163487&clcid=0x409*) can be used for more in-depth metadata design. Of extra benefit is the fact that the detailed worksheet can be directly imported (in Comma-Separated Value [CSV] format) into the Term Store Management Tool.

Successfully planning a term set involves four core activities: identifying each term set, identifying a term set owner, designing term set groups, and defining the term sets themselves.

Identifying term sets

Identifying what items should belong in a term set (and at what level) is often the hardest part of the entire metadata process. The sheer amount of metadata present in a business can be overwhelming, but there is an easy way to overcome the initial shock: Look for the pain points.

Specifically, you are looking for places that even a limited application of metadata could streamline processes and make information more readily searchable, such as the following:

- Custom columns, particularly those that enable the selection of one or more values (such as choice fields)
- Words or phrases that are being regularly used to tag an item (from folksonomy to taxonomy)
- Metadata that users often use to sort or filter items in a list or library
- Acronyms or abbreviations for a function or product
- Items that are, by definition, hierarchical in nature (for example, inventories)

Items that probably should not be included in a term set might include these:

- Items that have column metadata fields that have already been provided with the SharePoint framework (built-in columns)
- Boolean (yes/no) values
- Items that might have different values in different segments of a business
- Items that have no well-defined values

Identifying term set owners

A term set owner is the person or group responsible for the maintenance of terms in a particular term set. As an example, if a business has locations that are added and removed on a regular basis, the term set owner is the person who does the additions and deletions of terms from the term set.

In more formal term sets (global term sets, in particular), the term set owner is often not a single individual but a small team of people who are responsible for the overall correctness of the term set.

Determine term set groups

Term set groups define security for a particular term set; they also provide for the logical grouping of term sets. Earlier in this section, we combined the term sets of colors, sizes, and fabrics into a term set group.

Users can be designated as contributors for a term set, and these people can be enabled to manage a particular term set in the group. Additionally, individuals can be designated as term set group managers, enabling them to assign and remove permissions to a term set or sets as required.

Defining the term set

After owners are defined for a particular term set, they can either choose to define the term set on their own or designate contributors to a term set to more fully develop the term set. Defining a term set boils down to these three distinct questions:

- What terms belong in any given term set?
- How are terms organized with a term set?
- Who are designated contributors for a given term set?

Creating a new term set

There are at least two ways to begin the process of generating a new term set, and they both use the Term Store Management Tool.

SCAs/owners can find the Term Store Management Tool from any site in the site collection. To begin using the Term Store Management Tool do the following:

1. Click the Settings icon in the upper-right corner of the site.
2. When the drop-down menu appears, select Site Settings.
3. From the Site Settings page that appears, within the Site Administration section, select the Term Store Management link.

Farm administrators and designated term store administrators can find the Term Store Management Tool from within Central Administration. To begin using the Term Store Management Tool, follow these steps:

1. Open Central Administration.
2. In the Application Management section, select Manage Service Applications.
3. Look for the name of the MMS and select its link.
4. The Term Store Management Tool will appear.

Creating a term set from the Term Store Management Tool

Within the Term Set Management Tool, there are two panes. The leftmost pane is hierarchical and enables the administrator to navigate down through the following:

- The Taxonomy Term Store that is being administered (based on language)
- The name of the MMS instance (icon depicted as a house icon with a tag overlay)
- The name of a term set (icon depicted as a manila file folder with a tag overlay)

- The term set (depicted as a series of tags in a group
- To create a new term (depicted as a single tag)

To create the new term set, do the following:

1. Select an existing term set group and then click its drop-down arrow.

2. Note the options; you can do the following:

   A. Create a new term set.

   B. Import a term set (from a comma-delimited UTF-8 CSV file, generated with the detailed planning workbook).

   C. Delete a group (deletes the entire term set Group).

3. Selecting To create a new term set enables you to type a value for its name.

4. At this point, there are four tabs associated with your term set: General, Intended Use, Custom Sort, and Custom Properties.

5. On the General tab for the service application, you can specify the following:

   A. Term Set Name: Specifies the term set name

   B. Description: Enables you to type a description for the term set

   C. Owner: Enables you to choose a primary user or group to designate as an owner for the term set

   D. Contact: Enables you to specify an e-mail for term suggestions and feedback; without this value entered, the suggestion feature is disabled

   E. Stakeholders: Enables you to specify people and groups within the organization who should be notified before major changes are made to the term set

   F. Submission Policy: Enables the term set to be closed or opened; after it's closed, only metadata managers can add terms to the set

   G. Unique Identifier: Displays the GUID associated with this term set

6. On the Intended Use tab, you can specify the following:

   A. **Available For Tagging**   Enables the term set to be used by end users and content editors of sites

   B. **Use This Term Set For Site Navigation**   Enables the term set to be used for managed navigation

7. On the Custom Sort Order tab, you can specify either of the following:

   A. Use Default Sort Order According To The Current Language

   B. Use a Custom Sort Order

8. On the Custom Properties tab, you can create any new custom properties for use in the term set.

Objective summary

- A site collection is a group of sites that are functionally, navigationally, and administratively related to one another.
- Managed navigation uses a metadata structure to assign the navigational taxonomy of a site.
- A content type hub is a specific type of site that has been designated as the source that provides content types to other site collections.
- There are six major components to search in SharePoint 2013: Search Administration, Crawl, Content Processing, Analytics Processing, Indexing, and Query Processing.
- Regularly used keywords can be moved into term sets, allowing for central administration of terms.
- An information management policy is a set of rules that can be assigned to any given piece of content.

Objective review

Answer the following questions to test your knowledge of the information in this objective. You can find the answers to these questions and explanations of why each answer choice is correct or incorrect in the "Answers" section at the end of this chapter.

1. You are attempting to add new keywords to a SharePoint and receive a message that states The Site Does Not Contain A Default Keywords Store. How should you correct this issue?

    A. Add an enterprise keywords site column to the site's content types.

    B. In Central Administration, add an MMS application to the SharePoint farm.

    C. Edit the MMS Connection and then select This Service Application Is The Default Storage Location For Keywords.

    D. Activate the managed keyword service application in Central Administration.

2. You want to define a new information policy feature. The legal requirement for the document type requires that you produce and retain physical copies of each document. You want to use a policy feature that will be supported in the next version of SharePoint.

    Which of the following policy feature types should you choose?

    A. Retention

    B. Bar codes

    C. Labels

    D. Auditing

3. Within the managed metadata service, you want to designate a set of terms specifically for SharePoint navigation. What selection should you make within the Intended Use tab to accomplish this action?

    A. Use This Term Set For Managed Navigation

    B. Make Term Set Unavailable For Tagging

    C. Enable Team Site Navigation

    D. Use This Term Set For Site Navigation

Objective 1.2: Design a logical architecture

In the last objective, you designed the core informational elements for use within the farm. With this component of the plan in hand, you can now shift your focus onto determining the layout of technical components required to implement the newly generated informational design.

This objective focuses on the capabilities present in IIS and SharePoint, which enable you to determine the required structure to implement the logical design, including such topics as storage, authentication, URLs, web applications, and other components.

This objective covers how to:

- Plan application pools.
- Plan web applications.
- Plan for software boundaries.
- Plan content databases.
- Plan host header site collections.
- Plan zones and alternate access mapping.

Planning application pools

As you will discover in the planning for software boundaries section, there is a supported limit of 10 application pools per web server.

At first, it would seem that this number might be some sort of mistake; you see, if you were to build a basic SharePoint farm and run the Farm Configuration Wizard from Central Administration, you would see from IIS Manager that there are already 12 application pools in service before you've built your first web application.

Let's set aside the limits discussion for a moment and talk about what an application pool is used for.

How is an application pool used?

An application pool is a construct used to group web applications logically, based on a number of criteria such as authentication, performance, isolation, and configuration. Web applications contained in an application pool provide functionality for one or more web sites in an IIS farm.

Confused yet? Let's take a look at a SharePoint-specific example of how application pools, web applications, and sites interact.

If you build a SharePoint farm, activate the default service applications (manually or via the Farm Configuration Wizard) and then build the first site (using the defaults provided). You wind up with several application pools, even more web applications, and a few SharePoint-specific web sites (see Figure 1-26).

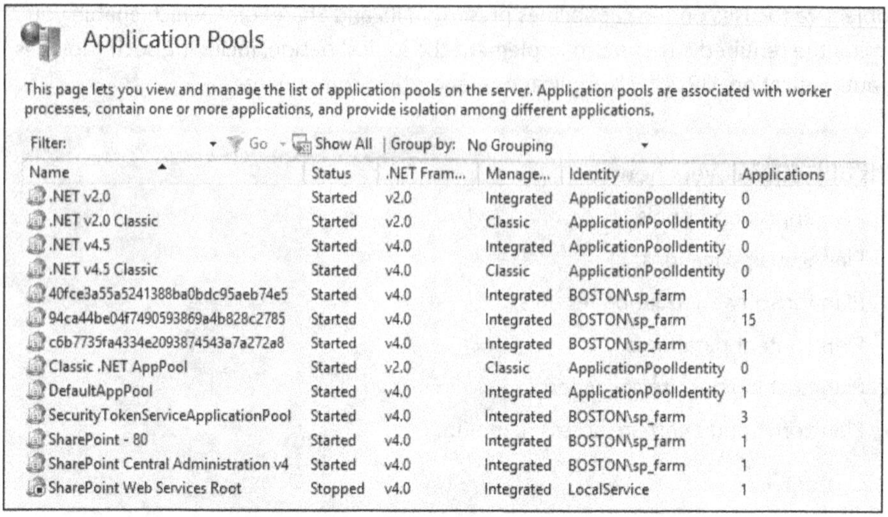
Application Pools
This page lets you view and manage the list of application pools on the server. Application pools are associated with worker processes, contain one or more applications, and provide isolation among different applications.
Filter:
Go
Show All
Group by: No Grouping
Name
Status
.NET Fram...
Manage...
Identity
Applications
.NET v2.0 Started v2.0 Integrated ApplicationPoolIdentity 0
.NET v2.0 Classic Started v2.0 Classic ApplicationPoolIdentity 0
.NET v4.5 Started v4.0 Integrated ApplicationPoolIdentity 0
.NET v4.5 Classic Started v4.0 Classic ApplicationPoolIdentity 0
40fce3a55a5241388ba0bdc95aeb74e5 Started v4.0 Integrated BOSTON\sp_farm 1
94ca44be04f7490593869a4b828c2785 Started v4.0 Integrated BOSTON\sp_farm 15
c6b7735fa4334e2093874543a7a272a8 Started v4.0 Integrated BOSTON\sp_farm 1
Classic .NET AppPool Started v2.0 Classic ApplicationPoolIdentity 0
DefaultAppPool Started v4.0 Integrated ApplicationPoolIdentity 1
SecurityTokenServiceApplicationPool Started v4.0 Integrated BOSTON\sp_farm 3
SharePoint - 80 Started v4.0 Integrated BOSTON\sp_farm 1
SharePoint Central Administration v4 Started v4.0 Integrated BOSTON\sp_farm 1
SharePoint Web Services Root Stopped v4.0 Integrated LocalService 1

FIGURE 1-26 Application pools supporting a SharePoint farm.

Looking at these application pools, we see that there is a SharePoint - 80 application pool. Filtering on this pool (by right-clicking the app pool and selecting view applications), you see that this pool hosts a single application for the SharePoint - 80 site (see Figure 1-27).

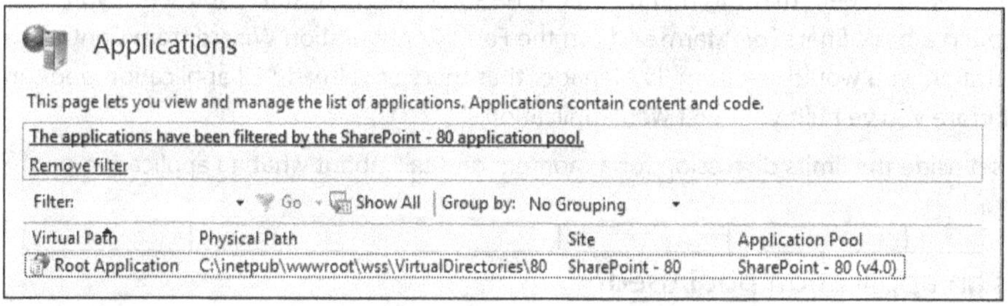
Applications
This page lets you view and manage the list of applications. Applications contain content and code.
The applications have been filtered by the SharePoint - 80 application pool.
Remove filter
Filter:
Go
Show All
Group by: No Grouping
Virtual Path
Physical Path
Site
Application Pool
Root Application C:\inetpub\wwwroot\wss\VirtualDirectories\80 SharePoint - 80 SharePoint - 80 (v4.0)

FIGURE 1-27 The root web application for the SharePoint - 80 site.

There is also another application pool that hosts a different application but is also providing services to the SharePoint - 80 site. Filtering instead on the SecurityTokenServiceApplicationPool, you see that it is linked to the SharePoint - 80 site as well as to the Central Administration and SharePoint Web Services sites (see Figure 1-28).

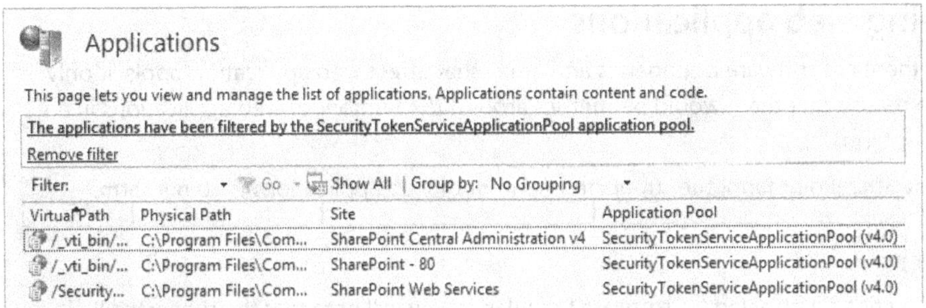

FIGURE 1-28 The SecurityTokenServiceApplicationPool and its associated sites.

Web application pool limits guidance

As a rule, you should seek to minimize the number of web application pools. Software boundary and limits guidance (which is covered shortly) states that no more than 10 web application pools exist in a farm.

There are two core reasons for this limitation: available random access memory (RAM) and usage characteristics.

Each web application pool adds about 100–200 megabytes (MB) of overhead to begin with plus the amount of memory required to run each site in the pool.

Before you add a new pool, consider whether an existing pool can be used to host any new web applications. The number of pools might not initially be an issue, but as SharePoint usage grows within your organization, you might find that the web servers in your farm begin to run short of available RAM.

A heavily trafficked web application pool can quickly generate a RAM load that can grow into the multigigabyte (GB) range (sometimes exceeding the 10 GB mark).

Considerations for building web applications

You might want to build a new web application pool for any of the following reasons:

- Grouping web applications that run with the same configuration settings
- Isolating web applications that require unique configuration settings
- Providing security by running a particular group of web sites under a closely monitored service account for auditing purposes
- Resource isolation:
  - To prevent an outage of the entire IIS application based on one or more misbehaving or failed web applications
  - For ISPs to separate application pools based on customer resource needs

Before adding a new web application, consider using Performance Monitor (perfmon.exe) to get a baseline of existing RAM usage. Monitoring a SharePoint environment is a topic that is covered in Chapter 5, "Maintain a core SharePoint environment."

Planning web applications

Because there are software boundaries and limits that affect web application pools, it only stands to reason that there would be metrics around the number of web applications in a SharePoint farm.

For any SharePoint farm, the supported number of web applications is 20 per farm.

> **EXAM TIP**
>
> In the section on planning for software boundaries, you will note that the supported limit for web applications in a farm is set to 20. This is not a per-web application pool limit, but a limit for the entirety of the SharePoint farm. As with the web application pools, this limitation is memory-dependent, and baseline RAM monitoring is recommended before increasing the web application count to that level.

Planning the web app configuration

Several configuration items must be considered when planning web applications in a new SharePoint farm. Recording each of these decisions on or before the new web application is implemented results in a streamlined, repeatable installation as well as providing documentary evidence of the installation processes that have occurred previously.

Although the name of the web application might seem trivial at first, developing a naming standard for both your web applications and the content databases that they interact with is a key first effort at documentation. There are few feelings worse than receiving that phone call after stopping/deleting the wrong web application during business hours.

Determining the purpose of a web application before it is implemented guides the direction of its configuration. Defining this purpose can be as easy as developing a set of questions such as the following:

- What group of users does this application serve (intranet, extranet, Internet)?
- How are users expected to authenticate?
- What type of navigation do users expect when they visit the site or site collections in this web application?

Although not technically part of a web application's design, the manner in which site collections will be created and deployed has a direct bearing on how a web application should be configured. There are two distinct choices:

- Host named site collections
- Path-based site collections

Configuration choices made at creation time for the web application have direct bearing on which type of site collections can be utilized within your new web application.

Host named site collections are discussed later in this chapter (and will be compared with path-based site collections).

Authentication provider and type

When a new web application is created, there are several choices available for authentication. Choosing which authentication methods will be available generally depends on the audience the web application will serve:

- Windows authentication
  - Integrated Windows authentication (NTLM or Kerberos)
  - Basic authentication
- Forms-based authentication
  - Using the ASP.NET membership and role provider
- Trusted identity provider
  - SAML token-based authentication

Anonymous access

Although not technically a form of authentication, enabling anonymous access for a web application enables users to retrieve content without the need for a user name/password combination.

Allowing anonymous access does not mean that content in a web application will be immediately available to users; it simply means that site administrators can enable anonymous authorization to site content.

This setting should be left on when using forms authentication mode because certain forms-aware client applications might not correctly authenticate without it.

Database server and authentication type for the web application

Working with the SQL DBA team, you should be able to determine which Microsoft SQL database server or instance should host your SharePoint content databases.

The SQL database administrator (DBA) will let you know which type of authentication is acceptable, but this authentication must be one of the following:

- Windows authentication (recommended)
- SQL authentication

Specifying a failover database server

There are currently three types of high availability (HA) solutions provided by SQL Server; however, the only one that SharePoint is aware of (the others are transparent) is SQL database mirroring.

When a SharePoint database is mirrored, SharePoint must not only know the name/instance of the principal server (where the database read/write transactions are occurring) but also the name/instance of the mirror server (the read-only copy of the database). If the mirrored database is failed over, SharePoint then knows the location of the alternative name/instance.

As stated previously, there are three SQL HA options available:

- SQL clustering (SQL 2008 R2 and 2012)
- SQL high availability groups (SQL 2012)
- SQL mirroring (SQL 2008 R2 and 2012)

> **IMPORTANT** **SQL MIRRORING HAS BEEN DEPRECATED AFTER SQL 2012**
>
> Although SQL mirroring is still supported in SQL 2012, it has been deprecated, meaning that it will not be supported in the next version of SQL. If you are creating a new SharePoint 2013 farm or upgrade, now might be a good time to consider one of the other options (high-availability groups are the preferred replacement for mirroring).

SQL database planning is discussed in greater detail later in this section.

Service application connections

SharePoint 2013 provides service application functionality (User Profile, Search, Excel Services, and so on) via a series of service application proxies.

These proxies are usually collected into a proxy group (the first one is called "default," appropriately enough), but it is possible to connect to one or more proxies by simply selecting a custom connection and selecting the check boxes of the proxies that you want to connect the new web application to.

Alternate Access Mapping (AAM) URLs and web application zones

Alternate Access Mapping (AAM) URLs are a mechanism that allows for a single site collection to be associated to multiple URLs.

Zones are logical constructs that define several different means of accessing the same web application. Each zone can have different types of authentication mechanisms based on how a user would be accessing the site.

Both AAMs and zones are covered later in this section.

Planning for software boundaries

Software boundaries can be interpreted as operational limitations for a system. Some limits are finite, with a maximum allowed value, whereas others exceed performance or recommended limitations.

Boundaries, thresholds, and limits

To better understand these limits, consider a new car. This car might have the following:

- Four doors (a boundary)
- A maximum weight recommendation (occupants and cargo) of 1,000 pounds (a threshold)
- A maximum engine rotations per minute (RPM) limitation as given by the tachometer (a limit)

The number of doors that the car possesses is a value that cannot be changed without significantly altering the car's design. Exceeding the weight recommendation probably won't cause the car to stop functioning, but will significantly affect both its performance and economy. Finally, exceeding the maximum RPM limitation is entirely possible, but the engine could fail and would surely not be warranted by the manufacturer.

Similar to our car analogy, SharePoint Server 2013 has three classes of software boundaries and limits: boundaries, thresholds, and supported limits.

Boundaries

A boundary is an absolute limit, meaning that the value given cannot be exceeded in the current version of SharePoint.

An example of this type of limit is the number of zones in a web application; there are always five: default, intranet, extranet, Internet, and custom.

Thresholds

A threshold has an initial value set, meaning that the value can be modified to a maximum value (boundary).

Before altering these values, consideration should be given as to whether your specific infrastructure can accommodate the increased load that might be caused by this change.

Supported limits

A supported limit for any particular configuration parameter is a set value based on testing conducted by Microsoft.

Although you can exceed supported limits, you might encounter unexpected results; these results could come in the form of diminished performance or unexpected behavior in the farm.

Boundary and limits overview

By the time SharePoint Server 2013 is released to manufacturing (RTM), it has gone through several development cycles. In addition to these development efforts, it has perhaps been vetted by Microsoft development and IT Pro teams, business users within Microsoft,

Technology Adoption Program (TAP) members from larger external corporations, selected external partners, and others.

A direct result of the internal and external testing and usage studies carried out by Microsoft is the sheer amount of metrics documented in this process. Operational characteristics are gathered and compiled for each major component of a SharePoint farm, and recommendations are documented for optimal performance characteristics.

> **MORE INFO**   **SOFTWARE BOUNDARIES AND LIMITS FOR SHAREPOINT 2013**
>
> Microsoft regularly updates a complete listing of the software boundaries and limits of SharePoint. The current software boundaries and limitations for SharePoint can be found on TechNet at *http://technet.microsoft.com/en-us/library/cc262787*.

Listed in the following sections is a subset of the recommended guidelines for major components of a SharePoint environment, along with their values and limit types. The sections shown do not include limits for SharePoint features such as Search, Managed Metadata, or Workflow (they can, however, be found in the software boundaries and limits TechNet article).

Web application limits

These limits include the following guidelines:

- **Web application**   This is a supported limit of fewer than 20 web applications per farm. Limit the number of web applications as much as possible, choosing instead to create additional host named site collections.

- **Zone**   This is a boundary limit of five zones per each web application and is hard-coded into the system; the zones include default, intranet, extranet, Internet, and custom.

- **Managed path**   This is a supported limit of 20 per web application; each managed path is cached on the web server, requiring additional CPU resources to process. Although exceeding this limit is possible, the system should be tested in depth to ensure no performance degradation.

- **Solution cache size**   This is a threshold limit of 300 MB per wen application. The InfoPath Forms Service keeps solutions in cache to avoid retrieving them from disk. When the cache size is exceeded, performance is degraded. This limit value can be changed using the Set-SPInfoPathFormsService PowerShell cmdlet.

Web server and application limits

These limits include the following guidelines:

- **Application pools**   This is a supported limit of 10 per web server; this number is a guideline that is heavily influenced by the following:
  - The amount of RAM available on the web servers.

- The usage characteristics for any given web application. A single highly active app pool can consume in excess of 10 GB of RAM.

Content database limits

These limits include the following guidelines:

- **Number of content databases** This is a supported limit of 500 per farm; exceeding this number does not tend to alter performance for end user operations on SharePoint:
  - It does negatively affect the performance of administrative operations (such as creating a new site collection).
  - If a large number of content databases are added to a farm, the recommendation is that PowerShell be favored over the web management interface for administering the web application.
- **Content database size** There are three supported limits:
  - For general usage scenarios, the supported limit is 200 GB per content database, with a limit of 100 GB recommended to ensure ease of backup and restore for site collections.
  - For all usage scenarios, the supported limit is 4 terabytes (TB) per content database, but you must be able to do the following:
    - Provide disk subsystem performance of 0.25 IOPS per GB minimum, with a preferred value of 2 IOPS per GB for optimal performance.
    - Have developed plans for high availability, disaster recovery, future capacity, and performance testing.
  - For document archive scenarios (only), there is no explicit content database limit; sites in these databases must be based on the document center or records center site templates:
    - As an average, less than 5 percent of the content in this database can be accessed and less than 1 percent modified or written.
    - Interactive elements such as alerts, workflows, link fix-ups, or item level security should not be used (content routing workflows are the exception).

> **MORE INFO** **ESTIMATING PERFORMANCE AND CAPACITY REQUIREMENTS FOR LARGE-SCALE DOCUMENT REPOSITORIES**
>
> Large document repositories, such as those found in the all usage and document archive scenarios of the preceding "Content database limits" section, should be constructed based on the guidelines found in the Estimate Performance and Capacity Requirements for Large Scale Document Repositories document at *http://technet.microsoft.com/en-us/library/ff608068.aspx*. This document was written for the 2010 version of SharePoint Server, but is still quite pertinent and will most likely be updated in the near future.

- **Content database items**   This is a supported (and tested) limit of 60 million items; exceeding this limit should include multiple content databases.
- **Site collections per content database**   This is a supported limit of 10,000 site collections maximum:
    - 2,500 nonpersonal site collections and 7,500 personal site collections.
    - 10,000 personal site collections.
    - This limitation has to do with upgrade times; larger numbers of site collections results in more difficult upgrades.
    - Content databases have a default warning and maximum levels of 2,000 and 5,000 sites, respectively.
    - Setting the warning and maximum levels for the number of sites in a content database can be done via Central Administration or the Set-SPContentDatabase commandlet with the -WarningSiteCount parameter.
- **Remote BLOB storage subsystem on Network Attached Storage (NAS)**   This is a boundary limit of 20 milliseconds maximum to the first byte response time from the NAS.

Site collection limits

These limits include the following guidelines:

- **Site collections per farm**   This is a supported limit of 750,000 sites (500,000 personal sites and 250,000 standard sites):
    - An excessive concentration of site collections within a single web application can place a substantial load on the memory allocated to a web server.
    - Search crawls across a large volume of site collections can also generate excessive memory loads on a web server.
    - As a safety measure, you should plan to configure a web application to recycle before memory on any web server falls beneath 2 GB.
- **Web sites per site collection**   This is a supported limit of 250,000 per site collection and speaks directly to the amount of sites that are nested beneath other sites in a particular site collection.
- **Site collection size**   This is a supported limit wherein a single site collection can utilize all the space afforded to it by the content database. As a result, the recommendation is that the content database (and by extension, the site collection) be limited to 100 GB.
- **Number of device channels per publishing site collection**   This is a boundary limit of 10 device channels.

List and library limits

These limits include the following guidelines:

- **List row size** This is a boundary limit of 8,000 bytes per row; 256 bytes are reserved for built-in columns, which leaves 7,744 bytes for end-user columns. The size per type of column is discussed in the section on column limits.

    - This limit can present itself when promoting a large amount of columns from an InfoPath form.

- **File size** This is a boundary limit of 2 GB; the default maximum file size is 50 MB but can be increased to 2 GB. Increasing file size to 2 GB can have a negative effect on farm performance.

- **Documents** This is a supported limit of 30 million documents per library; however, care should be given in advance about how documents will be presented with the use of nesting folders or views.

- **Major versions** This is a supported limit of 400,000 major versions of documents; exceeding this amount can cause issues with basic file operations (open, save, delete, version history, and so on).

- **Minor versions** This is a boundary limit of 511 minor file versions and cannot be exceeded.

- **Items** This is a supported limit of 30 million items per list; performance can be increased in large lists by way of views, and so on, although the limit can itself be affected by the following:

    - How many columns are in the list; large numbers of columns in a large list will negatively affect performance.

    - What the usage characteristics of the list are; large numbers of users reading and writing content to a large list will negatively affect performance.

- **Rows size limit** This is a supported limit of six table rows internal to the database used for a list or library item; so called "wide lists," which contain a large number of columns (see list row size on the previous page) might be wrapped over several table rows in a content database.

    - Six rows is the default size limit.

    - To accommodate more rows, farm administrators can alter the number of rows using PowerShell and the object model method SPWebApplication.MaxListItem-RowStorage.

- **Bulk operations** This is a boundary limit of 100 items per bulk operation; the user interface allows for the selection of and interaction with a maximum of 100 items in any one operation.

- **List view lookup threshold** This is a threshold limit of eight join operations per query; specifies the maximum number of joins per query (lookup, person/group, workflow status, and so on) and blocks any join requests beyond the limit.

- **List view threshold**   Specifies the maximum number of items that can be processed by a user during business hours. Outside this time window, queries are unrestricted.

  - List view threshold for users is a threshold limit of 5,000 items processed at any one time.

  - List view threshold for auditors and administrators is a threshold limit of 20,000 items processed at any one time.

- **Subsite**   This is a threshold limit of 2,000 per site view; enumerating subsites for a given site past the 2,000 limit (via the interface) does not perform well. This limitation also affects the all site content page and the tree view control.

- **Coauthoring in Word and PowerPoint (.docx, .pptx, and .ppsx files)**   This is a threshold limit of 10 concurrent editors per document; it is possible to have as many as 99 coauthors for any given document (this is a hard limit), but performance will degrade after 10 coauthors are editing the document.

- **Security scope**   This is a threshold limit of 1,000 per list; this is a maximum number and should not be exceeded.

> **MORE INFO**   **DESIGNING LARGE LISTS AND MAXIMIZING LIST PERFORMANCE**
>
> Lists and document libraries containing a large volume of items have the same performance characteristics and supported limits. As the amount of individual items increases, performance can be adversely affected. Microsoft provides prescriptive guidance for maximizing the performance of large lists and libraries in the "Designing large lists and maximizing list performance" document that can be found at *http://technet.microsoft. com/en-us/library/cc262813*. This document was written for the 2010 version of SharePoint Server but is still quite pertinent and will most likely be updated in the near future.

Page limits

These limits include the following guideline:

- **Web parts**   This is a threshold limit of 25 per wiki or web part page; this limit is an estimate because the complexity of the web parts determines how many can be used on a page before performance is affected.

Security limits

These limits include the following guidelines:

- **Number of SharePoint groups a user can belong to**   This is a supported limit of 5,000; this is not a hard limit, but follows the way Active Directory membership behaves. Exceeding this limit causes slower performance based on the amount of security checks required for an individual user.

- **Users in a site collection**   This is a supported limit of 2 million per site collection; if this number is to be exceeded, management of the site collection should be done via PowerShell instead of the user interface.

- **Active Directory principals/users in a SharePoint group**   This is a supported limit of 5,000 per SharePoint group; performance is the main consideration here because fetching user for permissions validation and rendering memberships can be adversely affected.

- **SharePoint groups**   This is a supported limit of 10,000 per site collection; beyond 10,000 groups, actions such as adding a user to a group, creating a new group, and rendering group views can take more time to process.

- **Security principal; size of the security scope**   This is a supported limit of 5,000 per Access Control List (ACL); every time the scope changes, there is a calculation that occurs. As the scope size increases, so does the amount of time required for the calculation.

EXAM TIP

There is a significant number of these metrics given for SharePoint 2013. It would be quite hard to memorize each limit and know whether it is a boundary, threshold, or limit (for the test); concentrate on the ones that have the largest impact—those that affect RAM, storage, and processor capacity.

Planning content databases

SharePoint administrators often become de facto SQL administrators as well; the level of SQL familiarity required by a SharePoint implementer is often fairly significant. SQL databases constitute an entire segment of the web/app/data SharePoint farm environment, so it only stands to reason that a SharePoint installation's health is heavily invested in the performance and storage characteristics of the SQL environment that supports it.

Software boundary considerations

In the previous section, there are some boundaries given for content databases:

- Five hundred content databases per farm (supported limit)
- General content database size recommendations:
  - 100 GB maximum recommended
  - 200 GB supported limit
- A supported limit of 4 TB per content database for archival content databases with very little read/write access
- No explicit limit for content databases housing document center or record center sites

If you examine these limits for a moment, you come to the realization that an environment approaching these levels would be quite large. A farm containing 500 databases with an average content database size of 50 GB each would place the SQL back-end storage requirement somewhere in the neighborhood of 25 TB of storage required.

EXAM TIP

In some organizations, the data tier of your SharePoint farm will be administered by one or more SQL database administrators. This team will most likely not be familiar with the specifications and limitations present in SharePoint 2013, so you will need to be able to explain these metrics to them.

A database of 50 GB in size is quite common. As the database continues to grow beyond this limit exceeding 100 GB in size, it will set off the SharePoint Health Analyzer rule: Some content databases are growing too large.

MORE INFO   SHAREPOINT HEALTH ANALYZER

In fact, there are two SharePoint Health Analyzer rules that have to do with database sizing. The first database has large amounts of unused space is a weekly check that databases that exceed 100 GB in size will set off the SharePoint Health Analyzer rule: Some content databases are growing too large.

Scaling a SharePoint implementation

A content database can house several site collections, but a site collection can reside only within a single content database; with this thought in mind, we begin to consider how to "scale-out" our environment.

Before contemplating the site collection taxonomy, you might first want to consider the lifecycle of site collections. Some site collections are fairly permanent, providing the structural backbone of your SharePoint environment; others might be quite temporary (a one-off collaborative site collection, for instance).

In an environment in which you, the SharePoint administrator, are responsible for managing growth, the initial goal is scalability. By scaling your SharePoint environment to multiple site collections, you now can control growth.

As shown in Figure 1-29, a content database is initially configured with six site collections:

1. Over time, one of the site collections begins to experience rapid growth and begins to cause the content database to increase in size.

2. The SharePoint farm administrator recognizes this growth and moves the larger site collection into its own content database to manage growth.

3. After the content database is moved, its growth can be restricted by setting maximum number of site collections in the database to 1.

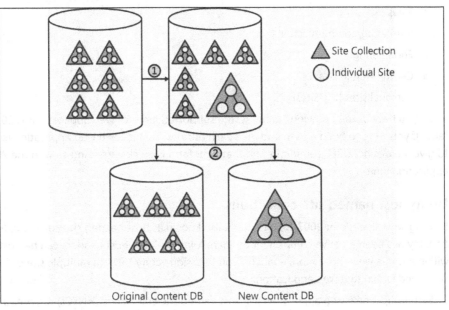

FIGURE 1-29 Moving a site collection into its own content database.

Planning host named site collections

This section and the one that follows, "Planning zones and Alternate Access Mapping," are closely related; not because one follows the other, but because the two of them put together result in a choice about how a user will ultimately access any particular URL within a Share-Point farm.

A little history

One of the primary reasons administrators used to build separate web applications for a SharePoint site was to enable a farm to have distinct URLs for different web applications. A business unit within an organization would request a particular URL for its function, such as hr.yoursharepointname.com for HR.

The farm administrator would then oblige by generating a new web application for the HR group and assigning it the hr.yoursharepointname.com host header. Other business units would find out about the new URL and begin to have the same requirement; soon the farm administrator could have several web applications:

- Corporate portal
- Human resources
- Information technology
- Accounting
- Operations

- Sales
- Marketing/communications
- Engineering
- Central Administration
- Personal sites (My Sites)

As you have seen in previous sections, the supported limit for web applications is 20 per farm. If you were to build a farm and give each business unit its own web application (simply to give it a distinct URL), you might find that your farm is quickly trending toward the 20 web application limit.

Using host named site collections

Starting with SharePoint 2007, host named (also known as host header) site collection functionality has been a native component of SharePoint. Multiple host headers can be hosted within a single web application, enabling you to assign vanity URLs to multiple site collections contained within that web application.

Setting up a new web application for host named site collections (HNSCs) requires a bit of forethought as well as some basic knowledge of PowerShell.

EXAM TIP

As of this writing, the default behavior of the New-SPWebApplication cmdlet is to create a web application in Windows classic authentication mode. This behavior can be averted by using the -AuthenticationProvider switch. Windows classic authentication mode is deprecated (read: not preferred/might be removed at a later date), and should not be used; claims authentication (Windows NTLM) should be used instead. PowerShell will dutifully warn you of the missing switch, but only after it has executed the cmdlet and created the web application in Windows classic mode.

When you create the new web application to contain the host named site collections, it is important to note that host headers are not assigned to the web application itself. Any host headers assigned within this web application will be assigned to the individual site collections.

When a new SharePoint installation is created, it often is the case that a new web application has also been created by default at TCP port 80 (called the Default Web Site). This site must be deleted as the new HNSC web application will need to respond to TCP port 80.

As with any other technology using host headers, DNS entries and load balancer configurations will be required for any new host named site collections.

The Central Administration interface for creating new web applications does not provide a way to build a new HNSC-based web application.

When the HNSC web application is created, a root site collection should also be created; this site collection should not be available for use, nor should it have a template assigned.

Assuming that the domain name for your SharePoint farm is something along the lines of yoursharepointname.com, you should request that your administrators place a wildcard (*) entry in DNS and point it to the IP address of your web server. Any requests that are made to this domain will then be referred to SharePoint.

EXAM TIP

Creating (and most of the maintenance duties for) host named site collections is done entirely in PowerShell.

Setting up host named site collections

Now that you know some of the caveats associated with host named site collections, let's run through some of the steps required to build a web application for use with SharePoint host named site collections.

Note that these steps are very manual for the purpose of instruction; it is recommended that these steps be converted to a PowerShell script or function for repeatability.

The following steps assume:

- The wildcard and host header DNS entries have been made by your DNS admins.
- You have already removed the default web site in IIS on each web server in your farm.
- You know the user name/password of the account that will run the web application service.
- You are logged in as the farm account or another account with the correct farm/DB permissions.

This example build uses the following names/values:

- Application pool name: Intranet Pool - 80
- Application pool managed service account: boston\sp_app
- Web application name: Boston SharePoint Content
- Web server URL: http://ws2012sp13
- ContentDB SharePoint_Content_Boston (this database will be automatically built in the PowerShell commands shown following)

To build the example HNSC web application, do the following:

1. Open a SharePoint 2013 Management Shell (PowerShell) as administrator (choose to run as administrator).

2. Set the variables for your example web application:

   A. $AP = Intranet Pool - 80

   B. $APAcct = boston\sp_app

   C. $APMail = spapp@boston.local

   D. $WA = Boston SharePoint Content

   E. $WSUrl = http://ws2012sp13

   F. $ContentDB = SharePoint_Content_Boston

3. Set the variable for claims authentication:

   A. $Provider = New-SPAuthenticationProvider

4. Create the example web application:

   A. New-SPWebApplication -ApplicationPool $AP -ApplicationPoolAccount $APAcct -Name $WA -Port 80 -AuthenticationProvider New-SPAuthenticationProvider -DatabaseName $ContentDB

Next, you need to build the empty (but necessary) site collection at the root of the web application:

1. Set the variables for the root site collection:

   A. $OAlias = **boston\troy**

   B. $OMail = **troy@boston.local**

2. Create the root site collection (note that there is no template assigned):

   A. New-SPSite -URL $WSUrl -ownerAlias $OAlias -owneremail $OMail

   To build a host named site collection, do the following:

3. Set the variables for the site collection. This example uses the same account as the admin account and e-mail, but you can specify a different owner alias and e-mail as appropriate:

   A. $hostName = **Boston Local**

   B. $hostUrl = **http://www.boston.local**

   C. New-SPSite -url $hostUrl -HostHeaderWebApplication $WSUrl -owneralias $OAlias -owneremail $OMail -template sts#0

When to not use host named site collections

Although creating host named site collections is the preferred choice for SharePoint 2013 installations, there are times when path-based site collections are more appropriate.

Distinct web applications might be preferable in the following situations:

- You want to provide greater security by provisioning separating web applications; optionally, each could run under its own managed account/password.
- You want to assign a completely different URL to a site that does not conform to the HNSC URL structure.

Path-based site collections might be preferable in the following situations:

- You intend to enable the self-service site creation functionality in a web application.
- You need to provide unique wildcard inclusions; wildcard inclusions in an HNSC-enabled web application are shared across all host name sites.

Planning zones and alternate access mappings

There are five zones available in SharePoint: default, intranet, extranet, Internet, and custom. While there is no functional difference (by default) between the zones, they provide a structure to configure access for different user segments accessing the same web application.

When a new SharePoint web application is created, its URL is stored in the default zone. If claims authentication is to be added along with another authentication mechanism, some consideration should be given to adding it to the default zone so the same URL can be used both inside the network and from outside the network.

> **IMPORTANT** **NTLM AUTHENTICATION AND SEARCH CRAWLS**
>
> At least one zone must be configured to enable NTLM authentication for the crawl component of search to be able to access content.

> ### Thought experiment
> #### Site collection implementation
>
> In the following thought experiment, apply what you've learned about this objective. You can find answers to these questions in the "Answers" section at the back of this chapter.
>
> In your organization, you have a few business groups that require separate vanity URLs for their portion of the intranet. Your SharePoint administrative staff is not well-versed in PowerShell but is comfortable with Central Administration. Additionally, you have a few business units that require the separation of content to meet legal and regulatory requirements. What type of site collection design might you use within this environment?

Objective summary

- A heavily trafficked web application pool can quickly generate a RAM load that can grow into the multi-GB range.
- There can be a maximum number of 500 content databases in a SharePoint farm.
- Host named site collections require configuration via PowerShell.
- A host named site collection should always have a root site collection, but this site collection should not be available for use or have a template assigned.

Objective review

Answer the following questions to test your knowledge of the information in this objective. You can find the answers to these questions and explanations of why each answer choice is correct or incorrect in the "Answers" section at the end of this chapter.

1. You want to build a navigational structure in which each site collection can have its own vanity URL. Which site collection designation should be used for the web application?

   A. Fully qualified domain name (FQDN) site collections

   B. Host named site collections

   C. Domain named site collections

   D. Path-based site collections

2. Which of the following SQL high availability (HA) solutions require configuration in SharePoint content databases?

   A. SQL log shipping

   B. SQL mirroring

   C. SQL high availability groups

   D. SQL clustering

3. Which of the following statements are true concerning web applications and application pools in a SharePoint environment? (Choose all that apply.)

   A. There is a threshold limit of 20 web applications per SharePoint farm.

   B. There is a supported limit of 20 web applications per SharePoint farm.

   C. There is a supported limit of 10 application pools per web server in a SharePoint farm.

   D. There is a threshold limit of 10 application pools per web server in a SharePoint farm.

Objective 1.3: Design a physical architecture

A key design characteristic of SharePoint Server is its scalability. Any given SharePoint installation can be designed for a small user intranet, a large enterprise, or a public web site. It can be focused on serving web page requests, dedicated to search services, or tuned for other applications such as Microsoft Excel or BCS.

One of the only constants in IT is change, and SharePoint is no exception to this rule. An effective SharePoint design accounts for the current and expected requirements of an organization. After the initial design is implemented, the SharePoint farm can then be modified and tuned to suit the changing requirements of the business.

> **This objective covers how to:**
> - Design a storage architecture.
> - Configure basic request management.
> - Define individual server requirements.
> - Define service topologies.
> - Plan server load balancing.
> - Plan a network infrastructure.

Designing a storage architecture

SharePoint Server farms are data-intensive, requiring both large storage capacities and solid in input/output (I/O) storage design to ensure the best performance possible. This back-end storage is attached to the SQL (data tier) instance of the SharePoint farm.

Three storage architectures are supported within a SharePoint environment: Direct Attached Storage (DAS), Storage Area Network (SAN), and Network Attached Storage (NAS). DAS and SAN storage architectures are fully supported; NAS storage is supported only for content databases configured to use Remote Blob Storage (RBS).

> **MORE INFO** **DESIGNING THE STORAGE SUBSYSTEM**
>
> Planning and configuring the storage layer of a SharePoint farm infrastructure can be a complex task. For more detailed information about each storage architecture, see the TechNet article "Storage and SQL Server Capacity Planning and Configuration" at *http://technet.microsoft.com/en-us/library/cc298801.aspx*.

Each storage architecture has an associated set of hardware and administrative costs; the storage type you choose often has to do with the hardware and administrative structure you have available within your enterprise.

Direct Attached Storage (DAS)

DAS describes an environment in which each server maintains its own discrete storage without benefit of a storage network. Modern servers support two distinct types of drives: Serial Attached SCSI (SAS) and Serial Attached ATA (SATA).

Choosing this type of storage has the following benefits and drawbacks:

- The initial setup and administration of DAS is pretty straightforward, requiring only the attachment of the storage hardware to the server(s).
- The future storage growth of this solution is limited to the available interconnects to the server's motherboard:
  - After there are no more connections available to the server backplane, the server must be replaced to allow for future growth.
  - After the I/O capacity of the motherboard is saturated, the server must be replaced with a larger server to allow for future growth.
- Long-term administration of the storage subsystems must be completed on a per-server basis, with no provision for centralized storage.
- Any remaining space available in the storage subsystem is unusable for other servers in the farm/enterprise.

Storage Area Network (SAN)

SAN utilizes a storage network to abstract the storage subsystem from the server hosts to which they are attached. The benefits of this abstraction are immediate: the storage subsystem can be centrally managed and expanded as desired.

The Fibre Channel connections between the storage and host are attached using either twisted-pair copper wire or fiber-optic cables. A host connected to the SAN uses a host-based adapter to transfer SCSI commands to the storage using the Fibre Channel Protocol (FCP) for transport.

Choosing this type of storage has the following benefits and drawbacks:

- Available storage within the SAN can be assigned as required to any participating host because there is no longer a 1:1 relationship between storage and host.
- SAN connectivity eases the configuration of cluster storage, enabling storage to be presented to and more easily moved back and forth between cluster nodes.
- The initial setup of the storage layer requires in-depth administrative knowledge of the storage vendor subsystem utilized in the SAN.
- Incorrect configuration of the SAN can have a far-reaching effect; degraded performance or corruption can occur when improper configuration occurs.
- SAN I/O metrics should be watched carefully to ensure that performance is not degraded by saturation of SAN connectivity.

Network Attached Storage (NAS)

NAS storage provides file-based data storage to other devices on the network. Connectivity and I/O metrics from such a system are often subpar when compared to DAS- or SAN-connected storage. As such, this type of storage is supported only for content databases that have been configured to utilize RBS.

Disk and RAID types

The types of disks chosen can have an effect on the performance of your storage subsystem. Additionally, the redundant array of independent disks (RAID) configuration of the drives can have a dramatic effect on the performance characteristics of storage.

SharePoint 2013 supports several types of disks:

- Small Computer System Interface (SCSI)
- Serial Advanced Technology Attachment (SATA)
- Serial Attached SCSI (SAS)
- Fibre Channel (FC)
- Integrated Drive Electronics (IDE)
- Solid State Drive (SSD)

Without going into on-disk caching, rotation speed, or other in-depth storage tuning discussions, you can pretty much break down this list in terms of newer, faster drive technologies (SSD, SAS, SATA, FC) and older legacy technologies (SCSI and IDE). Often, the type of drive you choose will simply come down to the available interface types provided by your storage subsystem.

SharePoint 2013 supports all RAID types, but the recommendation for best performance characteristics is to implement RAID 1+0 (also known as RAID 10).

This RAID type configures drives in a striped set of mirrored drives—the mirroring component provides fault tolerance, and the striped component maximizes performance. In such a system, multiple drives can sustain losses but the RAID does not fail unless a mirror loses all its drives.

Configuring basic request management

Traditional load balancing technologies enable incoming traffic to be routed to one or more SharePoint web servers. The amount of intelligence applied to these routing actions varies in scope from the most rudimentary types of routing (such as DNS round-robin) to advanced routing as seen in dedicated load balancing solutions.

Although it is possible to configure an external load balancer to understand the specific behaviors required for a SharePoint environment, such solutions can have shortcomings:

- Changes made at the load balancer level can have dramatic effects on the SharePoint farm, resulting in inconsistencies or outages.

- Changes made within the SharePoint farm but not reflected in the load balancer configuration (such as search crawler changes) can have a negative effect on performance.

For instance, consider a SharePoint farm that is both serving user requests and search crawls at the same time. Enough search requests might cause the SharePoint environment to have increased latency serving user requests; such a situation could result in a perceived outage, causing irregular work stoppages.

> **MORE INFO**   **CONFIGURING REQUEST MANAGER**
>
> There are several different ways in which Request Management can be configured. These configurations are discussed in the TechNet article "Configure Request Manager in Share-Point Server 2013" at *http://technet.microsoft.com/en-us/library/jj712708.aspx.*

Request Management versus throttling

Earlier versions of SharePoint included the notion of HTTP request throttling, in which the current state of each web server was evaluated, and incoming requests could be throttled before a server reached a nonresponsive status. The current health of a web server could be observed in the HTTP response within a header called X-SharePointHealthScore.

Request Management is a new form of intelligent request routing and throttling available within SharePoint 2013. Request Management can be enabled on a per web-application basis, enabling incoming requests to be evaluated against a set of rules to determine which web server (if any) will respond.

Deployment modes

There are two deployment modes for request management: dedicated and integrated.

Dedicated mode deployments are useful in larger environments and allow for the segmentation of request management activities away from the web servers servicing the requests.

In an integrated mode deployment, request management is handled directly on the web servers, meaning that any server running the SharePoint Foundation Web Application Service also has the Request Management service instance provisioned.

Throttling rules

An incoming HTTP request will first be evaluated by the throttling rules; if an incoming request matches a throttling rule, the request is refused immediately.

Throttling rules also have a couple of other options worth noting: Expiration and Threshold. The Expiration option enables you to set an expiration date and time for the rule; the Threshold option enables you to automatically remove a routing target (web server) if the health score exceeds the value you select (health scores from 0 to 10).

EXAM TIP

Unless otherwise specified, throttling is enabled by default on each web app created in the farm.

Throttling rules can be enabled or disabled using the -ThrottlingEnabled parameter of the Set-SPRequestManagementSettings cmdlet. Additional configuration for the throttling rules can be administered using the Get-/Set-SPThrottlingRule PowerShell cmdlet.

Routing rules and execution groups

Next to be evaluated are routing rules. These rules are accumulated into a series of three execution groups (0, 1, and 2). Group 0 is the highest level (evaluated first), followed by groups 1 and 2.

There are a couple of rather important things to know about execution group behavior:

- Routing rules that are not associated with an execution group are automatically associated with execution group 0.
- If an incoming request is matched by a rule within an execution group, no further rules or groups are evaluated and the request is routed and prioritized.

Unless otherwise specified, routing is enabled by default on each web app created in the farm.

Routing rules can be enabled or disabled using the -RoutingEnabled parameter of the Set-SPRequestManagementSettings cmdlet. Additional configuration for the throttling rules can be administered using the Get-/Set-SPThrottlingRule PowerShell cmdlet.

There are no PowerShell cmdlets for working with execution groups because they are configured along with the creation/administration of routing rules.

Rule syntax

Rules control the evaluation criteria for the throttling, prioritization, or routing of incoming HTTP requests. The criteria for each rule consist of match properties, match types, and match values. Each rule chooses a match property, assigns an operator to it, and then assigns a value for the match.

> **IMPORTANT THROTTLING AND ROUTING RULE SYNTAX**
>
> The syntax used for these rules is identical for both throttling and routing.

There are eight types of match properties that specify an HTTP header for the match values:

- CustomHeader
- Host
- HttpMethod
- IP
- SoapAction
- Url
- UrlReferrer
- UserAgent

There are four associated operators for the match:

- RegEx
- Equals
- Starts with
- Ends with

Rules criteria can be administered using the New-SPRequestManagementRuleCriteria cmdlet. This cmdlet enables an administrator to set the match properties, match types, and match values for throttling or routing rules.

Routing targets

Any machine running the SharePoint Foundation Web Application Service is a potential routing target (a machine that could service incoming HTTP requests). An appropriate server is selected via one of two weighting schemes: static- or health-weighted.

Static-weighted routing enables an administrator to predefine which servers will be more or less able to serve requests. This weighting is set by fault to a value of 1; changing this value to a lower integer value (say 0 or –1) will cause a server to be utilized less; changing the value to an integer value greater than 1 would cause a server to be considered "stronger" and thus more utilized.

For instance, in an environment in which servers are being refreshed (older servers being replaced by newer servers), the SharePoint web servers might not be identical in hardware configuration or resources. In such a situation, it might be preferable to assign a higher weight to a server with more resources while assigning a lower weight to a server that is older or less able to serve requests.

Unlike static-weighting routing, health-weighted routing is assigned by analyzing the health of a given server in the machine pool. Each server in a SharePoint environment has a health score, assigned by the SharePoint Health Analyzer, varying from a score of 0 (healthy) to 10 (unhealthy).

EXAM TIP

The deployment mode can be configured using the -RoutingWeightScheme switch of the Set-SPRequestManagementSettings cmdlet.

Machine pools

Machine pools are groupings of routing targets. Requests that match a given routing rule can be routed to a particular grouping of SharePoint web servers (instead of all of them), whereas requests that do not match a rule are routed to any available web server in the farm. Machine pools can be administered using the Get-/Set-SPRoutingMachinePool cmdlet.

Monitoring request management

There are a series of metrics that can be tracked within the Event Viewer to monitor the health of request management (see Table 1-2).

TABLE 1-2 Request management counters

Counter name	Description
Connections Current	The total number of connections that are currently open by Request Manager.
Connections Reused / Sec	The number of connections per second that are reused when the same client connection makes another request without closing the connection.
Routed Requests / Sec	The number of routed requests per second. The instance determines the application pool and server for which this counter tracks.
Throttled Requests / Sec	The number of throttled requests per second.
Failed Requests / Sec	The number of failed requests per second.
Average Processing Time	The time to process the request that is the time to evaluate all the rules and determine a routing target.
Last Ping Latency	The last ping latency (that is, Request Manager's PING feature) and the instance determine which application pool and machine target.
Connection Endpoints Current	The total number of endpoints that are connected for all active connections.
Routed Requests Current	The number of unfinished routed requests. The instance determines which application pool and machine target.

These metrics levels can be monitored in both the event and tracing logs using the Set-SPLogLevel PowerShell command. For instance, the following PowerShell command will increase the trace severity levels to verbose:

```
Set-SPLogLevel "Request Management" -TraceSeverity Verbose
```

Defining individual server requirements

The configuration of each server in your new SharePoint farm depends greatly on the topology you choose. If your environment is very small, you might start your design with a single server and then grow the farm to multiple servers as demand increases.

Interestingly enough, a single server installation of SharePoint requires significantly more memory and hard disk resources than a distributed server installation using more than one server. The reason for this requirement is rather straightforward: A single server installation really is two installations in one: a SharePoint server and a database server (either built-in or SQL).

The requirements you choose are also based on the version of SharePoint you are using. If you are installing SharePoint Foundation 2013, for instance, you might need as little as 8 GB of RAM to get started.

Single server installations

Single server installations of SharePoint are most often used for evaluation or development environments, not production. This approach should be used only in an environment with a limited number of users.

In such an environment, SharePoint and the built-in database or SQL server tend to contend for resources (particularly RAM), and the users' perception of the farm's performance might suffer as a result.

The following requirements do not really address items such as the storage space required for the databases and any other services (such as search indexes). The recommendation is to add a secondary drive for the storage of such information.

The basic requirements for a single server SharePoint farm depend greatly on the SharePoint installation chosen and are shown in Table 1-3.

TABLE 1-3 Single server hardware requirements

Installation Type	RAM	Processor	Hard Disk Space
Single Server SharePoint Foundation 2013 installation	8 GB	64-bit, 4 cores	80 GB for system drive
Single Server SharePoint Server 2013 installation	24 GB	64-bit, 4 cores	80 GB for system drive

Three tier server installations

Because we have determined that a single server is not the preferred installation for a production SharePoint farm, you should now learn about the hardware requirements for a tiered installation. In such an environment, the web and application tier servers are separated from the SQL servers and have different hardware requirements (see Table 1-4).

TABLE 1-4 Three tier server hardware requirements

Installation Type	RAM	Processor	Hard Disk Space
Web or application server in a three tier farm	12 GB	64-bit, 4 cores	80 GB for system drive
Database servers in a three tier farm	8 GB for small deployments; 16 GB for medium deployments	64-bit/4 cores for small deployments; 64-bit/8 cores for medium deployments	80 GB for system drive

Software requirements for single-server installations

The software requirements for members of a SharePoint farm are well defined and depend on the role of the server within the farm.

The minimum requirements for a single server with built-in database are the following:

- The 64-bit edition of Windows Server 2008 R2 Service Pack 1 (SP1) Standard, Enterprise, or Datacenter; or the 64-bit edition of Windows Server 2012 Standard or Datacenter.

- The SharePoint parsing process crashes in Windows Server 2008 R2 (KB 2554876).

- FIX: IIS 7.5 configurations are not updated when you use the ServerManager class to commit configuration changes (KB 2708075).
- Hotfix: ASP.NET (SharePoint) race condition in .NET 4.5 RTM:
  - Windows Server 2008 R2 SP1 (KB 2759112)
  - Windows Server 2012 (KB 2765317)
- The Setup program installs the following prerequisite for a single server with built-in database:
  - Microsoft SQL Server 2008 R2 SP1 Express Edition
- The Microsoft SharePoint Products Preparation Tool installs the following prerequisites for a single server with built-in database:
  - Web Server (IIS) Role
  - Application Server Role
  - Microsoft .NET Framework version 4.5
  - SQL Server 2008 R2 SP1 Native Client
  - Microsoft WCF Data Services 5.0
  - Microsoft Information Protection and Control Client (MSIPC)
  - Microsoft Sync Framework Runtime v1.0 SP1 (x64)
  - Windows Management Framework 3.0, which includes Windows PowerShell 3.0
  - Windows Identity Foundation (WIF) 1.0 and Microsoft Identity Extensions (previously named WIF 1.1)
  - Windows Server AppFabric
  - Cumulative Update Package 1 for Microsoft AppFabric 1.1 for Windows Server (KB 2671763)

Software requirements for web and application server installations

The minimum requirements for web and application servers in a farm are the following:

- The 64-bit edition of Windows Server 2008 R2 Service Pack 1 (SP1) Standard, Enterprise, or Datacenter; or the 64-bit edition of Windows Server 2012 Standard or Datacenter.
- The SharePoint parsing process crashes in Windows Server 2008 R2 (KB 2554876).
- FIX: IIS 7.5 configurations are not updated when you use the ServerManager class to commit configuration changes (KB 2708075).
- Hotfix: ASP.NET (SharePoint) race condition in .NET 4.5 RTM:
  - Windows Server 2008 R2 SP1 (KB 2759112)
  - Windows Server 2012 (KB 2765317)
- The Microsoft SharePoint Products Preparation Tool installs the following prerequisites for front-end web servers and application servers in a farm:

- Web Server (IIS) role
- Application Server role
- Microsoft .NET Framework version 4.5
- SQL Server 2008 R2 SP1 Native Client
- Microsoft WCF Data Services 5.0
- Microsoft Information Protection and Control Client (MSIPC)
- Microsoft Sync Framework Runtime v1.0 SP1 (x64)
- Windows Management Framework 3.0 which includes Windows PowerShell 3.0
- Windows Identity Foundation (WIF) 1.0 and Microsoft Identity Extensions (previously named WIF 1.1)
- Windows Server AppFabric
- Cumulative Update Package 1 for Microsoft AppFabric 1.1 for Windows Server (KB 2671763)

Software requirements for database server installations in a farm

The minimum requirements for database installations in a farm are as follows:

- One of the following:
  - The 64-bit edition of Microsoft SQL Server 2012
  - The 64-bit edition of SQL Server 2008 R2 Service Pack 1
- The 64-bit edition of Windows Server 2008 R2 Service Pack 1 (SP1) Standard, Enterprise, or Datacenter; or the 64-bit edition of Windows Server 2012 Standard or Datacenter.
- The SharePoint parsing process crashes in Windows Server 2008 R2 (KB 2554876).
- FIX: IIS 7.5 configurations are not updated when you use the ServerManager class to commit configuration changes (KB 2708075).
- Hotfix: ASP.NET (SharePoint) race condition in .NET 4.5 RTM:
  - Windows Server 2008 R2 SP1 (KB 2759112)
  - Windows Server 2012 (KB 2765317)
  - Microsoft .NET Framework version 4.5

Defining service topologies

Scaling a SharePoint 2013 installation requires planning for the distribution of service applications across the farm environment. Because each implementation differs in terms of the amount of data, services offered, and users supported, no single topology is appropriate for any given business.

The following topologies are by no means the only ones available, but they give guidance as topology starting farms for your design.

Smallest (practical) fault tolerant farm

In this farm type, each tier (web, application, and data) must provide fault tolerance. At the web tier, user requests are distributed across both servers using server load balancing (hardware- or software-based). The application layer servers each run all required service application roles.

> **IMPORTANT COMBINING THE WEB AND APPLICATION TIERS**
>
> Although you could technically collapse the web and application tiers into two servers instead of the four specified, performance would suffer considerably as demand increases for the services provided by the application tier.

The data tier for this farm is load balanced using Clustering, Mirroring, or SQL2012 AlwaysOn technologies (Availability Groups, Mirroring, or Clustering). All three tiers are shown in Figure 1-30.

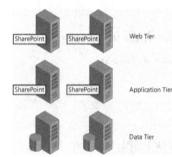

FIGURE 1-30 Smallest fault tolerant farm.

Search optimized farm

In a SharePoint environment that maintains a lot of content, search traffic can begin to produce a lot of traffic on the web servers. Segmenting the Crawl, Query, and Index components can improve the user experience, moving the search-centric activities onto dedicated servers.

In this configuration, a new web server is dedicated to the Crawl component in the web tier and the Query/Index components are moved onto their own fault tolerant server set (see Figure 1-31).

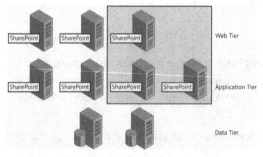

FIGURE 1-31 Search optimized farm.

Service application scaling

As the SharePoint environment continues to grow, a server can continue to be scaled out via server groups. Groupings of servers can be created at each tier based on the service applications or roles that will deliver. These groupings are logical (not configuration-based) in nature, giving administrators guidance about which set of servers should maintain a particular service application or role.

EXAM TIP

Know the roles and servers assigned at each tier of the smallest fault-tolerant SharePoint farm.

Planning server load balancing

A key part of HA, server load balancing provides technologies that can improve the resiliency of any IIS-based web farm, SharePoint included.

Server load balancing is a technology that has been around for over a decade. At a very basic level, the role of load balancing is simply to distribute incoming web requests across multiple web servers; you could do a very similar thing via round-robin DNS.

Any load balancer intended for use with SharePoint requires the capability to set up persistent/sticky/affinity sessions. Failure to properly configure affinity does not immediately manifest itself in problems, but causes problems with technologies such as Kerberos, SSL, and forms authentication.

Web tier load balancing

Web tier load balancing is accomplished via one of two technologies:

- Windows Network Load Balancing (NLB)
- Hardware load balancing

Windows Network Load Balancing (NLB) is a feature that can be activated from within the Add Roles And Features Wizard of Server Manager. This feature distributes incoming traffic across a series of web servers using the TCP/IP networking protocol.

In this type of load balancing, a virtual IP address is assigned to multiple servers at once. Although each web server is capable of responding to a single HTTP/HTTPS request, it is recommended that affinity be set up in load balancing so a user who starts a session with a particular web server stays with that server until the end of the session.

Because this is a built-in server feature, hardware and operating system resources are consumed in order for load balancing to operate, and this feature must be monitored along with the rest of the server functionality. As new web servers are added into the SharePoint farm, it is necessary for an administrator familiar with the load balancing services to configure this feature on any new server.

Although Windows NLB is quite durable, hardware load balancers are often preferred in larger enterprise server environments. These environments tend to acquire an administrator familiar with the specific skills required by the manufacturer of a dedicated load balancing system.

There are several reasons for building a dedicated load balancer layer within your organization:

- Centralized administration of load balancing.
- Performance impact of load balancing is not present on web servers.
- Multiple service types (Citrix, web servers, and so on) can be presented by the load balancing system.

Planning a network infrastructure

When planning the layout of a SharePoint farm, it is important to remember that the farm not only communicates with SharePoint users but also requires communications within the farm (to each tier) and communications to other servers in the network (such as Exchange or Lync servers). Effective network infrastructure planning requires that each of these connection types be considered in the overall design.

Interserver and end-user communication

There are two distinct types of network communication present within a SharePoint farm: user facing and interserver. Communications between servers within the farm can be quite intense at times; during these times, users might experience diminished performance if both types of communication take place across the same network interface.

As a result, servers in the web and application tiers of a SharePoint farm should have two distinct network interfaces:

- The first network interface card (NIC) handles user requests, routing traffic back and forth to users.
- The second NIC handles interserver connectivity, routing traffic back and forth between the SharePoint servers (web and app tier) and the data tier.

Network latency and stretched farms

Latency and bandwidth are concepts that go hand in hand. The best way to understand the relationship between these two is to imagine driving on a freeway. The speed limit (bandwidth) relates to how fast the traffic can travel on the freeway, whereas the traffic congestion present on the freeway can cause the commute time (latency) for any one car to increase.

SharePoint farm servers should be connected to each other with a minimum connectivity speed of 1 Gbps. Although it is possible to achieve this connection speed over a wide area network (WAN) connection, the network latency (time taken for a byte to travel from source to destination) often exceeds 1ms. Microsoft requires that the latency between SharePoint servers and the content database be less than 1 ms apart.

Unfortunately for system administrators, this latency requirement also prohibits the members of any one SharePoint farm from being located in two data centers (no matter how closely located these centers are). All servers belonging to a server farm must be physically located in the same datacenter to be supported.

Internet Protocol (IP) support in SharePoint 2013

SharePoint 2013 fully supports IPv6, the latest revision of the Internet Protocol. Microsoft recommends that you leave IPv6 enabled on your SharePoint servers; if your network does not support IPv6, IPv4 will be used as a default.

Thought experiment
Minimizing farm hardware expense

In the following thought experiment, apply what you've learned about this objective. You can find answers to these questions in the "Answers" section at the back of this chapter.

You are designing a small SharePoint environment to support 2000 users. Because this environment is heavily utilized for day-to-day operations and workflow, high-availability is a must. Additionally, there are several departments that make extensive use of features such as Excel Services.

You have rather stringent budget specifications and must weigh the value of purchasing server hardware against the cost of purchasing other equipment. What server layout approach should you propose and how might you address availability requirements?

Objective summary

- SharePoint supports three storage architectures: Direct Attached Storage (DAS), Storage Area Network (SAN), and Network Attached Storage (NAS).
- RAID 1+0 (RAID 10) storage offers the best performance in a SharePoint farm.

- Request Management can be enabled on a per-web application basis, enabling incoming requests to be evaluated against a set of rules to determine which web server (if any) will respond.
- Both Request Management routing and throttling are enabled by default in a SharePoint farm.
- SharePoint can be installed on the 64-bit versions of Windows 2008 R2 or Windows Server 2012.
- All servers in a SharePoint farm should be physically located in the same datacenter.

Objective review

Answer the following questions to test your knowledge of the information in this objective. You can find the answers to these questions and explanations of why each answer choice is correct or incorrect in the "Answers" section at the end of this chapter.

1. You want to utilize NAS storage within your SharePoint farm. Which of the following components are supported in this configuration?
   - **A.** Content databases
   - **B.** RBS
   - **C.** Configuration databases
   - **D.** Service application databases

2. You want to build a server farm specifically intended to handle incoming request management processing duties. Which deployment mode should you choose?
   - **A.** Affinity mode
   - **B.** Integrated mode
   - **C.** Dedicated mode
   - **D.** Throttling mode

3. The smallest fault-tolerant SharePoint 2013 farm should include how many servers?
   - **A.** 3 (one in each tier)
   - **B.** 4
   - **C.** 5
   - **D.** 6

Objective 1.4: Plan a SharePoint Online (Microsoft Office 365) deployment

Designing a modern SharePoint implementation requires knowledge of two distinct implementation types: on-premise and cloud-based. These two implementation types can be hybridized, allowing for a uniform experience for your corporate user located both on-premise and at remote offices (using SharePoint Online).

This objective covers how to:

- Evaluate service offerings.
- Plan service applications.
- Plan site collections.
- Plan customizations and solutions.
- Plan security for SharePoint Online.
- Plan networking services for SharePoint Online.

Evaluating service offerings

The previous Office 365 offering focused heavily on business clients in two subscription types: Small Business Plan (Plan P1) and two Midsize Business and Enterprise plans (Plan E1 and Plan E3). These types provided varying functionality, but focused on four core service offerings, all of which were cloud-based:

- Microsoft Exchange Online
- SharePoint Online
- Lync Online
- Microsoft Office Professional Plus

There are a total of four subscription types in this newest Office 365 platform. Small Business Premium and Enterprise continue to support business users; Home Premium and ProPlus extend the Office client in the cloud to the home and businesses that want to simply deploy Office without Exchange, SharePoint, and so on.

IMPORTANT SHAREPOINT IN OFFICE 365 SUBSCRIPTIONS

Neither Office 365 Home Premium nor Office 365 ProPlus includes any type of SharePoint offering in their subscription types. As in the previous Office 365, SharePoint is included within the Small Business and Enterprise subscription types and includes services that vary on the type of plan chosen.

SharePoint plans and subscription levels

Before discussing the major subscription types, it should be stated that there are individual plan levels that apply to the online components (SharePoint, Exchange, and Lync) within each subscription.

Although the combinations of plans, subscriptions, and levels can seem to be confusing (and occasionally overwhelming), the resulting customizability of each enables an organization to truly tailor the type of online environment that is required.

There are two plan levels that specifically apply to a SharePoint Online environment: Plan 1 and Plan 2. Additionally, Enterprise external users are also discussed as Enterprise levels (E1–E4 levels of SharePoint Online) allow for external collaboration with users not located within your organization.

> **MORE INFO** **PLANS, SUBSCRIPTIONS, AND LEVELS**
>
> A very thorough listing of each component's availability within each level of the SharePoint Online offering can be found at *http://technet.microsoft.com/en-us/library/jj819267.aspx*.

Office 365 Home Premium

The Home Premium subscription focuses on the availability of client services to users, providing access to Office 2013, SkyDrive, and Skype Services; it does not include Exchange Online, SharePoint Online, Lync Online, Project Online, or Visio Online services.

This subscription includes the following:

- The ability to install Office on up to five PCs, Macs, or tablets, shared among all users in the home
- Core Office applications: Microsoft Word, Excel, PowerPoint, and OneNote
- E-mail, publishing, and database applications: Microsoft Outlook, Publisher, and Access
- Office on Demand: Streaming versions of Office applications, requiring Windows 7 or 8 and an Internet connection
- Skype services, offering 60 minutes of free calling to 40-plus countries worldwide
- An additional 20 GB of SkyDrive online storage

Office 365 ProPlus

The ProPlus subscription focuses purely on the Microsoft Office client suite, omitting web-based services such as SharePoint, Exchange, and so on; if desired, these services can be purchased separately.

One of the more interesting components of this subscription is called Click-to-Run. Using this type of installation (instead of a traditional Windows Installer-based [*.msi]), users can begin using a program before it is completely downloaded.

This subscription includes the following:

- The ability to install Office on up to five PCs, Macs, or tablets per licensed user
- Core Office applications: Word, Excel, PowerPoint, and OneNote
- E-mail, publishing and database applications: Outlook, Publisher, and Access
- Unified communications and forms: Lync and InfoPath
- Office on Demand: Streaming versions of Office applications, requiring Windows 7 or 8 and an Internet connection
- Access to Enterprise features via Active Directory Domain Services (AD DS):
    - Single sign-on/identity federation
    - Active Directory synchronization
    - Domains

Office 365 Small Business Premium

Office Small Business Premium is the least-expensive subscription that offers SharePoint Online and is designed for small businesses with up to 10 employees. This subscription does not include either the Skype services or the additional SkyDrive storage granted by the Home Premium subscription, but does include the following:

- The ability to install Office on up to five PCs, Macs, or tablets per licensed user
- Core Office applications: Word, Excel, PowerPoint, and OneNote
- E-mail, publishing and database applications: Outlook, Publisher, and Access
- Unified communications and forms: Lync and InfoPath
- Office on Demand: Streaming versions of Office applications, requiring Windows 7 or 8 and an Internet connection
- A 25 GB Outlook mailbox, shared calendar, contact manager, scheduling, and task-list tools; and 10 GB of cloud-based storage (plus 500 MB per licensed user)
- The ability to set up, build, and maintain a public-facing web site with no additional hosting fees (SharePoint)
- Access to Lync Online (Plan 1)
- Access to SharePoint Online (Plan 1)
- Access to Exchange Online (Plan 1)

Office 365 Enterprise

The Enterprise subscription level of Office 365 is the top of the line, basically including the entire Office stack, both online and offline. This product provides functionality normally as-sociated with on-premise installations, including information rights management, federation, and enterprise records management.

This subscription includes the following:

- The ability to install Office on up to five PCs, Macs, or tablets per licensed user
- Core Office applications: Word, Excel, PowerPoint, and OneNote
- E-mail, publishing and database applications: Outlook, Publisher, and Access
- Unified communications and forms: Lync and InfoPath
- Office on Demand: Streaming versions of Office applications, requiring Windows 7 or 8 and an Internet connection
- A 25 GB Outlook mailbox, shared calendar, contact manager, scheduling and task-list tools, and 10 GB of cloud-based storage (plus 500 MB per licensed user)
- The ability to set up, build, and maintain a public-facing web site with no additional hosting fees (SharePoint)
- Access to Lync Online (Plan 2)
- Access to Exchange Online (Plan 2)
  - Data loss prevention that is compliant with regulatory standards
- Access to SharePoint Online (Plan 2), including the following:
  - Site mailboxes to enhance collaboration
  - Archiving, eDiscovery venter to identify, hold, and analyze information from Exchange, SharePoint, and Lync

---

EXAM TIP

Although it might seem trivial at first, knowing which functionality is available at each subscription level is a critical component of your Office 365 design and planning effort.

Planning service applications

Because SharePoint Online is a multitenant application within Office 365 (meaning that your SharePoint environment is contained in a series of farms that serve other Microsoft customers), there are some differences between the service applications that would be found in an on-premise environment and in SharePoint Online.

SharePoint services in Office 365

Not all SharePoint services in an on-premise installation of SharePoint have a matching analog within the SharePoint Online product line.

Table 1-5 shows a listing of the service applications found in SharePoint 2013 and the services available within SharePoint Online.

TABLE 1-5 SharePoint Online service comparison

Service Application	SharePoint Online Plan	Subscription Level	Note
Access Service	All plans	All levels	Not configurable
Access Service 2010	Not available	Not available	-----
App Management Service	All plans	All levels	-----
Business Data Catalog Service	Plan 2 only	E3 and E4 only	Configurable from the SharePoint Admin Center web site
Excel Service Application	Plan 2 only	E3 and E4 only	Not configurable
Machine Translation Service	All plans	All levels	Not configurable
PerformancePoint Service	Not available	Not available	-----
PowerPoint Automation Service	Not available	Not available	-----
Managed Metadata Service	All plans	All levels	Configurable from the SharePoint Admin Center web site
Search Service	All plans	All levels	Configurable from the SharePoint Admin Center web site
Secure Store Service	Plan 2 only	E3 and E4 only	Configurable from the SharePoint Admin Center web site
State Service	Not available	Not available	-----
User and Health Data Collection Service	Not available	Not available	The Office 365 admin console provides health information on a per-service basis
User Profile Service	All plans	All levels	Configurable from the SharePoint Admin Center web site
Visio Graphics Service	Plan 1 and 2	E1 through E4	-----
Word Automation Services	Not available	Not available	-----
Work Management Service	Not available	Not available	-----
Microsoft SharePoint Foundation Subscription Settings Service	Not available	Not available	-----

Planning site collections

Site collections in SharePoint Online are very similar to their on-premise counterparts. As we discussed at the beginning of this chapter, a site collection is nothing more than a grouping of sites that are functionally, navigationally, and administratively related to one another (see Figure 1-32).

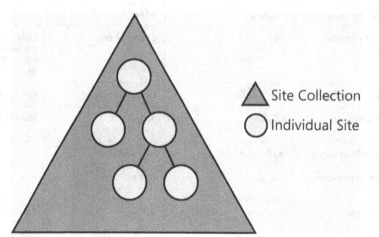

FIGURE 1-32 Sites within a site collection.

Site collection admin center

Creating a new SharePoint online site collection is accomplished within the Site Collections menu of the SharePoint admin center (see Figure 1-33).

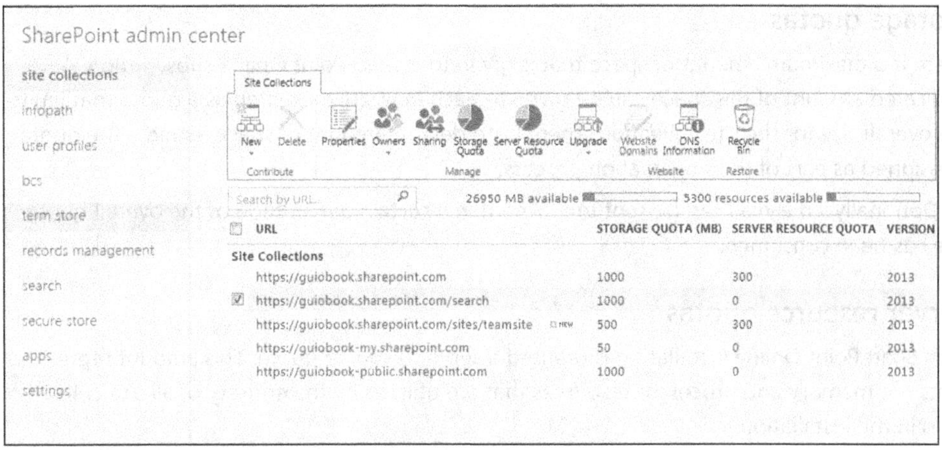

FIGURE 1-33 SharePoint admin center.

From this console, you can build a private site collection or a public web site.

Site collection types

Two types of site collections can be created within SharePoint Online: multiple private site collections and a single public web site.

- Each Office 365 subscription enables you to create a single public web site for your business; after this site has been created, the option to create it becomes grayed out.

- All SharePoint Online site collections (except the public web site) are initially created as private site collections. After creation, external users can be added to these site collections.

Before building a new site collection, you will want to consider factors such as the target audience of the site collection and how much data will be stored in the site collection.

Site collection administrators (SCAs)

In an on-premise SharePoint installation, each site collection has primary administrators and SCAs. Although others can be assigned the same permission levels, they do not receive SCA quota e-mail, for instance.

SharePoint Online site collections have a single designated SCA. This tenant administrator retains full control and is responsible for the administration of a site collection.

Other SCAs can be added as backups for the primary site collection admin. Additionally, external support partners can be given access to the site collection from a help desk or administrative perspective.

Storage quotas

There is a maximum amount of space that is given to a SharePoint Online subscription. A dedicated amount of this space can be given to each new site collection as a quota that limits the overall size for the site collection. There is no default amount of space issued—the quota is assigned as part of the site creation process.

Optionally, an e-mail can be sent to SCAs when a certain percentage of the overall quota size has been consumed.

Server resource quotas

Each SharePoint Online installation is granted a server resource quota. This amount represents the memory and processor resources that are utilized by the entirety of all site collections in the installation.

As a new site collection is created, it is assigned a percentage of the resources for use; the idea of this quota is to prohibit a single site collection from consuming all available resources within an installation. Adding new sandboxed solutions or apps to the site collection can cause this number to increase.

Sharing

Although site collections are created for private use, external users can be added to the permissions structure. These users can be granted reader, contributor, and even owner permissions.

Sharing is enabled on a per-site collection basis. Within the SharePoint admin console, there are three options for sharing:

- Don't Allow Sharing Outside Of Your Organization
- Allow External Users Who Accept Sharing Invitations And Sign In As Authenticated Users
- Allow Both External Users Who Accept Sharing Invitations And Anonymous Guest Links

After sharing is enabled, users can share an entire site or individual documents on a site. These users are fully authenticated, signing in with either a Microsoft account or a Microsoft Office 365 ID. If anonymous guest links have been enabled, users can share individual documents anonymously.

Planning customizations and solutions

As with an on-premise installation of SharePoint, SharePoint Online can be heavily modified to suit the requirements of your business users. These modifications can vary in scope from customizations produced for a small grouping of users to solutions that can be applied to major segments of your SharePoint Online environment.

There are three major customization levels present in a SharePoint farm: browser-based, tool-based, and developer-based.

Browser-based customizations

SharePoint users with the appropriate permission level can make customizations to any Share-Point site using nothing more than their web browser. These customizations do not require much technical expertise and are scoped to a particular site or site collection.

Browser-based customizations include the following:

- Changing the site theme to one of 18 available themes ("What's your style?")
- Adding a logo and description to your site ("Your site. Your brand.")
- Editing site pages, choosing customizing the appearance of web parts and other content to be displayed
- Altering the global and current navigation elements of a site
- Creating and altering the appearance of list and library views

Tool-based customizations

Sometimes the modifications available through the browser are not adequate; if the person making the changes is technically adept (but not a software developer), the next available option is using a tool-based customization.

These sorts of modifications are made using SharePoint tools such as InfoPath Designer for developing customized InfoPath forms; SharePoint Designer (SPD) for making more-detailed site modifications such as altering/creating page layouts and creating workflows; or any of the Office 2013 client tools such as Microsoft Access, Microsoft Excel, or Microsoft Visio 2013.

Developer-based customizations

The last option for making modifications to a SharePoint Online installation is to build custom code solutions. Solutions developed using Visual Studio 2012 can be activated on your Share-Point Online installation and run in the site's sandboxed solution environment.

Planning security for SharePoint Online

There are two aspects to securing any system: authentication and authorization.

Authentication versus authorization

Authentication is the process of determining the identity of a principal (a person trying to log in to your environment). When a principal tries to authenticate to a system, credentials are provided (such as a password) to verify the principal's identity.

Authorization is the process of verifying an authenticated user's access to a system. This access is usually associated with some sort of ACL.

When a user tries to access SharePoint Online, the user name is checked against the permissions of the site (either as an individual or as a member of a permissions group). If no permissions have been granted, access is denied to the site.

Office 365 authentication

There are two distinct authentication methods present in Office 365: Microsoft Online IDs and Federated IDs.

Microsoft IDs are issued and maintained by Microsoft—you might already have one of these in the form of an Office 365, Hotmail, SkyDrive, or Xbox Live account.

Using a Microsoft ID, a user can authenticate to multiple systems (Office 365 included) using a single user name and password.

Identity federation (also called single sign-on) is a mechanism for enabling users within your organization to use their standard Active Directory corporate user name and password to access Office 365.

Federation with Office 365 requires the use of Active Directory Federation Services (ADFS) 2.0. After this configuration has been completed, all identities are managed only on-premises.

EXAM TIP

Authentication is the process of determining the identity of a principal; authorization is the process of verifying an authenticated user's access to a system.

Planning networking services for SharePoint Online

With the arrival of Office 365, the ability to extend corporate SharePoint infrastructures to the cloud became reality. SharePoint 2010 provided basic federation between on-premise Active Directory and cloud authentication, but provided no further service connectivity.

SharePoint 2013 integration

SharePoint 2013 and the newest version of Office 365 now provide three levels of integration: domain federation, server-to-server (S2S) trust and identity management, and service integration.

- As with SharePoint 2010, federated authentication and account synchronization is available between on-premise Active Directory and Windows Azure Active Directory. Besides providing authentication services, Windows Azure also acts as a trusted token issuer between the two environments.

- Using the OAuth 2.0 protocol, a trusted communication channel is established between a SharePoint Online installation and SharePoint Server 2013. Additionally, federated users can be authenticated using this functionality.

- Services such as Search, BCS, and Duet Enterprise Online can now be integrated between SharePoint Server 2013 and SharePoint Online.

SharePoint hybrid topologies

There are three hybrid topologies that can be used to configure the relationship between on-premise and cloud installations of SharePoint. The authentication topology you choose will then determine the services you can support:

- One-way outbound supports SharePoint Server 2013 queries of online site collections, returning the federated results to the on-premise SharePoint Server 2013 search.

- One-way inbound supports SharePoint Online queries of on-premise SharePoint Server 2013 site collections, returning the federated results to SharePoint Online search. It also supports SharePoint Online BCS connectivity to an on-premise SharePoint BCS installation.

- Two-way (bidirectional) topology supports SharePoint Server 2013 Search, BCS, and Duet Enterprise Online connections between on-premise and cloud-based installations of SharePoint.

> **MORE INFO** **IMPLEMENTATION PHASES FOR SHAREPOINT HYBRIDIZATION**
>
> Configuring a hybrid on-premise and cloud-based installation of SharePoint requires a significant amount of planning and configuration effort. This effort is broken into three phases: configuration of the basic environment, identity management infrastructure, and service configuration. The hybridization of SharePoint is covered in the TechNet article "Hybrid for SharePoint Server 2013" at *http://technet.microsoft.com/en-us/library/jj838715. aspx.*

Thought experiment
Deploying the office client

In the following thought experiment, apply what you've learned about this objective. You can find answers to these questions in the "Answers" section at the back of this chapter.

Your organization is planning to move its core infrastructure to Office 365. Core services such as SharePoint and Exchange are required going forward. Management wants to absorb the cost of purchasing and deploying Office 2013 as part of the solution you propose. Which subscription of Office 365 would you select?

Objective summary

- Office Small Business Premium is the least-expensive subscription that offers Share-Point Online.
- A site collection is nothing more than a grouping of sites that are functionally, navigationally, and administratively related to one another.
- Only a single public web site can be created per Office 365 subscription.
- Three types of customization are present in SharePoint Online: browser-based, tool-based, and developer-based.
- Authentication to an Office 365 site can occur using one of two mechanisms: Microsoft IDs and Active Directory Federation System 2.0.

Objective review

Answer the following questions to test your knowledge of the information in this objective. You can find the answers to these questions and explanations of why each answer choice is correct or incorrect in the "Answers" section at the end of this chapter.

1. Which of the following Office 365 subscriptions include SharePoint Online as a component? (Choose all that apply.)

   A. Office 365 Home Premium

   B. Office 365 Small Business Premium

   C. Office 365 ProPlus

   D. Office 365 Enterprise

2. Which of the following services are not included in SharePoint Online? (Choose all that apply.)

   A. Word Automation Services

   B. Excel Calculation Services

   C. PerformancePoint Services

   D. Visio Graphics Services

3. Your Office 365 users complain that they cannot share the contents of their site collections with outside partners. Which section of the SharePoint admin center is appropriate for correcting this issue?

   A. Settings

   B. Search

   C. Apps

   D. Site collections

Chapter summary

- The MMS application is a required component for creating managed navigation hierarchies.

- A given retention policy requires at least one retention stage to be created, but can be composed of more than one retention stage (if required).

- Site collection policies are reusable; they can be exported from one site collection and imported to another for reuse.

- Structural navigation relies on the use of managed paths; metadata navigation relies on the use of a term set to create a navigational structure.

- The number of supported web applications in a farm is set to 20; this limit relies heavily on the amount of memory available to servers in the farm.

- A boundary is an absolute limit. A threshold is a limit that can be altered up to a maximum limit (but might affect performance). A supported limit is one that, if exceeded, might result in unexpected farm behavior.

- Use the -AuthenticationProvider switch with the New-SPWebApplication switch to avoid creating the web application in Windows Classic authentication mode.

- Regardless of the storage type used with SharePoint, it must meet two metrics: be capable of responding within 1 ms and of returning the first byte of data within 20 ms.

- The connection speed between all SharePoint servers in a farm must meet or exceed 1 Gbps. Additionally, the network latency between the web/application tiers and the data tier should be less than 1 ms.

- Authentication is the process of determining the identity of a principal; authorization is the process of verifying an authenticated user's access to a system.

Answers

Objective 1.1: Thought experiment

This is a two-part effort:

Because the navigational taxonomy is to be generated externally, you could create a sample CSV file to be given to the Corporate Communications group. This group could then generate the navigational terms for you to import into the term set.

After the navigational structure is complete, the Corporate Communications department would then need to generate a series of search terms to promote each of the major sites in search results. You would then generate a series of query rules that would render the appropriate promoted results on the search page.

Objective 1.1: Review

1. **Correct answer:** C

   A. **Incorrect:** An enterprise keywords site column is used for keyword storage, but will not cause the error.

   B. **Incorrect:** Although the MMS is indeed required, additional configuration steps are required.

   C. **Correct:** A default keywords term store must be selected in the MMS for enterprise keywords to be used.

   D. **Incorrect:** No Managed Keyword Service application exists in SharePoint 2013.

2. **Correct answer:** B

   A. **Incorrect:** The retention policy feature defines the lifecycle of content contained within SharePoint.

   B. **Correct:** The barcode policy feature is the only feature type that is both supported beyond SharePoint 2013 and useful for tracking physical documents.

   C. **Incorrect:** The labeling policy feature is a backward-compatible feature that works with printed documents; it is also deprecated, meaning that it will not be available in newer versions of SharePoint (beyond SharePoint 2013).

   D. **Incorrect:** The auditing policy feature defines monitoring of user document interactions, such as edits, deletions, and so on.

3. **Correct answer:** D

    A. **Incorrect:** Although managed navigation is the goal you are working toward, there is no menu item by this name within the Intended Use tab.

    B. **Incorrect:** Making a term set unavailable for tagging is an effective way to group terms together (for example, by an alphabetical grouping, such as A–F), but does not enable the term set for navigation.

    C. **Incorrect:** There is no option by this name in the Intended Use tab.

    D. **Correct:** The correct selection to enable managed navigation, it designates that a particular term set be used explicitly for the navigation of a site (or sites).

Objective 1.2: Thought experiment

In order to effectively maintain separation of content, you would most likely need to build a web application that uses separate security credentials and content databases. Although this requirement might not by itself preclude the use of host named site collections, the lack of PowerShell experience would be an issue as host named site collections cannot be created via the Central Administration interface.

Objective 1.2: Review

1. **Correct answer:** B

    A. **Incorrect:** Although host named site collections technically use FQDNs in DNS, this is not the correct designation for the site collection.

    B. **Correct:** Host named site collections allow for the assignment of vanity URLs to each site collection in a web application.

    C. **Incorrect:** There is no such thing as a domain named site collection.

    D. **Incorrect:** Path-based site collections are the alternative to host named site collections.

2. **Correct answer:** B

    A. **Incorrect:** SharePoint is not aware of content databases replicated via log shipping.

    B. **Correct:** Each content database in SharePoint can specify an alternative SQL server for use with mirroring.

    C. **Incorrect:** SharePoint is not aware of SQL availability groups.

    D. **Incorrect:** SharePoint is not aware of clustered SQL database servers.

3. **Correct answers:** B, D

    A. **Incorrect:** The limit of 20 web applications per SharePoint farm is a supported limit.

    B. **Correct:** There is a supported limit of 20 web applications per SharePoint farm.

    C. **Incorrect:** The limit of 10 application pools per web server in a SharePoint farm is a threshold limit.

    D. **Correct:** There is a threshold limit of 10 application pools per web server in a SharePoint farm.

Objective 1.3: Thought experiment

There are two key requirements present in this environment: budget and high-availability. If given the choice between buying a hardware load balancing solution and buying another piece or two of server hardware, the servers will most likely win out.

You will probably propose a three-tiered solution (to accommodate the Excel Services load) and have a pair of servers in each tier. Additionally, you will most likely use a SQL HA solution and install Windows NLB on your web tier versus spending money on a dedicated load balancer solution.

Objective 1.3: Review

1. **Correct answer:** B

    A. **Incorrect:** Content databases are not supported on NAS storage.

    B. **Correct:** RBS is fully supported on NAS storage.

    C. **Incorrect:** Configuration databases are not supported on NAS storage.

    D. **Incorrect:** Service application databases are not supported on NAS storage.

2. **Correct answer:** C

    A. **Incorrect:** There is no such mode in Request Management. Affinity has to do with server load balancing on the web tier.

    B. **Incorrect:** An integrated mode server farm handles request management policies along with all other operations on the web tier of the farm.

    C. **Correct:** A dedicated mode server farm exclusively handles request management policies in larger implementations of SharePoint.

    D. **Incorrect:** There is no such mode in Request Management. Throttling, although associated with request management, is accomplished via a series of rules.

3. **Correct answer:** D

   A. **Incorrect:** Three servers (one in each tier) would not provide any fault tolerance.

   B. **Incorrect:** Four servers would enable load balancing in two of the three tiers. Although you could technically collapse the web and application tiers, performance would suffer.

   C. **Incorrect:** Five servers would allow for load balancing in two of the three tiers.

   D. **Correct:** A six-server farm is the smallest practical design for load balancing in each tier.

Objective 1.4: Thought experiment

There are two distinct subscription plans in Office 365 that provide SharePoint and Exchange functionality: Office 365 Small Business Premium and Office 365 Enterprise. The ability to deploy Office as part of the solution is also provided with both of these subscription levels.

You will most likely narrow down the desired version of Office 365 based on the functionality required. For instance, if your office has more than 10 people, you should be considering the Office 365 Enterprise subscription as your solution.

Objective 1.4: Review

1. **Correct answers:** B, D

   A. **Incorrect:** Office 365 Home Premium does not include access to SharePoint Online.

   B. **Correct:** Office 365 Small Business Premium includes access to SharePoint Online.

   C. **Incorrect:** Office 365 ProPlus does not include access to SharePoint Online.

   D. **Correct:** Office 365 Enterprise includes access to SharePoint Online.

2. **Correct answers:** A, C

   A. **Correct:** Word Automation Services is not available in any SharePoint Online plan level.

   B. **Incorrect:** Excel Calculation Services is included in SharePoint Online.

   C. **Correct:** PerformancePoint Services is not available in any SharePoint Online plan level.

   D. **Incorrect:** Visio Graphics Services is included in SharePoint Online.

3. **Correct answer:** D

   A. **Incorrect:** Settings controls the general settings of your SharePoint Online subscription.

   B. **Incorrect:** Search controls the configuration of search in your SharePoint Online subscription.

   C. **Incorrect:** Apps controls the installation and configuration of applications installed from the Office App Store.

   D. **Correct:** Quotas are part of the configuration for site collections.

## CHAPTER 2

Plan security

Securing assets within a SharePoint environment is a multilayered process. This chapter begins with a discussion of how users become authenticated into the system and then progress into the authorization that is assigned in order to secure access to objects in the farm.

In addition to pure authentication and authorization, we will discuss how to go about setting up a secure infrastructure and assigning policies that will eventually result in a secure system.

Objectives in this chapter:

- Objective 2.1: Plan and configure authentication
- Objective 2.2: Plan and configure authorization
- Objective 2.3: Plan and configure platform security
- Objective 2.4: Plan and configure farm-level security

Objective 2.1: Plan and configure authentication

Authentication is a mechanism within a system that verifies the identity of the requestor as genuine; this mechanism has nothing to do with the assignment of rights or permissions. After a requestor has been authenticated, authorization can then be granted, providing access to system resources.

Authentication is required on three different occasions for on-premise installations of Microsoft SharePoint:

- **User authentication**   A user is trying to access SharePoint resources
- **App authentication**   An installed app is trying to access SharePoint resources
- **Server-to-server (S2S) authentication**   Two-way resource access between servers (Exchange/Lync/SharePoint) in the enterprise

SharePoint does not provide any authentication mechanism; it merely uses those provided by other systems. The Active Directory Domain Services (AD DS) provider is a good example of an authentication mechanism that can be used by SharePoint.

This objective covers how to:

- Plan and configure Windows authentication.
- Plan and configure identity federation.
- Configure claims providers.
- Configure server-to-server (S2S) intraserver and Open Authorization (OAuth) authentication.
- Plan and configure anonymous authentication.
- Configure connections to Access Control Service (ACS).

Planning and configuring Windows authentication

SharePoint 2013 web applications created via Central Administration are always created using claims authentication. Within claims authentication, there are four possible Windows authentication types available for users. These authentication options can be set via Windows PowerShell or on the Edit Authentication page (see Figure 2-1):

- NTLM
- Kerberos
- Basic authentication
- Digest authentication

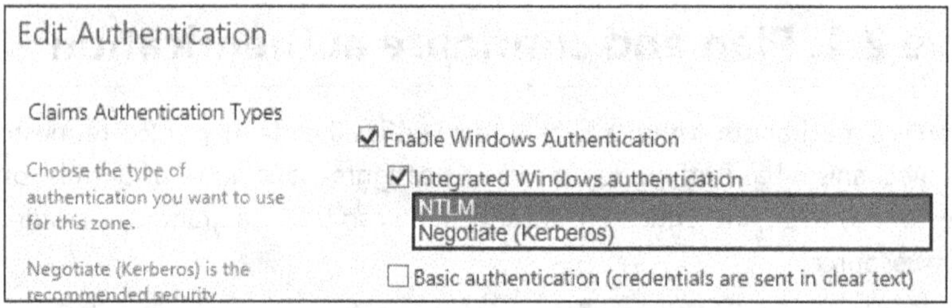

FIGURE 2-1 Windows authentication types.

As Figure 2-1 shows, it is possible to select one of the integrated Windows authentication options and also the basic authentication type at the same time for the same web application in the same zone. A user can then be authenticated by any of the available methods to the SharePoint web application.

Both the NTLM and Negotiate (Kerberos) authentication types are considered Windows integrated, meaning that the credentials of users who have logged on against an AD DS provider are automatically authenticated without the need for a new user name/logon prompt.

Integrated Windows authentication (NTLM)

The NT LAN Manager (NTLM) authentication type is the simpler of the two integrated Windows authentication mechanisms to configure; no extra effort is required from a SharePoint standpoint to make NTLM function correctly.

NTLM has a couple of advantages over Kerberos. Most of these benefits have to do with ease of use:

- NTLM authentication can still function when the computer making the request is outside the network or is a stand-alone computer.
- NTLM is much easier to set up and configure than its Kerberos counterpart.

There is a price to be paid for the NTLM simplicity:

- NTLM is an older, less secure authentication type, using a challenge/response mechanism for authentication that is less secure than Kerberos.

NTLM makes repeated round trips between Internet Information Services (IIS) and a domain controller, resulting in a performance loss from a SharePoint standpoint as well as an increased load on the domain controller:

- NTLM does not support delegation. If a user has authenticated to SharePoint and then needs to access another system through SharePoint (for instance, a SQL Server Reporting Services [SSRS] instance not located on the same server as SharePoint), the request will fail.

Integrated Windows authentication (Negotiate-Kerberos)

The Kerberos (Negotiate) authentication is the more secure of the two integrated Windows authentication types. The proper configuration of Kerberos authentication for SharePoint requires interaction and close coordination with the Active Directory and SQL support teams.

Kerberos requires more planning than its NTLM counterpart; however, this attention to structure provides wholesale performance and functional gains:

- Users authenticating to SharePoint are granted a ticket from the Key Distribution Center (KDC), which can be used to authenticate requests without repeated trips back and forth to the domain controller. This results in fairly significant performance gains over NTLM as well as a reduced load on domain controllers.
- The encryption mechanisms employed by Kerberos are significantly more secure than those present in NTLM.
- Delegation is supported by Kerberos. If users are authenticated and using SharePoint, they can make a request to a secondary system (such as SQL), and their credentials will be able to "double hop" to provide authentication to that system.

Basic authentication

Basic authentication is the least secure of the four Windows authentication types. This type of authentication is simple to configure, but is inherently insecure because credentials (user name and password) are passed over the wire in clear text.

Digest authentication

Digest authentication is more secure than basic authentication, and is similar to NTLM in that it uses a challenge/response mechanism. A calculated checksum component is stored on a domain controller that must match an MD5 checksum of the user's password at logon time.

If the user decides to visit more than one web application, he or she must reauthenticate (furnish user name/password) again.

Planning and configuring identity federation

As an organization's business needs change, it may become necessary to extend the use of an application such as SharePoint 2013 to members of another partner organization.

This business need is nothing new; organizations generally respond to this requirement by issuing user names and passwords to partner organization personnel.

This sort of arrangement is not without its share of headaches:

- The organization's IT staff must now be responsible for the maintenance and upkeep of their own users and also for users from external partners.

- Users from the external party must now keep track of one more set of credentials.

- Security becomes an issue because the partner organization may or may not let you know when users leave or change responsibilities.

Benefits of identity federation

With the advent of claims-based authentication, it is now possible to allow a partner organization user to maintain only one set of credentials, authenticating within their own environment to a Security Token Service (STS).

The application (in this case, SharePoint Server 2013) is configured to trust the STS of the partner organization STS. The user can then present this token to the application without need for further authentication.

Although you can create a new federation provider, the Active Directory Federation Services (ADFS) 2.0 provider fits the bill nicely, giving your organization's administrators a familiar mechanism for controlling external user access. ADFS not only enables your organization to federate users from another organization but also to provide an external authentication mechanism to nonpartner organization users.

EXAM TIP

Remember that users always authenticate to the identity provider within their organization to receive a Security Assertion Markup Language (SAML) token.

Basic identity federation

A basic federated identity process is shown in Figure 2-2. Prior to this process taking place, a couple of prerequisite actions have been taken:

- Your SharePoint farm's STS has been started.
- A trust is established between your SharePoint farm and your organization's federation provider (usually ADFS 2.0).
- A trust has been established between your organization's federation provider and another that belongs to the partner organization.

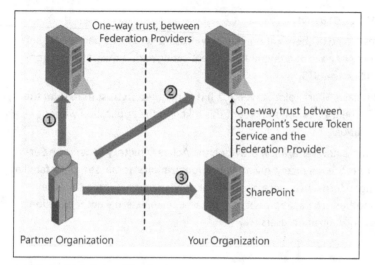

FIGURE 2-2 Basic federation identity.

Partner organization's users can gain access to SharePoint as follows:

1. The user authenticates to his or her organization's identity provider.

2. The user is returned a Security Assertion Markup Language (SAML) token that contains claims issued by the organization.

3. The user is redirected to your identity provider and receives a new SAML token with claims to be used within SharePoint.

4. The user is redirected to SharePoint, which validates the SAML token and then enables the user to access SharePoint using the permissions he or she is granted (authorization).

MORE INFO FEDERATED IDENTITY FOR SHAREPOINT APPLICATIONS

Although it is possible to have SharePoint directly set up trusts with external partner identity providers, it is much more manageable to configure the trust between identity providers. SharePoint may not be the only application that uses this relationship between organizations. For more information, see the MSDN article "Federated Identity for Share-Point Applications" at *http://msdn.microsoft.com/en-us/library/ff359110.aspx*. This article is part of a larger e-book titled *A Guide to Claims-based Identity and Access Control*, which can be found at *http://msdn.microsoft.com/en-us/library/ff423674.aspx*.

Configuring claims providers

For SharePoint 2013 to work with a trusted identity (claims) provider, there are several steps to be taken prior to setting up a web application. These steps occur on two different systems: the ADFS 2.0 server and the SharePoint 2013 Server farm.

EXAM TIP

In the next few steps, you will configure ADFS for use with SharePoint. The SharePoint web application that will use the trusted identity provider is required to use SSL.

Preparing ADFS for SharePoint 2013

Prior to configuring SharePoint for claims, some configuration has to be completed within ADFS:

1. Configure ADFS for a relying party. This step adds a relying party trust from the ADFS server to the SharePoint web application name, using the WS-Federation Passive protocol (the URL is defined as https://webappname/_trust/).

2. Configure a claim rule. This step determines which Lightweight Directory Access Protocol (LDAP) attributes (usually the e-mail address) are sent as claims and how they are mapped to the outgoing claim type (usually the User Principal Name [UPN]).

3. Export a token signing certificate. This step exports the public key (DER-encoded binary X.509) as a *.cer file for import into SharePoint.

IMPORTANT **EXPORTING MULTIPLE CERTIFICATES**

If you have one or more parent certificates within the chain that leads to your signing certificate, you must export them as well as the signing certificate.

Starting the Security Token Service (STS)

Depending on how you created the SharePoint Server 2013 farm, you may have not started the STS as part of your installation process. This service is required in order for claims to work correctly, and should be running on all SharePoint Servers in the farm.

To start the STS, repeat the following steps on each server in your farm:

1. Log on to your SharePoint Server console.

2. Open Internet Information Services Manager.

3. Expand the Application Pools section beneath the server name.

4. In the Application Pools pane, select SecurityTokenServiceApplicationPool.

5. In the Actions pane, select the Start link within the Application Pool Tasks section.

6. The application pool's status should now appear as Started, as shown in Figure 2-3.

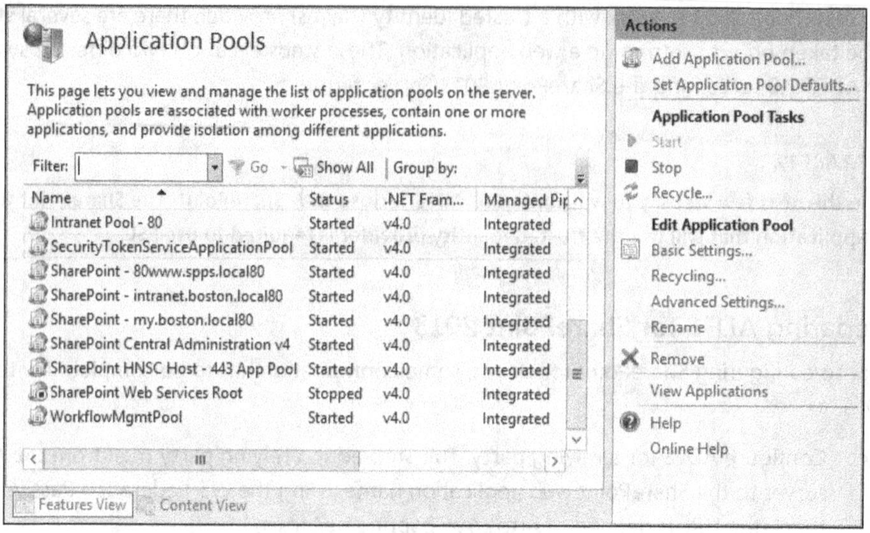

FIGURE 2-3 The STS application pool (started state).

Importing a token signing certificate

As with most of the more advanced SharePoint administrative tasks, the next few sections require configuration to be done in a Windows PowerShell window. To import one or more signing certificates, do the following:

1. Start a SharePoint 2013 Management Shell, remembering to run as administrator.

2. (Optional) If you had a root site in the certificate chain, you must import the parent certificate first before importing the signing certificate:

```
$parentcert = New-Object System.Security.Cryptography.X509Certificates.
X509Certificate2("<path to the parent certificate>")

New-SPTrustedRootAuthority -Name "Token Signing Cert Parent" -Certificate
$parentcert
```

3. Import the signing certificate provided to you by the ADFS administrator:

```
$signcert = New-Object System.Security.Cryptography.X509Certificates.
X509Certificate2("<path to the signing certificate>")

New-SPTrustedRootAuthority -Name "Token Signing Cert" -Certificate $signcert
```

4. If you display the contents of the certificate by typing in the variable name "$signcert" and clicking Enter, you see that the certificate shows the thumbprint and subject for this certificate (see Figure 2-4).

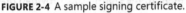

FIGURE 2-4 A sample signing certificate.

Defining a unique identifier for claims mapping

Next, you need to define mappings for the e-mail and UPN claims, as follows:

1. For the identity claim mapping (e-mail address), enter the following:

    ```
    $identityClaimMapping = New-SPClaimTypeMapping -IncomingClaimType "http://schemas.
    xmlsoap.org/ws/2005/05/identity/claims/emailaddress" -IncomingClaimTypeDisplayName
    "EmailAddress" -SameAsIncoming
    ```

2. For the UPN claim mapping, enter the following:

    ```
    $upnClaimMapping = New-SPClaimTypeMapping -IncomingClaimType "http://schemas.
    xmlsoap.org/ws/2005/05/identity/claims/upn" -IncomingClaimTypeDisplayName "UPN"
    -SameAsIncoming
    ```

    If you will set up S2S authentication (shown in the next section), you need to create additional mappings for both the role claim and primary security identifier (SID) mappings as well.

3. (Optional) For the role claim mapping, enter the following:

    ```
    $roleClaimMapping = New-SPClaimTypeMapping -IncomingClaimType "http://schemas.
    microsoft.com/ws/2008/06/identity/claims/role" -IncomingClaimTypeDisplayName
    "Role" -SameAsIncoming
    ```

4. (Optional) For the primary SID claim mapping, enter the following:

    ```
    $sidClaimMapping = New-SPClaimTypeMapping -IncomingClaimType "http://schemas.
    microsoft.com/ws/2008/06/identity/claims/primarysid" -IncomingClaimTypeDisplayName
    "SID" -SameAsIncoming
    ```

Creating the new authentication provider

Now that the claims mappings are complete, you can build the authentication provider that will be used in your SharePoint farm (trusted identity provider):

1. First, you define the trusted STS for a SharePoint farm ($realm), specifying the appropriate name for your web application ("PathBased" in the following example):

    ```
    $realm = "urn:sharepoint:Pathbased"
    ```

2. Next, you define a variable ($signInURL) for your ADFS server ("ws2012dc" in the following example):

    ```
    $signInURL = https://ws2012dc/adfs/ls
    ```

IMPORTANT **EXTERNAL USER LOGONS**

If you have users who navigate to SharePoint (directly) from outside your organization, they are prompted with a logon screen to redirect them to the sign-in URL provided previously. They can then authenticate and gain access to your SharePoint environment.

3. Finally, you create the new provider. In the following Windows PowerShell, insert your own values for the -Name and -Description values.

```
$ap = New-SPTrustedIdentityTokenIssuer -Name ADFS
-Description "Active Directory Federation Services" -realm
$realm -ImportTrustCertificate $signcert -ClaimsMappings
$emailClaimMapping,$upnClaimMapping,$roleClaimMapping,$sidClaimMapping -SignInUrl
$signInURL -IdentifierClaim $emailClaimmapping.InputClaimType
```

Selecting the authentication provider

Now that the provider is online, you can configure it for the appropriate web application:

1. From Central Administration, select Application Management.
2. On the Application Management page, click the URL area of your desired web application and then select the Authentication Providers icon on the ribbon (Security section, shown in Figure 2-5).

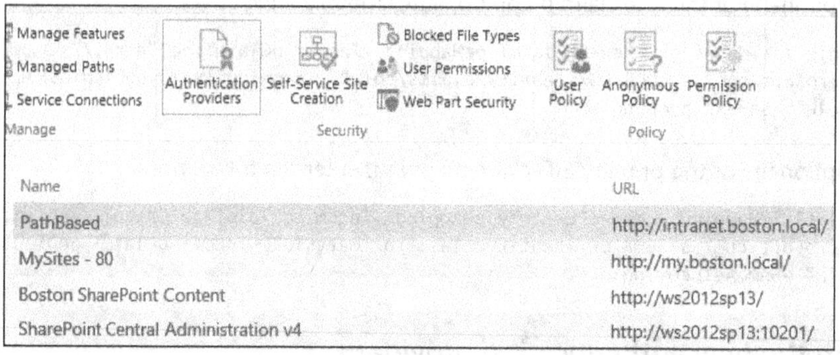

FIGURE 2-5 Selecting authentication providers.

3. Choose the appropriate zone for which you want to assign the new provider (see Figure 2-6).

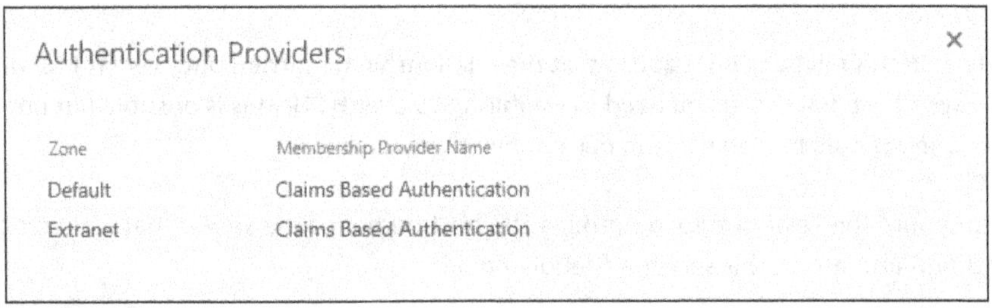

FIGURE 2-6 Selecting a zone.

4. The Trusted Identity Provider check box is now available for selection. Select Trusted Identity Provider and then check the box for the appropriate identity provider (see Figure 2-7).

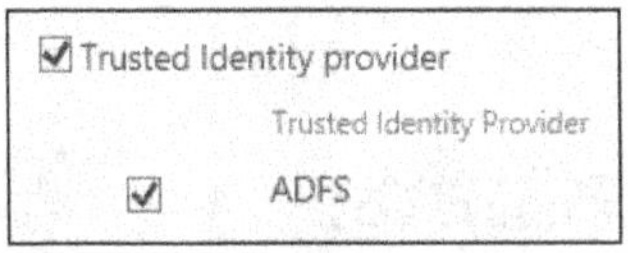

FIGURE 2-7 Selecting the trusted identity provider.

5. Scroll to the bottom of the page and click **Save** to commit your changes.

> **MORE INFO CONFIGURING SAML-BASED CLAIMS AUTHENTICATION**
>
> For more in-depth information concerning claims authentication in a SharePoint farm see the TechNet article "Configure SAML-based Claims Authentication with ADFS in SharePoint 2013" at *http://technet.microsoft.com/en-us/library/hh305235.aspx*.

Configuring server-to-server (S2S) intraserver and OAuth authentication

SharePoint 2013 utilizes the Open Authorization 2.0 (OAuth 2.0) protocol to add a number of new features, including ability to establish server-to-server (S2S) connections. S2S enables you to connect a SharePoint farm to another SharePoint Server farm, an Exchange installation, or a Microsoft Lync installation. Users can then authenticate into SharePoint and retrieve information from these other environments.

Configuring S2S between two SharePoint farms

When establishing this sort of relationship between SharePoint farms, one farm will be receiving S2S requests from the other. This relationship requires that the server sending the requests be configured to use HTTPS.

EXAM TIP

By default, this relationship requires that the relationship be carried out over HTTPS, which is always a best practice. If you need to establish S2S over HTTP, this is possible but not as secure, and should be done only in development environments.

To configure this relationship, determine the host name for the server that is sending the requests and also assign this server a friendly name:

1. Log on to the farm that will be receiving S2S requests.

2. Start a SharePoint 2013 Management Shell, remembering to run as administrator.

3. Enter the following Windows PowerShell command, replacing the host name and friendly name values:

```
New-SPTrustedSecurityTokenIssuer -MetadataEndpoint "https://<HostName>/_
layouts/15/metadata/json/1" -Name "<FriendlyName>"
```

> **MORE INFO** **CONFIGURING S2S BETWEEN SHAREPOINT 2013 FARMS**
>
> The configuration process for setting up S2S gets more complex based on the number of farms being interconnected and the way in which these connections are made. For more details about this process see the TechNet article "Configure Server-to-Server Authentication Between SharePoint 2013 Farms" at *http://technet.microsoft.com/en-us/library/ jj655400.aspx.*

Configuring S2S between SharePoint 2013 and Exchange 2013

S2S authentication between these two environments requires coordination between the administrators of each because the configuration of each system must be modified for Share-Point and Exchange to share resources.

There are three major steps involved in completing this configuration:

- Configuring the SharePoint 2013 Server to trust the Microsoft Exchange 2013 Server
- Configure permissions on the SharePoint 2013 Server for S2S
- Configure the Exchange 2013 Server to trust the SharePoint 2013 Server

EXAM TIP

Be familiar with the three distinct processes that go into establishing the relationship be-tween these two environments.

As usual, these configuration efforts take place in Windows PowerShell and require the use of Secure Sockets Layer (SSL) for communication between server environments.

To configure the SharePoint 2013 Server to trust the Exchange Server (completed by the SharePoint administrator), do the following:

1. Log on to the SharePoint Server.

2. Start a SharePoint 2013 Management Shell, remembering to run as administrator.

3. Set a variable for the SPTrustedSecurityTokenIssuer, similar to the step you took with ADFS earlier in this section. Fill in the ExchHostName field with the name or address of your Exchange 2013 Server and ExchFriendlyName with a friendly name for your Exchange 2013 Server:

```
New-SPTrustedSecurityTokenIssuer -MetadataEndpoint "https://<ExchHostName>/
autodiscover/metadata/json/1" -Name "<ExchFriendlyName>"
```

To configure the permissions on the SharePoint 2013 Server, run the following Windows PowerShell commands (completed by the SharePoint administrator):

1. Set a variable for Exchange and assign it the value of Get-SPTrustedSecurityTokenIssuer:

```
$exchange=Get-SPTrustedSecurityTokenIssuer
```

2. You can get the SPAppPrincipal for the SharePoint web app, assigning it to the $app variable. You also use the Get-SPSite cmdlet and assign its value to $site. The <hostname> value is the name or address of the SharePoint Server:

```
$app=Get-SPAppPrincipal -Site http://<HostName> -NameIdentifier $exchange.NameId
$site=Get-SPSite http://<HostName>
```

3. Finally, set the permission:

```
Set-SPAppPrincipalPermission -AppPrincipal $app -Site $site.RootWeb -Scope
sitesubscription -Right fullcontrol -EnableAppOnlyPolicy
```

To configure Exchange 2013 to trust the SharePoint Server, a Windows PowerShell script called Configure-EnterprisePartnerApplication is run (completed by the Exchange administrator):

1. Open the Exchange Management Shell.

2. Change to the Exchange Server script directory:

```
cd c:\'Program Files'\Microsoft\'Exchange Server'\V15\Scripts
```

3. Run the Windows PowerShell script, replacing the SPHostName value with the name of any SSL-enabled web application of the SharePoint farm:

```
.\Configure-EnterprisePartnerApplication.ps1 -AuthMetadataUrl
https://<SPHostName>/_layouts/15/metadata/json/1 -ApplicationType SharePoint
```

> **IMPORTANT** **TRUSTING ONE IS TRUSTING ALL**
>
> The trust that is shared between these two environments is not web-app specific. Establishing the trust from Exchange 2013 to one of the SharePoint 2013 web apps establishes a trust with all the web apps in the entire farm.

Configuring S2S between SharePoint 2013 and Lync Server 2013

S2S authentication between these two environments requires coordination between the administrators of each because the configuration of each system must be modified for SharePoint and Lync to share resources.

There are only two steps involved in completing this configuration:

- Configure the SharePoint 2013 Server to trust the Lync 2013 Server.
- Configure the Lync 2013 Server to trust the SharePoint 2013 Server.

These configuration efforts take place in Windows PowerShell and require the use of SSL for communication between server environments.

> **MORE INFO** **CONFIGURING S2S BETWEEN SHAREPOINT AND LYNC**
>
> If you want to know more about the process of connecting these two environments, visit the TechNet site "Configure Server-to-Server Authentication Between SharePoint 2013 and Lync Server 2013" at *http://technet.microsoft.com/en-us/library/jj670179.aspx*.

This configuration is still fairly basic from the SharePoint administrator standpoint. To configure the SharePoint 2013 Server to trust the Lync Server (completed by the SharePoint administrator), do the following:

1. Log on to the SharePoint Server.

2. Start a SharePoint 2013 Management Shell, remembering to run as administrator.

3. Set a variable for the SPTrustedSecurityTokenIssuer, similar to the step you took with ADFS and Exchange earlier in this section. Fill in the LyncHostName field with the name or address of your Lync 2013 Server and LyncFriendlyName with a friendly name for your Lync 2013 Server.

```
New-SPTrustedSecurityTokenIssuer -MetadataEndpoint "https://<LyncHostName>/
autodiscover/metadata/json/1" -Name "<LyncFriendlyName>"
```

To configure Lync 2013 to trust the SharePoint Server is quite a bit more involved than configuration is with Exchange (completed by the Exchange administrator):

1. Assign an S2S authentication certificate to Lync 2013.

2. Configure the Lync Server using the script found in the TechNet Article, "Configuring an On-Premises Partner Application for Microsoft Lync Server 2013" at *http://technet.microsoft.com/en-us/library/jj204975.aspx*.

3. In the script, change the sample lines containing the metadata URL string http://atl-sharepoint-001.litwareinc.com/jsonmetadata.ashx to read https://<NameAndPort>/_layouts/15/metadata/json/1, where the NameAndPort value is the host name/address and port of any SSL-enabled SharePoint Web Application.

Planning and configuring anonymous authentication

Anonymous is far and away the easiest method of authentication to plan for and implement. This authentication type enables a user to access a SharePoint web application (such as an Internet-facing web site) without being challenged for user name and password credentials.

As with the other types of authentication, anonymous authentication can be applied to the zone of a given web application. Each zone maintains its own list of which authentication types can be used.

To enable anonymous access to a web application, do the following:

1. From Central Administration, select Application Management.

2. On the Application Management page, click the URL area of your desired web application. From the ribbon, in the Security section, select the Authentication Providers icon on the ribbon (see Figure 2-8).

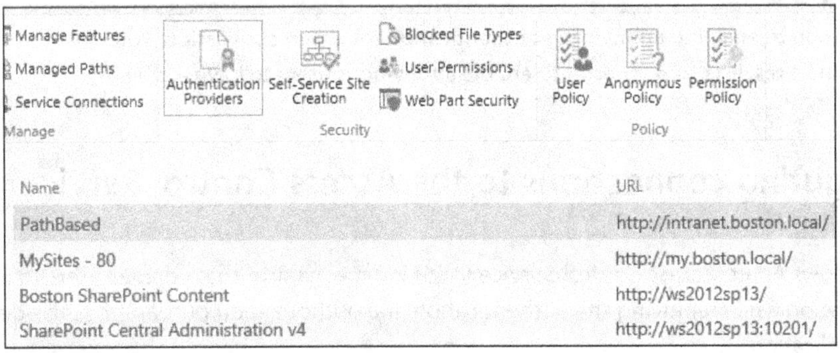

FIGURE 2-8 Selecting authentication providers.

3. Choose the appropriate zone for which you want to enable anonymous access (see Figure 2-9).

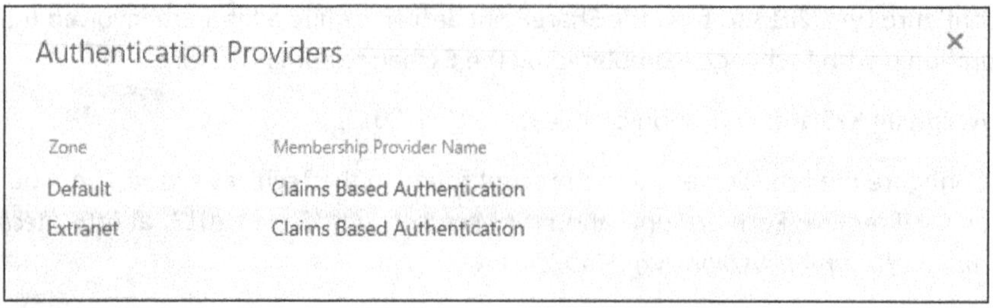

FIGURE 2-9 Selecting a zone.

4. On the Edit Authentication page, scroll to the section that reads Anonymous Access. Select the **Enable Anonymous Access** check box shown in Figure 2-10.

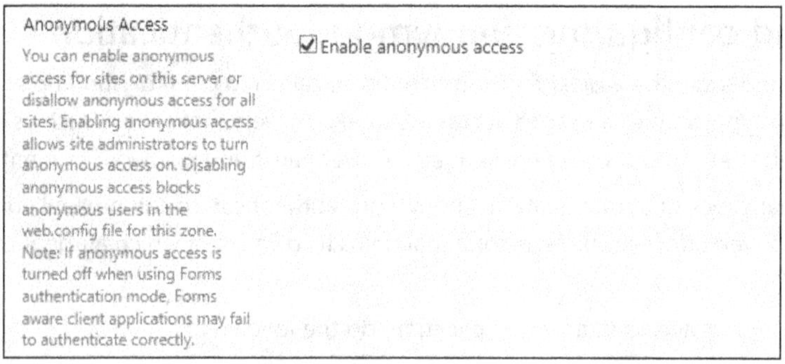

FIGURE 2-10 Enabling anonymous access.

5. Scroll to the bottom of the page and click **Save** to commit your changes.

EXAM TIP

In addition to enabling anonymous authentication for a web application, you must also configure sites, lists, and libraries to enable anonymous users to have access.

Configuring connections to the Access Control Service (ACS)

The Windows Azure Access Control Service (ACS) is a mechanism that enables users to access an application while removing the authentication and authorization burden from the design of the application.

IMPORTANT USING THE CURRENT VERSION OF ACS

There have been two versions of this service. The latest, v2.0, is free for use and is the only supported version.

ACS enables applications such as SharePoint 2013 to integrate with both Enterprise directories (such as Active Directory) and identity providers in the cloud such as Windows Live ID, Google, Yahoo!, and Facebook.

Using ACS for SharePoint authentication

As you saw in the section about using ADFS for authentication, there is a lot of configuration work that goes into creating simple authentication. Each organization that wants to federate has to designate an identity provider (usually ADFS); but that's just the beginning.

The organization that provides the SharePoint application functionality has to configure the relationship between SharePoint and its own identity provider; or worse yet, the relationship between SharePoint and all the partner identity providers.

> **IMPORTANT** **RECAPPING: ONE POINT OF CONTACT**
>
> For ease of administration, trust relationships should be established between your identity provider and those of your partner organizations, rather than between your application and the identity providers of your partner organization.

Configuring ACS for use with SharePoint 2013

To use ACS for SharePoint authentication, you have to run through a series of configuration steps. These steps establish and configure your company's ACS subscription (even though you have to subscribe to the trial, the use of the authentication component is still free on a continuous basis).

First, you need to create a new subscription at *http://www.windowsazure.com* for your company. After you have taken care of the subscription, it's time to configure ACS:

1. After you log on, you are redirected to the main page for the Select The Portal icon beneath your logon (see Figure 2-11).

FIGURE 2-11 Portal icon.

2. Create a namespace for your subscription. Select the Create A New Namespace link. Enter a Namespace Name and select the Region that you belong in (see Figure 2-12); then click the Check icon.

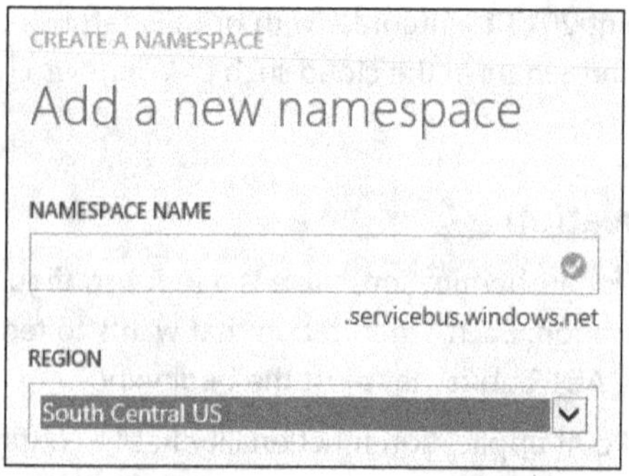

FIGURE 2-12 Adding a new namespace.

3. The completed namespace now appears in the Service Bus; click this link (indicated by an arrow) to continue.

4. Within the Service Bus, from the Management Tasks section, select the Manage Access Key link (see Figure 2-13).

Management tasks ⊘
Manage Access Key

FIGURE 2-13 Selecting Manage Access Key.

5. When the Connect To Your Namespace Page appears, select the Open ACS Management Portal link.

6. At this point, you need to configure one or more identity providers. Selecting this link under Trust Relationships shows existing identity providers (Windows Live ID, by default, shown in Figure 2-14).

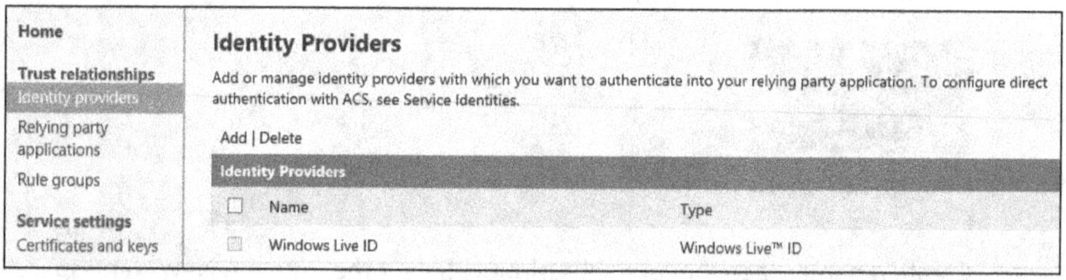

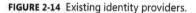

FIGURE 2-14 Existing identity providers.

7. Selecting the Add link enables you to see the Add Identity Provider page. There are several options available (see Figure 2-15):

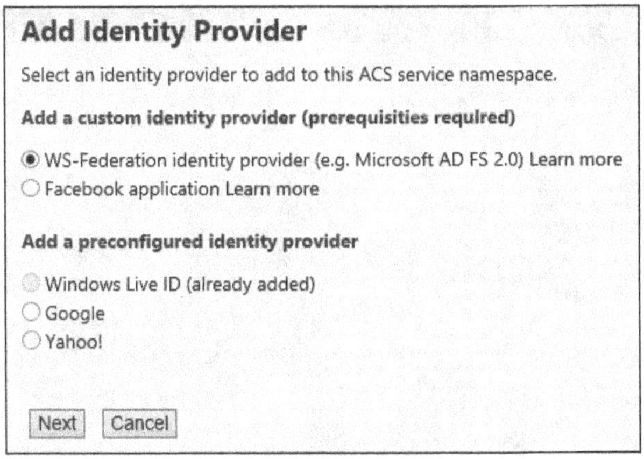

Add Identity Provider

Select an identity provider to add to this ACS service namespace.

Add a custom identity provider (prerequisities required)

◉ WS-Federation identity provider (e.g. Microsoft AD FS 2.0) Learn more
◯ Facebook application Learn more

Add a preconfigured identity provider

◯ Windows Live ID (already added)
◯ Google
◯ Yahoo!

[Next] [Cancel]

FIGURE 2-15 Adding an identity provider.

- Custom identity providers, such as WS-Federation and Facebook, require some additional configuration for use.

- Preconfigured identity providers (Windows Live ID, Google, and Yahoo!) require no extra configuration effort for use.

8. Select Relying Party Applications. The existing Service Bus is shown.

9. Selecting the Add link enables you to configure your SharePoint implementation as a relying party application. You need to specify the Name, Mode, Realm (https:// yourURL), Error URL (optional); what token format to use; and a configurable token lifetime (see Figure 2-16). Make a note of the Realm value; you will be using it again shortly.

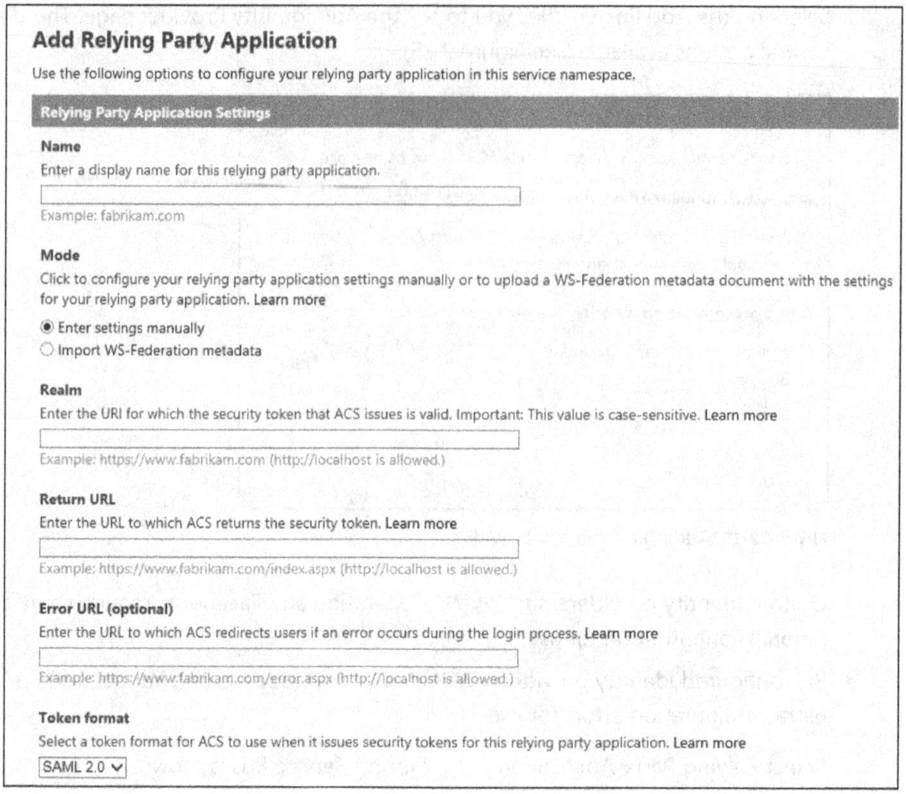

Add Relying Party Application

Use the following options to configure your relying party application in this service namespace.

Relying Party Application Settings

Name

Enter a display name for this relying party application.

[   ]

Example: fabrikam.com

Mode

Click to configure your relying party application settings manually or to upload a WS-Federation metadata document with the settings for your relying party application. Learn more

◉ Enter settings manually
○ Import WS-Federation metadata

Realm

Enter the URI for which the security token that ACS issues is valid. Important: This value is case-sensitive. Learn more

[   ]

Example: https://www.fabrikam.com (http://localhost is allowed.)

Return URL

Enter the URL to which ACS returns the security token. Learn more

[   ]

Example: https://www.fabrikam.com/index.aspx (http://localhost is allowed.)

Error URL (optional)

Enter the URL to which ACS redirects users if an error occurs during the login process. Learn more

[   ]

Example: https://www.fabrikam.com/error.aspx (http://localhost is allowed.)

Token format

Select a token format for ACS to use when it issues security tokens for this relying party application. Learn more

[SAML 2.0 ⌄]

FIGURE 2-16 Adding relying party application settings.

EXAM TIP

The capability to expire a token provides additional security for your SharePoint installation by disconnecting unused sessions. You may want to extend this value to 1200 seconds (10 minutes) for your SharePoint users, depending on how often you want them to log on.

10. Still on the Add Relying Party Application page, scroll down to the Authentication Settings and Token Signing Settings page, choosing values for the Identity Providers, Rule Groups, and Token Signing Settings sections.

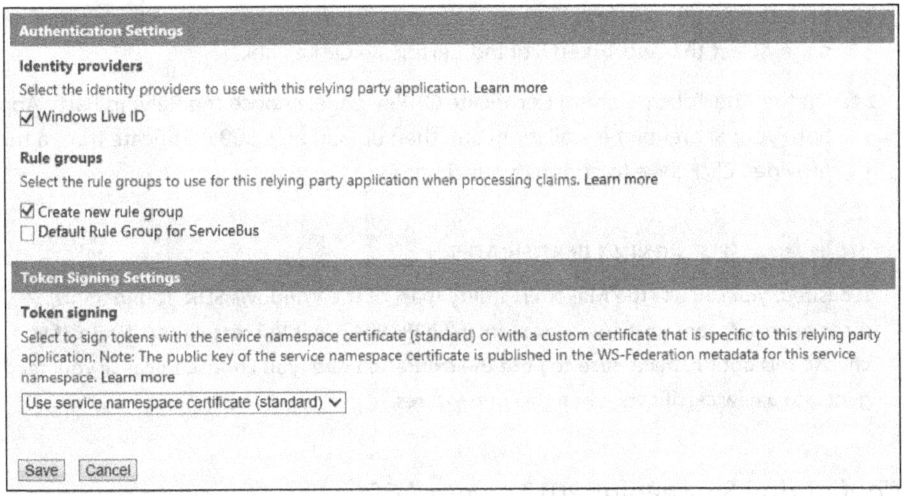

FIGURE 2-17 Choosing authentication and token signing settings.

11. Select the Rule Groups link and create a new rule group for your SharePoint application, specifying the Name and Relying Party Applications (SharePoint) to use this rule group. Click the Generate button to create rules for your selected providers (see Figure 2-18).

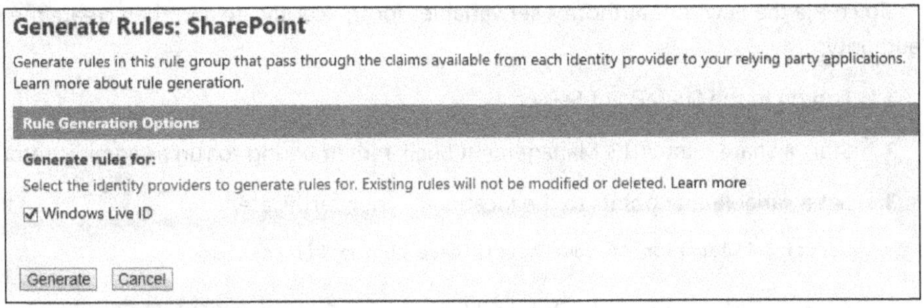

FIGURE 2-18 Generating rules for the identity providers.

12. A rule is created for each of your identity providers (see Figure 2-19). Click Save to commit your changes.

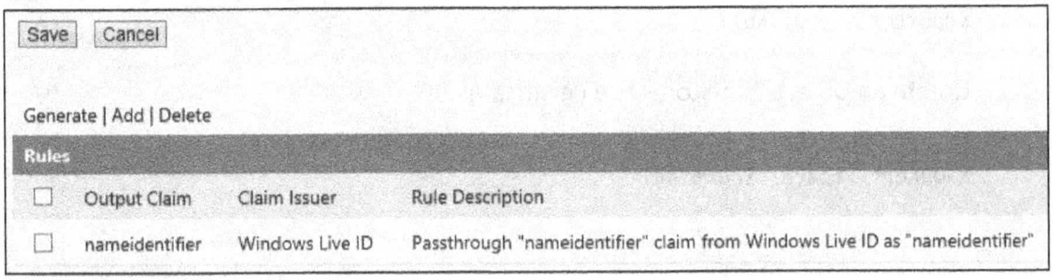

FIGURE 2-19 Generated rule(s).

13. Click the Certificates And Keys link in Service Settings. On the Certificates And Keys page, select the Add Token Signing Certificate Or Key link.

14. On the Add Token-Signing Certificate Or Key page, choose the Relying Party Application (your SharePoint installation) and then upload an x.509 certificate from a trusted provider. Click Save to commit your changes.

> **MORE INFO** **SELF-SIGNING CERTIFICATES**
>
> If desired, you can use the MakeCert utility (part of the Windows SDK, found at *http:// msdn.microsoft.com/en-us/windowsserver/bb980924.aspx*) to create a certificate. If you choose this option, make sure to note the expiration date you choose because you need to generate a new certificate when this one expires.

Configuring SharePoint 2013 to use ACS

As with the other claims-based connections, you now need to make claim mappings from ACS to SharePoint 2013. This claim mapping happens in three sections:

- Create a new trusted root authority
- Map the user principal name and email address fields
- Create a new trusted identity token issuer

To create the new root authority, set variables for the certificate and then create the root authority:

1. Log on to the SharePoint Server.

2. Start a SharePoint 2013 Management Shell, remembering to run as administrator.

3. Set a variable that points to the location of your certificate:

   ```
   $certloc="<location of your certificate on the file system>"
   ```

4. Set a variable that gets the Personal Information Exchange (PFX) certificate:

   ```
   $rootcert = Get-PfxCertificate $certloc
   ```

5. Create the new Trusted Root Authority:

   ```
   New-SPTrustedRootAuthority -name "ACS Token Signing Certificate" -certificate
   $rootcert | Out-Null
   ```

6. Create an object that stores the certificate:

   ```
   $cert = New-Object System.Security.Cryptography.X509Certificates.
   X509Certificate2($certloc)
   ```

7. Define the claims you will use (in this case, the UPN and Email Address):

```
$map1 = New-SPClaimTypeMapping -IncomingClaimType "http://schemas.xmlsoap.org/
claims/EmailAddress" -IncomingClaimTypeDisplayName "http://schemas.xmlsoap.org/
claims/EmailAddress" -SameAsIncoming

$map2 = New-SPClaimTypeMapping -IncomingClaimType "http://schemas.xmlsoap.org/
ws/2005/05/identity/claims/nameidentifier" -IncomingClaimTypeDisplayName "UPN"
-LocalClaimType "http://schemas.xmlsoap.org/ws/2005/05/identity/claims/upn"
```

8. Find the realm URL that you entered in the Relying Party Application screen of ACS and assign it to a variable:

```
$realm="https://<yoururl>"
```

9. Assign the sign-in URL for ACS, where the namespace value is the one you assign in Step 2 of your ACS account setup:

```
$signInUrl = "https://<namespace>.accesscontrol.windows.net/v2/wsfederation"
```

10. Finally, you create the token issuer:

```
$ap = New-SPTrustedIdentityTokenIssuer -Name "Azure ACS" -Description "Access
Control Services" -Realm $realm -ImportTrustCertificate $cert -ClaimsMappings
$map1,$map2 -SignInUrl $signInUrl -IdentifierClaim "http://schemas.xmlsoap.org/
ws/2005/05/identity/claims/nameidentifier"
```

Selecting the authentication provider

Now that the ACS configuration is complete, you can configure it for the appropriate web application:

1. From Central Administration, select Application Management.

2. On the Application Management page, click the URL area of your desired web application and then select the Authentication Providers icon on the ribbon (Security section, shown in Figure 2-20).

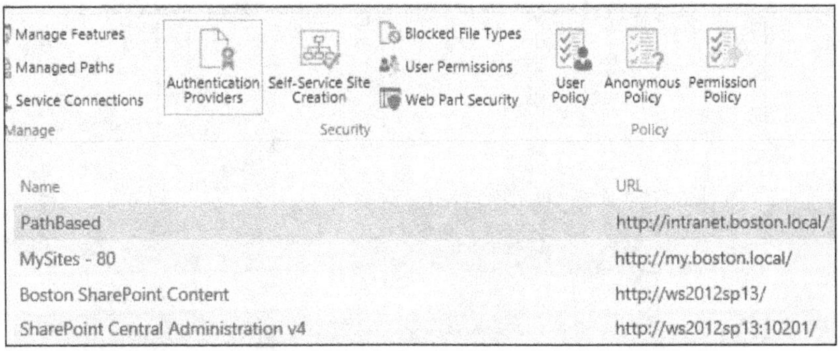

FIGURE 2-20 Selecting authentication providers.

3. Choose the appropriate zone for which you want to assign the new provider (see Figure 2-21).

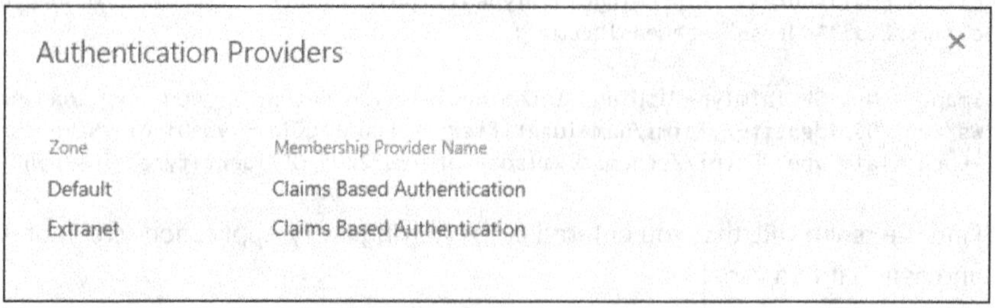

Authentication Providers ×

Zone	Membership Provider Name
Default	Claims Based Authentication
Extranet	Claims Based Authentication

FIGURE 2-21 Selecting a zone.

4. The Trusted Identity Provider check box is now available for selection. Select it and then choose the box for the appropriate identity provider (see Figure 2-22).

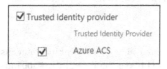

FIGURE 2-22 Selecting the trusted identity provider.

5. Scroll to the bottom of the page and click Save to commit your changes.

> **MORE INFO CONFIGURING ACS**
>
> This is by no means a definitive, end-to-end guide for creating the relationship between SharePoint and ACS. Although we have covered the basic steps, there is a lot of detail in items such as configuring the SSL certificate and defining the relying party (RP) application. For more detail on the configuration of ACS, see the MSDN article "Access Control Service 2.0" at *http://msdn.microsoft.com/en-us/library/hh147631.aspx*.

Objective summary

- Authentication verifies the identity of a requestor as genuine.
- Three kinds of authentication exist in SharePoint 2013: user, app, and S2S.
- SharePoint performs no authentication—ever.
- When a user authenticates to the identity provider within the organization, he or she receives a SAML token.
- OAuth is HTTPS-enabled by default. This configuration should not be changed for production environments.
- S2S can be configured between SharePoint, Exchange, and Lync farms.
- Anonymous authentication enables a user to access resources without being challenged for user name and password credentials.
- Anonymous authentication is specified at the zone level of a web application.
- Token lifetime is a setting used to automatically expire unused sessions.

Objective review

Answer the following questions to test your knowledge of the information in this objective. You can find the answers to these questions and explanations of why each answer choice is correct or incorrect in the "Answers" section at the end of this chapter.

1. Which of the following are considered integrated Windows authentication types? (Choose all that apply.)

   A. Basic authentication

   B. Forms authentication

   C. Kerberos authentication

   D. NTLM authentication

2. Which of the following authentication types are not claims-based? (Choose all that apply.)

   A. Windows classic authentication

   B. NTLM authentication

   C. Site collection authentication

   D. Forms authentication

3. Which of the following are supported configurations for S2S? (Choose all that apply.)

   A. SharePoint 2013 to Exchange 2013

   B. SharePoint 2013 to Lync 2013

   C. SharePoint 2013 to SQL Server 2012

   D. SharePoint 2013 to SharePoint 2013

4. At which of the following levels can anonymous authentication be configured in SharePoint? (Choose all that apply.)

   A. Zone

   B. Web application

   C. Site collection

   D. Site

Objective 2.2: Plan and configure authorization

After a user has been authenticated, he or she can then be validated when attempting to interact with resources in a web application; this validation process is called authorization.

> **This objective covers how to:**
> - Plan and configure SharePoint users and groups.
> - Plan and configure People Picker.
> - Plan and configure sharing.
> - Plan and configure permission inheritance.
> - Plan and configure anonymous access.
> - Plan web application policies.

Planning and configuring SharePoint users and groups

After users have been authenticated to a web application, they need to access the site collections contained within the web app. This access is granted via a series of permission levels that can be assigned to individual users or to SharePoint groups.

The optimal assignment of the permission structure goes something like this:

1. Individual permissions are assigned to a permission level.

2. One or more permission levels are assigned to a SharePoint group.

3. Users are assigned to the SharePoint group, receiving access based on the individual permissions.

EXAM TIP

It is not uncommon to see a user added to more than one group within a SharePoint site collection. As an example, consider a user who belongs to both the Visitors (Reader permissions) and Members (Contributor permissions) SharePoint groups for a site. This person will receive the greater of the two permission sets, thus having the permissions that are assigned to the Contributor permission level.

Individual permissions

SharePoint has a total of 33 individual permissions that control how a user interacts with a SharePoint site. These permissions are broken apart into three distinct levels:

- List permissions that apply only to lists and libraries
- Site permissions that apply to a particular site

- Personal permissions that apply to specialized objects such as personal views and personal web parts

Permission levels

As a SharePoint site is being created, a series of permission levels are created. The number and type of permission levels may vary, depending on the type of site created (for instance, there are a total of seven created for a Team Site, whereas there are 10 created for a Publishing Portal).

> **MORE INFO** **PERMISSION LEVELS IN SHAREPOINT 2013**
>
> For a complete list of permission levels and individual permissions see the TechNet article "User Permissions and Permission Levels in SharePoint 2013" at *http://technet.microsoft.com/en-us/library/cc721640.aspx*.

These permission levels are nothing more than an aggregation of the individual permissions available within the site collection. To view the permission levels on a site and the individual permissions assigned to each, follow these steps:

1. Navigate to your site.

2. From the Settings menu (gear icon), select Site Settings.

3. In the Users and Permissions section, select Site Permissions.

4. On the ribbon, select the Permission Levels icon (in the Manage section, shown in Figure 2-23).

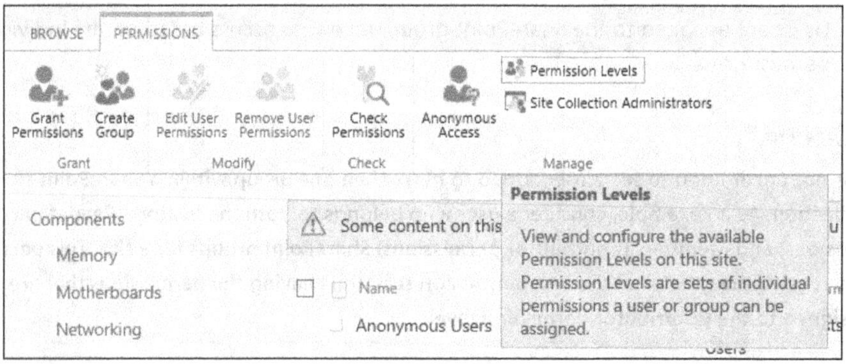

FIGURE 2-23 Selecting the Permissions Level icon.

5. When the Permission Levels screen appears, you see all the permissions levels available to the site and their descriptions (see Figure 2-24).

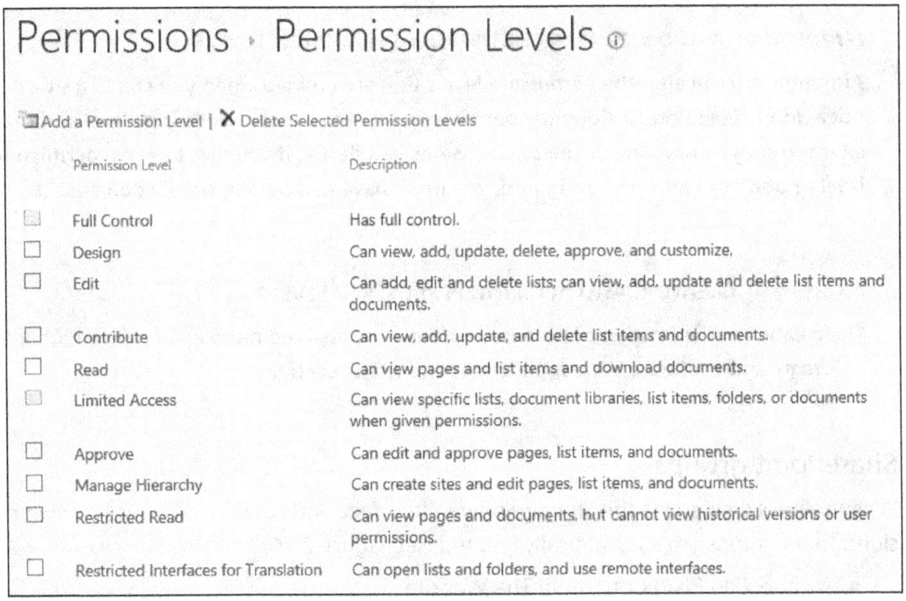

Permissions › Permission Levels ⓘ

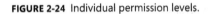
Add a Permission Level | ✕ Delete Selected Permission Levels

	Permission Level	Description
☐	Full Control	Has full control.
☐	Design	Can view, add, update, delete, approve, and customize.
☐	Edit	Can add, edit and delete lists; can view, add, update and delete list items and documents.
☐	Contribute	Can view, add, update, and delete list items and documents.
☐	Read	Can view pages and list items and download documents.
☐	Limited Access	Can view specific lists, document libraries, list items, folders, or documents when given permissions.
☐	Approve	Can edit and approve pages, list items, and documents.
☐	Manage Hierarchy	Can create sites and edit pages, list items, and documents.
☐	Restricted Read	Can view pages and documents, but cannot view historical versions or user permissions.
☐	Restricted Interfaces for Translation	Can open lists and folders, and use remote interfaces.

FIGURE 2-24 Individual permission levels.

6. If you select an individual permission level, you see the list of permissions that make up that permission level (see Figure 2-25).

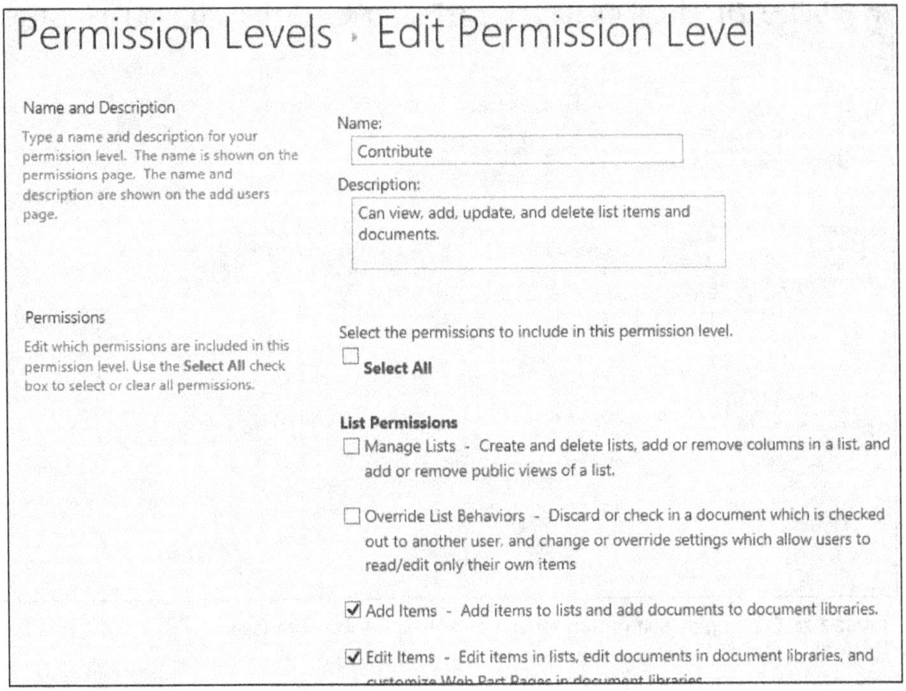

Permission Levels › Edit Permission Level

Name and Description

Type a name and description for your permission level. The name is shown on the permissions page. The name and description are shown on the add users page.

Name:

Contribute

Description:

Can view, add, update, and delete list items and documents.

Permissions

Edit which permissions are included in this permission level. Use the **Select All** check box to select or clear all permissions.

Select the permissions to include in this permission level.

☐ **Select All**

List Permissions

☐ Manage Lists - Create and delete lists, add or remove columns in a list, and add or remove public views of a list.

☐ Override List Behaviors - Discard or check in a document which is checked out to another user, and change or override settings which allow users to read/edit only their own items

☑ Add Items - Add items to lists and add documents to document libraries.

☑ Edit Items - Edit items in lists, edit documents in document libraries, and customize Web Part Pages in document libraries.

FIGURE 2-25 Editing a permission level.

IMPORTANT **AVOID ALTERING THE DEFAULT PERMISSION LEVELS**

Although you can alter the permission levels that are defined when you create a site, it is not a good idea to do so. Copy the permissions level to a new permissions level and then alter the copy to have the distinct permissions you desire. If you don't need a permission level or don't like how it's configured, you don't have to delete it; simply don't use it.

MORE INFO **CREATING AND ALTERING PERMISSION LEVELS**

The creation and alteration of permissions levels are covered more extensively in Chapter 4, "Create and configure Web applications and site collections."

SharePoint groups

When a site is created via the SharePoint web interface and configured to use its own permissions, three groups are automatically created (see Figure 2-26).

- Visitors Can Read Content In The Website
- Members Can Contribute Content In The Website
- Owners Have Full Control Over The Website

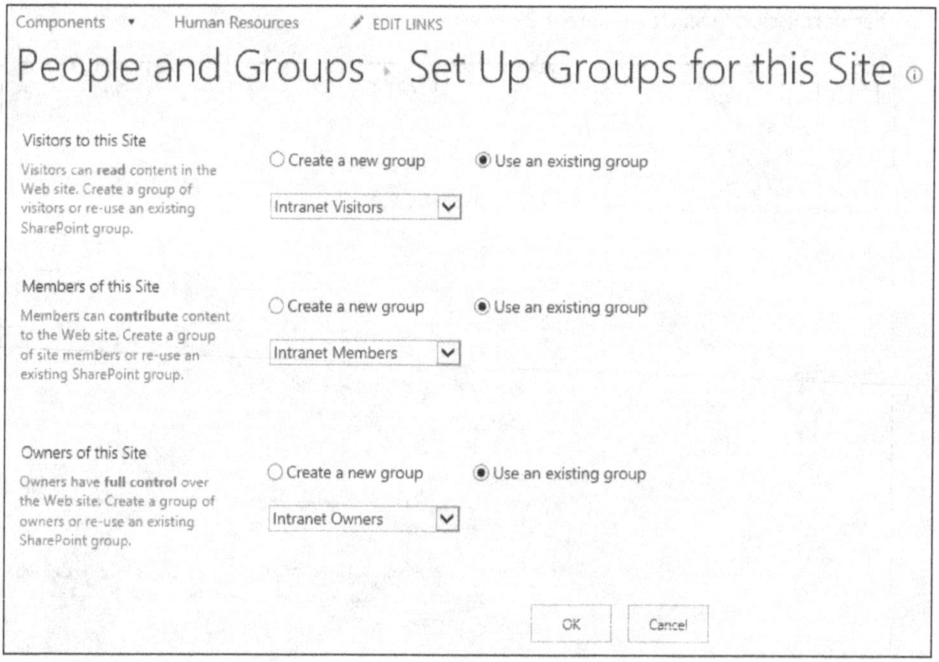

FIGURE 2-26 Creating default groups for SharePoint via the web interface.

Planning and configuring People Picker

People Picker is a web control that is used extensively throughout SharePoint 2013 to enable the selection of users, groups, and claims from a claims provider by the friendly name.

This control is configured at the zone level of a farm, enabling several levels of administrative granularity. As each zone is created, different authentication types are applied to the zone.

The People Picker control can be tailored to meet the needs of users in that zone. For instance, if you have users who were being authenticated over a forms-based authentication interface, you might choose to exclude Active Directory accounts from appearing in the People Picker.

Configuring People Picker properties

Administration of the People Picker web control is accomplished using the STSADM command along with getproperty (to retrieve values) and setproperty (to apply new values) operations.

The STSADM.exe command-line tool can be found at the following default location on any farm that has SharePoint installed:

```
%COMMONPROGRAMFILES%\Microsoft Shared\Web Server Extensions\15\Bin
```

EXAM TIP

There are no Windows PowerShell cmdlets for the configuration of People Picker in SharePoint 2013. All the properties that provide People Picker configuration are done via STSADM.

If you execute the STSADM -help setproperty (don't forget to run the command prompt as administrator), you find a total of nine property names that can be used to administer the People Picker web control. These property names are listed beneath the SharePoint virtual server properties section, and all begin with the "peoplepicker" prefix.

These property names are shown in Table 2-1.

TABLE 2-1 People Picker properties

Property name	Description
Peoplepicker-activedirectorysearchtimeout	Configures the time out when a query is issued to AD DS.
Peoplepicker-distributionlistsearchdomains	Restricts the search of a distribution list to a specific subset of domains.
Peoplepicker-nowindowsaccountsfornonwindows authenticationmode	Specifies not to search Active Directory when the current port is using forms-based authentication.
Peoplepicker-onlysearchwithinsitecollection	Displays only users who are members of the site collection.
Peoplepicker-peopleeditoronlyresolvewithinsite collection	Displays only users who are members of the current site collection.
Peoplepicker-searchadcustomfilter	Enables a farm administrator to specify a unique search query.
Peoplepicker-searchadcustomquery	Permits the administrator to set the custom query that is sent to Active Directory.
Peoplepicker-searchadforests	Permits a user to search from a second one-way trusted forest or domain.
Peoplepicker-serviceaccountdirectorypaths	Enables a farm administrator to manage the site collection that has a specific organizational unit (OU) setting as defined in the Setsiteuseraccountdirectorypath setting.

If you'd rather not type the full text of the -propertyname and -propertyvalue switches when running the STSADM command, you can instead substitute -pn and -pv, respectively.

> **MORE INFO** **USING STSADM TO CONFIGURE THE PEOPLE PICKER**
>
> There are many different scenarios for configuring the People Picker, most having to do with either configuring it for a particular authentication type or restricting the amount and type of results shown. In either event, the TechNet article "Configure People Picker in SharePoint 2013" details a lot of these options (and some LDAP magic). This article can be found at *http://technet.microsoft.com/en-us/library/gg602075.aspx*.

Planning and configuring sharing

Sometimes site owners may not be familiar with every user who accesses the site. Perhaps the team member is in the next office, but it is just as likely that he or she could be located half a world away in a different regional office.

Users in remote offices change, often without the site owner's knowledge. Sometimes they are added from other teams or perhaps they are a new hire. Personnel in the remote office can now "share" content in SharePoint 2013, recommending that a person be able to access information using one of the site's permission groups (Visitor, Member, and so on).

When the request is made, the site owner is notified of the request and can then choose whether to grant or reject the permission request.

Prerequisite configuration

In order for the sharing functionality to work, outbound e-mail must be properly configured in Central Administration so access requests can be routed and acknowledgements sent via e-mail.

In particular, the following settings must be configured (see Figure 2-27):

- Outbound SMTP Server
- From Address

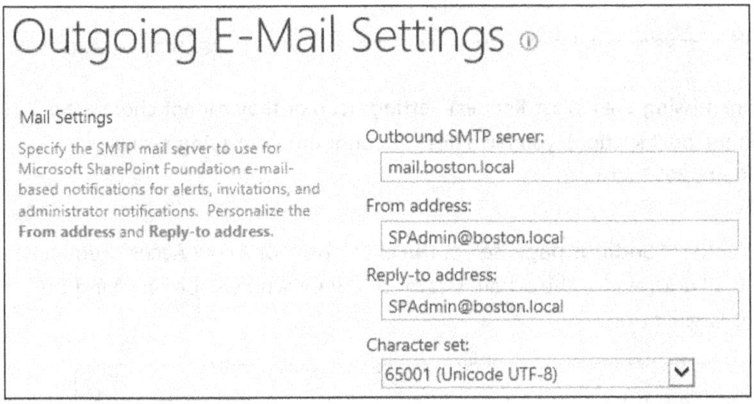

Outgoing E-Mail Settings ⓘ

Mail Settings
Specify the SMTP mail server to use for Microsoft SharePoint Foundation e-mail-based notifications for alerts, invitations, and administrator notifications. Personalize the **From address** and **Reply-to address.**

Outbound SMTP server:
mail.boston.local

From address:
SPAdmin@boston.local

Reply-to address:
SPAdmin@boston.local

Character set:
65001 (Unicode UTF-8)

FIGURE 2-27 Outgoing e-mail settings.

> **MORE INFO OUTGOING E-MAIL CONFIGURATION SETTINGS**
>
> More in-depth details for outgoing e-mail configuration settings are covered in Chapter 3, "Install and configure SharePoint farms."

Configuring a site for access requests

In order for sharing to take place within a site, it must be configured to enable access requests. This configuration is made on the Site Permissions page, as follows:

1. Navigate to your site.

2. From the Settings menu (gear icon), select Site Settings.

3. In the Users And Permissions section, select Site Permissions.

4. On the ribbon, select the Access Request Settings icon (in the Manage section, shown in Figure 2-28).

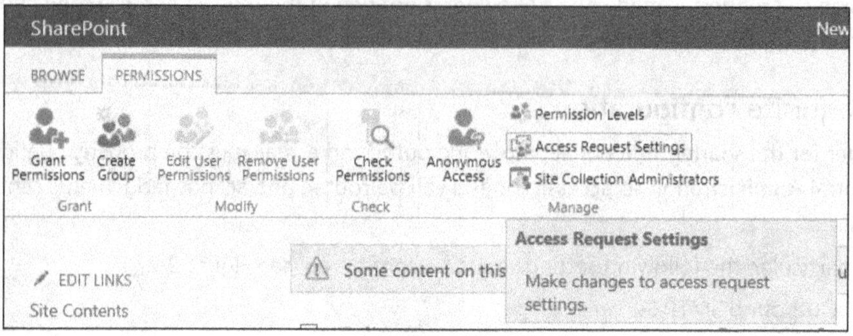

FIGURE 2-28 Selecting access request settings.

EXAM TIP

EXAM TIP

If your site owners are missing the Access Request Settings icon or they cannot choose the Share icon (shown in the next section), you have not yet configured outgoing e-mail settings for your SharePoint 2013 farm.

5. On the Access Requests Settings page, select the check box for Allow Access Requests and enter an e-mail address for the administrator or owner who will be receiving the e-mail addresses (see Figure 2-29).

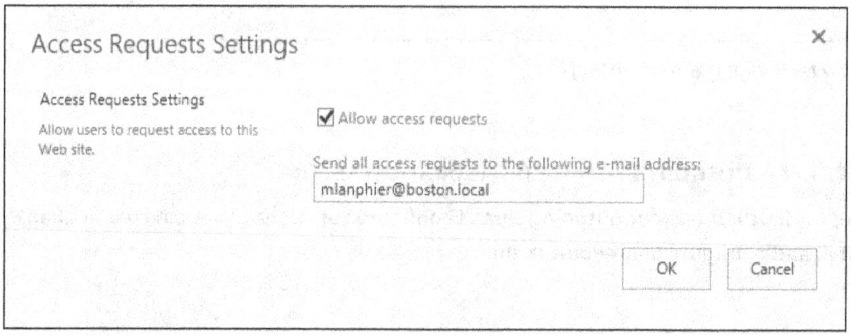

FIGURE 2-29 Allowing access requests.

6. Click OK to commit your changes.

Sharing site content from the site level

At this point, users can now share site content with other users. This invitation can be sent from the site level or from within a list or library. Follow these steps:

1. Select the Share link, located in the upper-right corner of the page next to the Follow icon (see Figure 2-30).

○ SHARE ☆ FOLLOW

FIGURE 2-30 Share link.

2. On the Share page, enter the name or e-mail address of the person being invited. Optionally, you can type a message.

3. Selecting the Show Options link enables you to select a different permission level for assignment to the user (instead of Contribute, as shown in Figure 2-31).

Share 'Human Resources'   ✕

👥 Shared with ⬜ Marlene Lanphier and ⬜ Troy Lanphier

Invite people to 'Contribute'

Marlene Lanphier x

Welcome to the Human Resources site

HIDE OPTIONS

☑ Send an email invitation

Select a group or permission level

Human Resources Members [Contribute]	⌄

[Share] [Cancel]

FIGURE 2-31 Sharing the Human Resources site.

4. Click Share to commit your changes.

Sharing site content from the list or library level

To share site content from the list or library level, follow these steps:

1. Open the ribbon for the library and locate the Shared With icon on the far right side (see Figure 2-32).

FIGURE 2-32 Shared With icon.

2. On the Shared With page, select the Invite People link.

3. On the Share page for the list or library, enter the name or e-mail address of the person being invited. Optionally, you can type a message.

4. Selecting the Show Options link enables you to select a different permission level for assignment to the user (instead of Contribute, as shown in Figure 2-33).

   Note that these permissions are different from those depicted in Figure 2-31.

Share 'Human Resources'   ✕

  Shared with ☐ Marlene Lanphier and ☐ Troy Lanphier

Invite people to 'Contribute'

Marlene Lanphier x

Welcome to the Human Resources site

HIDE OPTIONS

☑ Send an email invitation

Select a group or permission level

Human Resources Members [Contribute]   ⌄

Share   Cancel

FIGURE 2-33 Sharing the Documents library.

5. Click Share to commit your changes.

Planning and configuring permission inheritance

Permissions inheritance is often a sensitive subject. On the one hand, you want to provide the best security for the objects within a site collection; on the other, you want to ease the administrative burden by making the permission structure as flexible as possible while still providing effective permissions.

EXAM TIP

Breaking permission inheritance does not immediately change the effective permissions on the site, list, or library. A copy of the parent's permissions is made and applied to the object before permissions are split.

Common permission inheritance

Consider the objects in Table 2-2 and their permissions inheritance structure.

TABLE 2-2 Common permission inheritance

Securable Object	Description	Unique or Inherited Permissions
Intranet	Intranet home page	Unique
Intranet/ManagementTeam	Sensitive group	Unique
Intranet/ManagementTeam/BonusStructure	Sensitive data	Unique
Intranet/ManagementTeam/EmployeeSurveys	Nonsensitive data	Inherits from ManagementTeam
Intranet/NewsArticles	Intranet news	Inherited
Intranet/NewsArticles/DailyUpdates	Nonsensitive data	Inherited
Intranet/FieldGroup	Field team site	Inherited
Intranet/FieldGroup/ShopNotes	Nonsensitive data	Inherited
Intranet/FieldGroup/Clients	Sensitive data	Unique

Permissions in this series of objects have a few things in common:

- Permissions are assigned in as common a way as possible:
    - The News Articles and Field Group sites inherit permissions from the parent site (intranet)
    - The Daily Updates and Shop Notes libraries also inherit this permissions structure
    - The Employee Surveys list inherits its permissions from the ManagementTeam site
- Items that require unique permissions are separated from the overall structure
    - The Management Team site and its descendants
    - The Clients list under Field Group

Administration of this environment will be fairly simplistic because most levels inherit from their parent objects. No fine-grained permissions are required, easing administrative overhead.

Fine-grained permissions

If you took the same objects and collapsed some of the lists into one another, you may find that maintenance of the site becomes more involved.

TABLE 2-3 Fine-grained permissions

Securable Object	Description	Unique or Inherited Permissions
Intranet	Intranet home page	Unique
Intranet/ManagementTeam	Sensitive group	Unique
Intranet/ManagementTeam/DocumentLibrary	Sensitive and nonsensitive data	Inherited, but employee surveys must be individually secured
Intranet/NewsArticles	Intranet news	Inherited
Intranet/NewsArticles/DailyUpdates	Nonsensitive data	Inherited
Intranet/FieldGroup	Field team site	Inherited
Intranet/FieldGroup/DocumentLibrary	Sensitive and nonsensitive data	Inherited, but client documents must be individually secured

Permissions in this series of objects are more complex because the document libraries in the Field Group and Management Team sites now have documents that must be individually secured.

At first, this would not seem to be much of a problem. A new sensitive document (bonus structure or client document) could be secured, right? Absolutely; but the problem occurs when the document isn't secured properly or permissions for that series of documents change.

> **IMPORTANT** **SEARCH IS PERVASIVE**
>
> There's that one other technology that is so vital in SharePoint: search. Search is pervasive, browsing all the documents in the farm (unless told to do otherwise). When users search for a keyword, their permissions level is checked; if a bonus document is unsecured and the user searches for the word "performance," search might return back the bonus structure for an executive, thus revealing sensitive information.

MORE INFO **MORE ON PERMISSION LEVELS AND INHERITANCE**

More in-depth details for permission levels and inheritance are covered in Chapter 4.

Planning and configuring anonymous access

After a web application zone has been configured to enable anonymous authentication, the site owners within that application can then decide what level of authorization to grant to anonymous users.

Enabling anonymous access to a site

Enabling anonymous access to a site enables users to view the site without being challenged for a user name/password combination. All subsites, lists, and libraries that are configured to inherit permissions enable this level of access as well.

The following steps assume that you have already enabled anonymous authentication for the zone. To enable anonymous access at the site level, do the following:

1. Navigate to your site.
2. From the Settings menu (gear icon), select Site Settings.
3. In the Users and Permissions section, select Site Permissions.
4. On the ribbon, in the Manage section, select the Anonymous Access icon (see Figure 2-34).

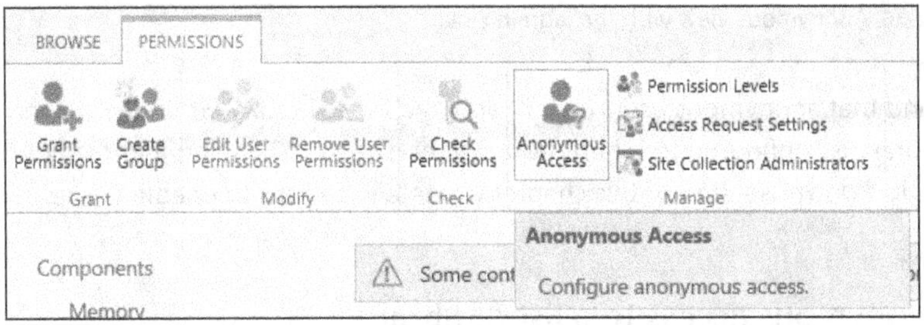

FIGURE 2-34 Anonymous Access icon.

5. On the Anonymous Access page, change the radio button in the Anonymous Access section to select the Entire Web Site option, as shown in Figure 2-35.

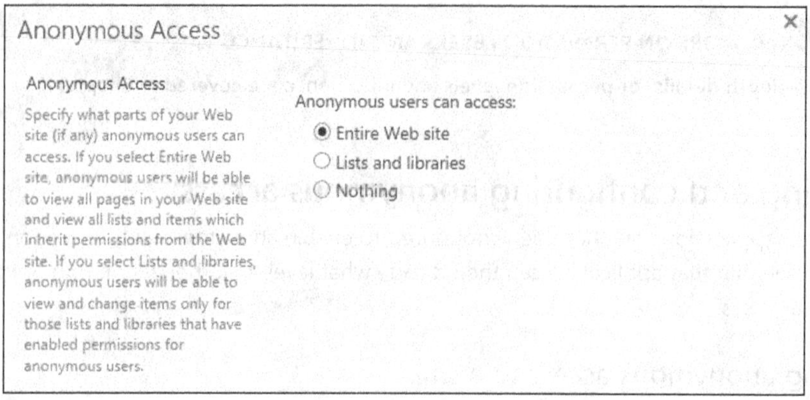

Anonymous Access   ✕

Anonymous Access

Specify what parts of your Web   Anonymous users can access:
site (if any) anonymous users can   ◉ Entire Web site
access. If you select Entire Web   ○ Lists and libraries
site, anonymous users will be able   ○ Nothing
to view all pages in your Web site
and view all lists and items which
inherit permissions from the Web
site. If you select Lists and libraries,
anonymous users will be able to
view and change items only for
those lists and libraries that have
enabled permissions for
anonymous users.

FIGURE 2-35 Anonymous Access: Entire Web Site.

6. Click OK to commit these changes.

7. When an anonymous user accesses the site, the site now appears without prompting for user name or password (see Figure 2-36).

SharePoint	Sign In ?
	☆ FOLLOW ⬚
S▷ Components ▾ Human Resources Search this site ▾ ⌕	
Home ⓘ	

FIGURE 2-36 Anonymous view with the Sign In Link.

8. If you find that anonymous users cannot access a list or library within the site, and the list or library is configured to inherit permissions, see the "Planning and configuring services lockdown" section of this chapter for details on how to enable this level of access.

Enabling anonymous access to a list or library

Enabling anonymous access to a list or library enables users to view only the particular list or library within the site. This means that anonymous users have to know the explicit URL to directly access the list or library content (there is no navigation available).

EXAM TIP

Authentication relies on the presence of a user name/password challenge. Credentials are never requested from anonymous users unless they attempt to access a location that is secured or choose to sign in to the SharePoint farm.

Additionally, there are differences in behavior for a list versus a library. A list enables an anonymous user to add, edit, delete, or view items; a library enables only an anonymous user to view items (this is a security measure).

The following steps assume that you have already enabled anonymous authentication for the zone, and that anonymous is not currently enabled at the site level. To enable anonymous access at the list or library level, do the following:

1. Navigate to your site.

2. From the Settings menu (gear icon), select Site Settings.

3. In the Users And Permissions section, select Site Permissions.

4. On the ribbon, in the Manage section, select the Anonymous Access icon (shown in Figure 2-37).

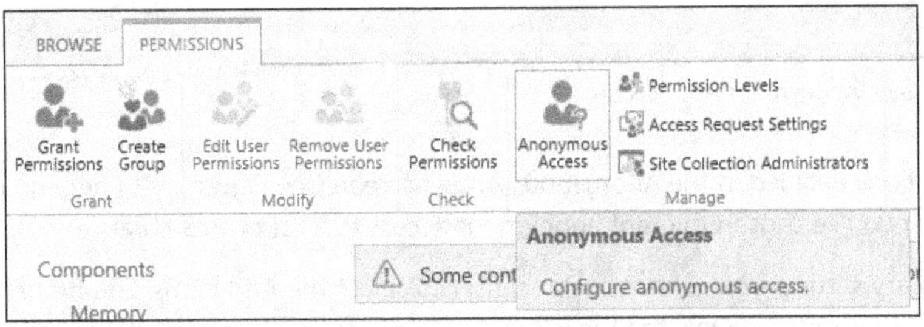

FIGURE 2-37 Anonymous Access icon.

5. On the Anonymous Access page, change the radio button in the Anonymous Access section to select the Lists And Libraries option, as shown in Figure 2-38.

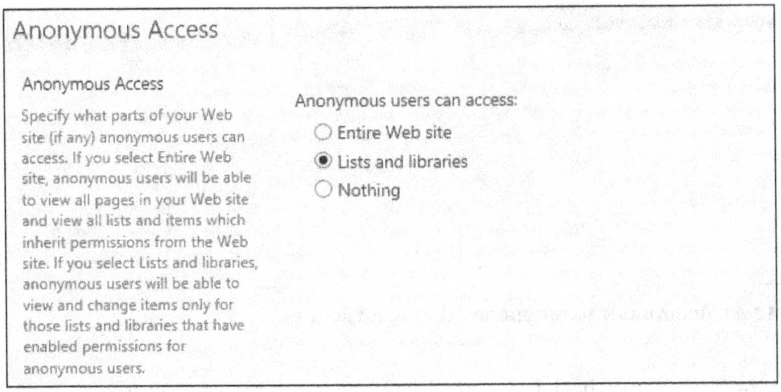

FIGURE 2-38 Anonymous access: Lists and libraries only.

At this point, all you have done is enabled lists and libraries in the site to permit anonymous access, nothing more. You must now break permissions inheritance from the parent site (where anonymous is disallowed) and then grant anonymous access to users for this list or library.

6. Break permissions inheritance for the list.

7. When you look at the ribbon for list permissions (on the Permissions tab), you can now confirm that unique permissions are applied to the list (the Delete Unique Permissions icon appears). In the Manage section of the ribbon, select the Anonymous Access icon (see Figure 2-39).

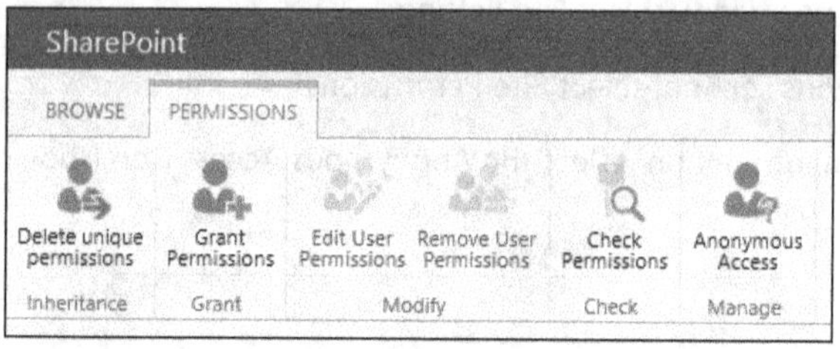

FIGURE 2-39 Anonymous Access icon.

8. The options enabled in the Anonymous Access screen (see Figure 2-40) depend on whether you've chosen to grant anonymous access to a list or to a library.

9. In a library setting, you cannot enable a user to select the Add Items, Edit Items, or Delete Items options. Only the View Items option is available for selection.

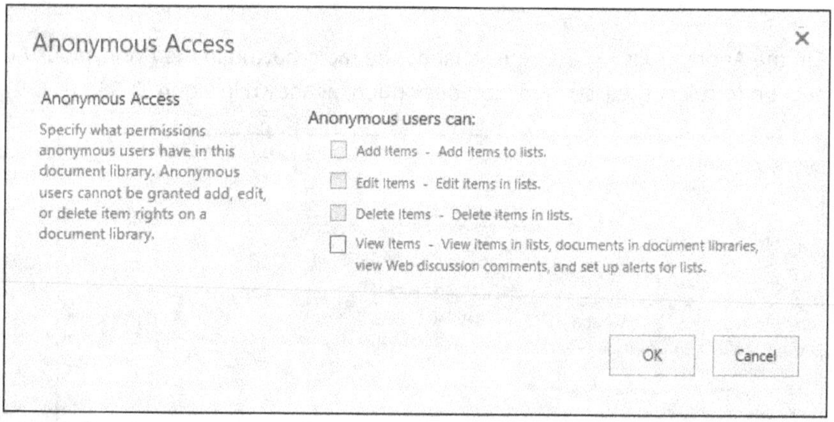

FIGURE 2-40 Anonymous access options (document library).

10. Select the View Items check box and click OK to commit your changes.

11. If you find that anonymous users cannot access a list or library within the site, and the list or library is configured to grant these permissions, see the "Planning and configuring services lockdown" section of this chapter for details on how to enable this level of access.

Planning and configuring web application policies

Web application policies are a way to control access for a web application from a global standpoint. This control can be utilized to allow or disallow permissions to all content within the web application.

There are three web application policies that can be configured on a per-web application basis: User Policy, Anonymous Policy, and Permission Policy (see Figure 2-41). These policies are configured in the Application Management (Manage Web Applications) section of Central Administration.

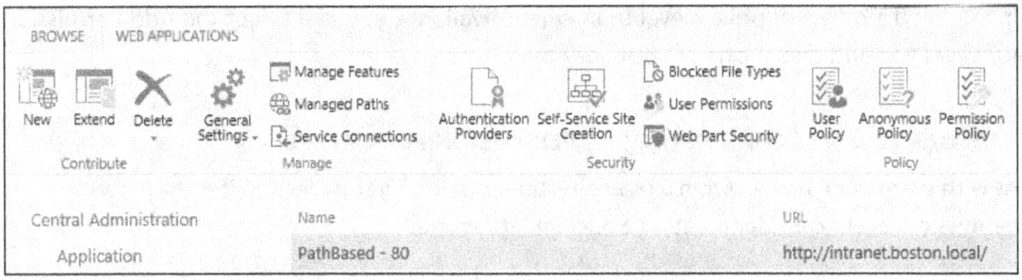

FIGURE 2-41 Web application policies (User, Anonymous, and Permission).

EXAM TIP

Know what the effect will be of altering each of these policies within a SharePoint farm, particularly those that deny users access.

Permission policy

Permission policies are used to specify the permission options available in user policy. You can think of them as permission groups that are scoped at the web application level (that's where they are applied, after all).

Selecting the Permission Policy icon shows the permission policy levels that are created out of the box (OOB), as shown in Figure 2-42).

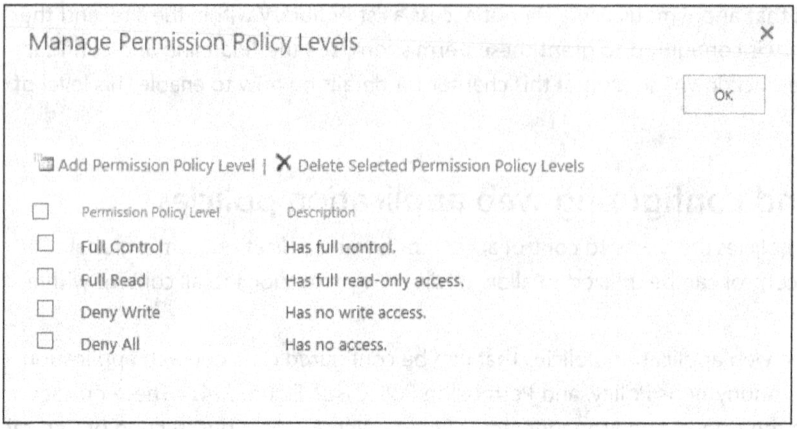

```
Manage Permission Policy Levels                                  ✕

                                                          OK


📋 Add Permission Policy Level | ✕ Delete Selected Permission Policy Levels

☐   Permission Policy Level      Description
☐   Full Control                 Has full control.
☐   Full Read                    Has full read-only access.
☐   Deny Write                   Has no write access.
☐   Deny All                     Has no access.
```

FIGURE 2-42 Permission policy levels.

If you need a different policy level than what's available, you can select the Add Permission Policy Level link and create one of your very own.

> **IMPORTANT DON'T CHANGE THE OOB PERMISSION POLICY LEVELS**
>
> As with permission levels within a site collection, it's not a good idea to alter these stock permission levels; consider creating a new one if required.

User Policy

Imagine that you had a legal requirement to enable an auditor access to review all content contained within a web application, regardless of the permissions assigned at the site collection or site levels. This sort of access could be provided within the User Policy, granting read permissions to the auditor at the User Policy level for the web application (on a temporary basis, of course).

Within the User Policy, you can choose to alter the access of one or more users at the web application level (see Figure 2-43). The users specified can be assigned permissions that you specify within the Permission Policy for the web application.

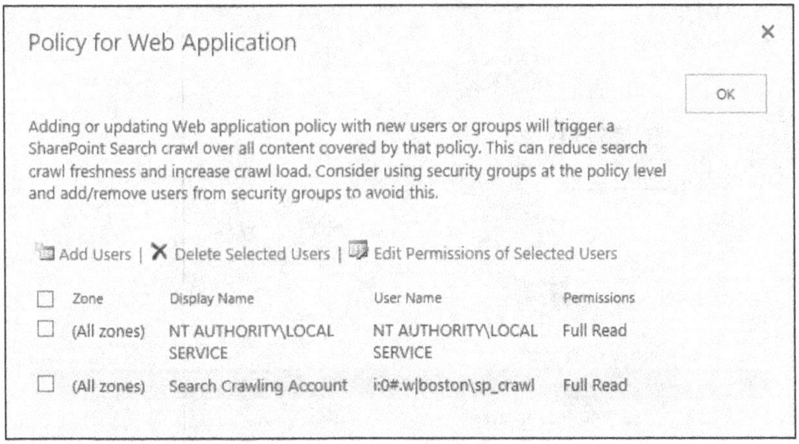

FIGURE 2-43 Managing the User Policy for a web application.

As indicated by the warning shown in the screen shot, changing the policy for a web application immediately kicks off a SharePoint search crawl, which may result in diminished performance for your users. Consider waiting until off-peak hours to alter a web application policy.

> **IMPORTANT SEARCH CRAWLS AND THE USER POLICY**
>
> As you can see, the search crawling account has been granted Full Read access to the web application. This permission level is required for the account to crawl content in each SharePoint web application. It is not recommended to alter this access in any way, including granting it Full Access, which would expose draft and unpublished documents, which should not appear within search results.

Anonymous policy

As another example, consider an organization that has a governance policy that states "No unauthenticated users can be allowed to upload or change content within a site," but still has a requirement to provide anonymous access to content on a read-only basis.

In the previous section, you saw that enabling anonymous access allowed site owners to enable access to Add, Edit, and Delete items, which would be against policy. Using the anonymous policy, you can choose on a zone by basis, whether anonymous users can be prevented from writing changes across a web application (Deny Write) or whether they have any access at all (Deny All). These options are shown in Figure 2-44.

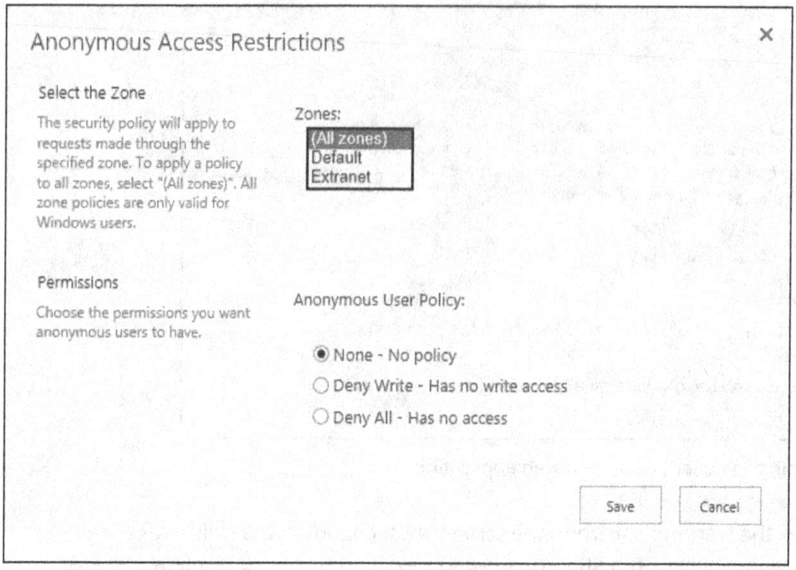

Anonymous Access Restrictions ✕

Select the Zone

The security policy will apply to requests made through the specified zone. To apply a policy to all zones, select "(All zones)". All zone policies are only valid for Windows users.

Zones:

(All zones)
Default
Extranet

Permissions

Choose the permissions you want anonymous users to have.

Anonymous User Policy:

◉ None - No policy
○ Deny Write - Has no write access
○ Deny All - Has no access

Save   Cancel

FIGURE 2-44 Managing the anonymous policy for a web application.

> ## Thought experiment
> ### Keeping an account active for auditing
>
> In the following thought experiment, apply what you've learned about this objective. You can find answers to these questions in the "Answers" section at the back of this chapter.
>
> You have been called in to take over for an administrator who was forcibly dismissed from his position. Management wants to have this person's account retained for legal reasons and must keep it active while audits are performed. You are required by management to ensure that this person can no longer access any web applications in your SharePoint installation.
>
> How might you proceed?

Objective summary

- Authorization is the act of user validation for accessing resources in a web application.
- There are 33 individual permissions that are broken apart into three permission levels: list, site, and personal.
- People Picker is configured using STSADM, property names, and property values.
- Avoid fine-grained permissions as much as possible when configuring permission inheritance structures.

- Anonymous access for libraries allows only view items; anonymous access for lists enables you to add, edit, delete, and view items.
- There are three distinct web application policies: User, Anonymous, and Permission.

Objective review

Answer the following questions to test your knowledge of the information in this objective. You can find the answers to these questions and explanations of why each answer choice is correct or incorrect in the "Answers" section at the end of this chapter.

1. Which of the following default groups is cannot be automatically set up during the provisioning of new SharePoint sites?

   A. Visitors

   B. Authors

   C. Members

   D. Owners

2. Which of the following Windows PowerShell cmdlets is used to configure People Picker?

   A. Set-PeoplePicker

   B. Set-PickerWebControl

   C. Get-PeoplePicker

   D. None of the above

3. At which levels can you choose to explicitly allow anonymous access (authorization)? (Choose all that apply.)

   A. Web application

   B. Web site

   C. Lists and libraries

   D. Individual item

4. Which of the following web application policies is responsible for setting up individual permission levels at the web app level? (Choose all that apply.)

   A. Permission Policy

   B. User Policy

   C. Anonymous Policy

   D. Inheritance Policy

Objective 2.3: Plan and configure platform security

Securing a SharePoint environment requires a significant amount of coordination between the networking, data, and SharePoint team at your organization. Configuration efforts vary in scope from altering core settings on your SharePoint web tier servers to altering SQL settings at the data tier, and enabling/disabling firewall configurations at the networking level. All these changes combine to form a more secure SharePoint implementation.

> **This objective covers how to:**
> - Plan and configure security isolation.
> - Plan and configure services lockdown.
> - Plan and configure general firewall security.
> - Plan and configure antivirus settings.
> - Plan and configure certificate management.

Planning and configuring security isolation

SharePoint is positioned in most organizations as the central nexus (or hub) for the presentation and aggregation of business knowledge. Content can be maintained within the SharePoint 2013 farm; it can just as easily be maintained in separate line of business applications and then presented by SharePoint.

Regardless of the content's original context, the fact that it can be presented in SharePoint has its pros and cons. On the one hand, information that was once stored in distinct, siloed systems is now readily available for use; on the other, information that may have been improperly secured in these disparate systems can be inadvertently exposed.

> **EXAM TIP**
>
> One of the key balances to be struck in defining isolation is between security and utility. Know not only the benefits of each isolation type but its drawbacks as well.

Security isolation requirements

This, then, is not so much a technical issue as a business process/legal issue. Dependencies such as how your business is organized, who the stakeholders are, and what your business purpose is can have far-ranging effects on the design outcome for your SharePoint farm.

For instance, if the SharePoint system being designed will be used to store medical information, knowledge management processes must be followed in order to comply with legal mandates. Failure to follow these mandates or to comply with auditing requirements could result in monetary and licensing penalties.

Even if your business does not have to comply with a heavy regulatory burden, you probably don't even have to go that far within your business to find reasons for considering security isolation. If you have employees, trade secrets, legal, or other boundaries, you may want to consider these design factors:

- **Farm architecture** Do you require more than one SharePoint farm to fully segregate the presentation of your data? Are there legal requirements for separating the data stores that support your SharePoint farm?

- **Web application layout** Legal, auditing, and human resources departments may require the creation of separate application pools.

- **Creating more than one search application** Your business may be penalized for exposing information via search that is improperly secured.

Physical isolation

In highly secure environments, you may want to secure a particular SharePoint farm at a separate site. This SharePoint site would participate in business operations, but would probably maintain its own web, application, and data tier servers.

Due to the nature of the data being stored in this environment, disaster recovery to a remote location may be required, making this environment immediately available in the case of a business continuity event. These events range in scope from an extended network outage event (in which the data services provider experiences a large-scale outage) to a flat-earth event (in which the site no longer exists or is irreparably damaged for the foreseeable future).

From an IRM point of view (covered in the next section), this environment should be configured to restrict rebroadcast (e-mail) and hard copy (printouts) for most users, requiring that auditing be fully enabled to track access to the data.

Users accessing this environment would likely be required to provide multiple layers of authentication, and this environment would be heavily secured from a networking point of view.

Service application isolation

SharePoint 2010 introduced the idea of service applications, which were the direct replacement for shared service providers. Each service application provides a connection (or proxy) that can be used by a web application to "subscribe" to the functionality provided by the particular service application.

A common example of this isolation is the separation of search information. Users that are privy to sensitive information, such as salaries and personal identification information, still require the use of search. In fact, search may be the key mechanism with which they can get work accomplished.

Creating a different search application for these folks enables them to use a particular search index in a web application without the exposure risk associated with sharing a search application.

Application pool isolation

An application pool can be used to host one or more URLs within a SharePoint environment. Each application pool can be configured to run as a distinct service account, meaning that you can allow this application to participate in the farm and still be compliant with many regulatory requirements.

This type of isolation is particularly useful in environments in which the application pool retains credentials from and access to sensitive line of business systems.

Web application and zone isolation

A distinct web application starts with a single URL, presented in the default zone. It is possible to extend this web application up to four more times, each time assigning a new URL and zone.

With zones now defined, the authentication mechanism for each zone in the web application can be chosen. Additionally, web application policies can be specified that will allow for administrative control over user access in each zone.

Data isolation

If supporting multiple physical environments is not feasible (or possible) within your organization, you may have to support distinct data tiers. Separating these data tiers may enable distinct teams to support environments that are more sensitive or require a higher level of availability.

Data isolation is particularly applicable to environments in which service level agreements and recovery time objectives differ based on the type of data being accessed from within a single SharePoint farm.

> *MORE INFO* **ARCHITECTURE PLANNING FOR SECURITY ISOLATION**
>
> Security isolation is applicable at every level of a SharePoint Design; both logical and physical considerations must be made in order to tailor the implementation to a particular need. Logical architecture is discussed in the TechNet article "Logical Architecture Components" at *http://technet.microsoft.com/en-us/library/cc263121.aspx*. Physical (services) architecture is discussed in the TechNet article "Services Architecture Planning" at *http://technet.microsoft.com/en-us/library/cc560988.aspx*.

Planning and configuring services lockdown

As the SharePoint Server product has matured, it has become better suited for use not only as an intranet and extranet platform but also for Internet use. The array of publishing features, ease of use, and scalability present in the platform makes for a versatile web site experience.

SharePoint has become a bigger security target as a result of this exposure and popularity. With detailed documentation readily available describing all the SharePoint's components and how they interact with one another, it falls to the administrator to secure Internet-facing SharePoint sites from external attacks.

EXAM TIP

As more and more SharePoint sites become externally facing, the need to secure anonymous resources from external search engines will become paramount. Be familiar with these settings, which really affect the underlying web.config file components of a SharePoint web application.

Using the Limited-Access User Permission Lockdown Mode feature

As you configure lists and libraries for anonymous access on a publishing site, you may run into a situation in which anonymous users cannot access lists and libraries, even though anonymous permissions have been granted.

This behavior is by design, as publishing sites have an activated feature called Limited-Access User Permission Lockdown Mode (see Figure 2-45).

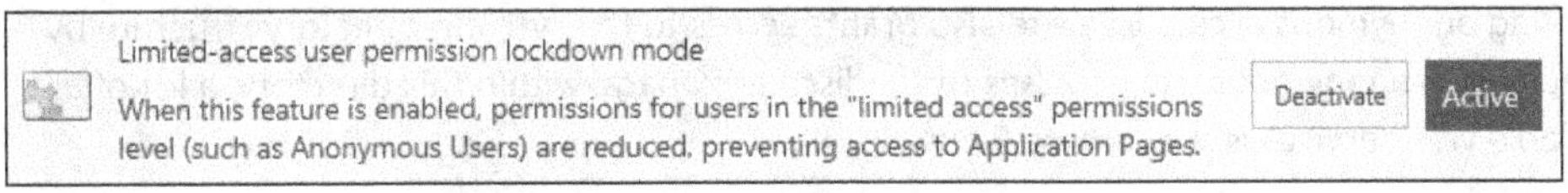

Limited-access user permission lockdown mode

When this feature is enabled, permissions for users in the "limited access" permissions level (such as Anonymous Users) are reduced, preventing access to Application Pages.   Deactivate   Active

FIGURE 2-45 Limited-Access User Permission Lockdown Mode feature.

> **MORE INFO USING LOCKDOWN MODE**
>
> For more details about what is included in lockdown mode, read the "Use Lockdown Mode" section of the TechNet article "Plan Security for an External Anonymous Access Environment" at *http://technet.microsoft.com/en-us/library/cc263468.aspx*.

The purpose of this feature is to secure application pages from being anonymously accessed. If this feature is deactivated, an anonymous user can get to pages that are stored in the _layouts folder of your site, such as _layouts/15/viewlsts.aspx (see Figure 2-46).

FIGURE 2-46 Anonymously available lists.

To check the status of this feature in Windows PowerShell, you can use the Get-SPFeature cmdlet:

```
Get-SPFeature -site http://<siteurl>
```

If the feature is displayed, it is active (see Figure 2-47).

FIGURE 2-47 ViewFormPagesLockdown feature is active.

If desired, you can disable the ViewFormPagesLockDown feature by running the following Windows PowerShell code:

```
$ViewFormPages = Get-SPFeature ViewFormPagesLockDown
Disable-SPFeature $ViewFormPages -url http://<siteurl>
```

Preventing anonymous access to web services

Granting anonymous access to a site also grants access to the _vti_bin directory structure by default. If an anonymous use accesses the spdisco.aspx page within this directory, a list of all available web services is shown (see Figure 2-48).

FIGURE 2-48 Anonymously accessed web services.

To change this behavior, you have to make a change in the web.config file of the desired web application on each web tier server.

> **IMPORTANT ALTERING WEB.CONFIG**
>
> Saving changes to the web.config file of a web application results in that web app being recycled to process the changes. Before making any changes, ensure that the site is not in production and make a backup copy of the web.config file.

For ease of location, place this code immediately above the </configuration> tag (the last tag in web.config):

```
<location path="_vti_bin">
  <system.web>
    <authorization>
      <deny users="?" />
    </authorization>
  </system.web>
</location>
```

The completed web.config entry is shown in Figure 2-49.

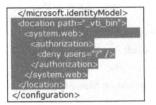

FIGURE 2-49 web.config changes.

After the web app has recycled, an anonymous user requesting pages within the _vti_bin folder requires authentication before any are displayed (see Figure 2-50). Only anonymous users are affected because all other users have previously been authenticated to the web app.

> **IMPORTANT** **BALANCING SECURITY VERSUS FUNCTIONALITY**
>
> Disabling these features makes the environment more secure by effectively "shrinking" the surface area of attack. Development for anonymous user functionality may require that these components be left available.

FIGURE 2-50 Authentication request.

Bundling these changes into a feature or scripting the modifications using Windows PowerShell makes the change more durable (storing these changes in the farm configuration database).

Avoiding manual changes has two distinct benefits:

- These changes are then capable of withstanding hotfixes and service packs, which this manual change may or may not survive.

- Storing these changes in the configuration database also means that the changes are automatically applied to new servers when they are added to the farm.

> **MORE INFO** **LOCKING DOWN SHAREPOINT**
>
> For more information regarding how to lock down SharePoint services, visit the "Locking Down Office SharePoint Server Sites" article at *http://technet.microsoft.com/en-us/library/ee191479.aspx*. As this is a SharePoint 2007 article; just remember that the _layouts folder is already secured by enabling the Limited-Access User Permission Lockdown Mode feature.

Planning and configuring general firewall security

Configuring the firewall policies for your SharePoint environment depends greatly on the level of control you want to have over detailed firewall configurations. You need to coordinate both with the networking team and the SQL team to ensure that the proper configurations are made at all levels of the SharePoint farm.

> **EXAM TIP**
>
> Know which components of your SharePoint environment should exist in the demilitarized zone (DMZ) between your back-end and front-end firewalls.

Network firewall settings

If you are in a larger environment, it may well be that firewalls are disabled on individual servers by group policy and instead enabled using dedicated networking hardware. If this is the case, ensure that you document all the TCP settings required at each tier of your farm and that you secure communications within your farm as much as possible (using HTTPS for communications vs. HTTP, for instance).

Web tier servers

If your SharePoint implementation will be externally facing, consider configuring two distinct networks per server: client-facing and intra-farm.

The web tier servers will most likely reside in a perimeter network, often called a demilitarized zone (DMZ), ahead of the back-end firewall but behind the front-end (Internet-facing) firewall and a load balancer. (Ideally, the load balancer also uses Network Address Translation [NAT] to provide further protection to your web servers).

- The client-facing connection should be configured to allow communications only via HTTPS on TCP Port 443. This should be the only port accessible through the Internet-facing firewall.

- The intrafarm connection does not allow any external connectivity; preferably being assigned to a different IP range altogether.

> **IMPORTANT** **SEARCH CRAWLS**
>
> Consider placing one or more extra web tier servers behind the back-end firewall. These servers can function as the web tier servers for internal users; they can also function as the crawl servers for search.

App tier servers

App tier servers should be placed inside the back-end firewall, not allowing any sort of external connectivity except the point-to-point relationship between the web- and app-tier servers.

Data tier servers

SQL Servers should obviously be located behind the back-end firewall. If a firewall is to be placed between the app- and data-tier servers, the TCP and User Datagram Protocol (UDP) connections between these servers need to be allowed through the firewall.

By default, these ports are TCP 1433 and UDP 1434, but your SQL administrator may decide instead to place your SharePoint data tier on its own named instance. If this is the case, he or she will most likely change the default ports used for connection. You have to make these ports available to all member servers in the SharePoint farm, passing them through any applicable firewalls.

> **MORE INFO** **PORTS AND PROTOCOLS**
>
> For a detailed list of the ports used by different services within the farm, visit the TechNet "Plan Security Hardening for SharePoint 2013" document at *http://technet.microsoft.com/en-us/library/cc262849.aspx*.

Planning and configuring antivirus settings

Most organizations deploy antivirus software to their client workstations; some also apply server-specific antivirus software to their back-end systems as an extra protective measure. As one of these back-end systems, SharePoint 2013 provides for integration of third-party antivirus software and its configuration within the Central Administration web site.

> **MORE INFO FOREFRONT FOR SHAREPOINT HAS BEEN DISCONTINUED**
>
> Microsoft has discontinued the on-premise version of Forefront for SharePoint (see *http://blogs.technet.com/b/server-cloud/archive/2012/09/12/important-changes-to-forefront-product-roadmaps.aspx*) for details. The last version made available is Forefront Protection 2010 for SharePoint, which will continue to be supported through December 31, 2015. This version works with SharePoint Server 2013.

SharePoint presents an interesting challenge to the designers of antivirus software because documents uploaded to a SharePoint instance are not directly stored on a file system; instead, they are stored within SQL tables as a Binary Large Object (BLOB).

The direct manipulation of SharePoint databases from SQL is not supported; this fact disallows the direct scanning of SharePoint content databases. Instead, Microsoft provides a SharePoint Virus Scan Engine (VSE) API, which enables third-party software to interact with SharePoint content databases.

Standard antivirus software typically scans documents in two ways:

- As a document is being copied to the system, it is checked for evidence of any malicious code.
- The file system of the system is scanned on a periodic basis to ensure that all existing documents on the file system remain free of malicious code.

SharePoint allows for similar functionality via third party antivirus solutions:

- As a document is being uploaded to or downloaded from SharePoint, it can be checked for evidence of any malicious code.
- Existing files contained with SharePoint content databases can be scanned on a periodic basis to ensure that all existing documents remain free of malicious code.

Implementing the antivirus configuration of your SharePoint installation is a fairly straight-forward process—there are few options to choose from, most of which have to do with controlling the performance impact of antivirus scans within your farm.

Configuring the antivirus settings of this farm is done from the Antivirus page of Central Administration, found at Central Administration → Security → General Security → Manage antivirus settings (see Figure 2-51).

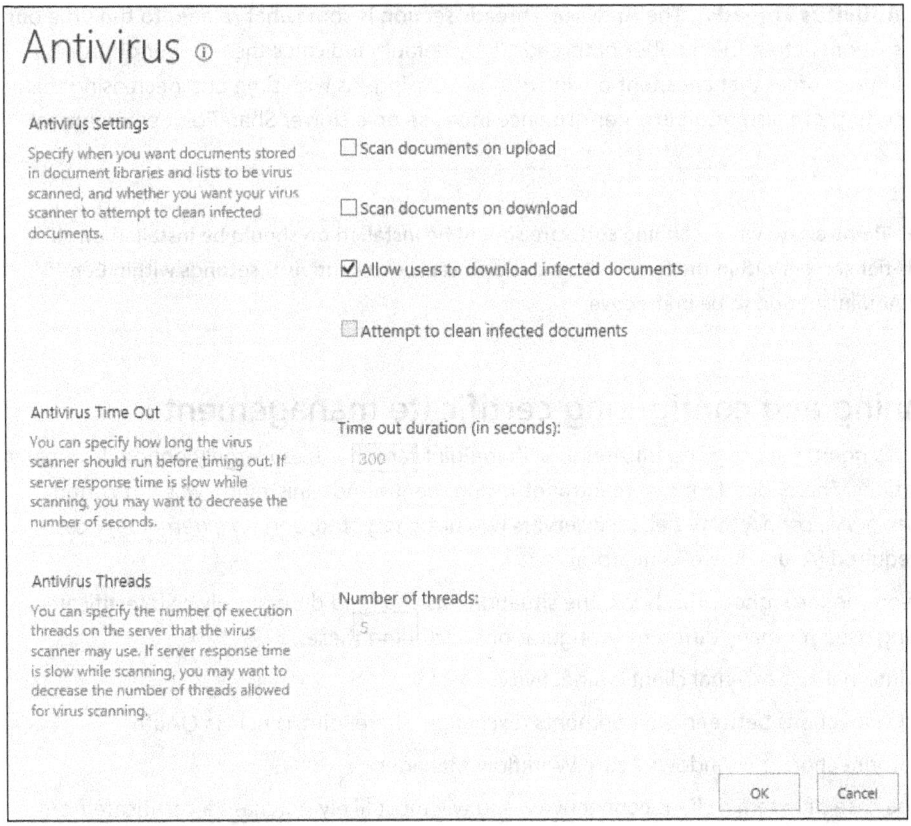

FIGURE 2-51 Antivirus settings (Central Administration).

From here, you can control the antivirus settings, time out, and thread count.

Within the Antivirus Settings section, you can choose any or all of the following:

- **Scan Documents On Upload** Scans documents on upload, preventing an infected file from ever being placed in a content database.

- **Scan Documents On Download** Scans documents on download, which causes the document to be scanned before it is downloaded.

- **Allow Users To Download Infected Documents** Enables users to download infected documents; this setting is most often used to troubleshoot virus-infected documents already in SharePoint.

- **Attempt To Clean Infected Documents** Enables the third-party antivirus solution to clean infected documents automatically.

- **Antivirus Time Out** Within the Antivirus Time Out section, you can specify the amount of time that can be spent before the virus scanner times out (default setting: 300 seconds/5 minutes). Decreasing this setting can result in a performance increase on a slower SharePoint environment.

- **Antivirus Threads** The Antivirus Threads section is somewhat related to the time out section, in that the number of threads (5 by default) indicates the number of processing resources that are spent on antivirus processing. As with time out, decreasing this setting can also result in a performance increase on a slower SharePoint environment.

Planning and configuring certificate management

Up to this point, the use of certificates in a SharePoint farm has been largely optional. In many installations, SharePoint farms were intranet-facing, Central Administration was not configured using SSL, connectivity between servers was not encrypted, and no external services were required (Azure, SharePoint Store).

As you see throughout this book, the situation has changed dramatically. SSL certificates are being used for many different configurations, including these:

- Internal and external client connectivity
- Connections between environments (Exchange/SharePoint/Lync) via OAuth
- Connections to Windows Azure Workflow Manager

In the case of external client connectivity, you will most likely purchase a certificate from a well-known SSL certificate provider; but in the other cases, you need to know the essentials for exporting, copying, and importing SSL certificates correctly.

In the following example, you will interact with the certificates used by two SharePoint farms as the relationship between them is established. This example will show you how to export and import both root and STS certificates in an interfarm setting.

Setting up for the trust creation

A trust relationship must be established between SharePoint farms that share service application functionality. In this relationship, one SharePoint farm (the "publisher") publishes a service application that can then be consumed by a different SharePoint farm (the "consumer").

This relationship is established in a secure fashion via the use of three distinct certificates:

- A root certificate, which is exported from the "consuming" farm

- An STS certificate, which is exported from the consuming farm
- Another root certificate, which is exported from the "publishing" farm

Exporting a root certificate (consuming farm)

Root certificates are exported using Windows PowerShell 3.0, as shown in the following steps:

1. Open the SharePoint 2013 Management Shell (run as administrator) on the consuming farm.

2. The Get-SPCertificateAuthority cmdlet is used to obtain the root certificate for the farm. If you simply run the cmdlet by itself, you see the certificate details (as shown in Figure 2-52), including an expiration date that is set far in the future.

```
PS C:\Users\sp_farm> get-spcertificateauthority

RootCertificate                : [Subject]
                                   CN=SharePoint Root Authority, OU=SharePoint,
                                 O=Microsoft, C=US

                                 [Issuer]
                                   CN=SharePoint Root Authority, OU=SharePoint,
                                 O=Microsoft, C=US

                                 [Serial Number]
                                   B48D6209B1B769AD454F3896F111787D

                                 [Not Before]
                                   11/7/2012 10:24:46 AM

                                 [Not After]
                                   12/31/9998 6:00:00 PM

                                 [Thumbprint]
                                   200E98DCAC54EA5FAC7C377C5BF158ABCBDFFB05

Name                           :
TypeName                       : Microsoft.SharePoint.Administration.SPCertificate
                                 Authority
```

FIGURE 2-52 Root certificate (consuming farm).

3. You can export the certificate to a file name (C:\ConsumingFarmRoot.cer):

```
$rootCert = (Get-SPCertificateAuthority).RootCertificate
$rootCert.Export("Cert") | Set-Content "C:\ConsumingFarmRoot.cer" -Encoding byte
```

Exporting an STS certificate (consuming farm)

As with the root certificate, the STS certificate can be exported using Windows PowerShell 3.0, as shown in the following steps:

1. Open the SharePoint 2013 Management Shell (run as administrator) on the consuming farm.

2. Using the Get-SPSecurityTokenServiceConfig cmdlet, you can obtain the STS certificate, this time storing it as C:\ConsumingFarmSTS.cer:

```
$stsCert = (Get-SPSecurityTokenServiceConfig).LocalLoginProvider.
SigningCertificate
$stsCert.Export("Cert") | Set-Content "C:\ConsumingFarmSTS.cer" -Encoding byte
```

Exporting a root certificate (publishing farm)

The process of exporting the root certificate on the publishing farm is identical to that on the consuming farm (with the exception of the file name, of course). Do the following:

1. Open the SharePoint 2013 Management Shell (run as administrator) on the publishing farm.

2. Export the certificate to a file name (C:\PublishingFarmRoot.cer):

```
$rootCert = (Get-SPCertificateAuthority).RootCertificate
$rootCert.Export("Cert") | Set-Content "C:\PublishingFarmRoot.cer" -Encoding byte
```

Preparing to establish the trust

You have to copy the files between farms, as follows:

- Copy the ConsumingFarmRoot.cer and ConsumingFarmSTS.cer files from the consuming farm to the publishing farm.

- Copy the PublishingFarmRoot.cer file from the publishing farm to the consuming farm.

Establishing the trust on the consuming farm

The trust is established on the consuming farm when the publishing farm's root certificate is imported (using the New-SPTrustedRootAuthority cmdlet). Follow these steps:

1. Open the SharePoint 2013 Management Shell (run as administrator) on the consuming farm.

2. Locate the publishing root certificate on the file system (C:\PublishingFarmRoot.cer).

3. Run the following Windows PowerShell to create the new Trusted Root Authority and call the farm PublishingFarm:

```
$trustCert = Get-PfxCertificate "C:\PublishingFarmRoot.cer"
New-SPTrustedRootAuthority "PublishingFarm" -Certificate $trustCert
```

4. Confirm the creation of the Trusted Root Authority using the Get-SPTrustedRootAuthority command (see Figure 2-53).

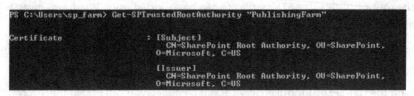

FIGURE 2-53 Verifying the Trusted Root Authority on the publishing farm.

Establishing the trust on the publishing farm

The trust is established on the Publishing farm when the Consuming farm's root certificate is imported (using the New-SPTrustedRootAuthority cmdlet).

1. Open the SharePoint 2013 Management Shell (run as Administrator) on the Publishing farm.

2. Locate the consuming root certificate on the file system (C:\ConsumingFarmRoot.cer).

3. Run the following Windows PowerShell to create the new Trusted Root Authority. Call the farm ConsumingFarm:

```
$trustCert = Get-PfxCertificate "C:\ConsumingFarmRoot.cer"
New-SPTrustedRootAuthority "ConsumingFarm" -Certificate $trustCert
```

4. Confirm the creation of the Trusted Root Authority using the Get-SPTrustedRootAuthority command (see Figure 2-54).

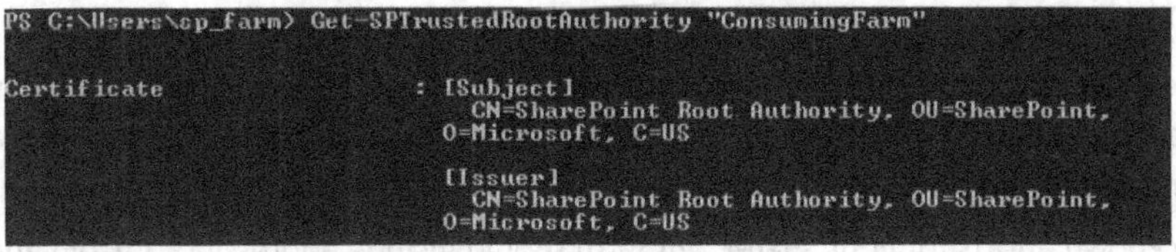

FIGURE 2-54 Verifying the consuming farm Trusted Root.

Importing the STS certificate on the publishing farm

The process of creating a trusted service token issuer also imports the STS certificate from the consuming farm. Follow these steps:

1. Open the SharePoint 2013 Management Shell (run as administrator) on the publishing farm.

2. Locate the consuming root certificate on the file system (C:\ConsumingFarmSTS.cer).

3. Run the following Windows PowerShell to create the new trusted service token issuer:

```
$stsCert = Get-PfxCertificate "c:\ConsumingFarmSTS.cer"
New-SPTrustedServiceTokenIssuer "ConsumingFarm" -Certificate $stsCert
```

Thought experiment

Farm security

In the following thought experiment, apply what you've learned about this objective. You can find answers to these questions in the "Answers" section at the back of this chapter.

You have been tasked with allowing anonymous access to your SharePoint farm. You must make the farm as secure as possible, addressing any weaknesses exposed on a publishing site. Existing users must continue to be able to authenticate as they do now.

How should you proceed?

Objective summary

- There are many levels at which security isolation can occur within SharePoint; some of the major ones include physical, service application, application pool, web application, zone, and data.
- Lockdown efforts for your SharePoint farm should include addressing _vti_bin and _layouts folder access for anonymous users.
- Web-tier servers should never be exposed directly to the Internet, but should be protected by a front-end firewall.
- A DMZ is the edge network that exists between the front-end (Internet-facing) and back-end firewalls.
- Virus scanning for a SharePoint document can occur on upload, download, or both.
- Trust relationships between farms require both root and STS certificates.

Objective review

Answer the following questions to test your knowledge of the information in this objective. You can find the answers to these questions and explanations of why each answer choice is correct or incorrect in the "Answers" section at the end of this chapter.

1. Which of the following features can be activated to disable anonymous access to the _layouts folder?

   A. Limited-Access User Permission Lockdown mode

   B. Forms Table Lockdown mode

   C. Layouts and Web Services Lockdown mode

   D. None of the above

2. In an Internet-facing SharePoint farm, which of the following SharePoint Server tiers does not require protection by a firewall?

    A. Web tier

    B. App tier

    C. Data tier

    D. None of the above

3. When can a document be scanned by a SharePoint-integrated antivirus solution? (Choose all that apply.)

    A. On upload

    B. At the end of a workflow

    C. During a workflow

    D. On download

4. Which of the following certificate types is part of establishing a trust between Share-Point farms? (Choose all that apply.)

    A. An STS certificate generated by the publishing farm

    B. A root certificate generated from the consuming farm

    C. An STS certificate generated from the consuming farm

    D. A root certificate generated by the publishing farm

Objective 2.4: Plan and configure farm-level security

The last objective focused on securing the farm from intrusion and data corruption from external sources. This objective focuses instead on how to secure the farm from the inside, assigning the appropriate administrative permissions and creating policies that help secure assets contained within the SharePoint infrastructure.

This objective covers how to:

- Plan rights management.
- Plan and configure delegated farm administration.
- Plan and configure delegated service application administration.
- Plan and configure managed accounts.
- Plan and configure blocked file types.
- Plan and configure web part security.

Planning rights management

Active Directory Rights Management Services (RMS) protect the intellectual capital of an enterprise. Built on Active Directory, these services enable the author of a document to determine its intended use, and disallow any unauthorized distribution or reproduction of the document's contents. This form of Information Rights Management (IRM) is supported by a server running the Active Directory RMS role.

In previous versions of SharePoint, enabling rights management required the installation of Active Directory RMS Client 2.0 on each web server in the farm. The RMS client is installed by default along with all the other SharePoint Server 2013 components, making the configuration and integration with RMS that much easier.

EXAM TIP

Understand the capabilities of RMS and what types of document and e-mail functionality it can secure.

To configure IRM within Central Administration, from Central Administration → Security → Information Policy → select Configure Information Rights Management. The Information Rights Management page appears, as shown in Figure 2-55.

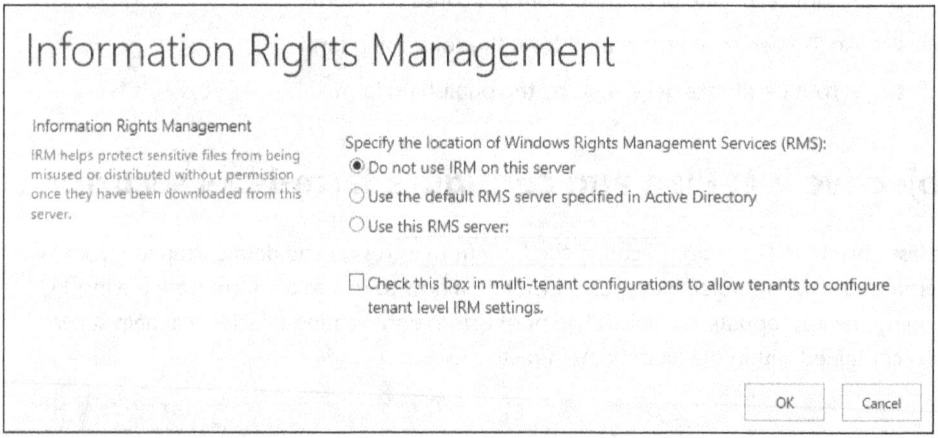

FIGURE 2-55 Information Rights Management page (Central Administration).

When implementing IRM, you have three choices for specifying the location of Windows RMS:

- Do Not Use IRM On This Server
- Use The Default RMS Server Specified In Active Directory
- Use A Particular RMS Server

The default configuration is Do Not Use IRM On This Server. If this setting has been selected, RMS are not available on the farm, period—not even for tenants.

The multitenant check box allows for per-tenant configurations of IRM settings. When this check box is selected, Windows PowerShell cmdlets can be used to enable/disable/configure IRM for each individual tenant, also allowing for the selection of a desired RMS server.

> **IMPORTANT** **MSIPC.DLL ERRORS WHEN ACTIVATING IRM**
>
> Choosing OK at this point (to save your IRM selections), you might receive an error that states The Required Active Directory Rights Management Service Client MSIPC.DLL Is Present But Could Not Be Configured Properly. If this is the case, the RMS server is probably not configured to enable the SharePoint web servers to access its ServerCertification.asmx page (found within the C:\Inetpub\Wwwroot\ADRMS_Wmcs\Certification\ file path on the RMS server). Contact your RMS administration team and have them grant both (a) read/execute on this file for each web server in your SharePoint farm and (b) read/execute for the Active Directory RMS service group of the RMS server.

Windows PowerShell administration for on-premise RMS is done via a total of four cmdlets:

- **Get-SPIRMSettings**   Returns the IRM settings
- **Get-SPSiteSubscriptionIRMConfig**   Returns the IRM settings for a specified tenant within the farm
- **Set-SPIRMSettings**   Sets the IRM settings
- **Set-SPSiteSubscriptionIRMConfig**   Sets the IRM settings for a specified tenant within the farm

Planning and configuring delegated farm administration

As your SharePoint implementation continues to grow in size, you may soon realize that having only one or two people responsible for farm administration becomes impractical. Perhaps you want to delegate the core maintenance of SharePoint to the members of a support team, some of whom are available on a 24x7 basis.

In a smaller environment such as this, it is likely that a small group of individuals have access to the server farm account and have been using it to accomplish administrative tasks. Although it has probably not caused an issue, allowing several people to have access to this credential set is simply not a good idea and does not comply with any sort of auditing requirements.

The server farm account has more responsibilities than just administration:

- It has full access to each of the databases in the SharePoint infrastructure (and the permission to create and delete more).
- It serves as the application pool identity for the Central Administration web site.
- It is the process account for the Windows SharePoint Services Timer Service.

Creating a farm administrator team

Delegating farm administrative tasks is a surprisingly easy process, consisting of one major step: Assigning users to the farm administrators group. After this permission has been assigned, the newly designated administrators have Full Control permissions to all servers in the farm and can be responsible for their general upkeep.

It is important to note that farm administrators have no local logon privileges to the SharePoint web-, application-, or data-tier servers. The extent of their administrative privilege stops at the Central Administrative level because they also cannot perform activities at the Windows PowerShell level (by default).

What these users can do is administer all the items they see in Central Administration: delegating service application permissions; administering managed accounts; and creating/ deleting/editing application pools, databases, and site collections are all within their control. Backups and restores are possible, even to the extent of backing up content databases without having to interact directly with SQL Server through SSMS.

Adding users to the farm administrators group

To add a user to the farm administrators group, follow these steps:

1. From Central Administration, select Security.

2. On the Security page, select the Manage The Farm Administrators group link.

3. The Farm Administrators group page appears, as shown in Figure 2-56.

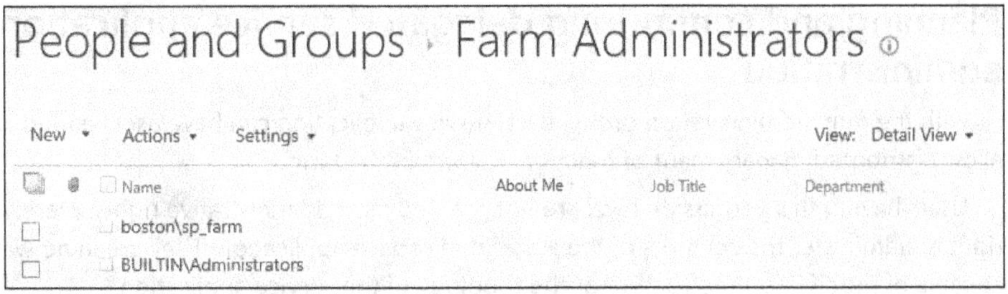

People and Groups › Farm Administrators ⓘ

New ▾	Actions ▾	Settings ▾			View: Detail View ▾
☐	📎 ☐ Name		About Me	Job Title	Department
☐		boston\sp_farm			
☐		BUILTIN\Administrators			

FIGURE 2-56 Farm administrators group.

EXAM TIP

By default, the local administrators group on a SharePoint Server has administrative privileges to the SharePoint farm, as shown in Figure 2-56 (BUILTIN\Administrators). In fact, they have more privilege than farm administrators because they can install and configure items from the command line (but are still subject to the shell admin limitations). Don't remove this group, but be sure that you know who in your organization is assigned to this group from an access auditing standpoint.

4. Enter one or more users and then type a welcome message (if desired). Optionally, you can choose to send an e-mail invitation with a link to the Central Administration site (see Figure 2-57).

Share 'Central Administration'   ✕

Add people to the Farm Administrators group

    Troy Lanphier x

    Welcome to the SharePoint Farm Administrators Group

HIDE OPTIONS

    ☑ Send an email invitation

                                                        [Share] [Cancel]

FIGURE 2-57 Adding users to the farm administrators group.

5. Click Share to complete this task.

Planning and configuring delegated service application administration

As with the farm administration group, each service application can have users added in to allow distributed management of functionality within the farm.

Users having this permission level are not granted farm administrative rights, merely the right to administer the contents of the associated service application. They are in no way capable of modifying the structure or the topology of the service application.

EXAM TIP

Become familiar with the different administrative levels in the more common service applications for delegation, such as the User Profile Service (UPA), Search Service, and Managed Metadata Service (MMS).

For instance, if you delegate the administration of search to an enterprise librarian who is charged with helping refine searchability within the farm, that person could not do the following:

- Add new search components
- Modify existing search components or topology
- Remove search components

The librarian can monitor, interact with, and configure settings for the Search Service application, however.

Adding administrators for a service application

In this example, you add a librarian to the Administrators group for a Search Service application in the farm. This person will have Full Control privileges for the service application.

To add the user to the service application's administrators group:

1. From Central Administration, select Application Management.

2. On the Application Management page, select the Manage Service Applications link.

3. On the Service Application page, click Search Service Application to highlight it.

4. On the Service Applications tab of the ribbon, select the Assign Administrators link, as shown in Figure 2-58.

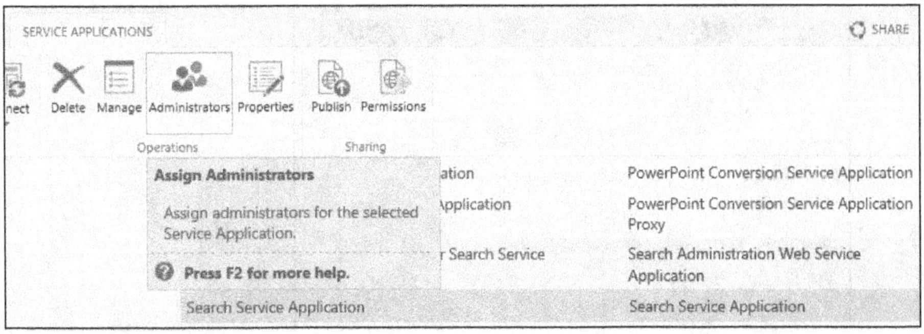

FIGURE 2-58 Assign Administrators icon.

5. On the Administrator For Search Service Application page, enter and validate the name of a user; then click Add (as shown in Figure 2-59).

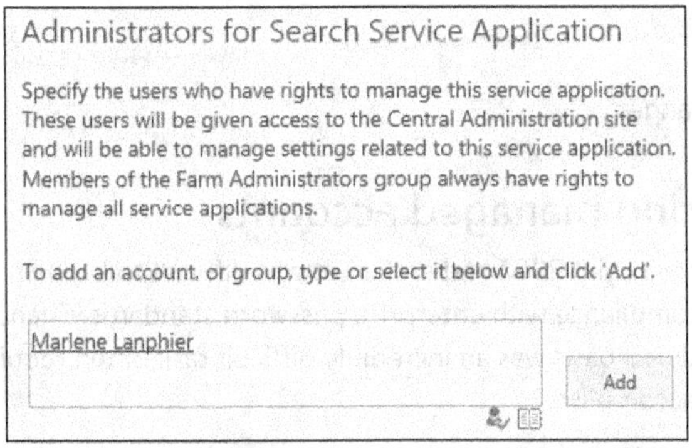

FIGURE 2-59 Adding an administrator.

6. Different permissions are available in each service application. For the Search Service application, two privilege levels are available: Full Control and Read (Diagnostics Pages Only). Selecting the Full Control permission level check box automatically assigns the Read permission level also (see Figure 2-60).

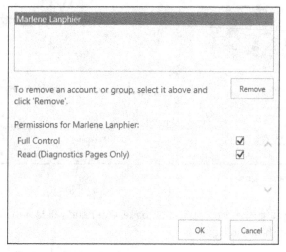

FIGURE 2-60 Permission levels.

7. Click OK to commit your changes.

Planning and configuring managed accounts

In earlier versions of SharePoint (SharePoint 2007 and earlier), it was difficult to keep Share-Point-specific service accounts in compliance with enterprise password standards. Changing the passwords on a regularly scheduled basis was an incredibly difficult task, often requiring farm outages (even brief ones) to accomplish.

SharePoint 2013 continues the concept of managed accounts first introduced in Share-Point 2010. A managed account is an Active Directory account (usually used as a service account) whose password is maintained within SharePoint.

> **IMPORTANT NOT ACTIVE DIRECTORY–MANAGED ACCOUNTS**
>
> If your organization uses the managed service account functionality found in Active Directory, you should exclude SharePoint-specific managed accounts from this policy because the password must be maintained from within SharePoint to function correctly. A password change that is accomplished outside of SharePoint results in an outage.

A SharePoint managed service account enables you to change the account credentials from within Central Administration. These passwords can either be changed manually (by an administrator) or automatically (by SharePoint) on a timed interval.

Creating a new managed account

When creating a new managed account, you specify an initial user name and password for the service account. This interface also enables you to configure automatic password changes.

To create a new managed account, follow these steps:

1. From Central Administration, select Security.

2. On the Security page, in the General Security section, select the Configure Managed Accounts link.

3. On the Managed Accounts page, select the Registered Managed Account link, as shown in Figure 2-61.

Managed Accounts

Register Managed Account

User name	Edit	Password change schedule	Next password change	Last password change	Remove
BOSTON\sp_farm				11/6/2012 3:43:13 PM	X
BOSTON\sp_app				12/10/2012 8:53:54 PM	X

FIGURE 2-61 Registering a new managed account.

4. On the Register Managed Accounts page, you can configure the registration of a new account and what automatic password change requirements you want to use (if any).

5. In the Account Registration section, enter a new User Name and Password for the Service Account Credentials (see Figure 2-62).

   If you need to check the password you entered, select the "eye" icon in the Password field.

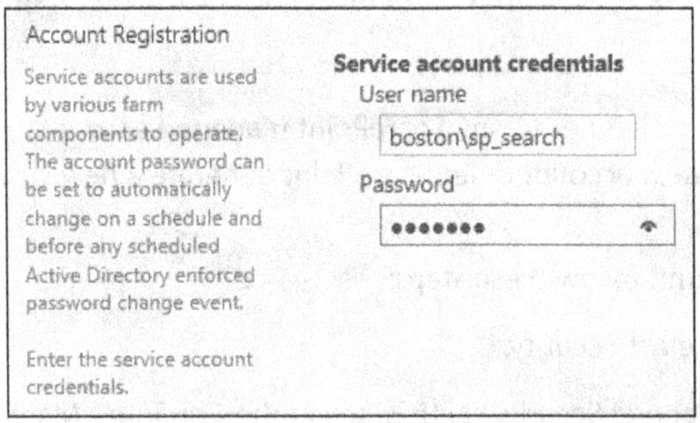

Account Registration

Service accounts are used by various farm components to operate. The account password can be set to automatically change on a schedule and before any scheduled Active Directory enforced password change event.

Enter the service account credentials.

Service account credentials
User name

boston\sp_search

Password

•••••••

FIGURE 2-62 Service account credentials.

6. In the Automatic Password Change section, you can choose to enable automatic password changes. You can also decide whether the system notifies the administrative time via e-mail and when the password change occurs (see Figure 2-63).

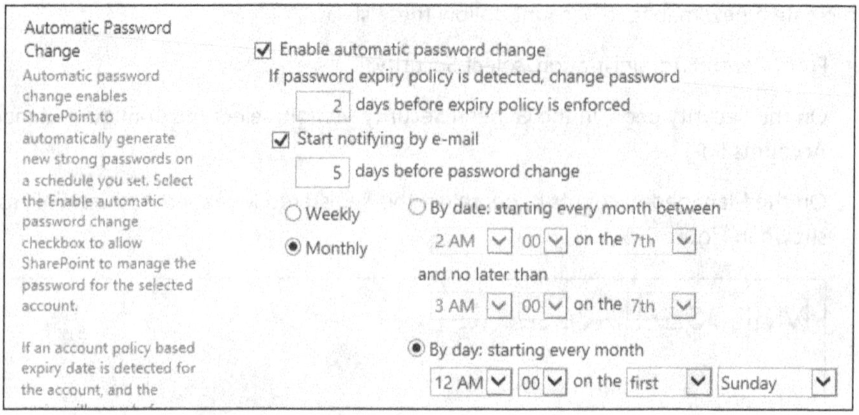

FIGURE 2-63 Automatic password change.

7. After you finish making changes to the new service account, click OK.

Editing an existing managed account

If you did not choose to have passwords automatically changed, you can still benefit from the concept of managed accounts. Perhaps your organization has a work day once per quarter wherein all passwords are changed and verified as part of a managed outage.

EXAM TIP

Because the service accounts are also Active Directory accounts, a distributed Active Directory team may not know to avoid changing passwords on your SharePoint service accounts. If this happens, know how to take the new credentials and apply them by editing the managed accounts.

This is a prime opportunity to make changes to any SharePoint managed accounts. You can choose a new password for each account or let SharePoint generate a new strong password.

To edit an existing managed account, follow these steps:

1. From Central Administration, select Security.

2. On the Security page, in the General Security section, select the Configure Managed Accounts link.

3. On the Managed Accounts page, select the managed account for which you want to make changes and click the Edit icon, as shown in Figure 2-64.

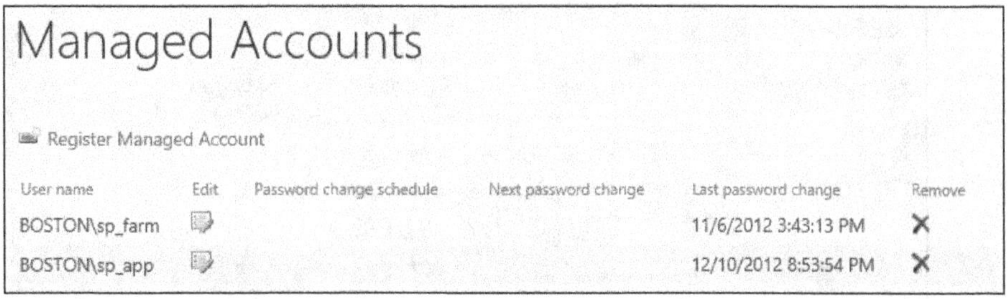

Managed Accounts

▧ Register Managed Account

User name	Edit	Password change schedule	Next password change	Last password change	Remove
BOSTON\sp_farm	▣			11/6/2012 3:43:13 PM	✕
BOSTON\sp_app	▣			12/10/2012 8:53:54 PM	✕

FIGURE 2-64 Editing a managed account.

4. In the Account Selection section, select the Managed Account whose password should be changed (see Figure 2-65).

Account Selection

Managed accounts are used by various farm components to operate.

Managed account
BOSTON\sp_app
BOSTON\sp_farm

FIGURE 2-65 Account selection.

5. In the Credential Management Section, you have three choices for resetting the password (see Figure 2-66):

- Have the system generate a new password.
- Set a new account password by entering and then confirming a password.
- Use an existing password. This option is particularly useful for environments in which the password is assigned to the service account as part of scheduled maintenance.

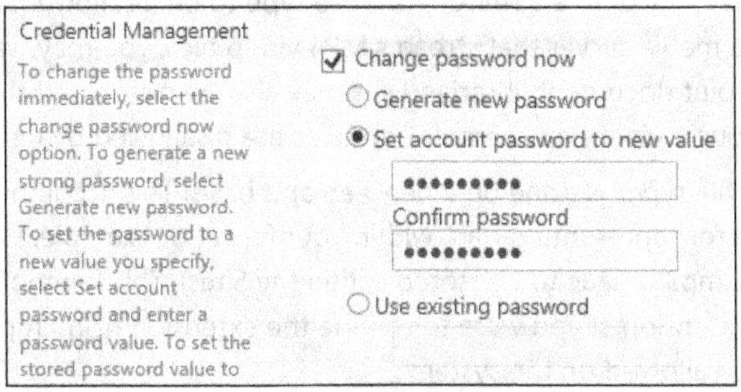

Credential Management

To change the password immediately, select the change password now option. To generate a new strong password, select Generate new password. To set the password to a new value you specify, select Set account password and enter a password value. To set the stored password value to

☑ Change password now
○ Generate new password
⦿ Set account password to new value
`●●●●●●●●●`
Confirm password
`●●●●●●●●●`
○ Use existing password

FIGURE 2-66 Changing service account credentials.

6. You can also cause an existing managed service account to automatically change its credentials (see Figure 2-67).

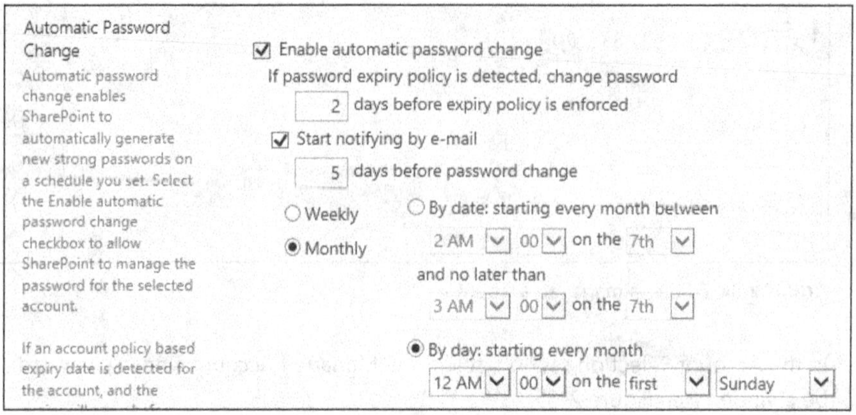

FIGURE 2-67 Automatic password change.

Planning and configuring blocked file types

As in previous versions, SharePoint 2013 enables an administrator to block certain file types from being uploaded into a SharePoint farm. In fact, there are several file extensions that are already disallowed within the Blocked File Types page of Central Administration.

MORE INFO **BLOCKED FILE TYPES**

For the current list of file types blocked by default, please visit the TechNet article "Manage Blocked File Types in SharePoint 2013" at *http://technet.microsoft.com/en-us/library/ cc262496.*

There are several scenarios that may define a reason for a file type to be disallowed. For instance, if your organization has a media server that streams MP4 video files, you may want to prevent their upload into SharePoint document libraries. Files may also be disallowed simply because they can contain malicious code (as an example, .exe files are disallowed by default).

The configuration of blocked file types is done on a per-web app basis. This accommodates design decisions you make for representing data within your farm (for example, not allowing music file types such as .mp3 or .aac to be stored within My Sites). This functionality simply works by examining the extension; if you were to change the extension from .mp3 to .txt, for instance, the file would be allowed on the system.

To add or remove a new blocked file type, go to the Blocked File Types page within Central Administration, found at Central Administration → Security → General Security → Define Blocked File Types (see Figure 2-68).

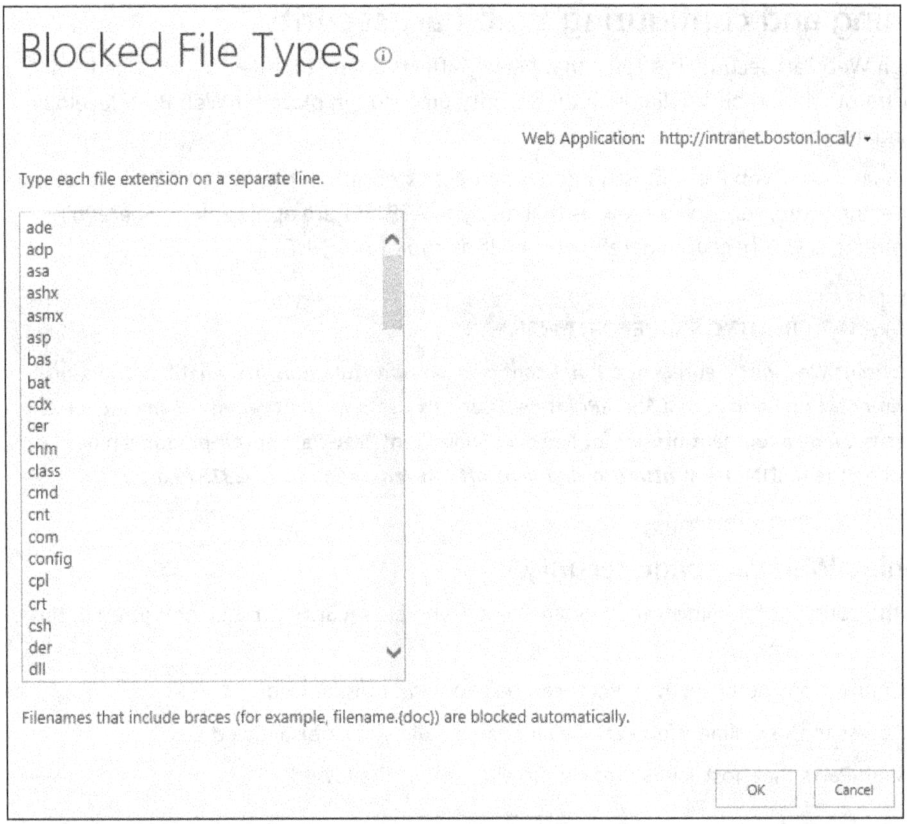

Blocked File Types ⓘ

Web Application: http://intranet.boston.local/ ▾

Type each file extension on a separate line.

```
ade
adp
asa
ashx
asmx
asp
bas
bat
cdx
cer
chm
class
cmd
cnt
com
config
cpl
crt
csh
der
dll
```

Filenames that include braces (for example, filename.{doc}) are blocked automatically.

OK   Cancel

FIGURE 2-68 Blocked File Types page (Central Administration).

On this page, you can do the following:

- Select an extension and delete its entry to "unblock" it.
- Add a new file extension in and it will be blocked. It is not required to add a new entry in alphabetical order, it will be reordered automatically once.

EXAM TIP

Newly blocked file types will have no effect on existing files already stored within a Share-Point web application. For instance, if there are already .mp3 files present in a given web application, blocking this file type prevents only the addition of new .mp3 files to document libraries within the web application.

Planning and configuring Web Part security

Although Web Part security is a topic that heavily affects SharePoint developers, SharePoint administrators should be familiar with the security protocols in place for Web Part development and implementation.

The SharePoint Web Part infrastructure is a direct extension of the ASP.NET Web Part infrastructure; therefore, security guidelines that apply to ASP.NET are applicable to SharePoint development as well because SharePoint is built on top of ASP.NET.

> **MORE INFO CREATING SHAREPOINT WEB PARTS**
>
> SharePoint Web Parts represent a significant portion of its functionality, enabling functional elements to be added to a SharePoint web page by users without requiring any technical expertise. A development primer for learning SharePoint Web Part development can be found on the MSDN site at *http://msdn.microsoft.com/en-us/library/ee231579.aspx*.

Assigning Web Part page security

Within the context of administration, SharePoint Web Part security can be configured in three ways:

- Connections between Web Parts can be allowed or disallowed
- Access to the Online Web Part Gallery can be allowed or disallowed
- Web Parts that host JavaScript can be allowed or disallowed

> **EXAM TIP**
>
> Web Part page security is assigned on a per-web application basis.

To change Web Part page security settings, do the following:

1. From Central Administration, select Application Management.

2. On the Web Applications List page, select the web application for which you want to make changes.

3. From the Web Applications tab Security section, select the Web Part Security icon (see Figure 2-69).

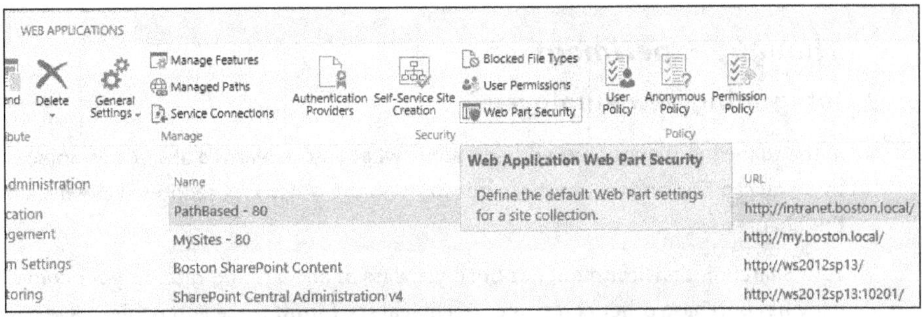

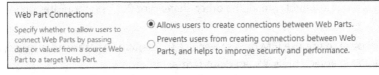

FIGURE 2-69 Web application Web Part security.

4. On the Security For Web Part Pages page, you can configure one of three options: Web Part Connections, Online Web Part Gallery, and Scriptable Web Parts.

5. In the Web Part Connections section, choose whether to allow connections between Web Parts (see Figure 2-70).

Web Part Connections

Specify whether to allow users to connect Web Parts by passing data or values from a source Web Part to a target Web Part.

◉ Allows users to create connections between Web Parts.
○ Prevents users from creating connections between Web Parts, and helps to improve security and performance.

FIGURE 2-70 Specifying Web Part connection settings.

6. In the Online Web Part Gallery section, choose whether or not to allow access to the Online Web Part Gallery (see Figure 2-71).

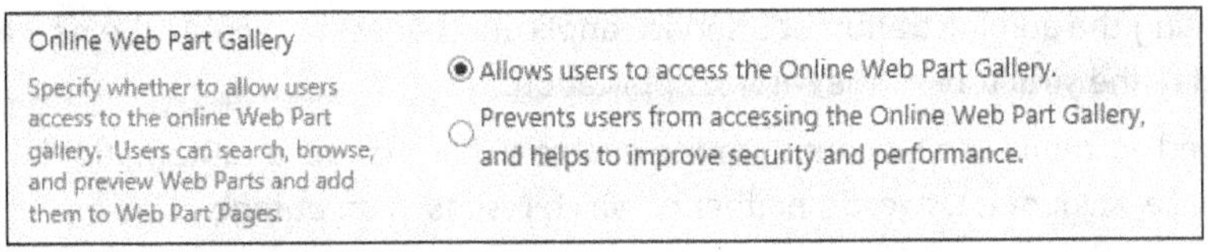

Online Web Part Gallery

Specify whether to allow users access to the online Web Part gallery. Users can search, browse, and preview Web Parts and add them to Web Part Pages.

◉ Allows users to access the Online Web Part Gallery.
○ Prevents users from accessing the Online Web Part Gallery, and helps to improve security and performance.

FIGURE 2-71 Specifying Online Web Part Gallery settings.

7. In the Scriptable Web Parts section (see Figure 2-72), choose whether to allow Web Parts to execute scripts (prevented by default).

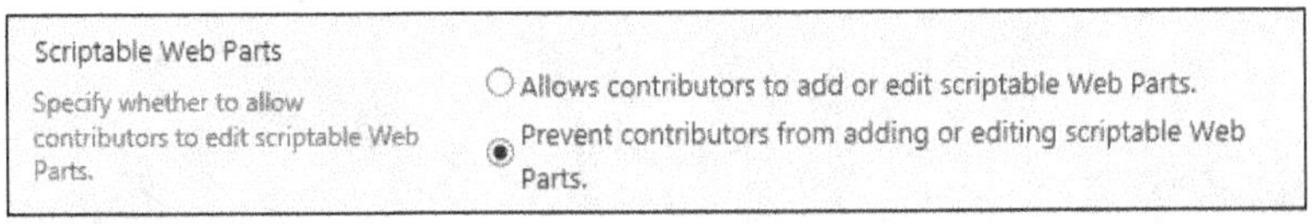

Scriptable Web Parts

Specify whether to allow contributors to edit scriptable Web Parts.

○ Allows contributors to add or edit scriptable Web Parts.
◉ Prevent contributors from adding or editing scriptable Web Parts.

FIGURE 2-72 Specifying scriptable Web Parts settings.

8. Click OK to commit your changes. If you prefer, you can click Restore Defaults to revert settings back to the factory default.

Objective summary

- The RMS client is installed with all the other SharePoint 2013 prerequisites on farm servers.
- You can choose to not use IRM on a server, use the default RMS server, or specify a particular RMS server. This is a SharePoint farm-wide setting.
- Users who are granted farm administrator membership do not possess access to run any sort of Windows PowerShell configurations within SharePoint.
- To grant a user account access to use Windows PowerShell, you must do so on a per-database basis using the Add-SPShellAdmin Windows PowerShell cmdlet.
- Delegating the administration of a service application does not enable the new admin to modify the structure of the service application.
- Managed accounts can be configured to enable either manual or automatic changes for service account passwords, neither of which results in an outage.
- File types are blocked by file extension. If a file existed prior to its type being blocked, no action is taken against it by the system.
- Web Part security is assigned at the web application level through Central Administration.

Objective review

Answer the following questions to test your knowledge of the information in this objective. You can find the answers to these questions and explanations of why each answer choice is correct or incorrect in the "Answers" section at the end of this chapter.

1. Which of the following options is available for using an RMS server in a SharePoint farm? (Choose all that apply.)

   A. Do Not Use IRM On This Server

   B. Use The Default RMS Server Specified In Active Directory

   C. Specify An Existing RMS Server

   D. All of the above

2. In a growing SharePoint farm, at what levels might you choose to delegate administration? (Choose all that apply.)

   A. Web application

   B. Farm

   C. Service application

   D. Zone

3. Which of the following statements are true concerning managed accounts? (Choose all that apply.)

   A. A system-generated password can be automatically provisioned

   B. An administrator can enter a new password

   C. An existing password can be used

   D. All of the above

4. Which of the following Web Part security settings has to do with the use of JavaScript in Web Parts?

   A. Web Part Connections

   B. Online Web Part Gallery

   C. Scriptable Web Parts

   D. None of the above

Chapter summary

- SharePoint 2013 requires the use of Windows PowerShell to configure Windows classic mode authentication (for backward compatibility).

- Users always authenticate to the identity provider in their organization to receive a Security Assertion Markup Language (SAML) token.

- Although you can reconfigure OAuth to use HTTP instead of HTTPS, doing so is insecure (HTTPS is the default).

- STSADM is used to configure the PropertyName (PN) and PropertyValues (PV) for the People Picker because there is no provision to administer this functionality in Windows PowerShell.

- If your site owners cannot configure access request settings, it is most likely because outgoing e-mail is not yet configured within your farm.

- Antivirus software for use with SharePoint must be installed on all web-tier servers in the farm.

- Web Part page security is assigned on a per-web application basis.

Answers

Objective 2.1: Thought experiment

Because you do not know the IT organizations that you might acquire, you can start with an ADFS 2.0 federation provider. You may, however, soon find this onerous to maintain, particularly if your partner organizations are as small as you expect.

Consider proposing a system whereby you use the Windows Azure ACS instead to allow for the centralized management of all federation efforts within your company.

Objective 2.1: Review

1. **Correct answers:** C, D

   A. **Incorrect:** Although basic authentication is a Windows authentication type, it is not integrated enabling user names and passwords to be passed through automatically.

   B. **Incorrect:** Forms authentication relies on ASP.NET and a back-end database to maintain authentication credentials.

   C. **Correct:** Negotiate (Kerberos) is a type of integrated Windows authentication.

   D. **Correct:** NTLM is a type of integrated Windows authentication.

2. **Correct answer:** A

   A. **Correct:** Windows classic is not claims-based, and must be configured from within Windows PowerShell.

   B. **Incorrect:** NTLM authentication is claims-based.

   C. **Incorrect:** There is no such authentication type.

   D. **Incorrect:** FBA is claims-based.

3. **Correct answers:** A, B, D

   A. **Correct:** This S2S configuration is supported.

   B. **Correct:** This S2S configuration is supported.

   C. **Incorrect:** You cannot use S2S to configure an OAuth relationship between Share-Point 2013 and SQL Server 2012.

   D. **Correct:** This S2S configuration is supported.

4. **Correct answer:** A

   A. **Correct:** Anonymous authentication is configured at the zone level only.

   B. **Incorrect:** Anonymous authentication cannot be configured at the web application level.

   C. **Incorrect:** Anonymous authentication cannot be configured at the site collection level.

   D. **Incorrect:** Anonymous authentication cannot be configured at the site level.

Objective 2.2: Thought experiment

Because the company cannot disable the account while it is being audited for access, the next best thing is to deny access on all SharePoint web applications.

This process is carried out on a web app by web app basis and requires you to specify this user account in the User policy, associating it with the Deny All permission level.

Objective 2.2: Review

1. **Correct answer:** B

   A. **Incorrect:** If selected, a visitors group can be created as part of the provisioning process.

   B. **Correct:** There is no such default group.

   C. **Incorrect:** If selected, a members group can be created as part of the provisioning process.

   D. **Incorrect:** If selected, an owners group can be created as part of the provisioning process.

2. **Correct answer:** D

   A. **Incorrect:** There is no such cmdlet.

   B. **Incorrect:** There is no such cmdlet.

   C. **Incorrect:** There is no such cmdlet.

   D. **Correct:** People Picker is configured using STSADM.

3. **Correct answers:** B, C

   A. **Incorrect:** You cannot allow anonymous access at the web application level.

   B. **Correct:** Anonymous access can be configured for the entire web site.

   C. **Correct:** Anonymous access can be configured for lists and libraries.

   D. **Incorrect:** Anonymous access cannot be configured for individual items.

4. **Correct answer:** A

    A. **Correct:** The Full Control, Full Read, Deny Write, and Deny All permission levels are created within this policy.

    B. **Incorrect:** The User policy associates individual users or groups with a permission level.

    C. **Incorrect:** The Anonymous policy maintains its own set of permissions.

    D. **Incorrect:** There is no such web application policy.

Objective 2.3: Thought experiment

You might begin by extending the web application that needs anonymous access using a different URL, which can be exposed through the firewall.

Next, you can secure the _vti_bin and _layouts folders in the extended web application's web.config file, and then allow anonymous authentication at the zone level and assign anonymous authorization at the site or site collection level.

Objective 2.3: Review

1. **Correct answer:** A

    A. **Correct:** If activated, this feature disallows access to the _layouts folder structure.

    B. **Incorrect:** There is no such feature.

    C. **Incorrect:** There is no such feature.

    D. **Incorrect:** Only the Limited-Access User Permission Lockdown mode feature disallows access.

2. **Correct answer:** D

    A. **Incorrect:** The web tier servers should, at the very least, be placed behind a front-end, Internet-facing firewall.

    B. **Incorrect:** This tier should never be exposed to the Internet and should be behind the DMZ and the back-end firewall.

    C. **Incorrect:** This tier should never be exposed to the Internet and should be behind the DMZ and the back-end firewall.

    D. **Correct:** No SharePoint server should be exposed directly to the Internet without an active firewall.

3. **Correct answers:** A, D

   A. **Correct:** A document can be scanned as part of the upload process.

   B. **Incorrect:** SharePoint cannot scan a document as part of a workflow operation.

   C. **Incorrect:** SharePoint cannot scan a document as part of a workflow operation.

   D. **Correct:** A document can be scanned as part of the download process.

4. **Correct answers:** B, C, D

   A. **Incorrect:** The "publishing" farm does not need to generate a secure token certificate.

   B. **Correct:** The "consuming" farm must generate a root certificate.

   C. **Correct:** The "consuming" farm must generate a secure token certificate.

   D. **Correct:** The "publishing" farm must generate a root certificate.

Objective 2.4: Thought experiment

There is a good chance that the companies you have purchased were already using Share-Point to some degree. This may mean that you have staff whose skills and experience vary in scope.

Consider designating some of the staff to maintain service applications, particularly those who already have experience in those services (search, managed metadata, and so on).

For those users who seem to possess some administrative skill, assign them as farm administrators, but grant them shell admin permissions only after you are assured of their readiness.

Objective 2.4: Review

1. **Correct answer:** D

   A. **Incorrect:** Partial answer.

   B. **Incorrect:** Partial answer.

   C. **Incorrect:** Partial answer.

   D. **Correct:** All three of these options are available.

2. **Correct answers:** B, C

   A. **Incorrect:** You cannot delegate administration at the zone level.

   B. **Correct:** You can delegate administration at the farm level.

   C. **Correct:** You can delegate administration at the farm level.

   D. **Incorrect:** You cannot delegate administration at the zone level.

3. **Correct answer:** D

   A. **Incorrect:** Partial answer.

   B. **Incorrect:** Partial answer.

   C. **Incorrect:** Partial answer.

   D. **Correct:** All three of these statements are true.

4. **Correct answer:** C

   A. **Incorrect:** Settings for Web Part connections do not have anything to do with the use of JavaScript in web parts.

   B. **Incorrect:** Settings for the Online Web Part Gallery do not have anything to do with the use of JavaScript in web parts.

   C. **Correct:** Scriptable Web Parts can have JavaScript contained in them.

   D. **Incorrect:** Only the Scriptable Web Parts settings have to do with using JavaScript in Web Parts.

## CHAPTER 3

Install and configure SharePoint farms

This chapter focuses on the installation of the server. By the end of the chapter, you will understand the core configuration of a SharePoint farm. With a firm design in hand and some install scripts, you can generate one or more SharePoint farms in a systematic and repeatable fashion.

Objectives in this chapter:

- Objective 3.1: Plan installation
- Objective 3.2: Plan and configure farm-wide settings
- Objective 3.3: Create and configure enterprise search
- Objective 3.4: Create and configure a Managed Metadata Service (MMS) application
- Objective 3.5: Create and configure a User Profile Service (UPA) application

Objective 3.1: Plan installation

In this section, we will cover the configuration steps required to set up a SharePoint farm at a very basic level. Establishing a core infrastructure plan that is both repeatable and well managed will help guide us toward the goal of a solid SharePoint installation.

This objective covers how to:

- Identify and configure installation prerequisites.
- Implement scripted deployment.
- Implement update slipstreaming.
- Plan and install language packs.
- Plan and configure SCPs.
- Plan installation tracking and auditing.

Identifying and configuring installation prerequisites

Before SharePoint 2013 binaries can be installed on a server, a series of installation prerequisites must be met. These prerequisites are a combination of installed software components (such as the Microsoft .NET Framework 4.5) and configuration changes to the server (adding the Application Server Role and Web Server Role).

Installation prerequisites

The list of installation prerequisites is dependent on the operating system version installed on the would-be SharePoint server. SharePoint 2013 will install on two different operating systems: Windows Server 2008 R2 and Windows Server 2012.

Because the Windows Server 2012 platform is newer, it already has a couple of the components preinstalled, as you can see in Table 3-1.

TABLE 3-1 Install prerequisites by operating system platform

Component or Configuration	Windows Server 2008 R2	Windows Server 2012
Microsoft .NET Framework 4.5	Installation required	Installed as part of the operating system
Windows Management Framework (WMF) 3.0	Installation required	Installed as part of the operating system
Application Server Role, Web Server (IIS) Role	Configuration required	Configuration required
Microsoft SQL Server 2008 R2 SP1 Native Client	Installation required	Installation required
Windows Identity Foundation (WIF) (KB 974405)	Installation required	Installation required
Microsoft Sync Framework Runtime v1.0 SP1 (x64)	Installation required	Installation required
Windows Server AppFabric	Installation required	Installation required
Microsoft Identity Extensions	Installation required	Installation required
Microsoft Information Protection and Control Client	Installation required	Installation required
Microsoft WCF Data Services 5.0	Installation required	Installation required
Cumulative update package 1 for Microsoft AppFabric 1.1 for Windows Server (KB2671763)	Installation required	Installation required

Windows Server 2012 already includes both the Microsoft .NET Framework 4.5 and Windows Management Framework (WMF) 3.0 components. When the prerequisite installer is run on a Windows Server 2012 platform, it checks to see whether these components are installed; if so, it skips their installation.

EXAM TIP

Although you should have familiarity with the prerequisites for the new SharePoint farm, concentrate on knowing which two roles are required for installation (Application Server Role, Web Server Role).

Server connectivity to the Internet

There are two distinct scenarios for running the prerequisite installer in SharePoint 2013: online and offline. In the online configuration, the server on which SharePoint 2013 will be installed has direct access to the Internet and can download the necessary components as part of the prerequisite installation process.

In environments that require a higher level of security, servers may not be allowed direct access to the Internet. In such a situation, the installation prerequisites can be downloaded in advance and copied to the server or copied to a central file share for distribution to multiple SharePoint 2013 server installations.

After the components have been downloaded, Windows PowerShell can be run to configure the Application Server and Web Server (IIS) Roles. Following this process, the prerequisite installer tool can be used to install the remaining components.

Installing and configuring prerequisites (online)

Prerequisites are installed as part of the SharePoint GUI experience. When the SharePoint 2013 splash screen appears, the first item in the Install section is Install Software Prerequisites (see Figure 3-1).

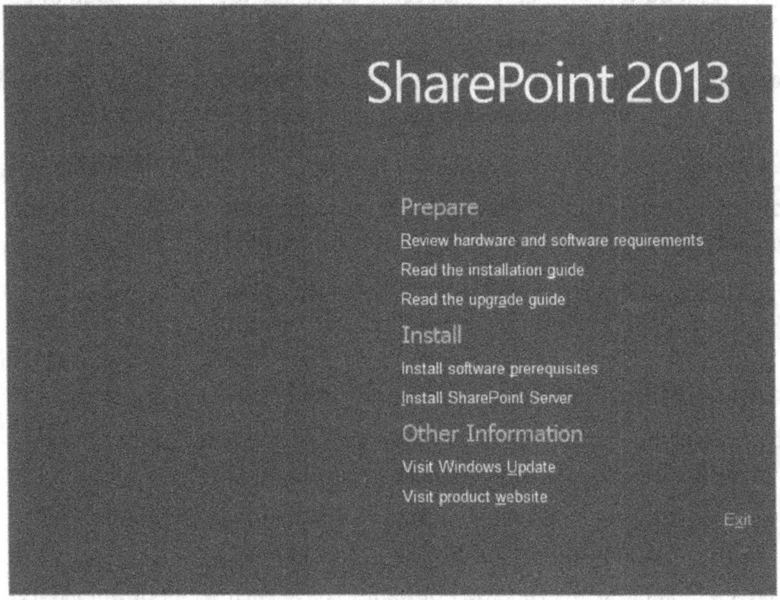

FIGURE 3-1 SharePoint 2013 installer splash screen.

Selecting the Install Software Prerequisites menu item immediately activates the prerequisite installer, as shown in Figure 3-2.

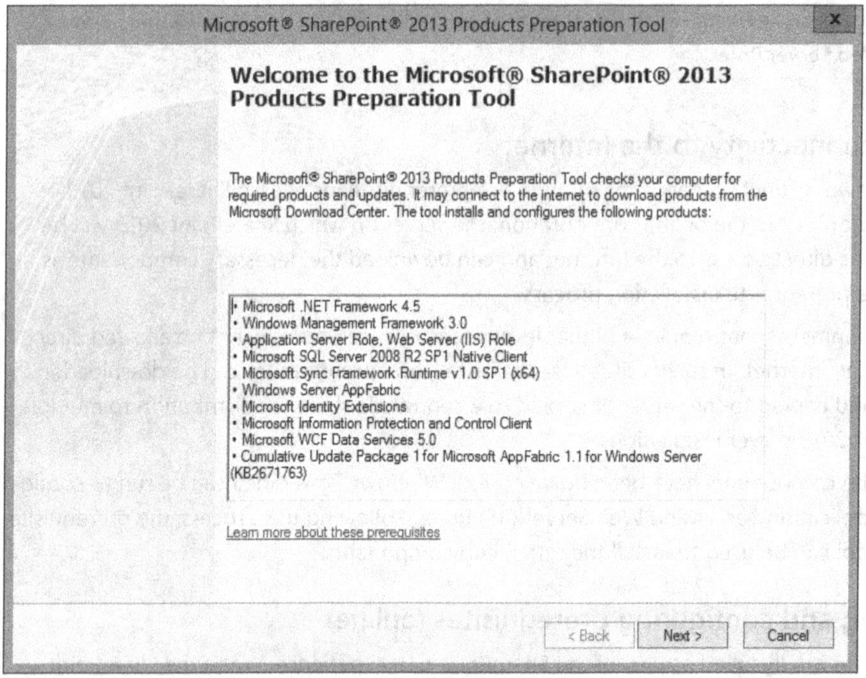

Welcome to the Microsoft® SharePoint® 2013 Products Preparation Tool

The Microsoft® SharePoint® 2013 Products Preparation Tool checks your computer for required products and updates. It may connect to the internet to download products from the Microsoft Download Center. The tool installs and configures the following products:

- Microsoft .NET Framework 4.5
- Windows Management Framework 3.0
- Application Server Role, Web Server (IIS) Role
- Microsoft SQL Server 2008 R2 SP1 Native Client
- Microsoft Sync Framework Runtime v1.0 SP1 (x64)
- Windows Server AppFabric
- Microsoft Identity Extensions
- Microsoft Information Protection and Control Client
- Microsoft WCF Data Services 5.0
- Cumulative Update Package 1 for Microsoft AppFabric 1.1 for Windows Server (KB2671763)

Learn more about these prerequisites

FIGURE 3-2 SharePoint 2013 Products Preparation Tool (online).

After you select the Next button and accept the license terms, the tool runs through three distinct steps:

1. The tool checks for the existence of the Microsoft .NET Framework 4.5 and Windows Management Framework 3.0 components. If they do not exist, they are installed.

2. The tool then installs both the Application Server Role and Web Server (IIS) Role.

   Note: The role installation requires a reboot of the server's operating system. After the reboot is complete, the tool resumes installation of the remaining components.

3. The remaining components are installed to the operating system, and the server is rebooted.

Downloading and installing prerequisites (offline)

It is also possible to install all the prerequisites with the server not connected to the Internet. Reasons for such a configuration might include the following:

- Your corporate IT policies may prevent you from downloading the prerequisites from the server. (The server cannot browse the Internet.)

- You have to create multiple servers and do not want to have each server download its own copy of the components.

The solution is to gather the components together into a centralized location and then install the prerequisites to each server as needed.

This type of installation involves two separate actions:

■ Installing and configuring the Application Server Role and Web Server (IIS) Role to the new servers via Windows PowerShell (requires Windows Server 2008 R2 or Windows Server 2012 media)

■ Creating a set of installation switches to run with the prerequisiteinstaller.exe tool; then downloading the components to a file share that is accessible by the new server

Installing and configuring the Application Role and Web Server Role is done via Windows PowerShell. Each of these roles is composed of a set of features. Before beginning this configuration, you need to mount the Windows Server installation disk in an available location (this example uses the D: drive).

To install the roles, do the following:

1. Mount the installation disk.

2. Open a Windows PowerShell window (run as Administrator).

3. Run the Import-Module ServerManager cmdlet.

4. Use the Add-WindowsFeature cmdlet to install each of the features, as shown in the following code snippet, specifying the source switch to the location in which you mounted the installation disk:

```
Add-WindowsFeature Net-Framework-Features,Web-Server,Web-WebServer,Web-Common-
Http,Web-Static-Content,Web-Default-Doc,Web-Dir-Browsing,Web-Http-Errors,Web-App-
Dev,Web-Asp-Net,Web-Net-Ext,Web-ISAPI-Ext,Web-ISAPI-Filter,Web-Health,Web-Http-
Logging,Web-Log-Libraries,Web-Request-Monitor,Web-Http-Tracing,Web-Security,Web-
Basic-Auth,Web-Windows-Auth,Web-Filtering,Web-Digest-Auth,Web-Performance,Web-
Stat-Compression,Web-Dyn-Compression,Web-Mgmt-Tools,Web-Mgmt-Console,Web-Mgmt-
Compat,Web-Metabase,Application-Server,AS-Web-Support,AS-TCP-Port-Sharing,AS-
WAS-Support, AS-HTTP-Activation,AS-TCP-Activation,AS-Named-Pipes,AS-Net-
Framework,WAS,WAS-Process-Model,WAS-NET-Environment,WAS-Config-APIs,Web-Lgcy-
Scripting,Windows-Identity-Foundation,Server-Media-Foundation,Xps-Viewer -Source
D:\sources\sxs
```

5. After the Add-WindowsFeature cmdlet has run, the server will advise you that it needs to restart. Type **shutdown /r** when you are ready, and the server will restart momentarily, as shown in Figure 3-3.

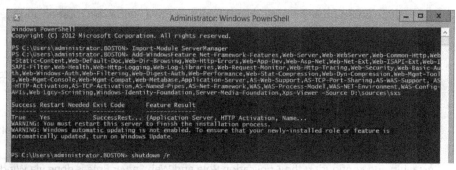

FIGURE 3-3 Add-WindowsFeature and Restart.

6. When the server restarts, it will complete the configuration.

Now that the roles have been configured, you need to download each software component to a central file share location that is accessible by the new server. The names and download locations for each component are shown in Table 3-2:

TABLE 3-2 Components and download locations

Component	Download address	File Downloaded
Microsoft .NET Framework 4.5	*http://go.microsoft.com/ fwlink/?LinkId=225702*	dotnetfx45_full_x86_x64.exe.
Windows Management Framework 3.0	*http://go.microsoft.com/fwlink/ p/?LinkId=273961*	Select Windows6.1-KB2506143-x64.msu.
Microsoft SQL Server 2008 R2 SP1 Native Client	*http://www.microsoft.com/en-us/ download/details.aspx?id=26728*	Select the appropriate sqlncli.msi file for your language. For English, the filename is 1033\x64\sqlncli.msi.
Windows Identity Foundation (KB 974405)	*http://go.microsoft.com/fwlink/ p/?LinkID=226830*	Windows6.1-KB974405-x64.msu.
Microsoft Sync Framework Runtime v1.0 SP1 (x64)	*http://go.microsoft.com/fwlink/ p/?LinkID=224449*	Synchronization.msi.
Windows Server AppFabric	*http://go.microsoft.com/ fwlink/?LinkId=235496*	WindowsServerAppFabricSetup_x64.exe.
Microsoft Identity Extensions	*http://go.microsoft.com/ fwlink/?LinkID=252368*	MicrosoftIdentityExtensions-64.msi.
Microsoft Information Protection and Control Client	*http://go.microsoft.com/fwlink/ p/?LinkID=219568*	setup_msipc_x64.msi.
Microsoft WCF Data Services 5.0	*http://www.microsoft.com/ en-us/download/confirmation. aspx?id=29306*	WcfDataServices.exe.
Cumulative Update Package 1 for Microsoft AppFabric 1.1 for Windows Server (KB2671763)	*http://www.microsoft.com/en-us/ download/details.aspx?id=29241*	Select AppFabric1.1-RTM-KB2671763-x86-*<XXX>*.exe where *<XXX>* indicates your language. For English, the file name is AppFabric1.1-RTM-KB2671763-x86-ENU.exe.

Again, if you are using Windows Server 2012, you can skip downloading the first two items because they are already installed in the operating system. All the other components in this list are required; SharePoint 2013 will not install without them.

> **IMPORTANT PREREQUISITE FILE LOCATION**
>
> The prerequisite installer expects these files to all be available in the same place. Do not place each file in its own directory; simply download each to the same folder as the rest.

Now that all the components have been downloaded, you can use the prerequisiteinstaller. exe file and some switches to install and configure each component. Running the prerequisit-einstaller.exe file (found at the root of your SharePoint installation media location) with the /? switch displays all the available switches, as shown in Figure 3-4.

```
***Command Line Options***
/continue - This is used to tell the installer that it is continuing from a restart
/unattended - No user interaction. Exit codes:
  0  - Success
  1  - Another instance of this application is already running
  2  - Invalid command line parameter(s)
  1001 - A pending restart blocks installation
  3010 - A restart is needed
  Other error codes - From the prerequisite installation that failed last
/? - Display this message

The installer installs from the file specified in the command line options below
where 'file' denotes the file to install from. If the option is not specified, it
downloads the file from the internet and installs. If the option is not applicable to
the current operating system, it ignores it.

/SQLNCli:file - Install Microsoft SQL Server 2008 R2 SP1 Native Client from file

/PowerShell:file - Install Windows Management Framework 3.0 from file

/NETFX:file - Install Microsoft .NET Framework 4.5 from file

/IDFX:file - Install Windows Identity Foundation (KB974405) from file

/Sync:file - Install Microsoft Sync Framework Runtime v1.0 SP1 (x64) from file

/AppFabric:file - Install Windows Server AppFabric from file

/IDFX11:file - Install Windows Identity Foundation v1.1 from file

/MSIPCClient:file - Install Microsoft Information Protection and Control client
from file

/WCFDataServices:file - Install Microsoft WCF Data Services from file

/KB2671763:file - Cumulative Update Package 1 for Microsoft AppFabric 1.1 for
Windows Server (KB2671763) from file
```

FIGURE 3-4 Prerequisiteinstaller.exe switches.

Each of these switches can be run individually, but they are most often batched together along with the appropriate file names (in the previous table) to install the components on each server. In the following example, a file share has been created on the \\WS2012DC server that contains all the component download files.

EXAM TIP

The prerequisiteinstaller.exe command can check for prerequisites as well as download and install them.

To begin the component installation process, follow these steps:

1. Mount the SharePoint 2013 media (D:\ in this example).
2. Type the following command and switch; then click Enter:
3. Note that the share location is specified in each switch (\\ws2012dc\prereq):

```
d:\Prerequisiteinstaller.exe /PowerShell:"\\ws2012dc\prereq\WINDOWS6.1-
KB2506143-x64.msu" /NETFX:"\\ws2012dc\prereq\dotNetFx45_Full_x86_x64.exe" /
IDFX:"\\ws2012dc\prereq\Windows6.1-KB974405-x64.msu" /sqlncli:"\\ws2012dc\
prereq\sqlncli.msi" /Sync:"\\ws2012dc\prereq\Synchronization.msi" /AppFabric:"\\
ws2012dc\prereq\WindowsServerAppFabricSetup_x64.exe" /IDFX11:"\\ws2012dc\prereq\
MicrosoftIdentityExtensions-64.msi" /MSIPCClient:"\\ws2012dc\prereq\setup_msipc_
x64.msi" /WCFDataServices:"\\ws2012dc\prereq\WcfDataServices.exe" /KB2671763:"\\
ws2012dc\prereq\AppFabric1.1-RTM-KB2671763-x64-ENU.exe"
```

4. The SharePoint 2013 Products Preparation Tool appears as if you are online (see Figure 3-5). Click Next and then accept the license agreement.

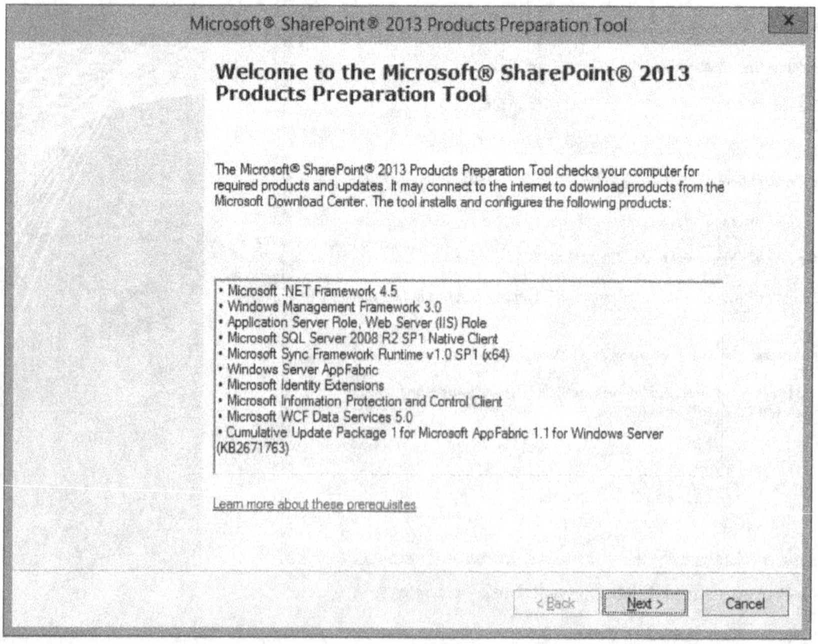

FIGURE 3-5 SharePoint 2013 Products Preparation Tool (offline).

5. The tool installs each of the components (if required).

6. When the installation completes, a summary screen appears that shows the completed installations (see Figure 3-6).

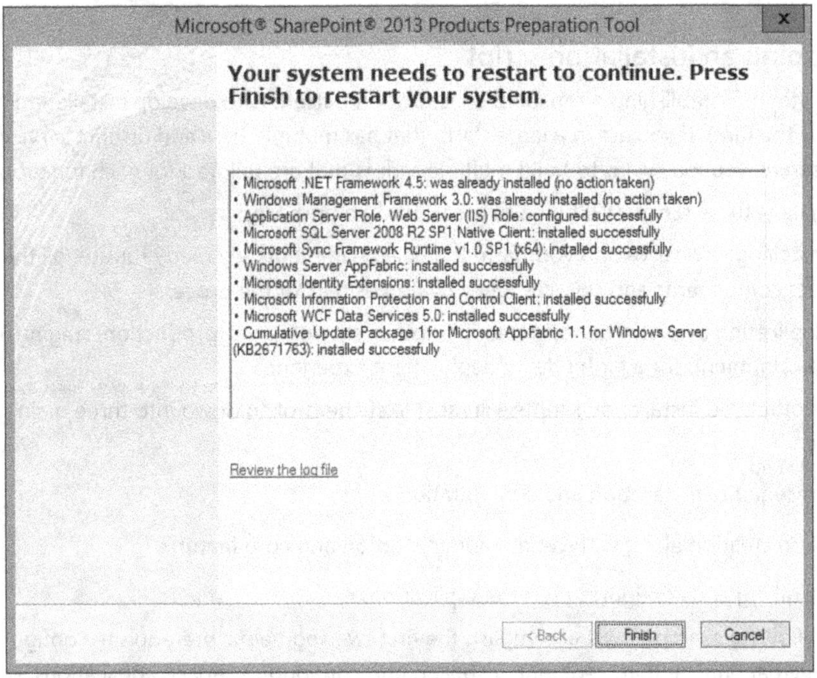

FIGURE 3-6 Installation complete; restart required.

7. Click Finish to immediately restart the server and complete the prerequisite installation.

Implementing scripted deployment

Installing a single server or small farm installation of SharePoint through the GUI is a pretty straightforward process. At a very high level, all you have to do is the following:

1. Install all the binaries from the installation media.

2. Download and install the prerequisites.

3. Execute the SharePoint 2013 Products Configuration Wizard.

4. Run the Farm Configuration Wizard.

At the end of this process, you will have a functional SharePoint farm; however, what you will also have is a farm that:

- Has GUIDs in each database name, for uniqueness
- May have more services activated than you want (depending on your selections in the Farm Configuration Wizard)

- Will activate all these services on each and every web and app tier server in the farm

Additionally, if you are not extremely careful about documenting your server build and configuration standard, you may end up configuring a newly added server in a way that is different from the other servers in the farm.

Developing an installation script

The first step of establishing a repeatable installation pattern is to develop installation scripts to deploy the farm. If you are in a larger farm that has multiple tiers and distinct services on a certain server, you may want to build multiple scripts that are tailored for each function.

Ultimately, these scripts will be quite useful for two purposes:

- Installing new servers to your farm that will be immediately ready for use (all the correct components and services are activated as part of the process).

- Replicating a certain tier of server in another environment (production, staging/test, development) for a high fidelity deployment experience.

Your completed installation scripts will most likely be broken down into three main segments:

1. Prerequisite installation and configuration

2. Farm creation along with central administration and core features

3. Installing and configuring service applications

The following examples will accomplish the first two segments: prerequisite configuration and farm creation. The third segment, installing and configuring service applications, is covered in several sections of this book, each of which applies to a particular service within the farm (Search, User Profiles, Managed Metadata, and so on).

> **MORE INFO** **CONFIGURING SERVICE APPLICATIONS VIA WINDOWS POWERSHELL**
>
> The Windows PowerShell creation and configuration of service applications within Share-Point 2013 is extensively documented and can be found within the article "Configure a Service Application by Using a Windows PowerShell Script" at *http://technet.microsoft.com/en-us/library/gg983005.aspx*.

Configuring the max degree of parallelism

On a SQL Server that has multiple processors, a single statement can be run in parallel across these processors. For a SharePoint installation, this value must be set to 1, indicating that no parallel processing activity can take place on the supporting instance.

Although this value can be configured within the SQL Server Management Studio (SSMS), either by running a T-SQL query or by changing settings on the instance, it is also possible for this function to be scripted via Windows PowerShell. This setting needs to be made only once on the database instance that supports your SharePoint 2013 farm.

The issue with including this in a script will be that neither your SharePoint installer account nor your farm account should have this level of permission; as a result, you will most likely need the SQL DBA to configure this value on your data tier before proceeding with the rest of the scripted actions.

EXAM TIP

Although SQL Server supports different settings for the Max Degree of Parallelism, SharePoint does not; the only valid value for this setting is 1.

Creating the farm

The initial farm creation is accomplished while logged in as the Setup user administrator account. This account requires the following:

- It must have domain user account permissions.
- It must be a member of the local administrators group on each server in the web and application tiers of the farm.
- It must be assigned to the securityadmin and dbcreator SQL security roles during any setup and configuration steps (including updates done after the initial setup).

The actual creation of the farm requires you to assign variables for the configuration database name, the database server, the administration content database, and the assignment of farm credentials:

```
# Add the PowerShell Snapin for SharePoint
Add-PSSnapin Microsoft.SharePoint.PowerShell -ErrorAction SilentlyContinue
# Prompt for the farm account password
$FarmCredential = Get-Credential -credential boston\sp_farm
# Prompt for the passphrase
$Passphrase = Read-Host -assecurestring "SP PassPhrase"
# Assign the other variables for the Config DB, Admin Content DB, and the Central Admin
TCP Port
$DbName = "SharePoint_Config"
$DbServer = "WS2012SP13"
$AdminContentDb = "SharePoint2013_Admin_Content"
$CAPort = "10201"
# Create Configuration Database
New-SPConfigurationDatabase -DatabaseName $DbName -DatabaseServer $DbServer
-AdministrationContentDatabaseName $AdminContentDb -FarmCredentials $FarmCredential
-Passphrase $Passphrase
```

IMPORTANT NEW CONFIGURATION DATABASES REQUIRE CONFIGURATION TIME

The New-SPConfigurationDatabase cmdlet can take quite a bit of time to execute—be patient.

Installing farm features and services

Next up, we must install the core components of the farm, including the help site collection files, available services, and available features:

```
# Install the Help Site Collection Files in the Current Farm
Install-SPHelpCollection -All
# Enforce Resource Security on the Local Server
Initialize-SPResourceSecurity
# Install and Provision Services on the Farm
Install-SPService
# Install Features from the Feature.xml file
Install-SPFeature -AllExistingFeatures
```

Creating the Central Administration Web Application

The last step in building the basic farm is to create the Central Administration Web Application and copy shared application data into the existing web application folders:

```
#Create Central Administration Web App
New-SPCentralAdministration -Port $CAPort -WindowsAuthProvider "NTLM"
#Copy Shared Application Data to Existing Web Application Folders
Install-SPApplicationContent
```

> **IMPORTANT CENTRAL ADMINISTRATION DOES NOT RUN IN CLAIMS MODE**
>
> If you look carefully at the New-SPCentralAdministration cmdlet's switches, you will notice something interesting: This web application uses Windows classic authentication.

Implementing patch slipstreaming

As with any software platform, SharePoint Server 2013 is constantly being updated. These updates often include security patches, bug remediation, as well as performance improvements (and the occasional new feature).

Updates come in one of three forms:

- **Critical on-demand (COD) hotfixes**   One-off patches, designed to be installed only when you are experiencing the particular issue(s) that the hotfix addresses.
- **Cumulative updates**   A collection of hotfixes that are released on a bimonthly basis, they can include both critical and noncritical hotfixes for your SharePoint installation.
- **Service packs**   The best-tested of the three update types, service packs are fully vetted groupings of corrective hotfixes (and sometimes new or improved features) that should be added to your farm.

In an existing SharePoint server farm, the application of patches is a fairly straightforward process. All that is required is for you to download the patch, apply it to each server, and then run the Configuration Wizard on each server.

As you grow your SharePoint installation from a single server to multiple servers in the web and application tiers, you may find that the process of installing the release to market (RTM) binaries and then applying updates becomes a more labor-intensive process.

The obvious solution is to find a way to apply patches in a cumulative fashion; that is, to download each patch and then extract it to a staging location for use by new servers in your SharePoint farm.

Preparing to slipstream patches

Slipstreaming patches requires a bit of typing because there is no built-in way to handle them from Central Administration. In essence, you will be building new installation media by accumulating the wanted updates and then storing them along with your original SharePoint installation media.

If you open your SharePoint installation media in Windows Explorer, you will see that there are several subdirectories present at the root directory. One of these subdirectories is called Updates, and it is the place where you will be extracting and updating your hotfixes, cumulative updates, and service packs (see Figure 3-7).

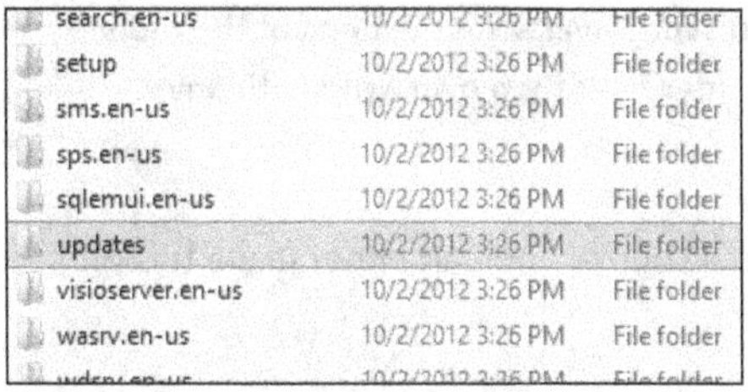

search.en-us	10/2/2012 3:26 PM	File folder
setup	10/2/2012 3:26 PM	File folder
sms.en-us	10/2/2012 3:26 PM	File folder
sps.en-us	10/2/2012 3:26 PM	File folder
sqlemui.en-us	10/2/2012 3:26 PM	File folder
updates	10/2/2012 3:26 PM	File folder
visioserver.en-us	10/2/2012 3:26 PM	File folder
wasrv.en-us	10/2/2012 3:26 PM	File folder
wdsrv.en-us	10/2/2012 3:26 PM	File folder

FIGURE 3-7 The Updates folder on the SharePoint installation media.

After this directory has been populated with updates, it can be automatically installed by the SharePoint Products Configuration Wizard as part of the installation process.

EXAM TIP

Understand the required commands to expand the media for each patch and how to add it to the Updates folder of your installation media, whether on CD/DVD or over a network share.

Creating slipstream installation media

Slipstreaming SharePoint installation media gives you a robust and repeatable way to configure multiple servers from one install source. This source is generally a network share that will
contain both the original SharePoint installation media and the updates you choose.

To prepare the slipstream media on a network share called \\WS2012DC\SPInstall, do the
following:

1. Copy the original SharePoint 2013 installation media to the SPInstall share.

2. If you have multiple updates you want to consolidate, extract each update, starting
   with the oldest update first. For each update, do this:

   A. Download the software update package

   B. Extract the update using the /extract switch; for example:

   ```
   sts2013-kb2752058-fullfile-x64-glb.exe /extract: \\ws2012dc\spinstall\updates
   ```

> **IMPORTANT LOAD FROM OLDEST TO NEWEST**
>
> As you may have guessed by now, the newer updates may overwrite portions of the older
> updates. Load the oldest media in to the updates folder first; then overwrite with any
> newer patches.

At this point, you should have a slipstreamed install source. You can either leave this on a
network share, or optionally burn it to a DVD.

Planning and installing language packs

SharePoint has built-in functionality to enable the use of multiple languages within a single
SharePoint installation. Each language that is supported within the farm requires the download of a distinct language pack. These packs are supported for use in both SharePoint Server
2013 and Project Server 2013 installations.

The following language packs are currently available for use in SharePoint 2013 platforms:

- Arabic
- Basque
- Bulgarian
- Catalan
- Chinese (Simplified)
- Chinese (Traditional)
- Croatian
- Czech
- Danish

- Dutch
- English
- Estonian
- Finnish
- French
- Galician
- German
- Greek
- Hebrew
- Hindi
- Hungarian
- Indonesian
- Italian
- Japanese
- Kazakh
- Korean
- Latvian
- Lithuanian
- Malay (Malaysia)
- Norwegian (Bokmål)
- Polish
- Portuguese (Brazil)
- Portuguese (Portugal)
- Romanian
- Russian
- Serbian (Cyrillic)
- Serbian (Latin)
- Slovak
- Slovenian
- Spanish
- Swedish
- Thai
- Turkish
- Ukranian
- Vietnamese

Downloading language packs

SharePoint Server 2013 language packs (applicable to both SharePoint Server 2013 and Project Server 2013) can be downloaded from the Microsoft Download Center at *http://www.microsoft.com/en-us/download/details.aspx?id=37140*.

EXAM TIP

No matter which language you download, the name of the file is always sharepointlanguagepack.exe (although the size changes), so it pays to store each language pack in its own directory to avoid confusion.

Downloading the language pack involves selecting the wanted language and then downloading the appropriate version of sharepointlanguagepack.exe (see Figure 3-8).

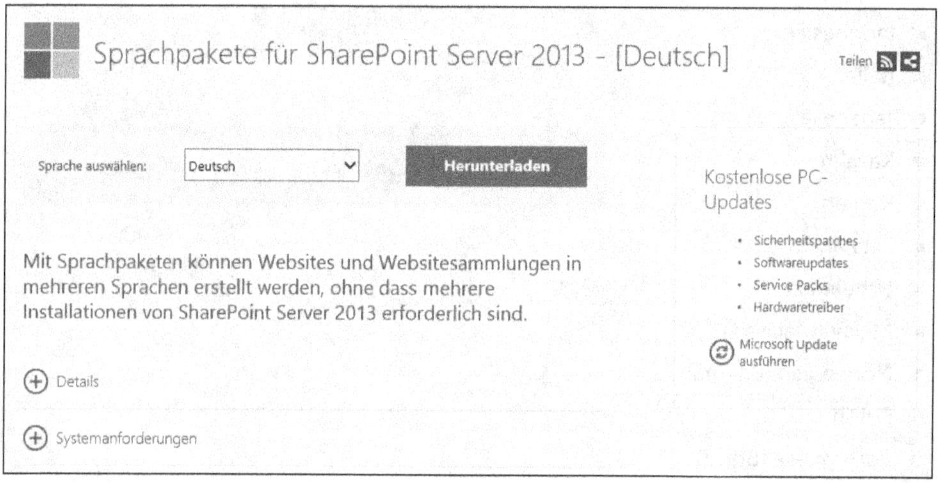

FIGURE 3-8 Selecting a language pack for download.

For instance, if you want to select the German language pack, do this:

1. Navigate to *http://www.microsoft.com/en-us/download/details.aspx?id=37140* (Microsoft Download Center).

2. Select the drop-down list box next to the Select Language field and choose German.

3. Wait a moment for the interface to display in the desired language (see Figure 3-9).

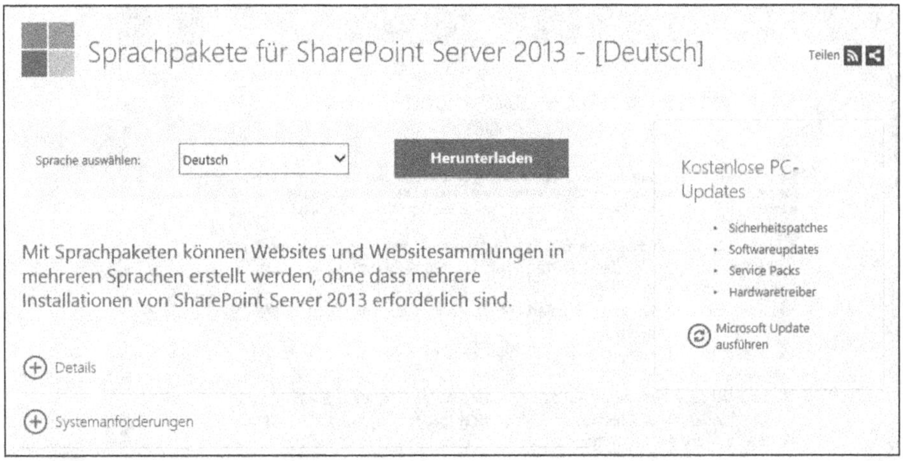

FIGURE 3-9 Selecting the Deutsch language pack.

4. Click the Download button to begin the download process (Herunterladen in German).

> **IMPORTANT** **INSTALL LANGUAGES DO NOT REQUIRE A LANGUAGE PACK**
>
> You never need to download a language pack for the language in which you installed SharePoint.

Installing a SharePoint 2013 language pack

Installing a SharePoint 2013 language pack is a simple process, save for one tiny detail: The installation procedure for the language pack is written in the designated language. For instance, the German installer appears in Figure 3-10.

FIGURE 3-10 German language pack installer.

As it happens, this is actually a minor detail; the interface is written pretty much the same regardless of the language you choose, so the install procedure goes like this:

1. Mount the serverlanguagepack.img file.

2. Run setup.exe.

3. Select the check box on the first screen, indicating that you accept the terms of this agreement.

4. Click the Weiter (Next) button to continue.

5. The installer will load the language pack into SharePoint.

6. After the install is complete, you will be prompted to run the Configuration Wizard (see Figure 3-11). If you have multiple servers, you need to install the language update on each one before running the wizard.

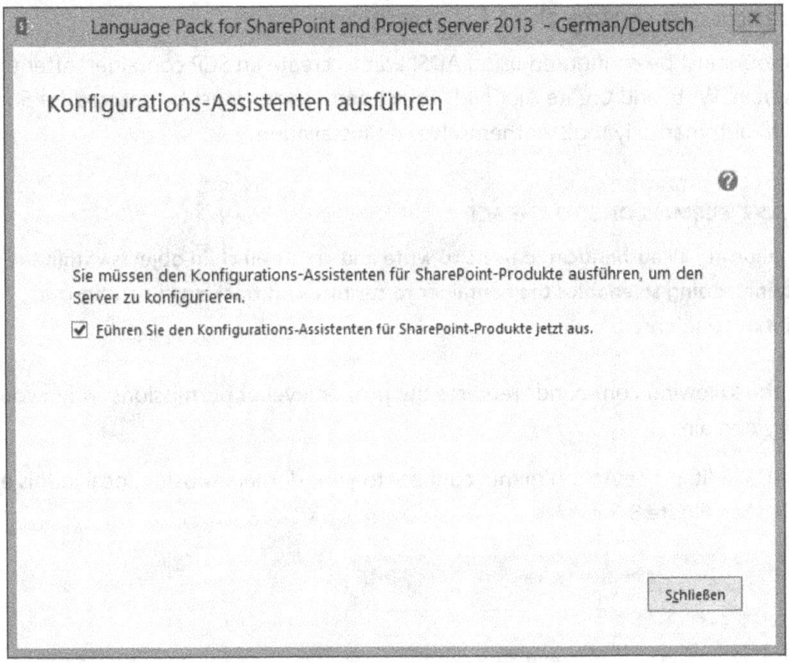

FIGURE 3-11 Running the Configuration Wizard (German).

> **IMPORTANT** **COMBINING MULTIPLE LANGUAGES IN THE INSTALL**
>
> If you have multiple languages to install, you can wait to run the Configuration Wizard until all have been individually installed.

Planning and configuring service connection points (SCPs)

Active Directory has a marker called a service connection point (SCP) that is set on a per-domain basis in an Active Directory container. If you have multiple domains that might contain SharePoint farms, you must configure the use of this marker in each domain to track these installations.

After SCP functionality is correctly set up, any new SharePoint farm created in the domain will automatically register itself. When the SharePoint Products Configuration Wizard is run on the farm, a marker will automatically be stored in the SCP container. This marker contains the address for the Application Discovery and Load Balancer Service (the Topology service application) for the farm.

Viewing this container using Active Directory Service Interfaces Editor (ADSI Edit) or querying it via Windows PowerShell enables you to view an accurate inventory of SharePoint installations in the domain. This inventory not only contains official installations of SharePoint but also any "rogue" installations that are present in the domain going forward.

Creating and configuring the SCP container

Active Directory must be configured using ADSI Edit to create an SCP container. After this container is built, Write and Create All Child Object permissions must be granted for Share-Point farms to automatically register themselves on installation.

> **IMPORTANT PERMISSIONS TO THE SCP**
>
> Consider allowing all authenticated users to write and create all child objects within the SCP container; doing so enables the container to capture and track any unauthorized SharePoint installations.

Running the following commands requires the proper level of permissions within your Active Directory domain:

1. Run ADSI Edit; in the Action menu, connect to your domain (boston.local in this example). See Figure 3-12.

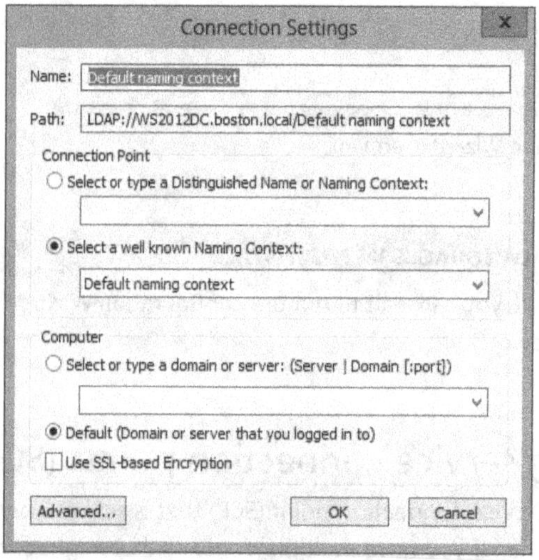

FIGURE 3-12 Connecting to a domain using the default naming context.

2. Expand the domain that you want to connect to and select CN=System.

3. Right-click in the white area of the details pane. From the New menu, select Object (see Figure 3-13).

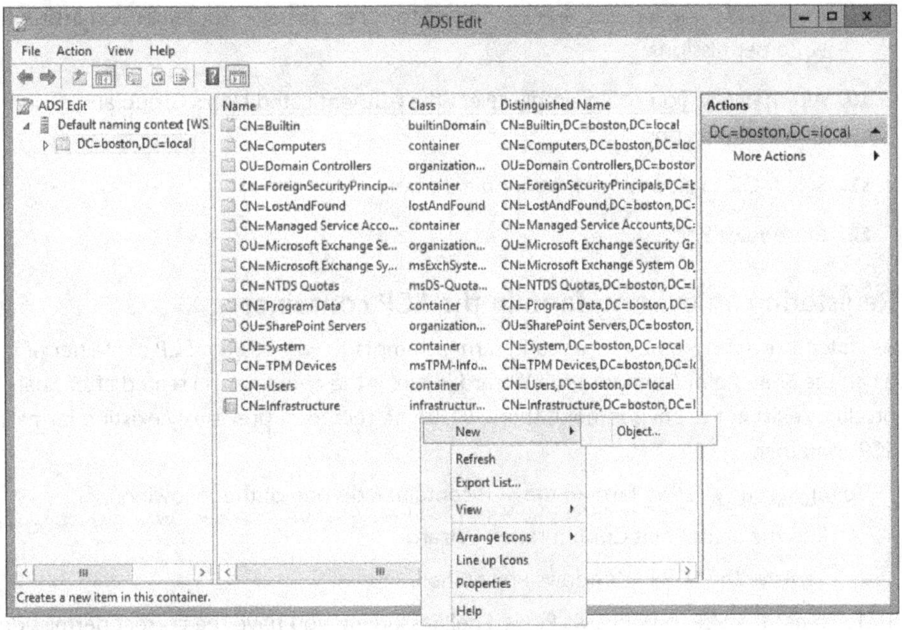

FIGURE 3-13 Creating a new object.

4. Select the Container class in the Create Object dialog box.

5. In the Value field, type **Microsoft SharePoint Products** and then click Next.

6. Click Finish. At this point, your new Active Directory container should appear in the details panel (see Figure 3-14).

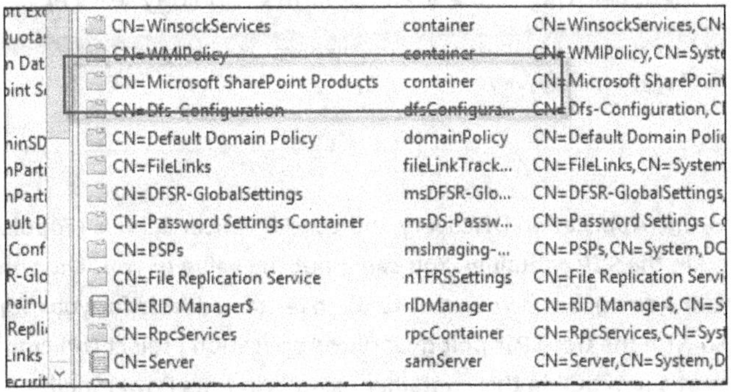

FIGURE 3-14 New Active Directory container for Microsoft SharePoint products.

7. Assign permissions to the container: right-click the container and select Properties.

8. Click Add on the Security tab.

9. Choose the appropriate users you want to access the SCP container and assign them write permissions.

10. Alternatively, you could simply select the Authenticated Users Group and assign it Write permissions.

11. Select OK to close the container dialog box.

12. Close ADSI Edit.

Registering an existing farm in the SCP container

As stated previously, a new or existing farm attempts to write to the SCP container (if it exists) when the SharePoint Configuration Wizard is run. If the container is created after SharePoint products exist in the environment, there will be no record of previously existing farms in the SCP container.

To register an existing farm in the SCP container, do one of the following:

- Run the SharePoint Configuration Wizard.
- Register the SCP in Windows PowerShell.

To create the SCP in Windows PowerShell (assuming you have the correct permissions), do the following:

1. Open the SharePoint 2013 Management Shell with administrative privileges.

2. (Optional) Run the following cmdlet to see whether the farm is already registered:

   ```
   Get-SPFarmConfig -ServiceConnectionPoint
   ```

3. Run the following cmdlet to register the farm in the SCP container (the URL shown is the uniform resource identifier [URI] of the example farm's Topology service):

   ```
   Set-SPFarmConfig -ServiceConnectionPointBindingInformation https://
   ws2012SP13:32844/Topology/topology.svc
   ```

EXAM TIP

By default, the address for the Application Discovery and Load Balancer Service (Topology service) of a farm is stored in the SCP container. You can input the value of your choosing (say, the address for Central Admin), but if you want to discover the address for your Topology service, you can do so with the Get-SPTopologyServiceApplication | select URI cmdlet. You should know how to set a new SCP in this container using Windows PowerShell.

Deleting a farm's SCP in Active Directory

You may decide that you need to remove the SCP for your farm from Active Directory. In theory, this should happen automatically when the last server is removed from a farm (effectively destroying it).

To remove the SCP for your farm, run the following cmdlet:

```
Set-SPFarmConfig -ServiceConnectionPointDelete
```

Planning installation tracking and auditing

Now that the SCP infrastructure has been created, you can utilize this functionality to effectively audit and manage any SharePoint installations in your domain. Each time a new farm is created, the SCP container will be updated with information about that new server.

EXAM TIP

Although you will most likely not be called on to inspect this container in Active Directory, you should know both the correct location in Active Directory where the SCPs are located (CN=Microsoft SharePoint Products) and the required permissions to write to this container.

Viewing SharePoint farm SCPs in ADSI Edit

In this example, we will view the Topology service content for a SharePoint 2013 farm that has registered in Active Directory. To view this information, do the following:

1. Open ADSI Edit.

2. Connect to your domain and then navigate to the System container (CN=System).

3. Within this container, select the Microsoft SharePoint Products container you previously created and expand it.

4. Entries for SharePoint farms appear with a GUID in the name field. Right-click this GUID and select Properties.

5. The address for the Topology service is shown (or another value if it is what you chose), as shown in Figure 3-15.

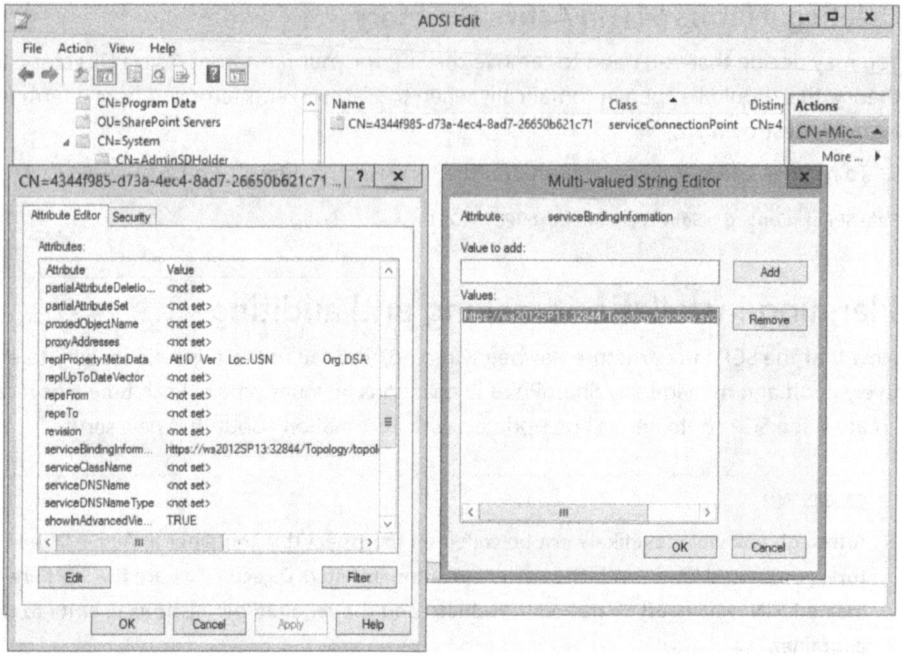

FIGURE 3-15 SCP information in ADSI Edit.

Viewing the SCP for a farm via Windows PowerShell

You may want to view to the SCP information for your current farm, which is readily available for your farm via Windows PowerShell. Follow these steps:

1. Open the SharePoint 2013 Management Shell, running as administrator.

2. Execute the following script:

```
Get-SPFarmConfig -ServiceConnectionPoint
```

> **MORE INFO** **RETRIEVING SCPS FROM ACTIVE DIRECTORY**
>
> These are by no means the only two ways of retrieving SCPs from Active Directory. In fact, you could execute a Lightweight Directory Access Protocol (LDAP) query against your domain or build a Windows PowerShell script that queries the Microsoft SharePoint Products container for SCPs. For more information, see the TechNet article "Track or Block SharePoint 2010 Installations" at *http://technet.microsoft.com/en-us/library/ff730261.aspx*.

Objective summary

- There are several software prerequisites for a SharePoint installation. Other prerequisites include the Application Server Role and Web Server (IIS) Role.
- Prerequisite checks, downloads, configuration, and installations are all handled by prerequisiteinstaller.exe, whether the server enables connectivity to the Internet or not.
- The max degree of parallelism setting in SQL to support a SharePoint 2013 farm is 1.
- Slipstreamed updates are made possible by downloading each component and then using the /extract switch to unpack the contents into the \updates folder for installation.
- Language pack installations are always shown in their native language.
- The container (CN) for SCPs is (most often) created in Active Directory by the domain administrator and must be called Microsoft SharePoint Products.
- The SCP value is stored within the SCP (which is a GUID) in the serviceBindingInformation attribute. By default, it is a link to the address of the Topology service of a farm.

Objective review

Answer the following questions to test your knowledge of the information in this objective. You can find the answers to these questions and explanations of why each answer choice is correct or incorrect in the "Answers" section at the end of this chapter.

1. Which of the following commands or cmdlets can used to install the Application Server Role and Web Server Role on a new server in preparation for a SharePoint installation? (Choose all that apply.)

   A. Get-SPPreReqInstaller

   B. Prerequisiteinstaller.exe

   C. Get-ServerRole

   D. Add-WindowsFeature

2. What is the proper value in SQL for the max degree of parallelism setting to support a SharePoint installation?

   A. 0

   B. 1

   C. Equal to the number of processor cores on the SQL Server

   D. Total amount of RAM/number of processor cores on the SQL Server

3. Which of the following commands can be run to install the Spanish version of the SharePoint language pack?

   A. Sharepointupdate.exe

   B. Prerequisiteinstaller.exe

   C. SPLanguagePack.exe

   D. Sharepointlanguagepack.exe

4. Which of the following tools are used by an Active Directory administrator to create the container for the SCP?

   A. Active Directory Users and Computers

   B. ADSIEdit.exe

   C. Get-ADContainer

   D. Set-ADContainer

Objective 3.2: Plan and configure farm-wide settings

After the initial installation of your SharePoint farm is complete, the next logical step is to configure some of the core farm services that are used across all web applications and sites.

> **This objective covers how to:**
> - Configure incoming and outgoing e-mail.
> - Plan and configure proxy groups.
> - Configure SharePoint designer settings.
> - Plan and configure a Corporate Catalog.
> - Configure Microsoft Office Web Apps integration.
> - Configure Azure Workflow server integration.

Configuring incoming and outgoing e-mail

There are two distinct facets to e-mail within SharePoint 2013: incoming and outgoing. Incoming e-mail enables users to store e-mail messages and attachments in lists and document libraries within the SharePoint farm; outgoing e-mail sends communications from SharePoint, both system and user-facing (such as alerts) in nature.

Incoming e-mail configuration tasks (basic scenario)

In the basic scenario, all incoming mail operations for SharePoint document libraries are handled from within the server farm. In other words, no Exchange interaction occurs within for this configuration.

To configure basic incoming e-mail, follow these steps:

1. Use the Add Features Wizard to install the SMTP server feature on the server that you intend to receive the incoming e-mail.

2. Enable incoming e-mail in Central Administration, System Settings using the automatic settings mode. Accept the default values.

3. (Optional) Configure directory managed service for this farm or choose to use the Directory Management Service present on another farm (this service is discussed in the following advanced scenario discussion).

4. Have your site collection administrator enable the incoming e-mail feature on the appropriate libraries and lists.

Incoming e-mail configuration tasks (advanced scenario)

When incoming e-mail is enabled in the advanced scenario, SharePoint site administrators can specify an e-mail address for use with a particular list or library (creating an alias in Active Directory). As in the basic scenario, users sending e-mail with attachments to this alias can effectively "drop" e-mail and attachments to these lists and libraries without requiring permissions or any sort of access to the library.

A timer job is responsible for picking up the incoming attachments and routing them to the appropriate document library. The service account associated with the timer job will also be responsible for the creation of e-mail aliases in Active Directory.

The configuration of incoming e-mail for a SharePoint farm requires five major steps, only two of which are executed by the SharePoint administrator (see Table 3-3).

TABLE 3-3 Incoming e-mail configuration tasks

Task	Completed By
Configure and add the Simple Mail Transport Protocol (SMTP) to the SharePoint 2013 server	SharePoint administrator
Create an organizational unit (OU) for storing e-mail aliases	Domain administrator
Create a Send Connector in Exchange	Exchange administrator
Configure incoming e-mail settings in SharePoint Central Administration	SharePoint administrator
Enable a document library to receive incoming e-mail	Site collection/Site/Library owner

First, the SMTP service should be added and configured on the SharePoint 2013 server. Only one server is required to host this role in the farm because it will be specified in Exchange as the smart host capable of processing incoming e-mail requests.

The server that hosts the SMTP service is generally located in the application tier, although any server in the web or app tier can be configured to handle incoming e-mail requests.

Installing and configuring the SMTP service consists of the following steps:

1. Add the SMTP feature from the Server Manager console.

2. Under Tools in Server Manager, open IIS 6.0 Manager.

Note: IIS 6.0 Manager is used to administer the SMTP service.

3. Expand the server and select SMTP Virtual Server (see Figure 3-16).

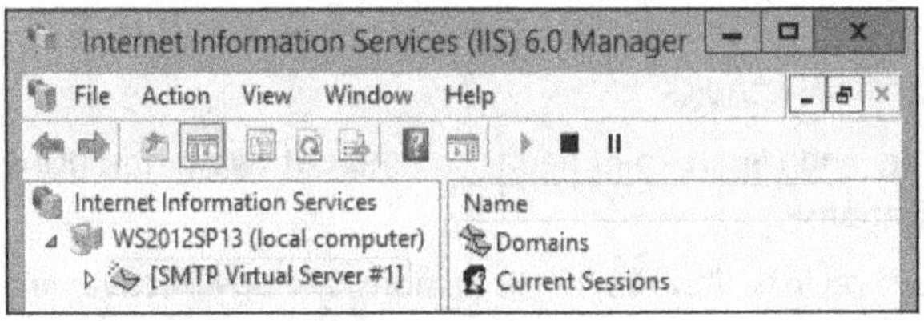

FIGURE 3-16 Selecting the SMTP virtual server.

4. From the Access tab, ensure that Anonymous authentication is enabled.

The Active Directory admin has to create an OU specifically for the retention of the aliases generated by libraries and lists. The timer job service account requires Create, Delegate, and Manage User Accounts permissions to be delegated for this OU.

EXAM TIP

If you don't know which account is running your timer service, look for the SharePoint timer service entry within Computer Management.

The Exchange administrator will need create and enable a Send Connector that routes e-mail to the SharePoint server (smart host).

Next, there are a series of tasks that the SharePoint administrator has to carry out in Central Administration. One of the major tasks is the configuration of a Directory Management service. Configuring this service enables closer integration between SharePoint and Exchange; in particular, the relationship established between e-mail distribution lists and SharePoint groups.

MORE INFO DIRECTORY MANAGEMENT SERVICE

For more information about the Directory Management service, see the TechNet article "Plan Incoming E-mail for a SharePoint Farm in SharePoint 2013" at *http://technet.microsoft.com/en-us/library/cc263260.aspx*.

To enable incoming e-mail in Central Administration for the advanced scenario:

1. Enable incoming e-mail in Central Administration, System Settings.

2. Select the Advanced Settings Mode radio button.

3. Choose whether to use the Directory Management Service along with selecting the appropriate options for its use.

4. Provide an incoming e-mail server display address.

5. Provide the location of the E-Mail Drop Folder used by the SMTP service.

Finally, have your site collection administrator enable the incoming e-mail feature on the appropriate libraries and lists to complete the incoming e-mail configuration.

Outgoing e-mail configuration tasks

Outgoing e-mail settings are used when SharePoint needs to send out two different types of e-mail to users: alerts and notifications.

- Alerts, which are generated on lists, libraries, or discussions, are an effective means of notifying users of content updates or changes.

- Notifications are a much broader grouping of e-mail that include items such as work-flow e-mail or nearing site collection quota limits.

Although the configuration of outgoing e-mail is much more straightforward than the configuration for incoming e-mail, you need the assistance of your organization's Exchange administrator to allow SMTP messages from your SharePoint server to be sent via Exchange.

To configure outgoing e-mail, follow these steps:

1. Ask your Exchange administrator to build a new Receive Connector that will receive e-mail sent from your SharePoint server (you have to provide the IP address of the SharePoint server that is providing the outbound e-mail function).

EXAM TIP

If the Receive Connector configuration does not occur, it is likely that your SharePoint environment cannot send outbound e-mail to your users.

2. Use the Add Features Wizard to install the SMTP server feature on the server that you intend to receive the incoming e-mail.

3. Enable incoming e-mail in Central Administration, System, specifying the following:

   A. Outbound SMTP server (provided by your Exchange administrator)

   B. From Address (the address that will show in the "from" field of the e-mail address)

   C. Reply-to Address (the address that you will monitor for user feedback)

   D. Character set (use the character set appropriate for your language)

4. Click OK to complete the configuration.

Planning and configuring proxy groups

A proxy group is a mechanism that defines the relationship between a web application and the proxy (or connection) for a service application. This proxy enables the web applications associated with the proxy group to consume services (MMS, UPA, and so on) from the service application.

In a newly created farm there is only one proxy group, which is called (appropriately enough) "default." More proxy groups can be created, providing for more granular segmentation of service application functionality within the farm.

EXAM TIP

If you create a new service application via Central Administration, by default it is automatically assigned to the default proxy group. Conversely, creating the service application (and its proxy) via Windows PowerShell does not automatically assign that service's application proxy to any of the available proxy groups (by default).

Assigning proxy groups to web applications

As an example, consider a larger enterprise installation. If you want to build a series of ad hoc collaborative sites under a particular web application (for example, http://teams.boston.local), you might want to prevent the use of Access Services in the application by following these steps:

1. Build a new proxy group called Ad Hoc.

2. Assign all the service application proxies to this group, except those for Access Services or Access Services 2010.

3. Associate the http://teams.boston.local web application to only the Ad Hoc proxy group.

Creating a new proxy group

New proxy groups are created from within Windows PowerShell only because there is no interface to create them in Central Administration. The following example creates a new proxy group for intranet use only:

1. Open a new SharePoint 2013 Management Shell, running as administrator.

2. To view the existing proxy groups, run the Get-SPServiceApplicationProxyGroup cmdlet and format the output in a table:

```
Get-SPServiceApplicationProxyGroup | Format-Table -wrap
```

3. The resulting output shows the existing proxy group (see Figure 3-17).

```
PS C:\Users\sp_farm> Get-SPServiceApplicationProxyGroup | Format-Table -wrap

FriendlyName                    Proxies                    DefaultProxies

[default]                       {Access Services,          {Access Services,
                                Access Services 2010,      Access Services 2010,
                                Secure Store Service,      Secure Store Service,
                                PowerPoint Conversion      PowerPoint Conversion
                                Service Application...}    Service
                                                           Application...}
```

FIGURE 3-17 Existing proxy group(s).

4. Now create the new proxy group "Intranet Only" by using the New-SPServiceApplica-tionProxyGroup cmdlet (see Figure 3-18).

FIGURE 3-18 Creating a new proxy group.

5. If you view the proxy groups now, the new one should appear. Note that it has no service application proxies associated with it (see Figure 3-19).

```
PS C:\Users\sp_farm> Get-SPServiceApplicationProxyGroup | Format-Table -Wrap
FriendlyName                  Proxies                      DefaultProxies
[default]                     (Access Services,            (Access Services,
                              Access Services 2010,        Access Services 2010,
                              Secure Store Service,        Secure Store Service,
                              PowerPoint Conversion        PowerPoint Conversion
                              Service Application...>      Service
                                                           Application...>
Intranet Only                 ()                           ()
```

FIGURE 3-19 All proxy groups.

Associating proxies to a proxy group (Windows PowerShell)

Associating a service application proxy with a proxy group in Windows PowerShell requires only a few lines of code. Although it might seem like a lot of typing, it would very easy to build several of these associations into a Windows PowerShell script, thereby saving a lot of configuration time in Central Administration.

EXAM TIP

A service application proxy can be associated with multiple proxy groups using Windows PowerShell. Also, a proxy group is not required to host each and every available service application available within the farm.

The following example associates the Access Services 2010 service application proxy to the "Intranet Only" proxy group via Windows PowerShell:

1. Use Get-SPServiceApplicationProxy with a where clause to obtain the identity of the Access Services 2010 proxy and assign it to a variable:

```
$SAProxy = Get-SPServiceApplicationProxy | ? {$_.DisplayName -eq "Access Services
2010"}
```

2. You can use this variable in the Add-SPServiceApplicationProxyGroupMember cmdlet to add the service application proxy to the "Intranet Only" proxy group:

```
Add-SPServiceApplicationProxyGroupMember "Intranet Only" -Member $SAProxy
```

3. The service application proxy now appears in the "Intranet Only" proxy group (see Figure 3-20).

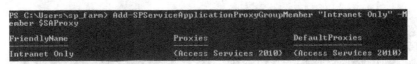

```
PS C:\Users\sp_farm> Add-SPServiceApplicationProxyGroupMember "Intranet Only" -M
ember $SAProxy

FriendlyName                 Proxies                  DefaultProxies

Intranet Only                <Access Services 2010>   <Access Services 2010>
```

FIGURE 3-20 Associated with the "Intranet Only" proxy group.

4. Use the Get-SPServiceApplicationProxyGroup cmdlet again; you can see that the Access Services 2010 service application proxy is associated with both the Default and Intranet Only proxy groups (see Figure 3-21).

```
PS C:\Users\sp_farm> Get-SPServiceApplicationProxyGroup | Format-Table -wrap

FriendlyName                 Proxies                  DefaultProxies

[default]                    <Access Services,        <Access Services,
                             Access Services 2010,    Access Services 2010,
                             Secure Store Service,    Secure Store Service,
                             PowerPoint Conversion    PowerPoint Conversion
                             Service Application...>  Service
                                                      Application...>
Intranet Only                <Access Services 2010>   <Access Services 2010>
```

FIGURE 3-21 Associated with both proxy groups.

Removing proxies from a proxy group (Windows PowerShell)

Removing a service application proxy from a proxy group in Windows PowerShell is also a straightforward process.

> **IMPORTANT REMOVING AN SERVICE APPLICATION GROUP RESULTS IN IMMEDIATE LOSS OF FUNCTION**
>
> Removing a service application proxy from a proxy group immediately removes that service's functionality from all associated web applications.

In this example, you remove the Access Services 2010 association completed in the previous step:

1. Use Get-SPServiceApplicationProxy with a where clause to obtain the identity of the Access Services 2010 proxy and assign it to a variable:

   ```
   $SAProxy = Get-SPServiceApplicationProxy | ? {$_.DisplayName -eq "Access Services 2010"}
   ```

2. Use the Remove-SPServiceApplicationProxyGroupMember cmdlet to disassociate the Access Services 2010 service application proxy from the "Intranet Only" proxy group. You will be prompted to confirm this action:

   ```
   Remove-SPServiceApplicationProxyGroupMember "Intranet Only" -Member $SAProxy
   ```

3. The "Intranet Only" proxy group no longer has any associated service proxies, as shown in Figure 3-22.

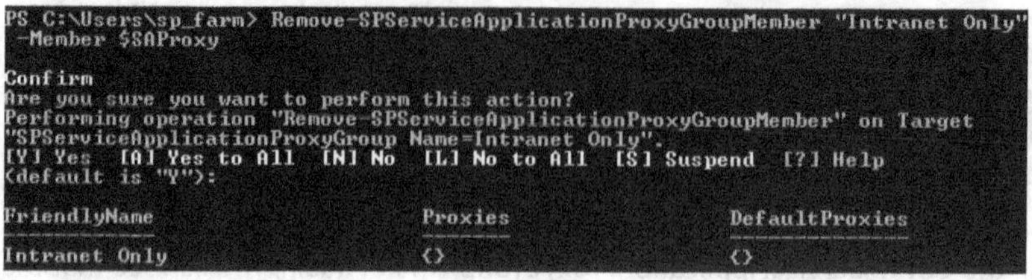

FIGURE 3-22 No service application proxies.

Configuring SharePoint Designer (SPD) settings

Microsoft SharePoint Designer (SPD) is a client application that enables the creation and modification of SharePoint sites, pages, and workflows. SPD offers users a powerful way to develop no-code solutions for use within a SharePoint farm environment and is free for download from the Microsoft Download Center at *http://www.microsoft.com/en-us/download/details.aspx?id=35491*.

As with any other capable tool, SharePoint Designer can be improperly used. Because of its tight integration with the SharePoint platform, SPD can provide great benefit to properly trained and trusted power users. In untrained or inexperienced hands, however, it can be inadvertently used to build poorly performing sites (or ones that no longer work at all).

An organization's governance decides who should have access to the tool and what the tool should be capable of doing within the environment. As the SharePoint admin, you should be able to advise the governance planners about what settings SPD has available within your SharePoint environment. These settings, along with controlling who can install SPD on their desktop, can go a long way in the proper administration and use of this tool.

SPD settings in Central Administration

SPD settings are controlled on a per-web application basis. Every time you build a new web application, you should evaluate the use of the web application to decide which options should be set (in accordance with your governance plan).

Configuring the SPD settings is fairly straightforward; simply select the check box of the appropriate selections (see Figure 3-23):

- **Allow SharePoint Designer To Be Used In This Web Application**   Enabling this setting disallows the use of SPD with this web application, regardless of which permissions the user holds.
- **Allow Site Collection Administrators To Detach Pages From The Site Template**   Detaching pages from the site template is also known as "customization" or "unghosting" the page. This change causes a customized copy of the page to be held in the content database rather than on the SharePoint web tier servers; having

pages in this state results in a performance penalty for rendering these custom pages. Enabling this setting disallows page detaching from the template.

- **Allow Site Collection Administrators To Customize Master Pages And Layout Pages** The effective customization of master pages and layout pages are some of the most important branding tasks that can be done on a publishing site. Enabling this setting precludes the customization of these page types.

- **Allow Site Collection Administrators To See The URL Structure Of Their Web Site** Enabling this setting precludes designers from seeing and interacting with the internal structure of their site.

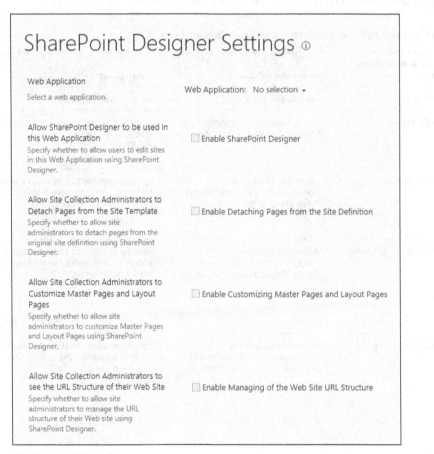

FIGURE 3-23 SPD settings.

Configuring SPD settings with Windows PowerShell

The SPD settings can be configured and viewed using the Set- and Get-SPDesignerSettings cmdlets in Windows PowerShell. For example, in order to set the SPD settings on the http://intranet.boston.local web application to enable the full use of SPD, you can type the following cmdlet and switches in Windows PowerShell:

```
Set-SPDesignerSettings -WebApplication http://intranet.boston.local -AllowDesigner $True
-AllowMasterPageEditing $True -AllowRevertFromTemplate $True -ShowURLStructure $True
```

The five switches for this cmdlet, which are shown in Table 3-4, are identical to the five items shown on the SPD settings page in Central Administration.

TABLE 3-4 Windows PowerShell Switches for Set-SPDesignerSettings

Windows PowerShell Switch	In Central Admin	Description
WebApplication	Web Application	Select a web application
AllowDesigner	Allow SharePoint Designer To Be Used In This Web Application	Specify whether to enable users to edit sites in this web application using SPD
AllowRevertFromTemplate	Allow Site Collection Administrators To Detach Pages From The Site Template	Specify whether to allow site administrators to detach pages from the original site definition using SPD
AllowMasterPageEditing	Allow Site Collection Administrators to Customize Master Pages and Layout Pages	Specify whether to allow site administrators to customize master pages and layout pages using SPD
ShowURLStructure	Allow Site Collection Administrators to See The URL Structure Of Their Web Site	Specify whether to allow site administrators to manage the URL structure of their web site using SPD

Planning and configuring a Corporate Catalog

SharePoint 2013 offers administrators the opportunity to enable a new application's infrastructure. Using this infrastructure, users in the enterprise can now browse the new SharePoint Store (see Figure 3-24).

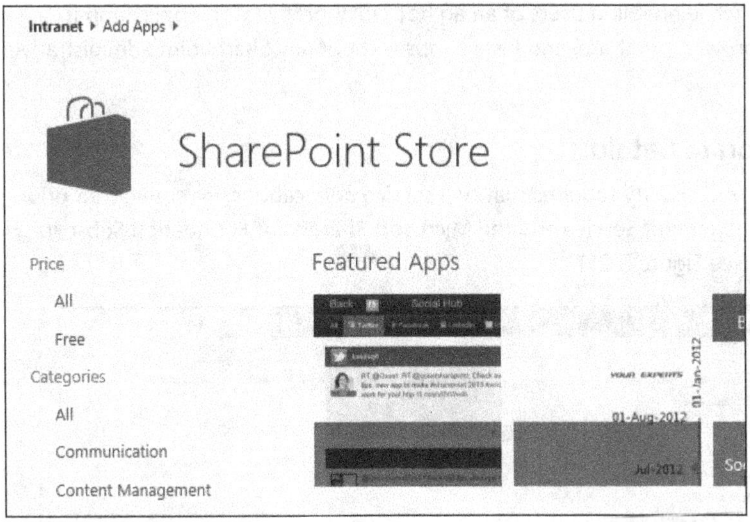

FIGURE 3-24 SharePoint Store.

If allowed by policy, users who possess the following permissions can purchase, download, and install apps to a site, provided they have the following permissions:

- Manage Web Site
- Create Subsites

> **IMPORTANT** **PERMISSIONS AND ASSOCIATED GROUPS**
>
> If these permissions look familiar, it is because they are assigned to people who have either Full Control or are members of the Site Owners group.

Corporate Catalogs (you may also see it called an App Catalog in some documentation) are the places where users in your enterprise can view apps for both Office and SharePoint. These catalogs are set up on a per-web application basis, meaning that you can configure different settings for your intranet versus your team site.

Administrative controls

The app store functionality supplied with SharePoint 2013 is fully adaptable to your governance plan and gives you the following administrative options for each catalog:

- To choose whether users can install their own apps from the SharePoint store
- To issue apps based on app requests (these requests can be viewed and responded to by the farm administrators and App Catalog site owners)
- To prepurchase apps and make them available for your users

Because the Corporate Catalog is scoped at the web application level, it is entirely possible to build an intranet with a tightly controlled series of apps that have been approved and meet governance standards while enabling users of an ad hoc collaborative web application to receive full access to browse, purchase, and install apps without any SharePoint administrative assistance.

Installing a Corporate Catalog

The SharePoint Store functionality requires that two service applications are configured prior to its use: the App Management Service and the Microsoft SharePoint Foundation Subscriptions Settings Service (see Figure 3-25).

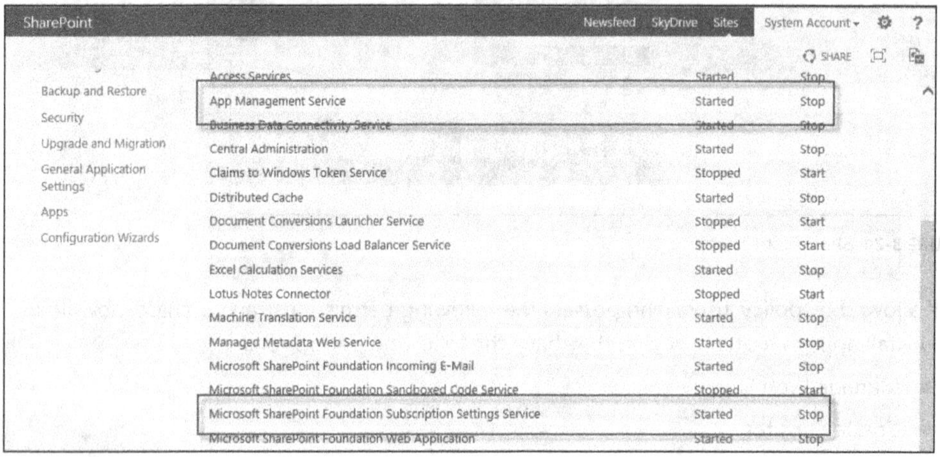

FIGURE 3-25 Required services.

> **MORE INFO** **SUBSCRIPTION SETTINGS SERVICE REQUIREMENTS**
>
> The Microsoft SharePoint Foundation Subscriptions Settings Service is not installed or configured as part of the Farm Configuration Wizard process. Setting up this service is a manual process that is covered in the TechNet article titled, "Configure an Environment for Apps for SharePoint (SharePoint 2013)" at *http://technet.microsoft.com/en-us/library/fp161236.aspx*.

Domain Name System (DNS) requirements

There are a series of requirements from a Domain Name System (DNS) standpoint that are necessary prior to the configuration of apps within SharePoint 2013:

- The DNS admin should be a domain name for the apps provider (for example, contosoapps.com).
- A CNAME alias needs to be made from the app domain to the SharePoint domain using a wildcard (for example, *.contosoapps.com, sharepoint.contoso.com).

- (Optional) If you will use HTTPS, a wildcard certificate needs to be created for the new app domain (https://*.contosoapps.com).

EXAM TIP

Although you may not be personally responsible for making DNS changes in your domain, knowing how these requirements are implemented enables you to better relate them to your DNS administrator.

Configuring SharePoint 2013 for apps

If services are online and the DNS configuration is in place, there are only a couple of administrative tasks that need to be done before users can begin using a Corporate Catalog:

- Creating the Corporate Catalog site collection
- Configuring the process for browsing, requesting, purchasing, and installing apps

To begin, let's create the Corporate Catalog site collection for a web application:

1. From Central Administration, select Apps.

2. On the Apps page under App Management, select Manage App Catalog. The App Catalog Site page appears.

3. Select the Create A New App Catalog Site radio button (see Figure 3-26).

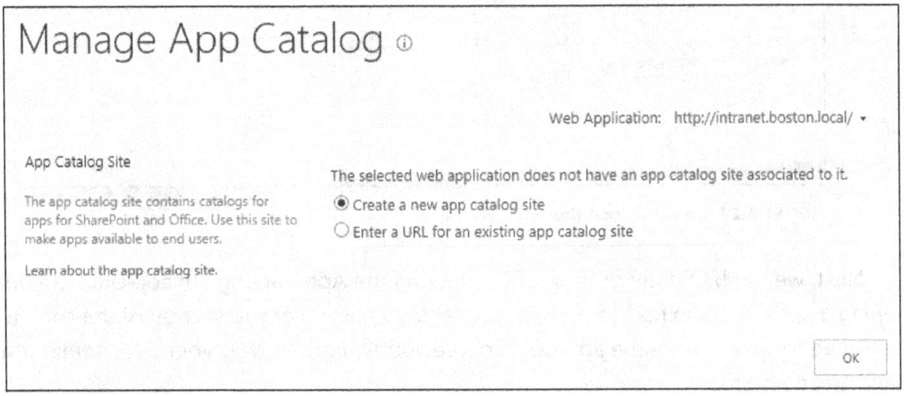

Manage App Catalog ⓘ

Web Application: http://intranet.boston.local/ ▾

App Catalog Site

The app catalog site contains catalogs for apps for SharePoint and Office. Use this site to make apps available to end users.

Learn about the app catalog site.

The selected web application does not have an app catalog site associated to it.

◉ Create a new app catalog site
○ Enter a URL for an existing app catalog site

OK

FIGURE 3-26 Manage App Catalog.

4. On the Create App Catalog page, you will create the site in the normal fashion. There are a couple of differences (see Figure 3-27):

  A. Select the web application.

  B. Add a title.

  C. Choose the address for the site (in this example, it is located beneath the /sites wildcard managed path at http://intranet.boston.local/sites/appcatalog.

D. Add a primary site collection administrator (SCA). (Difference #1: There is no secondary SCA.)

E. Choose end users (usually set to Everyone).

F. Difference #2: There is no template because this is specifically intended to be an App Catalog site.

G. Select a quota template as required and click OK to continue.

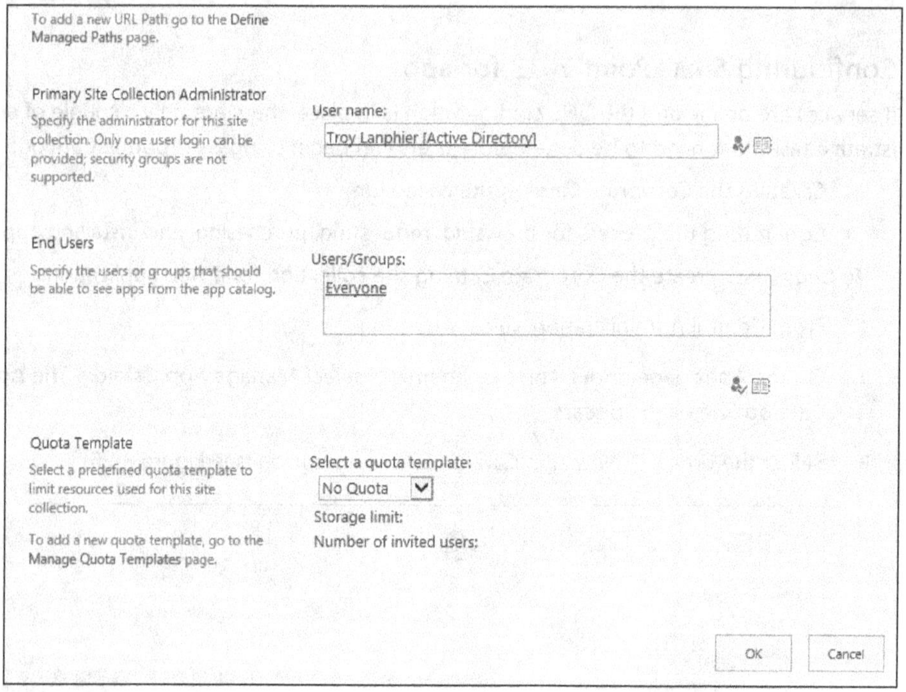

To add a new URL Path go to the **Define Managed Paths** page.

Primary Site Collection Administrator
Specify the administrator for this site collection. Only one user login can be provided; security groups are not supported.

User name:

Troy Lanphier [Active Directory]

End Users
Specify the users or groups that should be able to see apps from the app catalog.

Users/Groups:

Everyone

Quota Template
Select a predefined quota template to limit resources used for this site collection.

To add a new quota template, go to the Manage Quota Templates page.

Select a quota template:

No Quota ☑

Storage limit:

Number of invited users:

OK   Cancel

FIGURE 3-27 Can you spot the differences?

Next, we can begin the process of configuring the App Catalog. All app URLs are built along a pattern: <app prefix> - <app ID>.<app domain>. For this section of the configuration, we need to specify both the app domain (previously registered by your DNS administrator) and an app prefix.

1. From Central Administration, select Apps.

2. On the Apps page under App Management, select Configure App URLs.

> ***MORE INFO*** **MISCONFIGURATIONS IN THE SUBSCRIPTION SERVICE APP**
>
> **If you get an error at this point that reads The Subscription Settings service and corresponding application and proxy needs to be running in order to make changes to these settings," you most likely have a missing or misconfigured subscription service app or proxy. Configuration information can be found in the TechNet article "Configure an Environment for Apps for SharePoint" at *http://technet.microsoft.com/en-us/library/fp161236.aspx*.**

3. Add the app domain and your chosen app prefix to the Configure App URLs page and then click OK (see Figure 3-28).

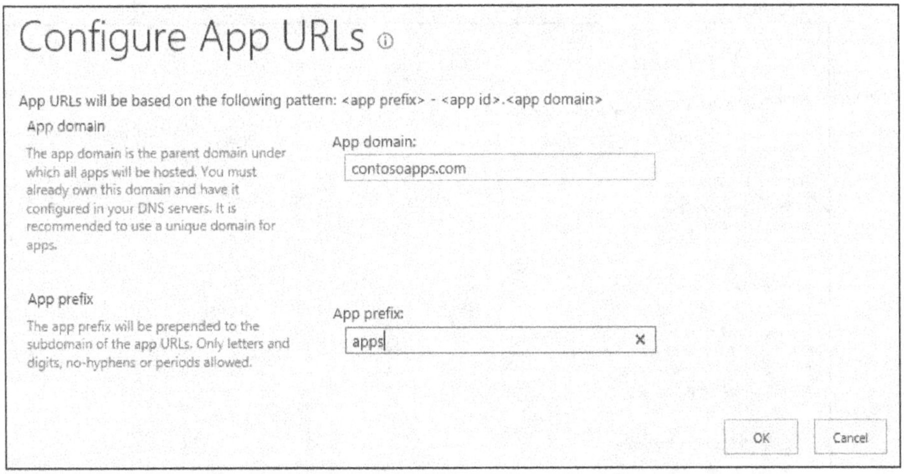

FIGURE 3-28 App URLs.

Configuring SharePoint Store settings

The last step in the configuration process is to decide how the SharePoint Store will behave for this web application. If disallowed from downloading and installing applications directly, users can still browse and request applications from the store.

Additionally, you must choose whether apps for Microsoft Office can also be browsed when users are viewing documents in the browser. To configure SharePoint Store settings, do the following:

1. In Central Administration, select Apps.
2. Within the SharePoint And Office Store section, note that you can purchase apps, manage any licenses purchased, and configure Store settings (see Figure 3-29). Let's configure the Store settings by clicking its link.

FIGURE 3-29 Apps menu within Central Administration.

3. Because the SharePoint Store settings are focused at the web application level, ensure that you choose the correct web app (see Figure 3-30).

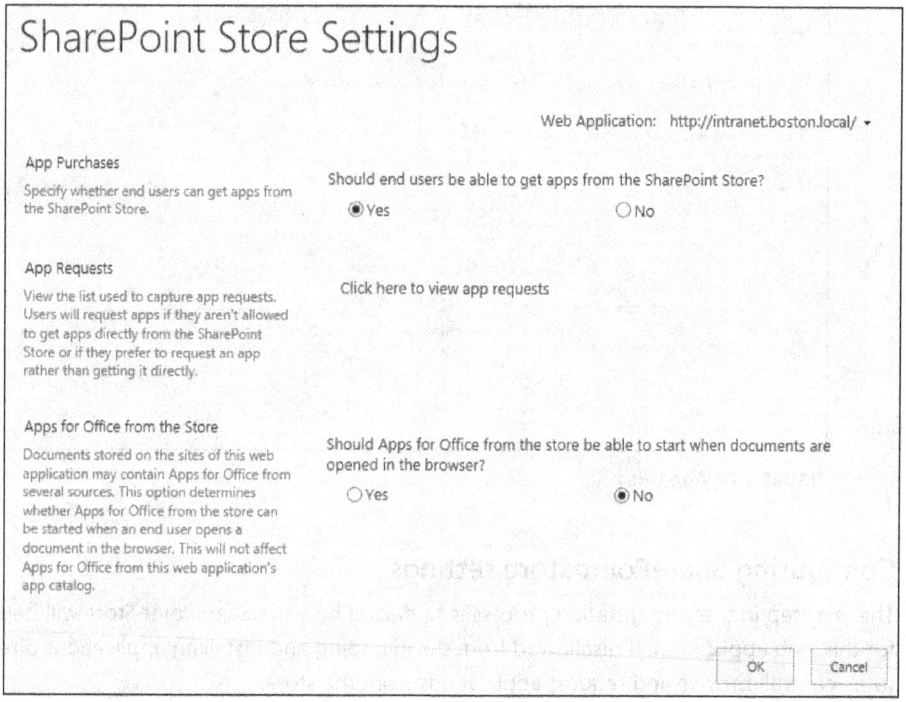

SharePoint Store Settings

Web Application: http://intranet.boston.local/ ▾

App Purchases

Specify whether end users can get apps from the SharePoint Store.

Should end users be able to get apps from the SharePoint Store?

◉ Yes   ○ No

App Requests

View the list used to capture app requests. Users will request apps if they aren't allowed to get apps directly from the SharePoint Store or if they prefer to request an app rather than getting it directly.

Click here to view app requests

Apps for Office from the Store

Documents stored on the sites of this web application may contain Apps for Office from several sources. This option determines whether Apps for Office from the store can be started when an end user opens a document in the browser. This will not affect Apps for Office from this web application's app catalog.

Should Apps for Office from the store be able to start when documents are opened in the browser?

○ Yes   ◉ No

OK   Cancel

FIGURE 3-30 SharePoint Store settings (default).

4. Choose from the following items:

   A. **App Purchases**   Decide whether or not users can purchase apps from the Share-Point Store.

   B. **App Requests**   A link that enables you to view any app requests made by your users.

C. **Apps For Office From The Store** Disabled by default, this setting enables you to choose whether or not Apps for Office starts when someone opens a document from the browser.

5. When your changes are complete, click OK.

Configuring Microsoft Office Web Apps integration

In SharePoint 2010, Office Web Apps was an optional component that could be licensed and installed into your existing SharePoint farm; this functionality could then be enabled to present Microsoft Office documents in a browser window (with no Office client installation required).

Office Web Apps 2013 is now a standalone product, meaning that it installs into its own farm and can even be load balanced. After the farm is installed and configured, it can be con-figured to support users who access Office files (Word, Excel, PowerPoint, and OneNote) files through SharePoint 2013, Lync 2013, Exchange 2013, shared folders, and web sites.

Integrating Office Web Apps 2013 with SharePoint 2013

After the Office Web Apps farm has been installed, integration with a SharePoint 2013 farm is done via Windows PowerShell. This integration is made possible via the Microsoft Web App Open Platform Interface (WOPI).

To integrate an Office Web Apps 2013 farm with a production SharePoint 2013 farm, do the following:

1. On a member server in the SharePoint farm, open a SharePoint 2013 Management Shell (run as administrator).

2. First, you must set up the binding to the Office Web Apps server name using the Fully Qualified Domain Name (FQDN). For example:

```
New-SPWOPIBinding -ServerName ws2012sp133.boston.local
```

3. Next, view the Office Web Apps Server zone by using the Get-SPWOPIZone cmdlet. The current zone should be set to "internal-https".

4. (Optional) If you have an environment that is both internal and external, alter the SP-WOPIZONE to be "external-https".

```
Set-SPWOPIZone -zone "external-https"
```

In a test environment, you may choose to use HTTP instead of HTTPS for your Office Web Apps setup. If so, you need to make a few more changes:

1. If you configured your Office Web Apps server to use HTTP instead of HTTPS (as is the case in this example), you must change the zone on your SharePoint server to match:

```
Set-SPWOPIZone -zone "internal-http"
```

2. Verify that this last setting took effect by running the Get-SPWOPIZone cmdlet again. The result should now read "internal-http" instead of "internal-https".

3. Finally, you have to change the AllowOAuthOverHttp setting to True for Office Web Apps to work using HTTP:

   A. Check to see if this is already enabled (True)

   B. If not, run the following cmdlets

   C. Verify that the setting is correct

Configuring Azure Workflow Server integration

SharePoint 2013 integrates with two different workflow engines. Existing SharePoint 2010 workflows continue to run under the Windows Workflow Foundation (WWF) engine, whereas new workflows can either be created in the 2010 WWF engine (for 2010 workflows) or in the new Azure Workflow engine (for 2013 workflows).

The Azure Workflow Manager does not install along with the rest of the SharePoint 2013 components; instead, it must be downloaded, installed, and configured before new SharePoint 2013 workflows can be built. This platform can be installed onto its own server farm or installed alongside a SharePoint 2013 server.

Note that it is not possible to integrate Azure Workflow services with SharePoint Foundation 2013.

In the following example, you will be downloading and installing the Azure Workflow Manager and installing it on a single server in the farm. This sample installation is very basic and does not provide for any sort of high availability or load balancing.

> **MORE INFO AZURE WORKFLOW MANAGER 1.0**
>
> For more detailed information about potential topologies and other installation topics, visit the Workflow Manager 1.0 site on MSDN at *http://msdn.microsoft.com/en-us/library/jj193528.aspx*.

After this installation process is complete, you will integrate the workflow engine with SharePoint Server 2013, enabling you to create a new SharePoint 2013 workflow.

Downloading Workflow Manager 1.0

All the Azure Workflow components can be found on the Microsoft Download Center site, listed under Workflow Manager 1.0 (*http://www.microsoft.com/en-us/download/details.aspx?id=35375*), as shown in Figure 3-31.

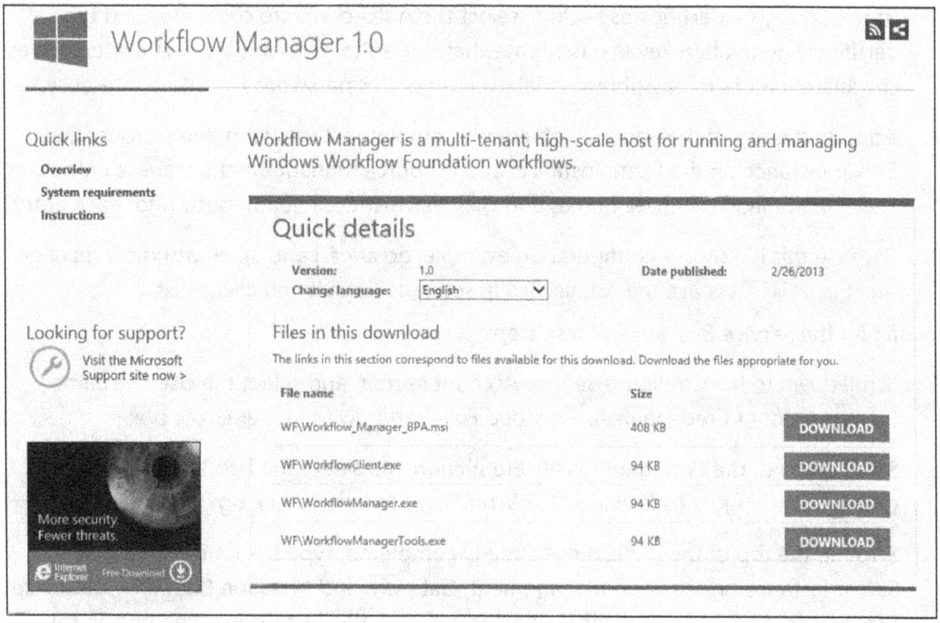

FIGURE 3-31 Downloading Workflow Manager 1.0.

Configuring a basic install of Workflow Manager

To begin the installation process, do the following:

1. In SSMS (data tier), grant the SharePoint install account the sysadmin server role.

2. Log on to the SharePoint server as the install account.

3. Download and run the WF\WorkflowManager.exe Web Platform Installer.

4. When the Workflow Manager 1.0 screen appears, click the Install button.

5. On the Prerequisites screen, choose whether to send setup and usage information to Microsoft; then select I Accept.

6. Choose whether to use Windows Update and select Continue.

7. At the Configure screen, select Continue.

8. Select Finish on the Web Platform Installer and close the installer down.

To configure Workflow Manager, follow these steps:

1. At the Welcome screen, select Configure Workflow Manager With Custom Settings.

2. Do not click the Test Connection buttons just yet. Scroll down to the Configure Service Account section and type the user ID and password for the service account you built in the previous steps.

3. In the Configure Certificates section, select the Auto-generate check box and type a certificate generation key (a passphrase that is used to generate the certificate, such as the SharePoint farm passphrase). Make a note of this password for future reference.

4. Scroll to the top of the page. If not already completed, type the name of your SQL Server instance on the Farm, Instance, and Resource Management Database entries. Leave the default database names and click the Test Connection button for each entry.

5. Because this is a simple configuration example, go ahead and allow workflow management over HTTP. Leave the Admin Group set at its default and click Next.

To configure the Service Bus, follow these steps:

1. Scroll down to the Configure Service Account section and select the Use The Same Service Account Credentials As Provided For Workflow Manager check box.

2. Scroll down to the Configure Certificate section and select the Use The Same Certificate Generation Key As Provided For Workflow Manager check box.

3. Scroll to the top of the page. If not already completed, type the name of your SQL Server instance on the Farm Management, Gateway, and Message Container Database entries. Leave the default database names and click the Test Connection button for each entry.

4. Leave the Admin Group set at its default and click Next.

5. On the summary screen, review the settings for both the Workflow Manager and Service Bus. Click the check button to complete the configuration.

6. Review the completed configuration and click the check icon.

Integrating SharePoint and Workflow Manager

After this installation, all that is left is to associate the workflow engine with SharePoint, which you can do via the Register-SPWorkflowService cmdlet. This command establishes a link between the workflow engine and any site connection in your farm and needs to be completed only once.

In the cmdlet, we specify a SPSite in the farm along with the workflow host URI specifying the name of the server and the TCP port (12290 for HTTPS or 12291 for HTTP, by default).

The completed cmdlet for the example is shown here:

```
register-spworkflowservice -spsite http://ws2012sp13" -WorkflowHostURI http://
ws2012sp13:12291 -AllowOAuthHttp
```

Thought experiment
E-mail and SharePoint sites

In the following thought experiment, apply what you've learned about this objective. You can find answers to these questions in the "Answers" section at the back of this chapter.

You are installing SharePoint and want to use both incoming and outgoing e-mail functionality with your farm. Members of your sales team regularly distribute the address of a library on the Internet as a drop box for a sales lead promotion.

What sort of setup options might you create for this environment?

Objective summary

- There are two scenarios for incoming mail: basic and advanced. Only the advanced scenario requires configuration on the Exchange environment.
- Regardless of scenario, the SharePoint server intended to receive incoming e-mail requires the SMTP service to be installed.
- Outgoing e-mail from SharePoint requires that your Exchange administrator have a new Receive Connector built for the transfer of e-mail to occur.
- Proxy groups are used to tie SharePoint web applications to the proxy or connection for each service application.
- SPD settings for a web application include whether it is enabled or disabled, whether SCAs can detach pages from the site template, whether SCAs can customize master pages and layout pages, and whether SCAs can see the URL structure of their web site.
- To configure the Apps functionality within a SharePoint farm, DNS changes need to be made that will enable the farm to connect to the Internet.

- A SharePoint farm connects to an Office Web Apps installation using WOPI.
- Azure Workflow components must be downloaded and installed to your SharePoint farm before any SharePoint 2013 workflows can be utilized.

Objective review

Answer the following questions to test your knowledge of the information in this objective. You can find the answers to these questions and explanations of why each answer choice is correct or incorrect in the "Answers" section at the end of this chapter.

1. Which of the following e-mail scenarios support the prevention of spam filtering and virus prevention through incoming e-mail connectivity to a list or library in SharePoint?

    A. Basic scenario

    B. List scenario

    C. Library scenario

    D. Advanced scenario

2. Which of the following cmdlets is used to create a new proxy group for use with service applications?

    A. Set-SPServiceApplicationProxyGroup

    B. Get-SPServiceApplicationProxyGroup

    C. Get-SPServiceApplicationProxy

    D. Add-SPServiceApplicationProxyGroupMember

3. Which of the following is the correct cmdlet to configure SPD settings within a web app?

    A. Set-SharePointDesigner

    B. Set-SPDesigner

    C. Set-SharePointDesignerSettings

    D. Set-SPDesignerSettings

4. Which of the following cmdlets is used to bind an Office Web Apps installation with a SharePoint farm?

    A. Set-NewWOPIBinding

    B. Set-NewSPBinding

    C. New-SPWOPIBinding

    D. New-WOPISPBinding

Objective 3.3: Create and configure enterprise search

Creating an effective Enterprise Search implementation is probably the most complex component of a SharePoint installation. Defining how Search will connect and extract information from disparate sources will require detailed administrative interaction with other system administrators to be successful.

> **This objective covers how to:**
> - Plan and configure a search topology.
> - Plan and configure content sources.
> - Plan and configure crawl schedules.
> - Plan and configure crawl rules.
> - Plan and configure crawl performance.
> - Plan and configure security trimming.

Planning and configuring a search topology

In SharePoint Server 2010, search came in two forms: Native and FAST. The native SharePoint Server search engine was a built-in component, providing one or more farms with a capable search engine. FAST search was an optional component that then could be purchased separately to further enhance the native search functionality.

The search engine in SharePoint Server 2013 is a natural progression from both of these search engines, including elements of each to deliver a robust, enterprise-level search experience.

> **IMPORTANT SHAREPOINT SERVER 2013 CALS AND SEARCH**
>
> The standard CAL of SharePoint Server includes only a subset of the FAST search functionality.

Search application topology

The search application topology has changed quite a bit in SharePoint 2013. Elements of both FAST search and the recently departed Web Analytics service application from SharePoint 2010 are now rolled up into the overall design of your search subsystem.

An out-of-the-box (OOB) SharePoint Server 2010 installation provided four search components: Search Administration, Crawl, Index, and Query Processing. In SharePoint Server 2013, there are now a total of six components present in the search application:

- **Crawl component** This component performs crawls of the content sources you specify, retrieving both metadata and crawled properties. This information is then propagated to the Content Processing component.

- **Content Processing component** This component transforms the crawled items before sending them on to the index component. Crawled properties are mapped to managed properties by this component; other information is also provided to the analytics processing component.

- **Analytics Processing component** This component has two major functions: analysis and reporting. It improves search relevance by analyzing the crawled items and how users interact with search results; it also creates search reports and recommendations.

- **Index component** This component has two major functions. This component receives items from the Content Processing component before writing them to the search index; it also handles both incoming and outgoing queries from the Query Processing component, retrieving information and returning result sets, respectively, to and from the search index.

- **Query Processing component** This component analyzes queries before passing them to the Index component for result set retrieval.

- **Search Administration component** This component does not have an active role in handling incoming or outgoing search requests; it only runs system processes pertaining to search and adds/initializes new search component instances.

Search application databases

A SharePoint Server 2010 farm possessed only three types of search application databases: Search Administration, Crawl, and Property. The functionality provided by the Web Analytics Staging and Reporting databases has now also been rolled into SharePoint 2013 search.

There are a total of four types of databases present in SharePoint 2013 Search:

- **Crawl database** This database stores tracking information and crawled items details; also crawl metrics (such as the last crawl time/ID).

- **Link database** This database stores information about search clicks as well as information extracted by the Content Processing component; both types of information are analyzed by the Analytics Processing component.

- **Analytics Reporting database** Reports are generated from the contents of this database, which include analysis statistics as well as the results of usage analysis.

- **Search Administration database** Stores all the Search Service Application settings; for example, the topology, rules, and mappings between crawled and managed properties.

Search topology requirements gathering

SharePoint 2013 search is capable of processing millions of items within the context of a single SharePoint farm. It goes without saying that careful design of the initial topology is essential.

Decision points for designing your SharePoint Search topology should include the following:

- High availability and fault tolerance
- Whether your farm is internally or externally facing (Enterprise, Internet, or both)
- Overall volume of content to be searched
- Client load on the farm, in terms of queries and page views per second

When you discuss the business need for high availability and fault tolerance, be prepared to decide whether every search component needs to be included in this requirement. For instance, if the analytics processing component were to fail, there would be no immediate outage; users would continue to be able to search within the farm.

The way you design your search topology may also depend on usage requirements for the farm. For instance, a farm that only faces the Internet may require that performance be focused on the Query Processing and Index components as the content corpus (body of content) does not change drastically. An enterprise intranet site may have just the opposite requirement due to the turnover in content, requiring that performance be focused on the Crawl and Content Processing components.

The sheer size of the content corpus may be an issue: If you are in a larger environment with thousands of people generating information to be included in the search, you may need to add an extra layer of application servers to your farm and alter the topology to make these servers focus the processing and delivery of search information.

Finally, client load (particularly on Internet-facing sites) may be an issue; if your SharePoint site hosts a large amount of content, you must deliver an outstanding search experience to provide your customers with the information they need. To do so, you may decide to break the index into multiple partitions and add servers that are specifically focused on providing query functionality.

MORE INFO **SEARCH ARCHITECTURE DIAGRAMS**

For more detailed examples of search architectures for both enterprise and Internet sites, visit the Microsoft Download Center to view the Internet Sites Search Architectures (*http://www.microsoft.com/en-us/download/details.aspx?id=30464*) and Enterprise Search Architectures (*http://www.microsoft.com/en-us/download/details.aspx?id=30383*) design sample documents.

Viewing the search application topology

You can view the search topology of a SharePoint Server 2013 search application from Central Administration. This topology map shows not only the members of the farm that host search but also the search components that they host within the farm and which database servers and databases are used by search.

To view the Search Administration Topology (see Figure 3-32), follow these steps:

1. Open the Central Administration web site.

2. Select Application Management.

3. In the Service Application section, select Manage Service Applications.

4. In the list of Service Applications, locate your Search Service Application and select it by name.

5. On the Search Administration page, scroll down to the Search Application Topology.

Search Application Topology

Server Name	Admin	Crawler	Content Processing	Analytics Processing	Query Processing	Index Partition 0
WS2012SP13	✓	✓	✓	✓	✓	✓

Database Server Name	Database Type	Database Name
WS2012SP13	Administration Database	Search_Service_Application_DB
WS2012SP13	Analytics Reporting Database	Search_Service_Application_AnalyticsReportingStoreDB
WS2012SP13	Crawl Database	Search_Service_Application_CrawlStoreDB
WS2012SP13	Link Database	Search_Service_Application_LinksStoreDB

Learn more about search topology

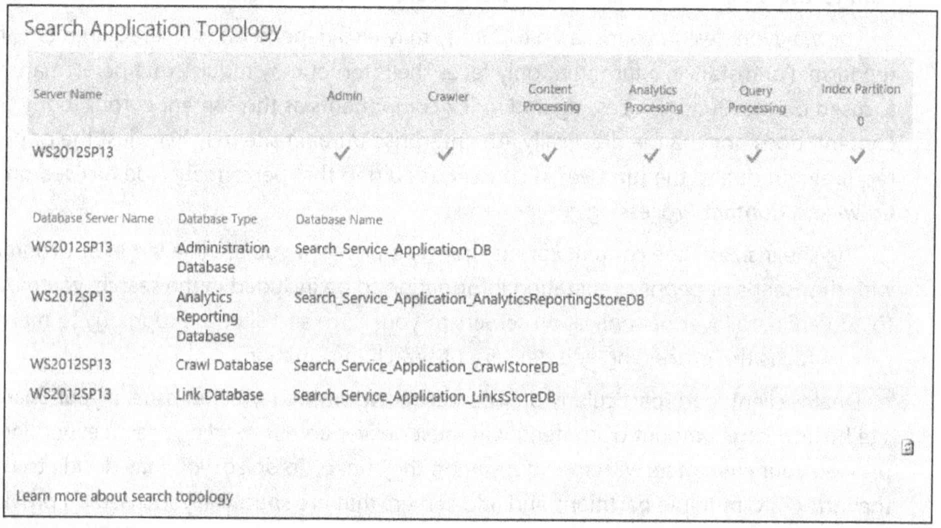

FIGURE 3-32 Search application topology.

This screen shows you the status of the search component(s) installed on each server in the farm:

- A green check mark indicates that the search component is running correctly.

- A yellow triangle indicates that the search component cannot perform all operations correctly.

- A red cross indicates that the search component is not running or that there are errors that prevent the component from running correctly.

Search topology changes

One of the largest administrative differences in SharePoint 2013 search has to do with changes in topology. In prior versions of SharePoint, these changes could be made from within Central Administration; in SharePoint 2013, topology changes must now be made from within Windows PowerShell.

If you installed your farm using the Configuration Wizard, all your search components will be installed on the server that hosts Central Administration. Although this is probably fine for small or development environments, you may want to change the topology for the purposes of improving SharePoint search performance within the farm.

There are two options for changing the search topology of a farm:

- If you have a new farm or one that has an empty index, you can directly change the topology in Windows PowerShell.

- If you have a farm with an existing index that you want to keep, you must do the following:

    - Clone the active search topology

    - Make changes to the cloned topology

    - Make the clone the active search topology for the farm

Changing the search topology (empty index)

With a fresh installation, you have the opportunity to alter the topology without too much effort. The key thing to note is that if you have a search index, the following steps are not to be used. Changing the search topology of a server that has already been in use is covered in the next section.

To verify that your farm has an empty index, scroll up on the Search Administration page to the System Status section. Within this section, locate the Searchable Items section and verify that there are 0 searchable items (see Figure 3-33).

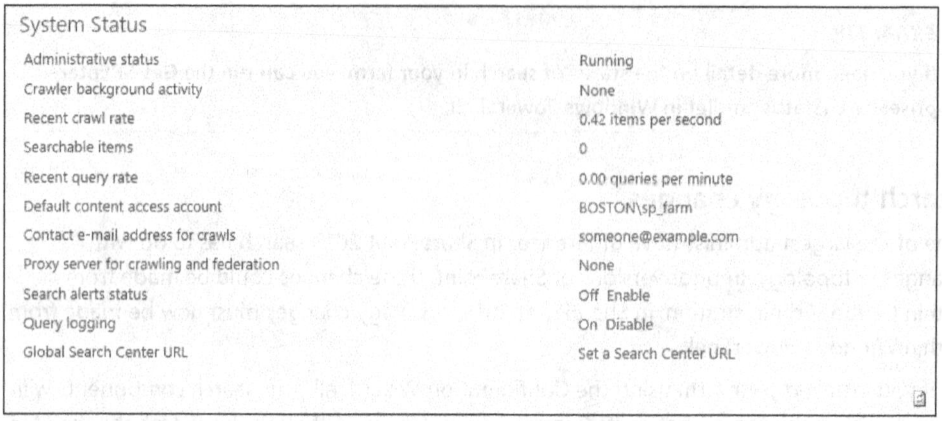

System Status

Administrative status	Running
Crawler background activity	None
Recent crawl rate	0.42 items per second
Searchable items	0
Recent query rate	0.00 queries per minute
Default content access account	BOSTON\sp_farm
Contact e-mail address for crawls	someone@example.com
Proxy server for crawling and federation	None
Search alerts status	Off Enable
Query logging	On Disable
Global Search Center URL	Set a Search Center URL

FIGURE 3-33 No searchable items found.

> **IMPORTANT EMPTYING THE INDEX RENDERS SEARCH TEMPORARILY UNUSABLE**
>
> Although you can choose to empty your index and then run these configuration steps, doing so will render search unusable for your users until you have completed a full crawl of your content sources. To reset the index, simply select the Index Reset link on the Search Application page.

If you have a farm with an empty index, you can use the following steps to alter the topology of your farm:

1. Assign the host name of each server to a variable using the Get-SPEnterpriseSearchServiceInstance cmdlet (the example server name shown is ws2012sp13):

   ```
   $hostA = Get-SPEnterpriseSearchServiceInstance -Identity "ws2013sp13"
   ```

2. (Note: Not the FQDN)

3. Start the Search instance on each of these hosts using the Start-SPEnterpriseSearchSer-viceInstance cmdlet:

   ```
   Start-SPEnterpriseSearchServiceInstance -Identity $hostA
   ```

4. Verify the status of search on each host using the Get-SPEnterpriseSearchServiceIn-stance cmdlet:

   ```
   Get-SPEnterpriseSearchServiceInstance -Identity $hostA
   ```

5. You must wait until the Status line reads Online (not Provisioning) for each host before proceeding (see Figure 3-34).

```
PS C:\Users\sp_farm> Get-SpEnterpriseSearchServiceInstance -Identity $hostA

TypeName    : SharePoint Server Search
Description : Index content and serve search queries
Id          : adcf4188-4ae1-43d7-93ee-9db3a851fa55
Server      : SPServer Name=WS2012SP13
Service     : SearchService Name=OSearch15
Role        : None
Status      : Online
```

FIGURE 3-34 Status is online.

6. Create a new search topology and set a reference using the Get-SPEnterpriseSearch-ServiceApplication and New-SPEnterpriseSearchTopology cmdlets, respectively:

```
$ssa = Get-SPEnterpriseSearchServiceApplication
$newTopology = New-SPEnterpriseSearchTopology -SearchApplication $ssa
```

7. Add the appropriate search components to the new topology using the appropriate cmdlets (you will be distributing them across multiple hosts, replacing $hostA with the appropriate server variable (see Table 3-5).

TABLE 3-5 Creating new components on the new topology

New Component Type	Windows PowerShell cmdlet
Admin component	New-SPEnterpriseSearchAdminComponent -SearchTopology $newTopology -SearchServiceInstance $hostA
Crawl component	New-SPEnterpriseSearchCrawlComponent -SearchTopology $newTopology -SearchServiceInstance $hostA
Content Processing component	New-SPEnterpriseSearchContentProcessingComponent -SearchTopology $new-Topology -SearchServiceInstance $hostA
Analytics Processing component	New-SPEnterpriseSearchAnalyticsProcessingComponent -SearchTopology $new-Topology -SearchServiceInstance $hostA
Query Processing component	New-SPEnterpriseSearchQueryProcessingComponent -SearchTopology $newTo-pology -SearchServiceInstance $hostA
Index component	New-SPEnterpriseSearchIndexComponent -SearchTopology $newTopology -SearchServiceInstance $hostA -IndexPartition 0

8. Activate the new search topology:

```
Set-SPEnterpriseSearchTopology -Identity $newTopology
```

(Note: This step takes a few moments to complete.)

9. Check the status of the new search topology:

```
Get-SPEnterpriseSearchTopology -SearchApplication $ssa
```

10. The status will show both active and inactive topologies. Make a note of the inactive Topology ID (see Figure 3-35).

```
PS C:\Users\sp_farm> Get-SPEnterpriseSearchTopology -SearchApplication $ssa

TopologyId     : bc92bf2a-8238-4da8-a06b-a363bde77f9f
CreationDate   : 11/28/2012 11:48:00 PM
State          : Inactive
ComponentCount : 6

TopologyId     : 7f4ece52-49b4-4a85-8c87-4f0684445124
CreationDate   : 3/7/2013 9:53:00 AM
State          : Active
ComponentCount : 6
```

FIGURE 3-35 Active and inactive topologies.

11. Verify the status of the new topology:

```
Get-SPEnterpriseSearchStatus -SearchApplication $ssa -Text
```

12. To remove the inactive search topology, you will use the Topology ID of the inactive topology and the Remove-SPEnterpriseSearchTopology cmdlet:

```
$ssa = Get-SPEnterpriseSearchServiceApplication
$topology = Get-SPEnterpriseSearchTopology -SearchApplication $ssa -Identity
bc92bf2a-8238-4da8-a06b-a363bde77f9f

Remove-SPEnterpriseSearchTopology -Identity $topology
```

13. Check the status of the new search topology; the inactive topology has been removed (see Figure 3-36).

```
PS C:\Users\sp_farm> Get-SPEnterpriseSearchTopology -SearchApplication $ssa

TopologyId     : 7f4ece52-49b4-4a85-8c87-4f0684445124
CreationDate   : 3/7/2013 9:53:00 AM
State          : Active
ComponentCount : 6
```

FIGURE 3-36 Only the active topology remains.

Changing the search topology (active index)

If you have an index that is populated on a farm (that you want to keep) and you need to change the topology, you must do the following:

- Clone the active search topology
- Make changes to the cloned topology
- Make the clone the active search topology for the farm

This example moves from one topology to another that is cloned and then altered:

1. Assign the host name of each server to a variable using the Get-SPEnterpriseSearchServiceInstance cmdlet (the example server name shown is ws2012sp13):

```
$hostA = Get-SPEnterpriseSearchServiceInstance -Identity "ws2013sp13"
```

(Note: Not the FQDN)

2. If you are adding new hosts to the search topology, start the Search instance on each of these hosts using the Start-SPEnterpriseSearchServiceInstance cmdlet:

```
Start-SPEnterpriseSearchServiceInstance -Identity $hostA
```

3. Verify the status of search on each host using the Get-SPEnterpriseSearchServiceInstance cmdlet:

```
Get-SPEnterpriseSearchServiceInstance -Identity $hostA
```

4. You must wait until the status line reads Online (not Provisioning) for each host before proceeding (see Figure 3-37).

FIGURE 3-37 Status is online.

5. Cloning the active topology is done by using the New-SPEnterpriseSearchTopology cmdlet:

```
$ssa = Get-SPEnterpriseSearchServiceApplication
$active = Get-SPEnterpriseSearchTopology -SearchApplication $ssa -Active
$clone = New-SPEnterpriseSearchTopology -SearchApplication $ssa -Clone
-SearchTopology $active
```

6. Running the Get-SPEnterpriseSearchTopology cmdlet at this point shows the existing active topology as well as its inactive clone (see Figure 3-38).

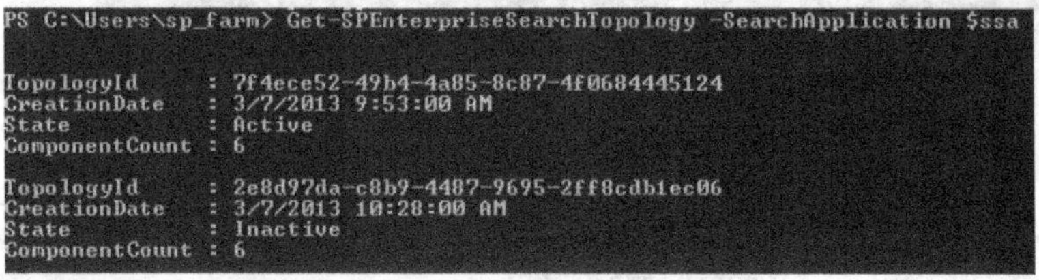

```
PS C:\Users\sp_farm> Get-SPEnterpriseSearchTopology -SearchApplication $ssa

TopologyId      : 7f4ece52-49b4-4a85-8c87-4f0684445124
CreationDate    : 3/7/2013 9:53:00 AM
State           : Active
ComponentCount  : 6

TopologyId      : 2e8d97da-c8b9-4487-9695-2ff8cdb1ec06
CreationDate    : 3/7/2013 10:28:00 AM
State           : Inactive
ComponentCount  : 6
```

FIGURE 3-38 Active topology and inactive topology (clone).

7. Assign the desired component to the appropriate host(s). Note that these Windows PowerShell commands are not identical to those in the previous section; you are addressing a clone instance instead of a new one (see Table 3-6).

TABLE 3-6 Creating new components on the cloned topology

New Component Type	Windows PowerShell cmdlet
Admin component	New-SPEnterpriseSearchAdminComponent -SearchTopology $clone -SearchServiceInstance $hostA
Crawl component	New-SPEnterpriseSearchCrawlComponent -SearchTopology $clone -SearchServiceInstance $hostA
Content Processing component	New-SPEnterpriseSearchContentProcessingComponent -SearchTopology $clone -SearchServiceInstance $hostA
Analytics Processing component	New-SPEnterpriseSearchAnalyticsProcessingComponent -SearchTopology $clone -SearchServiceInstance $hostA
Query Processing component	New-SPEnterpriseSearchQueryProcessingComponent -SearchTopology $clone -SearchServiceInstance $hostA
Index component	New-SPEnterpriseSearchIndexComponent -SearchTopology $clone -SearchServiceInstance $hostA -IndexPartition 0

8. Removing a component requires that you know its component ID. To get this information, run the Get-SPEnterpriseSearchComponent -SearchTopology $clone Windows PowerShell command (see Figure 3-39).

```
ComponentId : 0d899c3f-8435-43e9-97ec-6499b54620d3
TopologyId  : 2e8d97da-c8b9-4487-9695-2ff8cdb1ec06
ServerId    : b01d9e54-0ee8-4d73-ad4d-3e6f73e3e9cd
Name        : QueryProcessingComponent1
ServerName  : WS2012SP13

ComponentId : 7dbb5f36-e27e-4432-bec6-985df1c0962b
TopologyId  : 2e8d97da-c8b9-4487-9695-2ff8cdb1ec06
ServerId    : b01d9e54-0ee8-4d73-ad4d-3e6f73e3e9cd
Name        : ContentProcessingComponent1
ServerName  : WS2012SP13

PS C:\Users\sp_farm> Get-SPEnterpriseSearchComponent -SearchTopology $clone
```

FIGURE 3-39 Component ID of the Query Processing component.

9. Select the component ID you want to delete and use the Remove-SPEnterpriseSearchComponent cmdlet to remove it altogether. In this case, remove the QueryProcessing component from server WS2012SP13:

```
Remove-SPEnterpriseComponent -Identity 0d899c3f-8435-43e9-97ec-6499b54620d3
-SearchTopology $clone
```

10. To activate the new search topology, use the Set-SPEnterpriseSearchTopology cmdlet:

```
Set-SPEnterpriseSearchTopology -Identity $clone
```

(This step will take a few moments.)

11. Check the status of the new search topology:

```
Get-SPEnterpriseSearchTopology -SearchApplication $ssa
```

12. The status will show both the active (previously cloned) and inactive topologies. Make a note of the inactive topology ID (see Figure 3-40).

FIGURE 3-40 Active and inactive topologies (previous clone activated).

13. Verify the status of the new topology:

```
Get-SPEnterpriseSearchStatus -SearchApplication $ssa -Text
```

14. To remove the inactive search topology, use the topology ID of the inactive topology and the Remove-SPEnterpriseSearchTopology cmdlet:

```
$ssa = Get-SPEnterpriseSearchServiceApplication
$topology = Get-SPEnterpriseSearchTopology -SearchApplication $ssa -Identity
7f4ece52-49b4-4a85-8c87-4f0684445124
Remove-SPEnterpriseSearchTopology -Identity $topology
```

15. Check the status of the new search topology; the inactive topology has been removed (see Figure 3-41).

FIGURE 3-41 Only the active topology remains.

MORE INFO **ALTERING THE SEARCH TOPOLOGY OF A FARM**

For more details about altering the search topology of a farm, see the TechNet articles "Change the Default Search Topology in SharePoint Server 2013" at *http://technet.micro-soft.com/en-us/library/jj862356.aspx*; and "Manage Search Components in SharePoint Server 2013" at *http://technet.microsoft.com/en-us/library/jj862354.aspx*.

Planning and configuring content sources

A content source specifies settings that define what types of content to crawl, what start addresses are used, what priority the crawl has, and on what schedule the content is crawled.

Content source types

SharePoint 2013 enables eight types of content to be crawled in a content source (see Table 3-7).

TABLE 3-7 Content source types

Content Source Type	For This Content
SharePoint Sites	SharePoint content from SharePoint 2013, 2010, and 2007-based systems, including SharePoint Foundation and Search Server farms
Web Sites	Intranet- or Internet-based, non-SharePoint sites
File Shares	Information stored on file shares
Exchange Public Folders	Exchange Server content on 2013, 2010, and 2007 versions
Lotus Notes	Lotus Notes content (you must install and configure a connector before the Lotus Notes source type appears in the interface)
Documentum	EMC Documentum content (you must install and configure a connector before the Documentum source type appears in the interface)
Line of Business Data	Uses the Business Connectivity Service (BCS) to crawl other line of business applications
Custom Repository	Requires the development and installation of a custom connector

EXAM TIP

Know which content sources are available for use in a default setting: SharePoint Sites, Web Sites, File Shares, Exchange Public Folders, and (conditionally) Line of Business Data. The Line of Business Data content source type requires that at least one Business Data Connectivity (BDC) service application has been created.

MORE INFO **CREATING CUSTOM CONNECTORS**

For more information about creating a custom connector for use with SharePoint server, see the MSDN "Creating a Custom Indexing Connector" article at *http://msdn.microsoft. com/en-us/library/ff625806.aspx*.

Each content source type displayed in the search service application uses an indexing connector when crawling content. The BCS Connector Framework handles connections to the

Lotus Notes and Exchange Public Folder content source types; a standard series of protocol handlers handles connections to SharePoint sites, Web Sites, and File Shares.

> **MORE INFO** **DEFAULT INDEXING CONNECTORS**
>
> For a complete list of supported default connectors, see the TechNet article "Default Connectors in SharePoint Server 2013" at *http://technet.microsoft.com/en-us/library/jj219746.aspx.*

Planning and configuring crawl schedules

Content sources are most often configured to be crawled by SharePoint search on a frequent basis. The frequency with which they are crawled is set by the crawl schedule (see Figure 3-42).

Crawl Schedules

Select the crawl schedules for this content source.

Continuous Crawl is a special type of crawl that eliminates the need to create incremental crawl schedules and will seamlessly work with the content source to provide maximum freshness. Please Note: Once enabled, you will not be able to pause or stop continuous crawl. You will only have the option of disabling continuous crawl.

◉ Enable Continuous Crawls
◯ Enable Incremental Crawls
Incremental Crawl
| Every 4 hour(s) from 12:00 AM for 24 hour(s) every day, starting 3/6/2013 ▾ |
Edit schedule

Full Crawl
| At 12:00 AM every Mon, Wed, Fri, Sun of every week, starting 3/6/2013   ▾ |
Edit schedule

FIGURE 3-42 Content source crawl schedules.

There are three types of crawls available in SharePoint Server 2013: full, incremental, and a new type: continuous. Full and incremental crawls exist in the same form as they did within SharePoint 2010. The new crawl type, continuous, is available for use only with SharePoint Sites.

Full crawl

In a full crawl, all the content within a particular content source is crawled and then processed into the index. Depending on the volume of content to be crawled, this crawl could take hours or days, so full crawls are almost always scheduled for nonbusiness hours or weekends.

A full crawl can be scheduled to run monthly, weekly, or daily at a given time of day. It is also possible (though not recommended) to run the full crawl multiple times within a given day. You can also stagger the schedule using the Run Every/On option to crawl every x number of days (Daily setting), by choosing the days of the week in which to run the crawl (Weekly setting, shown in Figure 3-43), or by selecting a particular day to run the crawl each month (Monthly setting).

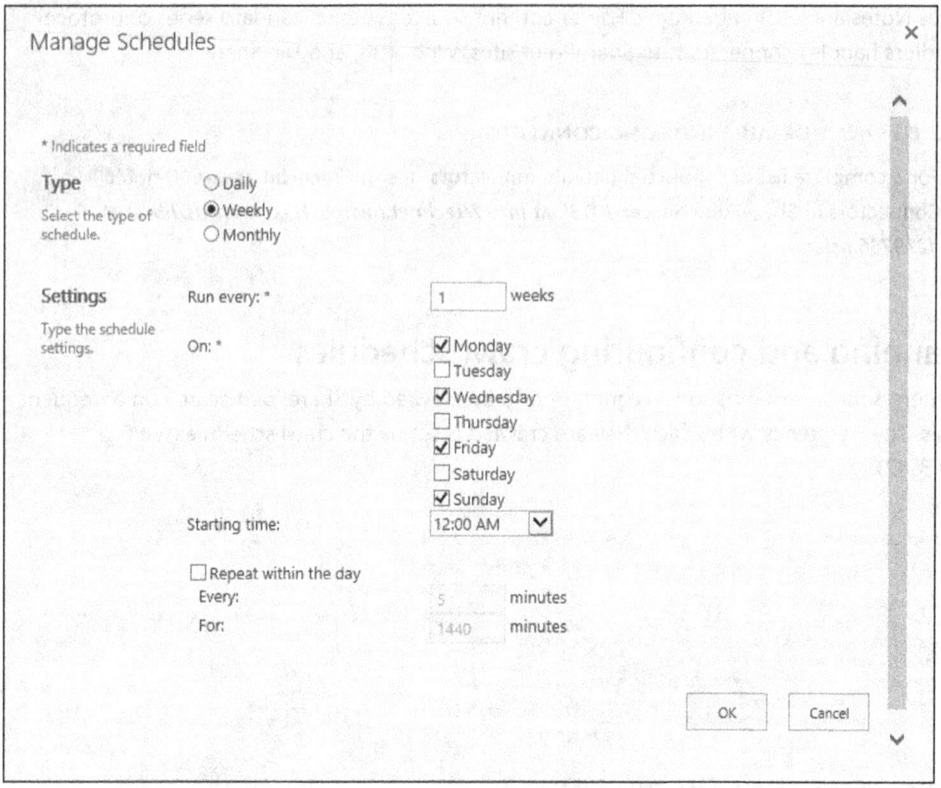

FIGURE 3-43 Managing the crawl schedule (Weekly setting).

There are several reasons for running a full crawl on a regular basis, including the following:

- Creating/re-creating the search index
- Correcting issues or corruption within the search index
- Detecting security changes made on a file share
- Capturing changes made by crawl rules (additions, deletions, modifications)
- Capturing new metadata mappings in search
- Capturing new server name mappings in search
- Credential changes for the crawl account
- Software changes (hotfixes, cumulative updates, service packs) applied to the farm

Incremental crawl

In an incremental crawl, changes made to the content within a particular content source are crawled and then processed into the index. An incremental crawl cannot be run alongside a full crawl; if a full crawl is taking an excessive amount of time to run, SharePoint waits to execute the next crawl until the first one completes.

An incremental crawl can be scheduled to run monthly, weekly, or daily at a given time of the day. Most often, an incremental crawl is scheduled a few times per day on every day of the week (again depending on the volume of content being crawled). The scheduling options for incremental crawls are identical to those of full crawls.

> **IMPORTANT CRAWL TYPES THAT CANNOT RUN SIMULTANEOUSLY**
>
> As with full crawls, no two incremental crawls can occur simultaneously. If a crawl is already running (full or incremental) and you schedule another to start before the first crawl completes, the new crawl is delayed.

Continuous crawl

SharePoint 2013 introduces the notion of continuous crawls. In a continuous crawl scenario, the index is constantly updated with new content as the content is added to a SharePoint site.

Continuous crawls are unique among the crawl types; they can run in parallel. One crawl of a content source can be in a running, incomplete state; another can start crawling the same content source (thus the name "continuous"). By default, continuous crawls kick off every 15 minutes; there is no way to schedule them in Central Administration.

You can use Windows PowerShell to either shorten or lengthen the crawl interval. In the following example, Local SharePoint Sites content source is set to crawl continuously and then the crawl interval is reset to 1 minute:

```
$searchapp = Get-SPEnterpriseSearchServiceApplication "Search Service Application"
$contentsource = Get-SPEnterpriseSearchCrawlContentSource -
SearchApplication $searchapp -Identity "Local SharePoint Sites"
$contentsource | Set-SPEnterpriseSearchCrawlContentSource -EnableContinuousCrawls $true
$searchapp.SetProperty("ContinuousCrawlInterval", 1)
```

Planning and configuring crawl rules

Crawl rules are used in conjunction with both content sources and search, but are applied to all content sources within the search service application. These rules have three functions:

- Exclude content from being crawled
- Crawl only a portion of content from a site that otherwise excludes it
- Specify authentication credentials

Crawl rules are added on the Add Crawl Rule page within the search service application. There are three sections to this page: (Rule) Path, Crawl Configuration, and Specify Authentication.

(Rule) path

This field captures the path that should be evaluated in this rule. The path should end with a final slash (front for a URL and back for a file share) and an asterisk (*), indicating a wildcard match (see Figure 3-44).

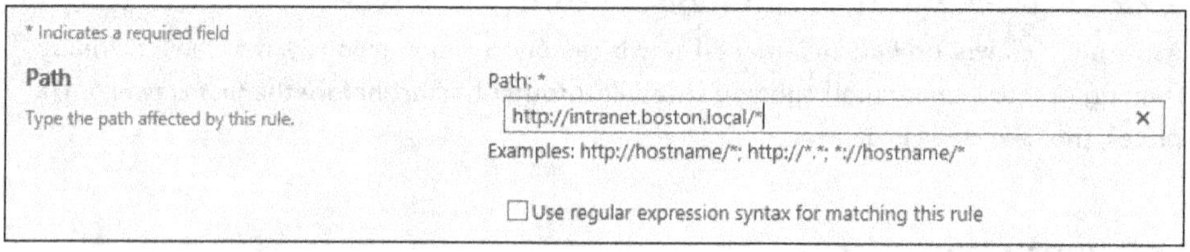

FIGURE 3-44 Rule path.

There exists an additional check box, Use Regular Expression Syntax For Matching This Rule, which can be used to craft a regular expression that would omit potentially sensitive items such as credit card or social security numbers across an assortment of SharePoint sites.

Crawl configuration

This section has two radio buttons (see Figure 3-45):

- Exclude All Items In This Path
- Include All Items In This Path

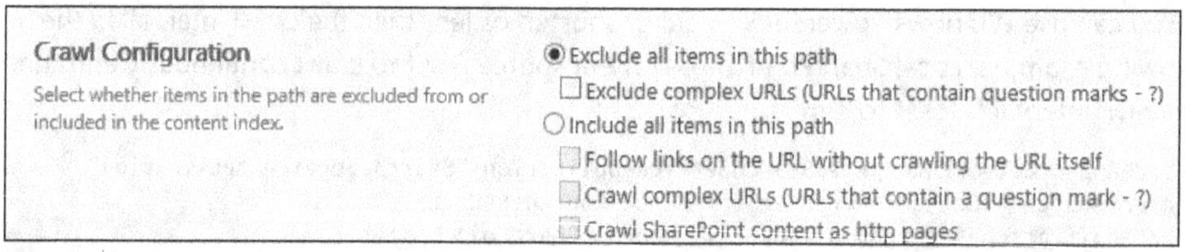

FIGURE 3-45 Crawl configuration.

- If you choose to exclude a path, you can optionally choose to only exclude complex URLs.
- If you choose to include a path, you can optionally choose to do the following:
  - Follow links on the URL without crawling the URL itself (only crawl child content)
  - Crawl complex URLs (URLs that contain a question mark: (?)
  - Crawl SharePoint content as HTTP pages

Specifying authentication

The authentication component of crawl rules is easily the most complex. There are six main options, each of which has a different configuration: Use The Default Content Access Account, Specify A Different Content Access Account, Specify Client Certificate, Specify FORM CREDENTIALS, Use Cookie For Crawling, and Anonymous Access.

- If you choose to use the default access account, no extra settings are required. This rule will crawl the content using the account specified in Search Administration.
- If you choose to specify a different content access account, you will be prompted for the account name and password. You can optionally choose to not allow basic authentication, which will prevent your password from being transmitted without encryption during the crawl.
- If you choose to specify a certificate, a drop-down list will appear with a list of available certificates.
- If you choose to specify form credentials (forms based authentication on the site being crawled), you will need to specify the logon address and enter credentials (user name and password).
- If you choose to use a cookie for crawling content, you can either obtain a cookie from a URL or specify one from your system.
- If you choose to access the site anonymously, no extra settings are required. This rule crawls the content without attempting to authenticate.

Rule evaluation order

Rules are evaluated on a per-URL basis; the first rule that a URL matches is the one that is evaluated—all others are ignored. Here are two rules that we will implement in SharePoint, written in plain English:

- Include the content contained in http://intranet.boston.local/sites/projectone/
- Exclude the content contained in http://intranet/boston.local/

To implement these rules in Central Administration, do the following:

1. Open Central Administration and select Application Management.

2. Select Manage Service Applications.

3. Click the name of your Search Application.

4. In the Quick Launch (Crawling section), select Crawl Rules.

5. Select New Crawl Rule.

   A. In the Path section, type **http://intranet.boston.local/sites/projectone/***.

   B. In the Crawl Configuration section, select Include All Items In This Path.

   C. In the Specify Authentication section, leave the default selected (Use The Default Content Access Account).

   D. Click OK.

6. Again select New Crawl Rule.

   A. In the Path section, type **http://intranet.boston.local/***.

   B. In the Crawl Configuration section, select Exclude All Items In This Path.

   C. The Specify Authentication radio button will be grayed out.

   D. Click OK.

At this point, your new rules should appear on the Manage Crawl Rules page (see Figure 3-46).

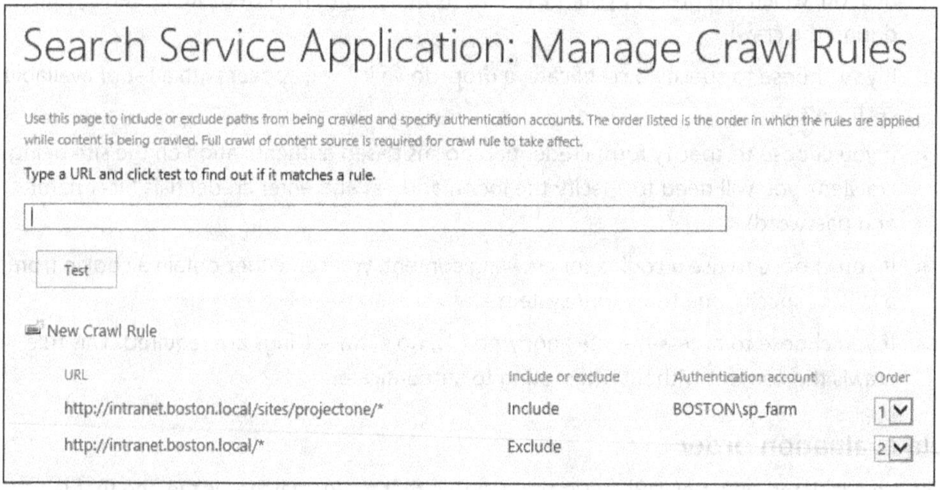

Search Service Application: Manage Crawl Rules

Use this page to include or exclude paths from being crawled and specify authentication accounts. The order listed is the order in which the rules are applied while content is being crawled. Full crawl of content source is required for crawl rule to take affect.

Type a URL and click test to find out if it matches a rule.

| | |

[Test]

New Crawl Rule

URL	Include or exclude	Authentication account	Order
http://intranet.boston.local/sites/projectone/*	Include	BOSTON\sp_farm	1 ▾
http://intranet.boston.local/*	Exclude		2 ▾

FIGURE 3-46 Completed crawl rules.

Now that the rules are in place, enter an address on the Manage Crawl Rules page to view how it will be evaluated (see Figure 3-47):

1. In the Type A URL box, type **http://intranet.boston.local/sites/projectone**.

2. Click Test.

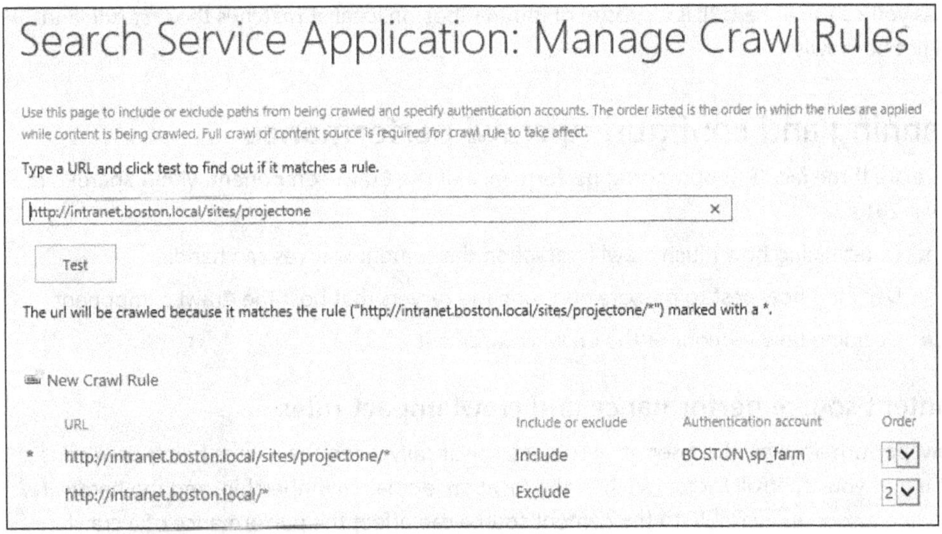

Search Service Application: Manage Crawl Rules

Use this page to include or exclude paths from being crawled and specify authentication accounts. The order listed is the order in which the rules are applied while content is being crawled. Full crawl of content source is required for crawl rule to take affect.

Type a URL and click test to find out if it matches a rule.

http://intranet.boston.local/sites/projectone	✕

[Test]

The url will be crawled because it matches the rule ("http://intranet.boston.local/sites/projectone/*") marked with a *.

📷 New Crawl Rule

	URL	Include or exclude	Authentication account	Order
*	http://intranet.boston.local/sites/projectone/*	Include	BOSTON\sp_farm	1 ⌄
	http://intranet.boston.local/*	Exclude		2 ⌄

FIGURE 3-47 The URL will be crawled.

The red indicator present in this screen shot indicates the first rule evaluated that matches the URL. In this case, the URL is to be included; any other URL under http://intranet.boston.local will match the other rule (#2) and will not be crawled.

Let's see what happens if the order is reversed (see Figure 3-48):

1. From the Order drop-down list for http://intranet.boston.local/*, select 1.

2. In the Type A URL box, type **http://intranet.boston.local/sites/projectone**.

3. Click Test.

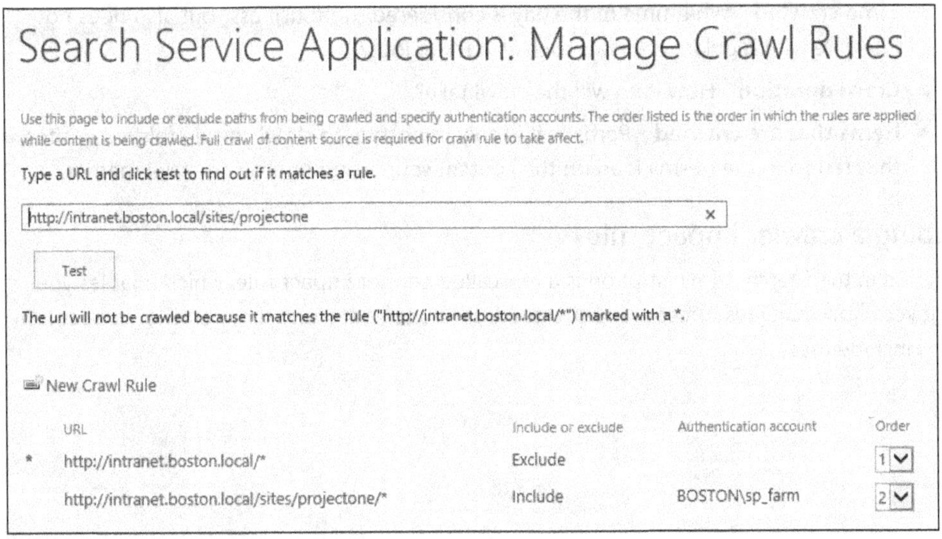

Search Service Application: Manage Crawl Rules

Use this page to include or exclude paths from being crawled and specify authentication accounts. The order listed is the order in which the rules are applied while content is being crawled. Full crawl of content source is required for crawl rule to take affect.

Type a URL and click test to find out if it matches a rule.

http://intranet.boston.local/sites/projectone	✕

[Test]

The url will not be crawled because it matches the rule ("http://intranet.boston.local/*") marked with a *.

📷 New Crawl Rule

	URL	Include or exclude	Authentication account	Order
*	http://intranet.boston.local/*	Exclude		1 ⌄
	http://intranet.boston.local/sites/projectone/*	Include	BOSTON\sp_farm	2 ⌄

FIGURE 3-48 The URL will not be crawled.

As you can see, the URL is a subsite of intranet.boston.local; it matches the first rule and will not be crawled.

Planning and configuring crawl performance

There are three facets of optimizing performance of the Crawl component within SharePoint Server 2013:

- Determining how much crawl interaction the content sources can handle
- Deciding how best to prepare and tune the servers that host the Crawl component
- Deciding how to monitor the Crawl component

Content source performance and crawl impact rules

Crawl performance can be a sensitive subject, specifically when the source being crawled is not under your control. Factors such as the location, domain membership, and the hardware/software resources available to the content source can affect the performance of a crawl.

Some of these sources may be located across a wide area network (WAN) segment; aggressively crawling these sources may cause diminished performance across the WAN segment, affecting the business.

Performance levels for content sources not located on the installation can be negatively affected by a well-provisioned Crawl component. If the SharePoint farm is crawling a content source so aggressively that it winds up diminishing performance on the content source, there is a very good chance that the crawl account will be temporarily (or perhaps permanently) disabled from accessing the content source.

Consider coordinating crawls with the administrator(s) of the "crawled" system for potential configuration changes like these:

- **Time crawled**   What time of the day is considered "nonbusiness" but also does not interfere with regular processes such as backup jobs?
- **Crawl duration**   How long will the crawl take?
- **Items that are crawled**   Perhaps it is only important to crawl certain folders or sites, thus reducing the overall load on the content source and improving crawl metrics.

Adding a crawler impact rule

Included in the Search Administration is a link called crawler impact rule, which enables you to govern how many resources are requested from a site at any one time. Crawler impact rule fields include these:

- **Site** The name of the site (not including the protocol).
- **Request Frequency** Indicates how the crawler will request documents from the site. From here you can choose to do either of the following:
  - Request up to the specified number of documents at a time and do not wait between requests (also specifying the number of simultaneous requests).
  - Request one document at a time and wait the specified time between requests (also specifying a time to wait in seconds).

Crawl component configuration recommendations

As you scale out your search topology, there are recommendations that will improve the performance of the Crawl component. These recommendations apply to both Enterprise (intranet) and Internet SharePoint installations:

- If you host the Crawl component along with other search components on a server, add an additional 8 gigabytes (GB) of random access memory (RAM) to the existing RAM requirement.
- The server that hosts the crawl component should have a 64-bit processor with 4 (or preferably 8) cores.
- A new crawl database should be added per every 20 million items crawled.
- For content sources that use continuous crawl for SharePoint Sites, consider using Windows PowerShell to alter the crawl interval to crawl once per minute.

> *MORE INFO* **SEARCH COMPONENT REQUIREMENTS**
>
> To see requirements specific to each search component, view the TechNet article "Scale Search for Performance and Availability in SharePoint Server 2013" at *http://technet.microsoft.com/en-us/library/jj219628.aspx*.

Monitoring crawl health reports

Crawl health reports are a series of graphical metrics that can be used to track the performance of the SharePoint Server 2013 Crawl component at a granular level. These metrics are broken into a seven report groupings, shown in Table 3-8.

TABLE 3-8 Crawl health reports

Report	Description
Crawl Rate	Provides two graphs: Crawl Rate Per Type and Crawl Rate Per Content Source. Provides a series of metrics: Crawled Documents per Second Total Items Modified Items Not Modified Items Security Items Deleted Items Retries Errors
Crawl Latency	Provides two graphs: Crawl Load (filtered by component) and Crawl Latency (filtered by content source and component). Crawl Load shows four metrics: Items In Crawler Queue Items Waiting to Submit to Content Processing Items Submitted to Content Processing Items Waiting to Commit (SQL) Crawl Latency shows four different metrics: Crawler Protocol Handler (PH) Repository SQL Time
Crawl Freshness	Provides a graph of freshness trending, showing item freshness by time interval. Provides a summary of freshness for each content source, showing its aggregate freshness and number of documents crawled.
CPU and Memory Load	Shows a summary of Total % CPU Usage and Total % Memory Usage, filterable by machine and time interval.
Content Processing Activity	Shows metrics for the Content Processing component: focusing on content sources, machines, Content Processing components, and content processing activity.
Crawl Queue	Shows the number of items in these two crawl queues: Links to Process (number of uncrawled URLs queued for crawling) Transactions Queued (number of uncrawled URLs queued to be processed in the crawl pipeline)
Continuous Crawl	Shows a graph of time in milliseconds vs. discovery time in minutes for these: Time in Links Table Time in Queue Table Crawler Time Protocol Handler Time Repository Time Content Pipeline Time SQL Time

Monitoring the crawl log

The crawl log tracks the status of crawled content, enabling you to troubleshoot and diagnose the search experience. Items that are monitored are the following:

- When and whether crawled content was added to the index

- Whether content is excluded by a crawl rule

- Whether an error caused the indexing of content to fail

Crawl log information is presented as a series of views. These views enable you to parse through the crawl information (see Table 3-9).

TABLE 3-9 Crawl log views

Crawl Log View	Description
Content Source	View a summary of items crawled on a per-content source basis
Host Name	View a summary of items crawled on a per-host basis
Crawl History	View a summary of crawl transactions completed during a crawl
Error Breakdown	View crawl errors, optionally filter by content source or host name
Databases	View the state of the crawl databases used by this search application
URL View	Search for documents that have been crawled

Planning and configuring security trimming

When viewed from a high level, search in SharePoint follows a very basic process:

1. A content source is crawled (including the permissions applied) and then processed into an index.

2. A user issues a search query, which returns a result set.

3. The result set is security trimmed before being returned to the user.

If a user is granted permission to access an item, the item then appears in the result set. This does not mean that the information wasn't there all along (the index certainly contained this data), but that it was simply "held back" from view at query time.

Content access accounts

SharePoint uses the notion of content access accounts when crawling content sources. These accounts are granted permission to access the appropriate content, which is then crawled, processed for content, and stored in the index.

Content access accounts should be ordinary Active Directory accounts; in fact, these accounts should specifically have no special privileges at all:

- They should not be the same account as that used for SharePoint setup or farm administration.

- They should not be the same account as those that run any of the application pools or services.

- They should not have local administrative access granted to any of the SharePoint or SQL member servers in the farm.

The reason we should care about the status of these accounts is their effect on security trimming and the Publishing model. One of the most important components of SharePoint 2013, Publishing can used for the lifecycle of items contained within a SharePoint site:

- An item is initially created and saved in draft mode.
- After the document is deemed to be ready for publication by its creator, it is submitted.
- If approvals are enabled, the item can be approved and then scheduled for publication.
- After the item is approved, it can be published immediately or scheduled for publication at a later date.

> **IMPORTANT** **UNPUBLISHED ITEMS**
>
> Items that are in draft mode, are not approved, or are not in a published state are unavailable in search results.

Content is accessed via two types of content access accounts: default and specific. The default access account is used to access the content present in the SharePoint farm, whereas specific access accounts can be used to access content in a particular content source.

Default content access account

The default content access account is used to access most of the content in the SharePoint installation. If you want, this account can also be assigned read permissions to other content sources; items crawled within these sources are also security trimmed as queries are issued by users.

The default content access account is shown (and can be assigned) from the System Status section of the Search Administration page (see Figure 3-49).

System Status	
Administrative status	Running
Crawler background activity	None
Recent crawl rate	0.07 items per second
Searchable items	413
Recent query rate	0.00 queries per minute
Default content access account	BOSTON\sp_farm
Contact e-mail address for crawls	someone@example.com
Proxy server for crawling and federation	None
Search alerts status	On Disable
Query logging	On Disable
Global Search Center URL	Set a Search Center URL

FIGURE 3-49 Default content access account in System Status.

As shown in Figure 3-49, this farm was set up using the sp_farm account (the farm account for this SharePoint installation). Due to its privilege level, the use of this service account as the content access account will result in draft versions of documents appearing in search (in other words, not trimmed). The account will need to be changed.

Changing the default content access account is a very basic process (see Figure 3-50):

1. Click the content access account name (in this case, BOSTON\sp_farm).

2. Type a new user name and password (you have to type the password twice).

3. Click OK.

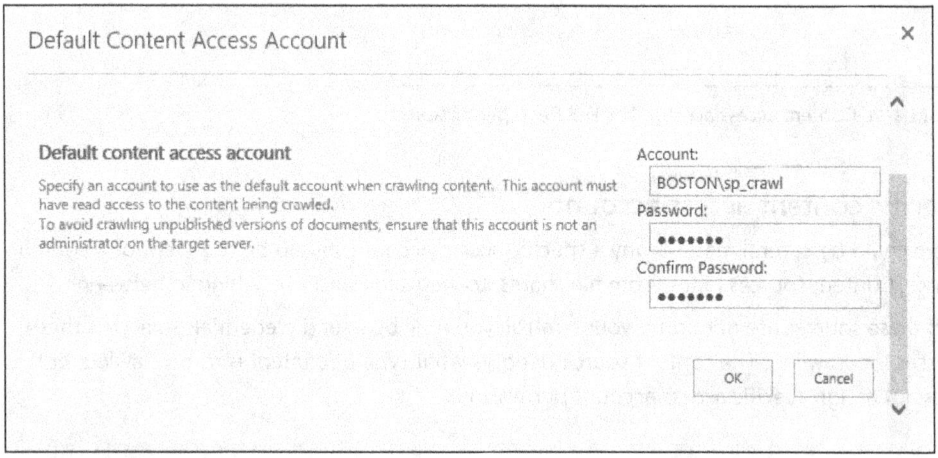

FIGURE 3-50 Default content access account.

After this account is designated as being the default content access account, it is assigned read permissions on all published content in a SharePoint farm on each Web Application in the farm. To view this access, do the following:

1. Open Central Administration and select Application Management.

2. In the Web Application section, select Manage Web Applications.

3. Select a Web Application and then select User Policy in the Policy section of the ribbon.

4. The content access account has Full Read permissions to the web application (see Figure 3-51). This permission level has no rights to any unpublished content in the farm.

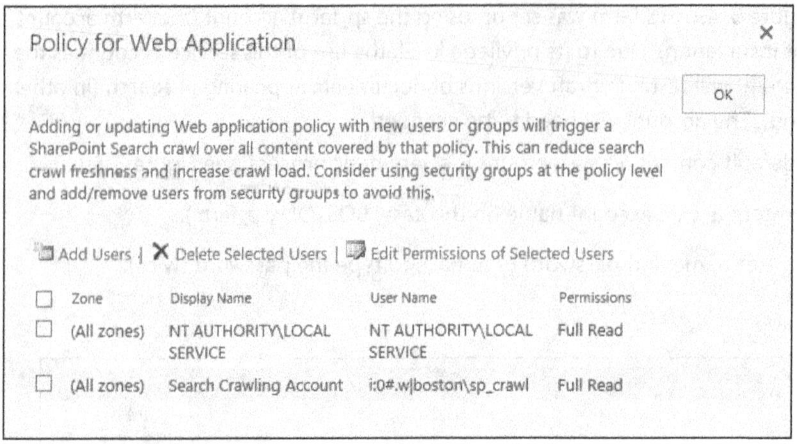

FIGURE 3-51 Content access account has Full Read permissions.

Specific content access accounts

There could be several reasons why a specific access account should be required for a content source. Content sources range from file shares, to web sites, and everything in between.

If these sources are not under your control, you may be issued credentials to access these sources for crawling. The content source denotes what type of content is to be crawled, but does not assign specific access account permissions.

> **EXAM TIP**
>
> **Specific content access accounts are assigned as part of crawl rules within the Specify Authentication section.**

Objective summary

- There are six major components in a SharePoint Server 2013 search application: Crawl, Content Processing, Analytics Processing, Index, Query Processing, and Search Administration.

- There are four search application databases in a SharePoint Server 2013 installation: Crawl, Link, Analytics Reporting, and Search Administration.

- The Web Analytics Staging and Reporting databases present in SharePoint 2010 have now been rolled into the search functionality present in SharePoint Server 2013.

- Topology changes are approached differently depending on whether the index is populated in a SharePoint 2013 farm.

- SharePoint 2013 uses an indexing connector to attach to distinct content sources within the environment. If you need additional connectors that are not supported OOB, they can be developed through the application programming interface (API) and imported into your farm.

- Continuous crawls work only on SharePoint Site content sources.

- Full and incremental crawls must complete before another can begin. Continuous crawls can overlap.

- Crawl rules are processed on a "first come, first served" basis. After the first rule is met, all others are ignored.

- Crawl performance affects both the farm and the performance levels of the crawl sources. Coordinate your search crawls with the administrators of those systems to allow for the best balance of performance on both systems.

Objective review

Answer the following questions to test your knowledge of the information in this objective. You can find the answers to these questions and explanations of why each answer choice is correct or incorrect in the "Answers" section at the end of this chapter.

1. You want to modify the search topology of your farm. The body of content is quite large and has generated a large index. Which of the following is a required action for this change?

   A. Mirroring the index

   B. Backing up the topology

   C. Cloning the index

   D. Cloning the topology

2. Which of the following content sources require additional configuration but are directly supported in a standard SharePoint Server 2013 search installation? (Choose all that apply.)

   A. Lotus Notes

   B. Documentum

   C. PeopleSoft

   D. SAP

3. Which of the following crawl types cannot be configured on the same content source? (Choose all that apply.)

   A. Differential

   B. Incremental

   C. Continuous

   D. Full

4. You receive a phone call from the remote site administrator of a small SharePoint server farm whose content you have been crawling. The site has been experiencing connectivity issues that occur only during working hours. Your requirement is that the content be kept as fresh as possible. What actions can you take to correct the issue? (Choose all that apply.)

   A. Disable all crawls

   B. Increase the continuous crawl interval

   C. Run a full crawl in the evening, but no other crawls

   D. Decrease the continuous crawl interval

Objective 3.4: Create and configure a Managed Metadata Service (MMS) application

The Managed Metadata Service (MMS) within a SharePoint farm provides a way to define taxonomical structures that can be carried out through the entire farm. These structures include term sets, which can be used for assigning metadata to lists/documents and controlling navigation, and content type hubs, which can be used to centralize and standardize the deployment of specific content types within your enterprise.

> **This objective covers how to:**
> - Configure proxy settings for managed service applications.
> - Configure content type hub settings.
> - Configure sharing term sets.
> - Plan and configure content type propagation schedules.
> - Configure custom properties.
> - Configure term store permissions.

Configuring proxy settings for managed service applications

The previous objective discussed proxy groups and how they are aligned with individual service application proxy connections. To review, each service application present in the farm maintains a connection/proxy that can be associated to a given connection or proxy group.

> **IMPORTANT PROXY VERSUS CONNECTION**
>
> The SharePoint interface refers to the relationship between a service application and the web application that consumes it as a "connection"; all other service applications refer to it as a "proxy." Regardless of how you refer to these connections, the relationship is still the same: The service app maintains its own connection that can be grouped with others and then connected to a web application for use.

Configuring proxy settings from Central Administration

In this example, you will add the MMS application (ManageMe2 in this example) to the Intranet Only proxy group defined earlier. At the same time, you will select a few more service application proxies and assign all to one of the web applications on the farm.

To reconfigure the web application and connection proxies, follow these steps:

1. Open Central Administration and then Application Management.

2. In the Service Applications section, select Configure Service Application Associations.

3. Note the current configuration, shown in Figure 3-52.

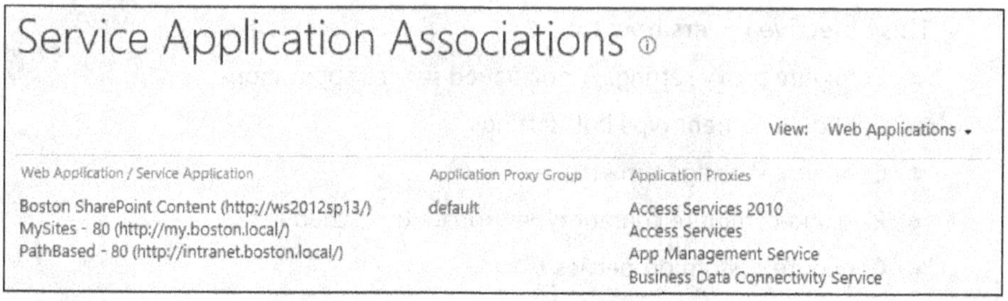

Service Application Associations ⓘ

View: Web Applications ▾

Web Application / Service Application	Application Proxy Group	Application Proxies
Boston SharePoint Content (http://ws2012sp13/) MySites - 80 (http://my.boston.local/) PathBased - 80 (http://intranet.boston.local/)	default	Access Services 2010 Access Services App Management Service Business Data Connectivity Service

FIGURE 3-52 Initial configuration.

4. Select the web application that you want to change (for example, http://intranet.bos-
ton.local).

5. From the drop-down menu, select Intranet Only (see Figure 3-53).

   Don't forget to scroll to the bottom of the page and click OK.

Configure Service Application Associations

Edit the following group of connections: | default / Intranet Only / [custom] |

Name	Type
✓ Access Services 2010	Access
✓ Access Services	Access

FIGURE 3-53 Selecting a new connection group.

6. The new configuration appears on the Services Application Associations page (see
Figure 3-54).

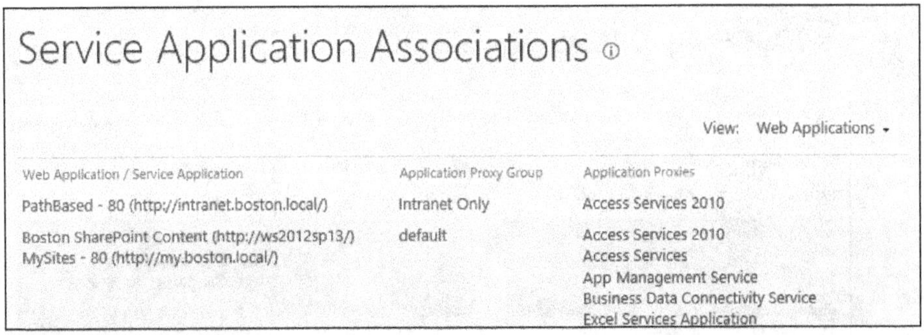

FIGURE 3-54 New association.

7. To change the application proxy and add services, click the name of the Application Proxy Group.

8. On the Configure Service Application Associations page, select the services that should be associated with this proxy (see Figure 3-55).

   Don't forget to scroll to the bottom of the page and click OK.

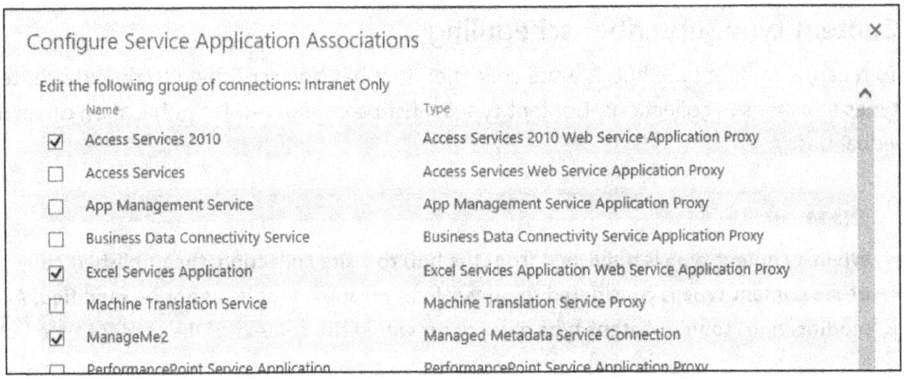

FIGURE 3-55 Configuring service applications.

9. The newly connected service applications appear on the Service Application Associations page, shown in Figure 3-56.

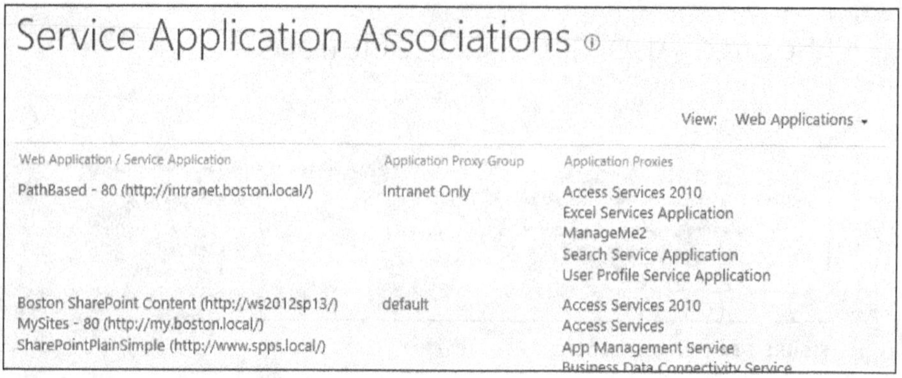

FIGURE 3-56 Completed application associations.

Configuring content type hub settings

Chapter 1 discussed the use of a content type hub within a SharePoint 2013 MMS application. You also created the relationship between the service application and a content type hub.

Content type subscriber scheduling

To recap, a content type hub is a site collection that has been specified to provide content types to other site collections. Content types must be configured for publication on an individual basis.

EXAM TIP

When a content type is published from the hub to a site collection, the published copy of the content type is considered to be "sealed," meaning that it cannot be modified. All modifications to this content type must occur within the context of the content type hub.

Publishing a newly created content type

The publication of content types stored in the hub is fully configurable from within the content type hub:

1. On the Content Type Hub page, select Site Settings (gear icon).

2. In the Web Designer Galleries section, select Site Content Types.

3. Select the link for your content type.

4. Select Manage Publishing For This Content Type.

5. The Content Type Publishing page appears (see Figure 3-57).

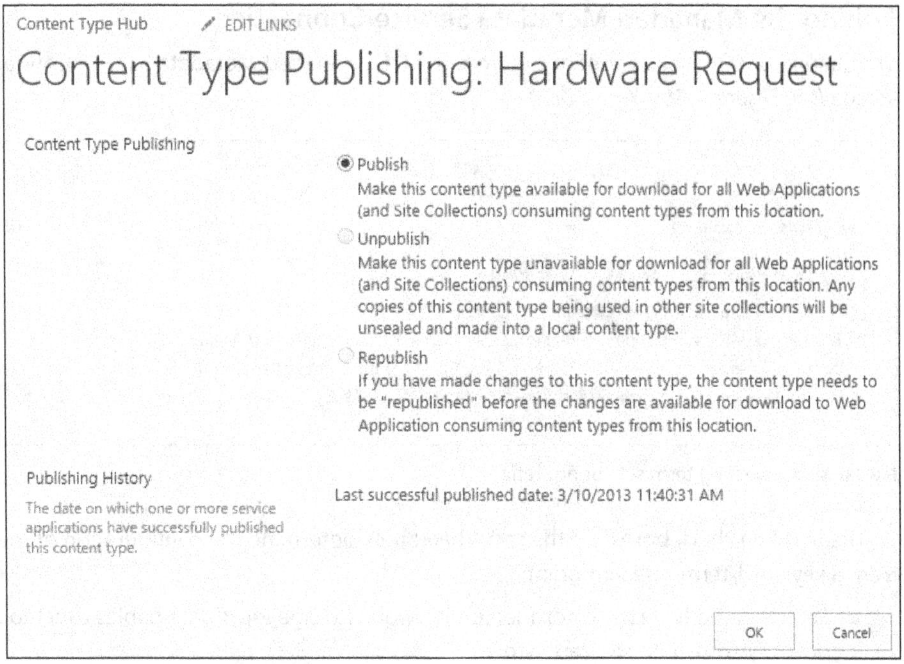

Content Type Hub   ✎ EDIT LINKS

Content Type Publishing: Hardware Request

Content Type Publishing

● Publish
Make this content type available for download for all Web Applications
(and Site Collections) consuming content types from this location.

○ Unpublish
Make this content type unavailable for download for all Web Applications
(and Site Collections) consuming content types from this location. Any
copies of this content type being used in other site collections will be
unsealed and made into a local content type.

○ Republish
If you have made changes to this content type, the content type needs to
be "republished" before the changes are available for download to Web
Application consuming content types from this location.

Publishing History

The date on which one or more service
applications have successfully published
this content type.

Last successful published date: 3/10/2013 11:40:31 AM

OK   Cancel

FIGURE 3-57 Content type publishing.

6. Choose from the following:

   A. Publish makes the content type available for use within all the web applications
   consuming content types from your hub.

   B. Unpublish makes the content type unavailable; also "unseals" each local copy of
   the content type.

   C. Republish publishes the newly updated changes to your content type.

> **IMPORTANT** **UNSEALING AND DISASSOCIATING CONTENT TYPES**
>
> Proceed with caution when you choose to unpublish a content type altogether. The act of
> unsealing the content type causes the content type in each site collection to become its
> own, freestanding entity. All changes made from that point on will be made within each
> distinct site collection.

7. Click OK to close this screen.

Configuring sharing term sets

A particular web application should have a default MMS application (known as the primary)
that enables users to enter and use keywords; this connection also provides the content hub
that is used for the web application.

Editing the Managed Metadata Service Connection

The sharing of term sets is configured from the Edit Managed Metadata Service Connection screen (see Figure 3-58).

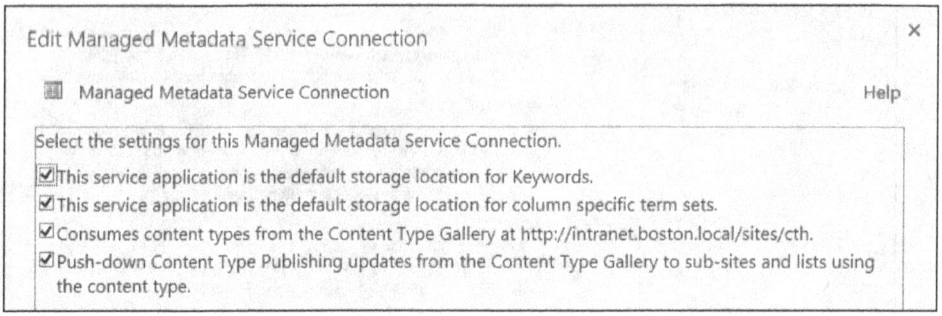

Edit Managed Metadata Service Connection   ×

    Managed Metadata Service Connection   Help

Select the settings for this Managed Metadata Service Connection.

☑ This service application is the default storage location for Keywords.
☑ This service application is the default storage location for column specific term sets.
☑ Consumes content types from the Content Type Gallery at http://intranet.boston.local/sites/cth.
☑ Push-down Content Type Publishing updates from the Content Type Gallery to sub-sites and lists using the content type.

FIGURE 3-58 Selecting term set configuration.

The first two check boxes are the focus here; they determine the configuration of the MMS from a keyword/term set standpoint:

- Selecting the first check box (default keyword storage location) enables users to store new keywords into this term store.

- Selecting the second check box (default term set location) enables site admins to create new term sets.

Web applications are often associated with more than one managed metadata web application; they can be used to create separate content type hubs. If you elect to have multiple web MMSs provided to a web application, leave these first two check boxes blank on all but the primary connection.

EXAM TIP

Do not make more than one connection the default keyword storage location for any one web app. And do not make more than one connection the default term set location for any one web application.

Planning and configuring content type propagation schedules

There are two types of timer jobs that control the flow and function of the content type hub:

- **Content Type Hub**   This is a singular job that controls the content type log maintenance and manages unpublished content types.

- **Content Type Subscriber**   If there are several web applications that are connected/proxied to the MMS, each is assigned a Content Type Subscriber job. This job retrieves content type packages from the hub and applies them to a local content type gallery.

Configuring the propagation schedule

The propagation of content types is controlled on a per-web application basis by the Content Type Subscriber timer job. To configure the propagation of a content type:

1. Open Central Administration and then select Monitoring.

2. On the Monitoring page, in the Timer Jobs section, select Review Job Definitions.

3. On the Job Definitions page, scroll down and select the Content Type Subscriber job for the intended web application.

4. Alter the Recurring Schedule for your job (see Figure 3-59).

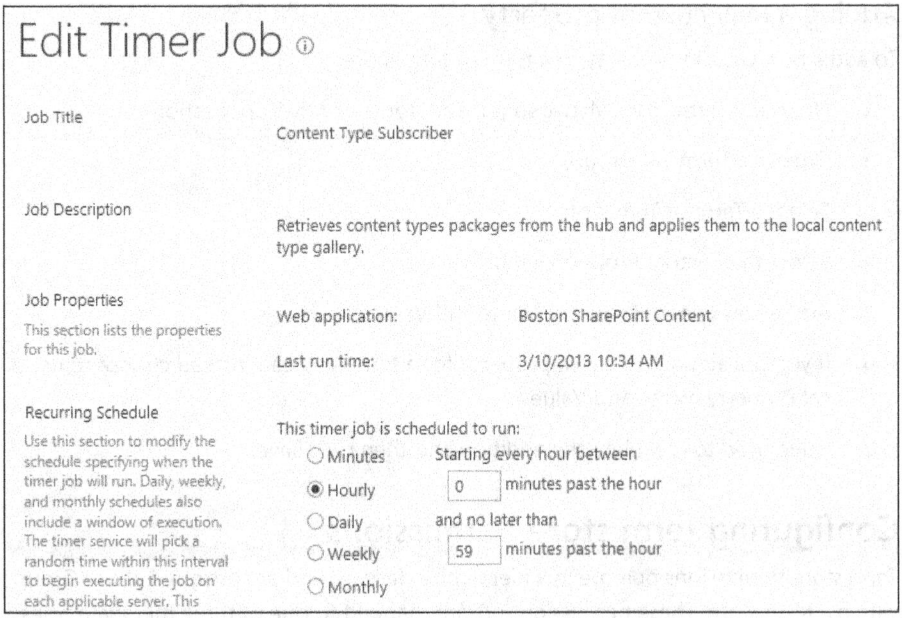

FIGURE 3-59 Altering the recurring schedule.

IMPORTANT **DISTRIBUTING THE SCHEDULE FOR TIMER JOBS**

The randomness of the time window is intentional and enables each SharePoint server in the farm to process the job within a certain window of time. This randomness is beneficial in that the farm can better balance the load caused by its timer jobs.

---

5. At the bottom of this page, you can choose one of the following options:

   A. Run Now starts the propagation cycle immediately.

   B. Disable disables the job (not recommended).

   C. OK accepts the changes you made to the propagation schedule.

   D. Cancel discards all the changes made to the propagation schedule.

Configuring custom properties

Custom properties can be added to an individual term or to a term set from within the Term Store Management Tool. These properties are useful for defining more-advanced term attributes, which can then be used to develop custom code solutions for displaying and sorting terms and term sets within a SharePoint 2013 installation. These properties can also be used in conjunction with the Term Property Web Part.

There are two distinct property types: shared and local. Local properties are available only for a particular term in a term set, whereas shared properties are useful on all reused or pinned instances of the term anywhere within the term store.

Adding a new custom property

To add a new custom property to a term or term store:

1. Open the Term Store Management Tool for your MMS application.

2. Expand a Term Set Group.

3. Select a Term or Term Set.

4. Select the Custom Properties tab.

5. Add a new Shared Property Name and Value.

6. If you are adding a custom property for a term, you can instead choose to use a Local Property Name and Value.

7. Select Add to complete the addition and then click Save.

Configuring term store permissions

Term store permissions operate in a hierarchical fashion and are assigned at the Group level within a term store. These permission sets are mapped to one of three metadata roles:

- Term Store Administrators can create new term set groups and assign users to the group manager or term store manager roles.

- Group Managers have contributor access and also can add users to the contributor role.

- Contributors have full permissions to edit terms and term set hierarchies within their term group.

EXAM TIP

Term store permissions for both Group Managers and Contributors are assigned at the term set group level. It is not possible to assign these permissions at the term set or individual term level.

Adding users to the Term Store Administrators role

The addition of new Term Store administrators is done at the Managed Metadata site level within the Term Store Management Tool.

1. Within Central Administration, select Application Management.
2. In the Service Applications section, select Manage Service Applications.
3. Select the link of your intended MMS application.
4. The General tab will appear for your MMS application. Add a new user into the Term Store Administrators box (see Figure 3-60).

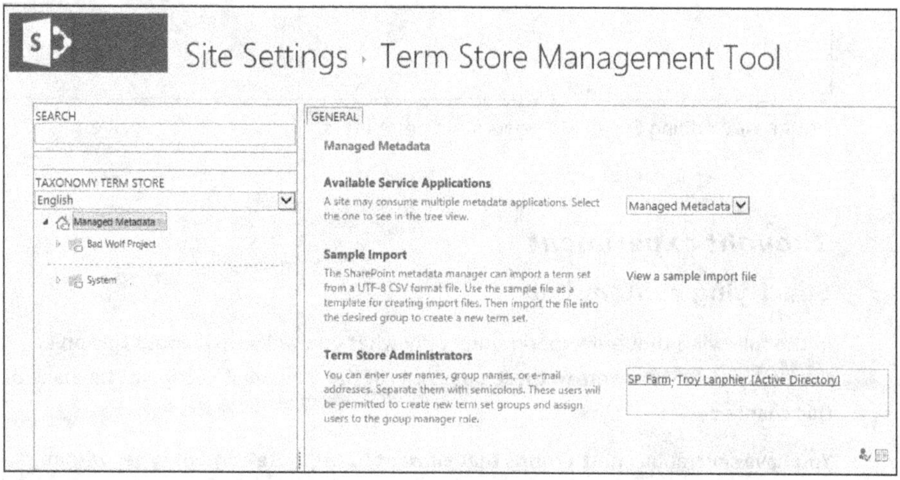

FIGURE 3-60 Adding a new Term Store Administrator.

5. Scroll to the bottom of the screen and click OK.

Adding users to Group Managers or Contributors roles

The addition of new Group Managers or Contributors is done at the term set Group level within the Term Store Management Tool.

1. Within Central Administration, select Application Management.
2. In the Service Applications section, select Manage Service Applications.
3. Select the link of your intended MMS application.

4. Choose the link for the term set group that you want to assign people to.

5. On the General Tab, you can now add Group Managers and/or Contributors (see Figure 3-61).

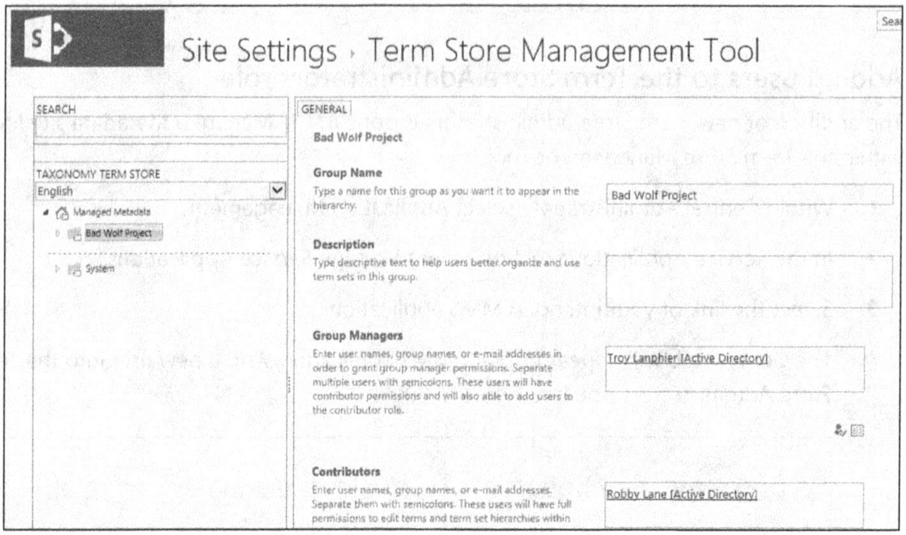

FIGURE 3-61 Adding Group Managers and Contributors.

Thought experiment

Specifying content hubs

In the following thought experiment, apply what you've learned about this objective. You can find answers to these questions in the "Answers" section at the back of this chapter.

You have several business groups that all want to promote content types within your farm. One of the key business requirements is that each business group must maintain its own content type hub.

How can you configure this arrangement?

Objective summary

- A single service application connection can be assigned to more than one proxy group at a time.
- A single web application can be assigned to only one proxy group at a time.
- A content type published from the content type hub to a site is considered "sealed" and cannot be altered.
- A content type that is unpublished "unseals" the content type on a site to which it was previously published.
- If multiple MMS Connections are applied to a single web app, only one MMS Connection should be the default keyword store and term set location.
- Content types are published by the Content Type Subscriber timer job.
- Term store roles include: Term Store Administrators, Group Managers, and Contributors.
- It is not possible to assign term store permissions at the term set or individual term levels.

Objective review

Answer the following questions to test your knowledge of the information in this objective. You can find the answers to these questions and explanations of why each answer choice is correct or incorrect in the "Answers" section at the end of this chapter.

1. Which of the following proxy/connection groups is used for one-off, ad hoc connectivity?

   A. Custom

   B. Default

   C. Direct

   D. Standby

2. Which of the following terms describes the status of a content type that has been published from the content type hub?

   A. Uncustomized

   B. Customized

   C. Sealed

   D. Unsealed

3. Which of the following terms describes the status of a content type that has been unpublished from the content type hub?

   A. Uncustomized

   B. Customized

C. Sealed

D. Unsealed

4. Which of the following MMS Connection options should be enabled for web applications that are already attached to another fully configured MMS Connection? (Choose all that apply.)

A. This Service Application Is The Default Storage Location For Keywords

B. This Service Application Is The Default Storage Location For Column Specific Term Sets

C. Consumes Content Types From The Content Type Gallery

D. Push-down Content Type Publishing Updates From The Content Type Gallery To Sub-Sites And Lists Using The Content Type

Objective 3.5: Create and configure a User Profile service (UPA) application

The User Profile service (UPA) application is a collection of databases and functionality focused on individual users in a SharePoint 2013 installation. This functionality can be limited in scope to a single farm or made available across multiple SharePoint farms in the enterprise.

This service is used to provide user profiles, profile synchronization with enterprise directory services, audiences, the My Site host and individual My Sites, and social notes and tagging.

> **This objective covers how to:**
> - Configure a UPA application.
> - Set up My Sites and My Site hosts.
> - Configure social permissions.
> - Plan and configure sync connections.
> - Configure profile properties.
> - Configure audiences.

Configuring a UPA

Configuring the UPA can be accomplished from either the Central Administration interface or Windows PowerShell cmdlets. Both configurations result in a series of three databases that are created along with the service application:

- Profile database stores profile information about individual users

- Synchronization database stores configuration and staging information for synchronizing profile data from enterprise directory services

- Social Tagging database stores social tags and notes associated with individual users' profile IDs

> **MORE INFO PLANNING WORKSHEETS FOR THE UPA**
>
> Because configuring the UPA can be complex, Microsoft provides a series of four worksheets to help configure this component. You can find them in the Microsoft Download Center at *http://www.microsoft.com/en-us/download/details.aspx?id=35404*.

Configuring the UPA from Central Administration

Configuring the UPA application from Central Administration will try to automatically associate the UPA with the default proxy group of the farm.

1. Manage Service Applications within Application Management.

2. In the Create group on the ribbon, from the New menu, select User Profile Service Application.

3. Assign a name to the new UPA.

4. In the Application Pool section, either select an existing application pool (one already created for services) or build a new application pool. Specify a managed account that should run this application pool (most often, this account runs all the service applications unless your security policy forbids it).

5. Type the configuration values for the Profile, Synchronization, and Social Tagging databases, using the following choices:

   A. Select an appropriate database name, following the conventions of your environment.

   B. For the authentication section, select Windows Authentication (recommended).

   C. If you are using mirroring, specify the name of your failover server.

6. Type the My Site host address and My Site Manage Path information.

7. You may not have this information yet. It's covered shortly and can be added in to the configuration after the UPA is created.

8. In the site naming section, choose a naming format that is best suited to your environment

9. Specify whether you want to associate the UPA with the default proxy group.

Configuring the UPA from Windows PowerShell

Configuring the UPA application from Windows PowerShell requires the use of two Windows PowerShell cmdlets:

- New-SPProfileServiceApplication enables you to specify the service application pool name and databases that you want to use for the new service application.

- New-SPProfileServiceApplicationProxy enables you to create a service application proxy/connection for use with the service application; this proxy is usually associated with the default proxy group.

EXAM TIP

Know how to specify a proxy group (including the default proxy group) in Windows PowerShell for a new service application.

Setting up My Sites and My Site hosts

By default, individual users can create their own My Sites from My Site hosts. This host is a specialized site collection that should be created at the root of a specialized web application.

Building the My Site host web application

Before a user can create a My Site, you must create a My Site host, which is a dedicated web application with a single site collection at its root.

> **IMPORTANT MY SITE, MY SITE PROVIDER, AND THE FARM CONFIGURATION WIZARD**
>
> If you create your farm and then run the Farm Configuration Wizard, it does not build the My Site host in its own web app. Instead, the My Site host exists as an explicit managed path under the "/my" URL. It causes all personal sites to be created under the main URL for the farm (for example, http://intranet.boston.local/my/personal/tlanphier). This is not a recommended configuration.

First, you have to create the new web application in which the My Site host will be located. The following example creates the new web application for the My Site host at http://my.boston.local:

1. Create a new web application from Central Administration using the following sample values (see Figure 3-62):

   A. Select the Create A New IIS Web site radio button.

   B. Name: MySites - 80.

   C. Port: 80 (unless you will be running your my sites over SSL at TCP Port 443).

   D. Type a host header value for the My Site (for example, my.boston.local).

E. This value has to be given to your DNS admin to build an entry that will point this FQDN to the farm's IP address.

F. Leave the default path unchanged: C:\inetpub\wwwroot\wss\VirtualDirectories\ my.boston.local80.

IIS Web Site	
Choose between using an existing IIS web site or create a new one to serve the Microsoft SharePoint Foundation application.	○ Use an existing IIS web site Default Web Site ▾
	● Create a new IIS web site Name
If you select an existing IIS web site, that web site must exist on all servers in the farm and have the same name, or this action will not succeed.	MySites - 80
	Port
	80
If you opt to create a new IIS web site, it will be automatically created on all servers in the farm. If an IIS setting that you wish to change is not shown here, you can use this option to create the basic site, then update it using the standard IIS tools.	Host Header
	my.boston.local
	Path
	wroot\wss\VirtualDirectories\my.boston.local80

FIGURE 3-62 IIS web site configuration.

2. Leave the Security Configuration, Claims Authentication Types, and Sign In Page URL sections unchanged.

3. Choose to create a new application pool or select one that is already in existence. If you choose to build a new app pool, you should use neither the setup nor the farm managed account, choosing instead to create a new one for web apps.

4. If you are using database mirroring, type a value for the Failover Database Server.

5. In the Service Application Connections section, choose a Service App Proxy (or you can choose [custom] and assign the connections/proxies one at a time).

6. Choose whether to join the Customer Experience Improvement Program and then click OK to build the new web app.

Building the site collection for the My Site host

Next, we need to build the My Site host. This is a special site collection that is created from the My Site Host template. Create a new site collection using the following sample values:

1. Web Application: http://my.boston.local.

2. Web Site Address: http://my.boston.local/.

3. It should be built at the root of the web application.

4. Note: Be sure that this selection does not point to a different managed path (such as /sites).

5. Select the My Site Host template from the Enterprise tab.

6. Click OK to complete the new site collection.

Enabling user self-provisioning of My Sites

After the My Site host and provider is set up, the web application for the My Sites provider must be configured to allow users to self-provision their own My Site.

1. In Application Management, select Manage Web Applications.

2. Select the My Site Web Application and then select Self-Service Site Creation on the ribbon.

3. In the Site Collections section, select the On radio button to allow users to create their own site collections. On the Quota drop-down menu, select Personal Site.

4. In the Start a Site section, choose one of the following:

   A. If you do not want users to have personal sites for site feeds, select the Be Hidden From Users radio button.

   B. If you want users to have personal sites for site feeds, select the Prompt Users To Create A Team Site Under: radio button. Do not change the URL (it should be pointing to the value you entered earlier; for example, http://my.boston.local/).

5. Click OK.

If you chose not to allow users to build personal sites, you are done. Otherwise, you need to provide permissions for users in the My Site web app.

1. In Permission Policy, add a Permission Policy Level named My Site User Permissions.

2. In Site Permissions, select the Grant option for Create Subsites and save the permission level.

3. In User Policy, select Add Users, All Zones.

4. Select Everyone to grant access to all your users.

Configuring My Sites in the UPA

The last step for My Sites is to add these settings to the UPA application:

1. Select the UPA application from Manage Service Applications (Application Management).

2. In the My Site Settings page, select My Site Settings and assign to it the following values:

   A. Preferred Search Center: (for example, http://intranet.boston.local/search).

   B. The My Site host created earlier: http://my.boston.local.

   C. If Exchange has been integrated with your farm, you can add the My Site host URL to Active Directory; otherwise this setting is grayed-out.

   D. Leave the Personal Site Location and Site Naming settings alone if they meet your requirements.

   E. Scroll down to the My Site Cleanup section.

   F. This field should be filled out. If a user leaves the company and his/her profile is deleted, this value is the person to whom their My Site is temporarily assigned for cleanup. If the Manager field is completed in Active Directory, this site is instead assigned to that individual.

   G. Click OK to complete the configuration.

Configuring social permissions

As in previous versions, a fully configured installation of SharePoint 2013 automatically provides full use of the personal and social features to everyone in the organization. These features are broken into three major components:

- Creating a personal site
- Following people and editing profiles
- Using tags and notes

If you want to alter these permissions, you can do so by managing the UPA application:

1. Manage the UPA application; in the People section, choose to Manage User Permissions.

2. Permissions will have automatically been granted to all authenticated users in your enterprise.

3. You can choose to allow or disallow any of the following components by clicking its check box (see Figure 3-63):

   A. Create Personal Site

   B. Follow People And Edit Profile

   C. Use Tags And Notes

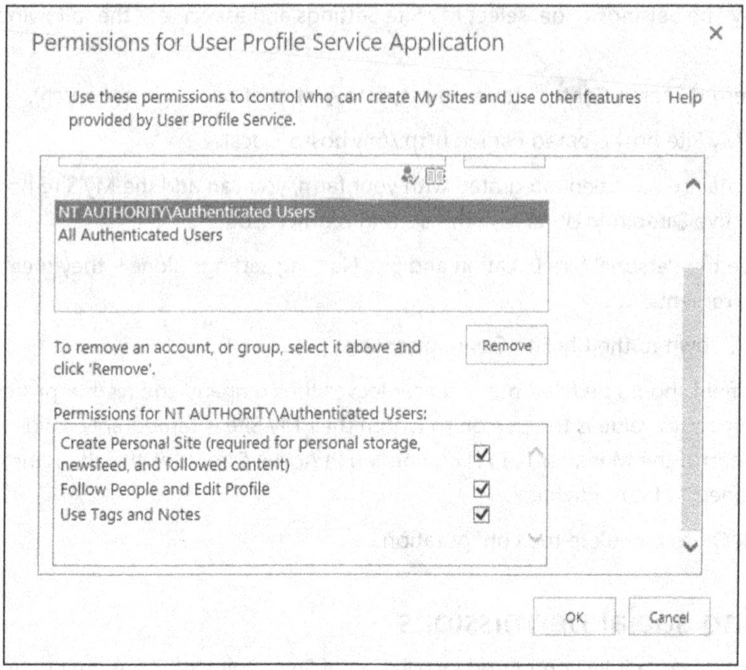

FIGURE 3-63 Permissions structure for UPA application.

4. Select the OK button to complete the configuration.

Planning and configuring sync connections

Synchronization between directory services and the SharePoint 2013 UPA application can happen in one of three ways:

- Using SharePoint profile synchronization
- Using SharePoint Active Directory import
- Enabling an external identity manager

> **IMPORTANT EXTERNAL IDENTITY MANAGEMENT**
>
> The third choice that appears in the menu, Enable External Identity Manager is useful if either you create a custom solution for creating user profiles or you want to remove user profile synchronization from the interface because your solution does not require it.

SharePoint profile synchronization

If you previously installed SharePoint 2010, you are no doubt familiar with the SharePoint profile synchronization process. This process enables fields from the SharePoint 2013 UPA to be mapped to directory service fields (often Active Directory).

This mapping can be configured as a two-way exchange, enabling metadata about users to be passed to and from the directory service from SharePoint 2013. Considered the "full-featured" option, it requires configuration on the part of the Active Directory administrator in order to be successful (if Active Directory is being used as the directory service).

MORE INFO ACTIVE DIRECTORY REPLICATION INSTRUCTIONS

Specific configuration instructions for configuring replication changes in Active Directory can be found in the TechNet article "Grant Active Directory Domain Services Permissions for Profile Synchronization in SharePoint Server 2013" at *http://technet.microsoft.com/en-us/library/hh296982.aspx*.

The following directory services are supported for this sync option:

- Active Directory Domain Services (AD DS) 2003 SP2 and upward
- Sun Java System Directory Server version 5.2
- Novell eDirectory version 8.7.3
- IBM Tivoli version 5.2

MORE INFO PROFILE SYNCHRONIZATION AND SUPPORTED DIRECTORY SERVICES

More information about profile synchronization for all these directory services can be found in the TechNet article "Plan Profile Synchronization for SharePoint Server 2013" at *http://technet.microsoft.com/en-us/library/ff182925.aspx*.

EXAM TIP

Although your domain administrator will be making the replication changes to Active Directory, you should be familiar with this process and also know what versions of Active Directory are supported for profile synchronization.

SharePoint Active Directory import

Considered the lighter-weight option for importing user profiles, the Active Directory Import option requires no configuration on the part of your Active Directory administrator. This operation is read-only, pulling information from Active Directory and populating it in the SharePoint UPA application.

This option, though not as complex or as powerful, does cause the import to be significantly faster. The lack of bidirectional functionality precludes this option from being useful for adding metadata about users from SharePoint profiles to Active Directory (such as phone numbers, addresses, and so on).

Configuring synchronization connections

Regardless of the import type chosen, you need to create synchronization connections for directory services to be synchronized to the UPA. This is done within the Synchronization Connections section of UPAs by the Create New Connection option.

Selecting this connection causes the Add New Synchronization Connection screen to appear (see Figure 3-64).

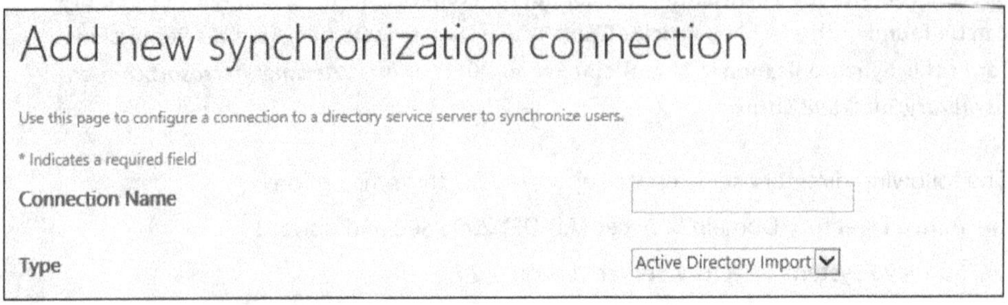

Add new synchronization connection

Use this page to configure a connection to a directory service server to synchronize users.

* Indicates a required field

Connection Name

Type   Active Directory Import ⌄

FIGURE 3-64 Add New Synchronization Connection name and type.

You specify the name and type for this connection; the connection type defaults to Active Directory Import unless you have specified other connection types (LDAP Directory, BCS, and so on).

Next, you configure the Connection Settings portion of the connection screen (see Figure 3-65).

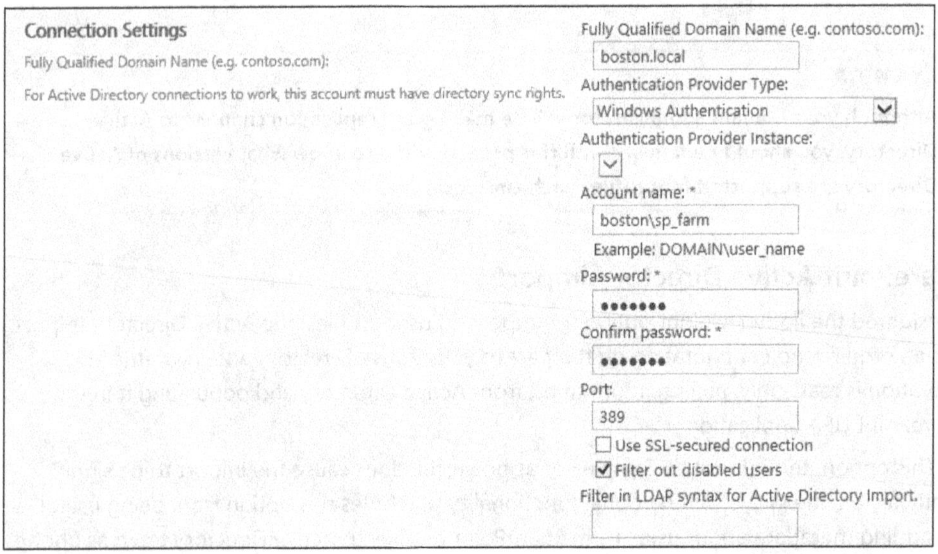

Connection Settings

Fully Qualified Domain Name (e.g. contoso.com):

For Active Directory connections to work, this account must have directory sync rights.

Fully Qualified Domain Name (e.g. contoso.com):
boston.local

Authentication Provider Type:
Windows Authentication ⌄

Authentication Provider Instance:
⌄

Account name: *
boston\sp_farm
Example: DOMAIN\user_name

Password: *
•••••••

Confirm password: *
•••••••

Port:
389
☐ Use SSL-secured connection
☑ Filter out disabled users
Filter in LDAP syntax for Active Directory Import.

FIGURE 3-65 Connection settings.

The Connection Settings fields enable you to specify the FQDN of the domain you are connecting to, along with the authentication types supported:

- Windows Authentication
- Forms Authentication
- Trusted Claims Provider Authentication

If you select either Forms or Claims Authentication, the Authentication Provider Instance populates with a list of available authentication providers.

Next you will be providing the credential that will access the directory store (user name and password). If you are using SharePoint profile synchronization (versus SharePoint Active Directory Import), the account you use for this step will require Replicate Directory permissions (or higher) in Active Directory.

The last fields within Connection Settings specify the TCP port used for the connection (389 for Active Directory, by default), whether you require an SSL-secured connection to your directory store, and whether you want to automatically filter out disabled users. At this point, you can also specify an LDAP query to further narrow the scope of your connection.

The Containers section of the Add New Synchronization Connection page enables you to focus your import on one or more OUs within a selected domain. Selecting the Populate Containers button fetches the directory structure, enabling you to select the OU(s) that you want to sync (see Figure 3-66).

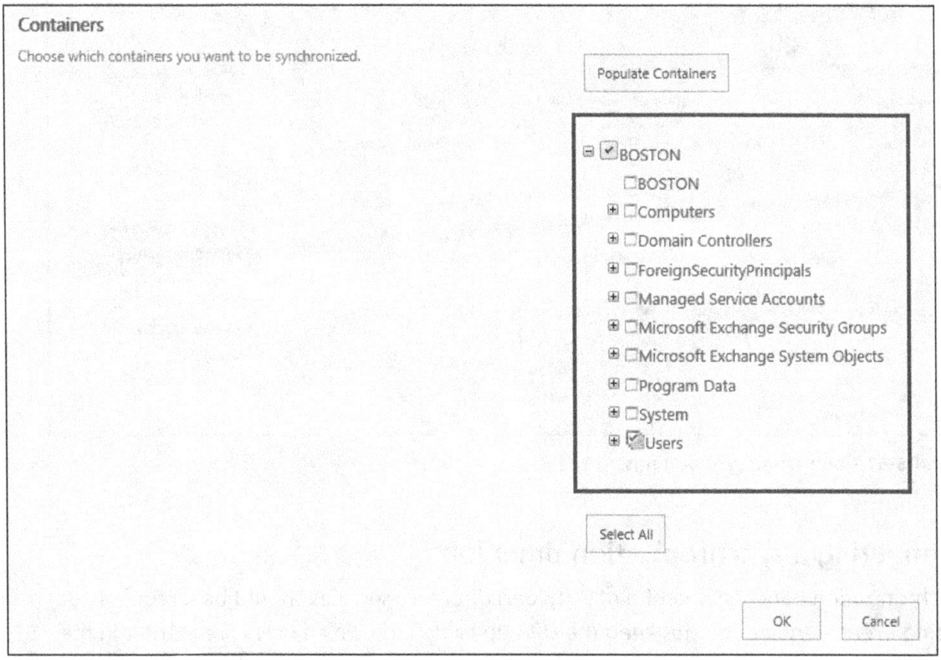

FIGURE 3-66 Directory containers.

Configuring synchronization settings

Synchronization settings configuration is accomplished within the Configure Synchronization Settings interface in the UPA application. There are three major options present in this configuration (see Figure 3-67):

- Synchronization Entities (radio button): Users And Groups or Users Only
- Synchronize BCS Connections (check box): Enables you to synchronize supplemental user profile information from Business Connectivity Services in addition to your standard import
- Synchronization Options:
    - Use SharePoint Profile Synchronization (heavyweight, bidirectional, slower)
    - User SharePoint Active Directory Import (lighter weight, unidirectional, faster)
    - Enable External Identity Manager (custom code or no sync required)

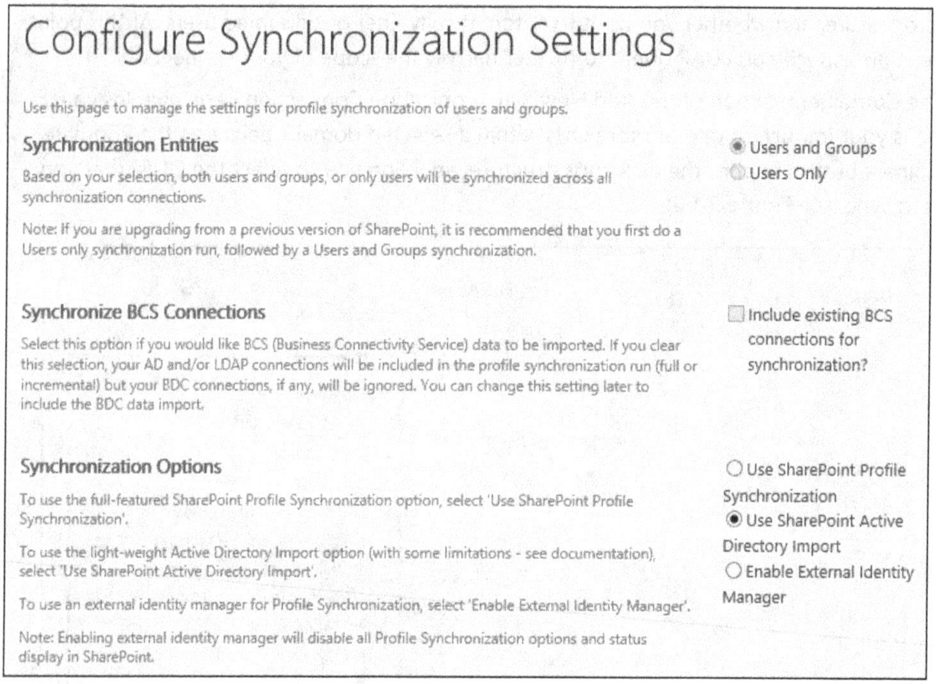

FIGURE 3-67 Configuring sync settings.

Configuring a synchronization timer job

Synchronization between SharePoint 2013 and directory services should be a regularly occurring event. Regular updates keep the UPA up to date on which users are current in the directory and any supporting metadata for those users that may have changed since the last import.

This update is maintained by the User Profile ActiveDirectory Import Job (see Figure 3-68).

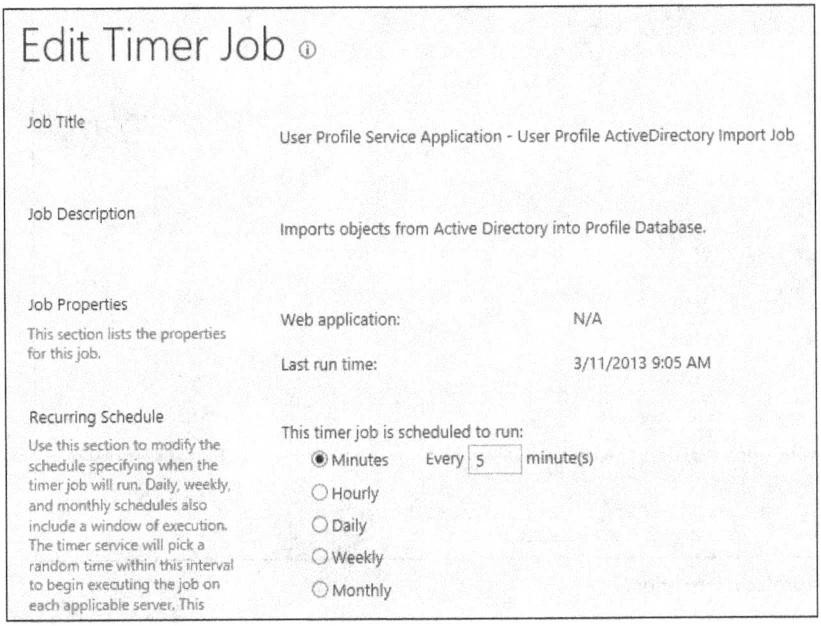

Edit Timer Job ⓘ

Job Title

User Profile Service Application - User Profile ActiveDirectory Import Job

Job Description

Imports objects from Active Directory into Profile Database.

Job Properties

This section lists the properties for this job.

Web application: N/A

Last run time: 3/11/2013 9:05 AM

Recurring Schedule

Use this section to modify the schedule specifying when the timer job will run. Daily, weekly, and monthly schedules also include a window of execution. The timer service will pick a random time within this interval to begin executing the job on each applicable server. This

This timer job is scheduled to run:

- ⦿ Minutes   Every 5   minute(s)
- ◯ Hourly
- ◯ Daily
- ◯ Weekly
- ◯ Monthly

FIGURE 3-68 User profile import timer job.

This timer job is identical to most, enabling you to specify a schedule on which the job should be run.

Configuring profile properties

The UPA application functionality is highly extensible; everything from custom code to BCS can be used to both input and output information from this component. As part of this extensibility, profile properties can be altered (and even added), providing much more detail about users in the enterprise.

Properties in a user profile

There are dozens of properties (93 by default, to be precise) about each user in SharePoint 2013; information contained in these properties varies in scope from system-required fields (security identifier [SID], account, claims, and other pieces of information) to more user-friendly metadata about users, such as their names and phone numbers. A sample user profile is shown in Figure 3-69.

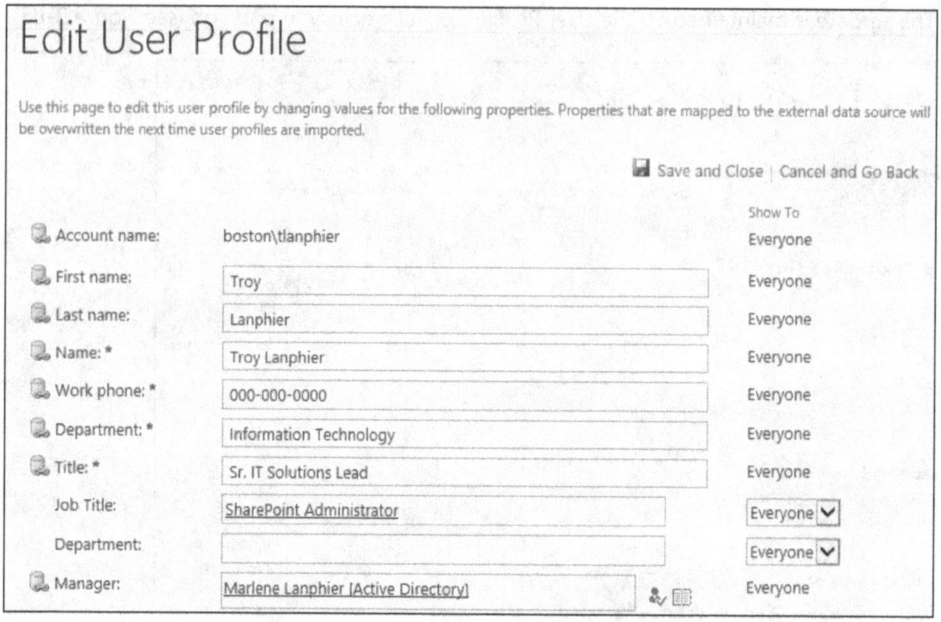

Edit User Profile

Use this page to edit this user profile by changing values for the following properties. Properties that are mapped to the external data source will be overwritten the next time user profiles are imported.

🖫 Save and Close | Cancel and Go Back

		Show To
🗄 Account name:	boston\tlanphier	Everyone
🗄 First name:	Troy	Everyone
🗄 Last name:	Lanphier	Everyone
🗄 Name: *	Troy Lanphier	Everyone
🗄 Work phone: *	000-000-0000	Everyone
🗄 Department: *	Information Technology	Everyone
🗄 Title: *	Sr. IT Solutions Lead	Everyone
Job Title:	SharePoint Administrator	Everyone ⌄
Department:		Everyone ⌄
🗄 Manager:	Marlene Lanphier [Active Directory] 👤 🏢	Everyone

FIGURE 3-69 User profile information.

In this profile, you can see the following:

- Property fields (Name, Work phone, Department, and so on)
- Active Directory mappings (indicated by the cylinder and link icon)
- Show To field

This last field is perhaps the most important. This field chooses one of five social levels that can be allowed to view a field (Only Me, My Colleagues, My Team, My Manager, and Everyone). The selection of a social level allows some profile information to be available to some, but not all, of your social levels. In Figure 3-69, you can see that some of these fields are selectable by the user (Job Title and Department), whereas others are not (Name, Work Phone).

As an example, consider your personal cell phone number. Odds are that some of your colleagues have it, and perhaps your manager does, too. But there would be no need (and this might even go against corporate policy) to have this number freely available to everyone in your organization.

Configuring profile properties

Using the Edit User Profile Property menu item from within Manage User Properties, you can change several property settings for each profile item. Fortunately, because there are dozens of choices and dozens of profile properties, several of these values are already preconfigured out of the box.

To configure a profile property:

1. Within the UPA application, select the Manage User Properties menu item.

2. Properties are grouped by sections, including the following:

    A. Basic Information (name, work phone, title, and so on)

    B. Contact Information (work e-mail, mobile phone, home phone, and so on)

    C. Details (past projects, skills, interests, and so on)

    D. Delegation (empty by default)

    E. Newsfeed Settings (e-mail notifications, people I follow)

    F. Language and Region (time zone, define your work week, and so on)

    G. Custom Properties (enables you to add new properties)

3. To alter a profile property, simply click its drop-down menu and click Edit. Most often, the items you will interact with are the mapping to Active Directory and the Policy Setting, which determines whether a user can change the setting and what the default privacy setting is.

> **IMPORTANT SEARCHABLE PROPERTIES**
>
> All these properties are searchable (but also security trimmed) within SharePoint, enabling the enterprise to track specific information such as individual certifications, status, and so on about a staff member.

Configuring audiences

Audiences are a mechanism in SharePoint that enables an enterprise to target specific content to users. This content can include links, lists, navigation, and other components.

A user's function within the company, membership in a security group, organizational hierarchy, and other relationships can be compiled within the UPA to enable content to be targeted to the appropriate user.

Security versus audiencing

At first glance, security and audiences might appear to be the same thing. A hyperlink that is not secured will not be seen by a particular user (or users). If you instead configure an audience on that very same hyperlink and do not include that same user or group of users in the compiled audience, the result appears to be the same: The link is not visible to those users.

This is where the similarity ends, however. If the link were secured, there would be no way to browse for the link or search for the link (for that group of users). On the other hand, a link that is targeted to a specific audience could be easily discovered via search (although it may not be as easy to find by browsing) for those same users.

So an audience is a promotional mechanism, a way to cause an item to appear when it is appropriate to the group of users viewing it. For example, if you have a global SharePoint installation, you more than likely have a different listing of holidays for each office in your enterprise. You can create an audience for each office and promote the appropriate holiday listing to that audience.

Managing audiences

New and existing audiences can be created and managed from the Manage Audiences link. Selecting this link causes the View Audiences page to appear (see Figure 3-70). From here, new audiences can be created or altered.

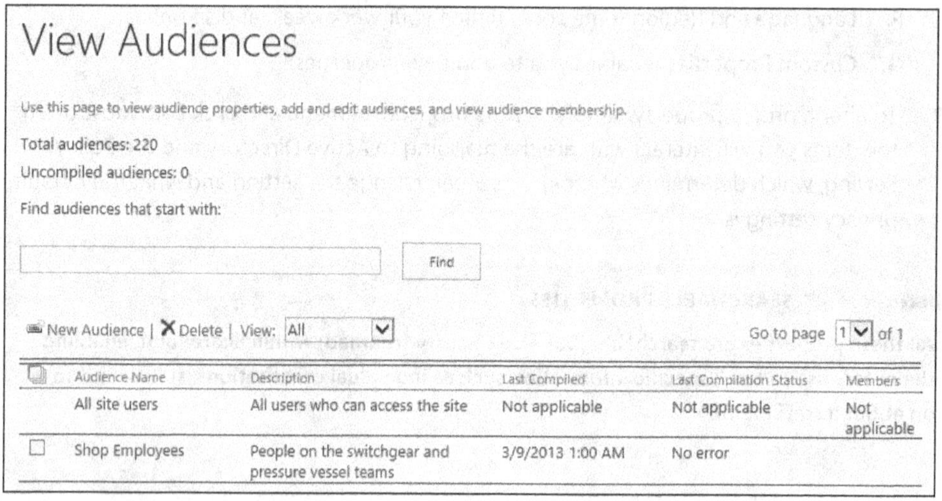

FIGURE 3-70 Viewing existing audiences.

Audiences are rule-based, meaning that they are compiled based on criteria you select during configuration. For instance, if you were to build an audience called Shop Employees (shown in Figure 3-70), you could build the audience to satisfy some or all the rules you specify (see Figure 3-71).

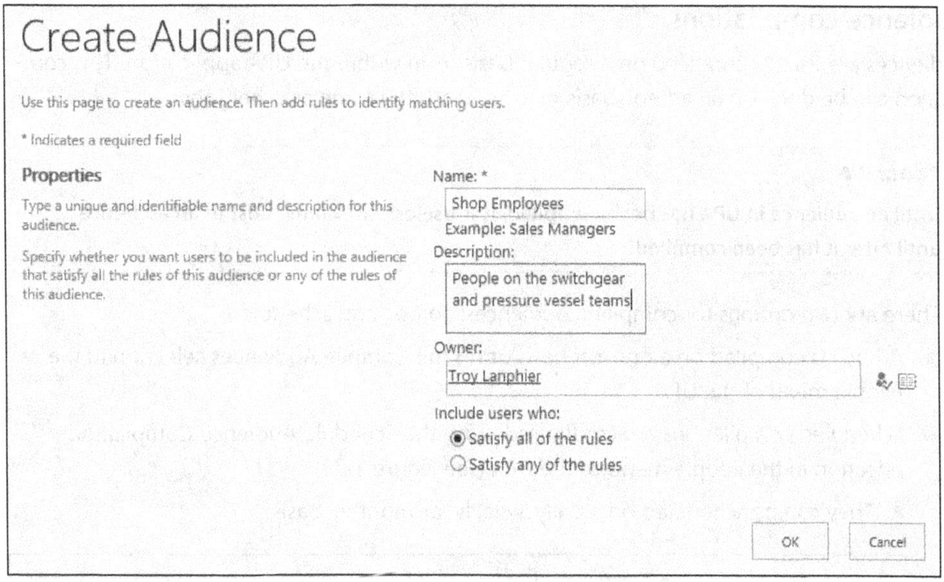

Create Audience

Use this page to create an audience. Then add rules to identify matching users.

* Indicates a required field

Properties

Type a unique and identifiable name and description for this audience.

Specify whether you want users to be included in the audience that satisfy all the rules of this audience or any of the rules of this audience.

Name: *

Shop Employees

Example: Sales Managers

Description:

People on the switchgear and pressure vessel teams

Owner:

Troy Lanphier

Include users who:

- Satisfy all of the rules
- Satisfy any of the rules

OK   Cancel

FIGURE 3-71 Creating a new audience.

From here, you can proceed to adding Operands, Operators, and Values to the rule. In this case, we look for users who report under Robby Lane, the shop manager (see Figure 3-72).

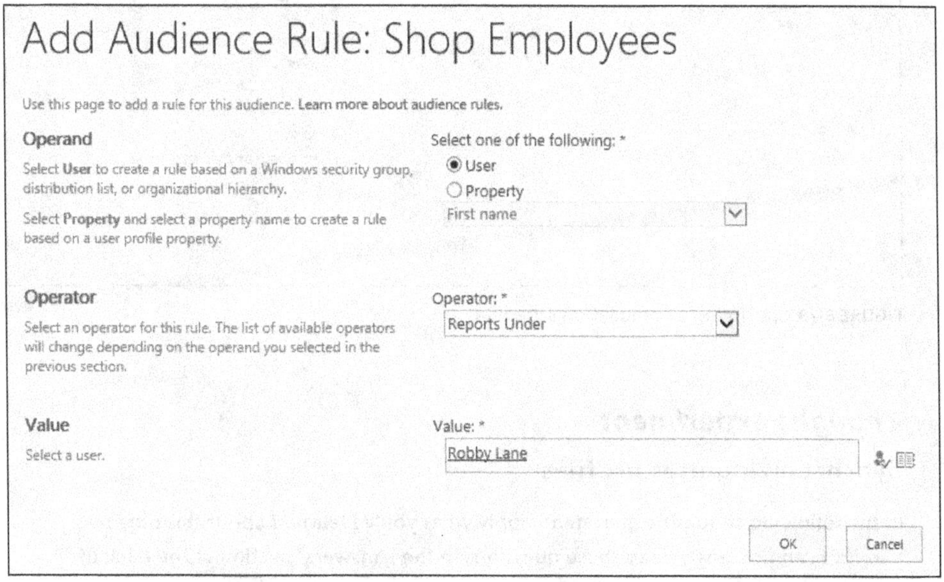

Add Audience Rule: Shop Employees

Use this page to add a rule for this audience. Learn more about audience rules.

Operand

Select **User** to create a rule based on a Windows security group, distribution list, or organizational hierarchy.

Select **Property** and select a property name to create a rule based on a user profile property.

Select one of the following: *

- User
- Property

First name

Operator

Select an operator for this rule. The list of available operators will change depending on the operand you selected in the previous section.

Operator: *

Reports Under

Value

Select a user.

Value: *

Robby Lane

OK   Cancel

FIGURE 3-72 Operands, operators, and values.

Audience compilations

Audiences are usually compiled on a regular basis from within the UPA application. This compilation can be done on an ad hoc basis or scheduled (the same as other jobs).

EXAM TIP

Until an audience in UPA has been compiled, it is useless; no values exist in an audience until after it has been compiled.

There are two options for compiling audiences: ad hoc and scheduled.

- Ad hoc is compiled on a one-off basis using the Compile Audiences selection in the People menu of the UPA.
- Scheduled compilations are configured using the Schedule Audience Compilation selection in the People menu of the UPA (see Figure 3-73).
    - They can be scheduled on a daily, weekly, or monthly basis.

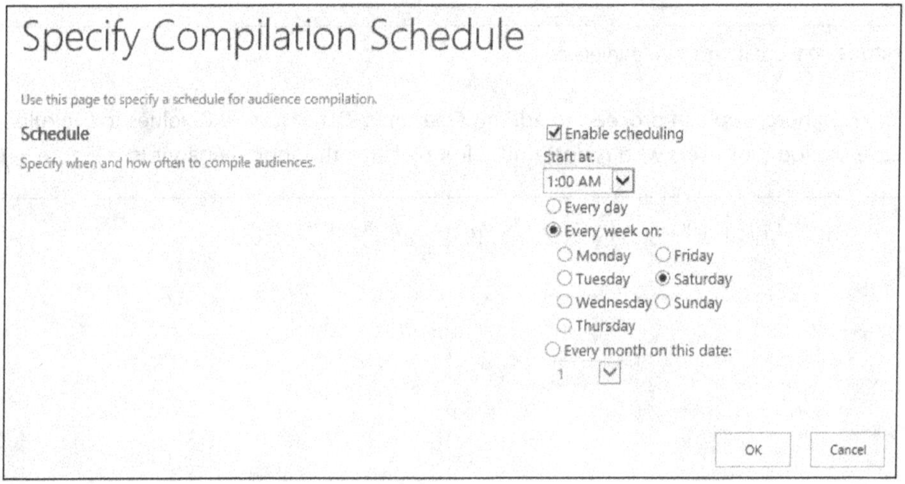

Specify Compilation Schedule

Use this page to specify a schedule for audience compilation.

Schedule

Specify when and how often to compile audiences.

☑ Enable scheduling

Start at:

[1:00 AM ▾]

○ Every day

⦿ Every week on:

   ○ Monday   ○ Friday

   ○ Tuesday   ⦿ Saturday

   ○ Wednesday ○ Sunday

   ○ Thursday

○ Every month on this date:

   1 [▾]

[OK]   [Cancel]

FIGURE 3-73 Specifying a compilation schedule.

Thought experiment
Synchronizing user profiles

In the following thought experiment, apply what you've learned about this objective. You can find answers to these questions in the "Answers" section at the back of this chapter.

You want to configure the UPA to synchronize user profile information from Active Directory. You intend to use profile synchronization versus the more basic Active Directory import. What actions might you recommend from a metadata standpoint?

Objective summary

- The UPA can be provisioned from within Central Administration or Windows Power-Shell.

- Configuring the farm using the Farm Configuration Wizard causes the My Site host to be installed beneath the /my Managed Path, rather than in its own web application.

- The My Site host is a custom template that should be installed at the root site of a web application for My Site use.

- If permitted to do so, users can self-provision their own My Site (Personal Site).

- The Manager field is used as the secondary site collection administrator for a user's My Site; if that person leaves, the manager is assigned permissions to the content after the user's account is disabled.

- Social permissions include Create a Personal Site, Follow People And Edit Profile, and Use Tags And Notes.

- There are two sync connection types present in SharePoint 2013: profile synchronization (more advanced), and Active Directory import (more basic).

- Profile synchronization can be configured against Active Directory, Sun Java Directory Server, Novell eDirectory, and IBM Tivoli.

- Active Directory import can use the following authentication types: Windows Authentication, Forms Authentication, and Trusted Claims Provider Authentication.

- An external identity manager can also be used for synchronization, but this would require custom development efforts.

- Audiencing does not provide any sort of security functionality.

- Audiences generated in UPAs must be compiled before use (preferably using a regularly scheduled job).

Objective review

Answer the following questions to test your knowledge of the information in this objective. You can find the answers to these questions and explanations of why each answer choice is correct or incorrect in the "Answers" section at the end of this chapter.

1. Which of the following directory services are supported for use with SharePoint 2013? (Choose all that apply.)

    A. Active Directory Domain Services 2000

    B. Sun Java System Directory Server 5.2

    C. Novell eDirectory version 8.7.3

    D. IBM Tivoli version 5.2

    E. All of the above

2. Which of the following authentication types is supported for use with SharePoint Active Directory import? (Choose all that apply.)

   A. Windows authentication

   B. Basic authentication

   C. Forms authentication

   D. Trusted Claims Provider authentication

3. Which is the correct TCP port used with Active Directory imports?

   A. TCP 1433

   B. TCP 80

   C. TCP 3389

   D. TCP 389

4. You have an audience that is working, but it displays stale or incomplete expected membership information. Which of the following items should you check?

   A. Audience rules

   B. Timer job for the synchronization service

   C. Compilation schedule

   D. All of the above

Chapter summary

- The Application Server Role and Web Server Role are required to prior to installing SharePoint binaries on a server.

- SharePoint requires that the supporting SQL Server instance have the max degree of parallelism property set to 1.

- A service application proxy can be associated with multiple proxy groups.

- Continuous crawls are available only for use with SharePoint sites.

- Content types that are published are considered to be "sealed" and cannot be modified.

- Term store permissions for Group Managers and Contributors are assigned only at the term set group level.

- Audiences created from within UPAs must be compiled prior to use.

Answers

This section contains the solutions to the thought experiments and answers to the lesson review questions in this chapter.

Objective 3.1: Thought experiment

For an environment that requires this level of control, you might decide that all configurations should be accomplished from a file share on the client network. Downloads of the SharePoint installation media and the supporting prerequisites can be placed in this file share.

A decision can be made regarding the updates that are supported for this installation and they can be applied to the updates folder, from oldest to newest.

Another folder can be created in in the share that lists a series of Windows PowerShell scripts for the installation of each tier and function of server (web tier, application tier, and so on).

Objective 3.1: Review

1. **Correct answers:** B, D

   A. **Incorrect:** There is no such cmdlet.

   B. **Correct:** Prerequisiteinstaller.exe is a command line installer from the SharePoint media that will download, configure, and install all the prerequisites for a Share-Point installation to a server, including the Application Role and the Web Server Role.

   C. **Incorrect:** There is no such cmdlet.

   D. **Correct:** When used to install the correct features, the Add-WindowsFeature cmd-let will install both the Application Role and Web Server Role.

2. **Correct answer:** B

   A. **Incorrect:** Setting the max degree of parallelism to 0 causes SQL to use a portion of the available processors to run a single statement (up to 64 total, depending on the edition of SQL server used).

   B. **Correct:** 1 is the proper setting for the max degree of parallelism for use with SharePoint and suppresses parallel plan generation in SQL.

   C. **Incorrect:** Although you could count the number of cores and manually specify that number as the max degree of parallelism, it would not be the correct value for use with SharePoint.

    D. **Incorrect:** This setting has nothing to do with the amount of RAM available to a system. Although you could count the number of cores and manually specify that number as the max degree of parallelism, it would not be the correct value for use with SharePoint.

3. **Correct answer:** D

    A. **Incorrect:** There is no such command.

    B. **Incorrect:** Prerequisiteinstaller.exe downloads and configures SharePoint prerequisites.

    C. **Incorrect:** There is no such command.

    D. **Correct:** Regardless of the language wanted, all language packs install using the SharePoint Languagepack.exe command. From that point on, all dialogue is in the language of the pack chosen.

4. **Correct answer:** B

    A. **Incorrect:** Active Users and Computers is used to administer the Active Directory structure.

    B. **Correct:** ADSI Edit is used to build the SCP container in Active Directory.

    C. **Incorrect:** There is no such cmdlet.

    D. **Incorrect:** There is no such cmdlet.

Objective 3.2: Thought experiment

SMTP would need to be configured in the SharePoint environment. Due to the sales team's requirements, the drop box e-mail could potentially receive a lot of spam and the occasional virus. You would most likely choose the Advanced connection scenario, requiring the Exchange administrator to create both Send and Receive connectors in Exchange.

Objective 3.2: Review

1. **Correct answer:** D

    A. **Incorrect:** Although a supported scenario, Basic provides no spam filtering or virus protection because incoming e-mail is not routed through an Exchange server.

    B. **Incorrect:** There is no such incoming e-mail scenario in SharePoint.

    C. **Incorrect:** There is no such incoming e-mail scenario in SharePoint.

    D. **Correct:** The Advanced scenario routes incoming e-mail first through Exchange before arriving at the SharePoint server. This configuration provides all the spam filtering and antivirus benefits Exchange has to offer.

2. **Correct answer:** A

   A. **Correct:** This cmdlet is the correct one for use in creating a new proxy group.

   B. **Incorrect:** The Get-SPServiceApplicationProxyGroup cmdlet is used to retrieve a listing of proxy groups.

   C. **Incorrect:** The Get-SPServiceApplicationProxy cmdlet is used to retrieve information about a service applications proxy.

   D. **Incorrect:** The Add-SPServiceApplicationProxyGroupMember cmdlet is used to add a new service application proxy to a proxy group.

3. **Correct answer:** D

   A. **Incorrect:** There is no such cmdlet.

   B. **Incorrect:** Prerequisiteinstaller.exe downloads and configures SharePoint prerequisites.

   C. **Incorrect:** There is no such command.

   D. **Correct:** The Set-SPDesignerSettings cmdlet is used to administer SPD settings for a given web app.

4. **Correct answer:** C

   A. **Incorrect:** There is no such cmdlet.

   B. **Incorrect:** There is no such cmdlet.

   C. **Correct:** The New-SPWOPIBinding cmdlet established the relationship between the SharePoint farm and the Office Web Apps instance. An easy way to remember the order is that the SharePoint farm is always connecting to the Office Web Apps farm.

   D. **Incorrect:** There is no such cmdlet.

Objective 3.3: Thought experiment

The additional load on the crawl and content processing components of your farm may cause you to add new servers in the application tier to meet the additional demand. Because you want to maintain the ever-growing index, you can alter the search topology by cloning the existing topology, altering the clone, and then switching it to be the active topology.

Objective 3.3: Review

1. **Correct answer:** D

   A. **Incorrect:** The index cannot be mirrored.

   B. **Incorrect:** There is no way to back up the search topology.

   C. **Incorrect:** The index cannot be cloned.

   D. **Correct:** Cloning the search topology enables its alteration; after it is configured, it can become the active topology.

2. **Correct answers:** A, B

   A. **Correct:** Lotus Notes is directly supported as a SharePoint Server 2013 content source.

   B. **Correct:** Documentum is directly supported as a SharePoint Server 2013 content source.

   C. **Incorrect:** PeopleSoft data is not directly supported as a SharePoint Server 2013 content source, although you may be able to crawl it via BCS.

   D. **Incorrect:** SAP data is not directly supported as a SharePoint Server 2013 content source, although you may be able to crawl it via BCS.

3. **Correct answers:** B, C

   A. **Incorrect:** There is no such crawl type in SharePoint Server 2013.

   B. **Correct:** Incremental crawls cannot be run alongside continuous crawls.

   C. **Correct:** Continuous crawls cannot be run alongside incremental crawls.

   D. **Incorrect:** Full crawls can be run alongside either incremental or continuous crawls.

4. **Correct answer:** B

   A. **Incorrect:** Disabling the crawls would result in the index becoming stale over time.

   B. **Correct:** Increasing the continuous crawl interval would ease the traffic traversing the WAN to this content source.

   C. **Incorrect:** Running a full crawl every evening may be functional, but would not keep the index as fresh as possible throughout the day.

   D. **Incorrect:** Decreasing the continuous crawl interval would result in an increase in traffic going across the WAN, potentially causing an outage for this location.

Objective 3.4: Thought experiment

Each content type hub could be stored in a distinct MMS application. The proxy for each MMS application could be connected to the web application for your site, but you would need to ensure that only one MMS app (probably none of the Business Unit MMS apps) hosts the keyword store and the term set location.

Objective 3.4: Review

1. **Correct answer:** A

   A. **Correct:** The custom connection is used to assign service application connections on a one-off basis.

   B. **Incorrect:** The default connection is used by default for all connections.

   C. **Incorrect:** There is no such connection group OOB.

   D. **Incorrect:** There is no such connection group OOB.

2. **Correct answer:** C

   A. **Incorrect:** The term "Uncustomized" does not describe the status of a published content type.

   B. **Incorrect:** The term "Customized" does not describe the status of a published content type.

   C. **Correct:** The term "Sealed" describes the status of a published content type.

   D. **Incorrect:** The term "Unsealed" does not describe the status of a published content type.

3. **Correct answer:** D

   A. **Incorrect:** The term "Uncustomized" does not describe the status of a published content type.

   B. **Incorrect:** The term "Customized" does not describe the status of a published content type.

   C. **Incorrect:** The term "Sealed" does not describe the status of a published content type.

   D. **Correct:** The term "Unsealed" describes the status of a published content type.

4. **Correct answers:** C, D

   A. **Incorrect:** Only one connected MMS should be the default storage location for keywords.

   B. **Incorrect:** Only one connected MMS should be the default storage location for column-specific term sets.

C. Correct: The content type gallery within each MMS can provide content type functionality.

D. Correct: The content type gallery within each MMS can provide content type functionality.

Objective 3.5: Thought experiment

The Manager field should be filled out in Active Directory; this field is used for the organization chart functionality as well as the disposition of My Sites for users who have left the company. Next, a review of the OOB user properties might be in order, deciding which of the fields would be suitable for one way versus two way synchronization with Active Directory. Finally, you might work with your Active Directory administrator to grant the replication permissions discussed in the article "Grant Active Directory Domain Services Permissions for Profile Synchronization in SharePoint Server 2013" at *http://technet.microsoft.com/en-us/library/hh296982.aspx*.

Objective 3.5: Review

1. **Correct answers:** B, C, D

   A. Incorrect: Active Directory Domain Services 2003 SP2 is the minimum level required for use with SharePoint 2013.

   B. Correct: This directory service is supported.

   C. Correct: This directory service is supported.

   D. Correct: This directory service is supported.

   E. Incorrect: Not all these directory services are supported.

2. **Correct answers:** A, C, D

   A. Correct: Windows Authentication is supported.

   B. Incorrect: Basic Authentication is not supported.

   C. Correct: Forms Authentication is supported.

   D. Correct: Trusted Claims Provider Authentication is supported.

3. **Correct answer:** D

   A. Incorrect: TCP 1433 is used with SQL Server default connections.

   B. Incorrect: TCP 80 is used with HTTP connections.

   C. Incorrect: TCP 3389 is used with RDP connections.

   D. Correct: TCP 389 is used with Active Directory connections.

4. **Correct answer:** D

    A. **Incorrect:** This is only one of the items to check.

    B. **Incorrect:** This is only one of the items to check.

    C. **Incorrect:** This is only one of the items to check.

    D. **Correct:** All of the above.

## CHAPTER 4

Create and configure web applications and site collections

After a new farm has been configured and provisioned, the next step is to start building web content. This content is placed within a series of site collections, stored in one or more content databases, and then presented via Internet Information Services (IIS).

After the site collections are created, security can be applied; this security enables proper access to content. Permissions-trimmed search then enables users to quickly locate appropriate content.

Some users may instead prefer to browse content from the site; effective taxonomy design by the SharePoint administration team allows for the navigation of content at a high level as well as the refinement of individual items on a site.

Objectives in this chapter:
- Objective 4.1: Provision and configure web applications
- Objective 4.2: Create and maintain site collections
- Objective 4.3: Manage site and site collection security
- Objective 4.4: Manage search
- Objective 4.5: Manage taxonomy

Objective 4.1: Provision and configure web applications

The web applications that support your SharePoint installation are the first component that your users encounter. An incorrectly configured web application can vary in experience from being entirely nonfunctional (misconfigured authentication mechanisms) to being functional but inconsistent (in the case of poorly configured alternate access mappings).

Configuring this level of the farm also becomes your first effort at maintaining effective security and governance mechanisms.

> **This objective covers how to:**
> - Create managed paths.
> - Configure HTTP throttling.
> - Configure list throttling.
> - Configure Alternate Access Mapping (AAM).
> - Configure an authentication provider.
> - Configure SharePoint Designer (SPD) settings.

Creating managed paths

As discussed in Chapter 1, "Design a SharePoint topology," managed paths are a mechanism that enables you to create a uniform navigational structure that relates multiple site collections together.

There are two distinct types of managed paths: wildcard and explicit:

- Wildcard managed paths enable one site collection to be the "implied" parent of several site collections using a wildcard path value (for example, http://URL/path/Site1, http://URL/path/Site2).
- Explicit managed paths enable one and only one site collection to be nested directly beneath another within a navigational structure (for example, http://URL/Site1).

EXAM TIP

There are a supported maximum number of managed paths per web application (20). Although it is possible to exceed this number, doing so places an extra processing load on the web tier servers in your farm.

Managed paths can either be created from within Central Administration or from Windows PowerShell (presumably as part of an automated deployment).

> *IMPORTANT* **CREATING MANAGED PATHS IN A HOST NAMED SITE COLLECTION**
>
> Creating a new managed path for a path-based site collection can be done via Central Administration without a problem. If you want to create a managed path within a host named site collection, however, you will be doing so using Windows PowerShell.

Create a managed path (Central Administration)

Managed paths are defined on a per–web application basis. From Central Administration, do the following:

1. Open Application Management.

2. On the Application Management page, select the Manage Web Applications link.

3. Select the web application you want to create managed paths for (click its line; for example, http://intranet.boston.local/).

4. When the ribbon activates, select the Managed Paths icon (see Figure 4-1).

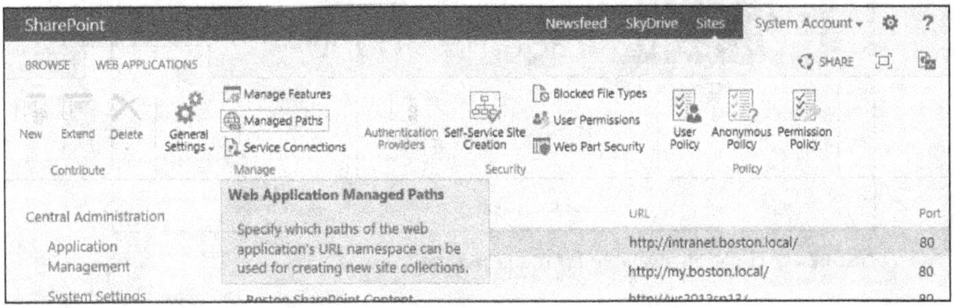

FIGURE 4-1 Selecting Managed Paths in the ribbon.

5. The Defined Managed Paths page appears, showing all existing paths. In the Add A New Path section, specify the name of a new managed path (see Figure 4-2).

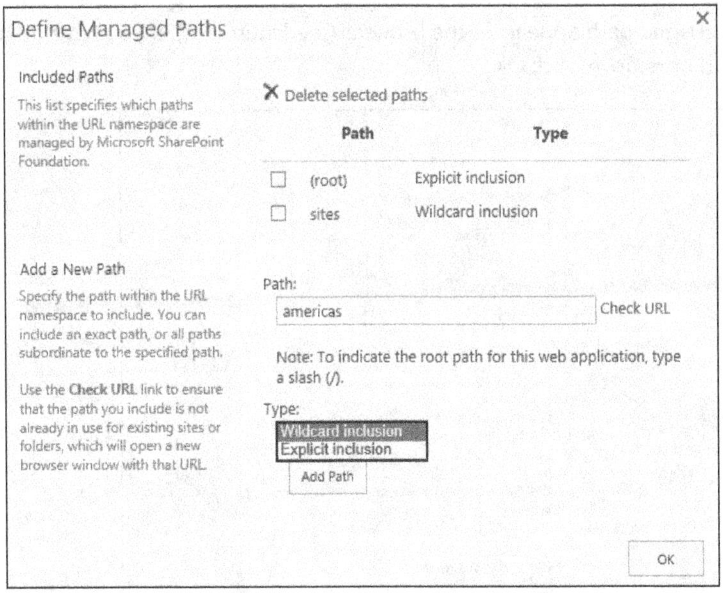

FIGURE 4-2 Defining managed paths.

6. Select the Check URL link to ensure that there are no existing sites or site collections occupying the intended specified path. A new browser window appears; if the window displays no site, the test is considered successful (see Figure 4-3).

FIGURE 4-3 Location available for managed path.

7. Close down the Page Not Found browser window and return to the Define Managed Paths window.

8. Select whether the new link is to be a wildcard inclusion (selected in this example) or an explicit inclusion; then select the Add Path button.

9. The new managed path appears in the browser (see Figure 4-4). If you have no more paths to add or remove, click OK.

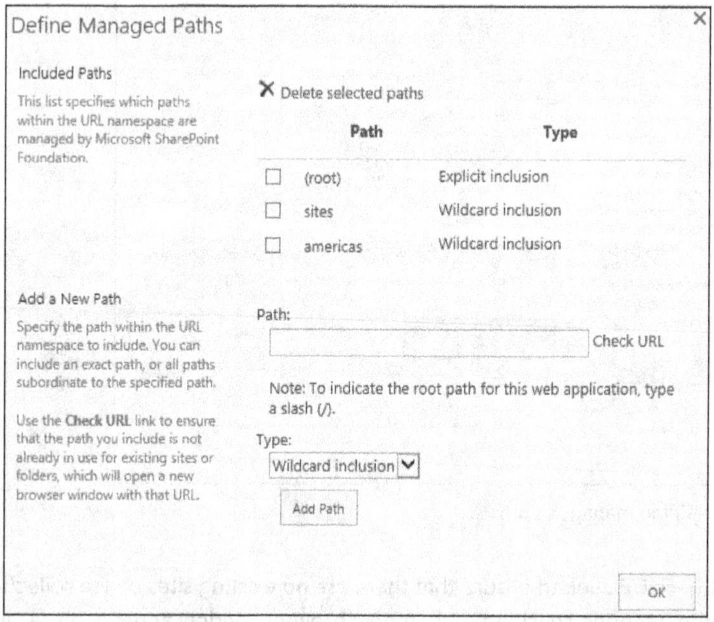

FIGURE 4-4 New managed path: Americas.

Remove a managed path (Central Administration)

Removing a managed path from Central Administration is a fairly simple task, using the same site in which paths are created.

> **IMPORTANT CHECK FOR NESTED SITE COLLECTIONS**
>
> Before removing a managed path, ensure that the site collections nested within it or beneath it have either been moved to a new location or removed altogether.

From Central Administration, follow these steps:

1. Open Application Management.

2. On the Application Management page, select the Manage Web Applications link.

3. Select the web application from which you want to remove managed paths (click its line; for example, http://intranet.boston.local/).

4. When the ribbon activates, select the Managed Paths icon (see Figure 4-5).

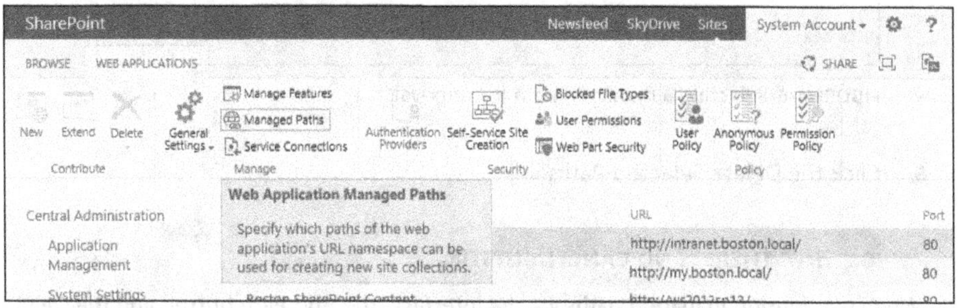

FIGURE 4-5 Selecting Managed Paths in the ribbon.

5. The Defined Managed Paths page appears, showing all existing paths. In the Included Paths section, select the check box for the managed path that is to be removed (see Figure 4-6).

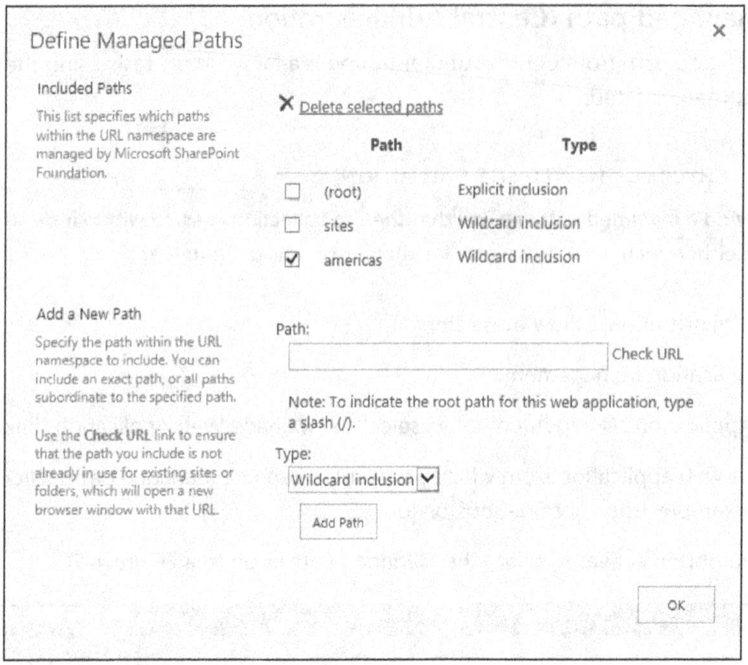

FIGURE 4-6 Selecting a managed path for removal.

6. Click the Delete Selected Paths link.

> **IMPORTANT** **THERE IS NO CANCEL BUTTON**
>
> When configuring managed paths via the interface, the Add Path button and the Delete Selected Paths link act in the same manner; that is to say, they have no confirmation action. After you have made your selection, that's it: The change is made.

7. The Defined Managed Paths page now shows the existing managed paths, with the Americas managed path removed. Click OK to close the window.

Create a managed path (Windows PowerShell)

Using Windows PowerShell cmdlets, you can create new managed paths in two simple steps. This Windows PowerShell path creation works for web applications that host both path-based and host named site collections.

In the following command, you create a wildcard inclusion (managed path) called Americas.

To create a managed path using Windows PowerShell, do the following:

1. Open a SharePoint 2013 Management Shell (Windows PowerShell), running as administrator.

2. Start by assigning a variable for your web application using the Get-SPWebApplication cmdlet:

```
$wa = Get-SPWebApplication -identity http://intranet.boston.local
```

3. Use the New-SPManagedPath cmdlet with the web application variable to build the managed path (note that if the explicit switch is not specified, this cmdlet will build a wildcard inclusion):

```
New-SPManagedPath "americas" -webapplication $wa
```

4. The finished cmdlets are shown in Figure 4-7.

FIGURE 4-7 Creating a managed path using Windows PowerShell.

EXAM TIP

If the web application you are using hosts host named site collections, do not forget to include the -HostHeader switch with your New-ManagedPath cmdlet; otherwise, it does not work correctly. Also, if the requirements for your new managed path indicate that you need to build an explicit inclusion, don't forget to add the -Explicit switch to the New-ManagedPath cmdlet.

Removing a managed path (Windows PowerShell)

Removing a managed path from a web application via Windows PowerShell is very similar to its creation.

In the following command, you remove a wildcard inclusion (managed path) called americas. To remove a managed path using Windows PowerShell, do the following:

1. Open a SharePoint 2013 Management Shell (Windows PowerShell), running as administrator.

2. Start by assigning a variable for your web application using the Get-SPWebApplication cmdlet:

```
$wa = Get-SPWebApplication -identity http://intranet.boston.local
```

3. (Optional) Display a list of existing managed paths using the Get-SPManagedPath cmdlet:

```
Get-SPManagedPath -webapplication $wa
```

4. Use the Remove-SPManagedPath cmdlet with the web application variable to remove the managed path from the web application:

```
Remove-SPManagedPath -identity "americas" -webapplication $wa
```

5. Confirm that you want to delete the managed path.

6. The finished cmdlets are shown in Figure 4-8.

FIGURE 4-8 Removing a managed path using Windows PowerShell.

Configuring HTTP throttling

HTTP throttling is a mechanism that SharePoint uses to reduce inbound connections when a server is overloaded. This feature was present in the 2010 version of SharePoint and is largely unchanged in SharePoint 2013.

When an HTTP request is made to a SharePoint server, the server evaluates its health against a couple of different performance counters by default: Memory (Available Mbytes) and ASP.NET (Requests Current). Each counter stores a series of 10 (by default) different values that determine a server's load (the health score, which varies from 1 to 10).

EXAM TIP

Know the difference between Request Management and HTTP throttling. Request Management enables you to proactively account for the performance capability of each web tier server, whereas HTTP throttling is a purely reactionary behavior on the part of an overloaded web tier server.

If a server's health score reaches a value of 10, the server stops responding to incoming requests until this score drops back down. The intervals for each counter can be seen on a per-web application basis using the Get-SPWebApplicationHttpThrottlingMonitor cmdlet, as shown in Figure 4-9.

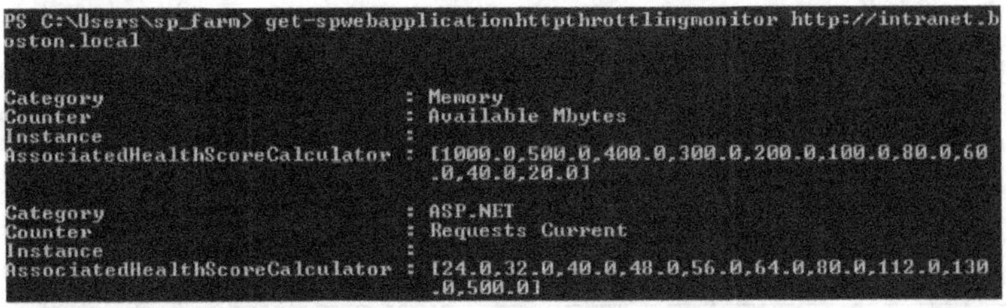

```
PS C:\Users\sp_farm> get-spwebapplicationhttpthrottlingmonitor http://intranet.b
oston.local

Category                         : Memory
Counter                          : Available Mbytes
Instance                         :
AssociatedHealthScoreCalculator  : [1000.0,500.0,400.0,300.0,200.0,100.0,80.0,60
                                   .0,40.0,20.0]

Category                         : ASP.NET
Counter                          : Requests Current
Instance                         :
AssociatedHealthScoreCalculator  : [24.0,32.0,40.0,48.0,56.0,64.0,80.0,112.0,130
                                   .0,500.0]
```

FIGURE 4-9 Using the Get-SPWebApplicationHttpThrottlingMonitor cmdlet to retrieve counter values.

Aside from adding and altering counter values, the only administration that can be done for this functionality is to enable or disable it on a per-web application basis.

Activate or deactivate HTTP throttling (Central Administration)

1. Open Application Management.

2. On the Application Management page, select the Manage Web Applications link.

3. Select the web application for which you want to configure HTTP throttling.

4. When the ribbon activates, select the drop-down list on the General Settings icon and then choose Resource Throttling (see Figure 4-10).

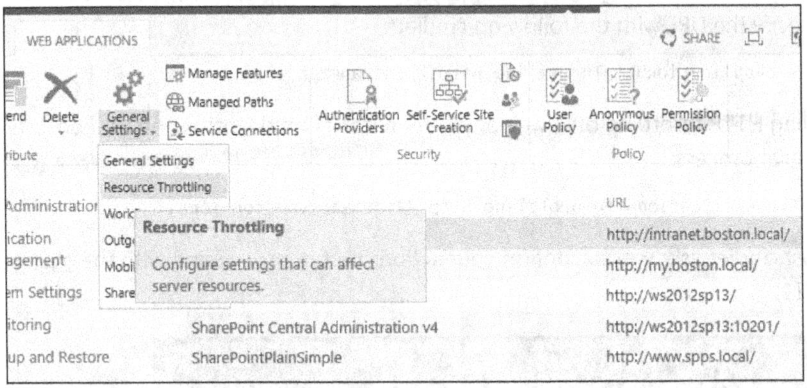

FIGURE 4-10 General Settings, Resource Throttling.

5. On the Resource Throttling page, scroll down to the HTTP Request Monitoring And Throttling section. From here, you can choose to activate or deactivate HTTP Request Throttling by selecting the appropriate radio button for On or Off (see Figure 4-11).

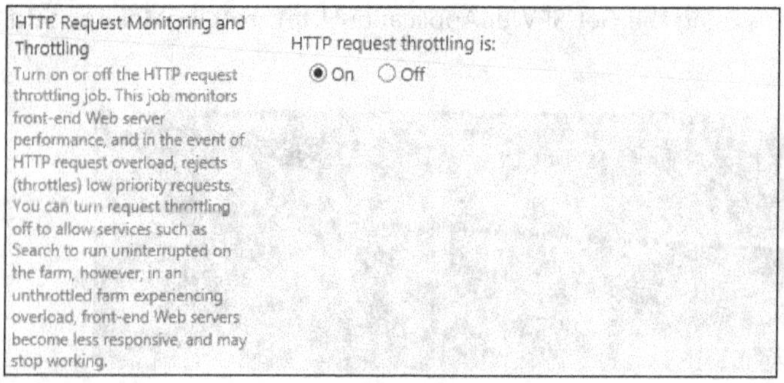

FIGURE 4-11 HTTP Request Monitoring And Throttling.

Activate or deactivate HTTP throttling (Windows PowerShell)

Windows PowerShell administration of HTTP throttling availability is done with two cmdlets, as shown in Table 4-1.

TABLE 4-1 Cmdlets for enabling/disabling HTTP throttling

Windows PowerShell Cmdlet	Function
Enable-SPWebApplicationHttpThrottling	Enables HTTP throttling for a given web application
Disable-SPWebApplicationHttpThrottling	Disables HTTP throttling for a given web application

To enable HTTP throttling on a web application (for example, http://intranet.boston.local), simply specify the URL with the following cmdlet:

```
Enable-SPWebApplicationHttpThrottling http://intranet.boston.local
```

Disabling HTTP throttling on a web application (for example, http://intranet.boston.local) is very similar process:

```
Disable-SPWebApplicationHttpThrottling http://intranet.boston.local
```

This last cmdlet asks you to confirm your actions before proceeding with the change (see Figure 4-12).

FIGURE 4-12 Confirming that you want to disable HTTP throttling.

Configuring list throttling

Any given SharePoint list or library can maintain literally millions of items (the supported number is 30 million). It goes without saying that any one user attempting the retrieval of large segment of these items in any one session would have a performance impact on the rest of the farm.

EXAM TIP

Be familiar with the appropriate list thresholds, particularly the List View Threshold (LVT) for users and the List View Lookup Threshold values.

List throttling was created with exactly this (potential) issue in mind. As a result, there are a series of metrics that can be controlled on a per web app basis (shown in Table 4-2):

TABLE 4-2 List thresholds

Resource Throttling Option	Default Threshold	Purpose
List View Threshold (LVT)	5,000 items	Specifies the maximum number of items that a database operation can involve at one time.
List View Threshold (Auditors and Administrators)	20,000 items	Specifies the maximum number of items that an object model database query can involve at one time for users to whom you grant sufficient permissions through security policy.
List View Lookup Threshold	8 fields	Specifies the maximum number of lookup, person/group, or workflow status fields that a database query can involve at one time.
List Unique Permissions Threshold	5000 unique permissions	Specifies the maximum number of unique permissions that a list can have at one time.

If your environment is not a 24×7 shop, you can additionally configure a daily time window for large queries. Obviously, such queries generate a significant load on the farm, so it is best to avoid backup and maintenance timeframes when specifying this window.

MORE INFO **DESIGNING LARGE LISTS AND MAXIMIZING LIST PERFORMANCE**

Because most of these numbers are considered thresholds within the "Software Boundaries and Limits for SharePoint 2013" document (*http://technet.microsoft.com/en-us/library/cc262787*), they can (technically) be exceeded. However, any modifications to these limits should be thoroughly considered and tested prior to implementation. Large lists and maximizing list performance are discussed in the TechNet document at *http://technet.microsoft.com/en-us/library/cc262813*.

Alter list throttling values

To alter list throttling values, follow these steps:

1. Open Application Management.

2. On the Application Management page, select the Manage Web Applications link.

3. Select the web application from which you want to remove managed paths (click its line; for example, http://intranet.boston.local/).

4. When the ribbon activates, select the drop-down list on the General Settings icon and then choose Resource Throttling (see Figure 4-13).

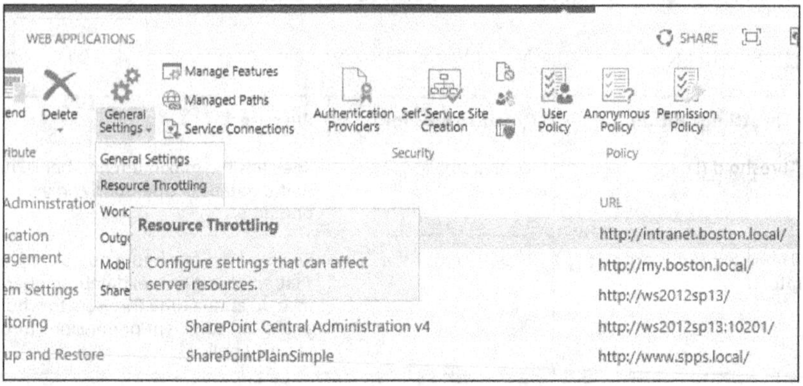

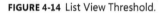

FIGURE 4-13 General Settings, Resource Throttling.

5. On the Resource Throttling page, the first section shown is the List View Threshold. The default value for this field is 5,000 operations at one time (see Figure 4-14).

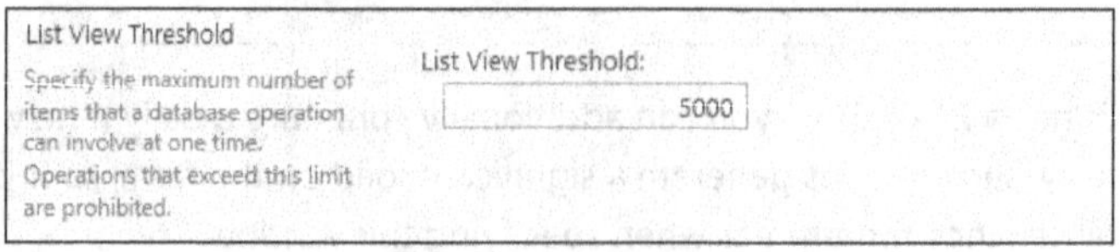

List View Threshold	
Specify the maximum number of items that a database operation can involve at one time. Operations that exceed this limit are prohibited.	List View Threshold: 5000

FIGURE 4-14 List View Threshold.

6. Next, you can choose whether to allow object model overrides of the standard list throttling limits and what those limits are. The default value is set to allow administrators and auditors to run larger queries during business hours, up to the limits specified in List View Threshold For Auditors And Administrators (the default value is 20,000 items queried at one time, as shown in Figure 4-15).

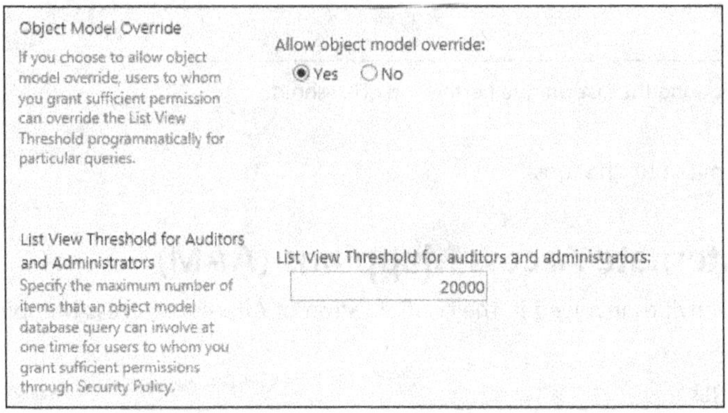

Object Model Override

If you choose to allow object model override, users to whom you grant sufficient permission can override the List View Threshold programmatically for particular queries.

Allow object model override:
◉ Yes   ○ No

List View Threshold for Auditors and Administrators

Specify the maximum number of items that an object model database query can involve at one time for users to whom you grant sufficient permissions through Security Policy.

List View Threshold for auditors and administrators:

20000

FIGURE 4-15 Object model override values for auditors and administrators.

7. The List View Lookup Threshold can be quite expensive from a performance standpoint. Essentially, it specifies the number of fields that are "joined" behind the scenes in an SQL query. The default value is set to 8 list view lookups (see Figure 4-16).

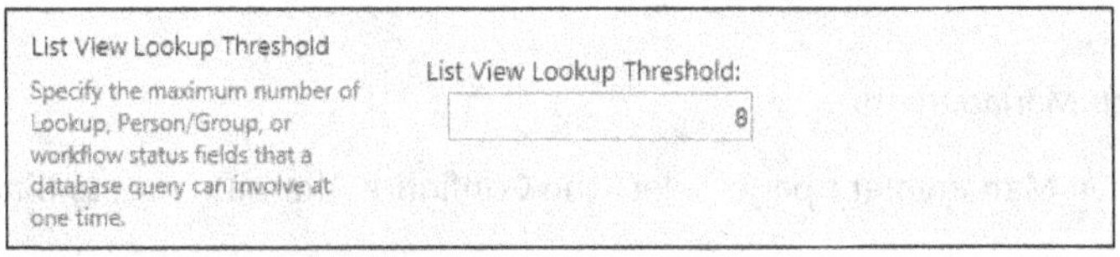

List View Lookup Threshold

Specify the maximum number of Lookup, Person/Group, or workflow status fields that a database query can involve at one time.

List View Lookup Threshold:

8

FIGURE 4-16 List View Lookup Threshold value.

8. The Daily Time Window For Large Queries entry enables you to allow a time window for nonauditors/admins to perform a large query (see Figure 4-17).

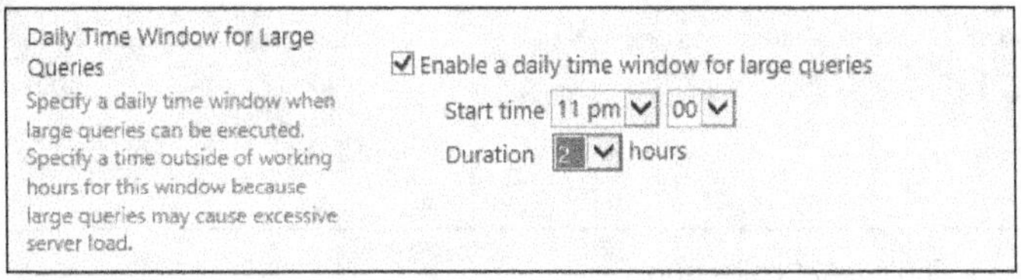

Daily Time Window for Large Queries

Specify a daily time window when large queries can be executed. Specify a time outside of working hours for this window because large queries may cause excessive server load.

☑ Enable a daily time window for large queries

Start time 11 pm ▼ 00 ▼
Duration   2 ▼ hours

FIGURE 4-17 Configuring the daily time window for large queries.

9. This might be useful for someone who is analyzing the contents of a large SharePoint list or library with Microsoft Access, for instance. This time window should be outside of normal operating hours and also not overlap maintenance windows.

10. The last configuration for list throttling is the List Unique Permissions Threshold (see Figure 4-18). This value specifies the maximum number of unique permissions that can be applied to any one list.

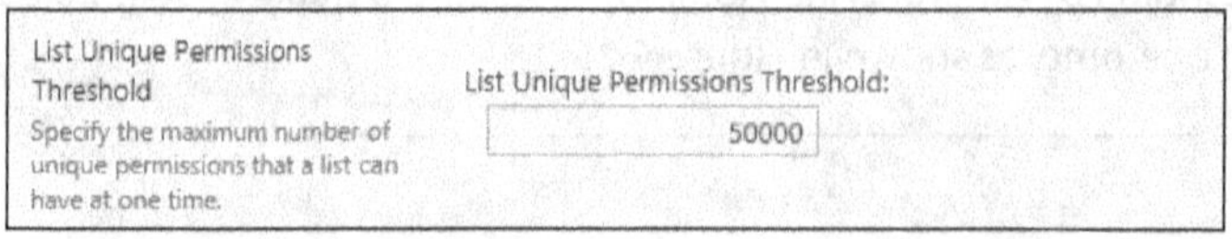

List Unique Permissions Threshold	List Unique Permissions Threshold:
Specify the maximum number of unique permissions that a list can have at one time.	50000

FIGURE 4-18 Configuring the List Unique Permissions Threshold.

11. Click OK to commit your changes.

Configuring Alternate Access Mappings (AAM)

There are three major activities involved in the configuration of Alternate Access Mapping (AAM):

- Editing public URLs
- Adding internal URLs
- Mapping to external resources

Edit public URLs

Each AAM collection has an associated grouping of public URLs. To configure these URLs, do the following:

1. Open Application Management.

2. On the Application Management page, select the Configure Alternate Access Mappings link.

3. Select the drop-down list to change to a different AAM collection (see Figure 4-19).

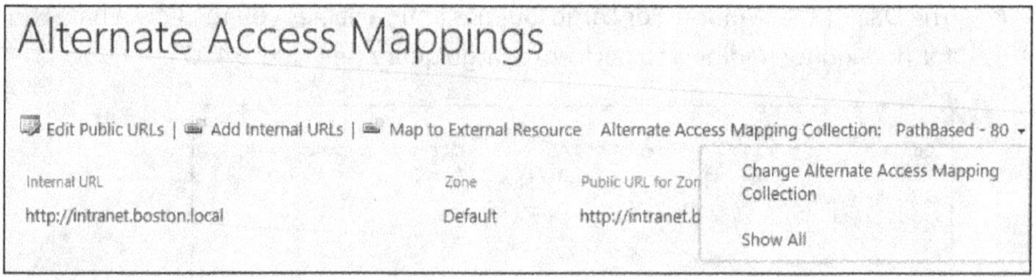

Alternate Access Mappings

Edit Public URLs | Add Internal URLs | Map to External Resource   Alternate Access Mapping Collection: PathBased - 80 ▾

Internal URL	Zone	Public URL for Zon	Change Alternate Access Mapping Collection
http://intranet.boston.local	Default	http://intranet.b	Show All

FIGURE 4-19 Choose a single AAM collection.

4. Select the Edit Public URLs link.

5. On the Edit Public Zone URLs page, enter the appropriate value for any of the five zones: Default, Intranet, Internet, Custom, or Extranet (see Figure 4-20). Click Save when you finish entering new zone URLs.

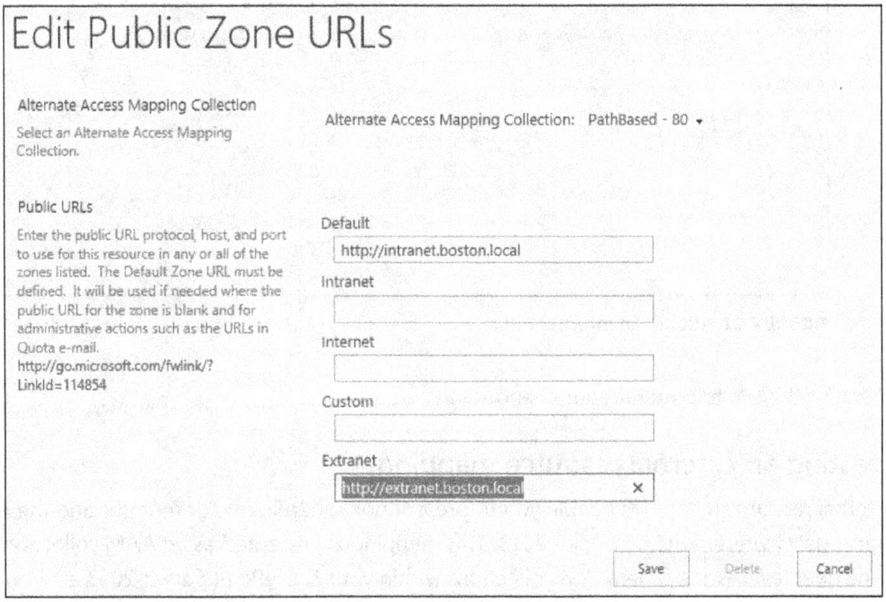

Edit Public Zone URLs

Alternate Access Mapping Collection

Select an Alternate Access Mapping Collection.

Alternate Access Mapping Collection: PathBased - 80 ▾

Public URLs

Enter the public URL protocol, host, and port to use for this resource in any or all of the zones listed. The Default Zone URL must be defined. It will be used if needed where the public URL for the zone is blank and for administrative actions such as the URLs in Quota e-mail.
http://go.microsoft.com/fwlink/?LinkId=114854

Default

http://intranet.boston.local

Intranet

Internet

Custom

Extranet

http://extranet.boston.local   ✕

Save   Delete   Cancel

FIGURE 4-20 Entering a new public zone URL (extranet).

6. The Alternate Access Mappings page appears again, this time indicating both of the public URLs for the PathBased - 80 Alternate Access Mapping Collection.

7. Click Save to commit your changes.

Adding internal URLs

Each AAM collection has an associated grouping of internal URLs. To configure these URLs, do the following:

1. Open Application Management.

2. On the Application Management page, select the Configure Alternate Access Mappings link.

3. Select the Add Internal URLs link.

4. On the Add Internal URLs page, select the desired AAM collection by choosing the drop-down link and selecting Change Alternate Access Mapping Collection (see Figure 4-21).

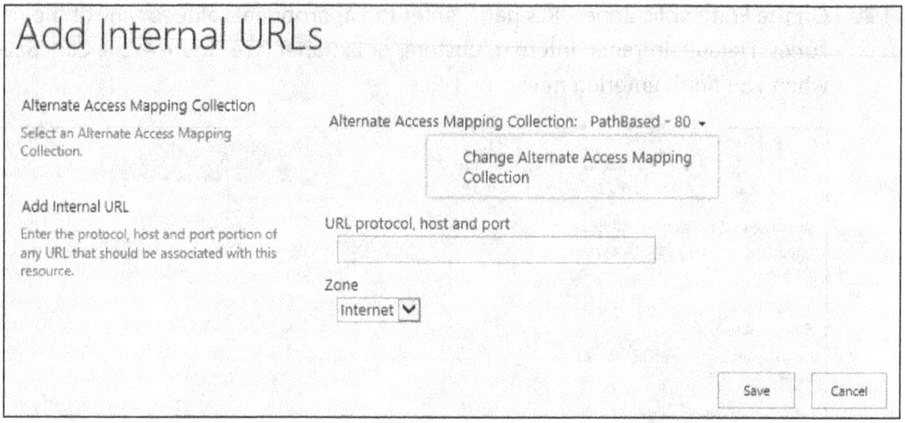

Add Internal URLs

Alternate Access Mapping Collection

Select an Alternate Access Mapping Collection.

Alternate Access Mapping Collection: PathBased - 80 ▾

Change Alternate Access Mapping Collection

Add Internal URL

Enter the protocol, host and port portion of any URL that should be associated with this resource.

URL protocol, host and port

Zone

Internet ▾

Save   Cancel

FIGURE 4-21 Adding an internal URL.

5. Click Save to commit your changes.

Creating an external resource mapping

External resource mappings enable you to present non–SharePoint content utilizing the AAM functionality present in SharePoint 2013. This mapping is presented as an AAM collection at the same peer level as the other AAM collections within your SharePoint Server 2013 environment.

To build a new external resource mapping (see Figure 4-22), do the following:

1. Open Application Management.

2. On the Application Management page, select the Configure Alternate Access Mappings link.

3. Select the Map To External Resource link.

4. On the Create External Resource Mapping page, create a new Resource Name and specify a URL for the zone.

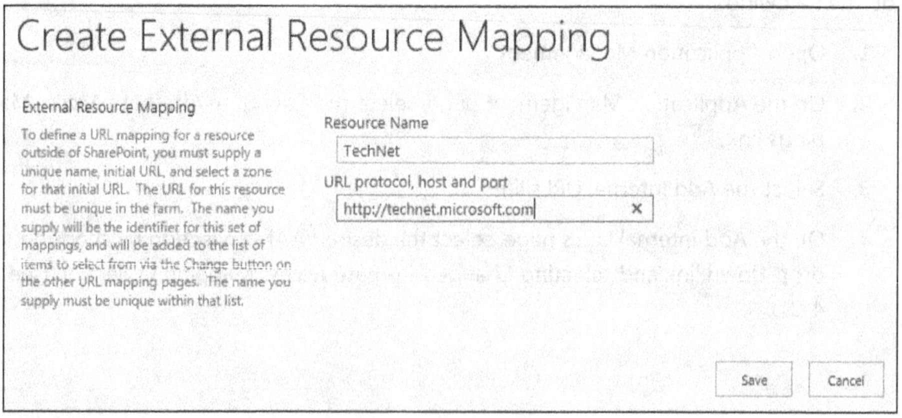

Create External Resource Mapping

External Resource Mapping

To define a URL mapping for a resource outside of SharePoint, you must supply a unique name, initial URL, and select a zone for that initial URL. The URL for this resource must be unique in the farm. The name you supply will be the identifier for this set of mappings, and will be added to the list of items to select from via the Change button on the other URL mapping pages. The name you supply must be unique within that list.

Resource Name

TechNet

URL protocol, host and port

http://technet.microsoft.com   ✕

Save   Cancel

FIGURE 4-22 External resource mapping.

5. Click Save to complete your changes.

6. The new AAM collection appears with the appropriate zone information (see Figure 4-23).

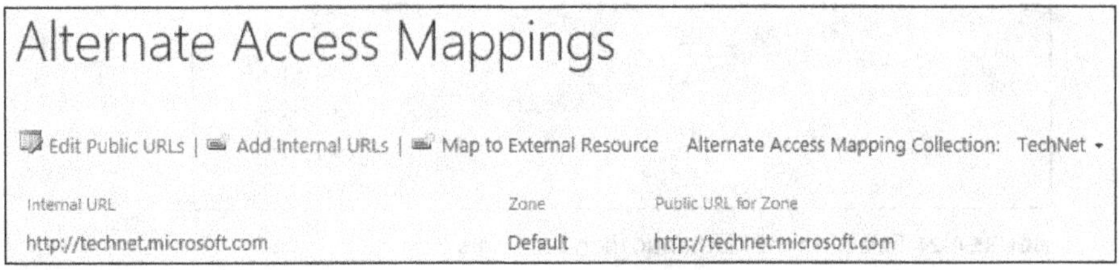

Alternate Access Mappings

🔲 Edit Public URLs | 🖿 Add Internal URLs | 🖿 Map to External Resource   Alternate Access Mapping Collection: TechNet ▾

Internal URL	Zone	Public URL for Zone
http://technet.microsoft.com	Default	http://technet.microsoft.com

FIGURE 4-23 New AAM collection for the external resource.

EXAM TIP

Although it is perfectly reasonable to point multiple URLs to the same web site in IIS (and supported in SharePoint), it is important to remember that SharePoint has to figure out how to map URLs and so on to the incoming requests. If you receive error messages in Event Viewer and Unified Logging Service (ULS) logs about missing AAM references, note what the inbound URL is and correct the AAM settings.

Configuring an authentication provider

Authentication providers are associated with particular zones within a web application. The types of providers available vary from none at all (enabling anonymous access only) to very customizable claims-based authentication using Security Assertion Markup Language (SAML) claims.

EXAM TIP

Although SharePoint 2013 still supports classic mode authentication for backward-compatibility purposes, this authentication mechanism does not work with several key components of SharePoint 2013. Use the Convert-SPWebApplication cmdlet to upgrade web apps that are using classic mode authentication to claims-based authentication.

To configure the authentication provider for a given web application, follow these steps:

1. Open Application Management in Central Administration.

2. On the Application Management page, select the Manage Web Applications link.

3. Select a web application (for example, http://intranet.boston.local); this action activates the ribbon.

4. Select the Authentication Providers icon, as shown in Figure 4-24.

FIGURE 4-24 Selecting the Authentication Providers icon.

5. The available zones for the web application appear in a new window (see Figure 4-25).

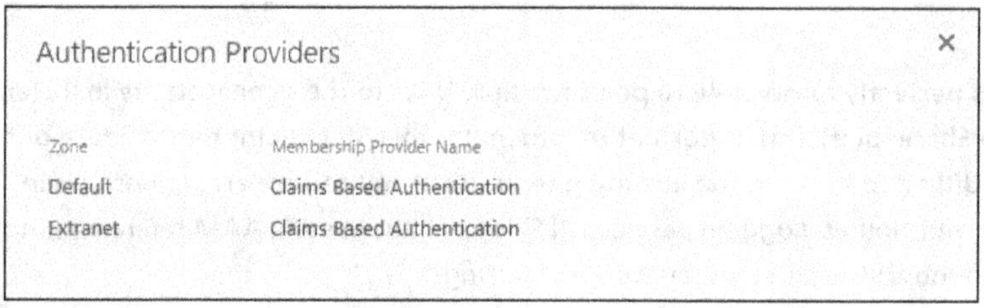

Authentication Providers   ✕

Zone	Membership Provider Name
Default	Claims Based Authentication
Extranet	Claims Based Authentication

FIGURE 4-25 Authentication providers by zone.

EXAM TIP

Each zone for a particular URL can (and most often does) have a different authentication provider. Be familiar with the three main types of user authentication methods: Windows claims (NTLM, Kerberos, and basic), SAML-based claims (using a trusted identity provider), and forms-based authentication (FBA) claims (using ASP.NET FBA).

---

6. For the zone you are configuring, decide whether anonymous access will be allowed. If so, select the Enable Anonymous Access check box (see Figure 4-26).

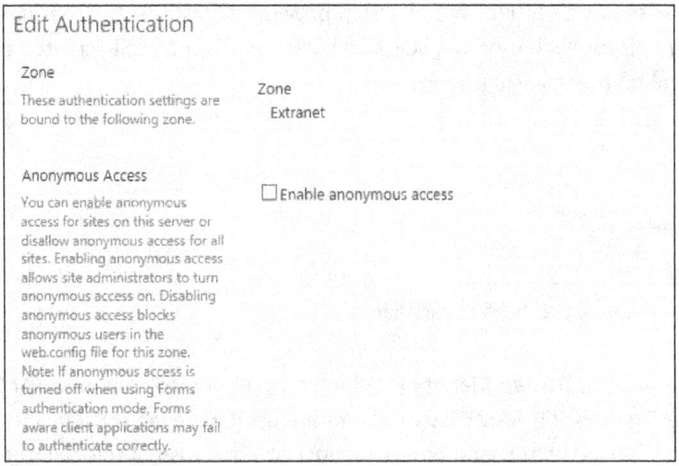

Edit Authentication

Zone

These authentication settings are bound to the following zone.

Zone
    Extranet

Anonymous Access

You can enable anonymous access for sites on this server or disallow anonymous access for all sites. Enabling anonymous access allows site administrators to turn anonymous access on. Disabling anonymous access blocks anonymous users in the web.config file for this zone. Note: If anonymous access is turned off when using Forms authentication mode, Forms aware client applications may fail to authenticate correctly.

☐ Enable anonymous access

FIGURE 4-26 Enabling anonymous access.

IMPORTANT ANONYMOUS ACCESS REQUIRED FOR FORMS AUTHENTICATION

If you are using forms-based authentication (FBA), anonymous access must be enabled so users can see the forms-based logon page.

7. Windows authentication is the default claims authentication type for a new web application created through the GUI. Within integrated Windows authentication, you get the choice of using NTLM or Kerberos for Windows authentication (see Figure 4-27).

IMPORTANT BASIC AUTHENTICATION SECURITY

Basic authentication is still a supported option in SharePoint 2013, but it has the same security issues: authentication credentials are sent in clear text over the wire.

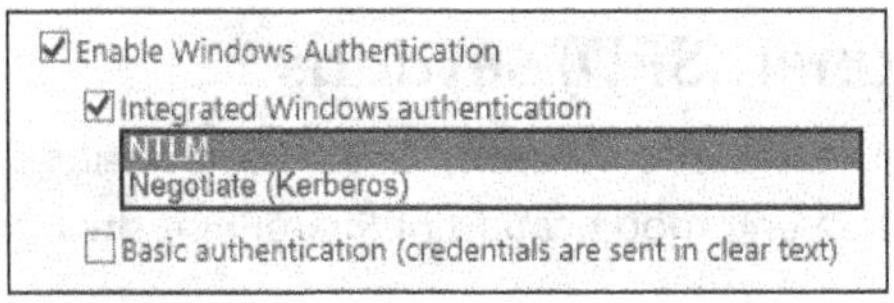

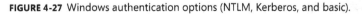

☑ Enable Windows Authentication
  ☑ Integrated Windows authentication
    NTLM
    Negotiate (Kerberos)
  ☐ Basic authentication (credentials are sent in clear text)

FIGURE 4-27 Windows authentication options (NTLM, Kerberos, and basic).

8. FBA requires the use of an ASP.NET membership provider and stores the user name/ password credentials for each user in a SQL database that is specifically created as part of this authentication mechanism (see Figure 4-28).

FIGURE 4-28 Forms-based authentication parameters.

9. The last option available, Trusted Identity Provider, enables you to configure SAML connections (see Figure 4-29). SAML-based claims are used when an outside authentication mechanism is used with SharePoint. The most common use of this claims type is for allowing Active Directory Federation Services (ADFS) connections to authenticate to SharePoint.

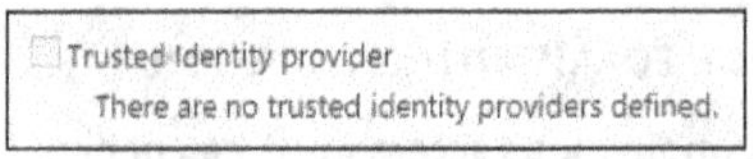

> ☐ Trusted Identity provider
>   There are no trusted identity providers defined.

FIGURE 4-29 Trusted identity provider.

> ***MORE INFO*** **AUTHENTICATION PROVIDER CONFIGURATION**
>
> As shown in the previous figures, differing levels of configuration effort are required to enable Kerberos, FBA, and SAML-based authentication. Each of these concepts is covered in the TechNet article "Configure Authentication Infrastructure in SharePoint 2013" at *http://technet.microsoft.com/en-us/library/jj219795.aspx*.

10. Click Save to cause all configuration changes to take effect.

Configuring SharePoint designer (SPD) settings

As discussed in Chapter 3, "Install and Configure SharePoint farms," SharePoint Designer (SPD) is a client application that allows for the creation and modification of SharePoint sites, pages, and workflows.

> ***EXAM TIP***
>
> Easily the most crucial configuration component for SPD, the customization/unghosting of pages can account for performance losses over time. Be familiar with what it means to cause a page to revert to its template.

Administrative control of SPD is controlled on a per-web application basis and enables four distinct configuration options:

- Enabling Or Disabling Sharepoint Designer Use On A Given Web Application
- Allowing Or Preventing Site Collection Administrators From Detaching Pages From The Site Template
- Allowing Or Preventing Site Collection Administrators From Customizing Master Pages And Layout Pages
- Allowing Or Preventing Site Collection Administrators From Seeing The Url Structure Of Their Web Site

After these selections are made, site collection administrators have more granular control at the site collection level for the use of SPD.

To configure SPD settings for a given web application, follow these steps:

1. Open Application Management in Central Administration.

2. On the Application Management page, select the Manage Web Applications link.

3. Select a web application (for example, http://intranet.boston.local); this action activates the ribbon.

4. From the General Settings drop-down list, choose SharePoint Designer (see Figure 4-30).

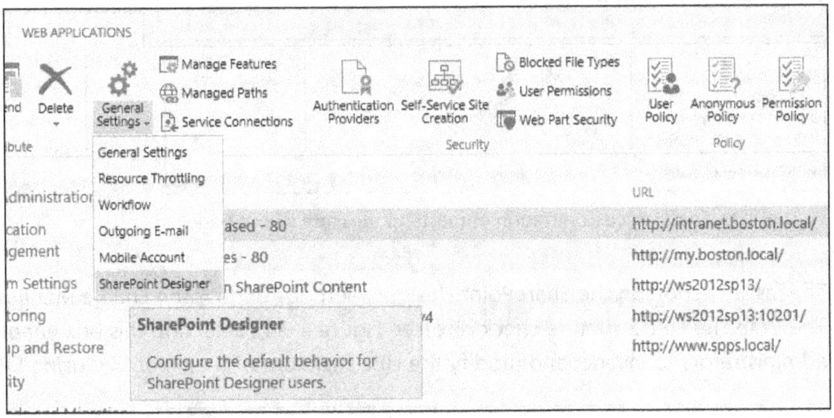

FIGURE 4-30 General settings for SPD.

5. The first selection on the SharePoint Designer settings page is the Enable SharePoint Designer check box. Selecting this box enables SPD to be used within this web application (see Figure 4-31).

FIGURE 4-31 Enabling the use of SPD in a web application.

6. The next selection on the SharePoint Designer settings page is the Enable Detaching Pages From The Site Definition check box (see Figure 4-32). Selecting this box enables the customization of a page from the site template, which can result in performance loss.

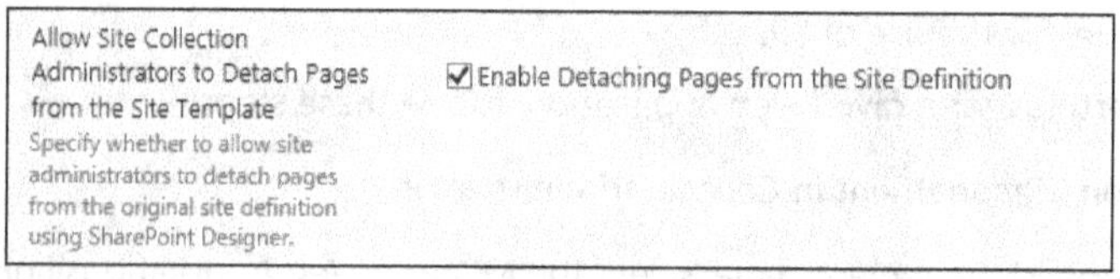

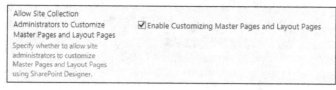

FIGURE 4-32 Enabling pages to be detached from the site definition.

7. The third selection on the SharePoint Designer settings page is the Enable Customizing Master Pages And Layout Pages check box (see Figure 4-33). Selecting this box enables customization of the individual master and layout pages, a key requirement in most SharePoint installations.

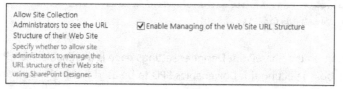

FIGURE 4-33 Enabling customization of master pages and layout pages.

8. The last selection on the SharePoint Designer settings page is the Enable Managing of The Web Site URL Structure check box (see Figure 4-34). Selecting this box enables site administrators to inspect and modify the URL structure of their web site using SPD.

FIGURE 4-34 Selecting Enable Managing Of The Web Site URL Structure.

9. Click OK to cause all configuration changes to take effect.

Objective summary

- There are two distinct types of managed paths: wildcard and explicit. Wildcard managed paths enable multiple site collections to be created beneath a single URL. Explicit managed paths allow only a single site collection to be created beneath the specified URL.

- Health values for a server range between 1 and 10; if the health score value reaches 10, HTTP throttling will cause the server to stop responding to inbound requests until the load eases and health improves.

- List throttling is used to help prevent excessive loads due to large queries during business hours. If desired, users can be allowed to submit larger queries during nonpeak hours.

- Three configuration activities occur within AAM: Editing Public URLs, Adding Internal URLs, and Mapping To External Resources.

- Although SharePoint 2013 still supports classic mode authentication for backward compatibility, the direction going forward is for web applications to be configured to use claims authentication.

- Anonymous access is a requirement for FBA; otherwise, users never see the logon page.

- SPD can be controlled on a per-web application basis.

Objective review

Answer the following questions to test your knowledge of the information in this objective. You can find the answers to these questions and explanations of why each answer choice is correct or incorrect in the "Answers" section at the end of this chapter.

1. What is the supported maximum number of managed paths for use in a SharePoint web application?

   A. 5

   B. 100

   C. 35

   D. 20

2. Which of the following values is the default maximum List View Lookup Threshold?

   A. 5,000

   B. 20,000

   C. 8

   D. 2,500

3. Which of the following authentication methods is required for use with FBA?

   A. anonymous

   B. basic

   C. Kerberos

   D. SAML

4. Which of the following settings are required to enable a designer to build a new page layout using SPD? (Choose all that apply.)

   A. Enable Detaching Pages From The Site Definition

   B. Enable Customizing Master Pages And Layout Pages

   C. Enable SharePoint Designer

   D. Enable Managing Of The Web Site URL Structure

Objective 4.2: Create and maintain site collections

Now that all your web applications are created, and users are capable of effective authentication to your web applications, it's time to turn your attention to configuring individual site collections within this environment. The initial architecture of the environment starts to take shape as site collections begin to follow one of two possible structural designs.

Additionally, well-governed provenance of self-service site collections enables users to begin to collaborate in a managed fashion.

> **This objective covers how to:**
> - Configure host header site collections.
> - Configure self-service site creation.
> - Maintain site owners.
> - Maintain site quotas.
> - Configure site policies.
> - Configure a team mailbox.

Configuring host header site collections

Host header (also called host named) site collections are created within a single web app. This web app can be provisioned via Central Administration or via Windows PowerShell, and must contain a created but unassigned site collection (no user access, no template assigned) at its root for SharePoint functionality (such as search) to work properly.

After this web application is in place, multiple Fully Qualified Domain Names (FQDNs) can access distinct site collections within the same web app. This functionality is analogous to the host header functionality contained within IIS that enables host headers to assign multiple FQDNs to multiple web sites that all utilize TCP Port 80.

There are three major components to configuring host header site collections: creating the host header web application, creating a blank top-level site within the web app, and creating host header site collections within the web app.

EXAM TIP

In order for search and other components to work effectively, there must be a root site collection in a host header web application. This site should only be created; it should never be configured or used.

Creating a host header web application

The new host header web application is created from Windows PowerShell and is usually the first new web application created (aside from Central Administration). It always occupies TCP Port 80 (for HTTP) or Port 443 (for HTTPS).

Before beginning this process, ensure that you have a service account created that will run your app pools. To create the host header web application (sample values are shown) follow these steps:

1. Assign variables for the web application name, authentication provider, app pool name, managed account credentials, and content database name:

```
$webApplicationName = "SharePoint HNSC Host - 80"
$authProvider = New-SPAuthenticationProvider
$appPoolName = "SharePoint HNSC Host - 80 App Pool"
$managedAccount = (Get-SPManagedAccount "boston\sp_app")
$contentDBName = "WSS_Content_HNSC"
```

2. Create the new web application. If you want to use Secure Sockets Layer (SSL) for HTTPS, you need to (1) change the $URL variable from HTTP to HTTPS, (2) specify the -SecureSocketsLayer switch as part of this next cmdlet, and (3) change the port number from 80 to 443:

```
New-SPWebApplication -Name $webApplicationName -AuthenticationProvider
$authProvider -ApplicationPool $AppPoolName -applicationPoolAccount
$ManagedAccount -Port 80 -Databasename $contentDBName
```

Creating a blank root site

A root site needs to exist at the entry point to the new web application. This new site is never accessed by users and should not have a template assigned to it.

Before beginning this process, run the Get-SPWebApplication cmdlet (see Figure 4-35). Record the URL shown for the host header site collection because you will be using it momentarily.

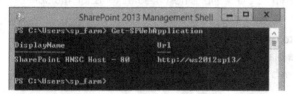

FIGURE 4-35 Running Get-SPWebApplication to find the URL.

To create the blank root site (sample values are again shown), do the following:

1. Assign variables for the root site collection name, site collection owner account and e-mail, and URL (from Get-SPWebApplication):

```
$rsName = "Root HNSC Site Collection"
$sco = "boston\tlanphier"
$scoEmail = "tlanphier@boston.local"
$url = "http://ws2012sp13"
```

2. Create the blank root site using the variables you defined:

```
New-SPSite -Name $rsName -Url $url -OwnerAlias $sco -OwnerEmail $scoEmail
```

Creating a host header site collection

The creation of a host header (also called host named) site collection is not possible from Central Administration; there is no functionality within the GUI to either create or remove a host header site collection.

Creating a new host header site collection via Windows PowerShell is almost as simple as creating a standard site collection; in fact, the only difference is the additional -HostHeader-WebApplication switch.

To create a new host header site collection (with sample values), follow these steps:

1. Assign variables for the host header site collection's URL, the host header web application, the owner account, and the owner e-mail. This example uses the standard team site template (STS#0):

   ```
   $hnscUrl = "http://customers.boston.local"
   $hhWebApp = get-spwebapplication "http://ws2012sp13"
   $owner = "boston\tlanphier"
   $ownerEmail = "tlanphier@boston.local"
   ```

2. Next, build the new site collection using the team site template:

   ```
   New-SPSite -url $hnscUrl -HostHeaderWebApplication $hhWebApp -owneralias $owner
   -owneremail $ownerEmail -template sts#0
   ```

When your configuration is complete, you should be able to open your new site collection in a web browser using the FQDN you specified for this site collection (see Figure 4-36).

FIGURE 4-36 Team site in a host header site collection.

Configuring self-service site creation (SSSC)

One of the key collaborative functionalities present in SharePoint has always been the capability to quickly build collaborative environments for use by individuals within the organization. This functionality has been a bit stymied, however, by the actual mechanisms present for building a new site. Should an individual user have to contact the help desk for a new site? If so, what is the turnaround time for this site?

One solution that has been used for this task is for collaborative sites to be created underneath a business unit's site collection. This tends to become a problem, however, when collaboration needs to involve more than one business unit.

Self-service site creation (SSSC) improvements

In previous versions of SharePoint, the governance factors for creating and retaining new collaborative site collections made the prospect of using this functionality unworkable for many organizations.

Other organizations saw both benefits and drawbacks to this feature; to make it suitable for their needs, they developed custom code that incorporated workflow and notifications to assist in creating and disposing of ad hoc collaborative sites.

As you will see shortly, SharePoint 2013 has made vast improvements in the "self-service" functionality of a farm. The link for self-service site collections (SSSCs) now appears only on a person's My Site, making the creation of new sites an easy process. The addition of the site policies now means that as the site collections are instantiated, not all have to obey the same disposition schedule or notification behavior.

Enabling an SSSC

Provisioning a new SSSC starts with the user's My Site. Within My Site, there is a tab called Sites. After My Site has been configured to create new sites, the link appears next to the search box (see Figure 4-37).

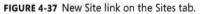

FIGURE 4-37 New Site link on the Sites tab.

To configure the My Site web application for SSSC, do the following:

1. Open Application Management in Central Administration.

2. On the Application Management page, select the Manage Web Applications link.

3. Click the URL name to highlight the line for your My Site web application.

4. In the ribbon, select the Self-Service Site Creation icon (see Figure 4-38).

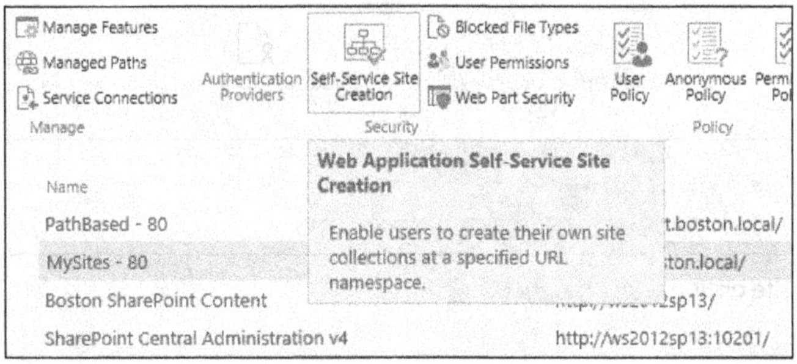

FIGURE 4-38 Configuring an SSSC.

5. The Site Collections section was previously configured for the creation of My Sites, so skip this section.

6. The Start A Site section has four options (see Figure 4-39):

   A. Be Hidden From Users hides the New Site link from a user's My Site.

   B. Prompt Users To Create A Team Site Under enables users to create a team site under a given path.

   C. Prompt Users To Create A Site Collection Under Any Managed Path enables users to create a new site collection beneath a specified managed path.

   D. Display The Custom Form At enables you to enter a customized page.

   E. This field can be set to the URL http://<web app>/_layouts/15/selfservicecreate. aspx.

EXAM TIP

Although the default behavior is to build self-service sites beneath the My Site web application, there is no reason why you cannot choose the URL of another web app for option D in the previous list. The only thing you must do in addition is to configure SSSC on the destination web app.

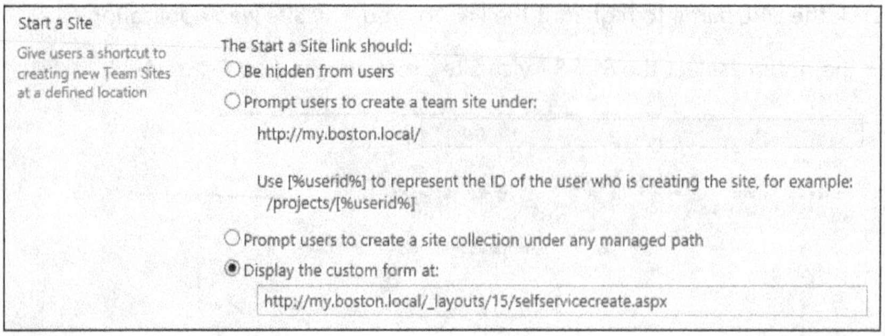

FIGURE 4-39 Start A Site options.

7. If you choose either of the "prompt" options, the Site Classification Settings and Require Secondary Contact options appear (see Figure 4-40).

    A. Site Classification Settings can be hidden from users, optional, or required. This functionality uses the site policies that you created earlier to enable the owner of the new site to tell you something about its function and the duration of time it will need to be used.

    B. It is highly recommended that Require Secondary Contact be set to On; if the site owner is unavailable to correct an issue in this site, the secondary can be called on to assist and has permission to do so.

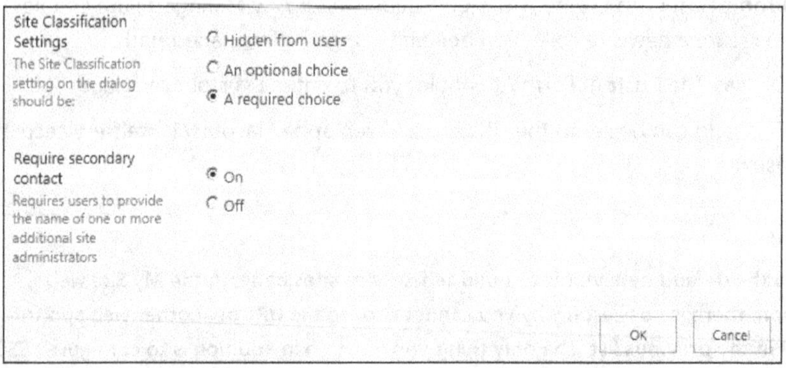

FIGURE 4-40 Site classification settings and secondary contact information.

8. When you have completed your selections, click OK to apply your changes.

Maintaining site owners

Each site collection within SharePoint 2013 has the capability to specify two site collection administrators (SCAs). These SCAs are the de facto owners of the site collection and are responsible for the administration of their site collection from a resourcing and permissioning standpoint.

Viewing and changing the SCAs is done through the same interface in Application Management, as follows:

1. Open Application Management in Central Administration.

2. On the Application Management page, select the Change Site Collection Administrators link.

3. In the Site Collection field, ensure that you have the correct site collection selected; then change the primary and secondary site collection administrator values (see Figure 4-41).

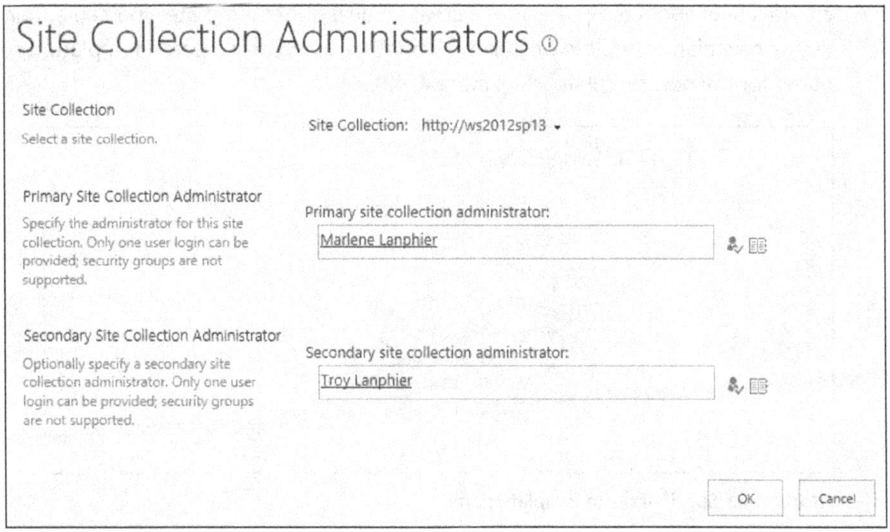

Site Collection Administrators ⓘ

Site Collection
Select a site collection.

Site Collection: http://ws2012sp13 ▾

Primary Site Collection Administrator
Specify the administrator for this site collection. Only one user login can be provided; security groups are not supported.

Primary site collection administrator:

Marlene Lanphier

Secondary Site Collection Administrator
Optionally specify a secondary site collection administrator. Only one user login can be provided; security groups are not supported.

Secondary site collection administrator:

Troy Lanphier

OK   Cancel

FIGURE 4-41 Primary and secondary site collection administrators.

4. Click OK to commit your changes.

Maintaining site quotas

Site quotas enable a SharePoint 2013 administrator to control the resource usage of site collections in a SharePoint farm. A site collection is allotted a particular amount of resources, and the administrator of that site is notified when the site has grown to consume a significant percentage of the overall space.

EXAM TIP

Users do not receive reminder e-mail if the SharePoint farm does not have outgoing e-mail configured and functional. Ensure that this service is available before placing any quota restrictions within your farm.

Site quota templates

Site quotas are assigned as new sites are built from Central Administration. Although it is possible to assign quotas on an individual basis to site collections in the farm, it is much easier to manage growth of a site via the use of site quota templates. To create a site quota template, follow these steps:

1. Open Application Management in Central Administration.
2. On the Application Management page, select the Specify Quota Templates link.
3. In the Template Name section, you can choose to either modify an existing template or create a new quota template. If you create a new quota template, you can either start with a new blank template or start with another previously created template. Specify a name for the new template (see Figure 4-42).

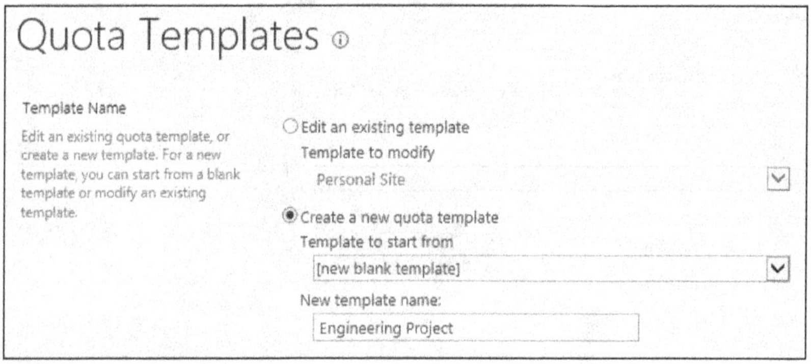

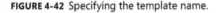

FIGURE 4-42 Specifying the template name.

4. The Storage Limit Values section has two check boxes intended to limit the maximum storage size and send a warning e-mail when a certain size limit is reached. Select either or both of these, populating values for each. A good rule of thumb is that the warning e-mail should be sent when the storage limit reaches 80 percent of the total storage maximum (see Figure 4-43).

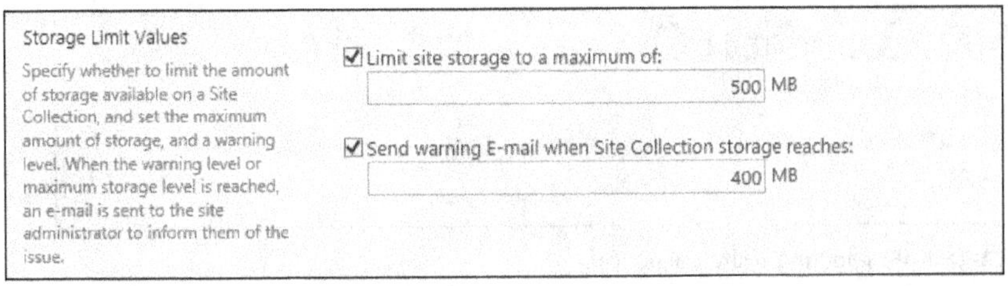

FIGURE 4-43 Storage limit values.

5. The last section of the quota template is called Sandboxed Solutions With Code Limits. As solutions are developed and deployed to the site collection, they consume sandbox resources, which are a number representing memory and processing cycles.

6. As with the storage limits, you can limit the maximum usage (on a daily basis) to a certain number of points and then set the warning e-mail to be sent out as you pass a certain resource value (see Figure 4-44).

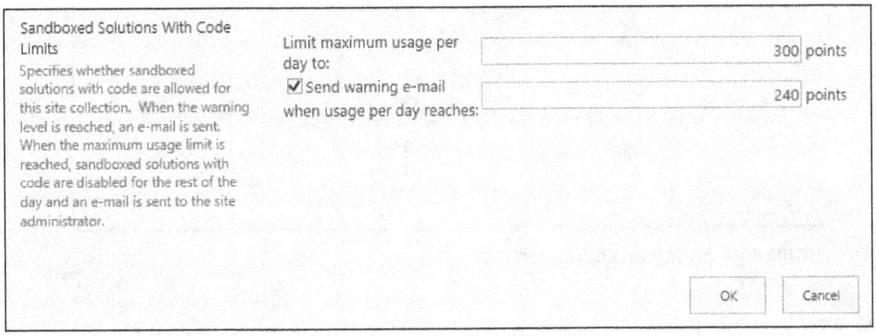

FIGURE 4-44 Sandboxed solutions quota values.

7. When you finish configuring your new quota template, click OK to commit your changes.

Assigning a quota to a site collection

After you have a series of quota templates built, assigning them is a straightforward process from Central Administration. To assign a site quota template to a site collection:

1. Open Application Management in Central Administration.

2. On the Application Management page, select the Configure Quotas And Locks link.

3. The first entry, Site Collection, lists the site collection to which the quota will be applied. If this is not the intended site collection, select the drop-down list next to the name of the current site collection and choose Change Site Collection (see Figure 4-45).

FIGURE 4-45 Selecting a site collection.

4. Scroll down to the Site Quota Information section (see Figure 4-46). In the Current Quota Template field, you can choose Individual Quota if you want to specify custom values for this site collection's quota; otherwise, select the desired quota template. Doing so causes all the values (which are identical to those in the quota template selection screen) to become grayed-out.

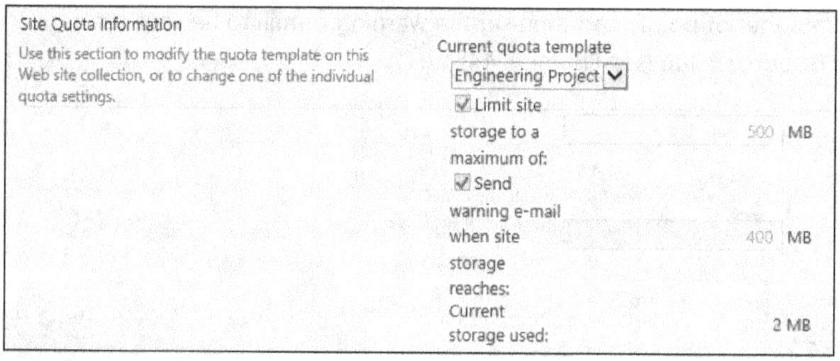

FIGURE 4-46 Selecting a quota template.

5. Scroll to the bottom of the page and click OK to commit your changes.

Configuring site policies

If you have been involved with SharePoint for any length of time, you may have run into sites that have been abandoned. There are several reasons why this can happen:

- The site was created along an organization structure that no longer applies.
- The site was created for a discontinued project and was abandoned along with the project.
- The site was left in place, but now hosts information that is out of date and no longer of value.
- Any way you cut it, a site that is not in use or is not useful as an archive should eventually be removed. This "trimming" effort is made possible by the use of site policies.

Site closures and deletions

In previous versions of SharePoint, the only disposition of a site from an automated stand-point was its eventual deletion. Although a site in SharePoint 2013 can still be automatically deleted; it can instead be set to a "closed" state.

A closed site is marked for eventual deletion, but its users can still modify the site and its content. A site that is in closed status no longer appears in locations that aggregate sites such as Outlook. If a site is closed, but the owner wants it to remain in use, he or she can go into the site settings menu and reopen the site.

Defining site policies

Site policies are defined at the site collection level. To create a new site policy (see Figure 4-47), do the following:

1. Navigate to the root site of your site collection.

2. From the Settings menu (gear icon), select Site Settings.

3. In the Site Collection Administration section, select Site Policies.

4. On the Site Policies page, select the Create link.

5. The Name and Description fields enable you to describe the intended use of the policy.

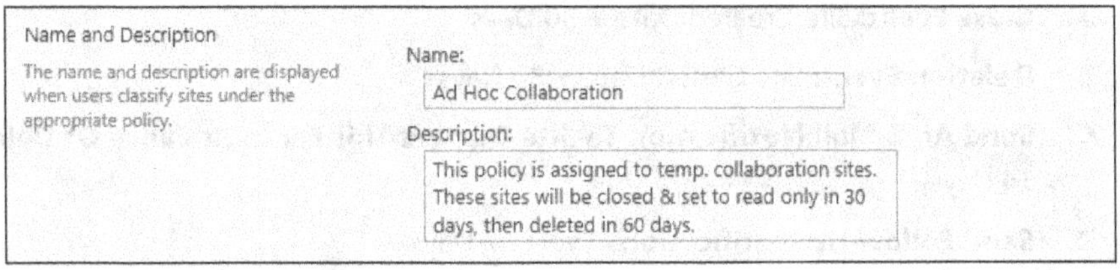

FIGURE 4-47 Name and description of the new policy.

As shown in Figure 4-48, the Site Closure And Deletion section describes what happens to the site (and its subsites) as a result of this policy. The options available are as follows:

- Do Not Close Or Delete Site Automatically
- Delete Sites Automatically
  - Specifies the deletion event date
  - (Optional) Send An Email Notification To Site Owners In Advance Of Deletion
  - (Optional) Send Follow-Up Notifications On A Timed Basis
  - (Optional) Allow The Site Owner To Postpone Imminent Deletion For A Fixed Period Of Time

- Close And Delete Sites Automatically
    - In addition to the options available for deleting sites, enables a site to be closed after a fixed period of time past its creation
- Set a site collection to read only when it is closed

1. Continuing the example policy, you will define a policy wherein the following conditions are met:

    A. Sites are closed and deleted automatically.

    B. The site should be closed 30 days after creation.

    C. The site should be deleted 30 days after site closure.

    D. E-mail is sent to the site owner 14 days prior to deletion and followed up every 7 days.

    E. Deletion of the site can be postponed for a maximum of 90 days (30 days to close, 30 days to delete, and 30 days delay on deletion).

2. The net result of these conditions indicates that a site could exist no longer than a theoretical maximum of 90 days.

3. In the site closure section, choose to have the policy close and delete sites automatically (see Figure 4-48).

    A. Close Event: Site Created Date + 30 Days

    B. Deletion Event: Site Closed Date + 30 Days

    C. Send An E-Mail Notification To Site Owners This Far In Advance Of Deletion: 14 Days

    D. Send Follow-Up Notifications Every: 7 Days

    E. Owners Can Postpone Imminent Deletion For: 30 Days

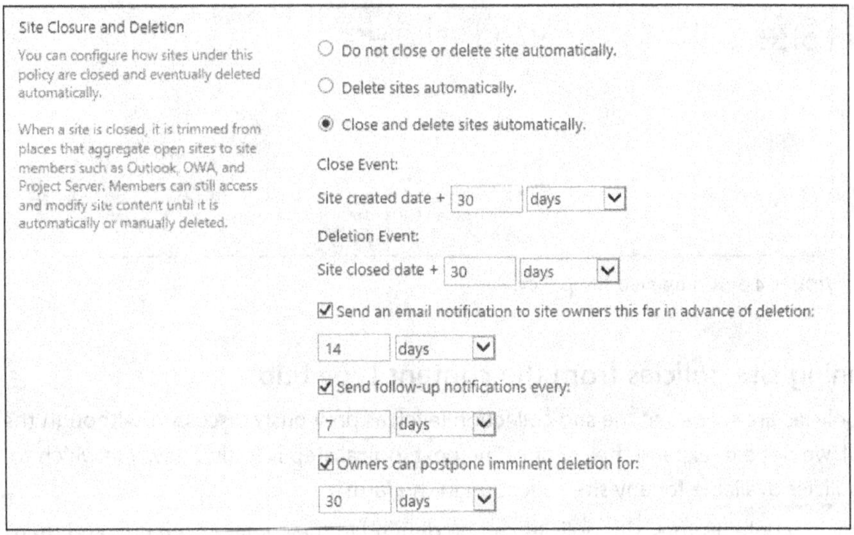

Site Closure and Deletion

You can configure how sites under this policy are closed and eventually deleted automatically.

When a site is closed, it is trimmed from places that aggregate open sites to site members such as Outlook, OWA, and Project Server. Members can still access and modify site content until it is automatically or manually deleted.

○ Do not close or delete site automatically.

○ Delete sites automatically.

● Close and delete sites automatically.

Close Event:

Site created date + [30] [days ▼]

Deletion Event:

Site closed date + [30] [days ▼]

☑ Send an email notification to site owners this far in advance of deletion:

[14] [days ▼]

☑ Send follow-up notifications every:

[7] [days ▼]

☑ Owners can postpone imminent deletion for:

[30] [days ▼]

FIGURE 4-48 Configuring site closure and deletion.

The Site Collection Closure section applies to the entirety of the site collection. If the root site of the site collection has this policy applied, the entirety of the site collection (the root site and all its subsites) is set to read only when the root site enters the "closed" state.

EXAM TIP

A site that has been closed is very different from a site that has been deleted.

Because this policy will be used exclusively for subsites, leave this check box deselected.

1. In the Site Collection Closure selection, leave the check box deselected.

2. Click OK to commit your changes (see Figure 4-49).

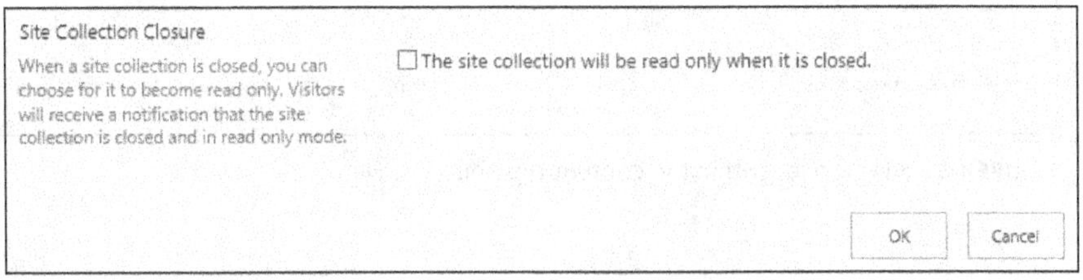

Site Collection Closure

When a site collection is closed, you can choose for it to become read only. Visitors will receive a notification that the site collection is closed and in read only mode.

☐ The site collection will be read only when it is closed.

OK   Cancel

FIGURE 4-49 Site Collection Closure section.

3. The completed policy appears within Site Policies. Note the importance of the Description field for describing the use of the site policy (see Figure 4-50). Also note the Publish Policy item, which will be discussed along with the content type hub.

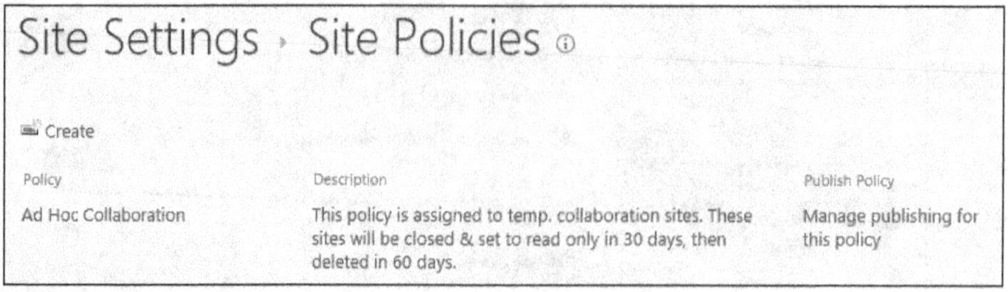

FIGURE 4-50 Completed site policy.

Defining site policies from the content type hub

Site policies are scoped at the site collection level, as previously discussed. Although they are useful, we need to expand their scope. The next logical step is to find a way in which to make site policies available for any site collection in the farm.

As with content types, site policies can be defined in the content type hub and then published. To create a new site policy that can be used for multiple site collections do the following:

1. Navigate to the content type hub for your farm (for example, http://intranet.boston. local/sites/cth).

2. Create a new site policy as you did in the previous section.

3. When the completed policy appears on the Site Policies page, select the link that reads Manage Publishing For This Policy (see Figure 4-51).

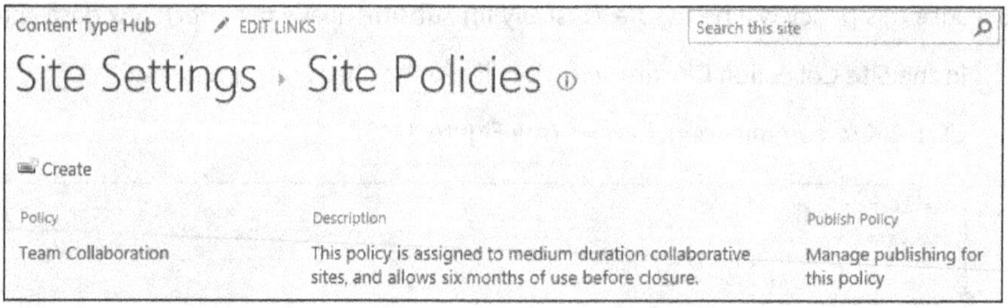

FIGURE 4-51 Site policies within the content type hub.

4. From the Content Type Publishing page for your site policy, you can choose to publish, unpublish, or republish the policy. The Publishing History section populates with the last date the policy was published.

5. Select the Publish radio button and then click OK (see Figure 4-52).

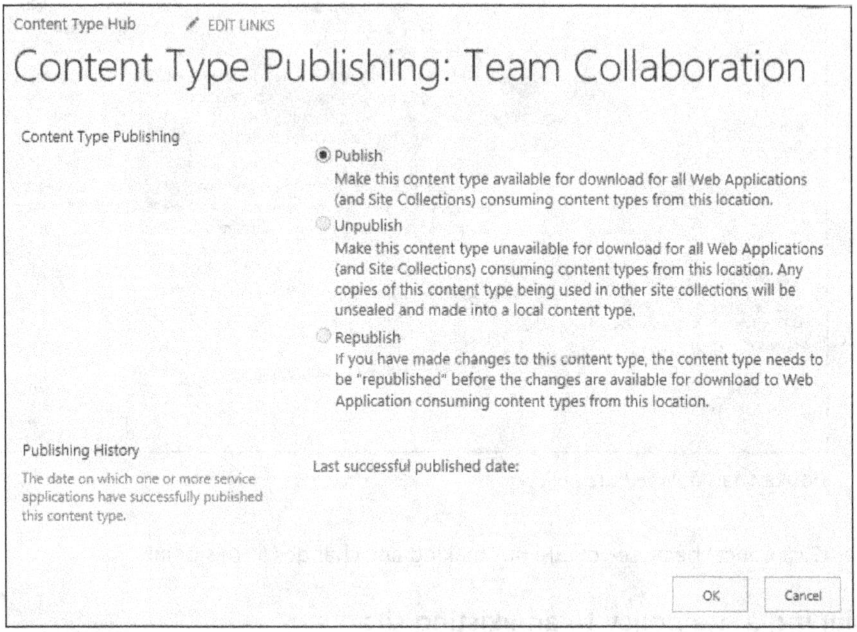

Content Type Hub   ✎ EDIT LINKS

Content Type Publishing: Team Collaboration

Content Type Publishing

◉ Publish
Make this content type available for download for all Web Applications (and Site Collections) consuming content types from this location.

○ Unpublish
Make this content type unavailable for download for all Web Applications (and Site Collections) consuming content types from this location. Any copies of this content type being used in other site collections will be unsealed and made into a local content type.

○ Republish
If you have made changes to this content type, the content type needs to be "republished" before the changes are available for download to Web Application consuming content types from this location.

Publishing History

The date on which one or more service applications have successfully published this content type.

Last successful published date:

| OK | Cancel |

FIGURE 4-52 Publishing the site policy.

6. Selecting the Manage Publishing For This Policy Link again from the Site Policies screen should show that the content type was successfully published (see Figure 4-53). Note that the only choices available at this point are to either unpublish or republish the site policy.

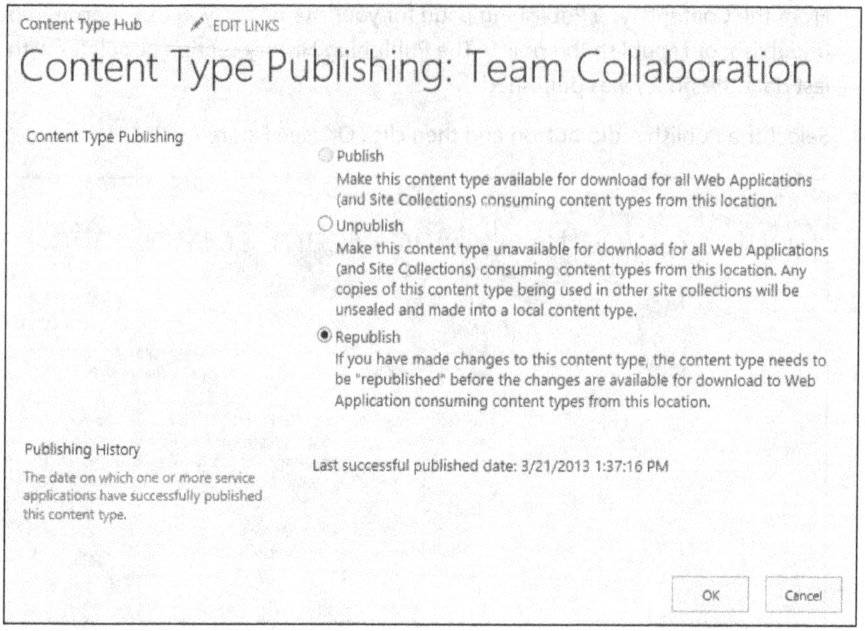

Content Type Hub   ✎ EDIT LINKS

Content Type Publishing: Team Collaboration

Content Type Publishing

○ Publish
Make this content type available for download for all Web Applications (and Site Collections) consuming content types from this location.

○ Unpublish
Make this content type unavailable for download for all Web Applications (and Site Collections) consuming content types from this location. Any copies of this content type being used in other site collections will be unsealed and made into a local content type.

◉ Republish
If you have made changes to this content type, the content type needs to be "republished" before the changes are available for download to Web Application consuming content types from this location.

Publishing History

The date on which one or more service applications have successfully published this content type.

Last successful published date: 3/21/2013 1:37:16 PM

OK   Cancel

FIGURE 4-53 Published site policy.

7. Click Cancel because you are not making any changes at this point.

Assigning a site policy to an existing site

As discussed in the "Configuring self-service site creation (SSSC)" section of this chapter, a policy can be selected for automatic application to any new self-service sites that are created. This is all well and good for self-service, but what about standard sites that are created by the site collection administrator or site owner?

Unfortunately, there is no simple way to assign the site policy as part of a new site's creation process, either via the GUI or via Windows PowerShell cmdlets. The good news is that it is easy to assign the site policy after the fact.

To assign a site policy to a site, follow these steps:

1. Open the site in your web browser.

2. From the Settings menu (gear icon), select Site Settings.

3. In the Site Administration section, select the Site Closure And Deletion link.

4. This page has three sections (see Figure 4-54):

   A. **Site Closure** A button that enables you to close the site immediately, thus removing it from aggregation.

   B. **Site Deletion** Indicates when the site will be deleted.

C. Site Policy Set by default to No Site Policy, this drop-down list enables you to choose a site policy for assignment to this site and its subsites.

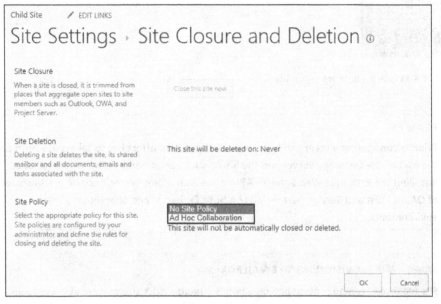

FIGURE 4-54 Selecting a site policy.

5. Select the appropriate site policy and click OK for it to take effect.

Configuring a team mailbox

One of the new features in SharePoint 2013 is the capability to build a team mailbox. This functionality enables users within a site to create a new mailbox for collaboration via Outlook.

From an IT perspective, things are as they should be because the newly created mailbox resides in Exchange rather than being hosted inside SharePoint. SharePoint uses a site feature called Site Mailbox to provision the necessary components.

After it is provisioned, you can not only view the site mailbox from within SharePoint (using Outlook Web Access) but also view your site documents from Outlook.

Creating the team mailbox

Initializing the site mailbox from within a team site is quite simple, requiring little technical ability. After SharePoint and Exchange are configured to work together (see the following Exam Tip), open your team site.

The Get Started With Your Site banner appears, located at the top of a team site. On the right side of the banner, there is an extra tile titled Keep Email In Context. Selecting this tile (see Figure 4-55) activates the Site Mailbox feature.

FIGURE 4-55 Site mailbox activation tile.

EXAM TIP

Prior to configuring a team mailbox, some configuration effort has to take place both on the part of the Exchange Server and the SharePoint Server admins. This effort includes installing the Exchange Web Services API on the SharePoint Server, and the establishment of OAuth Trust and Service permissions on both Exchange and SharePoint Server environments.

MORE INFO **PROVISIONING SITE MAILBOXES**

Site mailboxes can be provisioned only with Exchange 2013; the process of provisioning these mailboxes is detailed in the TechNet article "Configure Site Mailboxes in SharePoint Server 2013" at *http://technet.microsoft.com/en-us/library/jj552524.aspx*.

The Site Mailbox app appears, prompting you to add it to the team site. Selecting the Add It button completes the activation process (see Figure 4-56).

FIGURE 4-56 Activating the Site Mailbox app.

The Site Contents page appears, showing the newly added Site Mailbox app (see Figure 4-57). A Mailbox link also appears in the Recent section of the Current Navigation/Quick Links bar.

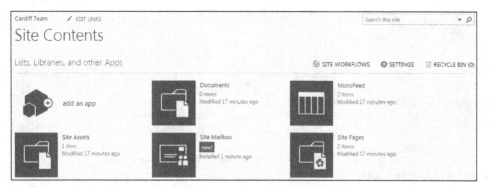

FIGURE 4-57 Site Contents page showing the new Site Mailbox app.

Selecting the Site Mailbox app begins the mailbox-creation process. A notice appears that tells you there may be a delay while the mailbox is being created (see Figure 4-58).

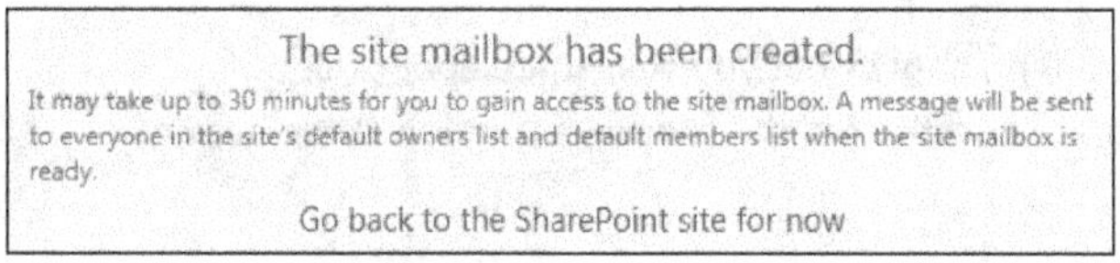

The site mailbox has been created.

It may take up to 30 minutes for you to gain access to the site mailbox. A message will be sent to everyone in the site's default owners list and default members list when the site mailbox is ready.

Go back to the SharePoint site for now

FIGURE 4-58 Site mailbox acknowledgment.

After returning to the SharePoint team site (and waiting for a bit), you can then select the Mailbox link to view your site mailbox. Notice that this functionality is actually being hosted by Outlook Web Access.

If this is the first time the e-mail is accessed, you need to select the appropriate language and time zone (see Figure 4-59).

Outlook Web App

Choose your preferred display language and home time zone below.

Language:
English (United States)

Time zone:
(UTC-06:00) Central Time (US & Canada)

⊕ save

FIGURE 4-59 Language and time zone selections for Microsoft Outlook Web App.

After the selections have been made, you will see a welcome e-mail in your Outlook team mailbox that indicates the e-mail address that should be sent to for people to read in the SharePoint site (see Figure 4-60).

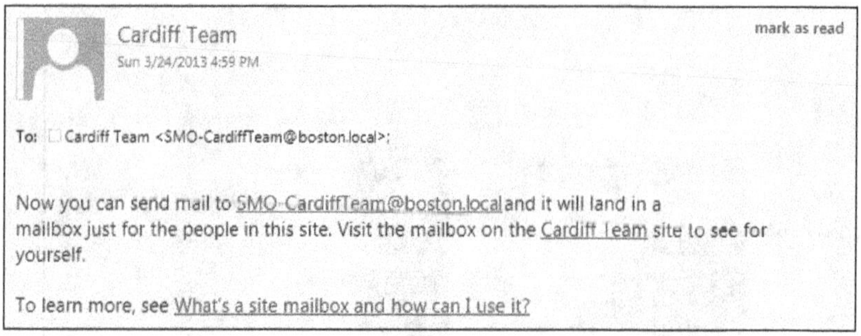

FIGURE 4-60 Welcome e-mail.

Thought experiment

Building a smaller implementation

In the following thought experiment, apply what you've learned about this objective. You can find answers to these questions in the "Answers" section at the back of this chapter.

You will be building a new SharePoint environment for a smaller organization. This organization has a limited IT staff; the IT administrator is comfortable with Central Administration but not Windows PowerShell. What sorts of site collections should you create for this environment?

Objective summary

- Host header site collections cannot be created via Central Administration; Windows PowerShell access is required.
- The -HostHeader switch is required when creating a new site collection within a host named/host header site collection.
- SSSCs are generally provisioned from a user's My Site.
- Primary and secondary site collection administrators receive notices about the status of their site collections; other site collection administrators and owners do not.
- Site policies are an effective mechanism for trimming unused sites from the SharePoint environment.
- Team mailboxes are presented via Outlook Web Application functionality.

Objective review

Answer the following questions to test your knowledge of the information in this objective. You can find the answers to these questions and explanations of why each answer choice is correct or incorrect in the "Answers" section at the end of this chapter.

1. Which of the following switches is required for use in creating host header site collections in Windows PowerShell?

    A. -HostNamed

    B. -HostHeaderSite

    C. -HostHeader

    D. -HNSC

2. Which of the following links is used from My Site to create a new SSSC?

    A. My Site

    B. Team Site

    C. New Site

    D. Self Service Site

3. Which of the following terms describes a site that is no longer made available via aggregation but is still available to its members?

    A. Closed

    B. Offline

    C. Unpublished

    D. Dormant

4. Which of the following Microsoft technologies is required for site mailboxes to be used? (Choose all that apply.)

    A. Microsoft Exchange

    B. Office web applications

    C. Outlook Web Access

    D. Outgoing e-mail

Objective 4.3: Manage Site and Site Collection Security

Securing a SharePoint installation can involve several different configuration levels. These levels vary in complexity from simply granting or removing access to a single item to deciding what applications should be run on a web application or what content can be displayed within a site.

> **This objective covers how to:**
> - Manage site access requests.
> - Manage app permissions.
> - Manage anonymous access.
> - Manage permission inheritance.
> - Configure permission levels.
> - Configure HTML field security.

Managing site access requests

As new users are added to the business, site collection administrators are not always kept informed of who needs access to a site or site collection. Permissions are not always granted to the appropriate sites.

New users then network with their peers to find out what components of the SharePoint environment are used for their work. When users visit a site to which they do not have permissions, they often see the message shown in Figure 4-61.

Sorry, this site hasn't been shared with you.

FIGURE 4-61 We truly are sorry...

Although this message is concise and to the point, it is not of much value to the person who needs access to the site. No phone number, no IM, not even an e-mail address to figure out just exactly who should be contacted to grant access to the site.

Fortunately, SharePoint administrators can make the user's interaction with this site a bit more practical by enabling access requests for the site, resulting in the user being able to ask permission to access the site.

Enabling site access requests

The first thing that is required for site access requests to work is outgoing e-mail; if this is not yet set up in your farm, you have to set it up before proceeding to configure site access requests.

After the outgoing e-mail is configured, you must visit the site and configure the access requests function:

1. Navigate to the site that you want to configure.

2. From the Settings menu (gear icon), select Site Settings.

3. In Site Settings, under Users And Permissions, select the Site Permissions link.

4. On the Permissions tab, select the Access Request Settings link (see Figure 4-62).

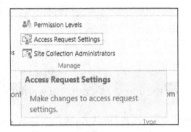

FIGURE 4-62 Access Request Settings icon.

5. On the Access Requests Settings page, determine whether access requests will be enabled (select or deselect the check box); then choose the e-mail address that will receive inbound requests (see Figure 4-63).

FIGURE 4-63 Allowing and directing requests.

6. Click OK to commit your changes.

EXAM TIP

Access requests are some of the few e-mail interactions that are not sent directly to a site collection administrator (by default). These e-mail messages are often sent to a group e-mail box because you can choose only a single e-mail address.

Managing site access requests

When a user visits the site now, the lack of permissions presents a different experience (see Figure 4-64).

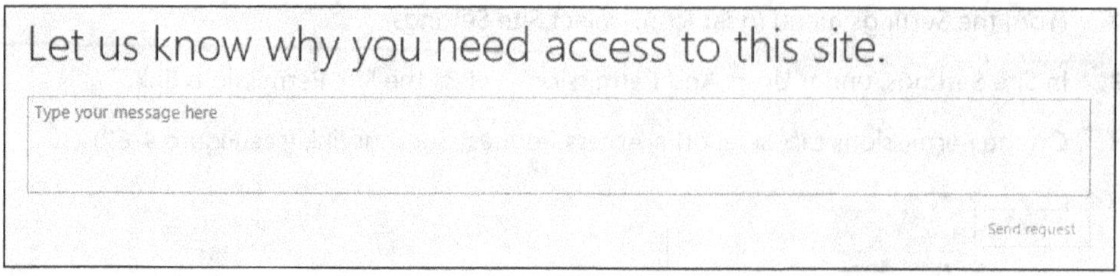

Let us know why you need access to this site.

Type your message here

Send request

FIGURE 4-64 Requesting access to a site.

1. An administrator visiting the permissions page for the site sees a pop-up warning (see Figure 4-65).

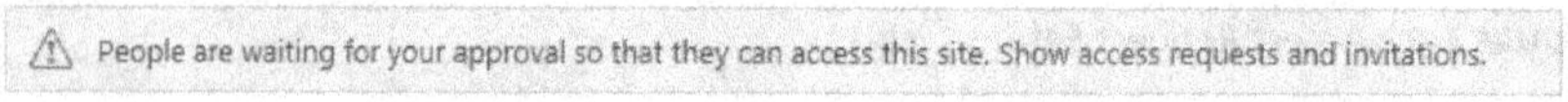

   ⚠ People are waiting for your approval so that they can access this site. Show access requests and invitations.

   FIGURE 4-65 Pending access approvals.

2. You can either click the link in the pop-up warning or select the Access Requests And Invitations link in Site Settings (see Figure 4-66).

Site Settings

Users and Permissions
People and groups
Site permissions
Access requests and invitations
Site collection administrators
Site app permissions

FIGURE 4-66 Access requests and invitations.

3. The submitted access requests now show in the library and can be acted upon (see Figure 4-67).

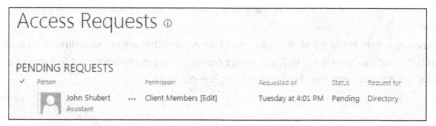

Access Requests ⓘ

PENDING REQUESTS

✓	Person	Permission	Requested on	Status	Request for
	John Shubert ••• Assistant	Client Members [Edit]	Tuesday at 4:01 PM	Pending	Directory

FIGURE 4-67 Pending access requests.

Managing app permissions

SharePoint 2013 introduces the notion of installing apps from the SharePoint Store to your SharePoint farm. If you've ever installed an app to your smartphone or tablet device, you are familiar with this process:

1. Find an app that would be useful in your SharePoint environment.

2. Purchase (they are sometimes free) and download/install the app to your environment.

3. Note the permission levels the app is requesting; decide whether to trust the app to possess those permissions.

4. Use the app on your SharePoint site.

EXAM TIP

Depending on the security considerations for your SharePoint farm, you may want to make the store available for users to view but review and approve any app before it is installed.

App permission requests

When an app is installed to your SharePoint farm, it requests one of four permission levels available in your farm (shown in Table 4-3):

TABLE 4-3 App permission requests

Permission Request	Description	Permissions Included
Read-Only	Enables apps to view pages, list items, and download documents.	View Items Open Items View Versions Create Alerts Use Self-Service Site Creation View Pages
Write	Enables apps to view, add, update, and delete items in existing lists and document libraries.	Read-Only permissions, plus: Add Items Edit Items Delete Items Delete Versions Browse Directories Edit Personal User Information Manage Personal Views Add/Remove Personal Web Parts Update Personal Web Parts
Manage	Enables apps to view, add, update, delete, approve, and customize items or pages within a web site.	Write permissions, plus: Manage Lists Add and Customize Pages Apply Themes and Borders Apply Style Sheets
Full Control	Enables apps to have full control within the specified scope.	All permissions

App permission request scopes

An app permission request can be assigned at any of four possible scopes within your SharePoint farm:

- SPSite defines the app permission request scope as a SharePoint 2013 site collection (site).
- SPWeb defines the app permission request scope as a SharePoint 2013 web site (web).
- SPList defines the app permission request scope as a SharePoint 2013 list.
- Tenancy defines the app permission request scope as a tenancy.

These scopes are hierarchical in nature: If an app is assigned permissions at one level, all levels that inherit from the parent also provide the same permissions. For example, if an app is granted permission to the SPSite scope, it also has the same permissions at the SPWeb and SPList scopes.

Scope types are expressed as uniform resource identifiers (URIs); the first three URIs begin with the http://sharepoint/content string. This URI indicates that these permissions are assigned to a content database within a SharePoint farm.

Each scope appends its type to the end of the URI (except Tenancy):

- SPSite appends the /sitecollection/ string to the end of the URI (http://sharepoint/content/sitecollection/)
- SPWeb appends the /sitecollection/web string to the end of the URI (http://sharepoint/content/sitecollection/web)
- SPList appends the /sitecollection/web/list string to the end of the URI (http://sharepoint/content/sitecollection/web/list)
- Tenancy follows the URI structure http://<sharepointserver>/<content>/<tenant>/

App authorization policies

To utilize an app requires two distinct permission sets: user and app. Depending on the policy assigned to the app, a policy that designates one or both of these sets must be assigned to the app in order for it to access a content database.

There are three distinct authorization policies available:

- User and app policy requires that both the permissions of the user and app be evaluated before authorization is granted to the content database.
- App-only policy requires that only the permissions of the app be evaluated before authorization is granted to the content database. This setting is used when the app does not act on behalf of the user.
- User-only policy requires that only the permissions of the user be evaluated before authorization is granted to the content database. This setting is used when users are accessing their own resources.

Managing anonymous access

Anonymous access is controlled at multiple levels within a SharePoint 2013 farm. As discussed, a web app must be configured to allow anonymous access before any site collections, sites, or content within the web application can be allowed to be accessed anonymously (see Figure 4-68).

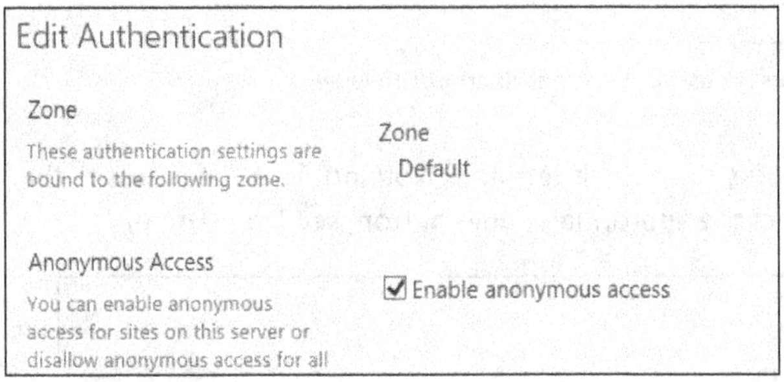

Edit Authentication

Zone

These authentication settings are bound to the following zone.

Zone
Default

Anonymous Access

You can enable anonymous access for sites on this server or disallow anonymous access for all

☑ Enable anonymous access

FIGURE 4-68 Enabling anonymous access at the web application level.

Enabling anonymous access at the web application level provides no access to any of the content within the web application; it merely allows users to authenticate to the web app. To access content within the web app, anonymous access needs to be added at the site collection, site, or list/library level.

EXAM TIP

Merely allowing anonymous access at the web application makes little difference to the content available within the web application. Be aware of how anonymous access is applied to each site or site collection and audit each web app occasionally. External search engines can be used for this task and quickly expose any security flaws you may have.

After anonymous permissions are assigned, any items that inherit permissions also inherit anonymous access.

To enable anonymous users to access a site collection/site, follow these steps:

1. Navigate to the site collection/site.

2. From the Settings menu (gear icon), select Site Settings.

3. In Site Settings, under Users And Permissions, select the Site Permissions link.

4. On the Permissions tab, select the Anonymous Access icon (see Figure 4-69).

FIGURE 4-69 Enabling anonymous access at the site collection/site level.

5. On the Anonymous Access page, the default setting is Nothing. To grant access to the web site or lists/libraries, select the appropriate radio button (see Figure 4-70).

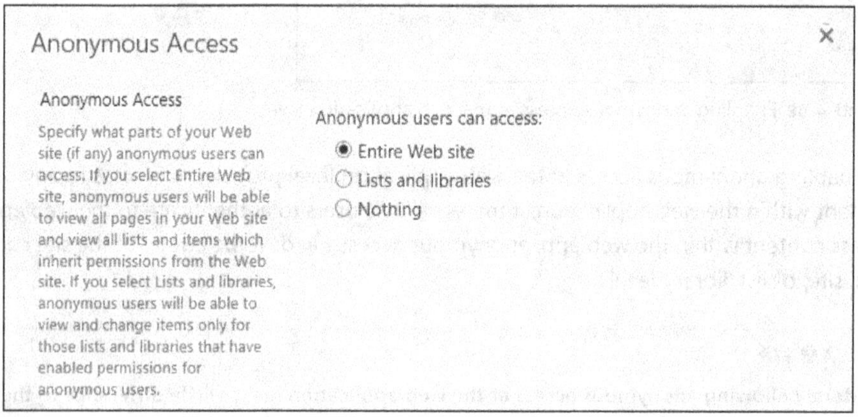

Anonymous Access   ×

Anonymous Access

Specify what parts of your Web   Anonymous users can access:
site (if any) anonymous users can
access. If you select Entire Web   ● Entire Web site
site, anonymous users will be able   ○ Lists and libraries
to view all pages in your Web site   ○ Nothing
and view all lists and items which
inherit permissions from the Web
site. If you select Lists and libraries,
anonymous users will be able to
view and change items only for
those lists and libraries that have
enabled permissions for
anonymous users.

FIGURE 4-70 Selecting the level of anonymous access.

Managing permission inheritance

Permission inheritance is a means of simplifying the administration of permissions on a site collection, site, list, or individual item. Instead of having to designate permissions on each and every item, you can configure inheritance (enabled by default) within a site or site collection.

Breaking permissions inheritance

By default, sites inherit their permissions from a site collection, whereas lists and libraries inherit permissions from the site they are contained within. More often than not, you will be breaking permissions inheritance rather than enabling it.

To stop permissions inheritance, follow these steps:

1. Navigate to the subsite.

2. From the Settings menu (gear icon), select Site Settings.

3. In Site Settings, under Users And Permissions, select the Site Permissions link.

4. Before proceeding, have a look at the permissions—they do not change. When you stop inheriting permissions from the parent, a copy of the permissions is applied to the child site.

5. On the ribbon, note the Manage Parent icon, indicating that the permissions that apply to this child site are set at the parent level. Select the Stop Inheriting Permissions icon to break inheritance (see Figure 4-71).

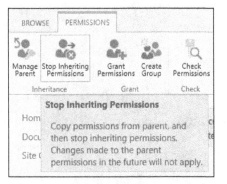

FIGURE 4-71 Stop inheriting permissions from the parent.

6. A pop-up window appears, notifying you that you will soon be creating unique permissions for this site and its subsites (see Figure 4-72). Click OK.

FIGURE 4-72 Creating unique permissions.

7. The next page that appears is Set Up Groups For This Site. This page offers you the chance to create new visitor (read privileges), members (change privileges), and owner (full privileges) groups for this site.

8. You can either choose to create a new groups or use existing groups as provided within the site collection (see Figure 4-73), but most often, you will create new members and owners, leaving the parent's visitors group (team site visitors) able to read the site.

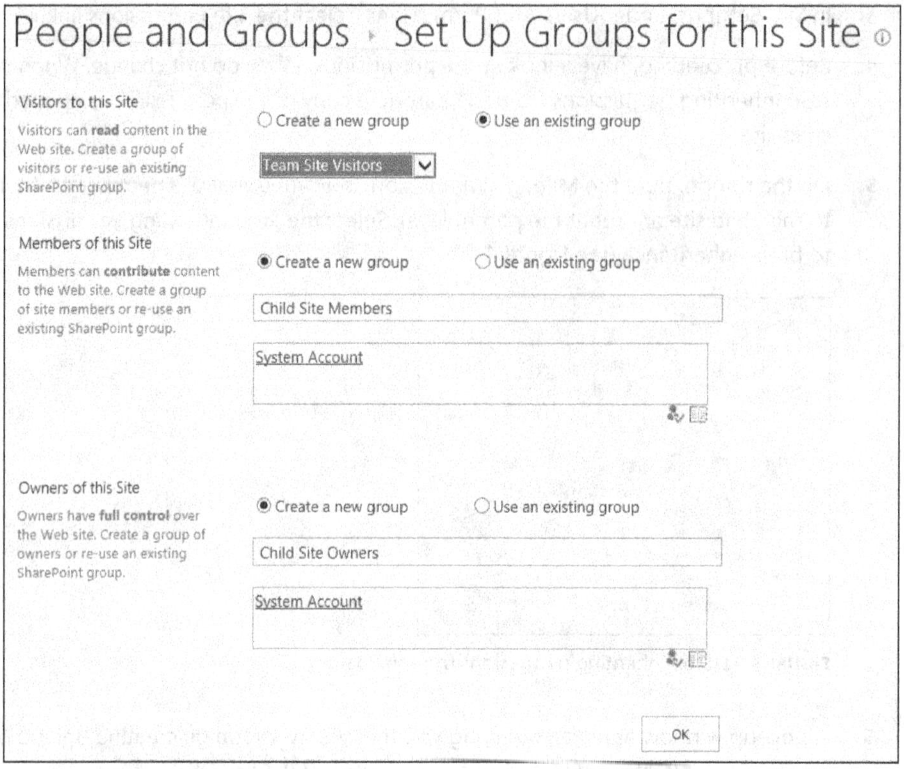

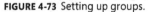

People and Groups › Set Up Groups for this Site ⓘ

Visitors to this Site

Visitors can **read** content in the Web site. Create a group of visitors or re-use an existing SharePoint group.

○ Create a new group   ◉ Use an existing group

[Team Site Visitors ▼]

Members of this Site

Members can **contribute** content to the Web site. Create a group of site members or re-use an existing SharePoint group.

◉ Create a new group   ○ Use an existing group

[Child Site Members]

[System Account]

Owners of this Site

Owners have **full control** over the Web site. Create a group of owners or re-use an existing SharePoint group.

◉ Create a new group   ○ Use an existing group

[Child Site Owners]

[System Account]

[OK]

FIGURE 4-73 Setting up groups.

9. Click OK to commit these changes.

Deleting unique permissions

At some point in the future, you may decide to "re-inherit" permissions from the parent site. This is done by using the Delete Unique Permissions command from the Permissions tab of the Site Permissions page.

> **EXAM TIP**
>
> It is very important to note that the act of re-inheriting permissions not only affects this site but also all sites beneath this level that inherit permissions from this site. You may inadvertently expose content if you apply these changes incorrectly.

To re-inherit permissions:

1. Navigate to the subsite.

2. From the Settings menu (gear icon), select Site Settings.

3. In Site Settings, under Users And Permissions, select the Site Permissions link.

4. Have a look at the permissions present before you revert the permissions to the parent; in the Permissions tab of the ribbon, select the Delete Unique Permissions icon (see Figure 4-74).

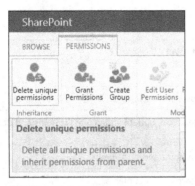

FIGURE 4-74 Deleting unique permissions.

5. Re-inheriting permissions can be tricky, as noted in Figure 4-75. Changes made at this level can cause newer permissions to be removed, causing a loss of access for some people in your organization. Click OK to proceed with your changes.

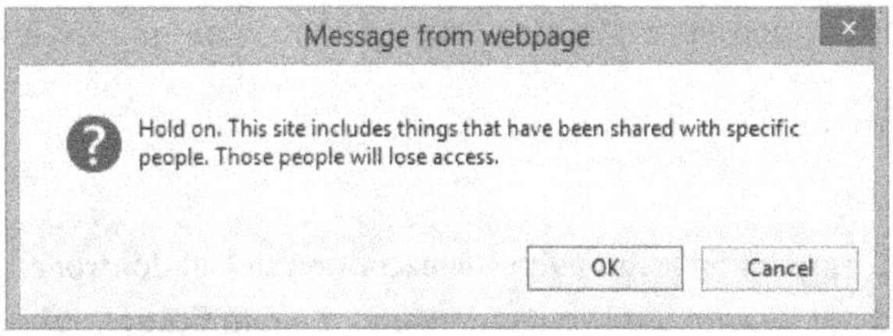

FIGURE 4-75 Deleting unique permissions can cause a loss of access.

6. Any unique groups that were previously created are now gone from this site. That does not mean that they cannot be added back in; just that they are removed for now.

> **IMPORTANT** **SITE GROUPS DON'T GET DELETED**
>
> If you created any specific groups as part of the "stop inheritance" process, these groups remain in the site collection until you delete them. You can simply choose to re-add these groups to the parent's permissions structure if appropriate.

Configuring permission levels

The previous section discussed the inheritance of permissions and showed how these permissions related to groups within a SharePoint site (from a high level). This section takes the discussion this a step further, showing how each of these groups is assigned a permission level that, in turn, is assigned a group of more granular permissions.

Default permission levels within a SharePoint site aggregate a series of permissions within each site collection; these permission levels can then be assigned to an individual or group. There are several out-of-the-box (OOB) permission levels, including those shown in Table 4-4.

TABLE 4-4 OOB permission levels

Permission Level	Users/Groups with this Permission Level
Full Control	Has full control.
Design	Can view, add, update, delete, approve, and customize.
Edit	Can add, edit and delete lists; can view, add, update and delete list items and documents.
Contribute	Can view, add, update, and delete list items and documents.
Read	Can view pages and list items and download documents.
Limited Access	Can view specific lists, document libraries, list items, folders, or documents when given permissions.
View Only	Can view pages, list items, and documents. Document types with server-side file handlers can be viewed in the browser but not downloaded.

Although these permission levels tend to cover most needs, SharePoint administrators are occasionally called on to alter existing permission levels or configure new permission levels within a site collection.

EXAM TIP

Although you can alter the OOB permission levels (with the exception of Full Control and Limited Access), doing so would not be wise until you understand the ramifications of such a change. For instance, you may decide that users holding the Contribute permission level should not be able to delete items (a fairly common request). Instead of altering the OOB permission Contribute permission level, consider building a similar permission level, perhaps called Contribute (No Delete), and assigning users to that permission level.

Adding a new permission level

As previously stated, it is a fairly common request to build a permission level similar, but not identical to, one of the OOB permission levels. In this example, we will view and document the existing rights of the Contribute permission level.

Let's begin by viewing the granular permissions present in the Contribute permission level:

1. Navigate to the top of the site collection where you want to build the new permission level.

2. From the Settings menu (gear icon), select Site Settings.

3. In Site Settings, under Users And Permissions, select the Site Permissions link.

4. In the ribbon, choose the Permissions tab and then select the Permission Levels icon and link (see Figure 4-76).

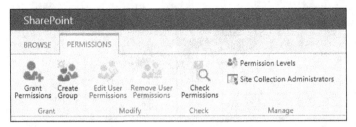

FIGURE 4-76 Permission Levels icon and link.

5. On the Permission Levels page, you see a series of permission levels, which can differ based on the type of site you have provisioned (team sites versus publishing sites, for instance). Note the existing permission levels and the fact that the Full Control and Limited Access levels cannot be changed (see Figure 4-77).

Home   Child Site   ✎ EDIT LINKS

Permissions › Permission Levels ⓘ

🗋 Add a Permission Level | ✖ Delete Selected Permission Levels

	Permission Level	Description
☐	Full Control	Has full control.
☐	Design	Can view, add, update, delete, approve, and customize.
☐	Edit	Can add, edit and delete lists; can view, add, update and delete list items and documents.
☐	Contribute	Can view, add, update, and delete list items and documents.
☐	Read	Can view pages and list items and download documents.
☐	Limited Access	Can view specific lists, document libraries, list items, folders, or documents when given permissions.
☐	View Only	Can view pages, list items, and documents. Document types with server-side file handlers can be viewed in the browser but not downloaded.

FIGURE 4-77 Existing permission levels and descriptions.

6. Because you will view the individual permissions present in the Contribute permission level, select its link.

7. The individual permissions that are present in each permission level are broken up into three major groups (see Figure 4-78):

A. List Permissions control a user's interaction with lists and libraries on the site.

B. Site Permissions control a user's interaction with the site.

C. Personal Permissions control a user's personal view of lists and web part pages.

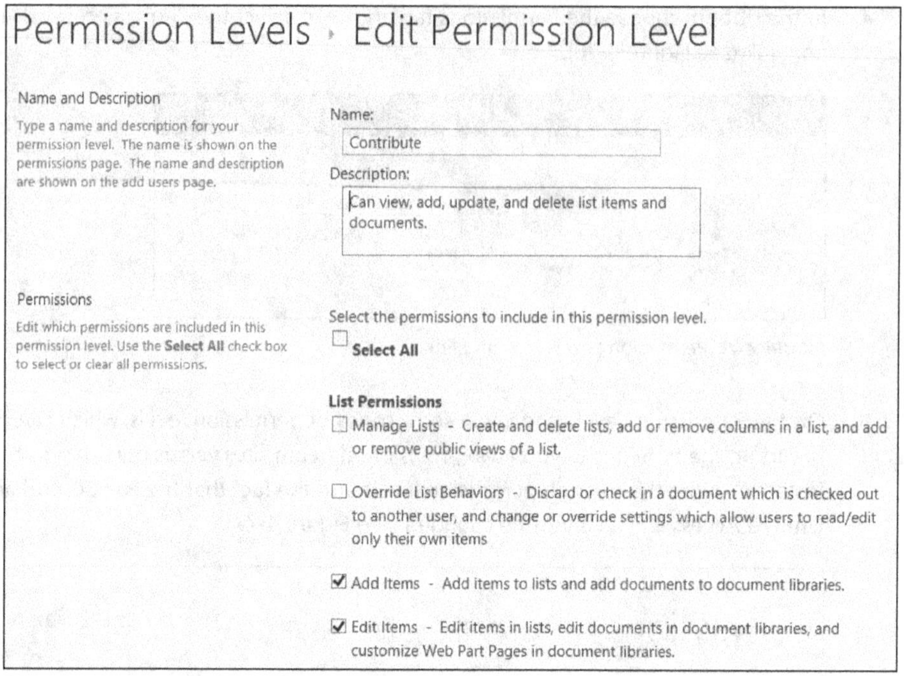

Permission Levels › Edit Permission Level

Name and Description

Type a name and description for your permission level. The name is shown on the permissions page. The name and description are shown on the add users page.

Name:

Contribute

Description:

Can view, add, update, and delete list items and documents.

Permissions

Edit which permissions are included in this permission level. Use the **Select All** check box to select or clear all permissions.

Select the permissions to include in this permission level.

☐ **Select All**

List Permissions

☐ Manage Lists - Create and delete lists, add or remove columns in a list, and add or remove public views of a list.

☐ Override List Behaviors - Discard or check in a document which is checked out to another user, and change or override settings which allow users to read/edit only their own items

☑ Add Items - Add items to lists and add documents to document libraries.

☑ Edit Items - Edit items in lists, edit documents in document libraries, and customize Web Part Pages in document libraries.

FIGURE 4-78 Individual permissions within the Contribute permission level.

8. Obviously, it might take you a while to document each of these permissions by hand. Fortunately, you don't have to: Scroll down to the bottom of the page and select the Copy Permission Level button (see Figure 4-79).

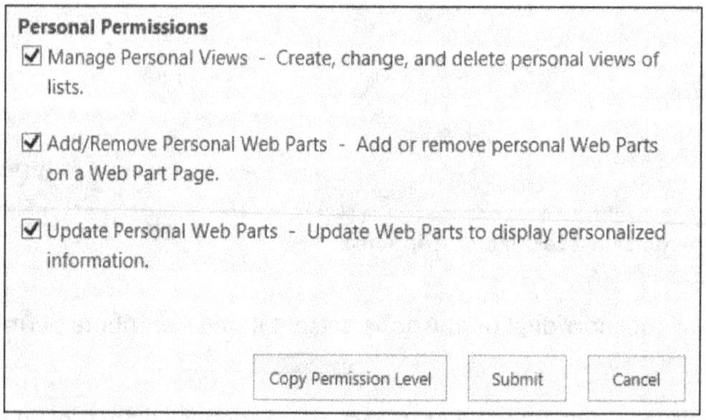

Personal Permissions

☑ Manage Personal Views - Create, change, and delete personal views of lists.

☑ Add/Remove Personal Web Parts - Add or remove personal Web Parts on a Web Part Page.

☑ Update Personal Web Parts - Update Web Parts to display personalized information.

| Copy Permission Level | Submit | Cancel |

FIGURE 4-79 Copy permission level.

9. For this example, you will copy Contribute, removing the users' ability to delete an item. Enter the following values in Name and Description (see Figure 4-80).

   A. **Name: Contribute (No Delete)**

   B. **Description: Can View, Add, And Update List Items And Documents**

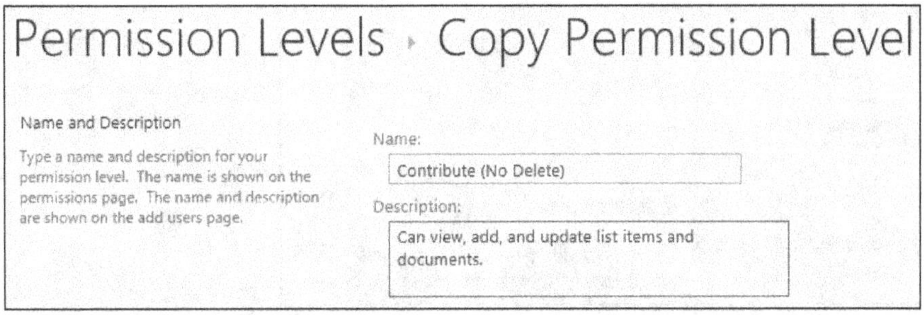

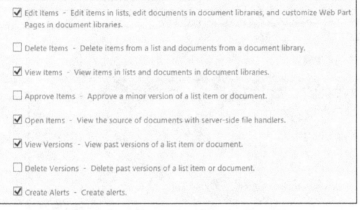

FIGURE 4-80 Adding name and description.

10. To remove the Delete capabilities present in the original permission level, deselect the Delete Items and Delete Versions permission check boxes (see Figure 4-81).

☑ Edit Items - Edit items in lists, edit documents in document libraries, and customize Web Part Pages in document libraries.

☐ Delete Items - Delete items from a list and documents from a document library.

☑ View Items - View items in lists and documents in document libraries.

☐ Approve Items - Approve a minor version of a list item or document.

☑ Open Items - View the source of documents with server-side file handlers.

☑ View Versions - View past versions of a list item or document.

☐ Delete Versions - Delete past versions of a list item or document.

☑ Create Alerts - Create alerts.

FIGURE 4-81 Deselecting the Delete Items and Delete Versions check boxes.

11. Scroll to the bottom of the page and click Create to commit your changes. Your new permission level is not ready for use (see Figure 4-82).

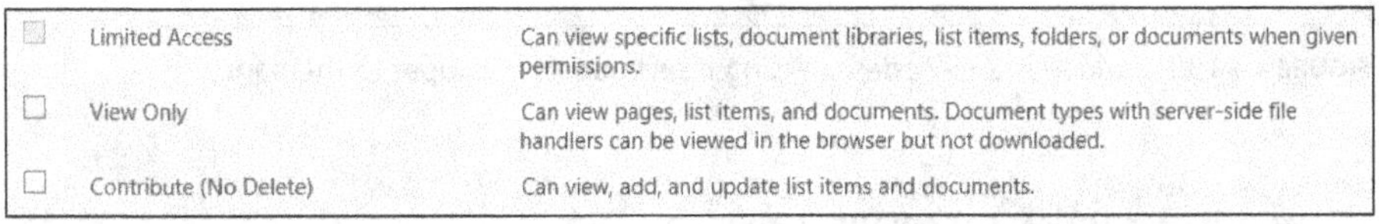

☐	Limited Access	Can view specific lists, document libraries, list items, folders, or documents when given permissions.
☐	View Only	Can view pages, list items, and documents. Document types with server-side file handlers can be viewed in the browser but not downloaded.
☐	Contribute (No Delete)	Can view, add, and update list items and documents.

FIGURE 4-82 New Contribute (No Delete) permission level.

Configuring HTML Field Security

SharePoint 2013 enables you to embed inline frames (iframes) into SharePoint sites that represent external web content. Embedding an iframe is done simply by editing a page and selecting the Embed Code icon in the ribbon (see Figure 4-83).

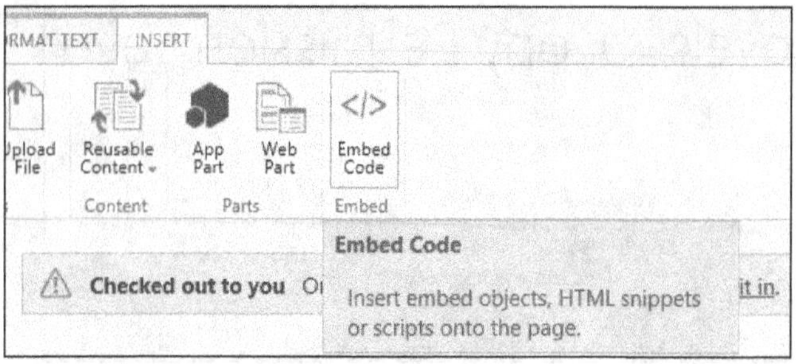

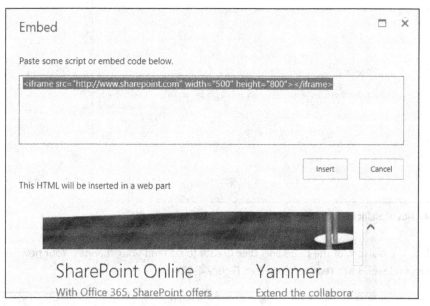

FIGURE 4-83 Embedding code.

After the code for the iframe has been entered (in this case, <iframe src="http://www.sharepoint.com" width="500" height="800"></iframe>), a preview appears in the Embed window (see Figure 4-84).

FIGURE 4-84 Embedded iframe code; selecting Insert adds the snippet to the page.

IMPORTANT WHEN NO PREVIEW APPEARS

If you enter code in the Embed window for an iframe, one of three things will happen: (1) The destination site will tell you that iframes are not allowed to reference the site; (2) the Embed preview will show you the contents of the site in preview; or (3) the Embed preview will show you nothing at all, indicating that you have an error in your iframe HTML code.

Selecting the Insert button will show you the finished Script Editor Web Part, which you can move to any point on the page (see Figure 4-85).

FIGURE 4-85 Script Editor web part.

HTML security levels

Within Site Settings, you can choose one of three HTML field security levels:

- Do Not Permit Contributors To Insert Iframes From External Domains Into Pages On This Site (default)
- Permit Contributors To Insert Iframes From Any External Domain Into Pages On This Site
- Permit Contributors To Insert Iframes From The Following List Of External Domains Into Pages On This Site (selected for this example)

EXAM TIP

It is possible (although not very likely) to cause a security breach by having an iframe represent content in a site that has been compromised. Choosing to limit your users to a particular subset of external domains is the best way to strike a balance between showing external content and showing none at all.

The last option enables you to determine the domains from which you allow iframes to be chosen. A sample listing of iframes is already chosen for you, but you can add others (see Figure 4-86).

Site Settings ⟩ HTML Field Security ⓘ

Allow external iframes

Specify whether contributors can insert external iframes in HTML fields on pages in this site. Iframes are commonly used on Web pages to show dynamic content from other web sites, like directions from a mapping site, or a video from a video site.

When using the list of allowed domains, note that all subdomains of the allowed domains are automatically trusted.

These settings do not affect content placed in scriptable Web Parts. Users who can add or edit scriptable Web Parts will be able to insert iframes pointing to any domain, regardless of the settings on this page.

○ Do not permit contributors to insert iframes from external domains into pages on this site.

○ Permit contributors to insert iframes from any external domain into pages on this site.

◉ Permit contributors to insert iframes from the following list of external domains into pages on this site:

Allow iframes from this domain:

| www.xbox.com ✕ | Add |

youtube.com
youtube-nocookie.com
player.vimeo.com
bing.com
office.microsoft.com
skydrive.live.com

FIGURE 4-86 Adding a new domain for use with iframes.

To commit the changes to the HTML Field Security settings, click OK.

Thought experiment
Dropping content into SharePoint

In the following thought experiment, apply what you've learned about this objective. You can find answers to these questions in the "Answers" section at the back of this chapter.

Your users request an anonymous dropbox (a site exposed to the Internet that could receive documentation). Prior to building and exposing the site, what sort of items should you consider for this environment?

Objective summary

- Enabling site access requests requires the configuration of outgoing e-mail within a SharePoint farm.

- Site access request e-mail messages are not sent to site collection administrators (by default).

- Site owners can view existing access requests and invite other users to access a site by selecting the access requests and invitations e-mail in Site Settings.

- Anonymous access is inherited; a site that is assigned anonymous access also assigns this permission level to any of its content (unless inheritance is blocked).
- Permission inheritance can be configured at any level within a site collection (site collection, site, list/library, individual item).
- A site's webmaster may choose to disallow iframes from representing content contained on their web site.

Objective review

Answer the following questions to test your knowledge of the information in this objective. You can find the answers to these questions and explanations of why each answer choice is correct or incorrect in the "Answers" section at the end of this chapter.

1. Which of the following services is required for use in configuring site access requests? (Choose all that apply.)

    A. Inbound email

    B. Outbound email

    C. Business Connectivity Services

    D. User Profile Services

2. Which of the following items can be individually secured for anonymous access?

    A. Web application

    B. Site or site collection

    C. Individual lists and libraries

    D. Individual items

3. At which of the following levels can you configure security inheritance? (Choose all that apply.)

    A. Web application

    B. Site or site collection

    C. Individual lists and libraries

    D. Individual items

4. Which of the following permission groups cannot have its permissions altered? (Choose all that apply.)

    A. Full Control

    B. Contribute

    C. Limited Access

    D. Read

Objective 4.4: Manage search

One of the cornerstone technologies present in SharePoint 2013, search is pervasive. The capability to search and render content can appear in navigation, filtering, search queries, and many other locations. Search is also capable of reaching across boundaries, surfacing content present in other line of business systems.

> **This objective covers how to:**
> - Manage result sources.
> - Manage query rules.
> - Manage display templates.
> - Manage Search Engine Optimization (SEO) settings.
> - Manage result types.
> - Manage a search schema.

Managing result sources

Result sources have two core functions:

- They are used to scope search results to a certain type of content or subset of search results.
- They are also used to federate queries with the local SharePoint index, a remote Share-Point index, OpenSearch, or a Microsoft Exchange Server index.

If you previously created search scopes in prior versions of SharePoint, result sources may seem a bit familiar. In fact, search scopes are deprecated, having been replaced outright by result sources.

EXAM TIP

Although search scopes are deprecated, they can still be viewed and used in queries. They cannot, however, be edited in SharePoint 2013; if you need to change a scope, you will instead need to replace it with a new result source that accomplishes the same function.

In SharePoint Server 2010, only the administrator of the Search service could configure federated locations for search. Within SharePoint Server 2013, this functionality has been expanded such that site collection administrators, site owners, and site designers can also create and configure result sources for use at the site collection and site levels. Search service administration privileges are still required for creating farm-scoped result sources.

Creating a new result source in SharePoint 2013

The creation of a new result source in SharePoint 2013 involves five tasks: providing general information, specifying a protocol, selecting a search result type, developing a query transform, and specifying credential information.

The following example walks through the creation of a farm-scoped result source capable of returning OneNote items in your farm:

1. Open Central Administration; within the Application Management section, select Manage Service Applications.

2. Click the link for your search service application.

3. In the Queries And Results section of the Search Administration page, select Result Sources.

4. On the Manage Result Sources page, select New Result Source.

5. In the General Information section, provide a name and description for your new result source (see Figure 4-87):

   A. **Name:** OneNote Files

   B. **Description:** Returns A List Of OneNote files Within This SharePoint Farm.

General Information

Names must be unique at each administrative level. For example, two result sources in a site cannot share a name, but one in a site and one provided by the site collection can.

Descriptions are shown as tooltips when selecting result sources in other configuration pages.

Name

OneNote Files

Description

Returns a list of OneNote files within this SharePoint farm.

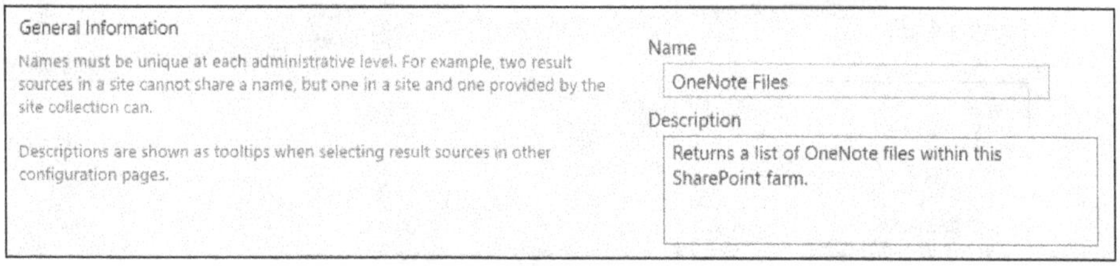

FIGURE 4-87 Name and description of the result source.

6. There are four protocol choices available: Local SharePoint (this farm), Remote SharePoint (a different farm), OpenSearch 1.0/1.1 (used to crawl OpenSearch compatible sources), and Exchange (used to crawl Exchange information).

7. Select the Local SharePoint protocol radio button (see Figure 4-88) because you are searching the current farm.

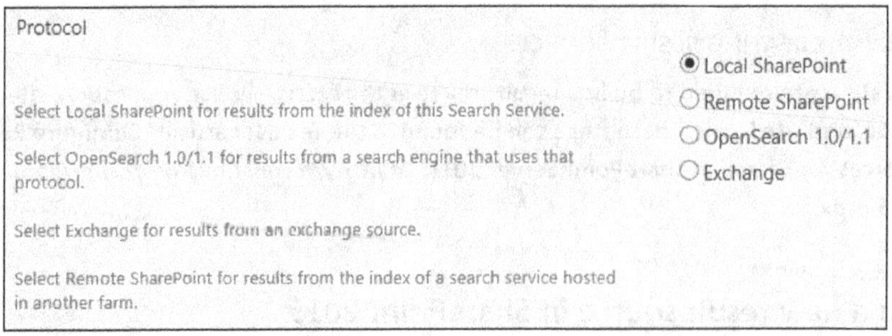

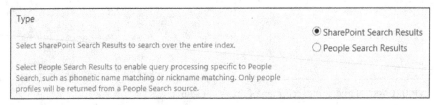

FIGURE 4-88 Protocol selections.

8. The Type section changes, based on the protocol you chose in the previous step. For the Local SharePoint protocol, two types of search results are available: SharePoint Search Results, which returns all results in the farm; and People Search Results, which returns only information about individuals. Select the SharePoint Search Results radio button (see Figure 4-89).

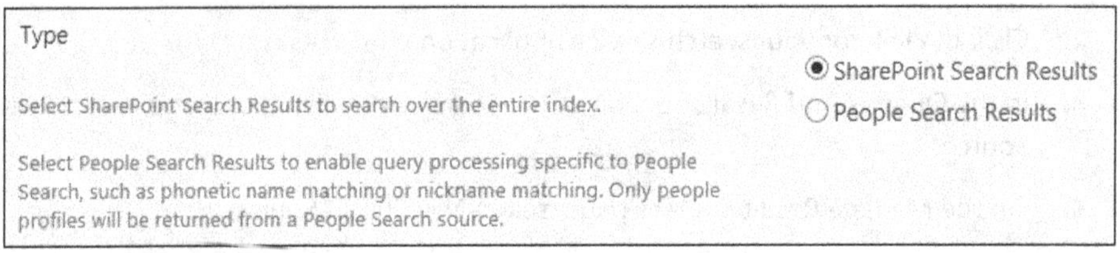

FIGURE 4-89 Selecting the search results type.

9. Easily the most complex task of this process; you can generate a query that is passed to the search engine by either launching the Query Builder tool or simply entering a query. The query is a fairly simple one, {searchTerms} fileextension=one, as shown in Figure 4-90.

FIGURE 4-90 Query Transform.

10. The last task, selecting credentials information, changes based on the protocol you select. For each protocol, the options available differ (see Figure 4-91):

A. **Local SharePoint** Choose Default Authentication or Basic Authentication

B. **Remote SharePoint** The choices are Default Authentication or SSO Id

C. **OpenSearch 1.0/1.1** Several choices exist, ranging from Anonymous to Basic, Digest, NTLM, Form, and Cookie Authentication

D. **Exchange** Specifies no credentials because it provides results via the SharePoint 2013 eDiscovery Center (required for use)

11. Select the Default Authentication credential radio button.

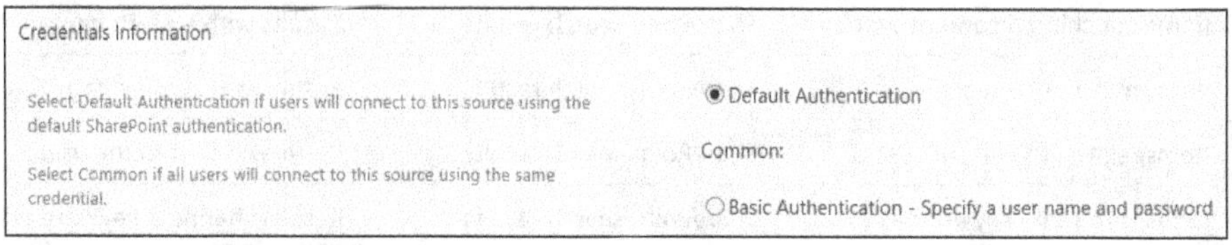

Credentials Information

Select Default Authentication if users will connect to this source using the default SharePoint authentication.

Select Common if all users will connect to this source using the same credential.

● Default Authentication

Common:

○ Basic Authentication - Specify a user name and password

FIGURE 4-91 Credentials Information.

12. Click Save to commit your changes. Your new result source will appear in the Defined For This Search Service section (see Figure 4-92).

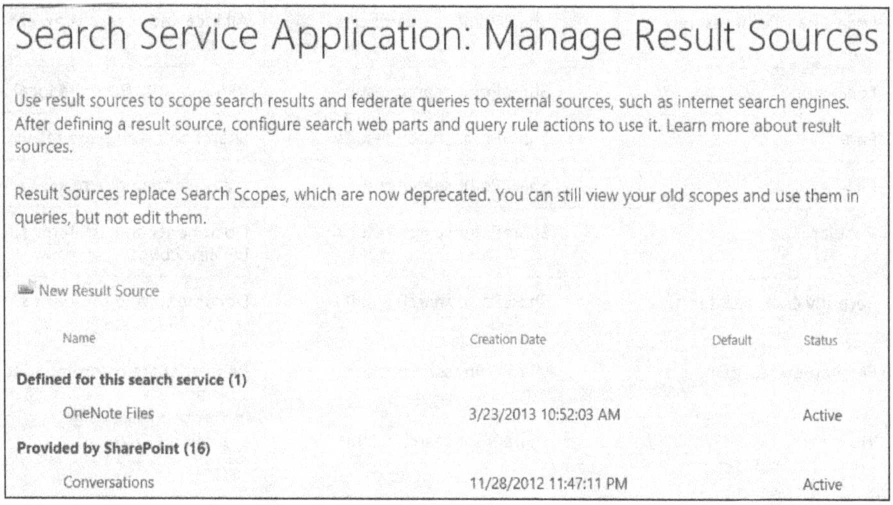

Search Service Application: Manage Result Sources

Use result sources to scope search results and federate queries to external sources, such as internet search engines. After defining a result source, configure search web parts and query rule actions to use it. Learn more about result sources.

Result Sources replace Search Scopes, which are now deprecated. You can still view your old scopes and use them in queries, but not edit them.

New Result Source

Name	Creation Date	Default	Status
Defined for this search service (1)			
OneNote Files	3/23/2013 10:52:03 AM		Active
Provided by SharePoint (16)			
Conversations	11/28/2012 11:47:11 PM		Active

FIGURE 4-92 New result source.

Predefined result sources in SharePoint 2013

There are a total of 16 built-in result sources provided by SharePoint 2013 (see Table 4-5). Each of these result sources uses the Local SharePoint protocol and a query transform to retrieve the appropriate content.

TABLE 4-5 Predefined result sources in SharePoint 2013

Name	Type	Description
Conversations	SharePoint search results	Results from conversation results and community sites
Documents	SharePoint search results	Office and PDF documents
Items matching a content type	SharePoint search results	Results with a given content type
Items matching a tag	SharePoint search results	Results with a given tag
Items related to current user	SharePoint search results	Results related to the user
Items with same keyword as this item	SharePoint search results	Results sharing a keyword with a given item
Local people results	People search results	People results from the profile database
Local reports and data results	SharePoint search results	Excel, ODC, RDL, and reports library results
Local SharePoint results	SharePoint search results	All local index results except people
Local video results	SharePoint search results	Video results from the local index
Pages	SharePoint search results	SharePoint web page results
Pictures	SharePoint search results	Picture and image result items
Popular	SharePoint search results	Documents and list items sorted by view count
Recently changed items	SharePoint search results	Documents and list items sorted by modified date
Recommended Items	SharePoint search results	Items that are recommended for a specific item
Wiki	SharePoint search results	SharePoint Wiki pages

Managing query rules

Query rules are used to promote certain search results, show blocks of additional results, or influence the ranking of search results. This functionality is made available not only to the search application administrator but also to the site collection and site administrators within a SharePoint farm.

Query rules can be defined at one of three possible levels:

- **Search service application**   Applies to all site collections in the web applications that consume the search service application
- **Site collection**   Applies to all sites within a particular site collection
- **Site**   Applies to a particular site

Creating a new query rule

A query rule is composed of three possible components: the query conditions that cause the rule to fire, the actions that occur when the rule is fired, and (optionally) the ability to provide a time window for when the rule is available to fire.

> **MORE INFO** **CREATING QUERY RULES**
>
> Specific steps are required to build a query rule at the search service application, site collection, and site levels. These steps can be found in the TechNet article "Manage Query Rules in SharePoint Server 2013" at *http://technet.microsoft.com/en-us/library/jj871676.aspx.*

Creating a new query rule at the search application level requires only a few steps to complete. In this example, you will build a new query rule that acts much like a best bet would have in prior versions of SharePoint. This rule will fire when the user queries for the following words:

- 401K
- Hiring
- Interviewing
- Retirement
- Termination

To create this example query rule at the search application level, follow these steps:

1. Open Central Administration; within the Application Management section, select Manage Service Applications.

2. Click the link for your search service application.

3. In the Queries And Results section of the Search Administration page, select Query Rules.

4. On the Manage Query Rules Page (see Figure 4-93), choose the drop-down list for the For What Context Do You Want To Configure Rules? field and select Local SharePoint Results (System). Next, select the New Query Rule link.

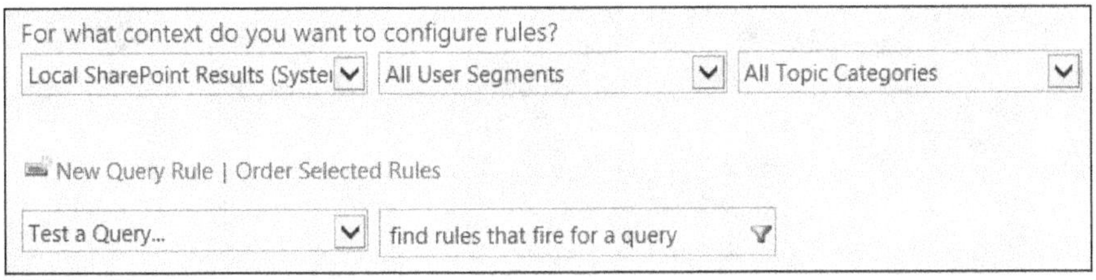

FIGURE 4-93 New query rule.

5. In the General Information field, type **Human Resources** for the Rule name.

6. In the Query Conditions section, choose the Query Matches Keyword Exactly drop-down value. In the field beneath the drop-down list, enter the following string of terms in the field (see Figure 4-94): **401K;hiring;interviewing;retirement;termination**

EXAM TIP

Be familiar with each of the query conditions and the potential effect they can have on the query rules.

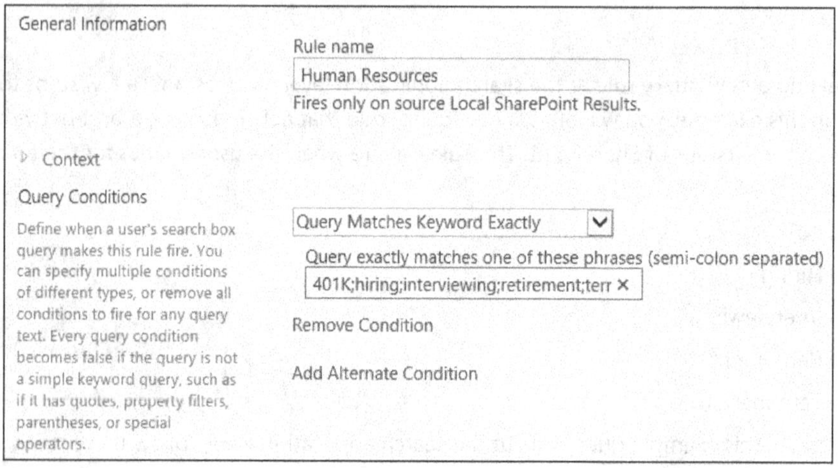

General Information

Rule name

Human Resources

Fires only on source Local SharePoint Results.

▷ Context

Query Conditions

Define when a user's search box query makes this rule fire. You can specify multiple conditions of different types, or remove all conditions to fire for any query text. Every query condition becomes false if the query is not a simple keyword query, such as if it has quotes, property filters, parentheses, or special operators.

Query Matches Keyword Exactly ⌄

Query exactly matches one of these phrases (semi-colon separated)

401K;hiring;interviewing;retirement;terr ✕

Remove Condition

Add Alternate Condition

FIGURE 4-94 General Information and Query Conditions sections.

7. In the Actions section, choose the Add Promoted Result link.

8. On the Add Promoted Result page, enter the following values for Title and URL (see Figure 4-95); then click Save:

- Title: **Human Resources**
- URL: **http://hr.boston.local**

You can also use this page to promote a banner instead of a plain link.

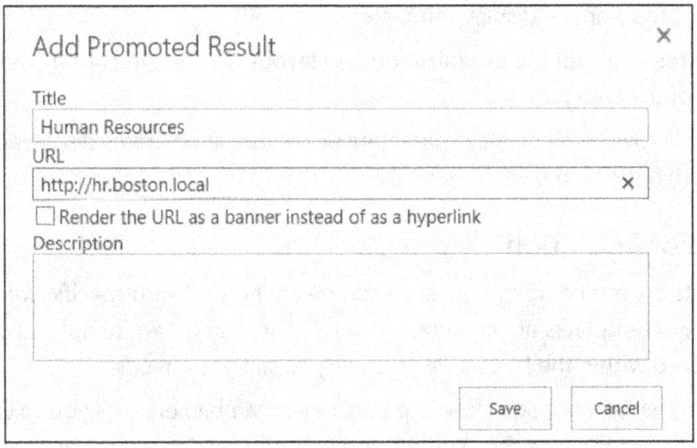

FIGURE 4-95 Add Promoted Result.

9. Click Save to commit your changes.

10. Users who search for a term present in the Query Conditions (Retirement) now see the promoted site (Human Resources—hr.boston.local), as shown in Figure 4-96).

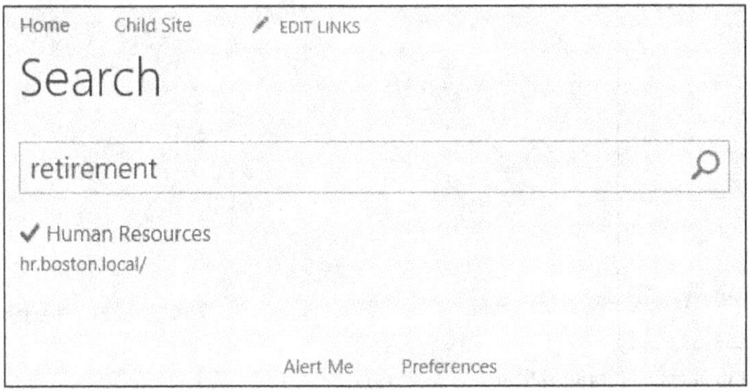

FIGURE 4-96 Search results.

Managing display templates

Search results in SharePoint 2013 are presented by a series of search-specific web parts. These web parts, in turn, rely on a series of display templates to control the formatting and presentation of search results.

> **IMPORTANT DISPLAY TEMPLATE AVAILABILITY**
>
> Display templates are available only for search-driven web parts.

There are two major groupings of display templates:

- **Control templates** Control the organization and layout of search results as well as the overall look of the web part

- **Item templates** Provide the display characteristics of individual items displayed in search results within the web part

Display template configuration

As new search web parts are added to a page, each can be configured with specific control and item templates. These templates are changeable; new control and item templates can also be defined and stored within the Master Page Gallery to suit your needs.

Editing the web part (the Content Search web part, in this example) enables you to configure its properties, as shown in Figure 4-97. Within the Display Templates section, you see the Control and Item template selection drop-down boxes.

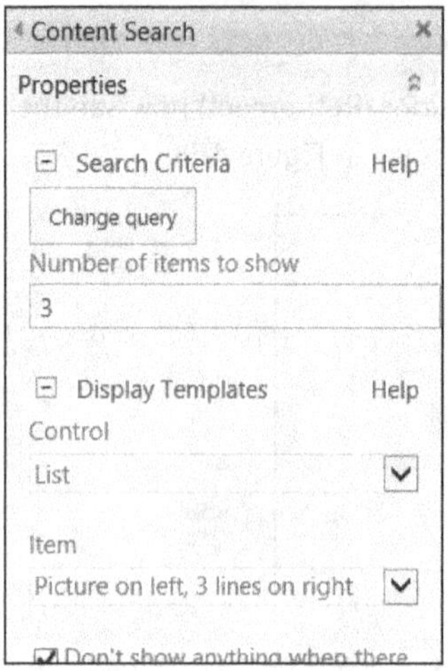

FIGURE 4-97 Web part properties (Content Search).

Note that you are looking at the List control template and the Picture On Left, 3 Lines On Right item template; you'll see them again in a few moments.

Although creating a new display template is beyond the scope of this section, we will walk through how to connect to the Master Page Library and see the place in which the templates are housed within each site collection.

Creating new display templates

The first step of building a new display template is locating its location within the SharePoint file system and mapping a location from your client system.

Display templates are housed within the Master Page Gallery of a SharePoint site. Probably the easiest way to document this location is to use Design Manager to tell you the location, as follows:

1. Navigate to the root site of your site collection.

2. From the Settings menu (gear icon), select Design Manager (see Figure 4-98).

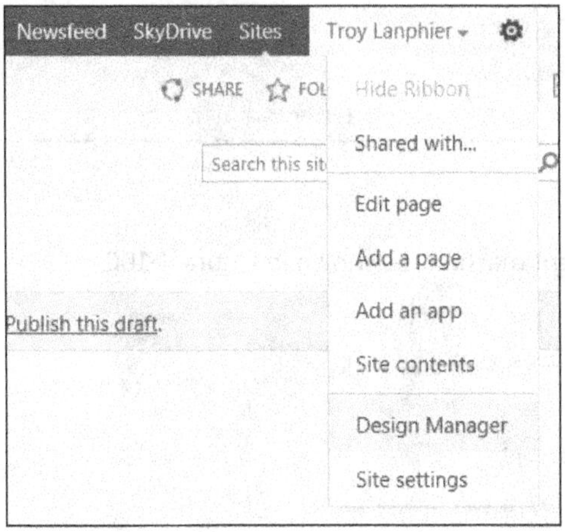

FIGURE 4-98 Design Manager selection.

EXAM TIP

If you look at your settings menu, but do not see the Design Manager link, there is a good chance that you do not have the publishing features activated in this site collection. These features are a requirement for much of the ease-of-design functionality in SharePoint Server 2013.

3. After the Design Manager page appears, select item 3, Upload Design Files (see Figure 4-99). The URL shown (http://intranet.boston.local/_catalogs/masterpage/) is the location of the Master Page Gallery. Copy this URL to your clipboard.

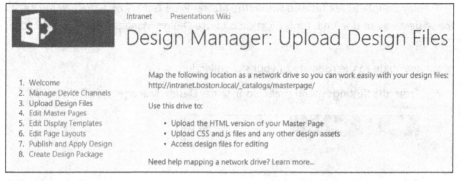

FIGURE 4-99 Master Page Gallery URL.

4. Map a network drive from your client machine, as shown in Figure 4-100.

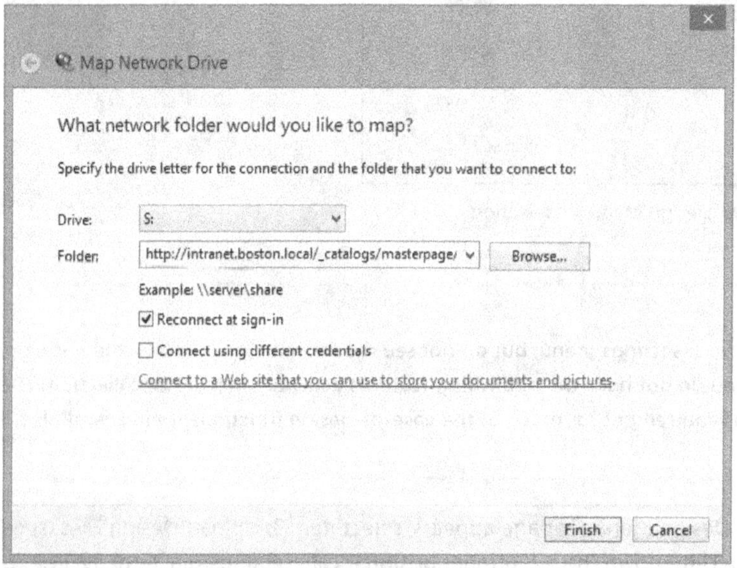

FIGURE 4-100 Mapping a drive to the Master Page Gallery.

5. In the newly mapped drive, open the Display Templates folder (see Figure 4-101). Note that the Content Web Parts, Filters, Search, and System folders each maintain both control and item templates (not shown).

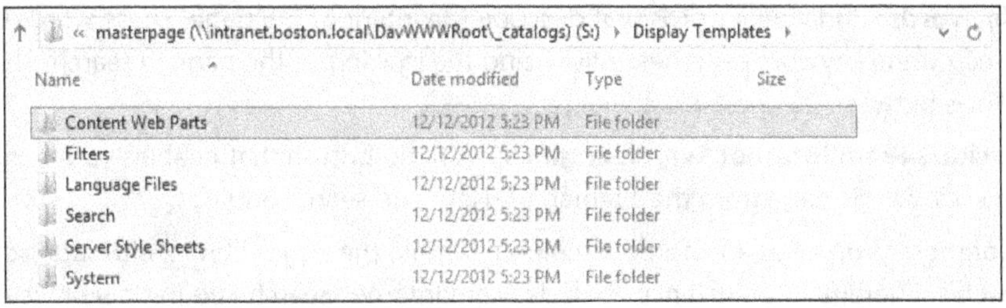

FIGURE 4-101 Display Templates folder.

6. Opening the Content Web Parts folder, you see a series of control and item templates. Among them are the Control_List and the Item_Picture3Lines templates, which correspond to the List and Picture On Left, 3 Lines On Right item templates you saw in the Search web part.

> **MORE INFO CREATING AND EDITING DISPLAY TEMPLATES**
>
> Creating display templates can be a fairly involved process. For more details on how to create a new display template, see the TechNet article "How To: Create a Display Template in SharePoint Server 2013" at *http://msdn.microsoft.com/en-us/library/jj945138.aspx*.

Managing Search Engine Optimization (SEO) settings

Previous versions of SharePoint did not provide any sort of built-in mechanism for controlling Search Engine Optimization (SEO). SharePoint Server 2013 now includes native, easy-to-configure, SEO support for publishing sites that can be administered by site collection administrators and site owners.

There are three distinct levels of SEO configuration within SharePoint 2013: publishing pages, site collection, and XML site mapping.

Configuring SEO properties for publishing pages

Each publishing page on a SharePoint site can be configured with a series of SEO properties:

- **Name** A name for the page that may appear in the URL.
- **Title** A phrase that may be used in search for keyword-based queries.
- **Browser Title** A friendly title for the page that may appear in the title bar of web browsers viewing the page (must be between 5 and 25 characters).
- **Meta Description** A description for the page that would appear on a search results page.

- **Keywords** Individual words that describe the intent of the page. These words will be used during keyword searches, influencing the ranking of the page in search. This field allows between 25 and 1024 characters.

- **Exclude From Internet Search Engines** A radio button that enables you to include or exclude this page from the sitemap (if used) and search engines.

Most of these properties are stored as columns within the Pages library, although some are mapped a bit differently (for instance, Exclude From Internet Search Engines becomes Hide From Internet Search Engines in the page's properties.

Additionally, you can use the last property, Exclude From Internet Search Engines, to both hide the page from an XML-generated site map as well as hiding it from search engines.

To configure SEO properties for a publishing page, do the following:

1. Check the page out.

2. On the ribbon, select the Page tab and then select the drop-down list for Edit Properties. Select the Edit SEO Properties menu item (see Figure 4-102).

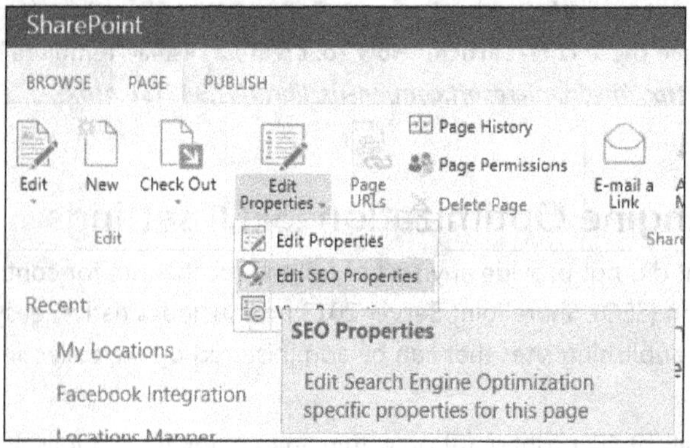

FIGURE 4-102 Selecting the Edit SEO Properties menu.

3. Change the values for the SEO Property fields and click OK to commit your changes. Note that changes made in this menu appear instantly on the site (such as changing the title of the page from Home to Intranet Home, as shown in Figure 4-103).

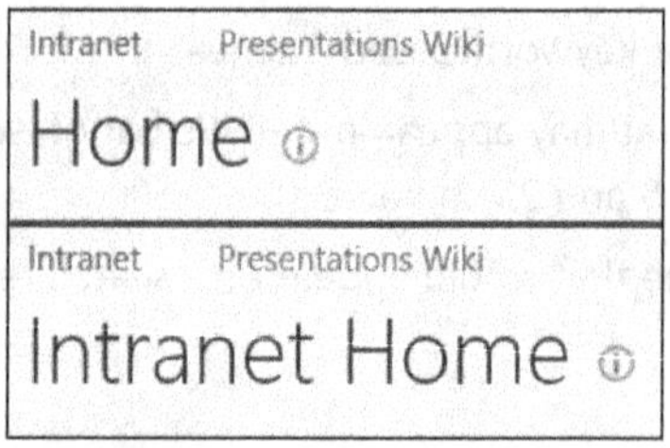

FIGURE 4-103 Before and after the title change in SEO settings.

4. Check your page back in and publish it for the change to take effect.

Configuring SEO settings for site collections

In addition to the SEO properties on publishing pages, SharePoint 2013 enables you to configure the following settings on a per-site collection basis:

- **Verify The Ownership Of This Site With Search Engines**   You can go to a search engine's webmaster tools page and request the appropriate <meta> tag that is specific to your URL.

- **Consolidate Link Popularity With Canonical URLs**   Allows you to specify filter link parameters that can help search engines combine the appropriate URLs on your site from a search metric point of view.

To configure SEO properties for a site collection, follow these steps:

1. Navigate to the root site of your site collection.

2. From the Settings menu (gear icon), select Site Settings.

3. In the Site Collection Administration section, select Search Engine Optimization Settings.

4. On the Search Engine Optimization Settings page, select the appropriate values for the two optimization settings sections and then click OK.

EXAM TIP

Be familiar with the structure of a meta tag and the way it can be added for your Internet–facing SharePoint site.

Configuring SEO for the XML site map

If you have a site that enables anonymous access, you can also enable the search engine Sitemap feature. This feature improves SEO of your site by automatically generating a sitemap on a regular basis that contains all the valid URLs in your web site.

Enabling this feature adds two additional fields to the SEO properties page, Sitemap Priority and Sitemap Change Frequency (see Figure 4-104).

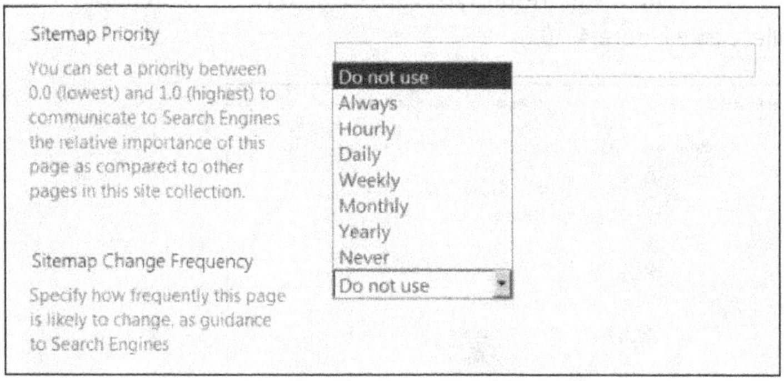

Sitemap Priority

You can set a priority between 0.0 (lowest) and 1.0 (highest) to communicate to Search Engines the relative importance of this page as compared to other pages in this site collection.

| Do not use |
| Always |
| Hourly |
| Daily |
| Weekly |
| Monthly |
| Yearly |
| Never |

Sitemap Change Frequency

Specify how frequently this page is likely to change, as guidance to Search Engines

Do not use

FIGURE 4-104 Sitemap Priority and Sitemap Change Frequency.

Sitemap Priority indicates the weighting (between 0.0 and 1.0) of the importance of one page over another within your site collection; the higher the number, the more important your page.

Sitemap Change Frequency enables you to tell the search engine how regularly you expect the page to change, to help improve search engine efficiency.

Managing result types

Result types evaluate a query based on a set of rules and then apply the appropriate display template. The display templates in use here are located in a different folder from the ones we used earlier in this section (located within the Content Web Parts folder).

EXAM TIP

Be familiar with the four different display templates folders and which affect the result type functionality.

When a query is made via search (for instance, a series of Microsoft Word documents), the result set that is returned is evaluated for the way the returned information should be presented. The Result Type defines the fields for evaluating the result set in terms of conditions and actions:

1. **Conditions**   For the Microsoft Word result set, two conditions are evaluated:

    A.   Which result source should the item match? (All sources)

    B.   What types of content should match? (Microsoft Word)

2. **Actions**   One action is applied, consisting of two parts:

    A.   What should these results look like? (Word item)

    B.   What is the appropriate display template URL? (~sitecollection/_catalogs/ masterpage/Display Templates/Search/Item_Word.js)

Display templates associated with result types

The display templates that are associated with result types are located in the Search folder within the Master Page Gallery (see Figure 4-105).

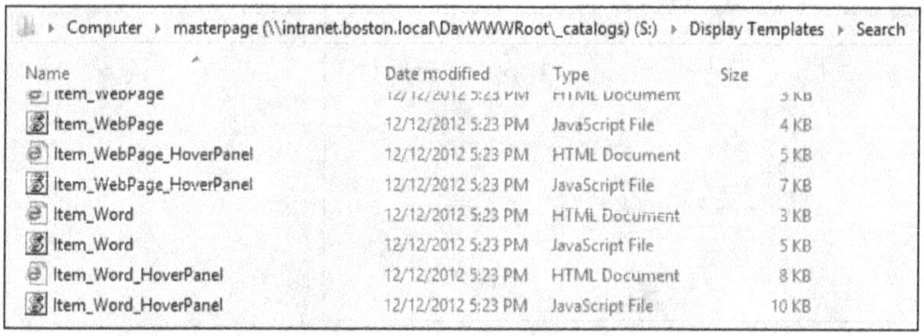

Name	Date modified	Type	Size
Item_WebPage	12/12/2012 5:23 PM	HTML Document	3 KB
Item_WebPage	12/12/2012 5:23 PM	JavaScript File	4 KB
Item_WebPage_HoverPanel	12/12/2012 5:23 PM	HTML Document	5 KB
Item_WebPage_HoverPanel	12/12/2012 5:23 PM	JavaScript File	7 KB
Item_Word	12/12/2012 5:23 PM	HTML Document	3 KB
Item_Word	12/12/2012 5:23 PM	JavaScript File	5 KB
Item_Word_HoverPanel	12/12/2012 5:23 PM	HTML Document	8 KB
Item_Word_HoverPanel	12/12/2012 5:23 PM	JavaScript File	10 KB

Computer ▸ masterpage (\\intranet.boston.local\DavWWWRoot_catalogs) (S:) ▸ Display Templates ▸ Search

FIGURE 4-105 Display templates for result types.

Managing a search schema

As a document is crawled, metadata is extracted as crawled properties. This metadata can include structured content (such as columnar metadata; for example: title, author) or unstructured content (such as keywords extracted from the body of the document).

In order for a user to be able to search on a piece of metadata, this crawled property must be mapped to a managed property. After this task is complete, queries can be performed against this metadata (such as looking up an item's order number, stored in a list column).

Viewing crawled and managed properties

To view the properties that have been crawled, do the following:

1. Open Central Administration and select Manage Service Applications In The Application Management section.

2. Select the link for your search service application.

3. Within the Queries And Results section, select the Search Schema link.

4. The first item displayed is Managed Properties (see Figure 4-106). From this page, you can selectively filter which managed property is shown and also see what Managed Properties are mapped to which crawled properties.

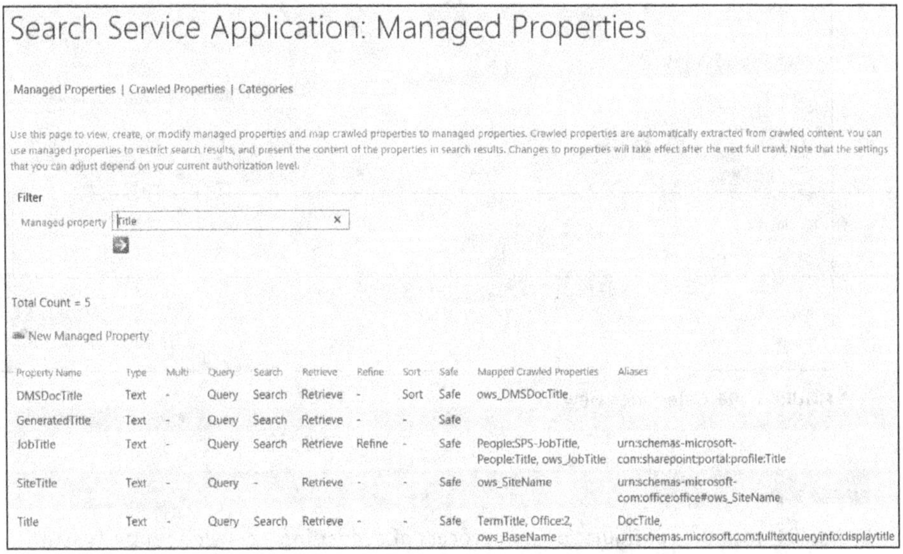

FIGURE 4-106 Managed Properties view.

5. Selecting the Crawled Properties link inverts the view. Selecting a category (such as People) then enables you to see which crawled properties are mapped to a particular managed property (see Figure 4-107).

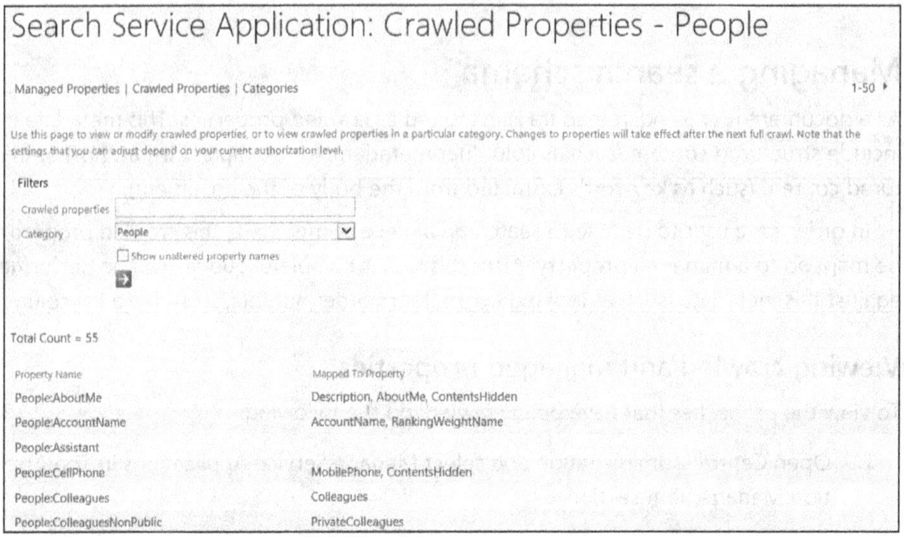

Search Service Application: Crawled Properties - People

Managed Properties | Crawled Properties | Categories   1-50 ▸

Use this page to view or modify crawled properties, or to view crawled properties in a particular category. Changes to properties will take effect after the next full crawl. Note that the settings that you can adjust depend on your current authorization level.

Filters

Crawled properties [ ]

Category [People ▾]

☐ Show unaltered property names

➡

Total Count = 55

Property Name	Mapped To Property
People:AboutMe	Description, AboutMe, ContentsHidden
People:AccountName	AccountName, RankingWeightName
People:Assistant	
People:CellPhone	MobilePhone, ContentsHidden
People:Colleagues	Colleagues
People:ColleaguesNonPublic	PrivateColleagues

FIGURE 4-107 Crawled Properties view.

6. The Categories selection enables you to see a summary of all available categories and the properties each possesses (see Figure 4-108).

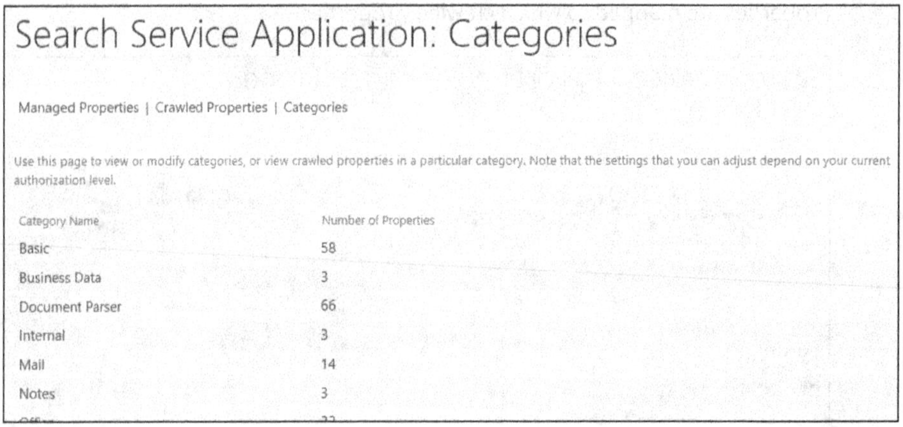

Search Service Application: Categories

Managed Properties | Crawled Properties | Categories

Use this page to view or modify categories, or view crawled properties in a particular category. Note that the settings that you can adjust depend on your current authorization level.

Category Name	Number of Properties
Basic	58
Business Data	3
Document Parser	66
Internal	3
Mail	14
Notes	3

FIGURE 4-108 Categories view.

EXAM TIP

Be familiar with the configuration and process of converting a crawled property to a managed property.

Objective summary

- Search scopes are deprecated in SharePoint 2013, having been replaced by result scopes.
- Creating a result type is composed of five tasks: providing general information, specifying a protocol, selecting a search result type, developing a query transform, and specifying credential information.
- Four protocol choices are available within result sources: Local SharePoint, Remote SharePoint, OpenSearch, and Exchange.
- Meta tags are used by SEO to help promote your Internet-facing SharePoint site.

Objective review

Answer the following questions to test your knowledge of the information in this objective. You can find the answers to these questions and explanations of why each answer choice is correct or incorrect in the "Answers" section at the end of this chapter.

1. Which of the following protocols can be used within a result source? (Choose all that apply.)

   A. SharePoint

   B. Exchange

   C. OpenSearch

   D. All of the above

2. At which of the following levels can you configure query rules? (Choose all that apply.)

   A. Search service application

   B. Site or site collection

   C. Web application

   D. All of the above

3. Which of the following folders houses the display templates for result types?

   A. Filters

   B. Search

   C. System

   D. Content Web Parts

4. Which of the following options is not available within the search service application for configuration?

   A. Managed properties

   B. Categories

   C. Filters

   D. Crawled properties

Objective 4.5: Manage taxonomy

Term sets contained within the Managed Metadata service work hand in glove with SharePoint 2013 search to accomplish functionality such as navigation and product catalogs. After the correct information has been located in search, term sets continue to provide benefit, enabling you to both refine search results and filter content within a list.

> **This objective covers how to:**
> - Manage site collection term set access.
> - Manage term set navigation.
> - Manage topic catalog pages.
> - Configure custom properties.
> - Configure search refinement.
> - Configure list refinement.

Managing site collection term set access

In SharePoint 2013, it's possible to have one site collection refer to another's term set. Of course, you could also generate the term set within the Managed Metadata Service application, but perhaps this level of availability (having the term set available across the entire farm) is not required.

> **EXAM TIP**
>
> **Although the designated site collections do indeed have read access to the original term set, they cannot change it.**

You may have a team that generates and maintains its own term set in one site collection, and then wants to provide that term set to several other site collections. This cross-site collection term set access is read-only, meaning that the sites allowed access are not themselves allowed to configure any new term sets or terms; however, the consuming site collections can bind and pin term sets from this group into their own term sets.

Configuring term set access in SharePoint 2013 can be done in a few steps, as follows:

1. Navigate to the root site of your site collection.
2. From the Settings menu (gear icon), select Site Settings.
3. In the Site Administration section, select Term Store Management.
4. Select the term set group for your site collection (see Figure 4-109).

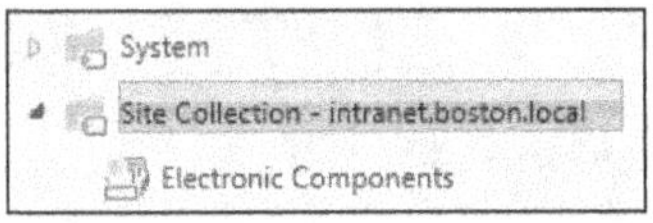

FIGURE 4-109 Selecting the site collection term set group.

5. Highlight the General tab for your term set group and scroll down to the Site Collection Access section.
6. Within the Site Collection Access section, enter the names of each site collection that should have access to this term set group (one per line, shown in Figure 4-110).

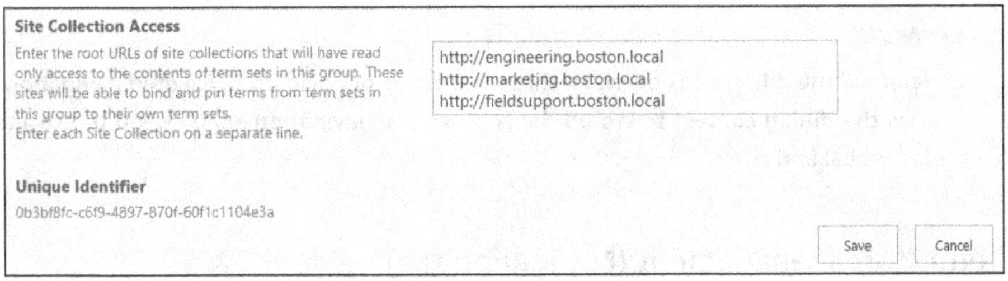

FIGURE 4-110 Site collection access.

7. Click Save to commit your changes.

Managing term set navigation

Configuring a site collection to use managed navigation requires the use of a new term set to house the navigational structure. This term set can then be configured to be used for site navigation, faceted navigation, or both (see Figure 4-111).

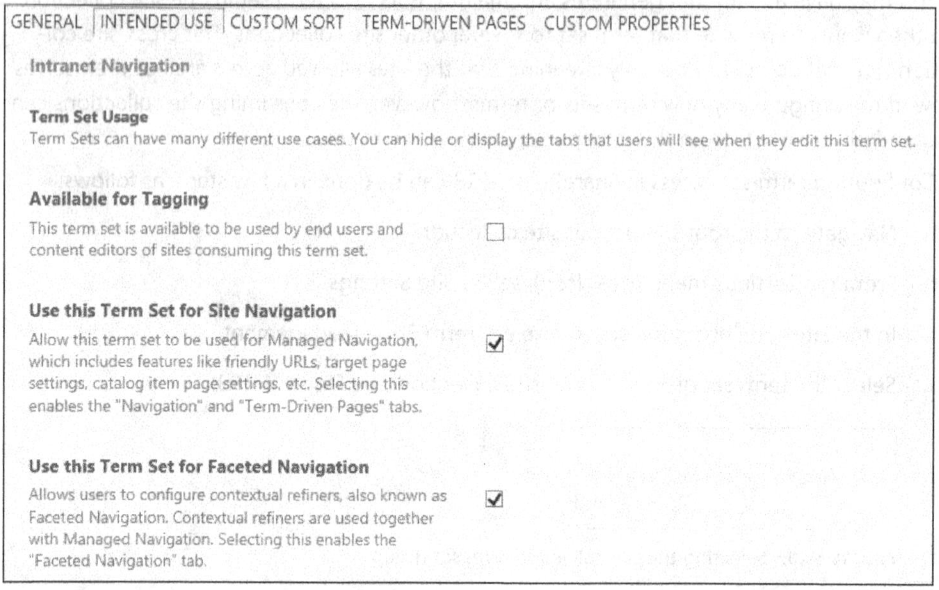

| GENERAL | INTENDED USE | CUSTOM SORT | TERM-DRIVEN PAGES | CUSTOM PROPERTIES |

Intranet Navigation

Term Set Usage
Term Sets can have many different use cases. You can hide or display the tabs that users will see when they edit this term set.

Available for Tagging
This term set is available to be used by end users and content editors of sites consuming this term set. ☐

Use this Term Set for Site Navigation
Allow this term set to be used for Managed Navigation, which includes features like friendly URLs, target page settings, catalog item page settings, etc. Selecting this enables the "Navigation" and "Term-Driven Pages" tabs. ☑

Use this Term Set for Faceted Navigation
Allows users to configure contextual refiners, also known as Faceted Navigation. Contextual refiners are used together with Managed Navigation. Selecting this enables the "Faceted Navigation" tab. ☑

FIGURE 4-111 Configuring a term set for navigational use.

Choosing to have a term set be used for site navigation activates both the Navigation and Term-Driven Pages tabs. After a term set is configured to be used as site navigation, its individual terms can function as navigation nodes.

EXAM TIP

Understand the differences between these two types of navigation. Faceted navigation has to do with refining content based on the context; site navigation enables you to use a term set for global and current navigation.

Term store management (Navigation tab)

Within the Navigation tab, the Navigation Node Appearance section enables you to configure how the node will appear in the global and current navigation of the site (see Figure 4-112):

1. You can choose to use the title as given by the term set or select the Customize check box and enter a more appealing name.

2. Editing the Navigation Hover Text enables more helpful information to be displayed when the user moves a mouse over the link.

3. The Visibility In Menus selection enables you to determine whether the link will be available to global navigation, current navigation, or both.

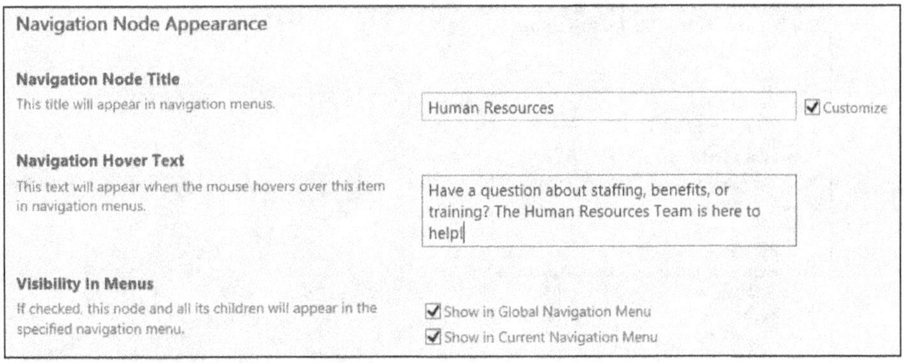

Navigation Node Appearance

Navigation Node Title
This title will appear in navigation menus.

Human Resources   ☑ Customize

Navigation Hover Text
This text will appear when the mouse hovers over this item in navigation menus.

Have a question about staffing, benefits, or training? The Human Resources Team is here to help!

Visibility In Menus
If checked, this node and all its children will appear in the specified navigation menu.

☑ Show in Global Navigation Menu
☑ Show in Current Navigation Menu

FIGURE 4-112 Navigation Node Appearance options.

Also located in the Navigation tab is the Navigation Node Type. This group of options enables you to specify whether the node is simply a link or header, or whether the node sends users to a term-driven page (see Figure 4-113):

4. If you choose the Simple Link Or Header radio button, you can either choose to enter the URL of a link or simply a header that can have links beneath it.

5. If you choose Term-Driven Page With Friendly URL, this node will be a friendly URL to a term-driven page (configured in the Term-Driven Pages tab).

Navigation Node Type

● **Simple Link or Header**
If you don't provide a URL here, this navigation node will be a text-only heading.

/hr   ✕   Browse...

○ **Term-Driven Page with Friendy URL**
This navigation node will be a friendly URL to a term-driven page. Switch to the "Term-Driven Page" tab to configure more options for this node type.

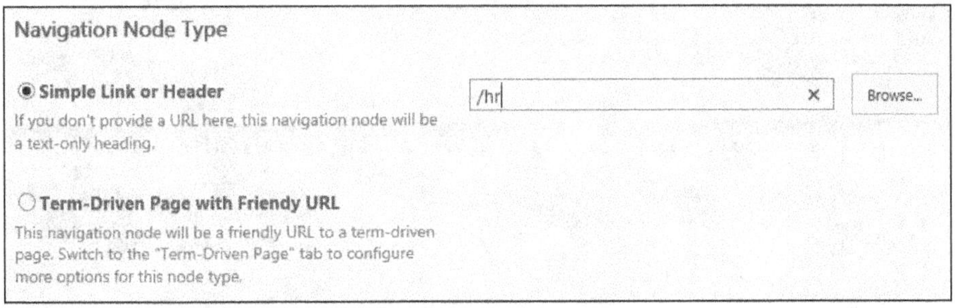

FIGURE 4-113 Navigation Node Type options.

Term-Driven Pages tab

Within the Term-Driven Pages tab, you can choose the Target Page Settings, Category Image, and Catalog Item Page settings. In the Target Page Settings (see Figure 4-114 and Figure 4-115), do the following:

1. You can change the friendly URL (FURL) to one that is perhaps easier to type by selecting the Customize check box and entering a new FURL name.

2. The Target Page Settings section enables you to choose both the target page for a term as well another one for children of the term.

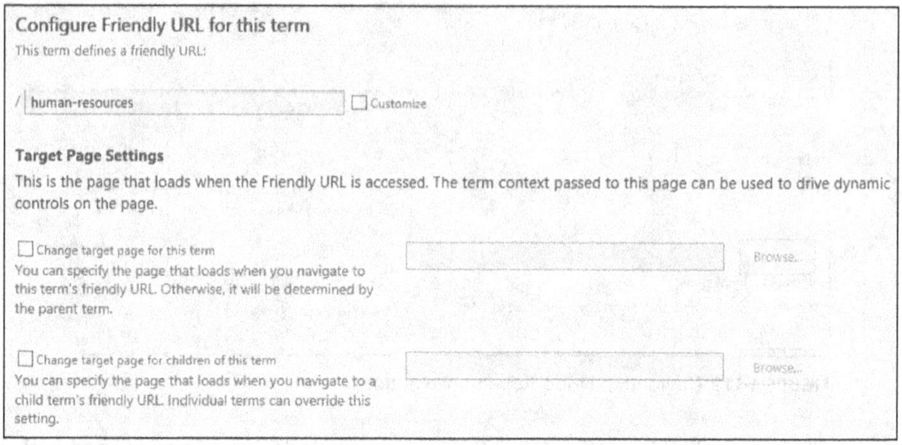

Configure Friendly URL for this term
This term defines a friendly URL:

/ | human-resources | ☐ Customize

Target Page Settings
This is the page that loads when the Friendly URL is accessed. The term context passed to this page can be used to drive dynamic controls on the page.

☐ Change target page for this term
You can specify the page that loads when you navigate to this term's friendly URL. Otherwise, it will be determined by the parent term. | | Browse...

☐ Change target page for children of this term
You can specify the page that loads when you navigate to a child term's friendly URL. Individual terms can override this setting. | | Browse...

FIGURE 4-114 Configuring the FURL and target page settings.

The Category Image section is used to display an image used to represent this term in the Term Property web part (see Figure 4-115).

If you are using the term as a catalog category (covered in the next section), the Catalog Item Page Settings enables you to choose both the Catalog Item Page for the category as well as another one for children of the category.

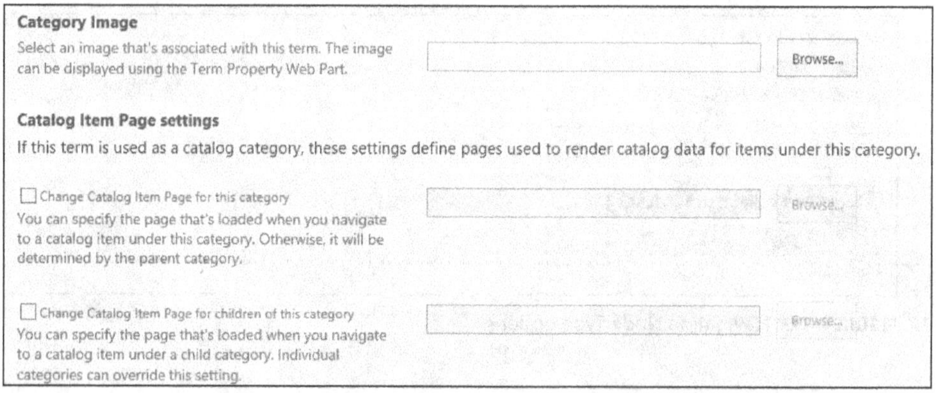

Category Image
Select an image that's associated with this term. The image can be displayed using the Term Property Web Part. | | Browse...

Catalog Item Page settings
If this term is used as a catalog category, these settings define pages used to render catalog data for items under this category.

☐ Change Catalog Item Page for this category
You can specify the page that's loaded when you navigate to a catalog item under this category. Otherwise, it will be determined by the parent category. | | Browse...

☐ Change Catalog Item Page for children of this category
You can specify the page that's loaded when you navigate to a catalog item under a child category. Individual categories can override this setting. | | Browse...

FIGURE 4-115 Configuring Category Image and Catalog Item Page settings.

Managing topic catalog pages

Topic catalog pages are used to render items within the products list on a product catalog site. These pages are used to show structured content in a consistent fashion across a Share-Point site.

Most often, these pages are used within the confines of a product catalog site. There are two distinct page types available:

- Category pages are used specifically to display a series of catalog items.
- Item pages (also called catalog item pages in some documentation) are used to display an item in detail.

EXAM TIP

Be familiar with the process of building a product catalog, assigning terms in the term set, and then allowing another publishing site to consume the result.

Assigning master pages to the category and item pages

Because these pages are standard publishing fare within SharePoint 2013, it only stands to reason that they follow the same structure that all other publishing pages do.

When a publishing site is initially configured to connect to a product catalog, the opportunity arises to specify the category and item page master pages.

To specify the catalog pages' master page as part of the connect-to-catalog process, do the following:

1. Navigate to the root site of your publishing site collection (not the product catalog).

2. From the Settings menu (gear icon), select Site Settings.

3. In the Site Administration section, choose the Manage Catalog Connections link.

4. On the Manage Catalog Connections page, select Connect To A Catalog.

5. On the Connect To Catalog page, select the Connect button for your product catalog (see Figure 4-116).

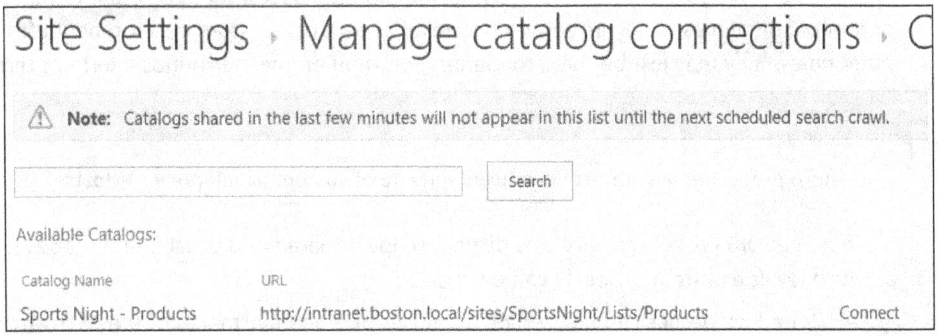

FIGURE 4-116 Connecting to a product catalog.

6. In Catalog Source Settings, scroll to the bottom of the page.

7. The last section of the page enables you to choose from the two OOB master page types (or use an existing one if you have it created). Category and item pages can also be configured within this section.

8. Select OK to complete the connection.

> **IMPORTANT CONFIGURING THE MASTER PAGE**
>
> When you initially make the connection between the product catalog site and the publishing site that consumes its navigational hierarchy, you have the chance to choose the master page for both category and item pages. Selecting Catalog Source Settings after the fact does not give you the opportunity to make the choice again.

Options within the Term-Driven Pages tab

As discussed in the term set navigation section, there are options available within the Term-Driven Pages tab that enable you to specify catalog page settings. These choices are just that—optional. Catalog pages work just fine without you making changes at this level.

The number of options available has to do with whether you are changing this setting at the term set or term level:

- If you are making this change at the term set level, your only option is to specify a custom page for the catalog item.

- If you are making this change at the term level, then you have two options: Change The Catalog Item Page For A Category, and also Change Catalog Item For Children of The Category.

Configuring custom properties

Within a term set, you can define properties that aren't a necessary part of the term, term set, or group. Sometimes these properties are useful as part of a custom development effort; at other times, they may just be there to identify information that surrounds a term or term set.

> **EXAM TIP**
>
> Custom properties are almost never used outside of custom development efforts.

These custom properties have two distinct scopes: Shared and Local; these scopes define at which levels a custom property can be applied:

- Shared properties can be used on all reuses of pinned instances of the term anywhere in the term store.

- Local properties can be used only for a term contained within the term set being configured.

Custom property configuration can differ based on the item. At the term set level, shared properties are the only configuration available; at the individual term level, both shared and local properties can be configured.

Custom property configuration

Configuration of a custom property is done within the Term Store Management Tool. To build a new custom property, follow these steps:

1. Navigate to the root site of your site collection.

2. From the Settings menu (gear icon), select Site Settings.

3. In the Site Administration section, select Term Store Management.

4. Expand your term set until you get to the desired location for your custom property.

5. Select the term/term set and then click the Custom Properties tab (see Figure 4-117).

6. Select the Add link and then enter values for the property name (either shared or local) and a matching value.

7. After you complete your changes, click Save.

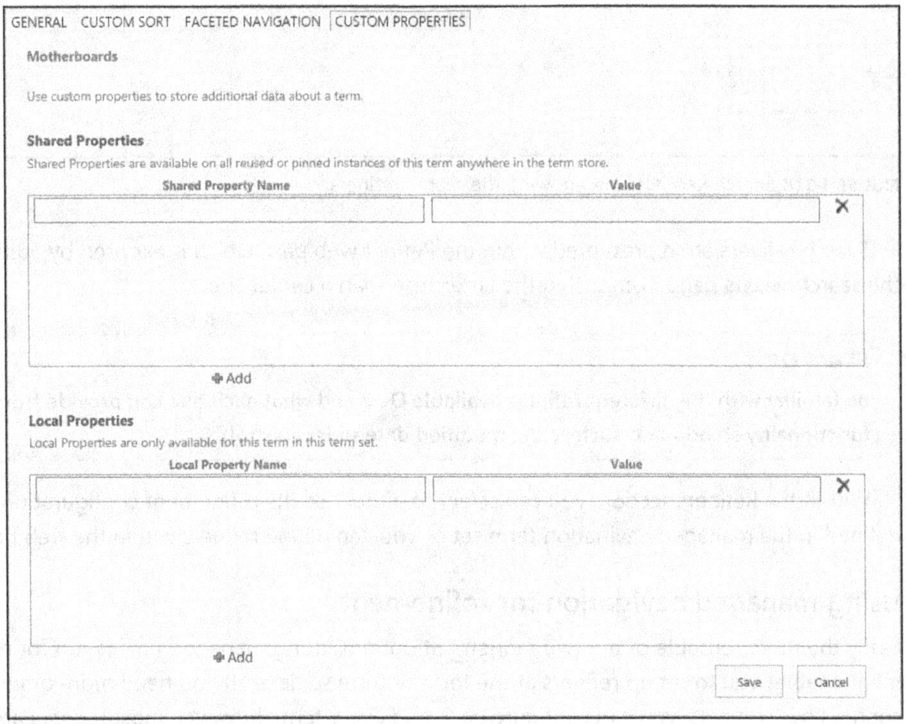

FIGURE 4-117 Custom Properties tab.

Configuring search refinement

When you issue a search query in SharePoint 2013, you not only get the returned results of your query but also a series of categories that you can use to narrow your search (shown on the left side of Figure 4-118) that are known as "search refiners."

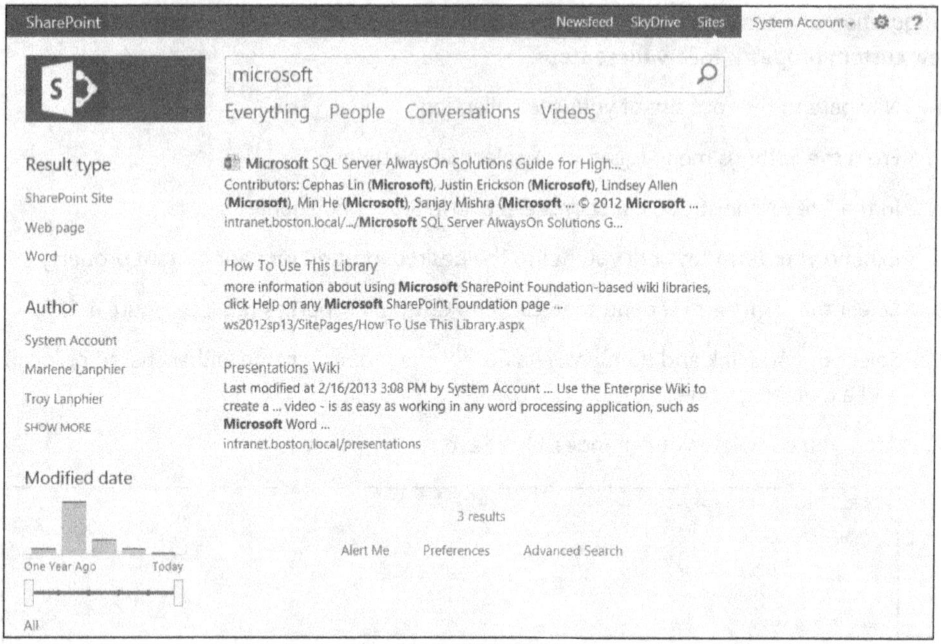

FIGURE 4-118 Search Results page, showing the search refiners.

Search refiners are represented within the Refiner web part, which is exposed by editing the search results page from within the Enterprise search center site.

> **EXAM TIP**
>
> **Be familiar with the different refiners available OOB and what each one can provide from a functionality standpoint (such as the modified date slider control).**

Within the Refiners section, you can select to either use the refinement configuration as defined in the managed navigation term set or you can define refiners within the web part.

Using managed navigation for refinement

Easily the more reusable of the two refinement options, using managed navigation for refinement enables you to set up refiners at the term or term set level. If you need more granular controls over refiners, you can configure each and every term; however, most refiners are applied at the term set level and then inherited by the individual terms.

To configure refiners within the managed navigation term set:

1. Navigate to the root site of your site collection.

2. From the Settings menu (gear icon), select Site Settings.

3. In the Site Administration section, select Term Store Management.

4. Expand your term set until you get to the desired location for your refiner to be applied and then select the term or term set.

5. Select the Faceted Navigation tab (see Figure 4-119). In this screen shot, the term selected already has custom refiners, but can add refiners as well.

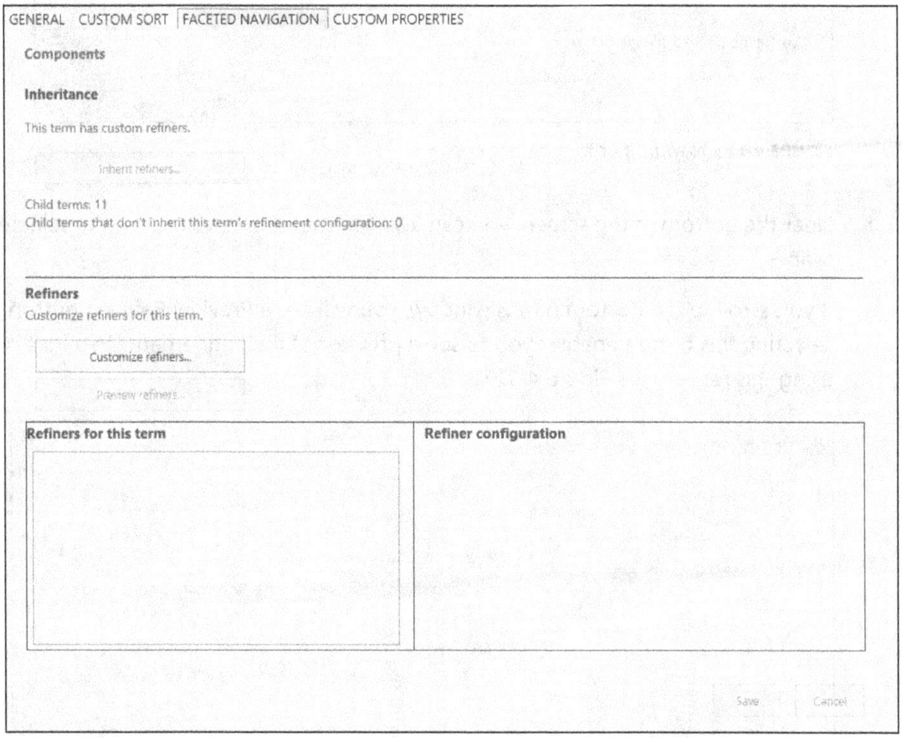

GENERAL   CUSTOM SORT   FACETED NAVIGATION   CUSTOM PROPERTIES

Components

Inheritance

This term has custom refiners.

Inherit refiners...

Child terms: 11
Child terms that don't inherit this term's refinement configuration: 0

Refiners
Customize refiners for this term.

Customize refiners...

Preview refiners

Refiners for this term   **Refiner configuration**

Save   Cancel

FIGURE 4-119 Refiners in managed navigation.

6. Select the Customize Refiners button. In this example, the suggested refiner Tags has been added to the Selected Refiners field (see Figure 4-120).

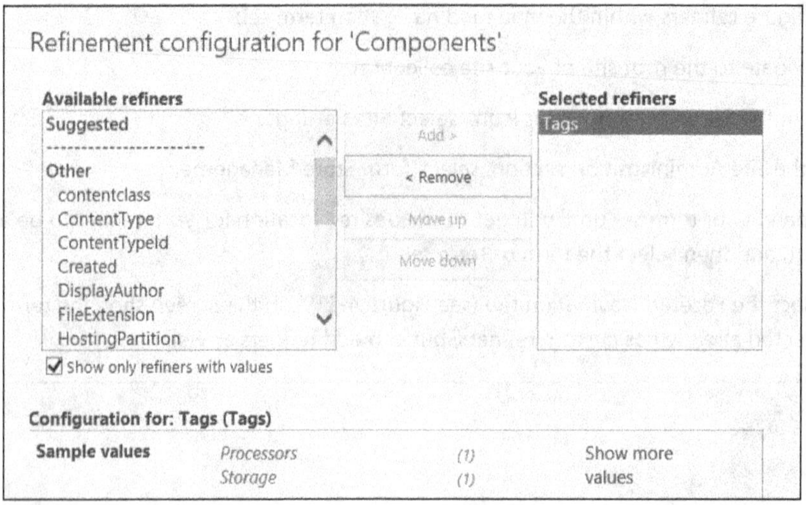

FIGURE 4-120 New refiner for components.

7. Near the bottom of the screen, you can also see the sample values for the selected refiner.

8. If you scroll to the bottom of this window, you will see a Preview Refiners button; selecting this button enables you to see a preview of the Refinement Web Part output using this refiner (see Figure 4-121).

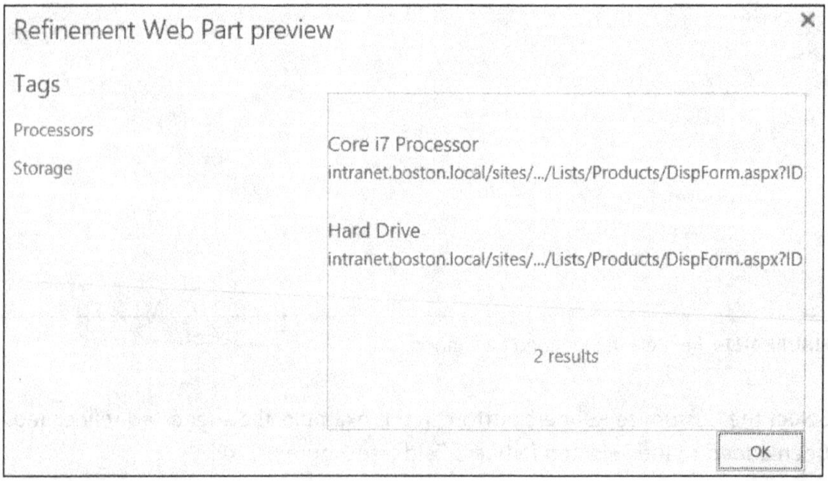

FIGURE 4-121 Refinement Web Part Preview.

9. If the result is satisfactory, click OK to close the preview window.

10. On the refinement configuration screen, verify your settings and click OK to commit them.

11. The completed refiners for the term now appear in the Faceted Navigation tab. Click Save to commit your changes.

12. Return to the site where you are configuring the Refinement web part and select the radio button titled Use The Refinement Configuration Defined In The Managed Navigation Term Set.

13. Click OK to close the Refiner web part.

EXAM TIP

Be familiar with the configuration steps required to configure a refiner both in the term set as well as a web part.

Using the web part refiners

Choosing your refiners within the web part enables you to make one-off refinement configurations.

To configure refinement directly within the web part, do the following:

1. Select the Choose Refiners button.

2. On the Refinement Configuration For 'Refinement' page, the Tags refiner has been added as in the previous set of steps.

3. Near the bottom of the page, select the Preview Refiners button. This opens the Refinement Web Part Preview window, showing the sample return based on the refiners chosen (see Figure 4-122).

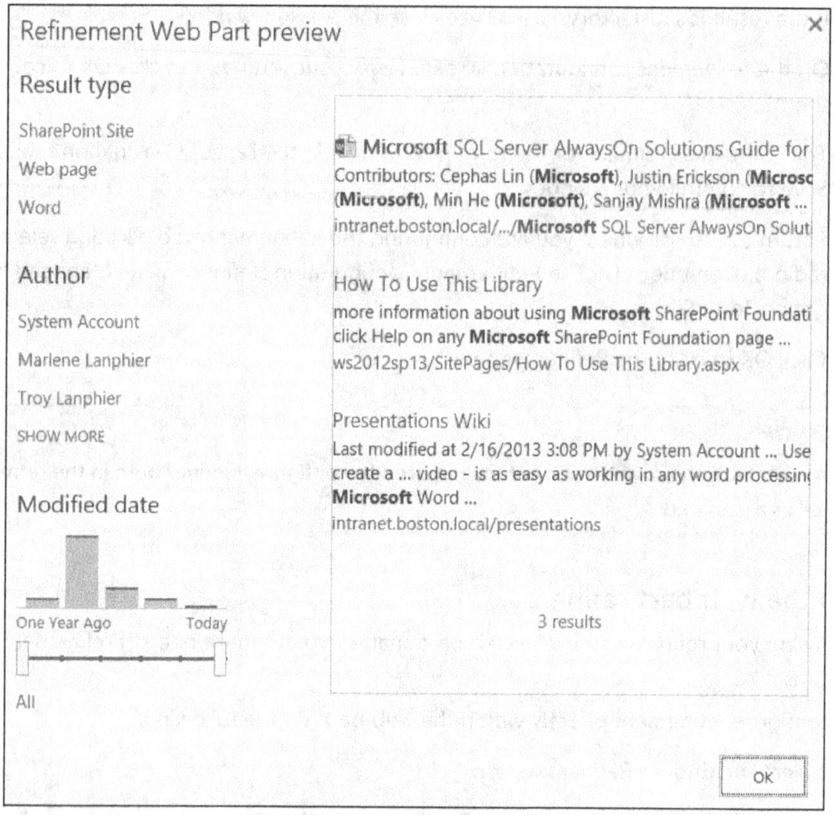

FIGURE 4-122 Refinement Web Part Preview.

4. If the result is satisfactory, select OK to close the preview window.

5. Close the refinement configuration page by selecting the OK button.

6. On the Refinement web part, click OK to close the web part.

7. Check the page back in and publish it, if required.

Configuring list refinement

The ability to refine items doesn't necessarily end with enterprise search; individual list and library items can also be refined because they are also part of the items indexed by search. This functionality is similar to views, in that particular items can be filtered and selected from the overall list.

Enabling list refinement is done via the list's settings page. In this example, we will add a couple of refiners to the Pages library of a publishing site:

1. Navigate to your list.

2. On the ribbon, select the Library Settings icon (see Figure 4-123).

Quick Step
Library Settings
Shared With
Workflow Settings
Settings

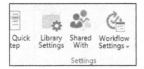

FIGURE 4-123 Library setting.

3. On the Settings page of your list/library, select the Metadata Navigation Settings link.

Within the metadata navigation settings for a list, you can configure one of three things: the list's navigation hierarchy, key filters for the list, and automatic column indexing. The last item, Indexing, is usually set to Automatically Manage Column Indices On This List, which results in improved query performance for the filtering and hierarchy used in this list.

4. In the Configure Key Filters section, you will add the Article Date and Created By fields to the Selected Key Filter Fields box, as shown in Figure 4-124.

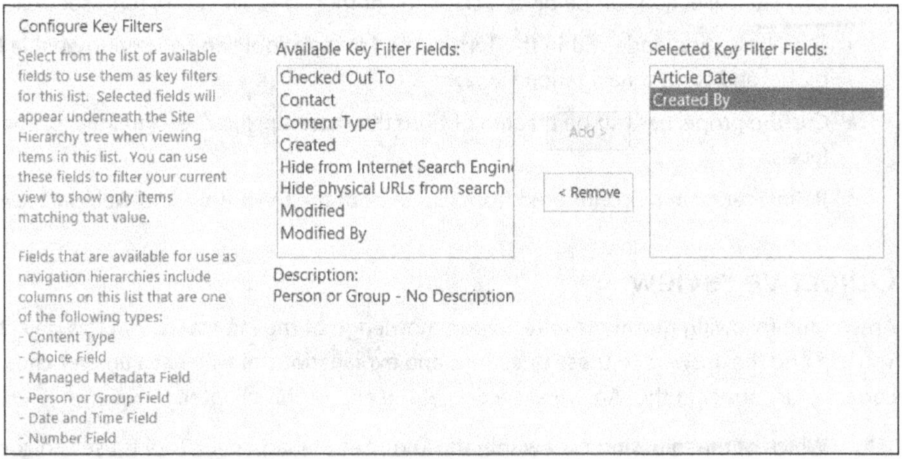
Configure Key Filters
Select from the list of available fields to use them as key filters for this list. Selected fields will appear underneath the Site Hierarchy tree when viewing items in this list. You can use these fields to filter your current view to show only items matching that value.
Fields that are available for use as navigation hierarchies include columns on this list that are one of the following types:
- Content Type
- Choice Field
- Managed Metadata Field
- Person or Group Field
- Date and Time Field
- Number Field
Available Key Filter Fields:
Checked Out To
Contact
Content Type
Created
Hide from Internet Search Engin
Hide physical URLs from search
Modified
Modified By
Add >
< Remove
Selected Key Filter Fields:
Article Date
Created By
Description:
Person or Group - No Description

FIGURE 4-124 Selecting key filter fields.

5. Click OK to commit your changes and then return to the library.

6. In the Quick Launch/Current Navigation section of the page (left column), there is now a Key Filters component added, which enables you to refine the contents of the library based on the Article Date or Created By columnar fields (see Figure 4-125).

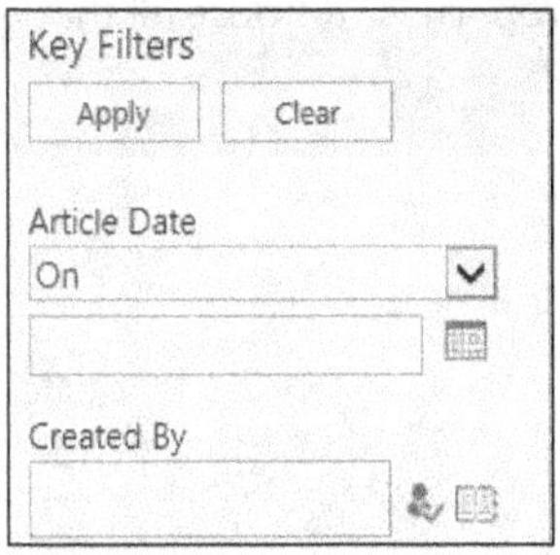
Key Filters
Apply
Clear
Article Date
On
Created By

FIGURE 4-125 List refinement.

Objective summary

- One site collection can be given access to another site collection's term set (read only).
- The Navigation node within the Term Store Manage Tool can be used to enable both global and current navigation via term sets.
- Custom properties can be created at both the shared properties and local properties levels.
- Refinement can be configured from within both the term store and web part levels.

Objective review

Answer the following questions to test your knowledge of the information in this objective. You can find the answers to these questions and explanations of why each answer choice is correct or incorrect in the "Answers" section at the end of this chapter.

1. Which of the following tabs within the Term Set Management Tool is used to configure a term set for navigation?

    A. General

    B. Term-Driven Pages

    C. Intended Use

    D. Custom Properties

2. Which of the following are valid scopes for custom properties? (Choose all that apply.)

    A. Shared properties

    B. Indexed properties

    C. Local properties

    D. All of the above

3. In which of the following can you configure a Search Refiner?

   A. Term store

   B. Navigation tab

   C. Custom properties

   D. Web part

4. At which of the following levels can list refiners be configured? (Choose all that apply.)

   A. Site level

   B. Site collection level

   C. List or library level

   D. Term Store level

Chapter summary

- There is a supported limit of 20 managed paths per web application in SharePoint 2013.

- A root site collection must be assigned to a host header web application; this site should not be configured or used (no template should be assigned).

- Only primary and secondary site collection administrators of a site collection receive e-mail notifications about site status and resourcing.

- Outgoing e-mail must be configured for users to receive e-mailed quota notifications.

- Exchange 2013 is required for team site mailbox creation.

- Search scopes are deprecated in SharePoint 2013, but can be viewed and used in queries.

- If Design Manager is not present in your site collection, it is most likely because you don't have the publishing features active in your site collection.

- Faceted navigation refines content based on context; site navigation can use a term set for both global and current navigation.

Answers

Objective 4.1: Thought experiment

Internally, you would probably use standard Windows authentication (either NTLM or Kerberos; claims-based, of course). For external users, you would most likely work with your Active Directory team to connect your SAML provider to its ADFS environment for authentication. It could then build you an OU that is appropriate for external users.

Objective 4.1: Review

1. **Correct answer:** D

   A. **Incorrect:** This value does not correspond to any of the effective limits.

   B. **Incorrect:** This value does not correspond to any of the effective limits.

   C. **Incorrect:** This value does not correspond to any of the effective limits.

   D. **Correct:** The supported limit is 20 managed paths per web application; although exceeding this limit is technically possible, it negatively affects performance.

2. **Correct answer:** C

   A. **Incorrect:** This is the maximum list view threshold.

   B. **Incorrect:** This is the maximum list view threshold for administrators and auditors.

   C. **Correct:** The default threshold for the list view lookup is eight fields.

   D. **Incorrect:** This value does not correspond to any of the effective limits.

3. **Correct answer:** A

   A. **Correct:** Anonymous authentication is required to see the logon page.

   B. **Incorrect:** Basic authentication provides no security.

   C. **Incorrect:** Kerberos is not for external use (no access to the Key Distribution Center).

   D. **Incorrect:** Claims authentication would work for external users, but FBA was specified.

4. **Correct answers:** B, C

   A. **Incorrect:** Detaching pages is not required.

   B. **Correct:** This setting is required.

   C. **Correct:** This setting is required.

   D. **Incorrect:** Management of the web site URL structure is not required.

Objective 4.2: Thought experiment

If the administrator is not very comfortable in Windows PowerShell, then he/she would most likely need to stick with path-based site collections, especially if this is a smaller environment.

Objective 4.2: Review

1. **Correct answer:** C
   - A. **Incorrect:** -HostNamed is not a valid switch.
   - B. **Incorrect:** -HostHeaderSite is not a valid switch.
   - C. **Correct:** -HostHeader is the correct switch used to create host header site collections.
   - D. **Incorrect:** -HNSC is not a valid switch.

2. **Correct answer:** C
   - A. **Incorrect:** The link is contained within a My Site.
   - B. **Incorrect:** Team Site is not the correct link.
   - C. **Correct:** New Site is the correct link.
   - D. **Incorrect:** Self Service Site is not the correct link.

3. **Correct answer:** A
   - A. **Correct:** A closed site is still available to its members.
   - B. **Incorrect:** There is no such site type.
   - C. **Incorrect:** There is no such site type.
   - D. **Incorrect:** There is no such site type.

4. **Correct answers:** A, C
   - A. **Correct:** Exchange provides the back-end mail store.
   - B. **Incorrect:** Office Web Applications is not a required technology.
   - C. **Correct:** Outlook Web Access presents the team mailbox in the SharePoint site.
   - D. **Incorrect:** Although this should be configured for the farm, it is not a component of team mailboxes.

Objective 4.3: Thought experiment

Rather than building a site and exposing it to the Internet, you might want to consider enabling inbound e-mail and mapping one or more Simple Mail Transport Protocol (SMTP) mailboxes to a library within a site. Doing so prevents external search engines from exposing all content contained within the site.

Objective 4.3: Review

1. **Correct answer:** B

    A. **Incorrect:** Inbound e-mail is not required for site access requests.

    B. **Correct:** Outbound e-mail is sent via the SharePoint system to the designated e-mail address for approval requests.

    C. **Incorrect:** Business Connectivity Services is not required for site access requests.

    D. **Incorrect:** User Profile Services is not required for site access requests.

2. **Correct answers:** B, C

    A. **Incorrect:** Although you can enable authentication at the web application level, you cannot provide authorization at this level.

    B. **Correct:** Sites and site collections can be secured for anonymous access.

    C. **Correct:** Individual lists and libraries can be secured for anonymous access.

    D. **Incorrect:** Although you can grant access to an individual item (by granting access to its parent), you cannot secure it individually.

3. **Correct answers:** B, C, D

    A. **Incorrect:** You cannot configure security inheritance at the web application level.

    B. **Correct:** You can configure security inheritance at the site or site collection level.

    C. **Correct:** You can configure security inheritance at the individual lists and libraries level.

    D. **Correct:** You can configure security inheritance at the individual item level.

4. **Correct answers:** A, C

    A. **Correct:** Full Control cannot be altered (grayed-out).

    B. **Incorrect:** Contribute can be altered.

    C. **Correct:** Limited Access cannot be altered (grayed-out).

    D. **Incorrect:** Read can be altered.

Objective 4.4: Thought experiment

You might start by building a new result source that is capable of selecting just a single type of file. Next, you could create a query rule that returns a particular result set that includes the file type you chose.

Objective 4.4: Review

1. **Correct answer:** D

    A. **Incorrect:** Partial answer – SharePoint is one of the available protocols.

    B. **Incorrect:** Partial answer – Exchange is one of the available protocols.

    C. **Incorrect:** Partial answer – OpenSearch is one of the available protocols.

    D. **Correct:** All three of these protocols can be used with a result source in a SharePoint farm.

2. **Correct answers:** B, C

    A. **Incorrect:** You cannot configure query rules at the search service application level.

    B. **Correct:** Query rules can be configured at the site or site collection level.

    C. **Correct:** Query rules can be configured at the web application level.

    D. **Incorrect:** Only answers B and C are correct.

3. **Correct answer:** C

    A. **Incorrect:** This folder does not house the display templates.

    B. **Incorrect:** This folder does not house the display templates.

    C. **Correct:** The System folder houses the display folders for result types.

    D. **Incorrect:** This folder does not house the display templates.

4. **Correct answer:** C

    A. **Incorrect:** Managed properties is an available option.

    B. **Incorrect:** Categories is an available option.

    C. **Correct:** Filters are not an available option for configuration within the search service application.

    D. **Incorrect:** Crawled properties is an available option.

Objective 4.5: Thought experiment

Because you do not know what the requirements are from a view-based standpoint, you cannot realistically hope to create several dozen views and have them be valid for any length of time.

Your best option is to have a series of custom refiners on the product list that would enable them to "slice and dice" the content in any fashion they find appropriate.

Objective 4.5: Review

1. **Correct answer:** C

   A. **Incorrect:** The General tab cannot be used to configure term sets for navigational use.

   B. **Incorrect:** The Term-Driven Pages tab cannot be used to configure term sets for navigational use.

   C. **Correct:** The Intended Use tab allows for the configuration of term sets for navigational use.

   D. **Incorrect:** The Custom Properties tab cannot be used to configure term sets for navigational use.

2. **Correct answer:** A, C

   A. **Correct:** Valid scope.

   B. **Incorrect:** The Indexed properties scope is not valid for custom properties.

   C. **Correct:** Valid scope.

   D. **Incorrect:** Only the Shared and Local properties scopes are valid for custom properties.

3. **Correct answers:** A, D

   A. **Correct:** Search refiners can be configured from within the Term Store.

   B. **Incorrect:** Cannot create a search refiner.

   C. **Incorrect:** Cannot create a search refiner.

   D. **Correct:** Search refiners can be configured from within a Web Part.

4. **Correct answers:** C

   A. **Incorrect:** List refiners cannot be configured at the site level.

   B. **Incorrect:** List refiners cannot be configured at the site collection level.

   C. **Correct:** List refiners are configured at the list or library level.

   D. **Incorrect:** List refiners cannot be configured at the Term Store level.

## CHAPTER 5

Maintain a core SharePoint environment

Up to this point, we've been talking about the preparations that go into creating a new SharePoint 2013 environment. Designing the topology, planning security, installing, and configuring the environment lead to the eventual completion of the implementation phase.

The implementation phase is not the end of the project but its beginning; moving forward, the environment will require careful maintenance, planning, and management to ensure continuing service to a growing user base.

In this chapter, we will focus on three major tasks: monitoring, tuning and optimization, and troubleshooting. Monitoring is concerned with the use of tools and metrics to minimize system failures or loss of performance. Tuning and optimization expands on these concepts, providing insight into how to optimize the performance of not only SharePoint, but SQL and Internet Information Services (IIS) as well. Troubleshooting is perhaps the most complex of these tasks and is concerned with establishing performance baselines as well as using both client and server tools to troubleshoot issues as they occur.

Objectives in this chapter:

- Objective 5.1: Monitor a SharePoint environment
- Objective 5.2: Tune and optimize a SharePoint environment
- Objective 5.3: Troubleshoot a SharePoint environment

Objective 5.1: Monitor a SharePoint environment

The first few steps after implementation are often the most critical. A sudden uptick in user adoption shortly arrives and may expose any design inconsistencies not discovered during performance testing. Previously defined service level agreements (SLAs) with the business may also be in effect, restricting the times that the system can be down for maintenance.

Ensuring reliability and performance levels during this period is a key requirement for user adoption of the new platform. Effective administration and monitoring of the SharePoint environment can capture events, addressing any misconfigurations or design shortfalls before they affect user adoption.

Defining monitoring requirements

Monitoring is the art of using instrumentation to analyze and predict the behaviors of a given system. Knowing what instrumentation is available and the expected values for each enables the administrator of a system to be able to adjust for performance idiosyncrasies of a system without experiencing any downtime.

Each new revision of SharePoint has introduced greater potential for monitoring at a more granular level than in previous versions. SharePoint 2013 continues this pattern by providing insight into the operations of major subsystems such as Microsoft SQL, ASP.NET, IIS, and other services.

Service guarantee metrics

In the planning stages of your farm design, you should have developed SLAs that define the service guarantee provided by the farm. This guarantee defines not only the times that a system can be up or down entirely but also the availability and enforceability of scheduled outage windows.

Within the SLA for your environment you will find terms such as "downtime," "scheduled downtime," and "uptime percentage." These metrics merely describe at a high level what the goals of monitoring are. For instance, within the Microsoft Office 365 SLA agreement for SharePoint Online, you will find definitions for the following:

- **Downtime** Defined as "Any period of time when users are unable to access SharePoint sites for which they have appropriate permissions."

- **Scheduled Downtime** Defined as "(i) Downtime within preestablished maintenance windows; or (ii) Downtime during major version upgrade." The SLA goes on to state that scheduled downtime is *not* considered downtime.

- **Monthly Uptime Percentage** Defined as being calculated "by taking the total number of minutes in a calendar month multiplied by the total number of users minus the total number of minutes of Downtime experienced by all users in a given calendar month, all divided by the total number of minutes in that calendar month multiplied by the total number of users."

Immediately after these definitions, the SLA goes on to define what service credit is offered in the event of monthly uptime percentage falling below 99.9% ("Three Nines"), 99% ("Two Nines"), and 95% ("One Nine").

Monitoring levels

Now you know what your monthly uptime percentage is (for example, three 9s would give you a maximum of approximately 24*60*.001, or 1.44 minutes per day of downtime) and what constitutes downtime, you can begin to monitor the SharePoint farm (or farms) to prevent these incidents.

A single SharePoint farm has three major levels at which it can be monitored (from largest to smallest):

- **Server level**   At this level, you will be monitoring the servers that constitute the farm:
  - Web tier servers
  - Application tier servers
  - SQL database servers
- **Service application level**   At this level, you will be monitoring all the services provided within the farm, such as Excel Calculation Services, User Profile services, and so on.
- **Site and site collection level**   At this level, you monitor all the sites and site collections contained within the farm.

***IMPORTANT* WHEN AN OUTAGE ISN'T A COMPLETE OUTAGE**

Remember that outages do not necessarily require the failure of an entire farm; an improperly deployed feature or a misconfigured service application can result in downtime for a considerable segment of the user base without rendering the entire farm inoperable.

Monitoring tools

There are four core tools that can be used to monitor SharePoint 2013 farms: Central Administration, Windows PowerShell, logs, and System Center 2012 Operations Manager.

Central Administration allows for the configuration and monitoring of the SharePoint logs as well as configuration of usage and health providers. Additionally, Health Analyzer runs a series of rules on a regular basis that check on the status of metrics such as these:

- Free disk space on both SharePoint and SQL servers
- Service issues such as problems with State service, InfoPath Forms Services, and Visio Graphics Service
- SQL-specific issues, such as overly large content databases, databases in need of upgrade, and the read/write status for a given database

MORE INFO SHAREPOINT HEALTH ANALYZER RULES

A complete list of all SharePoint Health Analyzer rules can be found on TechNet at *http://technet.microsoft.com/en-us/library/ff686816.aspx*.

Windows PowerShell focuses on the diagnostic capabilities found in the Unified Logging Service (ULS) logs. The ULS logs can be quite detailed in scope, meaning that quite literally hundreds and thousands of entries can be found on a given server. Using the Get-SPLogEvent cmdlet, you can view trace events by level, area, category, event ID, process, or message text.

EXAM TIP

Using the –MinimumLevel switch with Get-SPLogEvent enables you to look for events that are equal to or more severe than the level you specify. There are only two valid values: Error or Warning.

Additionally, you can pipe its output to the Out-GridView cmdlet to produce tabular log output in a graphical format (as shown in Figure 5-1), which can be easily refined and/or exported to an Excel spreadsheet for further analysis.

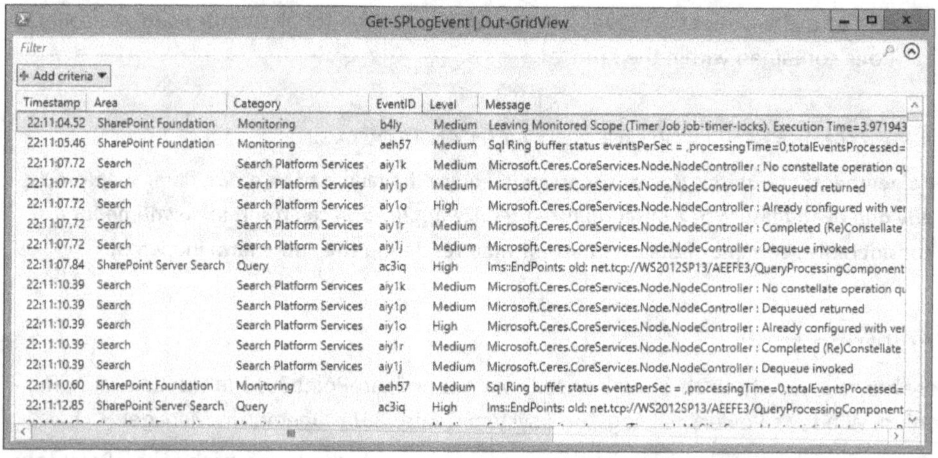

FIGURE 5-1 Using the Out-GridView cmdlet.

MORE INFO USING WINDOWS POWERSHELL TO VIEW DIAGNOSTIC LOGS

For a more detailed discussion of the use of Windows PowerShell for viewing diagnostic logs, see the TechNet article "View Diagnostic Logs in SharePoint 2013" at *http://technet.microsoft.com/en-us/library/ff463595.aspx*.

Logs for use with SharePoint monitoring come from two distinct sources. At the operating system level, you find the standard event logs, in which events that concern SharePoint and its supporting technologies (SQL, IIS, and so on) are recorded (primarily in the Application and System logs). As previously mentioned, SharePoint also records information in its own series of trace logs, otherwise known as the ULS logs.

Finally, if you have a larger SharePoint farm (or farms), you may find that the monitoring of each individual system is becoming time-centric, and that even the use of the usage and health providers is not enough to provide a complete picture of the systems required to support SharePoint.

For this purpose, Microsoft produces a product known as System Center 2012 Operations Manager. Using this toolset with the System Center Management Pack for SharePoint 2013 not only allows for the effective monitoring of multiple SharePoint farms and their component systems but also for the alerting and preventative actions required to assist in the maintenance of service level guarantees.

The System Center Monitoring Pack monitors both Microsoft SharePoint Server 2013 and Project Server 2013. It also monitors the following service applications:

- Access Services
- Business Data Connectivity (BDC)
- Security Token Service
- Managed Metadata Web Service
- Education Services
- Excel Services Application
- InfoPath Forms Services
- Performance Point Services
- Sandboxed Code Services
- Secure Store Services
- SharePoint Server Search
- Translation Services
- User Profile Service
- Visio Services
- Word Automation Service

Configuring performance counter capture

As your SharePoint installation grows in scope, you may want to evaluate the performance of one or more servers within the farm. Examining the performance level of each server in the farm from an operating system perspective is one way to predict areas in which more system resources or configuration changes are required.

One tool that can be used for this purpose is Performance Monitor (PerfMon), a native tool installed along with Windows Server. This tool enables you to monitor and capture metrics about your individual servers using a series of performance counters.

As SharePoint, SQL, and other applications are added to a server, performance counters for those applications are made available to PerfMon. These new counters describe additional performance and health metrics that are specific to the new application or its major components.

Starting a performance monitoring capture

To start a new performance capture, begin by opening PerfMon. In Windows Server 2012, you can do this by going to your Start screen and selecting the tile for PerfMon (see Figure 5-2).

FIGURE 5-2 Performance Monitor icon.

If you are having difficulty locating this app, there is another way to start PerfMon. Simply start a search and then type perfmon into your search box and select its icon (shown in Figure 5-3).

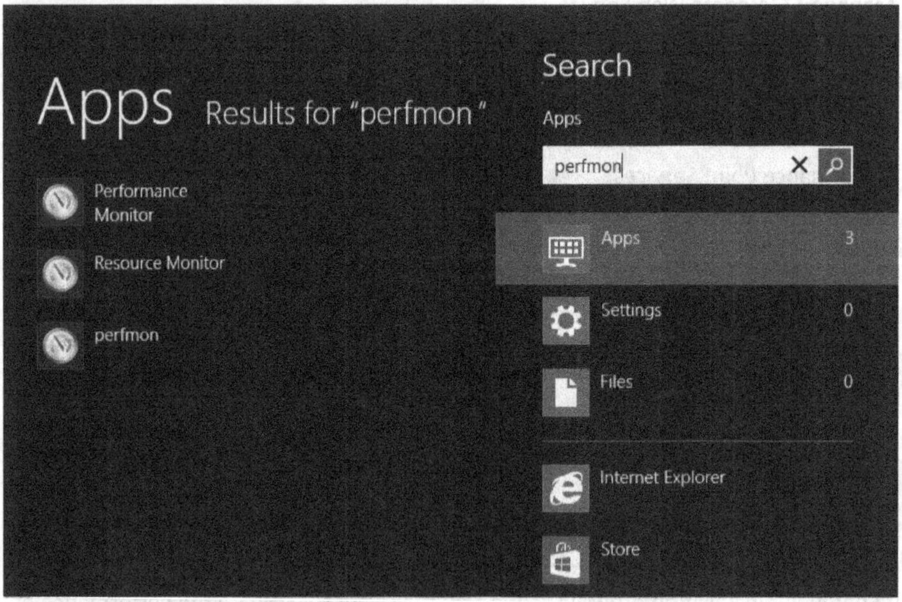

FIGURE 5-3 Finding PerfMon using search.

When Performance Monitor appears on the screen, there isn't a whole lot to it. To imme-diately begin using PerfMon, select the Performance Monitor menu item. A capture graph appears (as shown in Figure 5-4).

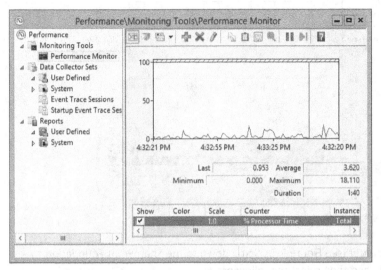

FIGURE 5-4 PerfMon default capture.

Still not too impressive, is it? At this point, PerfMon is capturing the %Processor Time per-formance counter over a 100-second (1:40 duration) interval.

Adding SharePoint counters to Performance Monitor

All sorts of SharePoint-specific counters can be added to a PerfMon capture. Counters are included for SharePoint, but other subsystems counters are also represented:

- Access Services (2010 and 2013 versions)
- InfoPath Forms Services
- Microsoft Office Web Apps
- Search
- Visio Services

Adding a counter to an existing performance capture is fairly straightforward:

1. Select the plus (+) icon in the toolbar (see Figure 5-5).

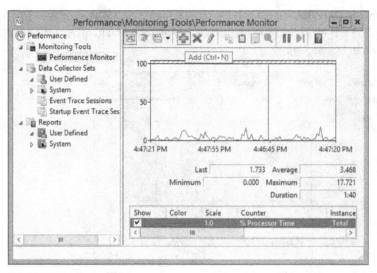

FIGURE 5-5 Adding a counter.

2. Add in a new counter (see Figure 5-6). Scroll down to the SharePoint Foundation category, expand it, and then select the following:

    A. **Health Score** displays the SharePoint Server Health Score

    B. **Current Page Requests** is the number of current requests in processing

3. In the Instances Of Select Object window, select <All Instances>.

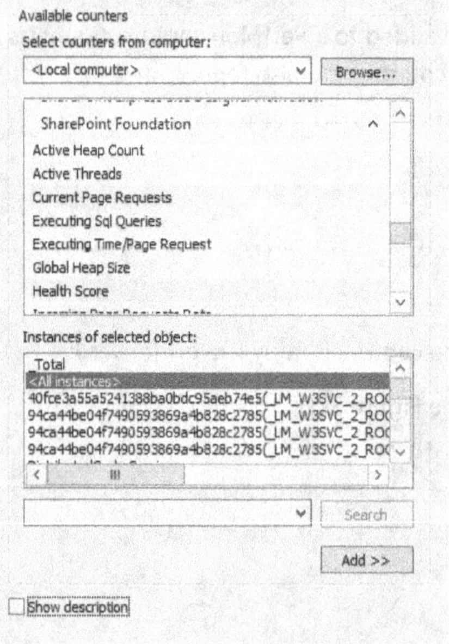

FIGURE 5-6 Adding SharePoint Foundation counters.

4. Select the Show Description check box in the lower-left corner and then select Add to add the counter. Finally, click OK to add the counter to Instances Of Select Object (see Figure 5-7).

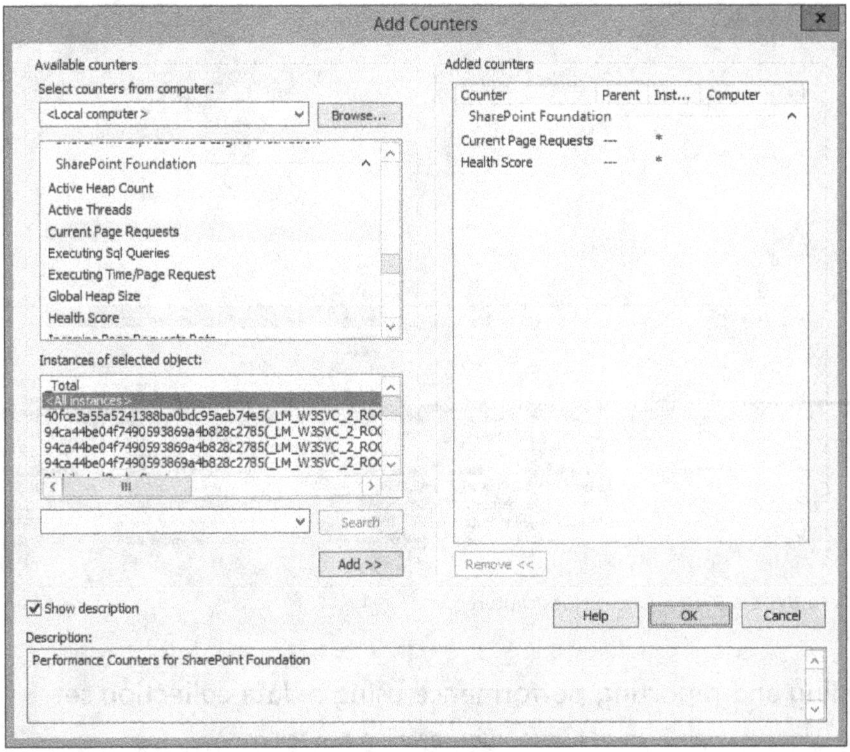

FIGURE 5-7 Counters are added.

IMPORTANT SHOWING THE DESCRIPTION FOR A COUNTER

One of the most valuable pieces of information in the Add Counters window is the often-overlooked Show Description check box. Selecting this box shows a description of what the counter actually does within the system.

---

5. The new values counters appear and are captured in the graph (see Figure 5-8).

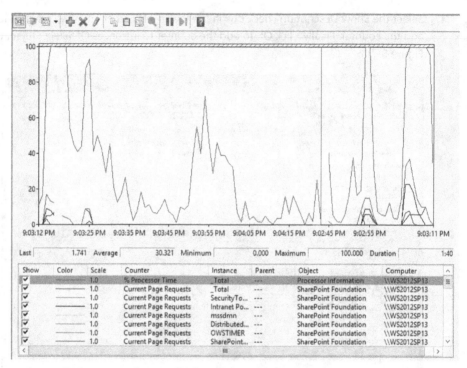

FIGURE 5-8 Performance values captured.

Building and reporting performance using a data collection set

The previous example is an ad hoc capture, meaning two things:

- Every time you start a new PerfMon session, you have to add the counters back in.
- There is no meaningful way to capture and replay the counters as they appear.

The next logical step is to build a data collector set to monitor the performance counters; then use the Reports feature of PerfMon to "replay" the log for review.

This example adds some basic performance counters used to monitor basic server performance:

1. Open Performance Monitor.

2. Within PerfMon, expand the Data Collector Sets group and select User Defined. From the New menu, right-click and select Data Collector Set (see Figure 5-9).

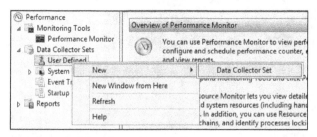

FIGURE 5-9 Creating a new data collector set.

3. Enter a name for your new data collector set, select Create Manually (Advanced), and then click Next (see Figure 5-10).

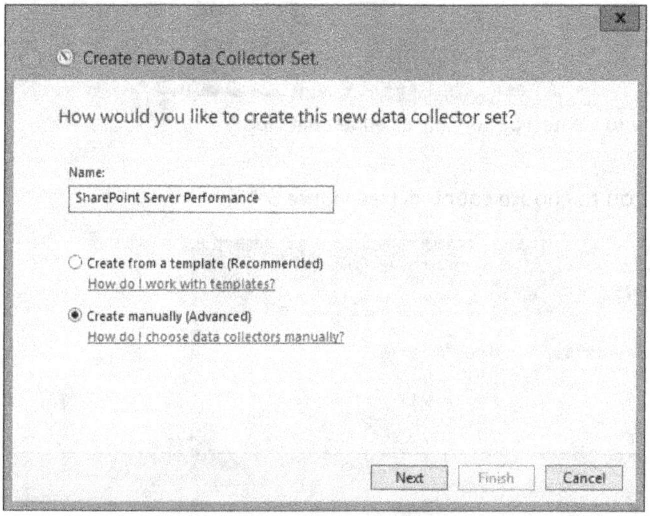

FIGURE 5-10 Naming the data collector set.

4. Choose to capture only performance counters and click Next (see Figure 5-11).

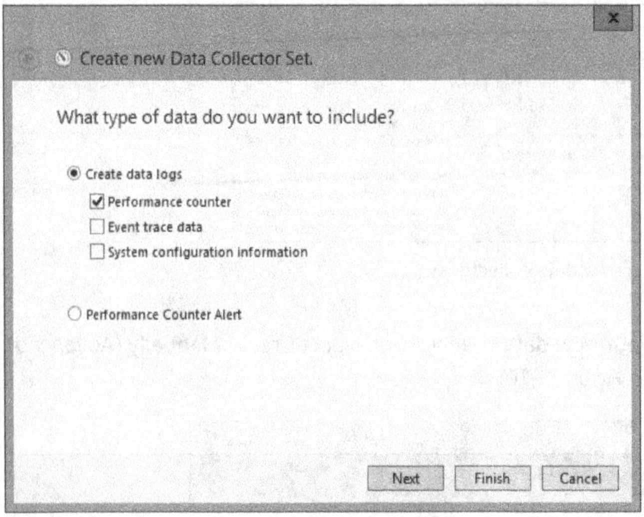

FIGURE 5-11 Choosing to create a performance counter data log.

5. Select the Add button to choose counters (see Figure 5-12).

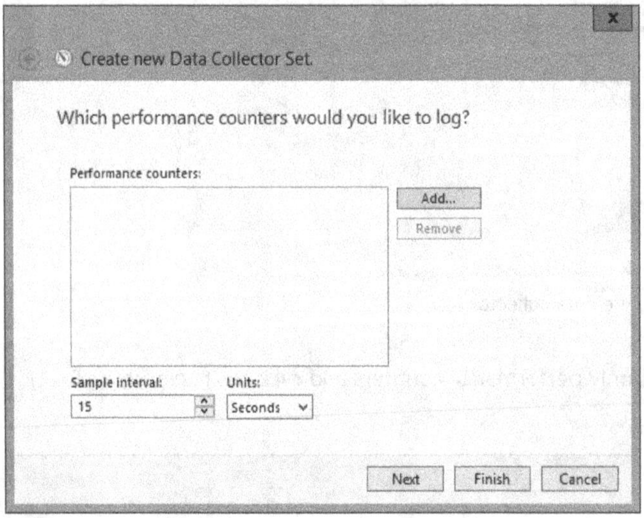

FIGURE 5-12 Selecting Add.

6. You will select five counters that are often used to check basic health of the server on which SharePoint is installed:

   A. % Processor Time shows processor usage over time

   B. Avg. Disk Queue Length shows the average number of both read and write requests that were queued for the selected disk during the sample interval

C. Available MBytes shows how much physical memory is available for allocation

D. % Used and % Used Peak Of Paging File shows the current and peak values for paging file used

7. Click OK to continue (see Figure 5-13).

EXAM TIP

The counters listed previously are those commonly used to troubleshoot core performance levels on a SharePoint server. Optimal values for the major performance counters can be found on TechNet at *http://technet.microsoft.com/en-us/library/ff758658.aspx*.

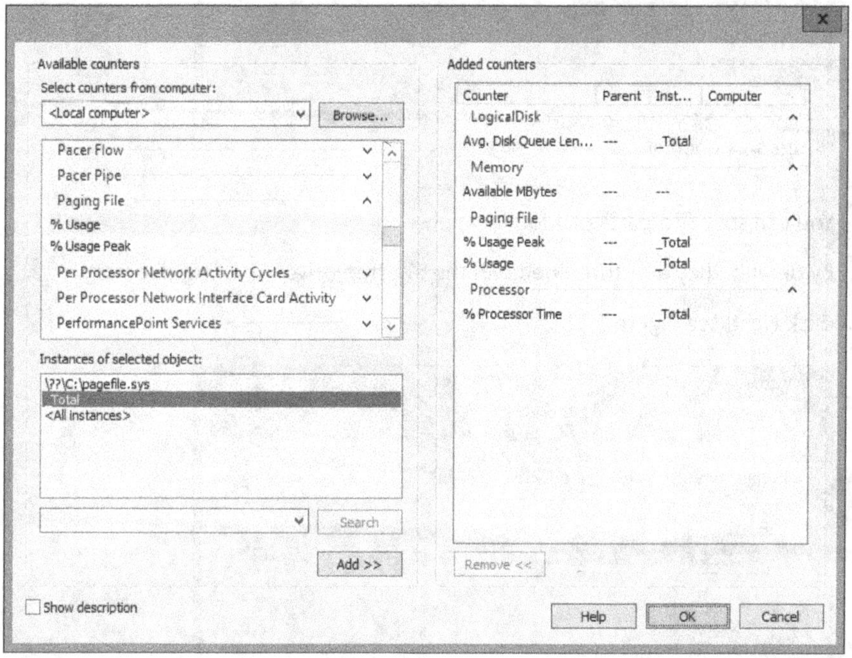

FIGURE 5-13 Selected performance counters.

8. The selected counters are displayed next. You might consider changing the sample interval (time between counter samples in seconds). Click Next to continue (see Figure 5-14).

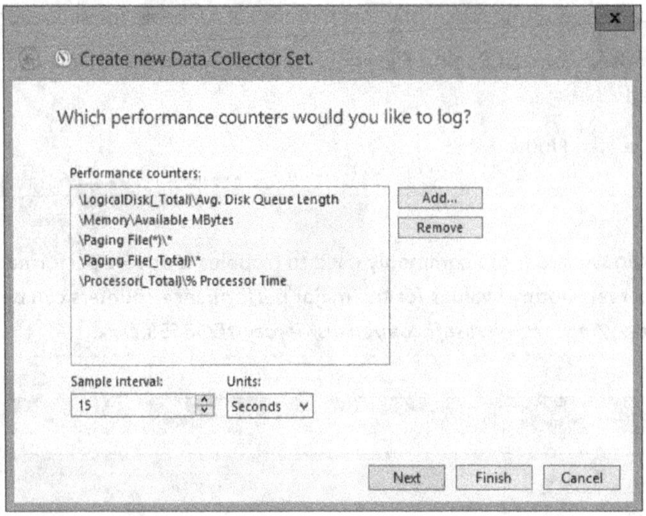

FIGURE 5-14 Counters added.

9. You can specify a particular log location.

10. By default, they are stored beneath the %systemdrive%\Perflog directory.

11. Click Next (see Figure 5-15).

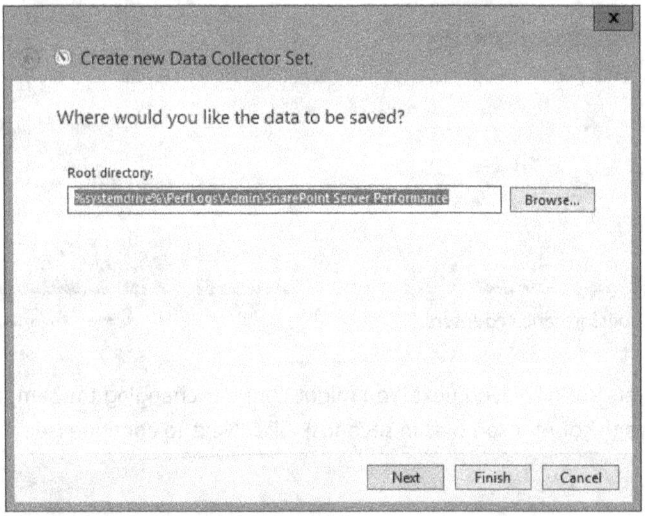

FIGURE 5-15 Save directory.

12. The final step in creating the new data collector set is to choose which account it runs under and selecting from a series of actions:

   A. Open Properties For This Data Collector Set enables you to specify additional selections for your log, such as its duration.

   B. Start This Data Collector Set Now saves and immediately starts the data collector set capture.

   C. Save And Close (selected) saves and then closes the capture.

13. Select Finish to complete this data collector set (see Figure 5-16).

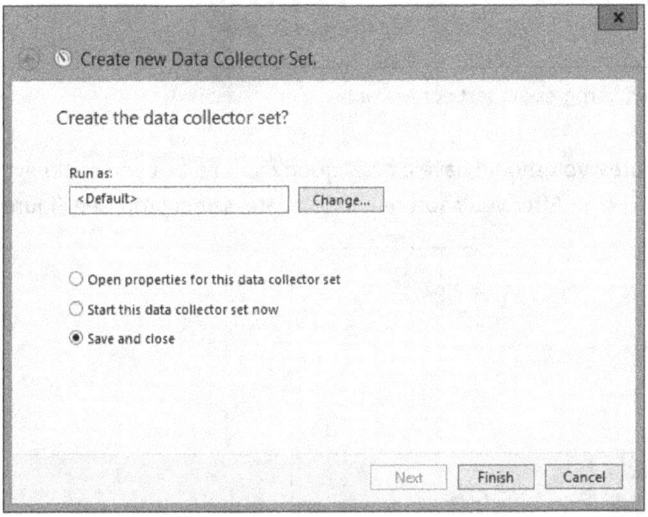

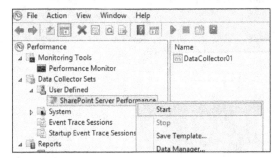

Create new Data Collector Set.

Create the data collector set?

Run as:
<Default>   Change...

○ Open properties for this data collector set
○ Start this data collector set now
● Save and close

Next   Finish   Cancel

FIGURE 5-16 Completed data collector set.

14. To begin the capture, simply right-click your data collector set and select Start (see Figure 5-17).

File Action View Window Help

Performance
  Monitoring Tools
    Performance Monitor
  Data Collector Sets
    User Defined
      SharePoint Server Performance
    System
    Event Trace Sessions
    Startup Event Trace Sessions
  Reports

Name
  DataCollector01

Start
Stop
Save Template...
Data Manager...

FIGURE 5-17 Start capture.

15. If you attempt to look at the report for your performance counter capture, it will show as Collecting Data until you stop the process (see Figure 5-18).

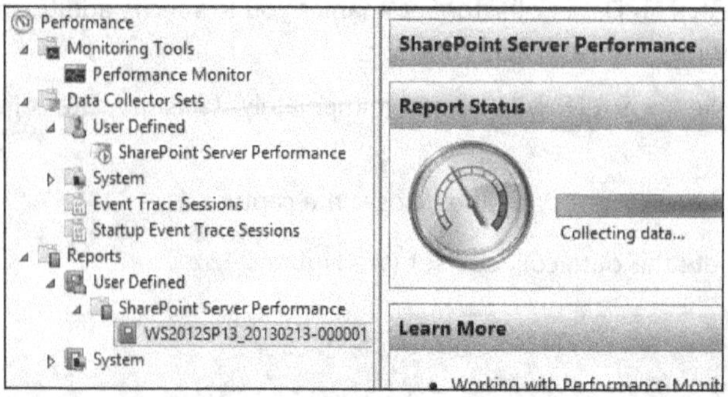

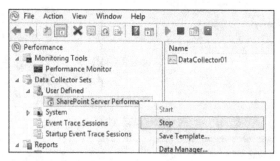

FIGURE 5-18 Capture in progress; report not available.

16. After about 5 minutes, you should have a fairly good capture, but you could extend this duration if you want. After you capture enough data, select Stop (see Figure 5-19).

FIGURE 5-19 Stopping a performance capture.

17. Selecting a report displays the metrics for a given time period along with some maximum, minimum, and average values (see Figure 5-20).

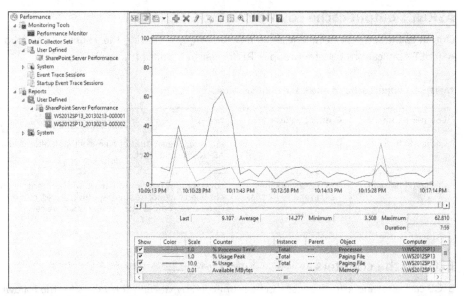

FIGURE 5-20 Performance Monitor report.

MORE INFO **SERVER PERFORMANCE COUNTER REFERENCE**

Basic server performance counters that are important for monitoring a SharePoint Server 2013 server are described in the TechNet article "Monitoring and Maintaining SharePoint Server 2013" at *http://technet.microsoft.com/en-us/library/ff758658.aspx*.

Configuring page performance monitoring

Page performance is dependent on a number of variables—whether the user has caching enabled on the desktop, whether the IIS web servers are caching artifacts such as graphic and text content, how SharePoint is caching information, and how quickly SQL Server can provide content to the SharePoint farm.

SharePoint makes use of three distinct caching mechanisms by default: ASP.NET output cache, BLOB cache, and the page object cache. Each of these caching mechanisms has a representative set of counters in Performance Monitor.

EXAM TIP

Although these caching mechanisms all enhance performance in a SharePoint farm, know which are enabled by default versus those that you must enable manually. Also know which types of items might be affected by each of the three cache types.

ASP.NET output cache counters

Output cache setting effectiveness can be monitored by viewing the values for the following ASP.NET Applications counter group in Performance Monitor (shown in Table 5-1).

TABLE 5-1 Output cache counters and optimal values

Counter name	Optimal Value	Notes
Cache API trim	0	Increases the amount of memory that is allocated to the ASP.NET output cache.
Cache API hit ratio	1 for read-only sites <1 for read-write sites	Low hit ratios have mostly to do with content that has not been cached, frequently edited pages, or customized cache profiles that prevent effective caching.

BLOB cache counters

BLOB cache setting effectiveness can be monitored by viewing the values for the following SharePoint Publishing cache counter group in Performance Monitor (shown in Table 5-2).

TABLE 5-2 BLOB cache counters and optimal values

Counter name	Optimal Value	Notes
Total number of cache compactions	0	A consistently high number indicates that the cache size is too small.
BLOB cache % full	< 80%	Values between 80% and 100% indicate that the cache size is too small.
Publishing cache flushes/second	0	When the cache is flushed, performance is negatively affected. Site owners may be performing actions on the sites that are causing the cache to be flushed. To improve performance during peak-use hours, make sure that site owners perform these actions only during off-peak hours.
Publishing cache hit ratio	1 for read-only sites <1 for read-write sites	Any time that unpublished or draft items are being interacted with, the read-write ratio is less than 1.

Page object cache counters

Object cache setting effectiveness can be monitored by viewing the values for the following SharePoint Publishing cache counter group in Performance Monitor (shown in Table 5-3).

TABLE 5-3 Object cache counters and optimal values

Counter name	Optimal Value	Notes
Total number of cache compactions	0	If this number is high, the cache size is too small for the data being requested. To improve performance, increase the size of the cache.
Publishing cache flushes/second	0	Site owners might be performing actions on the sites that are causing the cache to be flushed. To improve performance during peak-use hours, make sure that site owners perform these actions only during off-peak hours.
Publishing cache hit ratio	1 for read-only sites <1 for read-write sites	If the hit ratio starts to fall, either the cache has been flushed or a significant amount of content has been added to the site.

Configuring usage and health providers

Monitoring is an integral part of any IT administrator's job; although this person is occasionally called on to perform reactionary maintenance (fixing things that go wrong), the lion's share of duties should be focused on preventive administration. Monitoring logs and other metrics provided by the systems they support are a key component of long-term IT success.

SharePoint presents a special challenge from an administrative standpoint because it is dependent on a lot of other technologies such as SQL, IIS, ASP, the operating system, and SharePoint.

At any given time, a SharePoint administrator might need to know metrics such as these:

- How well IIS is serving pages
- If a member server's operating system is functioning correctly
- How a SQL server is meeting the data requirements placed on it by the SharePoint farm

Add monitoring several SharePoint servers into the mix, and there are a lot of logs to be checked, especially in a smaller IT team. Event Viewer, IIS logs, SQL logs, and SharePoint logs can be individually monitored, but each individual logging system paints only a partial picture of the health and well-being of a SharePoint farm.

Event selection

Although configuring the usage and health data collection for the farm, you will be given the opportunity to choose from a series of events to capture. Several of these events are chosen by default, although you can choose to deselect them before enabling the usage and health data provider to enhance performance.

Shown in Table 5-4 is a listing of events that can be logged along with their initial logging state.

TABLE 5-4 Potential logging events

Events to log	Enabled by default?
Analytics usage	Yes
App monitoring	Yes
App statistics	Yes
Bandwidth monitoring	No
Content export usage	Yes
Content import usage	Yes
Definition of usage fields for education telemetry	Yes
Definition of usage fields for microblog telemetry	Yes
Definition of usage fields for service calls	Yes
Definition of usage fields for SPDistributedCache calls	Yes
Definition of usage fields for workflow telemetry	Yes
Feature use	Yes
File I/O	Yes
Page requests	Yes
REST and client API action usage	Yes
REST and client API request usage	Yes
Sandbox request resource measures	Yes
Sandbox requests	Yes
SQL exceptions usage	No
SQL I/O usage	No
SQL latency usage	No
Task use	Yes
Tenant logging	No
Timer jobs	Yes
Tracks Access Services monitoring usage metrics	Yes
Tracks app database usage metrics	Yes
Tracks response times/processing time metrics for Access Services ADS and WFE subsystems	Yes
Tracks the CPU and memory usage characteristics of Access Services sessions	Yes

Events to log	Enabled by default?
User profile Active Directory import usage	Yes
User profile to SharePoint synchronization usage	Yes

Configuring usage and health data collection

A newly created SharePoint installation creates the usage and health data collection services, but does not activate or configure them by default. These services can affect performance; as a result, they should not be activated until after the farm is fully configured, but prior to user acceptance testing.

To display the usage and health data collection configuration, do the following:

1. Open Central Administration and select Monitoring.

2. On the Monitoring page, under the Reporting section header, select Configure Usage And Health Data Collection.

EXAM TIP

Be familiar with the steps required to both enable and configure usage and health providers—specifically how to schedule the log collection and select the events being captured.

There are six major components to the configuration of usage and health data collection:

- **Usage data collection** Choose to either enable or disable data collection (selected to be enabled by default).

- **Event selection** The selection of which events are to be captured within the logging database.

- **Usage data collection settings** Specifies the log file location on all SharePoint farm servers (set to %ProgramFiles%\Common Files\Microsoft Shared\Web Server Extensions\15\LOGS\ by default).

- **Health data collection** Choose whether or not to enable health data collection settings and edit the health logging schedule (if necessary).

- **Log collection schedule** Choose whether you want to edit the log collection schedule via the Usage Data Imports and Usage Data Processing timer jobs.

- **Logging database server** Displays the current database server and name for the logging database along with the authentication method used to connect to SQL (Windows authentication or SQL authentication).

The database server and name are intentionally grayed out; these values can be reconfigured via Windows PowerShell cmdlets.

After you have made your selections on this page, clicking OK button activates the usage and health data collection functionality.

> **MORE INFO** **USAGE AND HEALTH DATA COLLECTION FOR OTHER PRODUCTS**
>
> Usage and health data collection is not just for SharePoint; it can also be used to capture performance counters for the operating system (known as system counters) and SQL server counters. Obviously, special care should be taken to ensure that the logging database does not fill all its available space. The benefit of having these additional counters captured in the logging database is having a complete picture of your farm and all its members (including SQL server) for analysis as required. For more information on this functionality, see the TechNet article "Monitoring and Maintaining SharePoint Server 2013" at *http://technet. microsoft.com/en-us/library/ff758658.aspx*.

Logging database functionality

While installing your SharePoint farm, you specified a database to be stored in SQL for use in logging performance metrics. Individual metrics, captured by each member server of your SharePoint farm will be combined on a regular basis and stored in a series of partitioned tables within the logging database.

> **MORE INFO** **EXAMINING THE LOGGING DATABASE IN SQL SERVER MANAGEMENT STUDIO (SSMS)**
>
> This logging database is unlike any other in SharePoint 2013 because it is the only one created for the express purpose of querying via SQL Server Management Studio (SSMS). For more details about the views and stored procedures present within the logging database, see the article "View Data in the Logging Database in SharePoint 2013" at *http://technet. microsoft.com/en-us/library/jj715694.aspx*.

After the usage and health data collection has been configured in Central Administration, logged events are stored in a series of tables (partitioned by day), as shown in Figure 5-21. Each table has a total of 32 partitions, one for each possible day of a given month (31 days total) and another for the current day's logs (a specific partitioned table, which is known as _Partition0).

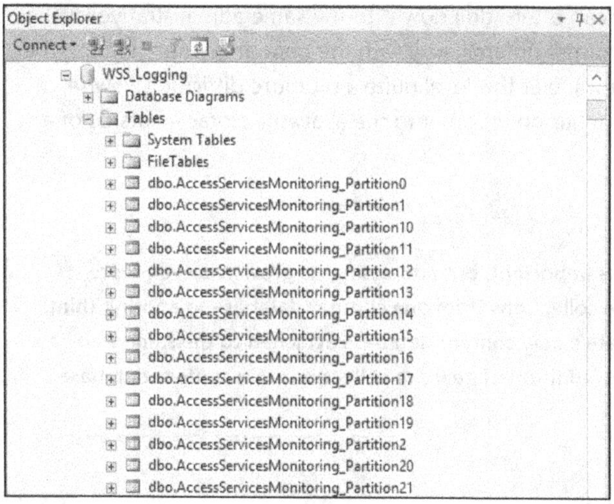

FIGURE 5-21 WSS_Logging database tables.

There are two timer jobs responsible for the collection and aggregation of logging data in a SharePoint farm:

- The Microsoft SharePoint Foundation usage data import timer job runs every five minutes by default and imports usage log files into the logging database.

- The Microsoft SharePoint Foundation usage data processing timer job runs once daily and expires usage data older than 30 days.

The usage data import timer job is fairly self-explanatory: All it does is extract logging data from every member of the farm and load this information into the logging database tables (by category) for further analysis. This information is temporarily stored in the _Partition0 table so logging information can be regularly added throughout the day.

At day's end, the usage data processing job accumulates and analyzes the current day's log information, removing it from _Partition0 and storing it in a different daily partition.

As an example, if today were the 10th of February and you selected the top 1,000 rows from the dbo.AccessServicesMonitoring_Partition10 table, you would be seeing logs from the 10th of January; today's logs would still be stored in the _Partition0 table until the date rolls over to February 11th. At that point, the logs for February 10th would be moved by the usage data processing timer job to the _Partition10 table, and the _Partition0 table would be reset.

Monitoring and forecasting storage needs

Predicting the storage requirements of SharePoint installation requires a combined effort on the part of the farm administrator and the site collection administrators. Each cannot only monitor storage, but also record the data growth rate for predicting future database size requirements.

Although the farm administrator can often "drill down" to the same administrative level as the site collection administrator, his or her unfamiliarity with the data or its retention requirement makes the administration of storage at this level quite a bit more difficult. Likewise, the site collection administrator often has no insight into the available storage outside of a particular site collection.

> ***EXAM TIP***
>
> **Monitoring the content database is important, but addressing its growth is even more important. Know how to move site collections from one content database to another (hint: Windows PowerShell), how to create a new content database attached to the same web application, and how to restrict the addition of new site collections to a content database that is already quite large.**

Monitoring content databases

Central Administration does not provide a method to farm administrators for reviewing the size of either content databases or site collections. Windows PowerShell, on the other hand, provides a couple of different cmdlets for reviewing SharePoint databases: Get-SPDatabase and Get-SPContentDatabase.

Get-SPDatabase is the more generic of the two commands and will retrieve information about all databases within a SharePoint farm: configuration, content, and service application. Running Get-SPDatabase with Out-GridView displays all the databases currently attached to this SharePoint farm, as shown in Figure 5-22.

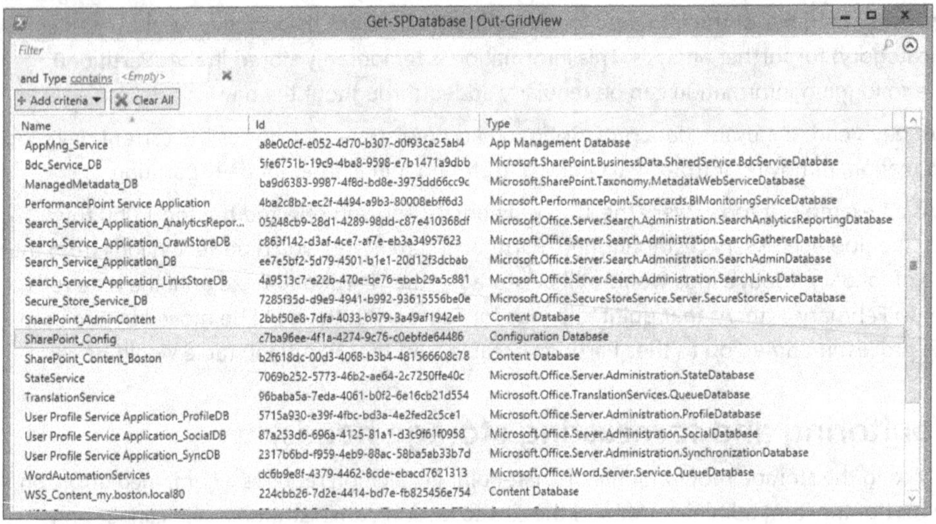

Name	Id	Type
AppMng_Service	a8e0c0cf-e052-4d70-b307-d0f93ca25ab4	App Management Database
Bdc_Service_DB	5fe6751b-19c9-4ba8-9598-e7b1471a9dbb	Microsoft.SharePoint.BusinessData.SharedService.BdcServiceDatabase
ManagedMetadata_DB	ba9d6383-9987-4f8d-bd8e-3975dd66cc9c	Microsoft.SharePoint.Taxonomy.MetadataWebServiceDatabase
PerformancePoint Service Application	4ba2c8b2-ec2f-4494-a9b3-80008ebff6d3	Microsoft.PerformancePoint.Scorecards.BIMonitoringServiceDatabase
Search_Service_Application_AnalyticsRepor...	05248cb9-28d1-4289-98dd-c87e410368df	Microsoft.Office.Server.Search.Administration.SearchAnalyticsReportingDatabase
Search_Service_Application_CrawlStoreDB	c863f142-d3af-4ce7-af7e-eb3a34957623	Microsoft.Office.Server.Search.Administration.SearchGathererDatabase
Search_Service_Application_DB	ee7e5bf2-5d79-4501-b1e1-20d12f3dcbab	Microsoft.Office.Server.Search.Administration.SearchAdminDatabase
Search_Service_Application_LinksStoreDB	4a9513c7-e22b-470e-be76-ebeb29a5c881	Microsoft.Office.Server.Search.Administration.SearchLinksDatabase
Secure_Store_Service_DB	7285f35d-d9e9-4941-b992-93615556be0e	Microsoft.Office.SecureStoreService.Server.SecureStoreServiceDatabase
SharePoint_AdminContent	2bbf50e8-7dfa-4033-b979-3a49af1942eb	Content Database
SharePoint_Config	c7ba96ee-4f1a-4274-9c76-c0ebfde64486	Configuration Database
SharePoint_Content_Boston	b2f618dc-00d3-4068-b3b4-481566608c78	Content Database
StateService	7069b252-5773-46b2-ae64-2c7250ffe40c	Microsoft.Office.Server.Administration.StateDatabase
TranslationService	96baba5a-7eda-4061-b0f2-6e16cb21d554	Microsoft.Office.TranslationServices.QueueDatabase
User Profile Service Application_ProfileDB	5715a930-e39f-4fbc-bd3a-4e2fed2c5ce1	Microsoft.Office.Server.Administration.ProfileDatabase
User Profile Service Application_SocialDB	87a253d6-696a-4125-81a1-d3c9f61f0958	Microsoft.Office.Server.Administration.SocialDatabase
User Profile Service Application_SyncDB	2317b6bd-f959-4eb9-88ac-58ba5ab33b7d	Microsoft.Office.Server.Administration.SynchronizationDatabase
WordAutomationServices	dc6b9e8f-4379-4462-8cde-ebacd7621313	Microsoft.Office.Word.Server.Service.QueueDatabase
WSS_Content_my.boston.local80	224cbb26-7d2e-4414-bd7e-fb825456e754	Content Database

FIGURE 5-22 Get-SPDatabase | Out-GridView.

Get-SPContentDatabase is more suitable to this task, focusing specifically on databases that possess SharePoint content. Using this command with Out-GridView narrows the items returned to simply content databases (shown in Figure 5-23).

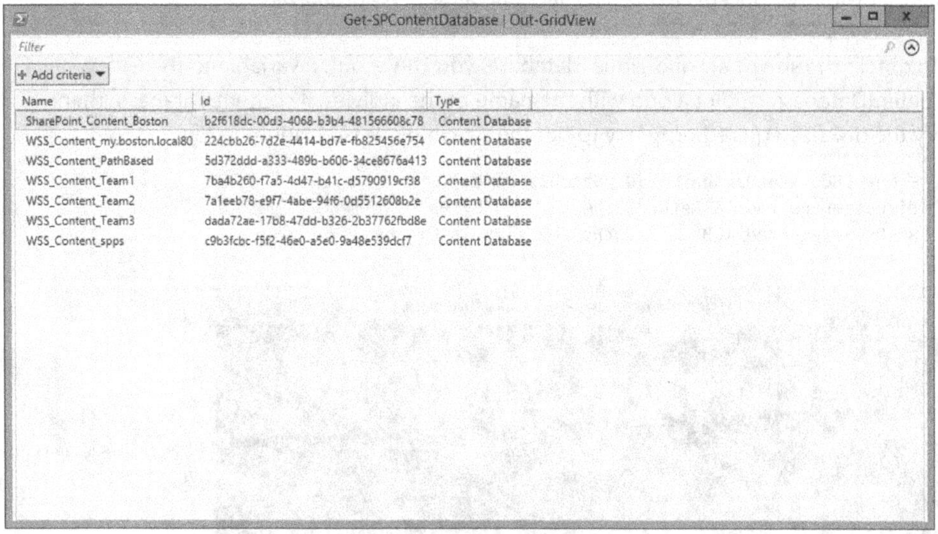

FIGURE 5-23 Content databases only (Get-SPContentDatabase).

Because a single web application may have multiple content databases, we can use the Get-SPContentDatabase cmdlet with the -webapplication switch to display all the content databases associated with a particular web application (see Figure 5-24).

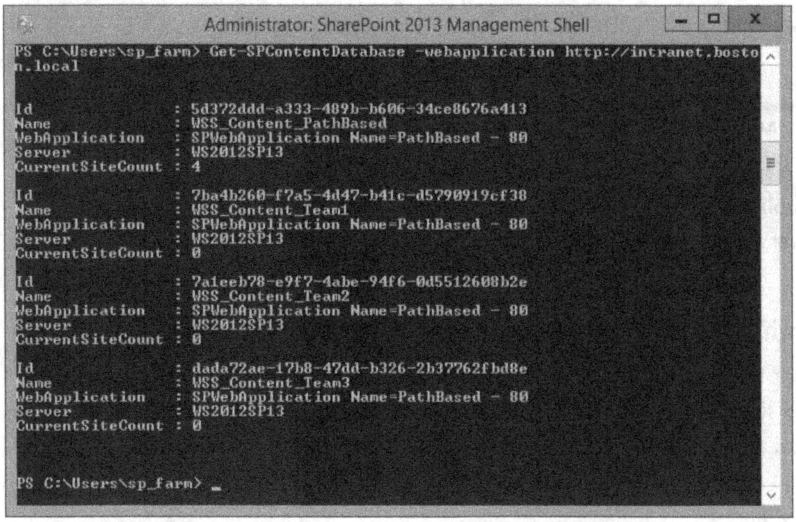

FIGURE 5-24 Get-SPContentDatabase with the -webapplication switch.

To obtain the size of any individual database, you can assign a variable to the Get-SPContentDatabase cmdlet along with the name of the individual content database; then query the disksizerequired property to get the size in bytes (see Figure 5-25):

```
$CDb = Get-SPContentDatabase -id <databasename>
$CDb.disksizerequired    à Returns the size in Bytes
$CDb.disksizerequired/1GB  à Returns the size in Gigabytes
```

FIGURE 5-25 Using the disksizerequired property.

> **NOTE A VERY SIMPLE EXAMPLE**
>
> Obviously, there are more sophisticated ways of retrieving the size of each content database, even grouping them by their associated web applications and URLs. This example was meant to be a very basic walkthrough.

Monitoring individual site collections via Windows PowerShell

Retrieving the size of a single site collection in Windows PowerShell is much less complicated than retrieving the size of an entire content database. The Get-SPSite Windows PowerShell cmdlet can be used along with the URL of the site collection to retrieve information about the site collection. Then you can determine the size of the site collection using the usage property (see Figure 5-26).

```
$site = get-spsite -identity http://intranet.boston.local
$site.usage
```

```
PS C:\Users\sp_farm> $site=Get-SPSite -identity http://intranet.boston.local
PS C:\Users\sp_farm> $site.usage

Storage          : 5385834
Bandwidth        : 0
Visits           : 0
Hits             : 0
DiscussionStorage : 0
```

FIGURE 5-26 Using the usage property (site collection sizing).

Monitoring site collection content

Site collection administrators can monitor the consumption of storage within their respective site collection by using the new Storage Metrics page. This page is located in the Site Collection Administration section of Site Settings, and shows a graphic representation of all content within the current site collection (see Figure 5-27).

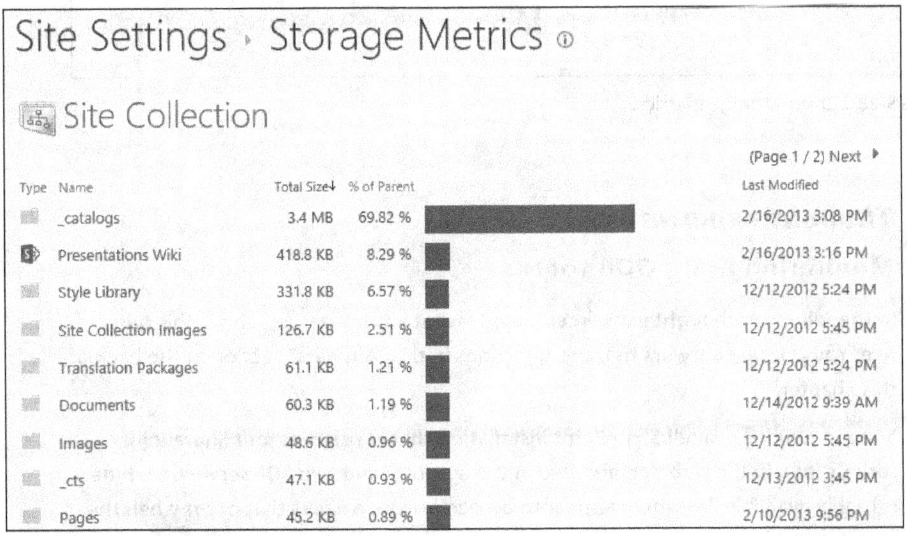

Site Settings ▸ Storage Metrics ⓘ

Site Collection

(Page 1 / 2) Next ▶

Type	Name	Total Size↓	% of Parent		Last Modified
	_catalogs	3.4 MB	69.82 %		2/16/2013 3:08 PM
	Presentations Wiki	418.8 KB	8.29 %		2/16/2013 3:16 PM
	Style Library	331.8 KB	6.57 %		12/12/2012 5:24 PM
	Site Collection Images	126.7 KB	2.51 %		12/12/2012 5:45 PM
	Translation Packages	61.1 KB	1.21 %		12/12/2012 5:24 PM
	Documents	60.3 KB	1.19 %		12/14/2012 9:39 AM
	Images	48.6 KB	0.96 %		12/12/2012 5:45 PM
	_cts	47.1 KB	0.93 %		12/13/2012 3:45 PM
	Pages	45.2 KB	0.89 %		2/10/2013 9:56 PM

FIGURE 5-27 Site collection storage metrics.

This report is far from being one-dimensional. From here, a site collection administration can drill down into the content of an individual site, retrieving its storage metrics (see Figure 5-28).

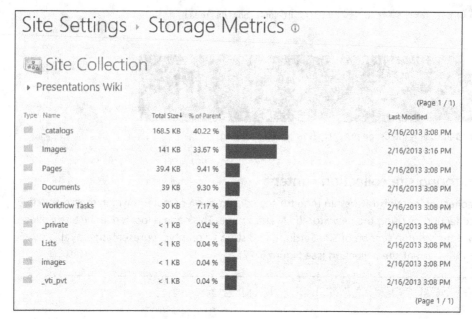

FIGURE 5-28 Subsite storage metrics.

> ### *Thought experiment*
> #### Monitoring using OOB tools
>
> In the following thought experiment, apply what you've learned about this objective. You can find answers to these questions in the "Answers" section at the back of this chapter.
>
> You are running a small SharePoint installation that consists of four SharePoint servers (two in the web tier, and two in the app tier) and two SQL servers. Each tier is highly available, but there appear to be performance issues that occur when the search crawls start.
>
> You want to be able to monitor and analyze logging information from each member of the farm in a single place. At this point, you have not as yet purchased any sort of monitoring solution, but do have an available SQL Server reporting services installation available. What options might you propose as a monitoring solution?

Objective summary

- SLAs define the service metrics used within a SharePoint farm; these agreements include definitions such as "downtime," "scheduled downtime," and "monthly uptime percentage," which describe the goals of monitoring within the farm.

- SharePoint farms provide performance counters that enable you to monitor the farm at three distinct levels: server, service application, and site/site collection.

- The Get-SPLogEvent cmdlet enables you to view trace log events (ULS logs) by level, area, category, event ID, process, or message text.

- System Center Management Pack for SharePoint 2013 works in conjunction with System Center 2012 Operations Manager to monitor both SharePoint Server 2013 and Project Server 2013 farms.

- Performance Monitor not only monitors Windows Server 2012 performance counters but also SharePoint counters for subsystems such as search, InfoPath Forms Services, and others.

- Page performance monitoring is dependent on the counters presented by the ASP.NET output cache, BLOB cache, object cache, and the Distributed Cache Service.

- The usage and health data collection service allows for the capture and centralization of SharePoint performance metrics within the logging database.

Objective review

Answer the following questions to test your knowledge of the information in this objective. You can find the answers to these questions and explanations of why each answer choice is correct or incorrect in the "Answers" section at the end of this chapter.

1. Which of the following can be configured within a data collector set? (Choose all that apply.)

   A. Performance counters

   B. Event trace data

   C. Service application databases

   D. System configuration information

2. How many web applications can be associated with a single content database in Share-Point?

   A. 0

   B. 1

   C. 2000

   D. 5000

3. Which of the following should you use to monitor the size of a single site within a site collection?

   A. $site=Get-SPSiteCollection

   B. $site.usage

   C. Get-SPDatabase -webapplication

   D. $site=get-spsite –identity http://<url>

   E. $site.usage

   F. Site settings, site collection administration, storage metrics

Objective 5.2: Tune and optimize a SharePoint environment

Creating an effective SharePoint environment isn't a one-size-fits-all task. Careful examination of how the farm is intended to be used often exposes perceived weaknesses in the original design. Add to that the changing requirements placed on the system by the user base, and you have a situation that is ripe with tuning potential.

The tuning and optimization portion of your project is the chance for you to tweak the underlying configuration of the farm, enabling you to both enhance performance metrics and avoid any limitations placed on the system by its original design.

This objective covers how to:

- Plan and configure SQL optimization.
- Execute database maintenance rules.
- Plan for capacity software boundaries.
- Estimate storage requirements.
- Plan and configure caching.
- Tune network performance.

Planning and configuring SQL optimization

SharePoint administrators often assume the role of itinerant (or occasional) SQL administrators because the performance of the data tier directly affects the performance of an entire SharePoint farm.

With this thought in mind, we approach the idea of planning and optimizing SQL for SharePoint use. Although your organization might already have a designated SQL database administrator, there is a good chance that this may be his or her first encounter with supporting the data tier of a SharePoint environment.

Knowing the behaviors, maintenance requirements, and performance characteristics of your content, configuration, and service application databases enables you to more clearly relate your desired strategy for long-term performance and growth goals to the SQL team.

Choosing a storage type

The type of storage configuration chosen for the SQL data tier will have a direct bearing on the performance of the completed SharePoint farm. In a server-based environment, storage is most often attached either directly to the server using Direct Attached Storage (DAS) or attached via a Storage Area Network (SAN).

EXAM TIP

Network Attached Storage (NAS) can be used for SharePoint storage, but this configuration is supported only for Remote Blob Storage (RBS).

In either type of storage implementation, the way in which these disks are organized and grouped together can have a direct bearing on performance.

Within a SharePoint farm, the design of the farm and which service applications or functions are to be implemented will determine what type of storage arrangement will be chosen.

There several factors to be considered:

- Is the service application or function more sensitive to read or write speeds? Is there a balance to be had between the two?
    - On an Internet site on which people consume a lot of data, but does not change often, you may want to focus on read speeds for your storage.
    - For a series of collaboration sites in which the data itself is changing on a regular basis, you might choose to balance read and write speeds.
    - For a service application such as search or for the TempDB of a SQL instance, you may want to focus on write speeds for your storage.
- Is the storage mechanism chosen more cost-prohibitive than need be?
    - A RAID 5 array (RAID configurations are discussed in the next section) containing five 100 gigabyte (GB) drives could store 400 GB of data (100 GB would be lost to maintain data parity). This array could withstand the failure of only a single drive; would have excellent read but poor write performance characteristics.
    - A RAID 10 array would require eight 100 GB drives to contain the same amount of storage (400 GB for the data; 400GB mirrored). This array would theoretically be able to withstand the failure of four drives (but only one per mirror set), and would offer both excellent read and write performance characteristics.

RAID configuration levels

Redundant array of independent disks (RAID) is a technology that uses either hardware or software to group and organize hard drives into one or more volumes. The RAID level chosen can meet one of two possible objectives:

- **Redundancy**   Allows for the grouping of drives to be able to withstand the failure of one or more individual drives within the group.

- **Performance**   Altering the arrangement and configuration of drives within the group results in performance gains.

> **REAL WORLD** **AVOIDING SOFTWARE RAID IN A PRODUCTION FARM**
>
> Although you can choose to use software RAID, it is not recommended to do so in a production, on-premise system because the operating system of the server to which the storage is attached is responsible for maintaining the RAID configuration. This maintenance consumes both memory and processor resources on the host system.

There are four RAID levels commonly used within the storage subsystems of a SharePoint farm (particularly within the data tier): 0, 1, 5, and 10.

- RAID Level 0 "striping" distributes the reads and writes across multiple physical drives (or spindles).

  - **Performance**   This arrangement offers the absolute best performance for both reads and writes in your storage subsystem.

  - **Redundancy**   This arrangement has absolutely no tolerance for any individual drive failures; if a single drive fails, the entire array is destroyed.

- RAID Level 1 "mirroring" utilizes an identical pair of disks or drive sets to ensure redundancy.

  - **Performance**   This arrangement offers the same read performance as RAID Level 0 (assuming the same number of physical disks/spindles), but write speed is reduced as the number of input/output (I/O) write operations per disk is doubled.

  - **Redundancy**   This arrangement can withstand the failure of a single drive or drive set.

- RAID Level 5 "block level striping with distributed parity" distributes reads and writes across all drives, but also writes parity in a distributed fashion across all drives.

  - **Performance**   This arrangement offers the same read performance as RAID Level 0, but it incurs a fairly steep write penalty as the parity operation increases write overhead.

  - **Redundancy**   This arrangement can withstand the failure of a single drive within the drive set.

Performance prioritization

Within a SQL data tier, there are four distinct groupings of databases and files you should consider from a performance perspective. The assignment of these groupings to different storage types can have a dramatic effect on performance.

Although you could theoretically put all your databases on a RAID 10 disk set, doing so would be wasteful from a cost standpoint and somewhat ineffective. Conversely, assigning write-heavy databases to a RAID 5 disk set would result in a heavy performance penalty.

The four groupings to consider are (in terms of priority from highest to lowest):

- TempDB files and transaction logs
    - If possible, assign these to RAID 10 storage
    - Allocate dedicated disks for TempDB
    - Number of TempDB files should be equal to the number of processor cores (hyper-threaded processors should be counted as one core)
    - All TempDB files should be the same size
    - An average write operation should require no more than 20 ms
- Database transaction log files
    - Should be on a separate volume from the data files
    - If possible, assign them to RAID 10 storage
    - Write-intensive
- Search databases
    - If possible, assign these to RAID 10 storage
    - Write-intensive
- Database data files
    - Can be assigned to RAID 5 storage with the understanding that writes may be slower (for better performance, consider using RAID 10 storage)
    - Read-intensive, especially useful for Internet-facing sites

Pregrowing content databases and logs

Pregrowth is the act of preemptively growing a content database (or its associated log file) to a designated initial size. This size can be an estimate of how big you might expect the database or log to grow because the database administrator (DBA) can also shrink the files somewhat if not all the space is eventually used.

Pregrowing a database has two benefits:

- A reduction in the amount of I/O because a database has to be expanded every time data is added
- A reduction in data disk fragmentation

Pregrowing the database is done from within SSMS; there is no way to configure initial size from within Central Administration.

To alter the size of a database or its associated log, do the following:

1. Open SSMS.

2. Locate your content database and right-click it; select Properties.

3. In the Select A Page Panel, select Files.

4. In the Database Files section (right panel), click within the Initial Size (MB) cell for your database or transaction log and change this value (see Figure 5-29).

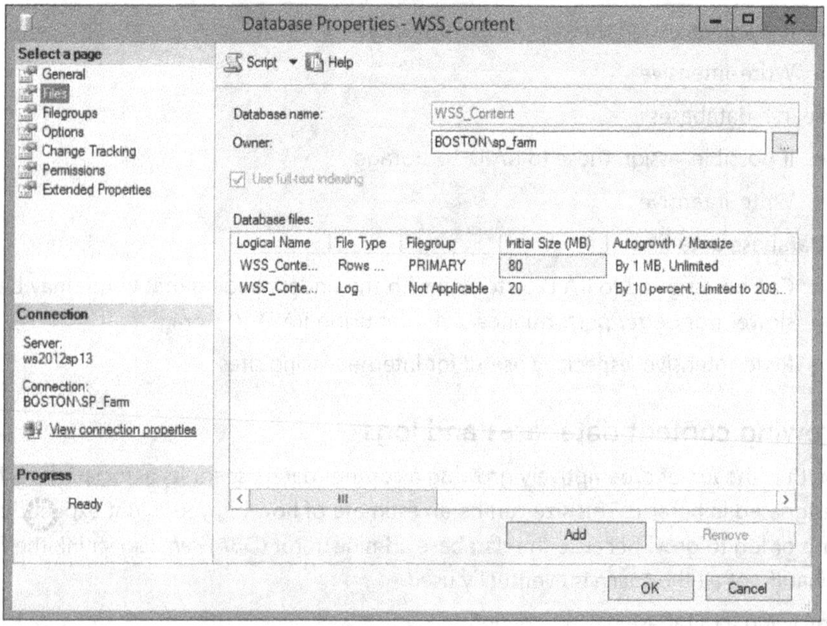

FIGURE 5-29 Database properties (initial size).

5. Click OK.

Configuring content database autogrowth

Autogrowth is the amount at which a database or its log grows after it reaches its current size limit. When a SharePoint content database is created from within Central Administration, its default autogrowth rate is set to 1 megabyte (MB).

As an example, if you had a database that was at its current size limit and you added a 10 MB file, the database file could be grown a total of 10 times before it could store the file. Imagine how much I/O this could generate multiplied over 1,000 files.

> **IMPORTANT** **THE MODEL DATABASE DOES NOT CONTROL AUTOGROWTH FOR SHAREPOINT DATABASES**
>
> The SQL model database (part of the system databases) cannot be used to control the autogrowth rate of newly created content databases. After its initial creation, consider modifying the rate at which a content database file grows after it is full.

To alter the size of a database or its associated log, follow these steps:

1. Open SSMS.

2. Locate your content database and right-click it; select Properties.

3. In the Select A Page panel, select Files.

4. In the Database files section (right panel), click the ellipsis box within the Autogrowth/Maxsize cell for your database or transaction log and change this value (see Figure 5-30).

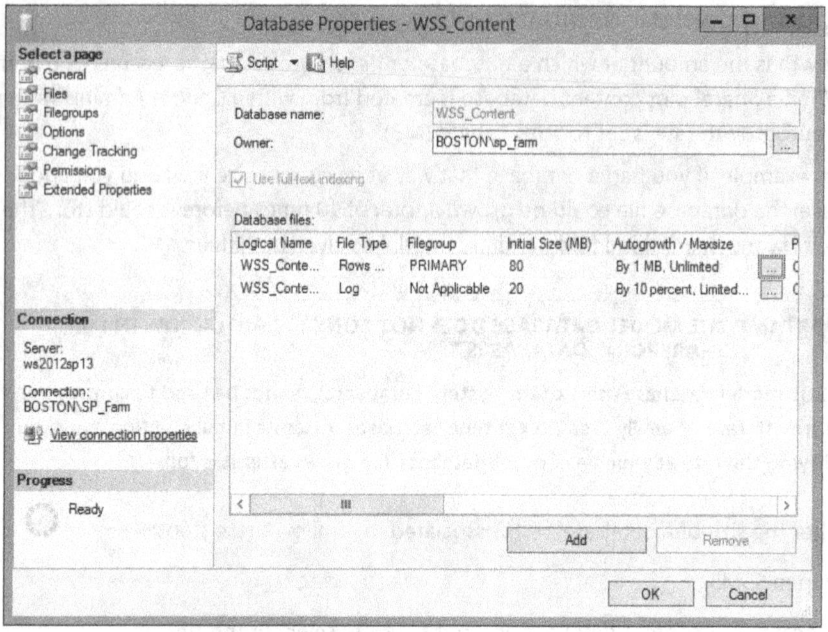

FIGURE 5-30 Autogrowth properties (starting value).

5. When the Change Autogrowth dialog box appears, you can select to configure file growth in percent or in megabytes (see Figure 5-31).

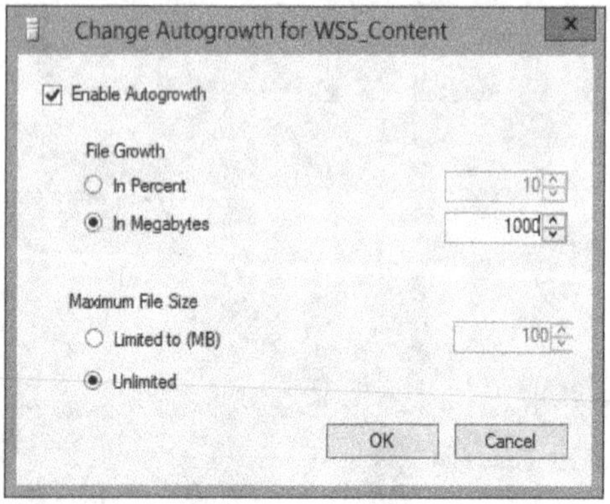

FIGURE 5-31 Changing autogrowth.

IMPORTANT **DO NOT LIMIT THE MAXIMUM FILE SIZE OF A SHAREPOINT DATABASE**

It is rarely a good idea to limit the maximum file size of a SharePoint content database or its associated transaction log. Doing so can have unintended results and appear as an error to your users if the size limit is reached.

6. The new value for autogrowth is shown in the Database Properties dialog box for your content database (see Figure 5-32).

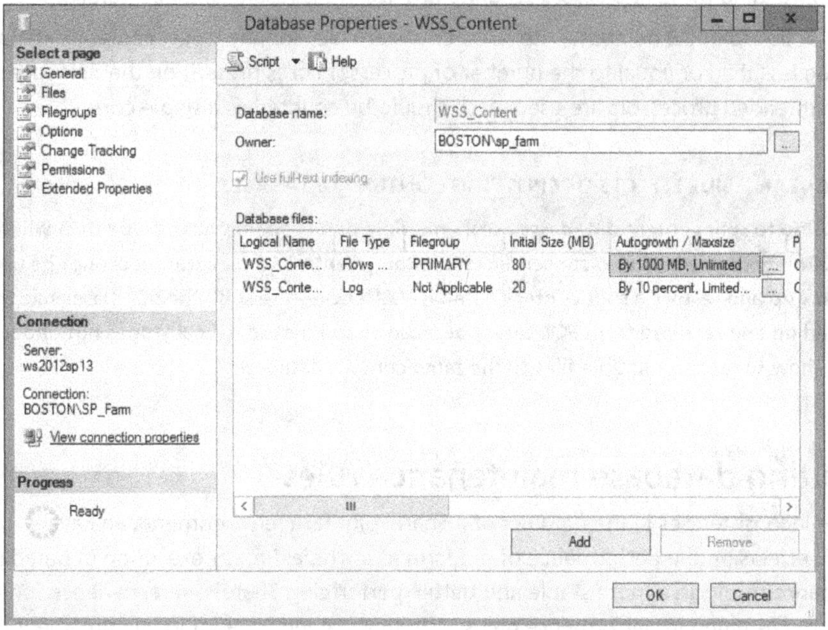

FIGURE 5-32 Autogrowth properties (final value).

7. Click OK.

One final note: Choosing to either adjust autogrowth rates or pregrow a database can trigger the SharePoint Health Analyzer rule called Database Has Large Amounts Of Unused Space. This message can be safely ignored because you intend to eventually fill the available space with data.

Specifically, this message will appear if the unused space is more than 20 percent of the disk space, and the unused space is greater than the autogrowth size plus 50 MB.

> **MORE INFO SHAREPOINT HEALTH ANALYZER RULES**
>
> A full list of all SharePoint Health Analyzer rules can be found in the TechNet article "SharePoint Health Analyzer Rules Reference (SharePoint 2013)" at *http://technet.microsoft.com/en-us/library/ff686816.aspx*.

Advanced content database performance

As content databases grow in size, their overall size can cause performance degradation. Depending on the content present in the database, separating the database into multiple smaller content databases may be impractical.

One of the potential solutions to this issue is to split a larger content database file into multiple smaller files that are still part of the same database. If you decide to go with this approach, spreading these files across separate physical disks results in far better I/O.

As with the TempDB database, the number of data files for any "split" content database should be less than or equal to the number of processor cores present on the database server. If hyper-threaded processors are used, each should be counted as a single core.

> **IMPORTANT** **SIDE EFFECTS OF SPLITTING CONTENT DATABASES**
>
> Choosing to split content databases across multiple database files has a side effect where SharePoint administration is concerned: SharePoint Central Administration cannot be used to back up and restore a split content database. After they are split, the databases must be backed up and restored from SQL server because SharePoint specifically does not understand how to restore multiple files to the same content database.

Executing database maintenance rules

Errors or inconsistencies in the data tier of a SharePoint farm environment can have dramatic effects on the performance of the farm as a whole. Proper execution of database maintenance results in a more stable and better-performing SharePoint experience for your users, often resulting in performance gains without the need for additional equipment or reconfiguration.

Health Analyzer rules

In previous versions of SharePoint, it was often necessary for either the SharePoint administrator or SQL DBA to perform index defragmentation and/or statistics maintenance. Health Analyzer rules were added (starting with SharePoint 2010) that addressed both defragmentation and statistics maintenance, removing these administrative tasks as regular maintenance items.

A Health Analyzer rules definition can be found in Central Administration in the Monitoring → Health → Review Rule Definitions menu. Within the Performance section, you see three rules that are all enabled and set to repair their related issues on a daily basis (see Table 5-5).

TABLE 5-5 Health rules for indexing and statistics

Health Rule	Schedule	Enabled	Repair Automatically
Databases used by SharePoint have fragmented indices	Daily	Yes	Yes
Databases used by SharePoint have outdated index statistics	Daily	Yes	Yes
Search: One or more crawl databases may have fragmented indices	Daily	Yes	Yes

Checking database consistency using DBCC CHECKDB

Running DBCC CHECKDB from SSMS executes a series of actions that check the logical and physical integrity of a selected database:

- Verifies the allocation structures in the database (equivalent to DBCC CHECKALLOC)
- Checks every table and view in the database to verify their logical and physical integrity (equivalent to DBCC CHECKTABLE)
- Verifies the consistency of the metadata in the database (equivalent to DBCC CHECK-CATALOG)

> **IMPORTANT** **AVOID RUNNING DBCC CHECKDB DURING PRODUCTION HOURS**
>
> DBCC CHECKDB can consume a lot of memory, I/O, and CPU resources; it is best to not run it during production hours. If you need to run this check against a production database that you suspect may be corrupt, you can back up the database, restore it to a different server, and then run the check there.

Executing a database consistency check

Performing a consistency check on a SharePoint database is done from SSMS, as follows:

1. Open SSMS.

2. Select the database that you intend to check for consistency; then right-click its name and select New Query.

3. Within the query window, type **DBCC CHECKDB** (see Figure 5-33) and select the Execute button.

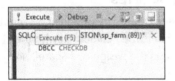

FIGURE 5-33 DBCC CHECKDB (Execute).

4. Optionally, you can include the WITH PHYSICAL_ONLY option to reduce CPU and memory usage on your system.

5. The database check runs and its output begins to appear in the Messages window (see Figure 5-34).

```
Messages
DBCC results for 'WSS_Content_spps'.
Service Broker Msg 9675, State 1: Message Types analyzed: 14.
Service Broker Msg 9676, State 1: Service Contracts analyzed: 6.
Service Broker Msg 9667, State 1: Services analyzed: 3.
Service Broker Msg 9668, State 1: Service Queues analyzed: 3.
Service Broker Msg 9669, State 1: Conversation Endpoints analyzed: 0.
Service Broker Msg 9674, State 1: Conversation Groups analyzed: 0.
Service Broker Msg 9670, State 1: Remote Service Bindings analyzed: 0.
Service Broker Msg 9605, State 1: Conversation Priorities analyzed: 0.
DBCC results for 'sys.sysrscols'.
There are 7111 rows in 66 pages for object "sys.sysrscols".
DBCC results for 'sys.sysrowsets'.
There are 409 rows in 4 pages for object "sys.sysrowsets".
```

FIGURE 5-34 DBCC results.

6. If everything is good in the database, you will see 0 allocation errors and 0 consistency errors (see Figure 5-35).

```
Messages
DBCC results for 'AllLinks'.
There are 1030 rows in 30 pages for object "AllLinks".
CHECKDB found 0 allocation errors and 0 consistency errors in database 'WSS_Content_spps'.
DBCC execution completed. If DBCC printed error messages, contact your system administrator.
```

FIGURE 5-35 DBCC results (no errors).

> **MORE INFO** **DATABASE MAINTENANCE FOR SHAREPOINT**
>
> For more detail about indexes and database consistency for SharePoint databases, have a look at the TechNet article titled "Database Maintenance for SharePoint 2010 Products" at *http://technet.microsoft.com/en-us/library/cc262731.aspx*.

Planning for capacity software boundaries

Boundaries are absolute limits within SharePoint that were created by design and cannot be exceeded. Although these boundaries are few in number when compared with the sheer quantity of options and settings available, they shape the design of a SharePoint infrastructure.

This boundary structure is present in many of the logical, hierarchical components of a SharePoint farm. Although not present in each level of the component hierarchy, boundaries exist in each of the following levels:

- Web applications
- Content databases
- Site collections
- Lists and libraries
- Search

- Business Connectivity Services (BCS)
- Workflows
- PerformancePoint Services
- Word Automation Services
- Office Web Application Service
- Project Server
- SharePoint apps
- Distributed Cache Service

> **MORE INFO** **MAJOR BOUNDARIES DISCUSSION**
>
> Only major boundaries will be explained in this section on a per-hierarchy basis. For more detail on the boundaries present in any given hierarchical level, see the TechNet article "Software Boundaries and Limits for SharePoint 2013" at *http://technet.microsoft.com/en-us/library/cc262787.aspx*.

Web application boundaries

Boundary: The number of zones defined for a farm is hard-coded to 5. Zones include Default, Intranet, Extranet, Internet, and Custom.

Note that the names of these zones are just that—names. With the exception of the Default zone (certain administrative functionality works only with this zone), all other zones are technically interchangeable. You can extend a web application to any of the zones and add the new name to DNS; the zone should work.

> **EXAM TIP**
>
> The URL of a host-named site collection is automatically considered to be in the Default zone.

Content database boundaries

Boundary: Time to first byte of any response from the Network Attached Storage (NAS) cannot exceed 20 milliseconds.

If you are using RBS on a NAS device, that device must be able to start responding with 20 ms to function with SharePoint.

Improving the network access to the NAS or replacing it altogether are the only remedies for this boundary.

Site collection limits

Boundary: The maximum number of device channels per publishing site collection is 10.

Device channels (new in SharePoint 2013) is a mechanism whereby an incoming request is mapped to a particular mobile device type. It enables a distinct master page to be applied to each device channel.

The remedy for this boundary is to support 10 or fewer distinct device channels, combining the support for a particular mobile device with that or another (finding a master page that works for both).

Major list and library limits

Boundary 1: Each list or library item can occupy only 8,000 bytes in total in the database. Two hundred fifty-six bytes are reserved for built-in columns, which leaves 7,744 bytes for end-user columns.

Column values promoted from within InfoPath (or defined within the list or library) consume space in SQL Server tables. The total size consumed has to do with the type of data being stored (String, Boolean, and so on), and if enough column values are used, a value can consume multiple rows in the table, which slows down performance.

Although it may take hundreds of columns to reach this boundary limit, it can happen nonetheless. The only choice of solutions is to change the type of data being captured (see Column Limits in the Boundaries and Limits document) or restrict the amount of columns in a list.

Boundary 2: The maximum file size in any list or library is limited to 2 GB.

The default maximum file size in SharePoint is 250 MB. Although this value is generally adequate for most uses, it occasionally has to be altered to accommodate larger files. The maximum upper limit for this file size is a hard limit of 2 GB.

Major search limits

Boundary 1: There is a hard limit of five crawl databases per search service application.

If you find that the crawl database is becoming I/O bound on your SQL server, and you cannot move it, one option is to add one or more additional crawl databases on the same SQL Server but on different I/O devices.

After you reach a total of five crawl databases, you must consider replacing one of the I/O devices, preferably one with the least I/O capability.

Boundary 2: There is a maximum size limit for documents pulled down by the crawler (3 MB for Excel documents; 64 MB for all others).

Each document in a content source is crawled and must be processed by search in SharePoint. Crawl will process only the first 3 MB of Excel documents and the first 64 MB of all other document types.

EXAM TIP

Although there are dozens of boundaries in SharePoint, there are a few that every administrator should know by heart. Maximum file size, zones in a farm, and crawl document size limits are all good metrics to be familiar with.

Estimating storage requirements

Because SharePoint is heavily dependent on SQL for its storage needs, the proper allocation of storage resources is a critical design element for the SharePoint farm. This design can be broken down into two major components, storage and I/O operations per second (IOPS).

Storage variables

Storage is simply the amount of available space configured for a particular database. If the database happens to be a content database, the overall size of the database can vary dramatically based on two features: recycle bins and auditing.

Recycle bins are enabled by default at both the site (web) and site collection (site) levels. A document that is deleted from a site occupies space in the associated content database until it is deleted from both the first and second stage recycle bins. If you foresee the need to delete many documents in the interest of reclaiming space, the documents must be deleted from both recycle bins.

Auditing can place a lesser storage demand on a content database. If you expect to use auditing in a particular content database, try to restrict the levels at which it is enabled rather than enabling auditing on entire site collections.

EXAM TIP

Recycle bins are some of the most straightforward and most misunderstood components in SharePoint. Knowing and understanding the behaviors of how a document moves from one stage recycle bin to another is key to understanding how documents that are "hidden" might be consuming space.

I/O operations per second (IOPS)

IOPS is the measure of how many input and output operations per second are available from your I/O subsystem (storage). The storage configuration influences both the read and write speeds available for use.

Stress testing a storage subsystem enables you to know the limits of your storage and also gives you an opportunity to tune it to your requirements. There are three main tools used for this purpose (see Table 5-6), each of which is free of charge:

TABLE 5-6 I/O subsystem testing tools

Tool	Provided By	Purpose	Download Location
SQLIO	Microsoft	Performance capacity (single I/O type at a time)	http://www.microsoft.com/en-us/download/details.aspx?id=20163
IOMeter	Open Source	Performance capacity (combination of I/O types at one time)	http://sourceforge.net/projects/iometer/
SQLIOSim	Microsoft	Simulates SQL I/O patterns	http://support.microsoft.com/kb/231619

> **MORE INFO** IOPS TESTING REFERENCE DOCUMENTATION
>
> For more details concerning IOPS testing using these tools, visit the MSDN page "SQL Server Best Practices Article" at *http://msdn.microsoft.com/en-us/library/cc966412.aspx*.

Estimating configuration storage and IOPS requirements

The SharePoint configuration database and Central Administration content database have meager storage requirements. Both databases use a negligible amount of space; you can safely plan for roughly 2 GB of configuration database storage and 1 GB of Central Administration content database storage. The configuration database will continue to grow over time, albeit in a very limited fashion (approximately 40 MB per 50,000 site collection.)

Estimating service application storage and IOPS requirements

Service applications vary wildly in the amount of storage and IOPS that they require. The largest consumer of service application resources is search, consuming the lion's share of available storage and IOPS resources. At the other end of the scale are the State, Word Automation, and PerformancePoint Service applications, each of which requires minimal IOPS and approximately 1 GB of allocated storage.

Table 5-7 shows a listing of each service application database and the given requirements.

> **MORE INFO** CAPACITY PLANNING
>
> This information is derived from the TechNet article "Storage and SQL Server Capacity Planning and Configuration" at *http://technet.microsoft.com/en-us/library/cc298801.aspx*.

Your environment may host multiples of the databases that display an asterisk (*).

TABLE 5-7 Service application storage and IOPS requirements

Service Application	Databases	Database Size (Approx.)	IOPS
Search	Search Admin	10 GB	Negligible
Search	Crawl (*)	.046 * total size of content databases	3,500 to 7,000 IOPS
Search	Property (*)	.015 * total size of content databases	2,000 IOPS
User Profile	Profile	1 MB per user profile	Not specified
User Profile	Synchronization	630 KB per user profile	Not specified
User Profile	Social Tagging	0.009 MB per tag, comment, or rating	Not specified
Managed Metadata	Managed Metadata	Not specified	Not specified
Web Analytics	Staging	Not specified	Not specified
Web Analytics	Reporting	Not specified	Not specified
Secure Store	Secure Store	5 MB per 1,000 credentials	Minimal
State	State	1 GB	Minimal
Word Automation	Word Automation	1 GB	Minimal
PerformancePoint	PerformancePoint	1 GB	Minimal

Estimating content database storage and IOPS requirements

In any SharePoint farm, the largest allotment of storage space is for the content. Every list, library, photo, media item, and more are all stored in one or more content databases. Effectively sizing these databases can be difficult, but building rough estimates for provisioning storage and then adjusting these estimates as demand increases is not difficult.

There is a formula that can be used to predict the amount of space required for any given database. Following is a description of the variables and their respective descriptions:

- **D** The expected number of documents in a content database
- **S** The average size of the documents to be stored
- **L** The number of list items (roughly three times the number of documents)
- **V** The number of retained versions for a document; the default value is 1 for the document
- **M** The estimated amount of metadata (a constant of 10 KB that can be adjusted if your environment is more metadata-intensive)

An estimate for the size of any given content database is the given by this formula:

```
Database Size = ((D * V) *S) + (M * (V * D)))
```

Using this formula to analyze the potential size of a content database with the following:

- 50,000 documents (D) expected
- 1,000 KB per document (S) average
- 10,000 list items (L) expected
- Five previous versions of a document (V) expected

This renders a maximum content database requirement of roughly the following:

((50000 * 5) * 1,000) + (10 * (5 * 50,000)) = 250 GB in size

This value should definitely be considered the "maximum" value because SharePoint 2013 stores the delta (changes) between versions of a document.

> **MORE INFO** **STORAGE PLANNING FOR SHAREPOINT 2013**
>
> For more detail about storage planning for SharePoint 2013, visit the TechNet article "Storage and SQL Server Capacity Planning and Configuration" at *http://technet.microsoft.com/en-us/library/cc298801.aspx*.

Planning and configuring caching

Caching within SharePoint 2013 is an effective mechanism for increasing the performance of page and content delivery to the requesting user. As stated earlier in this chapter, SharePoint uses a combination of three distinct technologies to deliver this enhanced performance: ASP.NET output cache, BLOB cache, and page output cache.

> **IMPORTANT** **ALTERING WEB.CONFIG DURING PRODUCTION HOURS**
>
> Some of the following configurations involve altering the web.config of a web application. When this file is saved after having been changed, it automatically recycles its associated web application, potentially disrupting service to your users. It is advisable to make these configuration changes after hours.

Planning and configuring the ASP.NET output cache

The output cache present in SharePoint 2013 stores several different versions of a rendered page; these versions are permissions-dependent, based on the permissions level of the person who is attempting to view the page. Settings for this cache can be configured at the site collection and site levels, and also configured for page layouts. Additionally, the web.config for a web application can be altered with the output cache profile settings. These settings will then override any settings made at the site collection level (or below).

Cache profiles

Prior to enabling the page output cache, you can review the site collection cache profiles that will be used in the output cache in the site settings of your site collection:

1. In Site Settings, select the Site Collection Administration section; under Site Collection, select Cache Profiles.

2. Four profiles exist by default (see Figure 5-36):

FIGURE 5-36 Output cache profiles.

A. **Disabled**   Caching is not enabled

B. **Public Internet (Purely Anonymous)**   Optimized for sites that serve the same content to all users with no authentication check

C. **Extranet (Published Site)**   Optimized for a public extranet in which no authoring takes place and no web parts are changed by the users

D. **Intranet (Collaboration Site)**   Optimized for collaboration sites (authoring, customization, and other write-intensive operations take place)

3. You can also create a new cache profile if none of these suits your needs.

Enabling the page output cache (web application level)

Enabling the page output cache at the web application level overrides all other page output cache settings at the site collection, site, or page layout levels.

To enable the page output cache:

1. Open Internet Information Services (IIS) Manager.

2. Select the web site that you want to configure (see Figure 5-37).

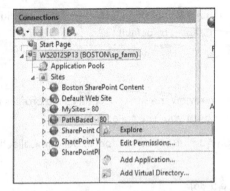

FIGURE 5-37 Explore virtual directory in IIS Manager.

3. Select the web.config and then open with the editor of your choice (see Figure 5-38).

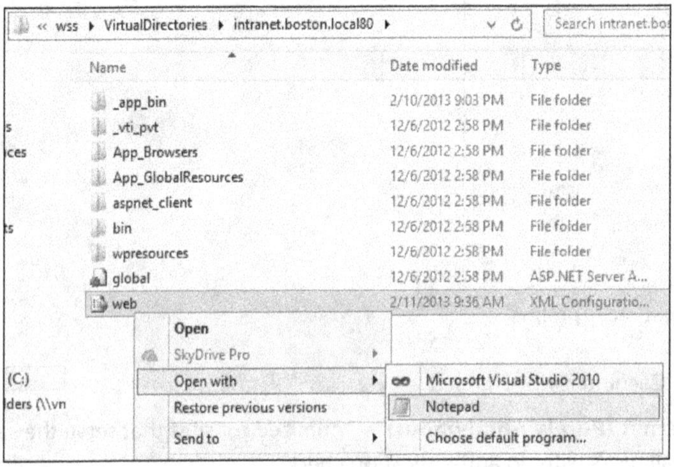

FIGURE 5-38 Editing web.config.

4. Search for the OutputCache Profiles XML entry:

```
<OutputCacheProfiles useCacheProfileOverrides="false" varyByHeader="" varyByParam="*"
varyByCustom="" varyByRights="true" cacheForEditRights="false" />
```

5. Change the useCacheProfileOverrides attribute from False to **True**.

6. Save and close the web.config file.

Enabling the page output cache (site collection level)

Enabling the page output cache within a publishing site collection is done within the Site Collection Administration menu.

1. In Site Settings, select the Site Collection Administration section and then select Site Collection Output Cache.

2. In the Output Cache section, choose to enable or disable the output cache.

3. In the Default Page Output Cache Profile section, you get the opportunity to choose from the cache profiles mentioned earlier:

    A. Anonymous Cache Profile: Choose from Disabled, Public Internet, Extranet, or Intranet

    B. Authenticated Cache Profile: Choose from Disabled, Extranet, or Intranet

4. Page Output Cache Policy enables you to delegate control of the cache policy:

    A. Whether publishing subsite owners can choose a different page output cache profile

    B. Whether page layouts can use a different page output cache profile

5. Debug Cache Information (optional) enables you to enable debug cache information on pages for troubleshooting cache contents.

6. Click OK to close the settings page.

Enabling the page output cache (subsite level)

If previously delegated by the site collection administrator, page output cache settings can be configured at the subsite level from the Site Administration menu.

1. In Site Settings, select the Site Administration section and then select Site Output Cache.

2. On the Publishing Site Output Cache page, you can choose the Page Output Cache Profiles:

    A. Anonymous Cache Profile can either inherit the parent site's profile or select a profile (Disabled, Public Internet, Extranet, or Intranet)

B.   Authenticated Cache Profile can either inherit the parent site's profile or select a profile (Disabled, Extranet, or Intranet)

   3.   Optionally, you can select the check box to apply these settings to all subsites.

   4.   Click OK to close the settings page.

Enabling the page output cache by page layout

If previously delegated by the site collection administrator, page output cache settings can be configured on a per-page layout basis from the Master Pages And Page Layouts menu.

   1.   In Site Settings, in the Web Designer Galleries section, select the Master Pages And Page Layouts section.

   2.   On the Master Page Gallery page, choose a page layout and then select its drop-down menu.

   3.   After selecting the Edit Properties value, you are presented with the properties page. Scroll down to the bottom and you can select either or both authenticated or anonymous cache profiles.

   4.   On the ribbon, in the Commit section, select the Save icon to close the settings.

Planning and configuring the BLOB cache

The BLOB (or Binary Large Object) cache is used to prestage branding (*.gif, *.jpg, *.css, *.js), image, sound, video, and other files that are stored in SQL as BLOBs. This is a disk-based caching technique that stores these items on the web tier servers within your farm.

The purpose of storing these items on the web tier is to directly benefit from not having to retrieve these larger files from the content databases stored on the SQL data tier.

This caching mechanism is enabled or disabled on each web tier server on a per-web application basis:

```
<BlobCache location="C:\BlobCache\14" path="\.(gif|jpg|jpeg|jpe|jfif|bmp|dib|tif|tiff|
themedbmp|themedcss|themedgif|themedjpg|themedpng|ico|png|wdp|hdp|css|js|asf|avi|
flv|m4v|mov|mp3|mp4|mpeg|mpg|rm|rmvb|wma|wmv|ogg|ogv|oga|webm|xap)$" maxSize="10"
enabled="false" />
```

There are a few settings in this piece of XML that are of interest:

- The BLOB cache location is not a typo; it is stored in "C:\BlobCache\14" by default. Although both the location and file folder details can be changed, the change should be uniform on all web tier servers.

- Path does not indicate the path on the file system, but instead the types of files (BLOB) that can be stored on the file system.

- The maxSize entry indicates the size in gigabytes (GB) for the BLOB cache; any changes to this value should be made uniformly on all web tier servers.

- The maxSize value should never be less than 10 GB, but can (and should) be grown to roughly 20 percent bigger than the expected BLOB content.

- Changing the enabled value from false to true activates the BLOB cache.

Planning and configuring the object cache

The object cache in SharePoint 2013 is used to store objects in the memory of the web tier SharePoint farm servers, thus reducing the amount of traffic between web tier servers and the SQL data tier. These objects—which include lists and libraries, site settings, and page layouts—are used by the publishing feature when it renders web pages on the site.

> **NOTE PUBLISHING FEATURE MUST BE ACTIVE**
>
> The use of the object cache requires that the publishing feature be active on your site. After the publishing feature is enabled, so too is the object cache (using default settings).

The object cache relies on a series of settings, which can be found at Site Settings, Site Collection Administration, Site Collection Object Cache (see Figure 5-39).

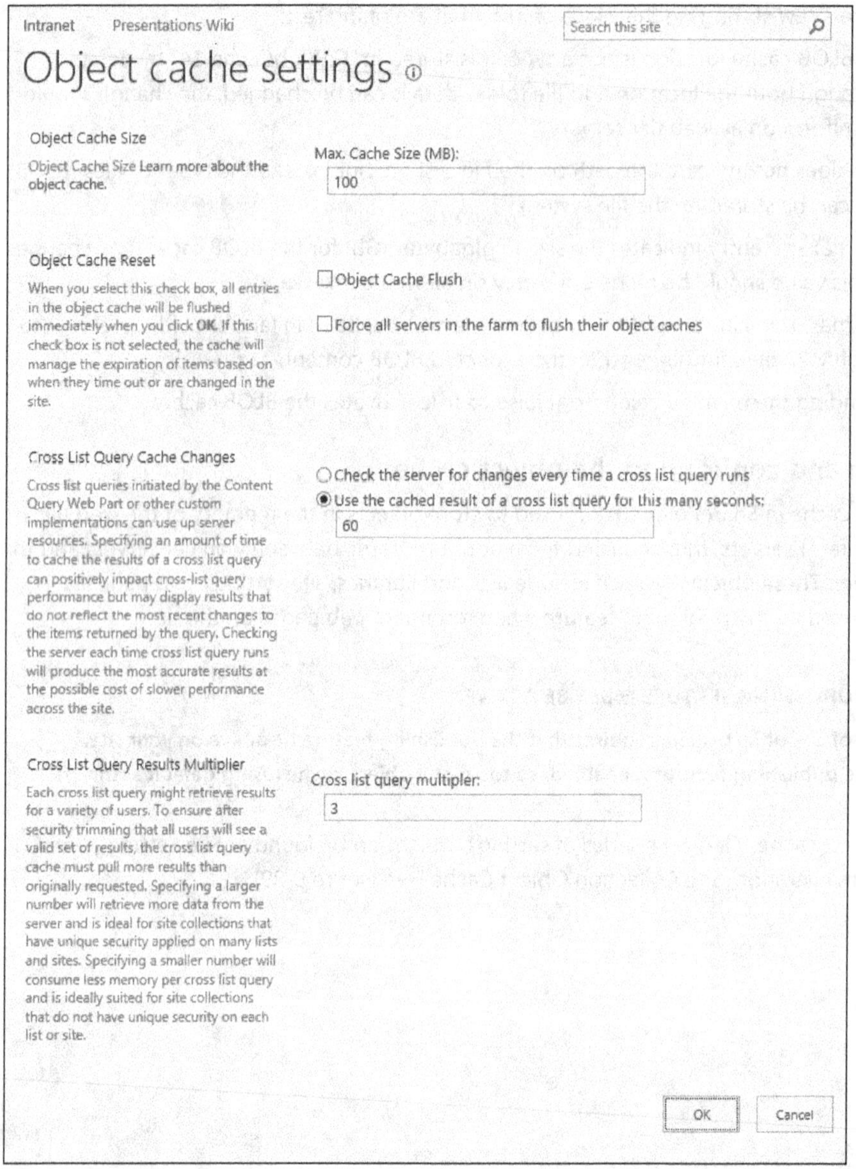

Search this site

Object cache settings

Object Cache Size

Object Cache Size Learn more about the object cache.

Max. Cache Size (MB):

100

Object Cache Reset

When you select this check box, all entries in the object cache will be flushed immediately when you click OK. If this check box is not selected, the cache will manage the expiration of items based on when they time out or are changed in the site.

☐ Object Cache Flush

☐ Force all servers in the farm to flush their object caches

Cross List Query Cache Changes

Cross list queries initiated by the Content Query Web Part or other custom implementations can use up server resources. Specifying an amount of time to cache the results of a cross list query can positively impact cross-list query performance but may display results that do not reflect the most recent changes to the items returned by the query. Checking the server each time cross list query runs will produce the most accurate results at the possible cost of slower performance across the site.

○ Check the server for changes every time a cross list query runs

◉ Use the cached result of a cross list query for this many seconds:

60

Cross List Query Results Multiplier

Each cross list query might retrieve results for a variety of users. To ensure after security trimming that all users will see a valid set of results, the cross list query cache must pull more results than originally requested. Specifying a larger number will retrieve more data from the server and is ideal for site collections that have unique security applied on many lists and sites. Specifying a smaller number will consume less memory per cross list query and is ideally suited for site collections that do not have unique security on each list or site.

Cross list query multipler:

3

OK   Cancel

FIGURE 5-39 Object cache settings.

1. In Site Settings, select the Site Collection Administration section and then select Site Collection Object Cache.

2. In the Object Cache Size section, specify the maximum cache size in MB (default is 100 MB). Remember that this cache space comes directly out of RAM of each server in your web tier.

3. In the Object Cache Reset section, you will normally leave these values unchecked. From here, you can not only flush the object cache of the current server (by selecting Object Cache Flush) but also that of the farm (by selecting Force All Servers In The Farm To Flush Their Object Cache).

4. In the Cross List Query Cache Changes section, you can configure the behavior of cross list queries, such as Content Query Web Parts. You have the choice of either precaching the results of such a query for a specified period of time (the default is 60 seconds) or forcing the server to check for changes every time a query is performed (which is more accurate from a results standpoint, but results in slower performance).

5. In the Cross List Query Results Multiplier section, you can choose a multiplier value ranging from 1 to 10 (where 3 is the default). This number should be increased if your site has unique security applied to many lists or libraries, but it can also be reduced if your site does not have as many unique permissions. A smaller multiplier uses less memory per query.

6. After you have made your selections, click OK.

> **NOTE CONTROLLING THE OBJECT CACHE WITH THE WEB.CONFIG FILE**
>
> The object cache size can also be controlled at the web application level by altering the web.config <ObjectCache maxSize="100" /> line.

Tuning network performance

Although there are significant networking improvements present in both the Windows Server 2008 and 2012 platforms, some minor alterations to your SharePoint 2013 network environment can result in significant performance gains.

Domain controllers and authentication

A SharePoint Server 2013 farm can potentially place a significant authentication load on domain controllers (DCs) within your network. As general guidance, Microsoft recommends that you deploy a new DC per every three web tier servers present in your SharePoint farm. It should be noted that the DC for this task should not be a read-only DC.

Hardware versus software load balancers

Microsoft includes the Microsoft Network Load Balancing (NLB) feature in Windows Server 2012. When active, this functionality presents a virtual IP address to the network for connections to the SharePoint web apps.

Each host in a Microsoft NLB arrangement must run the feature, which involves some overhead from an operating system perspective. If these servers are on the brink of being overcommitted already, this additional load could cause client connections to be slow or to cease altogether.

Consider installing and configuring a dedicated hardware-based NLB solution if the performance of your software NLB causes client connectivity issues.

Separating client and intrafarm network traffic

A SharePoint Server 2013 environment can start on only a single server and grow into an environment consisting of several servers in a three-tier environment. Depending on the arrangement chosen, a SharePoint environment could have client and intraserver traffic traversing the same interfaces, potentially disrupting or slowing services for SharePoint users.

Consider installing two network adapters on each web tier server:

- One connected to a client subnet/virtual LAN (VLAN): serves client requests
- The other connected to an intraserver subnet/VLAN: enables interserver connectivity

---

EXAM TIP

Network administration is not a core requirement for being a SharePoint administrator. Knowing how concepts such as subnets and VLANs can work to separate client and server communications, however, may be key to understanding a very simple way to improve SharePoint connectivity and performance.

Wide area network connectivity

If your clients are connecting across a wide area network (WAN), their connectivity to SharePoint may suffer from a higher-than-normal network latency. Using a WAN accelerator solution that is capable of shaping SharePoint network traffic improves the situation.

Thought experiment

Scaling resources for SharePoint growth

In the following thought experiment, apply what you've learned about this objective. You can find answers to these questions in the "Answers" section at the back of this chapter.

Your SharePoint farm has been experiencing a significant uptick in user adoption. Part of this growth has been due to a new Internet-facing web application; the other part is internal collaborative growth. Lately, users have begun to state that the environment is a bit slower than it was in the past. You initially stored all your content on RAID 5 storage, but are now considering splitting the storage back end so that portions support the Internet site while other portions support a heavily collaborative series of content databases. You have also begun refitting the web tier of your farm with more RAM and disk storage.

What sorts of changes might you consider to improve performance?

Objective summary

- Network Attached Storage (NAS) is supported only for use with Remote BLOB Storage (RBS).

- As a rule, performance priority should be given first to TempDB files and transaction logs, then database transaction log files, then search databases, and finally database data files.

- The model database can be used to configure the initial size of a newly created SharePoint content database, but not its autogrowth rate.

- Splitting a SharePoint content database into multiple database files is a supported (but advanced) way to enhance its performance level.

- A split-content database cannot be backed up or restored from within SharePoint Central Administration, but must instead be backed up from SSMS.

- Altering values for the ASP.NET output cache, BLOB cache, and object cache require additional memory and disk resources on the web tier servers and can result in a pronounced performance gain. Additional memory and disk resources are required on the web tier servers, however.

- The page output cache can be enabled and configured at the web application, site collection, site, or page layout levels.

- Separating client and intrafarm communications can result in a significant networking performance gain within your SharePoint farm.

Objective review

Answer the following questions to test your knowledge of the information in this objective. You can find the answers to these questions and explanations of why each answer choice is correct or incorrect in the "Answers" section at the end of this chapter.

1. You are building an Internet-facing publishing portal. Content will be infrequently added to this portal, but the majority of activity will be read-heavy. Which storage level offers the most cost-efficiencies while also providing the best performance characteristics and a layer of redundancy?

   A. RAID 0

   B. RAID 1

   C. RAID 5

   D. RAID 10

2. You have a limited amount of RAID 10 storage available due to expense. Because you are configuring the SQL data tier of the SharePoint farm, you must decide how best to utilize this fast storage. Which of the following database groupings makes the best use of RAID 10 storage?

   A. Database transaction log files

   B. Search databases

   C. TempDB files and transaction logs

   D. Database data files

3. Which of the following current tools cannot be used to estimate the capacity of a SQL 2008/2012 storage subsystem?

   A. SQLIO

   B. SQLIOStress

   C. SQLIOSim

   D. IOMeter

4. Which of the following ASP.NET cache profiles should be used for a collaborative site?

   A. Extranet

   B. Public Internet

   C. Disabled

   D. Intranet

Objective 5.3: Troubleshoot a SharePoint environment

Up to this point, your SharePoint project has been all about planning, configuring, and testing. A pristine new environment awaits and will soon provide SharePoint services to your user base.

Over the next few weeks, users will be added to your new farm. Any shortfalls in the original design can then be identified and documented as part of design tuning. If there are any errors or omissions in the design, they can be examined and remedied as part of the rollout process.

This objective covers how to:

- Establish baseline performance.
- Perform client-side tracing.
- Perform server-side tracing.
- Analyze usage data.
- Enable a Developer Dashboard.
- Analyze diagnostic logs.

Establishing baseline performance

Immediately after the implementation has been finalized, you have an opportunity to define the baseline performance of your SharePoint environment.

At this point, we are not talking about performance testing (what the system is capable of when it is working at maximum capacity) but rather what the nominal or expected operation of the system looks like from a logging standpoint.

The optimal goal is to have a statistical sampling of what the environment looks like as it adjusts to varying levels of user demand on a regular interval. For instance, odds are that a system is much busier at 09:00 on Monday than it is at 21:00 on Saturday (assuming a standard work week).

Baselining your SharePoint environment

In a SharePoint farm, there are three distinct tiers that should have a defined performance baseline:

- **Web tier**   Items to be monitored can include these:
    - Operating system metrics (processor, memory, network interface, and storage)
    - IIS metrics (process and ASP.NET metrics)
- **Application tier**   Items to be monitored can include these:
    - Operating system metrics (processor, memory, network interface, and storage)

- IIS metrics (process and ASP.NET metrics)
- Specific service application metrics (for functionality such as Excel Calculation Services, User Profile Services, and so on)
- **Data tier**   Items to be monitored can include these:
  - Operating system metrics (processor, memory, network interface, and storage)
  - SQL-specific counters (general statistics, user connections, and so on)

> **MORE INFO   SHAREPOINT 2013 PERFORMANCE COUNTERS**
>
> A listing of SharePoint 2013 performance counters can be found in the TechNet article "Monitoring and Maintaining SharePoint Server 2013" at *http://technet.microsoft.com/en-us/library/ff758658.aspx.*

Performance Monitor baseline captures

Although it is entirely possible to create and execute performance captures on an ad hoc basis, doing so does not give the retrieved metrics any consistency.

What used to be a fairly complex process of building the PerfMon capture and then scheduling it using an "AT" job is much easier in the newer versions of Windows Server.

The process of building a baseline performance monitor job consists of the following steps:

1.   Build a data collector set.

2.   Populate the data collector set with the desired performance counters to be retrieved and a desired sampling interval.

3.   Choose a desired storage location on the file system.

4.   (Optional) Save the data collector set as a template for use on your other systems.

5.   Create a series of schedules during which the PerfMon captures are to be run.

> **EXAM TIP**
>
> PerfMon is one of the most misunderstood and underutilized tools in Windows Server. Understanding not only how to capture point-in-time metrics but also how to capture a performance baseline over time is a must-have skill for an experienced SharePoint farm administrator.

Creating and scheduling PerfMon baseline captures

The following example builds a very basic data collector set, saves the set as a template for use on other systems, imports and utilizes the template on a new system, and finally schedules the performance counter captures.

To begin, let's first build the PerfMon data collector set, as follows:

1. Open Perfmon.exe.

2. Expand the Data Collector Sets section; from the New menu, select Data Collector Set (see Figure 5-40).

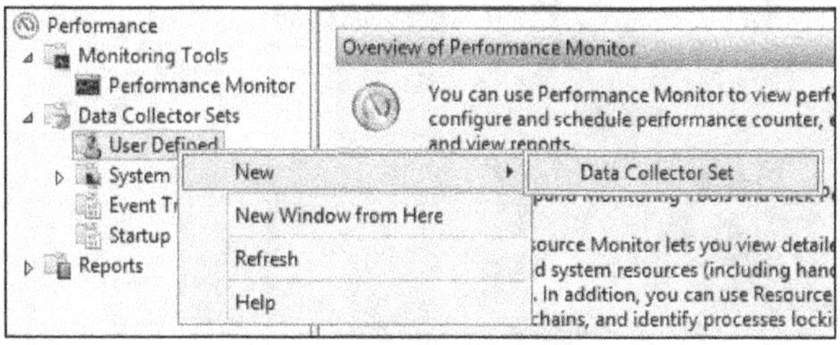

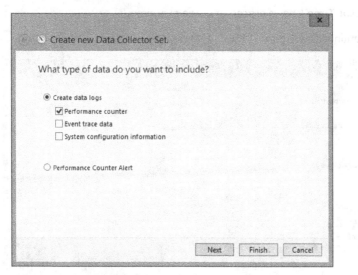

FIGURE 5-40 New data collector set.

3. On the Create New Data Collector Set page, select Create Data Logs and then select Performance Counter.

4. Click Next (see Figure 5-41).

FIGURE 5-41 Creating data logs (performance counter).

5. Select the Add button to begin the process of selecting a sample performance counter (see Figure 5-42).

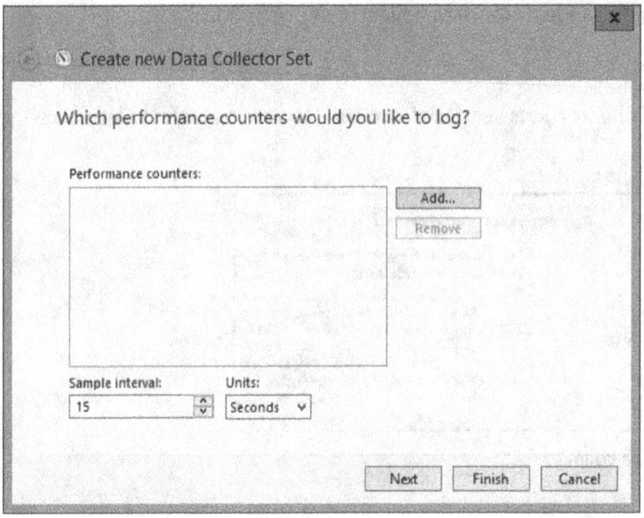

FIGURE 5-42 Adding performance counters.

6. Select only a single counter in this example:

    A. **% Processor Time** (shows processor usage over time)

7. Click OK to continue (see Figure 5-43).

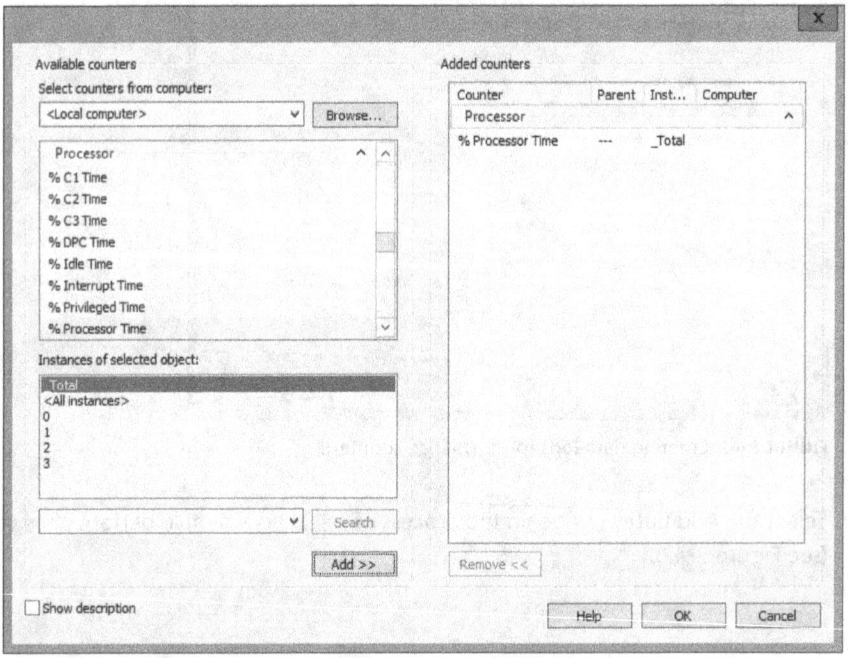

FIGURE 5-43 Example counter.

8. The selected counter is displayed next. You might consider changing the sample interval (the time between counter samples is set to 15 seconds by default). Click **Next** to continue (see Figure 5-44).

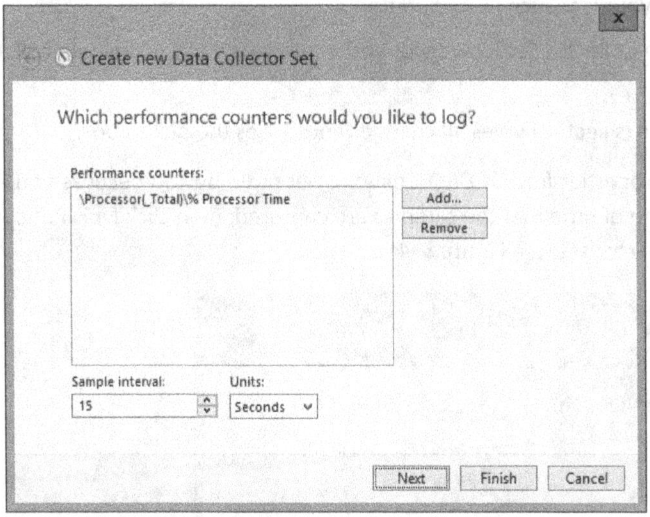

FIGURE 5-44 Example counter added.

9. You can specify a particular log location. By default, they are stored beneath the %systemdrive%\Perflog directory. Click Next (see Figure 5-45).

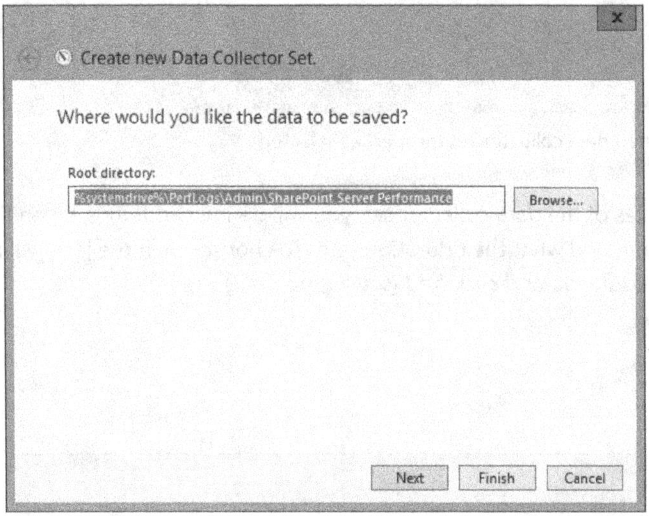

FIGURE 5-45 Choosing the save directory.

10. The final step of creating the new data collector set is to choose which account it runs under and selecting from a series of actions:

   A. Open Properties For This Data Collector Set enables you to specify additional selections for your log, such as its duration.

   B. Start This Data Collector Set Now saves and immediately starts the data collector set capture.

   C. Save And Close (selected) saves all changes and closes the dialog box.

11. Select the Open Properties for this Data Collector Set radio button because you want to limit the duration of time that the samples are captured; then click Finish to complete this data collector set (see Figure 5-46).

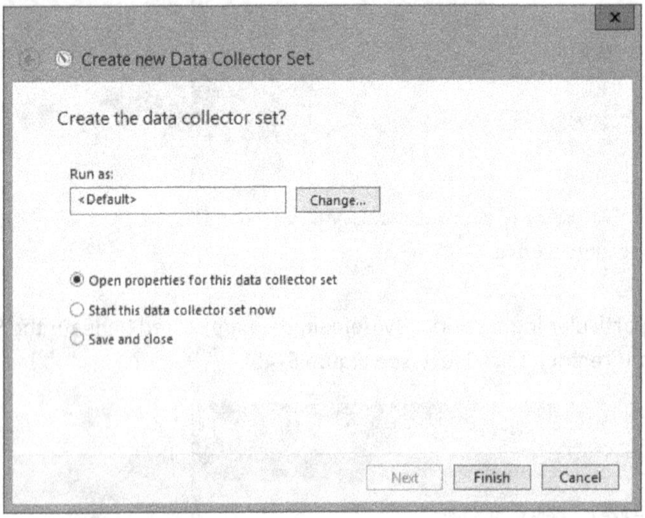

FIGURE 5-46 Completed data collector set (properties selected).

12. Within the properties of the data collector set, you will define two things: when the PerfMon jobs will run and what their durations are. To choose when the jobs will be run, select the Schedule tab and click Add (see Figure 5-47).

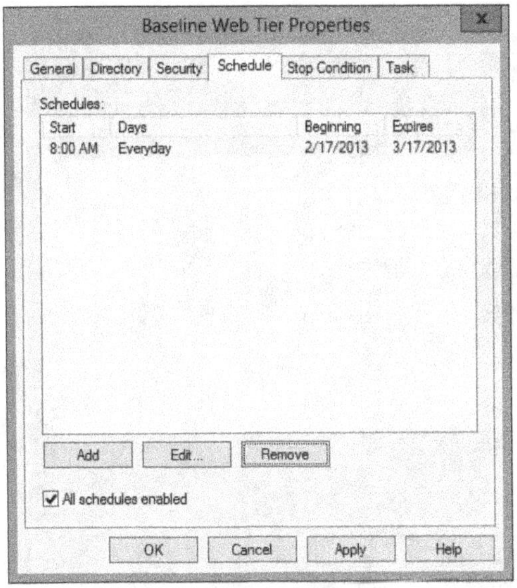

FIGURE 5-47 Adding to the schedule.

13. On the Folder Action screen, select start and stop dates for your baseline, along with the time the sample should be run and the days of the week on which it should be run. Click OK when the process is complete (see Figure 5-48).

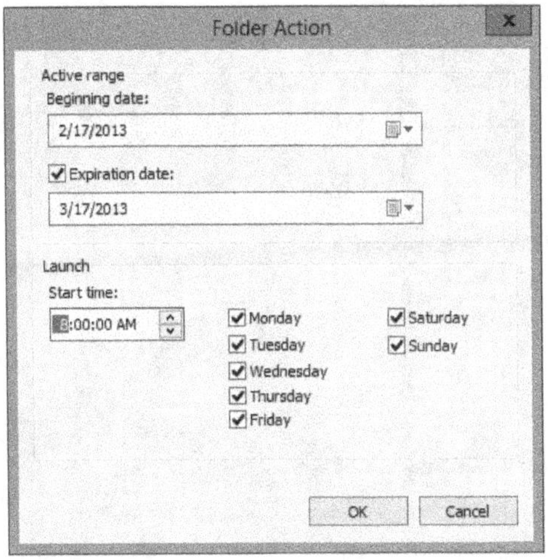

FIGURE 5-48 First baseline schedule entry.

14. Repeat this process, choosing all the times when you want to monitor throughout the day (see Figure 5-49).

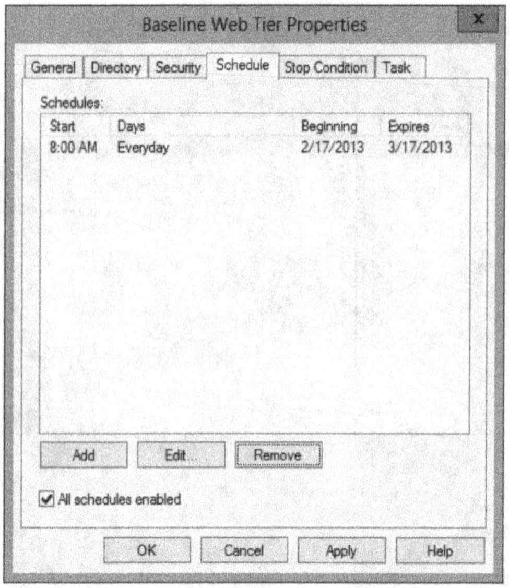

FIGURE 5-49 Baseline schedules.

15. Now that the schedules are built, all that remains is to set the duration of time that each captures information. On the Stop Condition tab, select the Overall Duration check box, and set the time length to 5 minutes. Click OK when complete (see Figure 5-50).

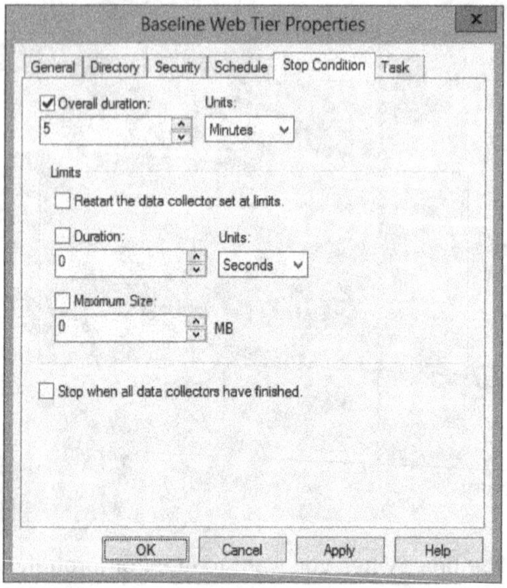

FIGURE 5-50 Stop condition.

Using a data collector set template

Now that the data collector set is defined, you can export it to a template for use with your other servers.

1. In Performance Monitor, select the collector set template and select Save Template (see Figure 5-51).

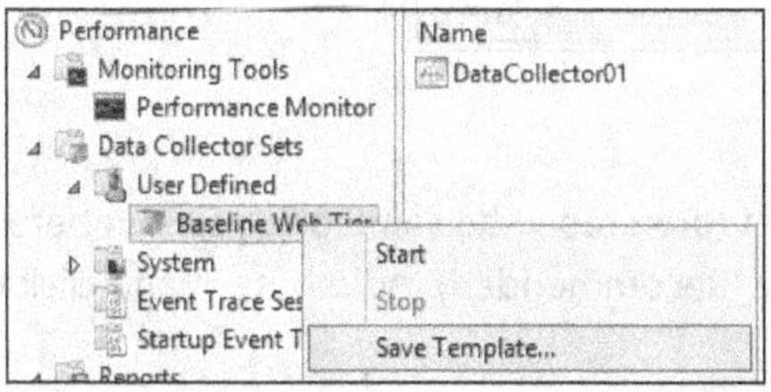

FIGURE 5-51 Saving the template.

2. By default, the templates are saved in C:\Windows\System32. If desired, choose a different location (perhaps on an available network share) and name the file before saving it (see Figure 5-52).

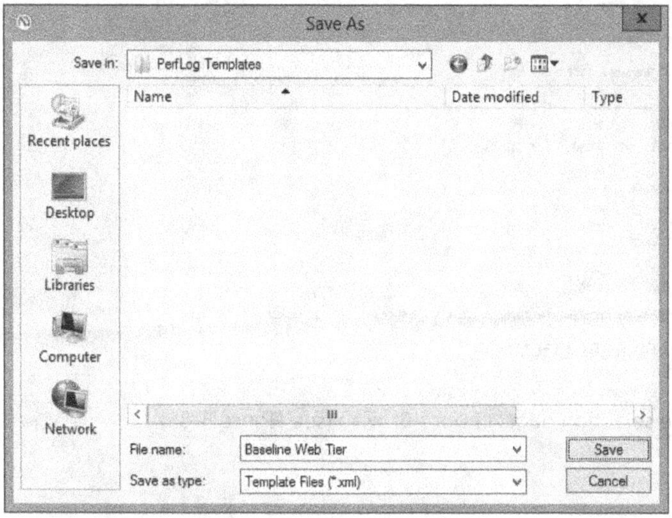

FIGURE 5-52 Choosing a template location.

3. Copy your template to the other server(s) you want to monitor. Open perfmon.exe on those servers and expand the Data Collector Sets icon.

4. Right-click User Defined. From the New menu, select Data Collector Set (see Figure 5-53).

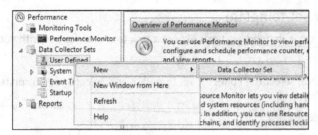

FIGURE 5-53 New data collector set.

5. Select a name for your data collector set (preferably the same one you had before); then select the Create From A Template (Recommended) radio button and click Next (see Figure 5-54).

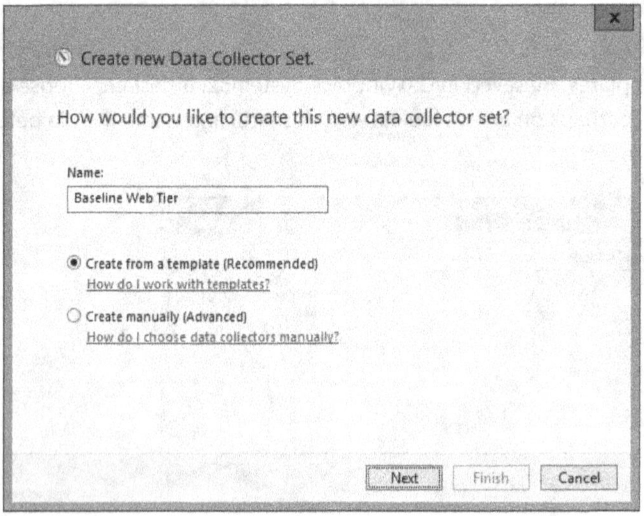

FIGURE 5-54 Creating from a template.

6. On the template selection page, choose Browse (see Figure 5-55).

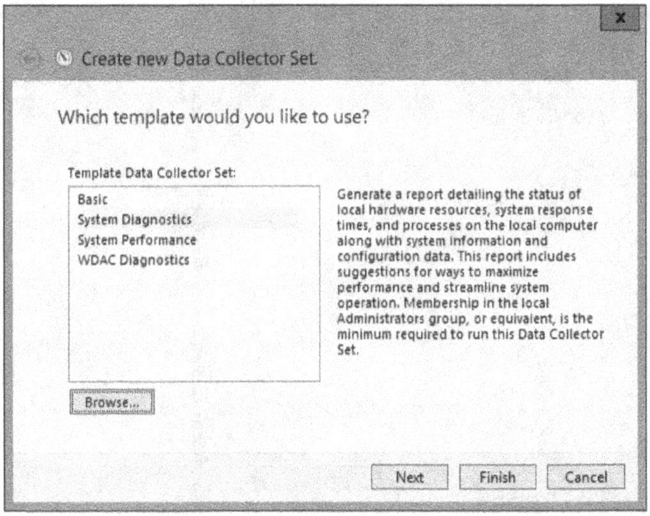

FIGURE 5-55 Browsing for a template.

7. Select the baseline web tier template you created previously and click Open (see Figure 5-56).

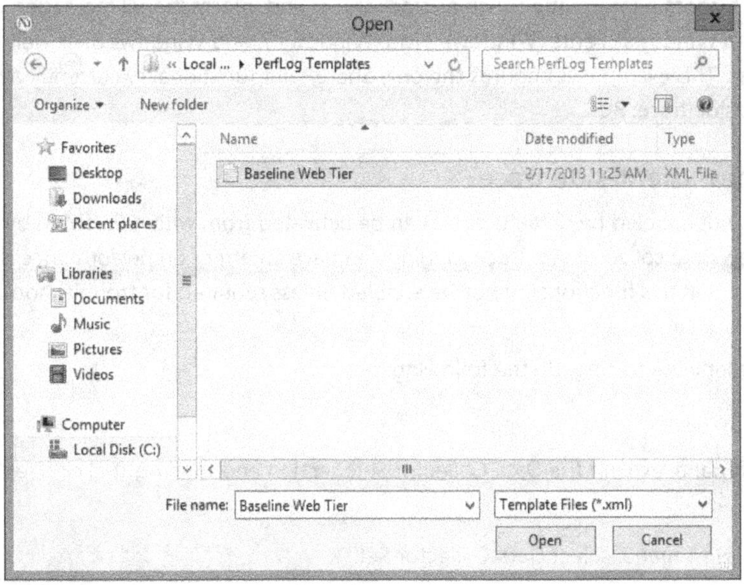

FIGURE 5-56 Baseline web tier template.

8. Click Finish to complete the new data collector set (see Figure 5-57).

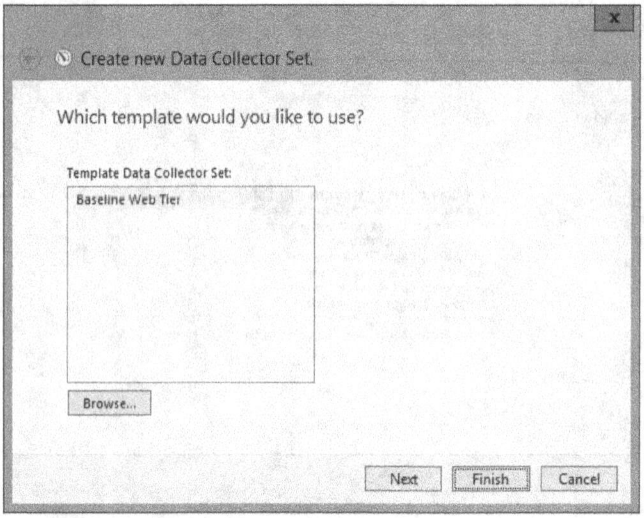

FIGURE 5-57 Finishing the process.

Performing client-side tracing

Trace logs, which contain information such as stack traces and informational messages, are available on both Windows clients (Windows Vista, Windows 7, and Windows 8) as well as Windows servers. This example configures the only SharePoint functionality currently available for a client-side trace: BCS.

Enabling a new client-side trace

Trace logging is not enabled by default, but it can be activated from within PerfMon by generating a new data collector set. Trace logging can have an effect on performance, so it is recommended that this functionality not be enabled unless required for troubleshooting efforts.

To perform client-site tracing, do the following:

1. Run perfmon.exe.

2. In the left pane, expand the Data Collector Sets section and then right-click User Defined.

3. From the New menu, select Data Collector Set.

4. When the Create New Data Collector Set dialog box appears, enter a name for the set and select the Create Manually (Advanced) radio button. Click Next.

5. On the What Type Of Data Do You Want To Include? page, leave the Create Data Logs radio button selected and select the Event Trace Data check box. Click Next.

6. On the Which Event Trace Providers Would You Like To Enable? page, select Add.

7. In the Event Trace Provider dialog box, scroll down and select the Microsoft-Office-Business Connectivity Services event trace provider and then click OK.

8. Returning to the Which Event Trace Providers Would You Like To Enable? screen, verify that your new provider is shown and then click Next.

9. On the Where Would You Like The Data To Be Saved? page, you can choose a new location or leave the default. Make a note of this location and then click Finish.

Running the new client trace

Now that the trace has been configured, it is available to run as desired from within PerfMon, as follows:

1. Run perfmon.exe.

2. In the left pane, expand Data Collector Sets and then expand User Defined, selecting your recently configured trace.

3. Right-click your data collector set and click Start.

4. Perform the BCS activities for which you want to capture trace data.

5. After you complete your activities, stop the trace by right-clicking the data collector set and clicking Stop.

Reviewing the client trace results

The results of the client trace can be reviewed from within Event Viewer. Follow these steps:

1. Run eventvwr.exe.

2. On the Action menu, select Open Saved Log.

3. In the Open Saved Log dialog box, navigate to the location in which you specified for the data to be saved when you created the data collector set.

4. Within this folder, you see one or more folders. The names of each of these folders begin with the machine name and then the year, month, and date in which the trace was performed. Expand this folder.

5. Within this folder is an *.etl file. Open this file in Event Viewer.

6. Correlation (activity) IDs are generated on both the server and the client when items are created, updated, or deleted in external data. The Correlation ID column may not appear by default.

7. To display the Correlation ID column, from the View menu, select Add/Remove Columns.

Performing server-side tracing

Server-side tracing is captured within the trace log on the SharePoint Server. Used in conjunction with client-side tracing, it is possible to watch a particular activity from both the server and the client's point of view.

Continuing with the previous example, BDC Services logging is already enabled on the SharePoint server. To configure its logging level, do the following:

1. Open Central Administration and select Monitoring.

2. In the Reporting section, select Configure Diagnostic Logging.

3. Expand the Business Connectivity Services entry and ensure that Business Data is set to at least the Medium trace level.

4. Analyze the ULS log entries, looking for information about two categories:

   A. BDC_Shared_Services

   B. SS_Shared_Service

Analyzing usage data

Using the built-in views provided in the logging database, you can review the different metrics that are captured in the SharePoint usage and health collection intervals. This information not only can be viewed in SSMS but can also be exported as a comma-separated value (*.csv) file to Microsoft Excel for further analysis.

EXAM TIP

SharePoint farm administrators are becoming more and more versatile. One of the key toolsets we are learning to master is the simple SSMS tool. Understand how to connect to a server, run a simple query, and view the result.

To begin viewing logging data in SSMS, do the following:

1. Open SSMS and connect to the SQL instance providing data services to your SharePoint farm (see Figure 5-58).

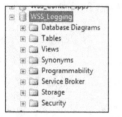

FIGURE 5-58 Connecting to a server.

2. Select the logging database and then select the plus (+) sign to show all its components (see Figure 5-59).

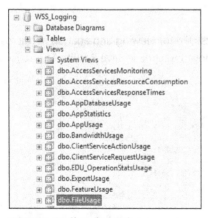

FIGURE 5-59 Expanded logging database.

3. Next, select a view for which you want to collect information (see Figure 5-60).

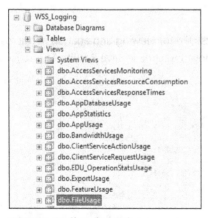

FIGURE 5-60 Choosing a view.

4. Right-click the view and choose Select Top 1000 Rows (see Figure 5-61).

FIGURE 5-61 Selecting the top 1,000 rows.

5. The SQL Query appears in the top pane, and the lower pane shows the query results (see Figure 5-62).

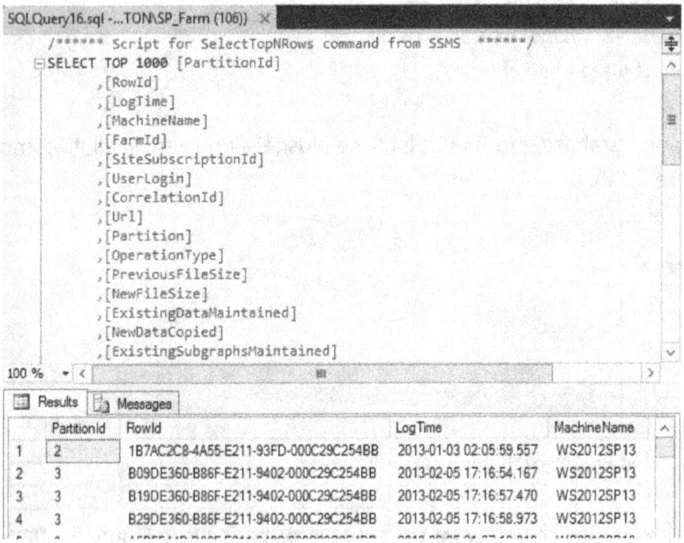

```
SQLQuery16.sql -...TON\SP_Farm (106)) ×
/****** Script for SelectTopNRows command from SSMS ******/
SELECT TOP 1000 [PartitionId]
    ,[RowId]
    ,[LogTime]
    ,[MachineName]
    ,[FarmId]
    ,[SiteSubscriptionId]
    ,[UserLogin]
    ,[CorrelationId]
    ,[Url]
    ,[Partition]
    ,[OperationType]
    ,[PreviousFileSize]
    ,[NewFileSize]
    ,[ExistingDataMaintained]
    ,[NewDataCopied]
    ,[ExistingSubgraphsMaintained]
```

	PartitionId	RowId	LogTime	MachineName
1	2	1B7AC2C8-4A55-E211-93FD-000C29C254BB	2013-01-03 02:05:59.557	WS2012SP13
2	3	B09DE360-B86F-E211-9402-000C29C254BB	2013-02-05 17:16:54.167	WS2012SP13
3	3	B19DE360-B86F-E211-9402-000C29C254BB	2013-02-05 17:16:57.470	WS2012SP13
4	3	B29DE360-B86F-E211-9402-000C29C254BB	2013-02-05 17:16:58.973	WS2012SP13

FIGURE 5-62 T-SQL query and results.

6. These results can now be exported to a *.csv file for viewing and analysis in Microsoft Excel. To begin, right-click the results window and choose Save Results As (see Figure 5-63).

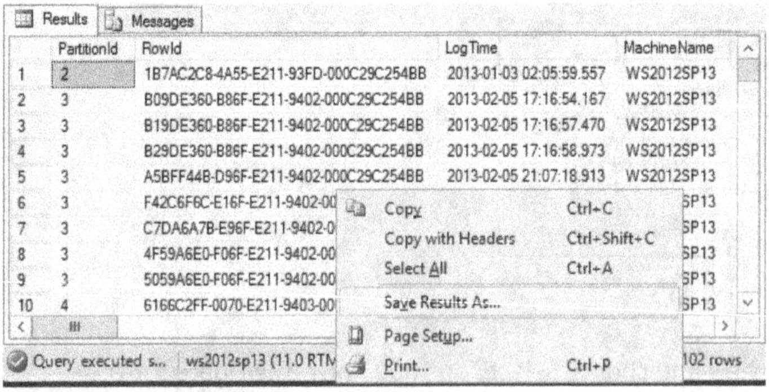

	PartitionId	RowId	LogTime	MachineName
1	2	1B7AC2C8-4A55-E211-93FD-000C29C254BB	2013-01-03 02:05:59.557	WS2012SP13
2	3	B09DE360-B86F-E211-9402-000C29C254BB	2013-02-05 17:16:54.167	WS2012SP13
3	3	B19DE360-B86F-E211-9402-000C29C254BB	2013-02-05 17:16:57.470	WS2012SP13
4	3	B29DE360-B86F-E211-9402-000C29C254BB	2013-02-05 17:16:58.973	WS2012SP13
5	3	A5BFF44B-D96F-E211-9402-000C29C254BB	2013-02-05 21:07:18.913	WS2012SP13
6	3	F42C6F6C-E16F-E211-9402-00	Copy	Ctrl+C	SP13
7	3	C7DA6A7B-E96F-E211-9402-00	Copy with Headers	Ctrl+Shift+C	SP13
8	3	4F59A6E0-F06F-E211-9402-00	Select All	Ctrl+A	SP13
9	3	5059A6E0-F06F-E211-9402-00			SP13
10	4	6166C2FF-0070-E211-9403-00	Save Results As...		SP13

Page Setup...

Query executed s... ws2012sp13 (11.0 RTM   Print...   Ctrl+P   102 rows

FIGURE 5-63 Saving results.

7. Choose a file name for the *.csv file and select Save (see Figure 5-64).

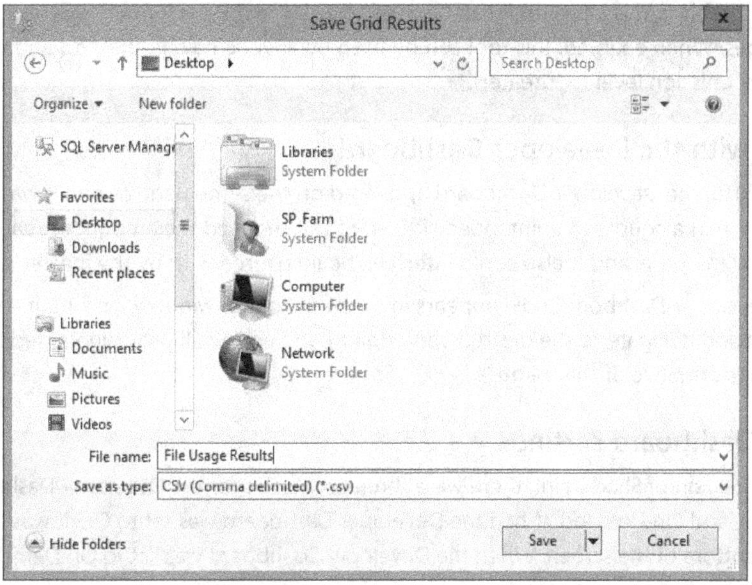

FIGURE 5-64 Choosing a name for the *.csv file.

8. Opening and importing the *.csv file in Excel enables you to display and interact with the data (see Figure 5-65).

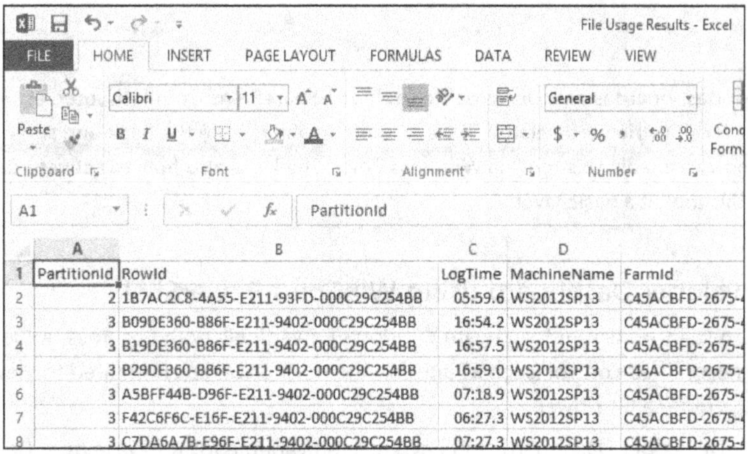

FIGURE 5-65 Usage and health data in Excel.

Enabling a Developer Dashboard

The Developer Dashboard is a tool that can be used to analyze the performance of your SharePoint pages. When enabled, this tool can be used by anyone having the Add and Customize Pages permission level (or greater).

Interaction with the Developer Dashboard

In SharePoint 2010, the Developer Dashboard appeared on the same page as one it was monitoring. This had a couple of unintended side effects: It reduced the amount of real estate available to view the page and it also could interfere/be interfered with by the master page.

The new Developer Dashboard now appears in its own browser window, making it easier to interact with and navigate to the desired SharePoint page while still providing a dedicated view into the performance of that page.

Developer Dashboard settings

In the previous version of SharePoint, there were three properties for the Developer Dashboard: Off (default), On, and On Demand. When the Developer Dashboard was set to On, it was constantly on the bottom of the screen. When the Developer Dashboard was set to On Demand, you had to select an icon to cause the Developer Dashboard to appear on the screen.

In SharePoint 2013, all three properties still exist in Windows PowerShell, but there are truly only two settings: Off and On. When you specify On, you are really specifying On Demand because you must select the Developer Dashboard icon in the ribbon to cause it to appear. If you choose On Demand, you receive the same result.

EXAM TIP

The Developer Dashboard is an indispensable tool for a SharePoint troubleshooter, especially because it can retrieve correlation IDs and their meaning from the back-end server. Understand how to enable this tool via Windows PowerShell and also how to activate/deactivate/use this tool at a basic level.

Enabling Developer Dashboard using Windows PowerShell

Although you can still use stsadm to activate Windows PowerShell, doing so does not let you exercise more fine-grained control (such as altering the permission level required to view the dashboard) and is quite a bit slower.

To enable the Developer Dashboard, you have to set a variable for the Developer Dashboard Settings object and then change its Properties:

```
$devdash=[Microsoft.SharePoint.Administration.SPWebService]::ContentService.
DeveloperDashboardSettings
$devdash.DisplayLevel = "On"
$devdash.Update()
```

To reverse the change, all you have to do to disable it is to set the DisplayLevel property to a value of Off and then do another Update().

Activating Developer Dashboard from a SharePoint page

When the Developer Dashboard is enabled, a new icon appears on the header to the right of Share, Follow, Sync, Edit, and Focus on Content links, as shown in Figure 5-66.

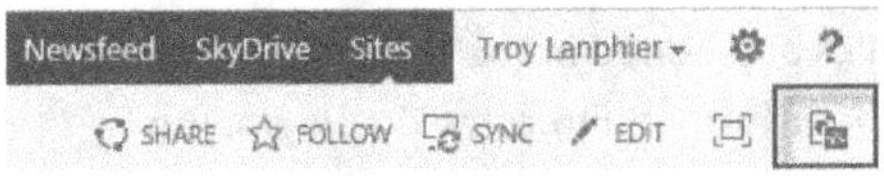

FIGURE 5-66 Developer Dashboard icon.

When this icon is selected, the Developer Dashboard appears in a new browser window. Selecting any of the HTTP GET Requests displays the overall metrics required for the particular page to be rendered, as shown in Figure 5-67.

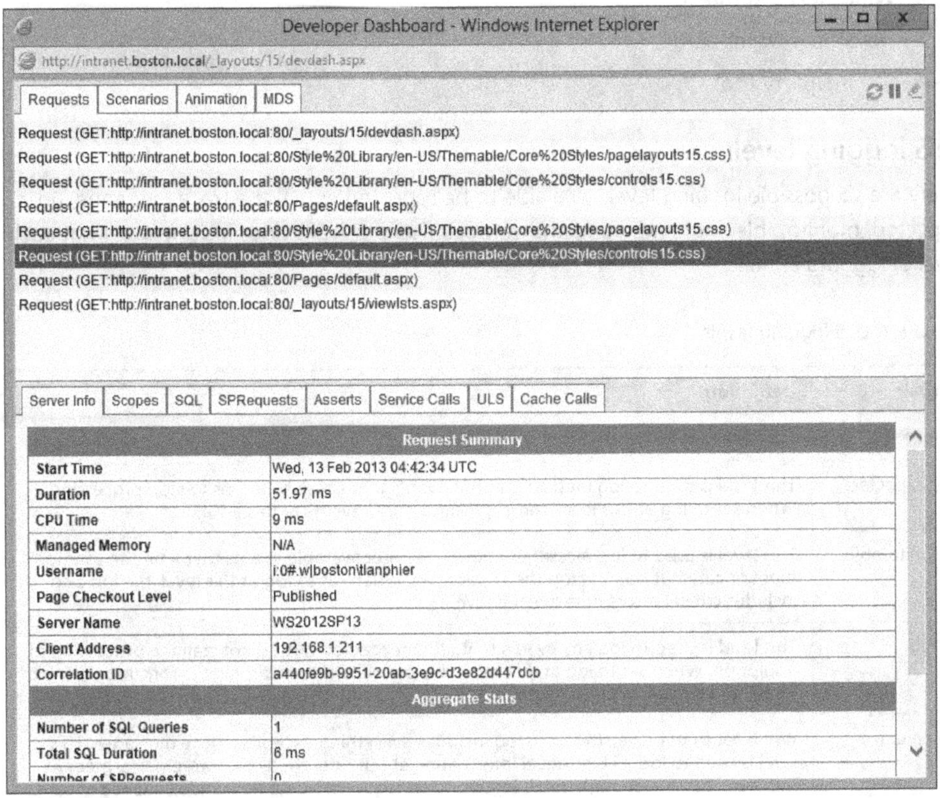

FIGURE 5-67 Developer Dashboard.

Analyzing diagnostic logs

Each server in a SharePoint farm maintains a series of diagnostics logs known as ULS logs, which are contained by default in %ProgramFiles%\Common Files\Microsoft Shared\Web Server Extensions\15\Logs and are saved by default in 30-minute increments.

> **NOTE ULS LOGGING FORMAT**
>
> ULS log files are in standard *.txt format. ULS log files are named in the format *servername-yyyymmdd-hhhh* where the hour indicated (in 24-hour format) indicates the beginning time of the log.

These logs are not available to be viewed through Central Administration, but can be viewed by using the following:

- A text editor such as Notepad
- Windows PowerShell
- Developer Dashboard
- A third-party tool

ULS logging levels

There are six possible logging levels available to be reported within the trace log: none, unexpected, monitorable, high, medium, and verbose. Table 5-8 provides insight into what each level of logging entails.

TABLE 5-8 ULS logging levels

Level	Definition
None	No trace logs are written to the file system.
Unexpected	This level is used to log messages about events that cause solutions to stop processing. When set to log at this level, the log includes only events at this level.
Monitorable	This level is used to log messages about any unrecoverable events that limit the solution's functionality but do not stop the application. When set to log at this level, the log also includes critical errors (unexpected level).
High	This level is used to log any events that are unexpected but do not stall the processing of a solution. When set to log at this level, the log will include warnings, errors (monitorable level), and critical errors (unexpected level).
Medium	When set to this level, the trace log includes everything except verbose messages. This level is used to log all high-level information about operations that were performed. At this level, there is enough detail logged to construct the data flow and sequence of operations. This level of logging can be used by administrators or support professionals to troubleshoot issues.
Verbose	When set to log at this level, the log includes messages at all other levels. Almost all actions that are performed are logged when you use this level. Verbose tracing produces many log messages. This level is typically used only for debugging in a development environment.

As the level of detail in the ULS logs increases (starting with none and working upward in detail toward verbose), each additional level of detail increases the corresponding amount of storage required to house all the log files.

Configuring ULS logs from Central Administration

Central Administration provides an easy-to-use interface for the configuration of event and ULS logs.

To configure the monitoring level, do the following:

1. Open Central Administration and select Monitoring.

2. In the Reporting section, select the Configure Diagnostic Logging link.

3. The Diagnostic Logging page appears. Within the Category section, you see three tiers of selections (see Figure 5-68). From here, you can make choices as follows:

    A. **All Categories**   The changes you make apply universally to every service

    B. **Individual Services**   The changes you make apply to the entire service (such as Access Services)

    C. **Category**   The changes you make apply only to a subcomponent of the individual service

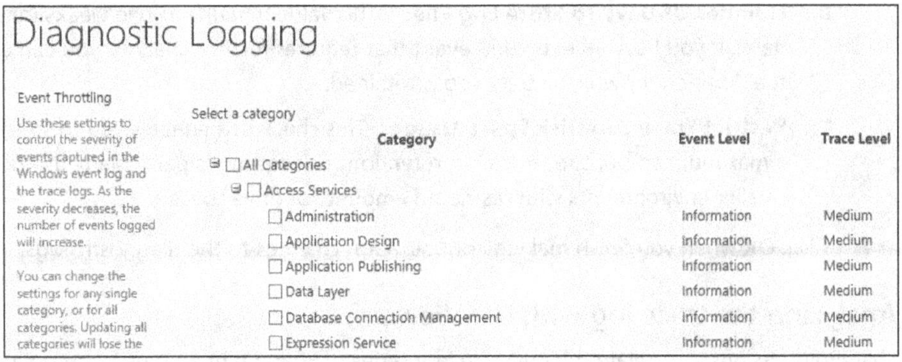

FIGURE 5-68 Diagnostic logging levels.

4. After you select the services you are interested in logging at a certain level, you can choose the least critical event you want to report for both the event level and trace level (ULS):

    A. Least Critical Event To Report To The Event Log (reset to default, none, critical, error, warning, information, verbose)

    B. Least Critical Event To Report To The Trace Log (reset to default, none, unexpected, monitorable, high, medium, verbose)

> **IMPORTANT** **VERBOSE LOGS AND STORAGE**
>
> A word of caution here. Setting verbose for the event log or trace log can quickly gener-
> ate large amounts of logging data, potentially filling your available drive space. This can
> be further amplified by selecting options such as All Categories, which enables this level of
> granularity for each and every category. If you have made changes to the logging settings
> and can't remember what exactly was done, you can always reset both the event log and
> trace log to the reset to default selection. It does not clear the log space, but does stop the
> addition of more log data.

5. Event Log Flood Protection enables the system to avoid the endless repetition of a
    particular event in the Windows event log. It is always a good idea to leave this value
    enabled.

6. The Trace Log section enables you to "catch" the system before it can completely fill a
    drive.

    A. **Path**   The trace log path is usually set to the default path, "%CommonProgram-
       Files%\Microsoft Shared\Web Server Extensions\15\LOGS\", which also happens to
       be the system drive. If you are expecting a large volume of log data, even tempo-
       rarily, consider moving the trace log until things return to normal.

    B. **Number Of Days To Store Log Files**   This value defaults to two weeks (or 14
       days). If you have an extended event that requires further analysis, you can change
       the duration for which a trace log is retained.

    C. **Restrict Trace Log Disk Space Usage**   This check box enables you to specify
       a maximum amount for trace log retention. This setting is particularly useful in
       smaller environments with restricted amounts of drive space.

7. Click **OK** when you finish making configuration changes to the diagnostic logs.

Analyzing the trace log with ULSViewer

SharePoint assigns a correlation log ID to every series of SharePoint actions taken on a particular farm member. These values take the form of a GUID and signify a "conversation" of
sorts, grouping together a sequence of actions.

There are several ways to analyze the trace logs on a server:

- Use Notepad or another text editor. You can open a trace log in Notepad and search
  for a correlation ID, but an entry for a particular sequence of events may be several
  lines long.

- Use Windows PowerShell. The Get-SPLogEvent cmdlet enables you to parse through a
  trace log to find correlation IDs.

- Use a third-party application. This example uses the ULSViewer application. This application is available from MSDN at *http://archive.msdn.microsoft.com/ULSViewer/Release/ProjectReleases.aspx*.

EXAM TIP

Regardless of how you choose to analyze the ULS logs/trace logs, knowing their function and being able to configure and evaluate them are key SharePoint skills.

Figure 5-69 indicates a particular issue when rendering a welcome page on a publishing site. This error appears every time a page load is attempted.

Sorry, something went wrong

An error occurred during the processing of /_catalogs/masterpage/seattle.master. Code blocks are not allowed in this file.

TECHNICAL DETAILS

GO BACK TO SITE

FIGURE 5-69 Failed page load.

To troubleshoot this issue, you can open the trace logs on the affected SharePoint Server.

IMPORTANT TRACE LOGS ARE SERVER-SPECIFIC

Each SharePoint server has its own copy of these trace logs. In a farm that has multiple web servers, you may need to analyze the trace logs on each server in order to locate an issue.

ULSViewer does not require any sort of installation mechanism; you merely download it and run it directly. Selecting and running ULSViewer.exe causes the ULS viewer to appear in a window (see Figure 5-70).

FIGURE 5-70 Opening the current trace log.

At this point, trace log messages begin to fill the ULS RealTime tab. You need to re-create the error, so let's attempt to load the errant page again (see Figure 5-71).

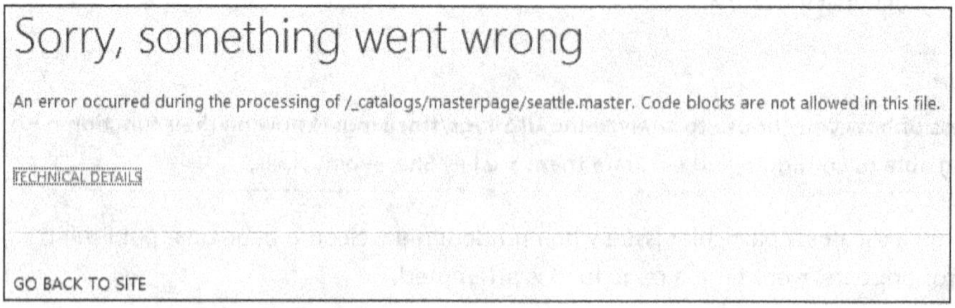

Sorry, something went wrong

An error occurred during the processing of /_catalogs/masterpage/seattle.master. Code blocks are not allowed in this file.

TECHNICAL DETAILS

GO BACK TO SITE

FIGURE 5-71 Page load still failing.

Selecting the Technical Details link shows the correlation ID GUID associated with this problem (see Figure 5-72). Select the first section of the GUID, right-click, and select Copy.

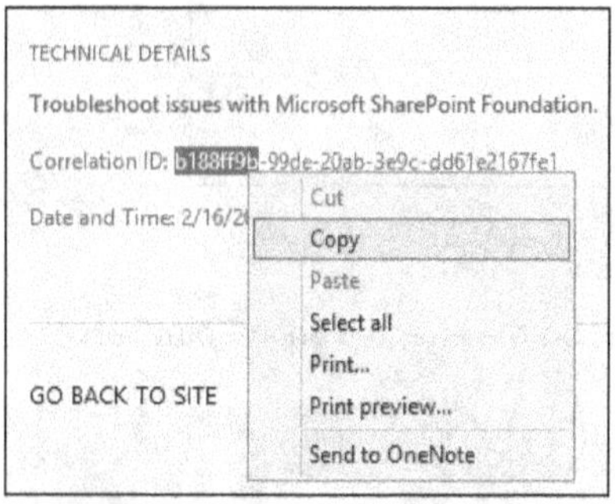

TECHNICAL DETAILS

Troubleshoot issues with Microsoft SharePoint Foundation.

Correlation ID: 6188ff9b-99de-20ab-3e9c-dd61e2167fe1

Date and Time: 2/16/2(

Cut
Copy
Paste
Select all
Print...
Print preview...
Send to OneNote

GO BACK TO SITE

FIGURE 5-72 Copy correlation ID GUID.

Although you can copy the entire GUID, it is not necessary because the first section should be enough to locate the error within the trace log.

Switching back to ULSViewer, select the Filter icon (see Figure 5-73).

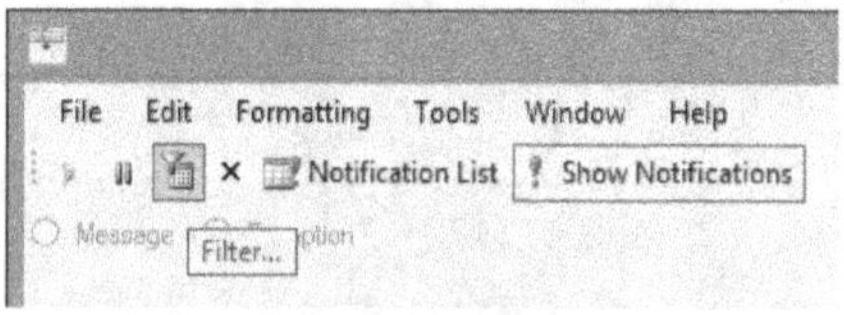

File   Edit   Formatting   Tools   Window   Help

× Notification List   Show Notifications

Message   Filter...   ption

FIGURE 5-73 Selecting the Filter icon.

Select the following values and then click OK (see Figure 5-74):

- Field, Correlation
- Operation, Contains
- Value, <partial GUID copied earlier>

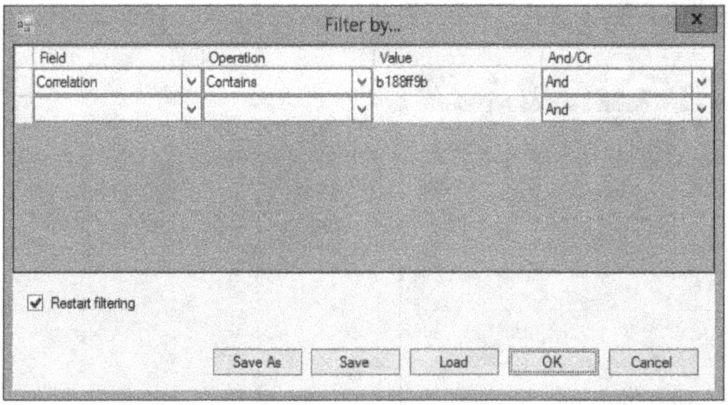

FIGURE 5-74 Filtering by correlation value.

When the grouping of correlation messages appears (see Figure 5-75), you can see the sequence of events both before and after the issue. In this case, the system has thrown an exception because the seattle.master page has a simple typo in it (compare the Unexpected error with the original error message shown when the page was loaded).

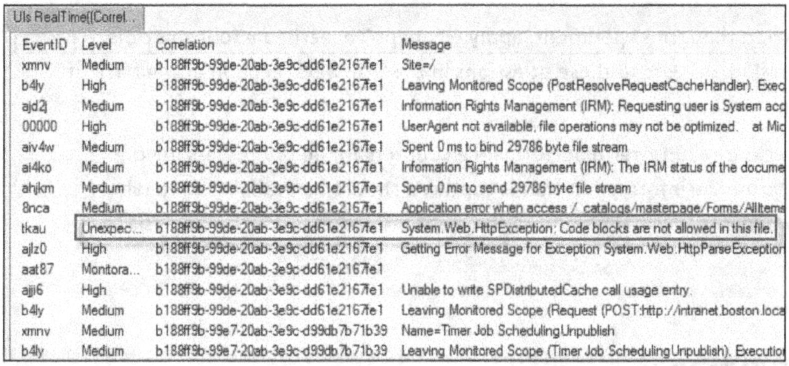

FIGURE 5-75 Unexpected error in ULS viewer.

Discarding the erroneous master page and reverting to the previous version corrected the issue (see Figure 5-76).

FIGURE 5-76 Corrected publishing page.

Objective summary

- A data collector set can be configured to capture performance counters on a regular basis for analysis.
- A data collector set created on one server can be saved as a template and then used on another server in the farm.
- Client-side tracing is available only for BCS.
- Server-site traces for BCS have matching activity IDs, also known as correlation IDs.
- The views in the SharePoint Usage and Health logging database can be analyzed and exported to Excel for further analysis.
- Although the Developer Dashboard has three settings (On, Off, and On Demand), there are effectively only two settings: Off and On Demand.
- The ULS log has six level settings: none, unexpected, monitorable, high, medium, and verbose.

Objective review

Answer the following questions to test your knowledge of the information in this objective. You can find the answers to these questions and explanations of why each answer choice is correct or incorrect in the "Answers" section at the end of this chapter

1. Which of the following actions are *not* steps of collecting a performance baseline?

    A. Building a data collector set

    B. Choosing a log storage location

    C. Checking the application event logs

    D. Creating a PerfMon schedule

2. Which of the following SharePoint services can benefit from client-side tracing?

    A. User Profile Services

    B. Search Services

    C. BCS

    D. InfoPath Services

3. SSMS interaction with which of the following SharePoint databases is supported?

    A. Logging

    B. User Profile Sync

    C. Search

    D. BDC

Chapter summary

- Monitoring a SharePoint environment can be done with one of several tools: Central Administration, Windows PowerShell, logs, and Systems Center 2012 Operations Manager.

- Caching performance can be improved by activating and configuring one or more different caching technologies: output cache, BLOB cache, and object cache.

- Usage and Health services enable SharePoint logging information to be centralized into a logging database.

- Data tier performance is highly dependent on the I/O characteristics of the SQL storage subsystem.

- Pregrowing and then configuring autogrowth for content databases can improve SQL performance by reducing I/O requests.

Answers

Objective 5.1: Thought experiment

Although each server can be monitored individually, it is often difficult to isolate a series of logged events as they occur across a group of SharePoint servers. Adding to this complexity is the requirement for monitoring processor, memory, and I/O on the SQL data tier.

There are at least two options available which will enable you to monitor the entirety of the farm: usage and health data collection services and System Center Monitoring Pack with Systems Center 2012 Operations Manager.

The first option enables data points to be captured within the logging database, where existing views (and newly created views) can be used for analysis.

The second option enables the monitoring of a SharePoint farm (and all its service applications) to be folded into an enterprise-wide monitoring effort using Systems Center 2012 Operations Manager.

Objective 5.1: Review

1. **Correct answers:** A, B, D

   A. **Correct:** Performance counters is a selection within the data collector set.

   B. **Correct:** Event trace data is a selection within the data collector set.

   C. **Incorrect:** Service application databases cannot be configured within a data collector set.

   D. **Correct:** System configuration information is a selection within the data collector set.

2. **Correct answer:** B

   A. **Incorrect:** A content database always belongs to a web application for it to be functional with SharePoint.

   B. **Correct:** A web application can host many content databases, but a content database can been associated only with a single web application.

   C. **Incorrect:** Each content database can be associated with only one web application.

   D. **Incorrect:** Each content database can be associated with only one web application.

3. **Correct answer:** D

   A. **Incorrect:** Get-SPSiteCollection is *not* a valid Windows PowerShell cmdlet for use with SharePoint.

   B. **Incorrect:** Get-SPDatabase –webapplication is used to display the content databases that are associated with a particular web application.

   C. **Incorrect:** $site.usage shows total space consumed for a given site collection.

   D. **Correct:** Storage metrics shows a graphical representation of the content within a site or subsite.

Objective 5.2: Thought experiment

A renewed web tier means that you can consider enabling output, BLOB, and object caching on your new servers. You may want to consider configuring the cache profiles for your different web applications.

   You may also want to configure the new storage as RAID 10 storage, which will be effective in supporting a heavily collaborative environment.

Objective 5.2: Review

1. **Correct answer:** C

   A. **Incorrect:** RAID 0 has excellent performance, but provides absolutely no redundancy.

   B. **Incorrect:** RAID 1 offers good performance and redundancy, but does not provide the best economy.

   C. **Correct:** RAID 5 provides good read performance, effective redundancy, and also provides the best economy.

   D. **Incorrect:** RAID 10 offers good performance and redundancy, but does not provide the best economy.

2. **Correct answer:** C

   A. **Incorrect:** Database transaction logs would not provide the best use, although performance would improve.

   B. **Incorrect:** Search databases can make very good use of this storage, but would not provide the best use from a performance perspective.

   C. **Correct:** TempDB Files and transaction logs would make the best use of this storage from a performance perspective.

   D. **Incorrect:** Database data files would benefit from the performance gain, but would not provide the best use from a performance perspective.

3. **Correct answer:** B

   A. **Incorrect:** SQLIO is used for testing performance capacity, one I/O type at a time.

   B. **Correct:** SQLIOStress is an older performance tool that was replaced by SQLIOSim.

   C. **Incorrect:** SQLIOSim is used for simulating SQL IO patterns.

   D. **Incorrect:** IOMeter is an open source tool that is used to test performance capacity with multiple I/O types at one time.

4. **Correct answer:** D

   A. **Incorrect:** This cache profile is optimized for a site in which users are authenticated, but no authoring or web part changes take place.

   B. **Incorrect:** This cache profile is optimized for anonymous users who receive the same content.

   C. **Incorrect:** Disabled indicates that no caching will take place.

   D. **Correct:** This cache profile is optimized for sites in which authoring, customization, and other write-intensive operations take place.

Objective 5.3: Thought experiment

First, you need to enable and configure the usage analysis service. After this is done, you can go into SSMS to open the logging database. Open the Views folder, select a view, and then run a SELECT statement to retrieve values. These values can then be exported to Microsoft Excel for analysis.

Objective 5.3: Review

1. **Correct answer:** C

   A. **Incorrect:** Building a data collector set is part of collecting a performance baseline.

   B. **Incorrect:** Choosing a log storage location is part of collecting a performance baseline.

   C. **Correct:** Event logs are not generally part of gathering a performance baseline.

   D. **Incorrect:** Creating a PerfMon schedule is part of collecting a performance baseline.

2. **Correct answer:** C

   A. **Incorrect:** User Profile Services do not provide for client-side tracing.

   B. **Incorrect:** Search Services do not provide for client-side tracing.

   C. **Correct:** BCS provide for client-side tracing.

   D. **Incorrect:** InfoPath Services do not provide for client-side tracing.

3. **Correct answer:** A

   A. **Correct:** SSMS interaction is supported only with the logging database.

   B. **Incorrect:** Direct interaction with the User Profile Sync database is *not* supported.

   C. **Incorrect:** Direct interaction with the Search database is *not* supported.

   D. **Incorrect:** Direct Interaction with the BDC database is *not* supported.

Index

N

About the Author

 TROY LANPHIER, MCT, MCSE, MCITP, MCTS, is a senior SharePoint Solutions developer and trainer, and has been working with the SharePoint family of products since 2003. When not writing about or working on SharePoint technologies, he can most likely be found at toy and collectible shows, working under the hood of a car, or enjoying the rides at Disneyland. Troy is a coauthor of *Microsoft SharePoint Foundation 2010 Inside Out.*

Exam Ref 70-331: Core Solutions of Microsoft SharePoint Server 2013

Troy Lanphier

ISBN: 978-0-7356-7808-8

4   16

Printed and bound in the United States of America.

Microsoft Press books are available through booksellers and distributors world-wide. If you need support related to this book, email Microsoft Press Book Support at mspinput@microsoft.com. Please tell us what you think of this book at *http://www.microsoft.com/learning/booksurvey*.

Microsoft and the trademarks listed at *http://www.microsoft.com/about/legal/en/us/IntellectualProperty/Trademarks/EN-US.aspx* are trademarks of the Microsoft group of companies. All other marks are property of their respective owners.

Acquisitions and Developmental Editor: Kenyon Brown
Production Editor: Kara Ebrahim
Editorial Production: Box Twelve Communications
Technical Reviewer: Kyle Davis
Copyeditor: Box Twelve Communications
Indexer: Box Twelve Communications
Cover Design: Twist Creative • Seattle
Cover Composition: Karen Montgomery
Illustrator: Rebecca Demarest

To Marlene—none of this would be possible without you believing in me.

To Mom, for teaching me perseverance.

To Dad, for teaching me to learn by experience.

—TROY LANPHIER